Intermediate Microeconomics

A Modern Approach

Fifth Edition

Intermediate Microeconomics

A Modern Approach

Fifth Edition

Hal R. Varian

University of California at Berkeley

W. W. Norton & Company • New York • London

FIFTH EDITION

Editor: Ed Parsons
Associate Managing Editor: Jane Carter
Project Editor: Kate Barry
Production Manager: Roy Tedoff
Editorial Assistant: Mark Henderson
TEXnician: Hal Varian

ISBN 0-393-97370-0

W. W. Norton & Company, Inc., 500 Fifth Avenue, New York, N.Y. 10110
http://www.wwnorton.com
W. W. Norton & Company, Ltd., 10 Coptic Street, London WC1A 1PU

4 5 6 7 8 9 0

To Carol

CONTENTS

3 Preferences

4 Utility

5 Choice

6 Demand

7 Revealed Preference

8 Slutsky Equation

9 Buying and Selling

10 Intertemporal Choice

11 Asset Markets

12 Uncertainty

13 Risky Assets

14 Consumer's Surplus

15 Market Demand

16 Equilibrium

17 Auctions

18 Technology

19 Profit Maximization

20 Cost Minimization

21 Cost Curves

22 Firm Supply

23 Industry Supply

24 Monopoly

25 Monopoly Behavior

26 Factor Markets

27 Oligopoly

28 Game Theory

29 Exchange

30 Production

31 Welfare

32 Externalities

33 Law and Economics

34 Information Technology

35 Public Goods

36 Asymmetric Information

Mathematical Appendix

PREFACE

The success of the first four editions of *Intermediate Microeconomics* has pleased me very much. It confirmed my belief that the market would welcome an analytic approach to microeconomics at the undergraduate level.

My aim in writing the first edition was to present a treatment of the methods of microeconomics that would allow students to apply these tools on their own and not just passively absorb the predigested cases described in the text. I have found that the best way to do this is to emphasize the fundamental conceptual foundations of microeconomics and to provide concrete examples of their application rather than to attempt to provide an encyclopedia of terminology and anecdote.

A challenge in pursuing this approach arises from the lack of mathematical prerequisites for economics courses at many colleges and universities. The lack of calculus and problem-solving experience in general makes it difficult to present some of the analytical methods of economics. However, it is not impossible. One can go a long way with a few simple facts about linear demand functions and supply functions and some elementary algebra. It is perfectly possible to be analytical without being excessively mathematical.

The distinction is worth emphasizing. An analytical approach to economics is one that uses rigorous, logical reasoning. This does not necessarily imply the use of advanced mathematical methods. The language of mathematics certainly helps to ensure a rigorous analysis, and using it is undoubtedly the best way to proceed when possible, but it may not be appropriate for all students.

Many undergraduate majors in economics are students who *should* know calculus, but don't—at least, not very well. For this reason I have kept calculus out of the main body of the text. However, I have provided complete calculus appendices to many of the chapters. This means that the calculus methods are there for the students who can handle them, but they do not pose a barrier to understanding for the others.

I think that this approach manages to convey the idea that calculus is not just a footnote to the argument of the text, but is instead a deeper way to examine the same issues that one can also explore verbally and graphically. Many arguments are much simpler with a little mathematics, and all economics students should learn that. In many cases I've found that with a little motivation, and a few nice economic examples, students become quite enthusiastic about looking at things from an analytic perspective.

There are several other innovations in this text. First, the chapters are generally very short. I've tried to make most of them roughly "lecture size," so that they can be read at one sitting. I have followed the standard order of discussing first consumer theory and then producer theory, but I've spent a bit more time on consumer theory than is normally the case. This is not because I think that consumer theory is necessarily the most important part of microeconomics; rather, I have found that this is the material that students find the most mysterious, so I wanted to provide a more detailed treatment of it.

Second, I've tried to put in a lot of examples of how to use the theory described here. In most books, students look at a lot of diagrams of shifting curves, but they don't see much algebra, or much calculation of any sort for that matter. But it is the algebra that is used to solve problems in practice. Graphs can provide insight, but the real power of economic analysis comes in calculating quantitative answers to economic problems. Every economics student should be able to translate an economic story into an equation or a numerical example, but all too often the development of this skill is neglected. For this reason I have also provided a workbook that I feel is an integral accompaniment to this book. The workbook was written with my colleague Theodore Bergstrom, and we have put a lot of effort into generating interesting and instructive problems. We think that it provides an important aid to the student of microeconomics.

Third, I believe that the treatment of the topics in this book is more accurate than is usually the case in intermediate micro texts. It is true that I've sometimes chosen special cases to analyze when the general case is too difficult, but I've tried to be honest about that when I did it. In general, I've tried to spell out every step of each argument in detail. I believe that the discussion I've provided is not only more complete and more accurate than usual, but this attention to detail also makes the arguments easier to understand than the loose discussion presented in many other books.

There Are Many Paths to Economic Enlightenment

There is more material in this book than can comfortably be taught in one semester, so it is worthwhile picking and choosing carefully the material that you want to study. If you start on page 1 and proceed through the chapters in order, you will run out of time long before you reach the end of the book. The modular structure of the book allows the instructor a great deal of freedom in choosing how to present the material, and I hope that more people will take advantage of this freedom. The following chart illustrates the chapter dependencies.

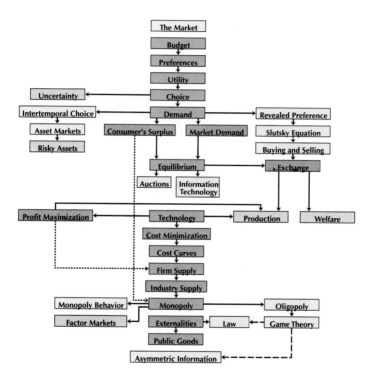

The dark colored chapters are "core" chapters—they should probably be covered in every intermediate microeconomics course. The light-colored chapters are "optional" chapters: I cover some but not all of these every semester. The gray chapters are chapters I usually don't cover in my course, but they could easily be covered in other courses. A solid line going from Chapter A to Chapter B means that Chapter A should be read before chapter B. A broken line means that Chapter B requires knowing some material in Chapter A, but doesn't depend on it in a significant way.

I generally cover consumer theory and markets and then proceed directly to producer theory. Another popular path is to do exchange right after consumer theory; many instructors prefer this route and I have gone to some trouble to make sure that this path is possible.

Some people like to do producer theory before consumer theory. This is possible with this text, but if you choose this path, you will need to supplement the textbook treatment. The material on isoquants, for example, assumes that the students have already seen indifference curves.

Much of the material on public goods, externalities, law, and information can be introduced earlier in the course. I've arranged the material so that it is quite easy to put it pretty much wherever you desire. For example, the material on antitrust law fits naturally in with the discussion of monopoly; tort law can be used to illustrate ideas of efficiency; and criminal law can be used to illustrate consumer choice problems.

Similarly, the material on public goods can be introduced as an illustration of Edgeworth box analysis. Externalities can be introduced right after the discussion of cost curves, and topics from the information chapter can be introduced almost anywhere after students are familiar with the approach of economic analysis.

Changes for the Fifth Edition

The major addition is a chapter on auctions. Given the interest in the FCC spectrum auctions and online auctions, this seemed like a natural topic. As a bonus, this chapter comes relatively early in the book so that students can study this material roughly halfway through the course.

In the last edition I added a chapter on information technology and I have continued to develop that material in this edition. The newspapers never tire of telling us that we now live in an "information society." Although everyone talks about the information economy, few have attempted to do serious analysis of the issues. In this chapter I describe some economic models of information networks, of switching costs, and of rights management for information goods. The point is to show how standard economic techniques of the sort developed in this book can lend significant insight into these issues.

The Test Bank and Workbook

The workbook, *Workouts in Intermediate Microeconomics,* is an integral part of the course. It contains hundreds of fill-in-the-blank exercises that lead the students through the steps of actually applying the tools they have learned in the textbook. In addition to the exercises, *Workouts* contains a collection of short multiple-choice quizzes based on the workbook problems in each chapter. Answers to the quizzes are also included in *Workouts.* These quizzes give a quick way for the student to review the material he or she has learned by working the problems in the workbook.

But there is more ... instructors who have adopted *Workouts* for their course can make use of the test-item file offered with the textbook. The test-item file contains several alternative versions of each *Workouts* quiz. The questions in these quizzes use different numerical values but the same internal logic. They can be used to provide additional problems for students to practice on, or to give quizzes to be taken in class. Grading is quick and reliable because the quizzes are multiple choice and can be graded electronically.

In our course, we tell the students to work through all the quiz questions for each chapter, either by themselves or with a study group. Then during the term we have a short in-class quiz every other week or so, using the alternative versions from the test-item file. These are essentially the Workouts quizzes with different numbers. Hence, students who have done their homework find it easy to do well on the quizzes.

We firmly believe that you can't learn economics without working some problems. The quizzes provided in *Workouts* and in the test-item file make the learning process much easier for both the student and the teacher.

The Production of the Book

The entire book was typeset by the author using TEX, the wonderful type-setting system designed by Donald Knuth. TEX gives the author complete control over the structure and appearance of a document; it is especially convenient for text involving mathematics. I used the standard Unix tools `emacs` for editing and `rcs` for version control. I used Tom Rokicki's TEX system including his previewer, `TeXView`, and print driver, `dvips`. I used `makeindex` for the index, and Trevor Darrell's `psfig` software for inserting the diagrams.

The book design was by Nancy Dale Muldoon, with some modifications by Roy Tedoff and the author. Kate Barry was the manuscript editor, and Ed Parsons coordinated the whole effort in his capacity as editor.

Acknowledgments

Several people contributed to this project. First, I must thank my editorial assistants for the first edition, John Miller and Debra Holt. John provided many comments, suggestions, and exercises based on early drafts of this text and made a significant contribution to the coherence of the final product. Debra did a careful proofreading and consistency check during the final stages and helped in preparing the index.

The following individuals provided me with many useful suggestions and comments during the preparation of the first edition: Ken Binmore (University of Michigan), Mark Bagnoli (Indiana University), Larry Chenault (Miami University), Jonathan Hoag (Bowling Green State University), Allen Jacobs (M.I.T.), John McMillan (University of California at San Diego),

Hal White (University of California at San Diego), and Gary Yohe (Wesleyan University). In particular, I would like to thank Dr. Reiner Buchegger, who prepared the German translation, for his close reading of the first edition and for providing me with a detailed list of corrections. Other individuals to whom I owe thanks for suggestions prior to the first edition are Theodore Bergstrom, Jan Gerson, Oliver Landmann, Alasdair Smith, Barry Smith, and David Winch.

My editorial assistants for the second edition were Sharon Parrott and Angela Bills. They provided much useful assistance with the writing and editing. Robert M. Costrell (University of Massachusetts at Amherst), Ashley Lyman (University of Idaho), Daniel Schwallie (Case-Western Reserve), A. D. Slivinskie (Western Ontario), and Charles Plourde (York University) provided me with detailed comments and suggestions about how to improve the second edition.

In preparing the third edition I received useful comments from the following individuals: Doris Cheng (San Jose), Imre Csekó (Budapest), Gregory Hildebrandt (UCLA), Jamie Brown Kruse (Colorado), Richard Manning (Brigham Young), Janet Mitchell (Cornell), Charles Plourde (York University), Yeung-Nan Shieh (San Jose), John Winder (Toronto). I especially want to thank Roger F. Miller (University of Wisconsin), David Wildasin (Indiana) for their detailed comments, suggestions, and corrections.

The fifth edition benefited from the comments by Kealoah Widdows (Wabash College), William Sims (Concordia University), Jennifer R. Reinganum (Vanderbilt University), and Paul D. Thistle (Western Michigan University).

Berkeley
January 1999

Intermediate Microeconomics

A Modern Approach

Fifth Edition

CHAPTER **1**

THE MARKET

The conventional first chapter of a microeconomics book is a discussion of the "scope and methods" of economics. Although this material can be very interesting, it hardly seems appropriate to *begin* your study of economics with such material. It is hard to appreciate such a discussion until you have seen some examples of economic analysis in action.

So instead, we will begin this book with an *example* of economic analysis. In this chapter we will examine a model of a particular market, the market for apartments. Along the way we will introduce several new ideas and tools of economics. Don't worry if it all goes by rather quickly. This chapter is meant only to provide a quick overview of how these ideas can be used. Later on we will study them in substantially more detail.

1.1 Constructing a Model

Economics proceeds by developing **models** of social phenomena. By a model we mean a simplified representation of reality. The emphasis here is on the word "simple." Think about how useless a map on a one-to-one scale would be. The same is true of an economic model that attempts to describe every aspect of reality. A model's power stems from the elimination of irrelevant detail, which allows the economist to focus on the essential features of the economic reality he or she is attempting to understand.

Here we are interested in what determines the price of apartments, so we want to have a simplified description of the apartment market. There is a certain art to choosing the right simplifications in building a model. In general we want to adopt the simplest model that is capable of describing the economic situation we are examining. We can then add complications one at a time, allowing the model to become more complex and, we hope, more realistic.

The particular example we want to consider is the market for apartments in a medium-size midwestern college town. In this town there are two sorts of apartments. There are some that are adjacent to the university, and others that are farther away. The adjacent apartments are generally considered to be more desirable by students, since they allow easier access to the university. The apartments that are farther away necessitate taking a bus, or a long, cold bicycle ride, so most students would prefer a nearby apartment ... if they can afford one.

We will think of the apartments as being located in two large rings surrounding the university. The adjacent apartments are in the inner ring, while the rest are located in the outer ring. We will focus exclusively on the market for apartments in the inner ring. The outer ring should be interpreted as where people can go who don't find one of the closer apartments. We'll suppose that there are many apartments available in the outer ring, and their price is fixed at some known level. We'll be concerned solely with the determination of the price of the inner-ring apartments and who gets to live there.

An economist would describe the distinction between the prices of the two kinds of apartments in this model by saying that the price of the outer-ring apartments is an **exogenous variable**, while the price of the inner-ring apartments is an **endogenous variable**. This means that the price of the outer-ring apartments is taken as determined by factors not discussed in this particular model, while the price of the inner-ring apartments is determined by forces described in the model.

The first simplification that we'll make in our model is that all apartments are identical in every respect except for location. Thus it will make sense to speak of "the price" of apartments, without worrying about whether the apartments have one bedroom, or two bedrooms, or whatever.

But what determines this price? What determines who will live in the inner-ring apartments and who will live farther out? What can be said about the desirability of different economic mechanisms for allocating apartments? What concepts can we use to judge the merit of different assignments of apartments to individuals? These are all questions that we want our model to address.

1.2 Optimization and Equilibrium

Whenever we try to explain the behavior of human beings we need to have a framework on which our analysis can be based. In much of economics we use a framework built on the following two simple principles.

The optimization principle: People try to choose the best patterns of consumption that they can afford.

The equilibrium principle: Prices adjust until the amount that people demand of something is equal to the amount that is supplied.

Let us consider these two principles. The first is *almost* tautological. If people are free to choose their actions, it is reasonable to assume that they try to choose things they want rather than things they don't want. Of course there are exceptions to this general principle, but they typically lie outside the domain of economic behavior.

The second notion is a bit more problematic. It is at least conceivable that at any given time peoples' demands and supplies are not compatible, and hence something must be changing. These changes may take a long time to work themselves out, and, even worse, they may induce other changes that might "destabilize" the whole system.

This kind of thing can happen ... but it usually doesn't. In the case of apartments, we typically see a fairly stable rental price from month to month. It is this *equilibrium* price that we are interested in, not in how the market gets to this equilibrium or how it might change over long periods of time.

It is worth observing that the definition used for equilibrium may be different in different models. In the case of the simple market we will examine in this chapter, the demand and supply equilibrium idea will be adequate for our needs. But in more general models we will need more general definitions of equilibrium. Typically, equilibrium will require that the economic agents' actions must be consistent with each other.

How do we use these two principles to determine the answers to the questions we raised above? It is time to introduce some economic concepts.

1.3 The Demand Curve

Suppose that we consider all of the possible renters of the apartments and ask each of them the maximum amount that he or she would be willing to pay to rent one of the apartments.

Let's start at the top. There must be someone who is willing to pay the highest price. Perhaps this person has a lot of money, perhaps he is very lazy and doesn't want to walk far ... or whatever. Suppose that this person is willing to pay $500 a month for an apartment.

If there is only one person who is willing to pay $500 a month to rent an apartment, then if the price for apartments were $500 a month, exactly one apartment would be rented—to the one person who was willing to pay that price.

Suppose that the next highest price that anyone is willing to pay is $490. Then if the market price were $499, there would still be only one apartment rented: the person who was *willing* to pay $500 would rent an apartment, but the person who was willing to pay $490 wouldn't. And so it goes. Only one apartment would be rented if the price were $498, $497, $496, and so on ... until we reach a price of $490. At that price, exactly two apartments would be rented: one to the $500 person and one to the $490 person.

Similarly, two apartments would be rented until we reach the maximum price that the person with the *third* highest price would be willing to pay, and so on.

Economists call a person's maximum willingness to pay for something that person's **reservation price**. The reservation price is the highest price that a given person will accept and still purchase the good. In other words, a person's reservation price is the price at which he or she is just indifferent between purchasing or not purchasing the good. In our example, if a person has a reservation price p it means that he or she would be just indifferent between living in the inner ring and paying a price p and living in the outer ring.

Thus the number of apartments that will be rented at a given price p^* will just be the number of people who have a reservation price greater than or equal to p^*. For if the market price is p^*, then everyone who is willing to pay at least p^* for an apartment will want an apartment in the inner ring, and everyone who is not willing to pay p^* will choose to live in the outer ring.

We can plot these reservation prices in a diagram as in Figure 1.1. Here the price is depicted on the vertical axis and the number of people who are willing to pay that price or more is depicted on the horizontal axis.

Another way to view Figure 1.1 is to think of it as measuring how many people would want to rent apartments at any particular price. Such a curve is an example of a **demand curve**—a curve that relates the quantity demanded to price. When the market price is above $500, zero apartments will be rented. When the price is between $500 and $490, one apartment will be rented. When it is between $490 and the third highest reservation price, two apartments will be rented, and so on. The demand curve describes the quantity demanded at each of the possible prices.

The demand curve for apartments slopes down: as the price of apartments decreases more people will be willing to rent apartments. If there are many people and their reservation prices differ only slightly from person to

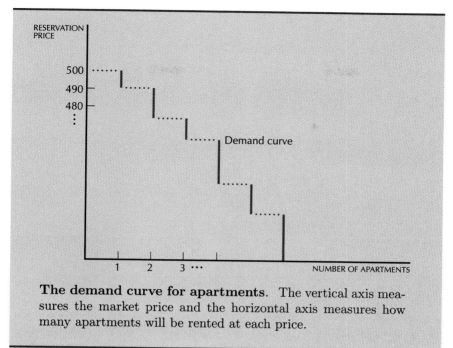

The demand curve for apartments. The vertical axis measures the market price and the horizontal axis measures how many apartments will be rented at each price.

Figure
1.1

person, it is reasonable to think of the demand curve as sloping smoothly downward, as in Figure 1.2. The curve in Figure 1.2 is what the demand curve in Figure 1.1 would look like if there were many people who want to rent the apartments. The "jumps" shown in Figure 1.1 are now so small relative to the size of the market that we can safely ignore them in drawing the market demand curve.

1.4 The Supply Curve

We now have a nice graphical representation of demand behavior, so let us turn to supply behavior. Here we have to think about the nature of the market we are examining. The situation we will consider is where there are many independent landlords who are each out to rent their apartments for the highest price the market will bear. We will refer to this as the case of a **competitive market**. Other sorts of market arrangements are certainly possible, and we will examine a few later.

For now, let's consider the case where there are many landlords who all operate independently. It is clear that if all landlords are trying to do the best they can and if the renters are fully informed about the prices the landlords charge, then the equilibrium price of all apartments in the inner ring must be the same. The argument is not difficult. Suppose instead that there is some high price, p_h, and some low price, p_l, being charged

Demand curve for apartments with many demanders.
Because of the large number of demanders, the jumps between
prices will be small, and the demand curve will have the conventional smooth shape.

for apartments. The people who are renting their apartments for a high
price could go to a landlord renting for a low price and offer to pay a rent
somewhere between p_h and p_l. A transaction at such a price would make
both the renter and the landlord better off. To the extent that all parties
are seeking to further their own interests and are aware of the alternative
prices being charged, a situation with different prices being charged for the
same good cannot persist in equilibrium.

But what will this single equilibrium price be? Let us try the method
that we used in our construction of the demand curve: we will pick a price
and ask how many apartments will be supplied at that price.

The answer depends to some degree on the time frame in which we are
examining the market. If we are considering a time frame of several years,
so that new construction can take place, the number of apartments will
certainly respond to the price that is charged. But in the "short run"—
within a given year, say—the number of apartments is more or less fixed.
If we consider only this short-run case, the supply of apartments will be
constant at some predetermined level.

The **supply curve** in this market is depicted in Figure 1.3 as a vertical
line. Whatever price is being charged, the same number of apartments will
be rented, namely, all the apartments that are available at that time.

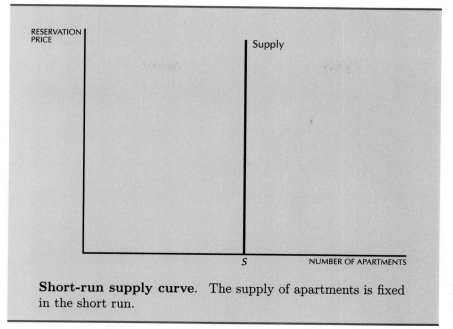

Short-run supply curve. The supply of apartments is fixed in the short run.

Figure
1.3

1.5 Market Equilibrium

We now have a way of representing the demand and the supply side of the apartment market. Let us put them together and ask what the equilibrium behavior of the market is. We do this by drawing both the demand and the supply curve on the same graph in Figure 1.4.

In this graph we have used p^* to denote the price where the quantity of apartments demanded equals the quantity supplied. This is the **equilibrium price** of apartments. At this price, each consumer who is willing to pay at least p^* is able to find an apartment to rent, and each landlord will be able to rent apartments at the going market price. Neither the consumers nor the landlords have any reason to change their behavior. This is why we refer to this as an *equilibrium:* no change in behavior will be observed.

To better understand this point, let us consider what would happen at a price other than p^*. For example, consider some price $p < p^*$ where demand is greater than supply. Can this price persist? At this price at least some of the landlords will have more renters than they can handle. There will be lines of people hoping to get an apartment at that price; there are more people who are willing to pay the price p than there are apartments. Certainly some of the landlords would find it in their interest to raise the price of the apartments they are offering.

Similarly, suppose that the price of apartments is some p greater than p^*.

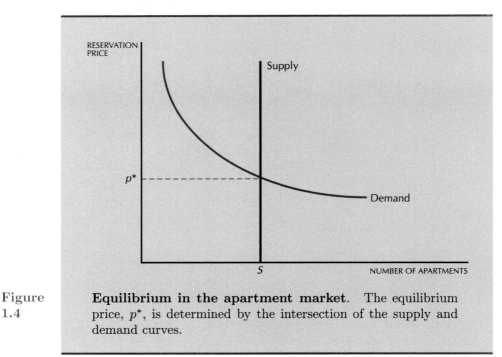

Figure 1.4

Equilibrium in the apartment market. The equilibrium price, p^*, is determined by the intersection of the supply and demand curves.

Then some of the apartments will be vacant: there are fewer people who are willing to pay p than there are apartments. Some of the landlords are now in danger of getting no rent at all for their apartments. Thus they will have an incentive to lower their price in order to attract more renters.

If the price is above p^* there are too few renters; if it is below p^* there are too many renters. Only at the price of p^* is the number of people who are willing to rent at that price equal to the number of apartments available for rent. Only at that price does demand equal supply.

At the price p^* the landlords' and the renters' behaviors are compatible in the sense that the number of apartments demanded by the renters at p^* is equal to the number of apartments supplied by the landlords. This is the equilibrium price in the market for apartments.

Once we've determined the market price for the inner-ring apartments, we can ask who ends up getting these apartments and who is exiled to the farther-away apartments. In our model there is a very simple answer to this question: in the market equilibrium everyone who is willing to pay p^* or more gets an apartment in the inner ring, and everyone who is willing to pay less than p^* gets one in the outer ring. The person who has a reservation price of p^* is just indifferent between taking an apartment in the inner ring and taking one in the outer ring. The other people in the inner ring are getting their apartments at less than the maximum they would be willing to pay for them. Thus the assignment of apartments to renters is determined by how much they are willing to pay.

1.6 Comparative Statics

Now that we have an economic model of the apartment market, we can begin to use it to analyze the behavior of the equilibrium price. For example, we can ask how the price of apartments changes when various aspects of the market change. This kind of an exercise is known as **comparative statics**, because it involves comparing two "static" equilibria without worrying about how the market moves from one equilibrium to another.

The movement from one equilibrium to another can take a substantial amount of time, and questions about how such movement takes place can be very interesting and important. But we must walk before we can run, so we will ignore such dynamic questions for now. Comparative statics analysis is only concerned with comparing equilibria, and there will be enough questions to answer in this framework for the present.

Let's start with a simple case. Suppose that the supply of apartments is increased, as in Figure 1.5.

Increasing the supply of apartments. As the supply of apartments increases, the equilibrium price decreases.

Figure 1.5

It is easy to see in this diagram that the equilibrium price of apartments will fall. Similarly, if the supply of apartments were reduced the equilibrium price would rise.

Let's try a more complicated—and more interesting—example. Suppose that a developer decides to turn several of the apartments into condominiums. What will happen to the price of the remaining apartments?

Your first guess is probably that the price of apartments will go up, since the supply has been reduced. But this isn't necessarily right. It is true that the supply of apartments to rent has been reduced. But the *demand for apartments* has been reduced as well, since some of the people who were renting apartments may decide to purchase the new condominiums.

It is natural to assume that the condominium purchasers come from those who already live in the inner-ring apartments—those people who are willing to pay more than p^* for an apartment. Suppose, for example, that the demanders with the 10 highest reservation prices decide to buy condos rather than rent apartments. Then the new demand curve is just the old demand curve with 10 fewer demanders at each price. Since there are also 10 fewer apartments to rent, the new equilibrium price is just what it was before, and exactly the same people end up living in the inner-ring apartments. This situation is depicted in Figure 1.6. Both the demand curve and the supply curve shift left by 10 apartments, and the equilibrium price remains unchanged.

Figure 1.6

Effect of creating condominiums. If demand and supply both shift left by the same amount the equilibrium price is unchanged.

Most people find this result surprising. They tend to see just the reduction in the supply of apartments and don't think about the reduction in demand. The case we've considered is an extreme one: *all* of the condo purchasers were former apartment dwellers. But the other case—where none of the condo purchasers were apartment dwellers—is even more extreme.

The model, simple though it is, has led us to an important insight. If we want to determine how conversion to condominiums will affect the apartment market, we have to consider not only the effect on the supply of apartments but also the effect on the demand for apartments.

Let's consider another example of a surprising comparative statics analysis: the effect of an apartment tax. Suppose that the city council decides that there should be a tax on apartments of $50 a year. Thus each landlord will have to pay $50 a year to the city for each apartment that he owns. What will this do to the price of apartments?

Most people would think that at least some of the tax would get passed along to apartment renters. But, rather surprisingly, that is not the case. In fact, the equilibrium price of apartments will remain unchanged!

In order to verify this, we have to ask what happens to the demand curve and the supply curve. The supply curve doesn't change—there are just as many apartments after the tax as before the tax. And the demand curve doesn't change either, since the number of apartments that will be rented at each different price will be the same as well. If neither the demand curve nor the supply curve shifts, the price can't change as a result of the tax.

Here is a way to think about the effect of this tax. Before the tax is imposed, each landlord is charging the highest price that he can get that will keep his apartments occupied. The equilibrium price p^* is the highest price that can be charged that is compatible with all of the apartments being rented. After the tax is imposed can the landlords raise their prices to compensate for the tax? The answer is no: if they could raise the price and keep their apartments occupied, they would have already done so. If they were charging the maximum price that the market could bear, the landlords couldn't raise their prices any more: none of the tax can get passed along to the renters. The landlords have to pay the entire amount of the tax.

This analysis depends on the assumption that the supply of apartments remains fixed. If the number of apartments can vary as the tax changes, then the price paid by the renters will typically change. We'll examine this kind of behavior later on, after we've built up some more powerful tools for analyzing such problems.

1.7 Other Ways to Allocate Apartments

In the previous section we described the equilibrium for apartments in a competitive market. But this is only one of many ways to allocate a resource; in this section we describe a few other ways. Some of these may sound rather strange, but each will illustrate an important economic point.

The Discriminating Monopolist

First, let us consider a situation where there is one dominant landlord who owns all of the apartments. Or, alternatively, we could think of a number of individual landlords getting together and coordinating their actions to act as one. A situation where a market is dominated by a single seller of a product is known as a **monopoly**.

In renting the apartments the landlord could decide to auction them off one by one to the highest bidders. Since this means that different people would end up paying different prices for apartments, we will call this the case of the **discriminating monopolist**. Let us suppose for simplicity that the discriminating monopolist knows each person's reservation price for apartments. (This is not terribly realistic, but it will serve to illustrate an important point.)

This means that he would rent the first apartment to the fellow who would pay the most for it, in this case $500. The next apartment would go for $490 and so on as we moved down the demand curve. Each apartment would be rented to the person who was willing to pay the most for it.

Here is the interesting feature of the discriminating monopolist: *exactly the same people will get the apartments as in the case of the market solution,* namely, everyone who valued an apartment at more than p^*. The last person to rent an apartment pays the price p^*—the same as the equilibrium price in a competitive market. The discriminating monopolist's attempt to maximize his own profits leads to the same allocation of apartments as the supply and demand mechanism of the competitive market. The amount the people *pay* is different, but who gets the apartments is the same. It turns out that this is no accident, but we'll have to wait until later to explain the reason.

The Ordinary Monopolist

We assumed that the discriminating monopolist was able to rent each apartment at a different price. But what if he were forced to rent all apartments at the same price? In this case the monopolist faces a tradeoff: if he chooses a low price he will rent more apartments, but he may end up making less money than if he sets a higher price.

Let us use $D(p)$ to represent the demand function—the number of apartments demanded at price p. Then if the monopolist sets a price p, he will rent $D(p)$ apartments and thus receive a revenue of $pD(p)$. The revenue that the monopolist receives can be thought of as the area of a box: the height of the box is the price p and the width of the box is the number of apartments $D(p)$. The product of the height and the width—the area of the box—is the revenue the monopolist receives. This is the box depicted in Figure 1.7.

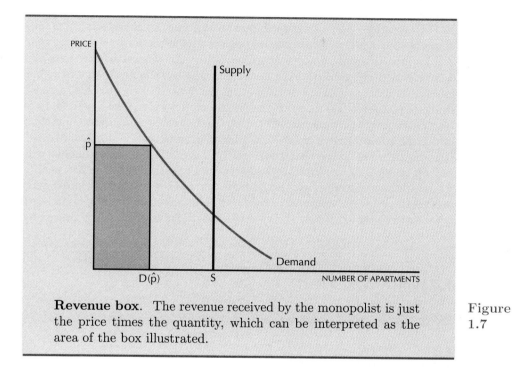

Revenue box. The revenue received by the monopolist is just the price times the quantity, which can be interpreted as the area of the box illustrated.

Figure
1.7

If the monopolist has no costs associated with renting an apartment, he would want to choose a price that has the largest associated revenue box. The largest revenue box in Figure 1.7 occurs at the price $\hat{p}$. In this case the monopolist will find it in his interest *not* to rent all of the apartments. In fact this will generally be the case for a monopolist. The monopolist will want to restrict the output available in order to maximize his profit. This means that the monopolist will generally want to charge a price that is higher than the equilibrium price in a competitive market, p^*. In the case of the ordinary monopolist, fewer apartments will be rented, and each apartment will be rented at a higher price than in the competitive market.

Rent Control

A third and final case that we will discuss will be the case of rent control. Suppose that the city decides to impose a maximum rent that can be charged for apartments, say p_{max}. We suppose that the price p_{max} is less than the equilibrium price in the competitive market, p^*. If this is so we would have a situation of **excess demand**: there are more people who are willing to rent apartments at p_{max} than there are apartments available. Who will end up with the apartments?

The theory that we have described up until now doesn't have an answer to this question. We can describe what will happen when supply equals demand, but we don't have enough detail in the model to describe what will happen if supply doesn't equal demand. The answer to who gets the apartments under rent control depends on who has the most time to spend looking around, who knows the current tenants, and so on. All of these things are outside the scope of the simple model we've developed. It may be that exactly the same people get the apartments under rent control as under the competitive market. But that is an extremely unlikely outcome. It is much more likely that some of the formerly outer-ring people will end up in some of the inner-ring apartments and thus displace the people who would have been living there under the market system. So under rent control the same number of apartments will be rented at the rent-controlled price as were rented under the competitive price: they'll just be rented to different people.

1.8 Which Way Is Best?

We've now described four possible ways of allocating apartments to people:

- The competitive market.
- A discriminating monopolist.
- An ordinary monopolist.
- Rent control.

These are four different economic institutions for allocating apartments. Each method will result in different people getting apartments or in different prices being charged for apartments. We might well ask which economic institution is best. But first we have to define "best." What criteria might we use to compare these ways of allocating apartments?

One thing we can do is to look at the economic positions of the people involved. It is pretty obvious that the owners of the apartments end up with the most money if they can act as discriminating monopolists: this would generate the most revenues for the apartment owner(s). Similarly the rent-control solution is probably the worst situation for the apartment owners.

What about the renters? They are probably worse off on average in the case of a discriminating monopolist—most of them would be paying a higher price than they would under the other ways of allocating apartments.

Are the consumers better off in the case of rent control? Some of them are: the consumers *who end up getting the apartments* are better off than they would be under the market solution. But the ones who didn't get the apartments are *worse off* than they would be under the market solution.

What we need here is a way to look at the economic position of all the parties involved—all the renters *and* all the landlords. How can we examine the desirability of different ways to allocate apartments, taking everybody into account? What can be used as a criterion for a "good" way to allocate apartments taking into account *all* of the parties involved?

1.9 Pareto Efficiency

One useful criterion for comparing the outcomes of different economic institutions is a concept known as Pareto efficiency or economic efficiency.[1] We start with the following definition: if we can find a way to make some people better off without making anybody else worse off, we have a **Pareto improvement**. If an allocation allows for a Pareto improvement, it is called **Pareto inefficient**; if an allocation is such that no Pareto improvements are possible, it is called **Pareto efficient**.

A Pareto inefficient allocation has the undesirable feature that there is some way to make somebody better off without hurting anyone else. There may be other positive things about the allocation, but the fact that it is Pareto inefficient is certainly one strike against it. If there is a way to make someone better off without hurting anyone else, why not do it?

The idea of Pareto efficiency is an important one in economics and we will examine it in some detail later on. It has many subtle implications that we will have to investigate more slowly, but we can get an inkling of what is involved even now.

Here is a useful way to think about the idea of Pareto efficiency. Suppose that we assigned the renters to the inner- and outer-ring apartments randomly, but then allowed them to sublet their apartments to each other. Some people who really wanted to live close in might, through bad luck, end up with an outer-ring apartment. But then they could sublet an inner-ring apartment from someone who was assigned to such an apartment but who didn't value it as highly as the other person. If individuals were assigned randomly to apartments, there would generally be some who would want to trade apartments, if they were sufficiently compensated for doing so.

For example, suppose that person A is assigned an apartment in the inner ring that he feels is worth $200, and that there is some person B in the outer ring who would be willing to pay $300 for A's apartment. Then there is a

---

[1] Pareto efficiency is named after the nineteenth-century economist and sociologist Vilfredo Pareto (1848–1923) who was one of the first to examine the implications of this idea.

"gain from trade" if these two agents swap apartments and arrange a side payment from B to A of some amount of money between $200 and $300. The exact amount of the transaction isn't important. What is important is that the people who are willing to pay the most for the apartments get them—otherwise, there would be an incentive for someone who attached a low value to an inner-ring apartment to make a trade with someone who placed a high value on an inner-ring apartment.

Suppose that we think of all voluntary trades as being carried out so that all gains from trade are exhausted. The resulting allocation must be Pareto efficient. If not, there would be some trade that would make two people better off without hurting anyone else—but this would contradict the assumption that all voluntary trades had been carried out. An allocation in which all voluntary trades have been carried out is a Pareto efficient allocation.

1.10 Comparing Ways to Allocate Apartments

The trading process we've described above is so general that you wouldn't think that anything much could be said about its outcome. But there is one very interesting point that can be made. Let us ask who will end up with apartments in an allocation where all of the gains from trade have been exhausted.

To see the answer, just note that anyone who has an apartment in the inner ring must have a higher reservation price than anyone who has an apartment in the outer ring—otherwise, they could make a trade and make both people better off. Thus if there are S apartments to be rented, then the S people with the highest reservation prices end up getting apartments in the inner ring. This allocation is Pareto efficient—anything else is not, since any other assignment of apartments to people would allow for some trade that would make at least two of the people better off without hurting anyone else.

Let us try to apply this criterion of Pareto efficiency to the outcomes of the various resource allocation devices mentioned above. Let's start with the market mechanism. It is easy to see that the market mechanism assigns the people with the S highest reservation prices to the inner ring—namely, those people who are willing to pay more than the equilibrium price, p^*, for their apartments. Thus there are no further gains from trade to be had once the apartments have been rented in a competitive market. The outcome of the competitive market is Pareto efficient.

What about the discriminating monopolist? Is that arrangement Pareto efficient? To answer this question, simply observe that the discriminating monopolist assigns apartments to exactly the same people who receive apartments in the competitive market. Under each system everyone who is willing to pay more than p^* for an apartment gets an apartment. Thus the discriminating monopolist generates a Pareto efficient outcome as well.

Although both the competitive market and the discriminating monopolist generate Pareto efficient outcomes in the sense that there will be no further trades desired, they can result in quite different distributions of income. Certainly the consumers are much worse off under the discriminating monopolist than under the competitive market, and the landlord(s) are much better off. In general, Pareto efficiency doesn't have much to say about distribution of the gains from trade. It is only concerned with the *efficiency* of the trade: whether all of the possible trades have been made.

What about the ordinary monopolist who is constrained to charge just one price? It turns out that this situation is not Pareto efficient. All we have to do to verify this is to note that, since all the apartments will not in general be rented by the monopolist, he can increase his profits by renting an apartment to someone who doesn't have one at *any* positive price. There is some price at which both the monopolist and the renter must be better off. As long as the monopolist doesn't change the price that anybody else pays, the other renters are just as well off as they were before. Thus we have found a **Pareto improvement**—a way to make two parties better off without making anyone else worse off.

The final case is that of rent control. This also turns out not to be Pareto efficient. The argument here rests on the fact that an arbitrary assignment of renters to apartments will generally involve someone living in the inner ring (say Mr. In) who is willing to pay less for an apartment than someone living in the outer ring (say Ms. Out). Suppose that Mr. In's reservation price is $300 and Ms. Out's reservation price is $500.

We need to find a Pareto improvement—a way to make Mr. In and Ms. Out better off without hurting anyone else. But there is an easy way to do this: just let Mr. In sublet his apartment to Ms. Out. It is worth $500 to Ms. Out to live close to the university, but it is only worth $300 to Mr. In. If Ms. Out pays Mr. In $400, say, and trades apartments, they will both be better off: Ms. Out will get an apartment that she values at more than $400, and Mr. In will get $400 that he values more than an inner-ring apartment.

This example shows that the rent-controlled market will generally not result in a Pareto efficient allocation, since there will still be some trades that could be carried out after the market has operated. As long as some people get inner-ring apartments who value them less highly than people who don't get them, there will be gains to be had from trade.

1.11 Equilibrium in the Long Run

We have analyzed the equilibrium pricing of apartments in the **short run**—when there is a fixed supply of apartments. But in the **long run** the supply of apartments can change. Just as the demand curve measures the number of apartments that will be demanded at different prices, the supply curve measures the number of apartments that will be supplied at different prices.

The final determination of the market price for apartments will depend on the interaction of supply and demand.

And what is it that determines the supply behavior? In general, the number of new apartments that will be supplied by the private market will depend on how profitable it is to provide apartments, which depends, in part, on the price that landlords can charge for apartments. In order to analyze the behavior of the apartment market in the long run, we have to examine the behavior of suppliers as well as demanders, a task we will eventually undertake.

When supply is variable, we can ask questions not only about who gets the apartments, but about how many will be provided by various types of market institutions. Will a monopolist supply more or fewer apartments than a competitive market? Will rent control increase or decrease the equilibrium number of apartments? Which institutions will provide a Pareto efficient number of apartments? In order to answer these and similar questions we must develop more systematic and powerful tools for economic analysis.

Summary

1. Economics proceeds by making models of social phenomena, which are simplified representations of reality.

2. In this task, economists are guided by the optimization principle, which states that people typically try to choose what's best for them, and by the equilibrium principle, which says that prices will adjust until demand and supply are equal.

3. The demand curve measures how much people wish to demand at each price, and the supply curve measures how much people wish to supply at each price. An equilibrium price is one where the amount demanded equals the amount supplied.

4. The study of how the equilibrium price and quantity change when the underlying conditions change is known as comparative statics.

5. An economic situation is Pareto efficient if there is no way to make some group of people better off without making some other group of people worse off. The concept of Pareto efficiency can be used to evaluate different ways of allocating resources.

REVIEW QUESTIONS

1. Suppose that there were 25 people who had a reservation price of $500, and the 26th person had a reservation price of $200. What would the demand curve look like?

2. In the above example, what would the equilibrium price be if there were 24 apartments to rent? What if there were 26 apartments to rent? What if there were 25 apartments to rent?

3. If people have different reservation prices, why does the market demand curve slope down?

4. In the text we assumed that the condominium purchasers came from the inner-ring people—people who were already renting apartments. What would happen to the price of inner-ring apartments if all of the condominium purchasers were outer-ring people—the people who were not currently renting apartments in the inner ring?

5. Suppose now that the condominium purchasers were all inner-ring people, but that each condominium was constructed from two apartments. What would happen to the price of apartments?

6. What do you suppose the effect of a tax would be on the number of apartments that would be built in the long run?

7. Suppose the demand curve is $D(p) = 100 - 2p$. What price would the monopolist set if he had 60 apartments? How many would he rent? What price would he set if he had 40 apartments? How many would he rent?

8. If our model of rent control allowed for unrestricted subletting, who would end up getting apartments in the inner circle? Would the outcome be Pareto efficient?

CHAPTER **2**

BUDGET CONSTRAINT

The economic theory of the consumer is very simple: economists assume that consumers choose the best bundle of goods they can afford. To give content to this theory, we have to describe more precisely what we mean by "best" and what we mean by "can afford." In this chapter we will examine how to describe what a consumer can afford; the next chapter will focus on the concept of how the consumer determines what is best. We will then be able to undertake a detailed study of the implications of this simple model of consumer behavior.

2.1 The Budget Constraint

We begin by examining the concept of the **budget constraint**. Suppose that there is some set of goods from which the consumer can choose. In real life there are many goods to consume, but for our purposes it is convenient to consider only the case of two goods, since we can then depict the consumer's choice behavior graphically.

We will indicate the consumer's **consumption bundle** by (x_1, x_2). This is simply a list of two numbers that tells us how much the consumer is choosing to consume of good 1, x_1, and how much the consumer is choosing to consume of good 2, x_2. Sometimes it is convenient to denote the consumer's bundle by a single symbol like X, where X is simply an abbreviation for the list of two numbers (x_1, x_2).

We suppose that we can observe the prices of the two goods, (p_1, p_2), and the amount of money the consumer has to spend, m. Then the budget constraint of the consumer can be written as

$$p_1 x_1 + p_2 x_2 \leq m. \qquad (2.1)$$

Here $p_1 x_1$ is the amount of money the consumer is spending on good 1, and $p_2 x_2$ is the amount of money the consumer is spending on good 2. The budget constraint of the consumer requires that the amount of money spent on the two goods be no more than the total amount the consumer has to spend. The consumer's *affordable* consumption bundles are those that don't cost any more than m. We call this set of affordable consumption bundles at prices (p_1, p_2) and income m the **budget set** of the consumer.

2.2 Two Goods Are Often Enough

The two-good assumption is more general than you might think at first, since we can often interpret one of the goods as representing everything else the consumer might want to consume.

For example, if we are interested in studying a consumer's demand for milk, we might let x_1 measure his or her consumption of milk in quarts per month. We can then let x_2 stand for everything else the consumer might want to consume.

When we adopt this interpretation, it is convenient to think of good 2 as being the dollars that the consumer can use to spend on other goods. Under this interpretation the price of good 2 will automatically be 1, since the price of one dollar is one dollar. Thus the budget constraint will take the form

$$p_1 x_1 + x_2 \leq m. \qquad (2.2)$$

This expression simply says that the amount of money spent on good 1, $p_1 x_1$, plus the amount of money spent on all other goods, x_2, must be no more than the total amount of money the consumer has to spend, m.

We say that good 2 represents a **composite good** that stands for everything else that the consumer might want to consume other than good 1. Such a composite good is invariably measured in dollars to be spent on goods other than good 1. As far as the algebraic form of the budget constraint is concerned, equation (2.2) is just a special case of the formula given in equation (2.1), with $p_2 = 1$, so everything that we have to say about the budget constraint in general will hold under the composite-good interpretation.

2.3 Properties of the Budget Set

The **budget line** is the set of bundles that cost exactly m:

$$p_1 x_1 + p_2 x_2 = m. \tag{2.3}$$

These are the bundles of goods that just exhaust the consumer's income.

The budget set is depicted in Figure 2.1. The heavy line is the budget line—the bundles that cost exactly m—and the bundles below this line are those that cost strictly less than m.

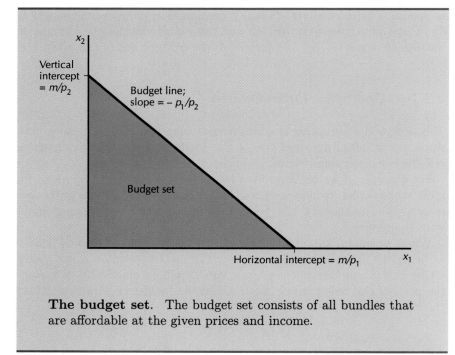

Figure
2.1
The budget set. The budget set consists of all bundles that are affordable at the given prices and income.

We can rearrange the budget line in equation (2.3) to give us the formula

$$x_2 = \frac{m}{p_2} - \frac{p_1}{p_2} x_1. \tag{2.4}$$

This is the formula for a straight line with a vertical intercept of m/p_2 and a slope of $-p_1/p_2$. The formula tells us how many units of good 2 the consumer needs to consume in order to just satisfy the budget constraint if she is consuming x_1 units of good 1.

Here is an easy way to draw a budget line given prices (p_1, p_2) and income m. Just ask yourself how much of good 2 the consumer could buy if she spent all of her money on good 2. The answer is, of course, m/p_2. Then ask how much of good 1 the consumer could buy if she spent all of her money on good 1. The answer is m/p_1. Thus the horizontal and vertical intercepts measure how much the consumer could get if she spent all of her money on goods 1 and 2, respectively. In order to depict the budget line just plot these two points on the appropriate axes of the graph and connect them with a straight line.

The slope of the budget line has a nice economic interpretation. It measures the rate at which the market is willing to "substitute" good 1 for good 2. Suppose for example that the consumer is going to increase her consumption of good 1 by Δx_1.[1] How much will her consumption of good 2 have to change in order to satisfy her budget constraint? Let us use Δx_2 to indicate her change in the consumption of good 2.

Now note that if she satisfies her budget constraint before and after making the change she must satisfy

$$p_1 x_1 + p_2 x_2 = m$$

and

$$p_1(x_1 + \Delta x_1) + p_2(x_2 + \Delta x_2) = m.$$

Subtracting the first equation from the second gives

$$p_1 \Delta x_1 + p_2 \Delta x_2 = 0.$$

This says that the total value of the change in her consumption must be zero. Solving for $\Delta x_2 / \Delta x_1$, the rate at which good 2 can be substituted for good 1 while still satisfying the budget constraint, gives

$$\frac{\Delta x_2}{\Delta x_1} = -\frac{p_1}{p_2}.$$

This is just the slope of the budget line. The negative sign is there since Δx_1 and Δx_2 must always have opposite signs. If you consume more of good 1, you have to consume less of good 2 and vice versa if you continue to satisfy the budget constraint.

Economists sometimes say that the slope of the budget line measures the **opportunity cost** of consuming good 1. In order to consume more of good 1 you have to give up some consumption of good 2. Giving up the opportunity to consume good 2 is the true economic cost of more good 1 consumption; and that cost is measured by the slope of the budget line.

---

[1] The Greek letter Δ, delta, is pronounced "del-ta." The notation Δx_1 denotes the change in good 1. For more on changes and rates of changes, see the Mathematical Appendix.

2.4 How the Budget Line Changes

When prices and incomes change, the set of goods that a consumer can afford changes as well. How do these changes affect the budget set?

Let us first consider changes in income. It is easy to see from equation (2.4) that an increase in income will increase the vertical intercept and not affect the slope of the line. Thus an increase in income will result in a *parallel shift outward* of the budget line as in Figure 2.2. Similarly, a decrease in income will cause a parallel shift inward.

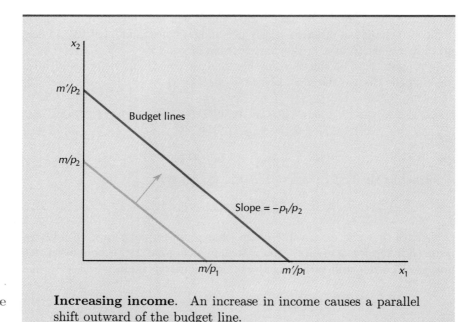

Figure
2.2

Increasing income. An increase in income causes a parallel shift outward of the budget line.

What about changes in prices? Let us first consider increasing price 1 while holding price 2 and income fixed. According to equation (2.4), increasing p_1 will not change the vertical intercept, but it will make the budget line steeper since p_1/p_2 will become larger.

Another way to see how the budget line changes is to use the trick described earlier for drawing the budget line. If you are spending all of your money on good 2, then increasing the price of good 1 doesn't change the maximum amount of good 2 you could buy—thus the vertical intercept of the budget line doesn't change. But if you are spending all of your money on good 1, and good 1 becomes more expensive, then your consumption of good 1 must decrease. Thus the horizontal intercept of the budget line must shift inward, resulting in the tilt depicted in Figure 2.3.

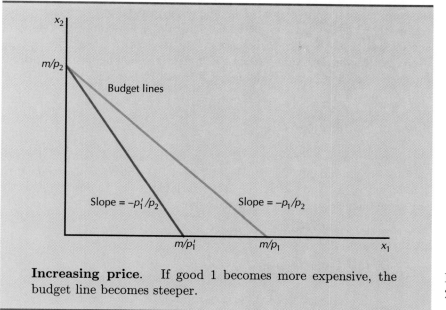

x_2

m/p_2

Budget lines

Slope = $-p_1'/p_2$

Slope = $-p_1/p_2$

m/p_1'

m/p_1

x_1

Increasing price.   If good 1 becomes more expensive, the budget line becomes steeper.

Figure 2.3

What happens to the budget line when we change the prices of good 1 and good 2 at the same time? Suppose for example that we double the prices of both goods 1 and 2. In this case both the horizontal and vertical intercepts shift inward by a factor of one-half, and therefore the budget line shifts inward by one-half as well. Multiplying both prices by two is just like dividing income by 2.

We can also see this algebraically. Suppose our original budget line is

$$p_1 x_1 + p_2 x_2 = m.$$

Now suppose that both prices become t times as large. Multiplying both prices by t yields

$$t p_1 x_1 + t p_2 x_2 = m.$$

But this equation is the same as

$$p_1 x_1 + p_2 x_2 = \frac{m}{t}.$$

Thus multiplying both prices by a constant amount t is just like dividing income by the same constant t. It follows that if we multiply both prices by t *and* we multiply income by t, then the budget line won't change at all.

We can also consider price and income changes together. What happens if both prices go up and income goes down? Think about what happens to the horizontal and vertical intercepts. If m decreases and p_1 and p_2 both increase, then the intercepts m/p_1 and m/p_2 must both decrease. This means that the budget line will shift inward. What about the slope of the budget line? If price 2 increases more than price 1, so that $-p_1/p_2$ decreases (in absolute value), then the budget line will be flatter; if price 2 increases less than price 1, the budget line will be steeper.

2.5 The Numeraire

The budget line is defined by two prices and one income, but one of these variables is redundant. We could peg one of the prices, or the income, to some fixed value, and adjust the other variables so as to describe exactly the same budget set. Thus the budget line

$$p_1 x_1 + p_2 x_2 = m$$

is exactly the same budget line as

$$\frac{p_1}{p_2} x_1 + x_2 = \frac{m}{p_2}$$

or

$$\frac{p_1}{m} x_1 + \frac{p_2}{m} x_2 = 1,$$

since the first budget line results from dividing everything by p_2, and the second budget line results from dividing everything by m. In the first case, we have pegged $p_2 = 1$, and in the second case, we have pegged $m = 1$. Pegging the price of one of the goods or income to 1 and adjusting the other price and income appropriately doesn't change the budget set at all.

When we set one of the prices to 1, as we did above, we often refer to that price as the **numeraire** price. The numeraire price is the price relative to which we are measuring the other price and income. It will occasionally be convenient to think of one of the goods as being a numeraire good, since there will then be one less price to worry about.

2.6 Taxes, Subsidies, and Rationing

Economic policy often uses tools that affect a consumer's budget constraint, such as taxes. For example, if the government imposes a **quantity tax**, this means that the consumer has to pay a certain amount to the government for each unit of the good he purchases. In the U.S., for example, we pay about 15 cents a gallon as a federal gasoline tax.

How does a quantity tax affect the budget line of a consumer? From the viewpoint of the consumer the tax is just like a higher price. Thus a quantity tax of t dollars per unit of good 1 simply changes the price of good 1 from p_1 to $p_1 + t$. As we've seen above, this implies that the budget line must get steeper.

Another kind of tax is a **value** tax. As the name implies this is a tax on the value—the price—of a good, rather than the quantity purchased of a good. A value tax is usually expressed in percentage terms. Most states in the U.S. have sales taxes. If the sales tax is 6 percent, then a good that is priced at \$1 will actually sell for \$1.06. (Value taxes are also known as **ad valorem** taxes.)

If good 1 has a price of p_1 but is subject to a sales tax at rate τ, then the actual price facing the consumer is $(1 + \tau)p_1$.[2] The consumer has to pay p_1 to the supplier and τp_1 to the government for each unit of the good so the total cost of the good to the consumer is $(1 + \tau)p_1$.

A **subsidy** is the opposite of a tax. In the case of a **quantity subsidy**, the government *gives* an amount to the consumer that depends on the amount of the good purchased. If, for example, the consumption of milk were subsidized, the government would pay some amount of money to each consumer of milk depending on the amount that consumer purchased. If the subsidy is s dollars per unit of consumption of good 1, then from the viewpoint of the consumer, the price of good 1 would be $p_1 - s$. This would therefore make the budget line flatter.

Similarly an ad valorem subsidy is a subsidy based on the price of the good being subsidized. If the government gives you back \$1 for every \$2 you donate to charity, then your donations to charity are being subsidized at a rate of 50 percent. In general, if the price of good 1 is p_1 and good 1 is subject to an ad valorem subsidy at rate σ, then the actual price of good 1 facing the consumer is $(1 - \sigma)p_1$.[3]

You can see that taxes and subsidies affect prices in exactly the same way except for the algebraic sign: a tax increases the price to the consumer, and a subsidy decreases it.

Another kind of tax or subsidy that the government might use is a **lump-sum** tax or subsidy. In the case of a tax, this means that the government takes away some fixed amount of money, regardless of the individual's behavior. Thus a lump-sum tax means that the budget line of a consumer will shift inward because his money income has been reduced. Similarly, a lump-sum subsidy means that the budget line will shift outward. Quantity taxes and value taxes tilt the budget line one way or the other depending

---

[2] The Greek letter τ, tau, rhymes with "wow."

[3] The Greek letter σ is pronounced "sig-ma."

on which good is being taxed, but a lump-sum tax shifts the budget line inward.

Governments also sometimes impose *rationing* constraints. This means that the level of consumption of some good is fixed to be no larger than some amount. For example, during World War II the U.S. government rationed certain foods like butter and meat.

Suppose, for example, that good 1 were rationed so that no more than $\overline{x}_1$ could be consumed by a given consumer. Then the budget set of the consumer would look like that depicted in Figure 2.4: it would be the old budget set with a piece lopped off. The lopped-off piece consists of all the consumption bundles that are affordable but have $x_1 > \overline{x}_1$.

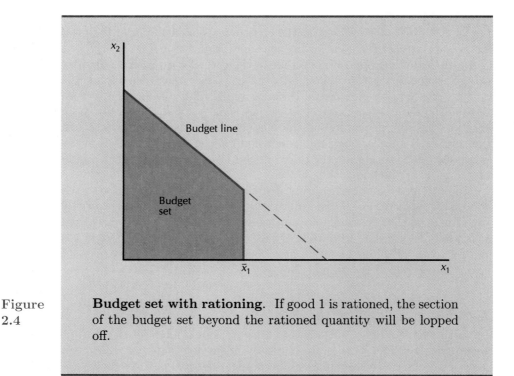

Figure
2.4

Budget set with rationing. If good 1 is rationed, the section of the budget set beyond the rationed quantity will be lopped off.

Sometimes taxes, subsidies, and rationing are combined. For example, we could consider a situation where a consumer could consume good 1 at a price of p_1 up to some level $\overline{x}_1$, and then had to pay a tax t on all consumption in excess of $\overline{x}_1$. The budget set for this consumer is depicted in Figure 2.5. Here the budget line has a slope of $-p_1/p_2$ to the left of $\overline{x}_1$, and a slope of $-(p_1 + t)/p_2$ to the right of $\overline{x}_1$.

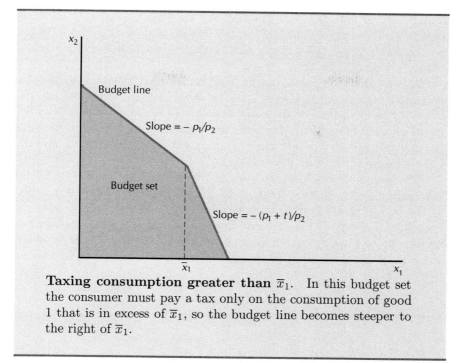

Taxing consumption greater than $\bar{x}_1$. In this budget set
the consumer must pay a tax only on the consumption of good
1 that is in excess of $\bar{x}_1$, so the budget line becomes steeper to
the right of $\bar{x}_1$.

Figure
2.5

EXAMPLE: The Food Stamp Program

Since the Food Stamp Act of 1964 the U.S. federal government has provided
a subsidy on food for poor people. The details of this program have been
adjusted several times. Here we will describe the economic effects of one
of these adjustments.

Before 1979, households who met certain eligibility requirements were
allowed to purchase food stamps, which could then be used to purchase food
at retail outlets. In January 1975, for example, a family of four could receive
a maximum monthly allotment of $153 in food coupons by participating in
the program.

The price of these coupons to the household depended on the household
income. A family of four with an adjusted monthly income of $300 paid
$83 for the full monthly allotment of food stamps. If a family of four had
a monthly income of $100, the cost for the full monthly allotment would
have been $25.[4]

The pre-1979 Food Stamp program was an ad valorem subsidy on food.
The rate at which food was subsidized depended on the household income.

---

[4] These figures are taken from Kenneth Clarkson, *Food Stamps and Nutrition*, American Enterprise Institute, 1975.

The family of four that was charged $83 for their allotment paid $1 to receive $1.84 worth of food (1.84 equals 153 divided by 83). Similarly, the household that paid $25 was paying $1 to receive $6.12 worth of food (6.12 equals 153 divided by 25).

The way that the Food Stamp program affected the budget set of a household is depicted in Figure 2.6A. Here we have measured the amount of money spent on food on the horizontal axis and expenditures on all other goods on the vertical axis. Since we are measuring each good in terms of the money spent on it, the "price" of each good is automatically 1, and the budget line will therefore have a slope of −1.

If the household is allowed to buy $153 of food stamps for $25, then this represents roughly an 84 percent (= 1 − 25/153) subsidy of food purchases, so the budget line will have a slope of roughly −.16 (= 25/153) until the household has spent $153 on food. Each dollar that the household spends on food up to $153 would reduce its consumption of other goods by about 16 cents. After the household spends $153 on food, the budget line facing it would again have a slope of −1.

Figure 2.6

Food stamps. How the budget line is affected by the Food Stamp program. Part A shows the pre-1979 program and part B the post-1979 program.

These effects lead to the kind of "kink" depicted in Figure 2.6. Households with higher incomes had to pay more for their allotment of food stamps. Thus the slope of the budget line would become steeper as household income increased.

In 1979 the Food Stamp program was modified. Instead of requiring that households purchase food stamps, they are now simply given to qualified households. Figure 2.6B shows how this affects the budget set.

Suppose that a household now receives a grant of $200 of food stamps a month. Then this means that the household can consume $200 more food per month, regardless of how much it is spending on other goods, which implies that the budget line will shift to the right by $200. The slope will not change: $1 less spent on food would mean $1 more to spend on other things. But since the household cannot legally sell food stamps, the maximum amount that it can spend on other goods does not change. The Food Stamp program is effectively a lump-sum subsidy, except for the fact that the food stamps can't be sold.

2.7 Budget Line Changes

In the next chapter we will analyze how the consumer chooses an optimal consumption bundle from his or her budget set. But we can already state some observations here that follow from what we have learned about the movements of the budget line.

First, we can observe that since the budget set doesn't change when we multiply all prices and income by a positive number, the optimal choice of the consumer from the budget set can't change either. Without even analyzing the choice process itself, we have derived an important conclusion: a perfectly balanced inflation—one in which all prices and all incomes rise at the same rate—doesn't change anybody's budget set, and thus cannot change anybody's optimal choice.

Second, we can make some statements about how well-off the consumer can be at different prices and incomes. Suppose that the consumer's income increases and all prices remain the same. We know that this represents a parallel shift outward of the budget line. Thus every bundle the consumer was consuming at the lower income is also a possible choice at the higher income. But then the consumer must be at least as well-off at the higher income as at the lower income—since he or she has the same choices available as before plus some more. Similarly, if one price declines and all others stay the same, the consumer must be at least as well-off. This simple observation will be of considerable use later on.

Summary

1. The budget set consists of all bundles of goods that the consumer can afford at given prices and income. We will typically assume that there are only two goods, but this assumption is more general than it seems.

2. The budget line is written as $p_1x_1 + p_2x_2 = m$. It has a slope of $-p_1/p_2$, a vertical intercept of m/p_2, and a horizontal intercept of m/p_1.

3. Increasing income shifts the budget line outward. Increasing the price of good 1 makes the budget line steeper. Increasing the price of good 2 makes the budget line flatter.

4. Taxes, subsidies, and rationing change the slope and position of the budget line by changing the prices paid by the consumer.

REVIEW QUESTIONS

1. Originally the consumer faces the budget line $p_1x_1 + p_2x_2 = m$. Then the price of good 1 doubles, the price of good 2 becomes 8 times larger, and income becomes 4 times larger. Write down an equation for the new budget line in terms of the original prices and income.

2. What happens to the budget line if the price of good 2 increases, but the price of good 1 and income remain constant?

3. If the price of good 1 doubles and the price of good 2 triples, does the budget line become flatter or steeper?

4. What is the definition of a numeraire good?

5. Suppose that the government puts a tax of 15 cents a gallon on gasoline and then later decides to put a subsidy on gasoline at a rate of 7 cents a gallon. What net tax is this combination equivalent to?

6. Suppose that a budget equation is given by $p_1x_1 + p_2x_2 = m$. The government decides to impose a lump-sum tax of u, a quantity tax on good 1 of t, and a quantity subsidy on good 2 of s. What is the formula for the new budget line?

7. If the income of the consumer increases and one of the prices decreases at the same time, will the consumer necessarily be at least as well-off?

CHAPTER **3**

PREFERENCES

We saw in Chapter 2 that the economic model of consumer behavior is very simple: people choose the best things they can afford. The last chapter was devoted to clarifying the meaning of "can afford," and this chapter will be devoted to clarifying the economic concept of "best things."

We call the objects of consumer choice **consumption bundles**. This is a complete list of the goods and services that are involved in the choice problem that we are investigating. The word "complete" deserves emphasis: when you analyze a consumer's choice problem, make sure that you include all of the appropriate goods in the definition of the consumption bundle.

If we are analyzing consumer choice at the broadest level, we would want not only a complete list of the goods that a consumer might consume, but also a description of when, where, and under what circumstances they would become available. After all, people care about how much food they will have tomorrow as well as how much food they have today. A raft in the middle of the Atlantic Ocean is very different from a raft in the middle of the Sahara Desert. And an umbrella when it is raining is quite a different good from an umbrella on a sunny day. It is often useful to think of the "same" good available in different locations or circumstances as a different good, since the consumer may value the good differently in those situations.

However, when we limit our attention to a simple choice problem, the relevant goods are usually pretty obvious. We'll often adopt the idea described earlier of using just two goods and calling one of them "all other goods" so that we can focus on the tradeoff between one good and everything else. In this way we can consider consumption choices involving many goods and still use two-dimensional diagrams.

So let us take our consumption bundle to consist of two goods, and let x_1 denote the amount of one good and x_2 the amount of the other. The complete consumption bundle is therefore denoted by (x_1, x_2). As noted before, we will occasionally abbreviate this consumption bundle by X.

3.1 Consumer Preferences

We will suppose that given any two consumption bundles, (x_1, x_2) and (y_1, y_2), the consumer can rank them as to their desirability. That is, the consumer can determine that one of the consumption bundles is strictly better than the other, or decide that she is indifferent between the two bundles.

We will use the symbol $\succ$ to mean that one bundle is **strictly preferred** to another, so that $(x_1, x_2) \succ (y_1, y_2)$ should be interpreted as saying that the consumer **strictly prefers** (x_1, x_2) to (y_1, y_2), in the sense that she definitely wants the x-bundle rather than the y-bundle. This preference relation is meant to be an operational notion. If the consumer prefers one bundle to another, it means that he or she would choose one over the other, given the opportunity. Thus the idea of preference is based on the consumer's *behavior*. In order to tell whether one bundle is preferred to another, we see how the consumer behaves in choice situations involving the two bundles. If she always chooses (x_1, x_2) when (y_1, y_2) is available, then it is natural to say that this consumer prefers (x_1, x_2) to (y_1, y_2).

If the consumer is **indifferent** between two bundles of goods, we use the symbol $\sim$ and write $(x_1, x_2) \sim (y_1, y_2)$. Indifference means that the consumer would be just as satisfied, according to her own preferences, consuming the bundle (x_1, x_2) as she would be consuming the other bundle, (y_1, y_2).

If the consumer prefers or is indifferent between the two bundles we say that she **weakly prefers** (x_1, x_2) to (y_1, y_2) and write $(x_1, x_2) \succeq (y_1, y_2)$.

These relations of strict preference, weak preference, and indifference are not independent concepts; the relations are themselves related! For example, if $(x_1, x_2) \succeq (y_1, y_2)$ and $(y_1, y_2) \succeq (x_1, x_2)$ we can conclude that $(x_1, x_2) \sim (y_1, y_2)$. That is, if the consumer thinks that (x_1, x_2) is at least as good as (y_1, y_2) *and* that (y_1, y_2) is at least as good as (x_1, x_2), then the consumer must be indifferent between the two bundles of goods.

Similarly, if $(x_1, x_2) \succeq (y_1, y_2)$ but we know that it is *not* the case that $(x_1, x_2) \sim (y_1, y_2)$, we can conclude that we must have $(x_1, x_2) \succ (y_1, y_2)$. This just says that if the consumer thinks that (x_1, x_2) is at least as good as (y_1, y_2), and she is not indifferent between the two bundles, then it must be that she thinks that (x_1, x_2) is strictly better than (y_1, y_2).

3.2 Assumptions about Preferences

Economists usually make some assumptions about the "consistency" of consumers' preferences. For example, it seems unreasonable—not to say contradictory—to have a situation where $(x_1, x_2) \succ (y_1, y_2)$ and, at the same time, $(y_1, y_2) \succ (x_1, x_2)$. For this would mean that the consumer strictly prefers the x-bundle to the y-bundle ... and vice versa.

So we usually make some assumptions about how the preference relations work. Some of the assumptions about preferences are so fundamental that we can refer to them as "axioms" of consumer theory. Here are three such axioms about consumer preference.

Complete. We assume that any two bundles can be compared. That is, given any x-bundle and any y-bundle, we assume that $(x_1, x_2) \succeq (y_1, y_2)$, or $(y_1, y_2) \succeq (x_1, x_2)$, or both, in which case the consumer is indifferent between the two bundles.

Reflexive. We assume that any bundle is at least as good as itself: $(x_1, x_2) \succeq (x_1, x_2)$.

Transitive. If $(x_1, x_2) \succeq (y_1, y_2)$ and $(y_1, y_2) \succeq (z_1, z_2)$, then we assume that $(x_1, x_2) \succeq (z_1, z_2)$. In other words, if the consumer thinks that X is at least as good as Y and that Y is at least as good as Z, then the consumer thinks that X is at least as good as Z.

The first axiom, completeness, is hardly objectionable, at least for the kinds of choices economists generally examine. To say that any two bundles can be compared is simply to say that the consumer is able to make a choice between any two given bundles. One might imagine extreme situations involving life or death choices where ranking the alternatives might be difficult, or even impossible, but these choices are, for the most part, outside the domain of economic analysis.

The second axiom, reflexivity, is trivial. Any bundle is certainly at least as good as an identical bundle. Parents of small children may occasionally observe behavior that violates this assumption, but it seems plausible for most adult behavior.

The third axiom, transitivity, is more problematic. It isn't clear that transitivity of preferences is *necessarily* a property that preferences would have to have. The assumption that preferences are transitive doesn't seem compelling on grounds of pure logic alone. In fact it's not. Transitivity is a hypothesis about people's choice behavior, not a statement of pure logic. Whether it is a basic fact of logic or not isn't the point: it is whether or not it is a reasonably accurate description of how people behave that matters.

What would you think about a person who said that he preferred a bundle X to Y, and preferred Y to Z, but then also said that he preferred Z to X? This would certainly be taken as evidence of peculiar behavior.

More importantly, how would this consumer behave if faced with choices among the three bundles X, Y, and Z? If we asked him to choose his most preferred bundle, he would have quite a problem, for whatever bundle he chose, there would always be one that was preferred to it. If we are to have a theory where people are making "best" choices, preferences must satisfy the transitivity axiom or something very much like it. If preferences were not transitive there could well be a set of bundles for which there is no best choice.

3.3 Indifference Curves

It turns out that the whole theory of consumer choice can be formulated in terms of preferences that satisfy the three axioms described above, plus a few more technical assumptions. However, we will find it convenient to describe preferences graphically by using a construction known as **indifference curves**.

Consider Figure 3.1 where we have illustrated two axes representing a consumer's consumption of goods 1 and 2. Let us pick a certain consumption bundle (x_1, x_2) and shade in all of the consumption bundles that are weakly preferred to (x_1, x_2). This is called the **weakly preferred set**. The bundles on the boundary of this set—the bundles for which the consumer is just indifferent to (x_1, x_2)—form the **indifference curve**.

We can draw an indifference curve through any consumption bundle we want. The indifference curve through a consumption bundle consists of all bundles of goods that leave the consumer indifferent to the given bundle.

One problem with using indifference curves to describe preferences is that they only show you the bundles that the consumer perceives as being indifferent to each other—they don't show you which bundles are better and which bundles are worse. It is sometimes useful to draw small arrows on the indifference curves to indicate the direction of the preferred bundles. We won't do this in every case, but we will do it in a few of the examples where confusion might arise.

If we make no further assumptions about preferences, indifference curves can take very peculiar shapes indeed. But even at this level of generality, we can state an important principle about indifference curves: *indifference curves representing distinct levels of preference cannot cross*. That is, the situation depicted in Figure 3.2 cannot occur.

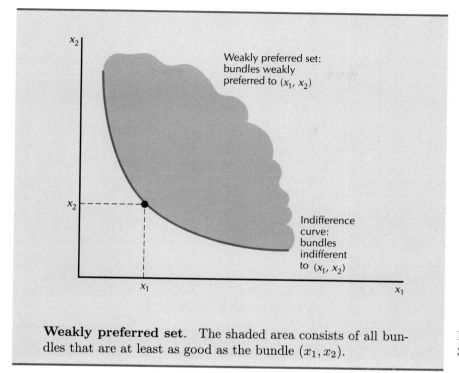

Figure
3.1

Weakly preferred set. The shaded area consists of all bundles that are at least as good as the bundle (x_1, x_2).

In order to prove this, let us choose three bundles of goods, X, Y, and Z, such that X lies only on one indifference curve, Y lies only on the other indifference curve, and Z lies at the intersection of the indifference curves. By assumption the indifference curves represent distinct levels of preference, so one of the bundles, say X, is strictly preferred to the other bundle, Y. We know that $X \sim Z$ and $Z \sim Y$, and the axiom of transitivity therefore implies that $X \sim Y$. But this contradicts the assumption that $X \succ Y$. This contradiction establishes the result—indifference curves representing distinct levels of preference cannot cross.

What other properties do indifference curves have? In the abstract, the answer is: not many. Indifference curves are a way to describe preferences. Nearly any "reasonable" preferences that you can think of can be depicted by indifference curves. The trick is to learn what kinds of preferences give rise to what shapes of indifference curves.

3.4 Examples of Preferences

Let us try to relate preferences to indifference curves through some examples. We'll describe some preferences and then see what the indifference curves that represent them look like.

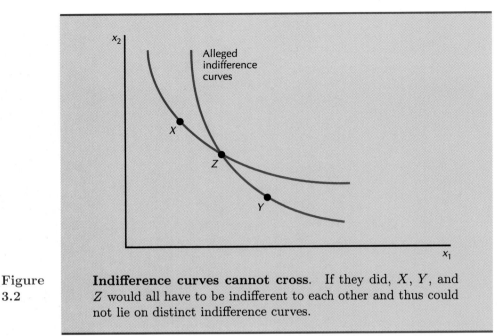

Figure
3.2

Indifference curves cannot cross. If they did, X, Y, and Z would all have to be indifferent to each other and thus could not lie on distinct indifference curves.

There is a general procedure for constructing indifference curves given a "verbal" description of the preferences. First plop your pencil down on the graph at some consumption bundle (x_1, x_2). Now think about giving a little more of good 1, Δx_1, to the consumer, moving him to $(x_1 + \Delta x_1, x_2)$. Now ask yourself how would you have to *change* the consumption of x_2 to make the consumer indifferent to the original consumption point? Call this change Δx_2. Ask yourself the question "For a given change in good 1, how does good 2 have to change to make the consumer just indifferent between $(x_1 + \Delta x_1, x_2 + \Delta x_2)$ and (x_1, x_2)?" Once you have determined this movement at one consumption bundle you have drawn a piece of the indifference curve. Now try it at another bundle, and so on, until you develop a clear picture of the overall shape of the indifference curves.

Perfect Substitutes

Two goods are **perfect substitutes** if the consumer is willing to substitute one good for the other at a *constant* rate. The simplest case of perfect substitutes occurs when the consumer is willing to substitute the goods on a one-to-one basis.

Suppose, for example, that we are considering a choice between red pencils and blue pencils, and the consumer involved likes pencils, but doesn't care about color at all. Pick a consumption bundle, say $(10, 10)$. Then for this consumer, any other consumption bundle that has 20 pencils in it is just as good as $(10, 10)$. Mathematically speaking, any consumption bundle (x_1, x_2) such that $x_1 + x_2 = 20$ will be on this consumer's indifference curve through $(10, 10)$. Thus the indifference curves for this consumer are all parallel straight lines with a slope of -1, as depicted in Figure 3.3. Bundles with more total pencils are preferred to bundles with fewer total pencils, so the direction of increasing preference is up and to the right, as illustrated in Figure 3.3.

How does this work in terms of general procedure for drawing indifference curves? If we are at $(10, 10)$, and we increase the amount of the first good by one unit to 11, how much do we have to change the second good to get back to the original indifference curve? The answer is clearly that we have to decrease the second good by 1 unit. Thus the indifference curve through $(10, 10)$ has a slope of -1. The same procedure can be carried out at any bundle of goods with the same results—in this case all the indifference curves have a constant slope of -1.

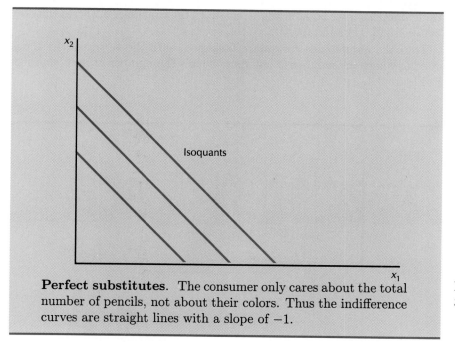

Perfect substitutes. The consumer only cares about the total number of pencils, not about their colors. Thus the indifference curves are straight lines with a slope of -1.

Figure 3.3

The important fact about perfect substitutes is that the indifference curves have a *constant* slope. Suppose, for example, that we graphed blue pencils on the vertical axis and *pairs* of red pencils on the horizontal axis. The indifference curves for these two goods would have a slope of -2, since the consumer would be willing to give up two blue pencils to get one more *pair* of red pencils.

In the textbook we'll primarily consider the case where goods are perfect substitutes on a one-for-one basis, and leave the treatment of the general case for the workbook.

Perfect Complements

Perfect complements are goods that are always consumed together in fixed proportions. In some sense the goods "complement" each other. A nice example is that of right shoes and left shoes. The consumer likes shoes, but always wears right and left shoes together. Having only one out of a pair of shoes doesn't do the consumer a bit of good.

Let us draw the indifference curves for perfect complements. Suppose we pick the consumption bundle $(10, 10)$. Now add 1 more right shoe, so we have $(11, 10)$. By assumption this leaves the consumer indifferent to the original position: the extra shoe doesn't do him any good. The same thing happens if we add one more left shoe: the consumer is also indifferent between $(10, 11)$ and $(10, 10)$.

Thus the indifference curves are L-shaped, with the vertex of the L occurring where the number of left shoes equals the number of right shoes as in Figure 3.4.

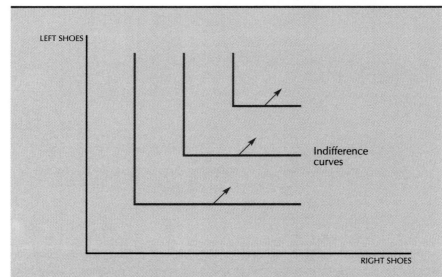

Figure
3.4

Perfect complements. The consumer always wants to consume the goods in fixed proportions to each other. Thus the indifference curves are L-shaped.

Increasing both the number of left shoes and the number of right shoes at the same time will move the consumer to a more preferred position, so the direction of increasing preference is again up and to the right, as illustrated in the diagram.

The important thing about perfect complements is that the consumer prefers to consume the goods in fixed proportions, not necessarily that the proportion is one-to-one. If a consumer always uses two teaspoons of sugar in her cup of tea, and doesn't use sugar for anything else, then the indifference curves will still be L-shaped. In this case the corners of the L will occur at (2 teaspoons sugar, 1 cup tea), (4 teaspoons sugar, 2 cups tea) and so on, rather than at (1 right shoe, 1 left shoe), (2 right shoes, 2 left shoes), and so on.

In the textbook we'll primarily consider the case where the goods are consumed in proportions of one-for-one and leave the treatment of the general case for the workbook.

Bads

A **bad** is a commodity that the consumer doesn't like. For example, suppose that the commodities in question are now pepperoni and anchovies—and the consumer loves pepperoni but dislikes anchovies. But let us suppose there is some possible tradeoff between pepperoni and anchovies. That is, there would be some amount of pepperoni on a pizza that would compensate the consumer for having to consume a given amount of anchovies. How could we represent these preferences using indifference curves?

Pick a bundle (x_1, x_2) consisting of some pepperoni and some anchovies. If we give the consumer more anchovies, what do we have to do with the pepperoni to keep him on the same indifference curve? Clearly, we have to give him some extra pepperoni to compensate him for having to put up with the anchovies. Thus this consumer must have indifference curves that slope up and to the right as depicted in Figure 3.5.

The direction of increasing preference is down and to the right—that is, toward the direction of decreased anchovy consumption and increased pepperoni consumption, just as the arrows in the diagram illustrate.

Neutrals

A good is a **neutral good** if the consumer doesn't care about it one way or the other. What if a consumer is just neutral about anchovies?[1] In this case his indifference curves will be vertical lines as depicted in Figure 3.6.

---

[1] Is anybody neutral about anchovies?

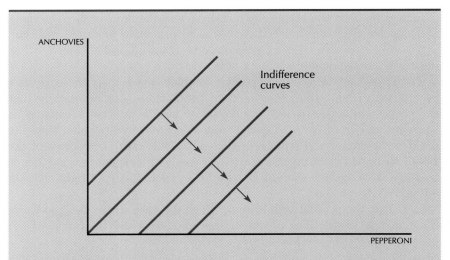

Figure
3.5

Bads. Here anchovies are a "bad," and pepperoni is a "good"
for this consumer. Thus the indifference curves have a positive
slope.

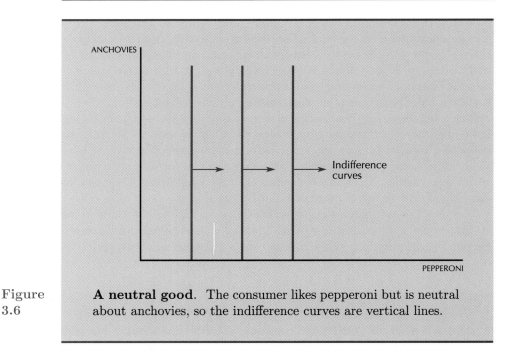

Figure
3.6

A neutral good. The consumer likes pepperoni but is neutral
about anchovies, so the indifference curves are vertical lines.

He only cares about the amount of pepperoni he has and doesn't care at
all about how many anchovies he has. The more pepperoni the better, but
adding more anchovies doesn't affect him one way or the other.

Satiation

We sometimes want to consider a situation involving **satiation**, where there is some overall best bundle for the consumer, and the "closer" he is to that best bundle, the better off he is in terms of his own preferences. For example, suppose that the consumer has some most preferred bundle of goods $(\overline{x}_1, \overline{x}_2)$, and the farther away he is from that bundle, the worse off he is. In this case we say that $(\overline{x}_1, \overline{x}_2)$ is a **satiation** point, or a **bliss** point. The indifference curves for the consumer look like those depicted in Figure 3.7. The best point is $(\overline{x}_1, \overline{x}_2)$ and points farther away from this bliss point lie on "lower" indifference curves.

Satiated preferences.   The bundle $(\overline{x}_1, \overline{x}_2)$ is the satiation point or bliss point, and the indifference curves surround this point.

Figure 3.7

In this case the indifference curves have a negative slope when the consumer has "too little" or "too much" of both goods, and a positive slope when he has "too much" of one of the goods. When he has too much of one of the goods, it becomes a bad—reducing the consumption of the bad good moves him closer to his "bliss point." If he has too much of both goods, they both are bads, so reducing the consumption of each moves him closer to the bliss point.

Suppose, for example, that the two goods are chocolate cake and ice cream. There might well be some optimal amount of chocolate cake and ice cream that you would want to eat per week. Any less than that amount would make you worse off, but any more than that amount would also make you worse off.

If you think about it, most goods are like chocolate cake and ice cream in this respect—you can have too much of nearly anything. But people would generally not voluntarily *choose* to have too much of the goods they consume. Why would you choose to have more than you want of something? Thus the interesting region from the viewpoint of economic choice is where you have *less* than you want of most goods. The choices that people actually care about are choices of this sort, and these are the choices with which we will be concerned.

Discrete Goods

Usually we think of measuring goods in units where fractional amounts make sense—you might on average consume 12.43 gallons of milk a month even though you buy it a quart at a time. But sometimes we want to examine preferences over goods that naturally come in discrete units.

For example, consider a consumer's demand for automobiles. We could define the demand for automobiles in terms of the time spent using an automobile, so that we would have a continuous variable, but for many purposes it is the actual number of cars demanded that is of interest.

There is no difficulty in using preferences to describe choice behavior for this kind of discrete good. Suppose that x_2 is money to be spent on other goods and x_1 is a **discrete good** that is only available in integer amounts. We have illustrated the appearance of indifference "curves" and a weakly preferred set for this kind of good in Figure 3.8. In this case the bundles indifferent to a given bundle will be a set of discrete points. The set of bundles at least as good as a particular bundle will be a set of line segments.

The choice of whether to emphasize the discrete nature of a good or not will depend on our application. If the consumer chooses only one or two units of the good during the time period of our analysis, recognizing the discrete nature of the choice may be important. But if the consumer is choosing 30 or 40 units of the good, then it will probably be convenient to think of this as a continuous good.

3.5 Well-Behaved Preferences

We've now seen some examples of indifference curves. As we've seen, many kinds of preferences, reasonable or unreasonable, can be described by these simple diagrams. But if we want to describe preferences in general, it will be convenient to focus on a few general shapes of indifference curves. In

A discrete good. Here good 1 is only available in integer amounts. In panel A the dashed lines connect together the bundles that are indifferent, and in panel B the vertical lines represent bundles that are at least as good as the indicated bundle.

Figure
3.8

this section we will describe some more general assumptions that we will typically make about preferences and the implications of these assumptions for the shapes of the associated indifference curves. These assumptions are not the only possible ones; in some situations you might want to use different assumptions. But we will take them as the defining features for **well-behaved indifference curves**.

First we will typically assume that more is better, that is, that we are talking about *goods*, not bads. More precisely, if (x_1, x_2) is a bundle of goods and (y_1, y_2) is a bundle of goods with at least as much of both goods and more of one, then $(y_1, y_2) \succ (x_1, x_2)$. This assumption is sometimes called **monotonicity** of preferences. As we suggested in our discussion of satiation, more is better would probably only hold up to a point. Thus the assumption of monotonicity is saying only that we are going to examine situations *before* that point is reached—before any satiation sets in—while more *still is* better. Economics would not be a very interesting subject in a world where everyone was satiated in their consumption of every good.

What does monotonicity imply about the shape of indifference curves? It implies that they have a *negative* slope. Consider Figure 3.9. If we start at a bundle (x_1, x_2) and move anywhere up and to the right, we must be moving to a preferred position. If we move down and to the left we must be moving to a worse position. So if we are moving to an *indifferent* position, we must be moving either left and up or right and down: the indifference curve must have a negative slope.

Second, we are going to assume that averages are preferred to extremes. That is, if we take two bundles of goods (x_1, x_2) and (y_1, y_2) on the same indifference curve and take a weighted average of the two bundles such as

$$\left(\frac{1}{2}x_1 + \frac{1}{2}y_1, \frac{1}{2}x_2 + \frac{1}{2}y_2\right),$$

then the average bundle will be at least as good as or strictly preferred to each of the two extreme bundles. This weighted-average bundle has the average amount of good 1 and the average amount of good 2 that is present in the two bundles. It therefore lies halfway along the straight line connecting the x–bundle and the y–bundle.

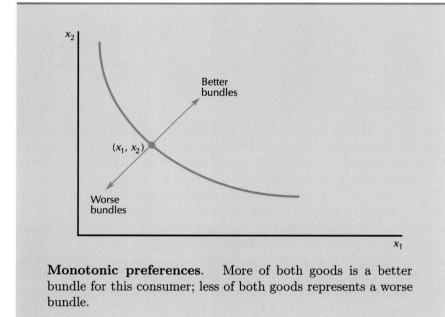

Figure
3.9

Monotonic preferences. More of both goods is a better bundle for this consumer; less of both goods represents a worse bundle.

Actually, we're going to assume this for any weight t between 0 and 1, not just $1/2$. Thus we are assuming that if $(x_1, x_2) \sim (y_1, y_2)$, then

$$(tx_1 + (1-t)y_1, tx_2 + (1-t)y_2) \succeq (x_1, x_2)$$

for any t such that $0 \leq t \leq 1$. This weighted average of the two bundles gives a weight of t to the x-bundle and a weight of $1 - t$ to the y-bundle. Therefore, the distance from the x-bundle to the average bundle is just a fraction t of the distance from the x-bundle to the y-bundle, along the straight line connecting the two bundles.

What does this assumption about preferences mean geometrically? It means that the set of bundles weakly preferred to (x_1, x_2) is a **convex set**. For suppose that (y_1, y_2) and (x_1, x_2) are indifferent bundles. Then, if averages are preferred to extremes, all of the weighted averages of (x_1, x_2) and (y_1, y_2) are weakly preferred to (x_1, x_2) and (y_1, y_2). A convex set has the property that if you take *any* two points in the set and draw the line segment connecting those two points, that line segment lies entirely in the set.

Figure 3.10A depicts an example of convex preferences, while Figures 3.10B and 3.10C show two examples of nonconvex preferences. Figure 3.10C presents preferences that are so nonconvex that we might want to call them "concave preferences."

Various kinds of preferences. Panel A depicts convex preferences, panel B depicts nonconvex preferences, and panel C depicts "concave" preferences.

Figure 3.10

Can you think of preferences that are not convex? One possibility might be something like my preferences for ice cream and olives. I like ice cream and I like olives ... but I don't like to have them together! In considering my consumption in the next hour, I might be indifferent between consuming 8 ounces of ice cream and 2 ounces of olives, or 8 ounces of olives and 2 ounces of ice cream. But either one of these bundles would be better than consuming 5 ounces of each! These are the kind of preferences depicted in Figure 3.10C.

Why do we want to assume that well-behaved preferences are convex? Because, for the most part, goods are consumed together. The kinds of preferences depicted in Figures 3.10B and 3.10C imply that the consumer would prefer to specialize, at least to some degree, and to consume only one of the goods. However, the normal case is where the consumer would want to trade some of one good for the other and end up consuming some of each, rather than specializing in consuming only one of the two goods.

In fact, if we look at my preferences for *monthly* consumption of ice cream and olives, rather than at my immediate consumption, they would tend to look much more like Figure 3.10A than Figure 3.10C. Each month I would prefer having some ice cream and some olives—albeit at different times—to specializing in consuming either one for the entire month.

Finally, one extension of the assumption of convexity is the assumption of **strict convexity**. This means that the weighted average of two indifferent bundles is *strictly* preferred to the two extreme bundles. Convex preferences may have flat spots, while *strictly* convex preferences must have indifferences curves that are "rounded." The preferences for two goods that are perfect substitutes are convex, but not strictly convex.

3.6 The Marginal Rate of Substitution

We will often find it useful to refer to the slope of an indifference curve at a particular point. This idea is so useful that it even has a name: the slope of an indifference curve is known as the **marginal rate of substitution (MRS)**. The name comes from the fact that the MRS measures the rate at which the consumer is just willing to substitute one good for the other.

Suppose that we take a little of good 1, Δx_1, away from the consumer. Then we give him Δx_2, an amount that is just sufficient to put him back on his indifference curve, so that he is just as well off after this substitution of x_2 for x_1 as he was before. We think of the ratio $\Delta x_2/\Delta x_1$ as being the *rate* at which the consumer is willing to substitute good 2 for good 1.

Now think of Δx_1 as being a very small change—a marginal change. Then the rate $\Delta x_2/\Delta x_1$ measures the *marginal* rate of substitution of good 2 for good 1. As Δx_1 gets smaller, $\Delta x_2/\Delta x_1$ approaches the slope of the indifference curve, as can be seen in Figure 3.11.

When we write the ratio $\Delta x_2/\Delta x_1$, we will always think of both the numerator and the denominator as being small numbers—as describing *marginal* changes from the original consumption bundle. Thus the ratio defining the MRS will always describe the slope of the indifference curve: the rate at which the consumer is just willing to substitute a little more consumption of good 2 for a little less consumption of good 1.

One slightly confusing thing about the MRS is that it is typically a *negative* number. We've already seen that monotonic preferences imply that indifference curves must have a negative slope. Since the MRS is the numerical measure of the slope of an indifference curve, it will naturally be a negative number.

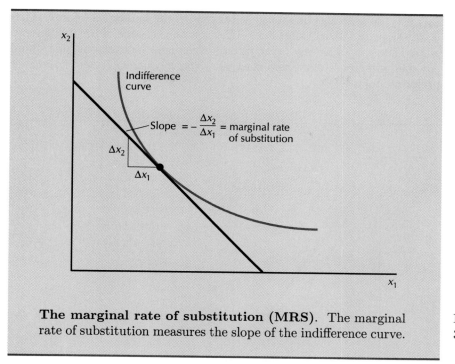

The marginal rate of substitution (MRS). The marginal rate of substitution measures the slope of the indifference curve.

Figure
3.11

The marginal rate of substitution measures an interesting aspect of the consumer's behavior. Suppose that the consumer has well-behaved preferences, that is, preferences that are monotonic and convex, and that he is currently consuming some bundle (x_1, x_2). We now will offer him a trade: he can exchange good 1 for 2, or good 2 for 1, in any amount at a "rate of exchange" of E.

That is, if the consumer gives up Δx_1 units of good 1, he can get $E\Delta x_1$ units of good 2 in exchange. Or, conversely, if he gives up Δx_2 units of good 2, he can get $\Delta x_2/E$ units of good 1. Geometrically, we are offering the consumer an opportunity to move to any point along a line with slope $-E$ that passes through (x_1, x_2), as depicted in Figure 3.12. Moving up and to the left from (x_1, x_2) involves exchanging good 1 for good 2, and moving down and to the right involves exchanging good 2 for good 1. In either movement, the exchange rate is E. Since exchange always involves giving up one good in exchange for another, the exchange *rate E* corresponds to a *slope* of $-E$.

We can now ask what would the rate of exchange have to be in order for the consumer to want to stay put at (x_1, x_2)? To answer this question, we simply note that any time the exchange line *crosses* the indifference curve, there will be some points on that line that are preferred to (x_1, x_2)—that lie above the indifference curve. Thus, if there is to be no movement from

(x_1, x_2), the exchange line must be tangent to the indifference curve. That is, the slope of the exchange line, $-E$, must be the slope of the indifference curve at (x_1, x_2). At any other rate of exchange, the exchange line would cut the indifference curve and thus allow the consumer to move to a more preferred point.

Figure
3.12
Trading at an exchange rate. Here we are allowing the consumer to trade the goods at an exchange rate E, which implies that the consumer can move along a line with slope $-E$.

Thus the slope of the indifference curve, the marginal rate of substitution, measures the rate at which the consumer is just on the margin of trading or not trading. At any rate of exchange other than the MRS, the consumer would want to trade one good for the other. But if the rate of exchange equals the MRS, the consumer wants to stay put.

3.7 Other Interpretations of the MRS

We have said that the MRS measures the rate at which the consumer is just on the margin of being willing to substitute good 1 for good 2. We could also say that the consumer is just on the margin of being willing to "pay" some of good 1 in order to buy some more of good 2. So sometimes you hear people say that the slope of the indifference curve measures the **marginal willingness to pay**.

If good 2 represents the consumption of "all other goods," and it is measured in dollars that you can spend on other goods, then the marginal-willingness-to-pay interpretation is very natural. The marginal rate of substitution of good 2 for good 1 is how many dollars you would just be willing to give up spending on other goods in order to consume a little bit more of good 1. Thus the MRS measures the marginal willingness to give up dollars in order to consume a small amount more of good 1. But giving up those dollars is just like paying dollars in order to consume a little more of good 1.

If you use the marginal-willingness-to-pay interpretation of the MRS, you should be careful to emphasize both the "marginal" and the "willingness" aspects. The MRS measures the amount of good 2 that one is *willing* to pay for a *marginal* amount of extra consumption of good 1. How much you actually *have* to pay for some given amount of extra consumption may be different than the amount you are willing to pay. How much you have to pay will depend on the price of the good in question. How much you are willing to pay doesn't depend on the price—it is determined by your preferences.

Similarly, how much you may be willing to pay for a large change in consumption may be different from how much you are willing to pay for a marginal change. How much you actually end up buying of a good will depend on your preferences for that good and the prices that you face. How much you would be willing to pay for a small amount extra of the good is a feature only of your preferences.

3.8 Behavior of the MRS

It is sometimes useful to describe the shapes of indifference curves by describing the behavior of the marginal rate of substitution. For example, the "perfect substitutes" indifference curves are characterized by the fact that the MRS is constant at -1. The "neutrals" case is characterized by the fact that the MRS is everywhere infinite. The preferences for "perfect complements" are characterized by the fact that the MRS is either zero or infinity, and nothing in between.

We've already pointed out that the assumption of monotonicity implies that indifference curves must have a negative slope, so the MRS always involves reducing the consumption of one good in order to get more of another for monotonic preferences.

The case of convex indifference curves exhibits yet another kind of behavior for the MRS. For strictly convex indifference curves, the MRS—the slope of the indifference curve—decreases (in absolute value) as we increase x_1. Thus the indifference curves exhibit a **diminishing marginal rate of**

substitution. This means that the rate at which a person is just willing to trade x_1 for x_2 decreases as we increase the amount of x_1. Stated in this way, convexity of indifference curves seems very natural: it says that the more you have of one good, the more willing you are to give some of it up in exchange for the other good. (But remember the ice cream and olives example—for some pairs of goods this assumption might not hold!)

Summary

1. Economists assume that a consumer can rank various consumption possibilities. The way in which the consumer ranks the consumption bundles describes the consumer's preferences.

2. Indifference curves can be used to depict different kinds of preferences.

3. Well-behaved preferences are monotonic (meaning more is better) and convex (meaning averages are preferred to extremes).

4. The marginal rate of substitution (MRS) measures the slope of the indifference curve. This can be interpreted as how much the consumer is willing to give up of good 2 to acquire more of good 1.

REVIEW QUESTIONS

1. If we observe a consumer choosing (x_1, x_2) when (y_1, y_2) is available one time, are we justified in concluding that $(x_1, x_2) \succ (y_1, y_2)$?

2. Consider a group of people A, B, C and the relation "at least as tall as," as in "A is at least as tall as B." Is this relation transitive? Is it complete?

3. Take the same group of people and consider the relation "strictly taller than." Is this relation transitive? Is it reflexive? Is it complete?

4. A college football coach says that given any two linemen A and B, he always prefers the one who is bigger and faster. Is this preference relation transitive? Is it complete?

5. Can an indifference curve cross itself? For example, could Figure 3.2 depict a single indifference curve?

6. Could Figure 3.2 be a single indifference curve if preferences are monotonic?

7. If both pepperoni and anchovies are bads, will the indifference curve have a positive or a negative slope?

8. Explain why convex preferences means that "averages are preferred to extremes."

9. What is your marginal rate of substitution of $1 bills for $5 bills?

10. If good 1 is a "neutral," what is its marginal rate of substitution for good 2?

11. Think of some other goods for which your preferences might be concave.

CHAPTER 4

UTILITY

In Victorian days, philosophers and economists talked blithely of "utility" as an indicator of a person's overall well-being. Utility was thought of as a numeric measure of a person's happiness. Given this idea, it was natural to think of consumers making choices so as to maximize their utility, that is, to make themselves as happy as possible.

The trouble is that these classical economists never really described how we were to measure utility. How are we supposed to quantify the "amount" of utility associated with different choices? Is one person's utility the same as another's? What would it mean to say that an extra candy bar would give me twice as much utility as an extra carrot? Does the concept of utility have any independent meaning other than its being what people maximize?

Because of these conceptual problems, economists have abandoned the old-fashioned view of utility as being a measure of happiness. Instead, the theory of consumer behavior has been reformulated entirely in terms of **consumer preferences**, and utility is seen only as a *way to describe preferences*.

Economists gradually came to recognize that all that mattered about utility as far as choice behavior was concerned was whether one bundle had a higher utility than another—how much higher didn't really matter.

Originally, preferences were defined in terms of utility: to say a bundle (x_1, x_2) was preferred to a bundle (y_1, y_2) meant that the x-bundle had a higher utility than the y-bundle. But now we tend to think of things the other way around. The *preferences* of the consumer are the fundamental description useful for analyzing choice, and utility is simply a way of describing preferences.

A **utility function** is a way of assigning a number to every possible consumption bundle such that more-preferred bundles get assigned larger numbers than less-preferred bundles. That is, a bundle (x_1, x_2) is preferred to a bundle (y_1, y_2) if and only if the utility of (x_1, x_2) is larger than the utility of (y_1, y_2): in symbols, $(x_1, x_2) \succ (y_1, y_2)$ if and only if $u(x_1, x_2) > u(y_1, y_2)$.

The only property of a utility assignment that is important is how it *orders* the bundles of goods. The magnitude of the utility function is only important insofar as it *ranks* the different consumption bundles; the size of the utility difference between any two consumption bundles doesn't matter. Because of this emphasis on ordering bundles of goods, this kind of utility is referred to as **ordinal utility**.

Consider for example Table 4.1, where we have illustrated several different ways of assigning utilities to three bundles of goods, all of which order the bundles in the same way. In this example, the consumer prefers A to B and B to C. All of the ways indicated are valid utility functions that describe the same preferences because they all have the property that A is assigned a higher number than B, which in turn is assigned a higher number than C.

Different ways to assign utilities.

Table 4.1

Bundle	U_1	U_2	U_3
A	3	17	-1
B	2	10	-2
C	1	.002	-3

Since only the ranking of the bundles matters, there can be no unique way to assign utilities to bundles of goods. If we can find one way to assign utility numbers to bundles of goods, we can find an infinite number of ways to do it. If $u(x_1, x_2)$ represents a way to assign utility numbers to the bundles (x_1, x_2), then multiplying $u(x_1, x_2)$ by 2 (or any other positive number) is just as good a way to assign utilities.

Multiplication by 2 is an example of a **monotonic transformation**. A monotonic transformation is a way of transforming one set of numbers into another set of numbers in a way that preserves the order of the numbers.

We typically represent a monotonic transformation by a function $f(u)$ that transforms each number u into some other number $f(u)$, in a way that preserves the order of the numbers in the sense that $u_1 > u_2$ implies $f(u_1) > f(u_2)$. A monotonic transformation and a monotonic function are essentially the same thing.

Examples of monotonic transformations are multiplication by a positive number (e.g., $f(u) = 3u$), adding any number (e.g., $f(u) = u + 17$), raising u to an odd power (e.g., $f(u) = u^3$), and so on.[1]

The rate of change of $f(u)$ as u changes can be measured by looking at the change in f between two values of u, divided by the change in u:

$$\frac{\Delta f}{\Delta u} = \frac{f(u_2) - f(u_1)}{u_2 - u_1}.$$

For a monotonic transformation, $f(u_2) - f(u_1)$ always has the same sign as $u_2 - u_1$. Thus a monotonic function always has a positive rate of change. This means that the graph of a monotonic function will always have a positive slope, as depicted in Figure 4.1A.

Figure 4.1

A positive monotonic transformation. Panel A illustrates a monotonic function—one that is always increasing. Panel B illustrates a function that is *not* monotonic, since it sometimes increases and sometimes decreases.

---

[1] What we are calling a "monotonic transformation" is, strictly speaking, called a "positive monotonic transformation," in order to distinguish it from a "negative monotonic transformation," which is one that *reverses* the order of the numbers. Monotonic transformations are sometimes called "monotonous transformations," which seems unfair, since they can actually be quite interesting.

If $f(u)$ is *any* monotonic transformation of a utility function that represents some particular preferences, then $f(u(x_1, x_2))$ is also a utility function that represents those same preferences.

Why? The argument is given in the following three statements:

1. To say that $u(x_1, x_2)$ represents some particular preferences means that $u(x_1, x_2) > u(y_1, y_2)$ if and only if $(x_1, x_2) \succ (y_1, y_2)$.
2. But if $f(u)$ is a monotonic transformation, then $u(x_1, x_2) > u(y_1, y_2)$ if and only if $f(u(x_1, x_2)) > f(u(y_1, y_2))$.
3. Therefore, $f(u(x_1, x_2)) > f(u(y_1, y_2))$ if and only if $(x_1, x_2) \succ (y_1, y_2)$, so the function $f(u)$ represents the preferences in the same way as the original utility function $u(x_1, x_2)$.

We summarize this discussion by stating the following principle: *a monotonic transformation of a utility function is a utility function that represents the same preferences as the original utility function.*

Geometrically, a utility function is a way to label indifference curves. Since every bundle on an indifference curve must have the same utility, a utility function is a way of assigning numbers to the different indifference curves in a way that higher indifference curves get assigned larger numbers. Seen from this point of view a monotonic transformation is just a relabeling of indifference curves. As long as indifference curves containing more-preferred bundles get a larger label than indifference curves containing less-preferred bundles, the labeling will represent the same preferences.

4.1 Cardinal Utility

There are some theories of utility that attach a significance to the magnitude of utility. These are known as **cardinal utility** theories. In a theory of cardinal utility, the size of the utility difference between two bundles of goods is supposed to have some sort of significance.

We know how to tell whether a given person prefers one bundle of goods to another: we simply offer him or her a choice between the two bundles and see which one is chosen. Thus we know how to assign an ordinal utility to the two bundles of goods: we just assign a higher utility to the chosen bundle than to the rejected bundle. Any assignment that does this will be a utility function. Thus we have an operational criterion for determining whether one bundle has a higher utility than another bundle for some individual.

But how do we tell if a person likes one bundle twice as much as another? How could you even tell if *you* like one bundle twice as much as another?

One could propose various definitions for this kind of assignment: I like one bundle twice as much as another if I am willing to pay twice as much for it. Or, I like one bundle twice as much as another if I am willing to run twice as far to get it, or to wait twice as long, or to gamble for it at twice the odds.

There is nothing wrong with any of these definitions; each one would give rise to a way of assigning utility levels in which the magnitude of the numbers assigned had some operational significance. But there isn't much right about them either. Although each of them is a possible interpretation of what it means to want one thing twice as much as another, none of them appears to be an especially compelling interpretation of that statement.

Even if we did find a way of assigning utility magnitudes that seemed to be especially compelling, what good would it do us in describing choice behavior? To tell whether one bundle or another will be chosen, we only have to know which is preferred—which has the larger utility. Knowing how much larger doesn't add anything to our description of choice. Since cardinal utility isn't needed to describe choice behavior and there is no compelling way to assign cardinal utilities anyway, we will stick with a purely ordinal utility framework.

4.2 Constructing a Utility Function

But are we assured that there is any way to assign ordinal utilities? Given a preference ordering can we always find a utility function that will order bundles of goods in the same way as those preferences? Is there a utility function that describes any reasonable preference ordering?

Not all kinds of preferences can be represented by a utility function. For example, suppose that someone had intransitive preferences so that $A \succ B \succ C \succ A$. Then a utility function for these preferences would have to consist of numbers $u(A)$, $u(B)$, and $u(C)$ such that $u(A) > u(B) > u(C) > u(A)$. But this is impossible.

However, if we rule out perverse cases like intransitive preferences, it turns out that we will typically be able to find a utility function to represent preferences. We will illustrate one construction here, and another one in Chapter 14.

Suppose that we are given an indifference map as in Figure 4.2. We know that a utility function is a way to label the indifference curves such that higher indifference curves get larger numbers. How can we do this?

One easy way is to draw the diagonal line illustrated and label each indifference curve with its distance from the origin measured along the line.

How do we know that this is a utility function? It is not hard to see that if preferences are monotonic then the line through the origin must intersect every indifference curve exactly once. Thus every bundle is getting a label, and those bundles on higher indifference curves are getting larger labels— and that's all it takes to be a utility function.

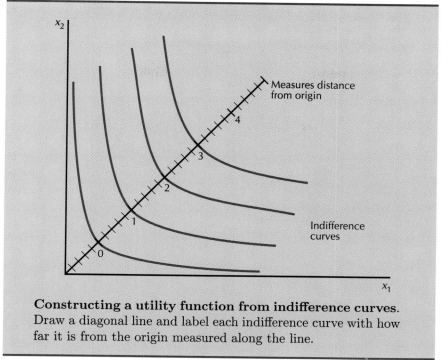

Constructing a utility function from indifference curves.
Draw a diagonal line and label each indifference curve with how
far it is from the origin measured along the line.

Figure
4.2

This gives us one way to find a labeling of indifference curves, at least as
long as preferences are monotonic. This won't always be the most natural
way in any given case, but at least it shows that the idea of an ordinal utility
function is pretty general: nearly any kind of "reasonable" preferences can
be represented by a utility function.

4.3 Some Examples of Utility Functions

In Chapter 3 we described some examples of preferences and the indifference curves that represented them. We can also represent these preferences
by utility functions. If you are given a utility function, $u(x_1, x_2)$, it is relatively easy to draw the indifference curves: you just plot all the points
(x_1, x_2) such that $u(x_1, x_2)$ equals a constant. In mathematics, the set of
all (x_1, x_2) such that $u(x_1, x_2)$ equals a constant is called a **level set**. For
each different value of the constant, you get a different indifference curve.

EXAMPLE: Indifference Curves from Utility

Suppose that the utility function is given by: $u(x_1, x_2) = x_1 x_2$. What do
the indifference curves look like?

We know that a typical indifference curve is just the set of all x_1 and x_2 such that $k = x_1 x_2$ for some constant k. Solving for x_2 as a function of x_1, we see that a typical indifference curve has the formula:

$$x_2 = \frac{k}{x_1}.$$

This curve is depicted in Figure 4.3 for $k = 1, 2, 3 \cdots$.

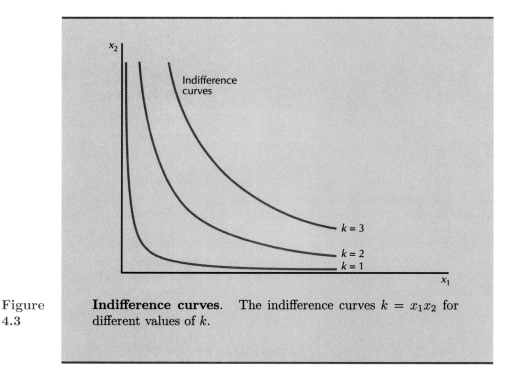

Figure 4.3

Indifference curves. The indifference curves $k = x_1 x_2$ for different values of k.

Let's consider another example. Suppose that we were given a utility function $v(x_1, x_2) = x_1^2 x_2^2$. What do its indifference curves look like? By the standard rules of algebra we know that:

$$v(x_1, x_2) = x_1^2 x_2^2 = (x_1 x_2)^2 = u(x_1, x_2)^2.$$

Thus the utility function $v(x_1, x_2)$ is just the square of the utility function $u(x_1, x_2)$. Since $u(x_1, x_2)$ cannot be negative, it follows that $v(x_1, x_2)$ is a monotonic transformation of the previous utility function, $u(x_1, x_2)$. This means that the utility function $v(x_1, x_2) = x_1^2 x_2^2$ has to have exactly the same shaped indifference curves as those depicted in Figure 4.3. The labeling of the indifference curves will be different—the labels that were $1, 2, 3, \cdots$ will now be $1, 4, 9, \cdots$—but the set of bundles that has $v(x_1, x_2) =$

9 is exactly the same as the set of bundles that has $u(x_1, x_2) = 3$. Thus $v(x_1, x_2)$ describes exactly the same preferences as $u(x_1, x_2)$ since it *orders* all of the bundles in the same way.

Going the other direction—finding a utility function that represents some indifference curves—is somewhat more difficult. There are two ways to proceed. The first way is mathematical. Given the indifference curves, we want to find a function that is constant along each indifference curve and that assigns higher values to higher indifference curves.

The second way is a bit more intuitive. Given a description of the preferences, we try to think about what the consumer is trying to maximize— what combination of the goods describes the choice behavior of the consumer. This may seem a little vague at the moment, but it will be more meaningful after we discuss a few examples.

Perfect Substitutes

Remember the red pencil and blue pencil example? All that mattered to the consumer was the total number of pencils. Thus it is natural to measure utility by the total number of pencils. Therefore we provisionally pick the utility function $u(x_1, x_2) = x_1 + x_2$. Does this work? Just ask two things: is this utility function constant along the indifference curves? Does it assign a higher label to more-preferred bundles? The answer to both questions is yes, so we have a utility function.

Of course, this isn't the only utility function that we could use. We could also use the *square* of the number of pencils. Thus the utility function $v(x_1, x_2) = (x_1 + x_2)^2 = x_1^2 + 2x_1 x_2 + x_2^2$ will also represent the perfect-substitutes preferences, as would any other monotonic transformation of $u(x_1, x_2)$.

What if the consumer is willing to substitute good 1 for good 2 at a rate that is different from one-to-one? Suppose, for example, that the consumer would require *two* units of good 2 to compensate him for giving up one unit of good 1. This means that good 1 is *twice* as valuable to the consumer as good 2. The utility function therefore takes the form $u(x_1, x_2) = 2x_1 + x_2$. Note that this utility yields indifference curves with a slope of -2.

In general, preferences for perfect substitutes can be represented by a utility function of the form

$$u(x_1, x_2) = ax_1 + bx_2.$$

Here a and b are some positive numbers that measure the "value" of goods 1 and 2 to the consumer. Note that the slope of a typical indifference curve is given by $-a/b$.

Perfect Complements

This is the left shoe–right shoe case. In these preferences the consumer only cares about the number of *pairs* of shoes he has, so it is natural to choose the number of pairs of shoes as the utility function. The number of complete pairs of shoes that you have is the *minimum* of the number of right shoes you have, x_1, and the number of left shoes you have, x_2. Thus the utility function for perfect complements takes the form $u(x_1, x_2) = \min\{x_1, x_2\}$.

To verify that this utility function actually works, pick a bundle of goods such as $(10, 10)$. If we add one more unit of good 1 we get $(11, 10)$, which should leave us on the same indifference curve. Does it? Yes, since $\min\{10, 10\} = \min\{11, 10\} = 10$.

So $u(x_1, x_2) = \min\{x_1, x_2\}$ is a possible utility function to describe perfect complements. As usual, any monotonic transformation would be suitable as well.

What about the case where the consumer wants to consume the goods in some proportion other than one-to-one? For example, what about the consumer who always uses 2 teaspoons of sugar with each cup of tea? If x_1 is the number of cups of tea available and x_2 is the number of teaspoons of sugar available, then the number of correctly sweetened cups of tea will be $\min\{x_1, \frac{1}{2}x_2\}$.

This is a little tricky so we should stop to think about it. If the number of cups of tea is greater than half the number of teaspoons of sugar, then we know that we won't be able to put 2 teaspoons of sugar in each cup. In this case, we will only end up with $\frac{1}{2}x_2$ correctly sweetened cups of tea. (Substitute some numbers in for x_1 and x_2 to convince yourself.)

Of course, any monotonic transformation of this utility function will describe the same preferences. For example, we might want to multiply by 2 to get rid of the fraction. This gives us the utility function $u(x_1, x_2) = \min\{2x_1, x_2\}$.

In general, a utility function that describes perfect-complement preferences is given by

$$u(x_1, x_2) = \min\{ax_1, bx_2\},$$

where a and b are positive numbers that indicate the proportions in which the goods are consumed.

Quasilinear Preferences

Here's a shape of indifference curves that we haven't seen before. Suppose that a consumer has indifference curves that are vertical translates of one another, as in Figure 4.4. This means that all of the indifference curves are just vertically "shifted" versions of one indifference curve. It follows that the equation for an indifference curve takes the form $x_2 = k - v(x_1)$, where k is a different constant for each indifference curve. This equation says that the height of each indifference curve is some function of x_1, $-v(x_1)$, plus a constant k. Higher values of k give higher indifference curves. (The minus sign is only a convention; we'll see why it is convenient below.)

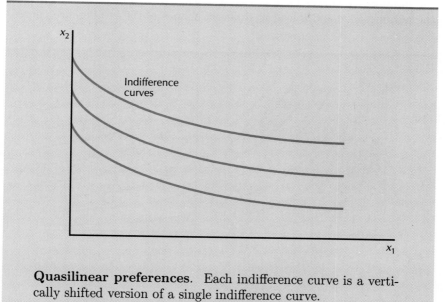

Quasilinear preferences. Each indifference curve is a vertically shifted version of a single indifference curve.

Figure 4.4

The natural way to label indifference curves here is with k—roughly speaking, the height of the indifference curve along the vertical axis. Solving for k and setting it equal to utility, we have

$$u(x_1, x_2) = k = v(x_1) + x_2.$$

In this case the utility function is linear in good 2, but (possibly) nonlinear in good 1; hence the name **quasilinear utility**, meaning "partly linear" utility. Specific examples of quasilinear utility would be $u(x_1, x_2) = \sqrt{x_1} + x_2$, or $u(x_1, x_2) = \ln x_1 + x_2$. Quasilinear utility functions are not particularly realistic, but they are very easy to work with, as we'll see in several examples later on in the book.

Cobb-Douglas Preferences

Another commonly used utility function is the **Cobb-Douglas** utility function

$$u(x_1, x_2) = x_1^c x_2^d,$$

where c and d are positive numbers that describe the preferences of the consumer.[2]

The Cobb-Douglas utility function will be useful in several examples. The preferences represented by the Cobb-Douglas utility function have the general shape depicted in Figure 4.5. In Figure 4.5A, we have illustrated the indifference curves for $c = 1/2, d = 1/2$. In Figure 4.5B, we have illustrated the indifference curves for $c = 1/5, d = 4/5$. Note how different values of the parameters c and d lead to different shapes of the indifference curves.

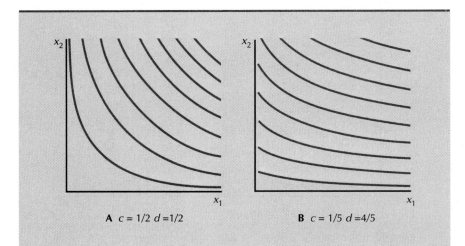

A $c = 1/2$ $d = 1/2$ **B** $c = 1/5$ $d = 4/5$

Figure
4.5

Cobb-Douglas indifference curves. Panel A shows the case where $c = 1/2$, $d = 1/2$ and panel B shows the case where $c = 1/5$, $d = 4/5$.

Cobb-Douglas indifference curves look just like the nice convex monotonic indifference curves that we referred to as "well-behaved indifference curves" in Chapter 3. Cobb-Douglas preferences are the standard example of indifference curves that look well-behaved, and in fact the formula describing them is about the simplest algebraic expression that generates well-behaved preferences. We'll find Cobb-Douglas preferences quite useful to present algebraic examples of the economic ideas we'll study later.

Of course a monotonic transformation of the Cobb-Douglas utility function will represent exactly the same preferences, and it is useful to see a couple of examples of these transformations.

---

[2] Paul Douglas was a twentieth-century economist at the University of Chicago who later became a U.S. senator. Charles Cobb was a mathematician at Amherst College. The Cobb-Douglas functional form was originally used to study production behavior.

First, if we take the natural log of utility, the product of the terms will become a sum so that we have

$$v(x_1, x_2) = \ln(x_1^c x_2^d) = c \ln x_1 + d \ln x_2.$$

The indifference curves for this utility function will look just like the ones for the first Cobb-Douglas function, since the logarithm is a monotonic transformation. (For a brief review of natural logarithms, see the Mathematical Appendix at the end of the book.)

For the second example, suppose that we start with the Cobb-Douglas form

$$v(x_1, x_2) = x_1^c x_2^d.$$

Then raising utility to the $1/(c+d)$ power, we have

$$x_1^{\frac{c}{c+d}} x_2^{\frac{d}{c+d}}.$$

Now define a new number

$$a = \frac{c}{c+d}.$$

We can now write our utility function as

$$v(x_1, x_2) = x_1^a x_2^{1-a}.$$

This means that we can always take a monotonic transformation of the Cobb-Douglas utility function that make the exponents sum to 1. This will turn out to have a useful interpretation later on.

The Cobb-Douglas utility function can be expressed in a variety of ways; you should learn to recognize them, as this family of preferences is very useful for examples.

4.4 Marginal Utility

Consider a consumer who is consuming some bundle of goods, (x_1, x_2). How does this consumer's utility change as we give him or her a little more of good 1? This rate of change is called the **marginal utility** with respect to good 1. We write it as MU_1 and think of it as being a ratio,

$$MU_1 = \frac{\Delta U}{\Delta x_1} = \frac{u(x_1 + \Delta x_1, x_2) - u(x_1, x_2)}{\Delta x_1},$$

that measures the rate of change in utility (ΔU) associated with a small change in the amount of good 1 (Δx_1). Note that the amount of good 2 is held fixed in this calculation.[3]

---

[3] See the appendix to this chapter for a calculus treatment of marginal utility.

This definition implies that to calculate the change in utility associated with a small change in consumption of good 1, we can just multiply the change in consumption by the marginal utility of the good:

$$\Delta U = MU_1 \Delta x_1.$$

The marginal utility with respect to good 2 is defined in a similar manner:

$$MU_2 = \frac{\Delta U}{\Delta x_2} = \frac{u(x_1, x_2 + \Delta x_2) - u(x_1, x_2)}{\Delta x_2}.$$

Note that when we compute the marginal utility with respect to good 2 we keep the amount of good 1 constant. We can calculate the change in utility associated with a change in the consumption of good 2 by the formula

$$\Delta U = MU_2 \Delta x_2.$$

It is important to realize that the magnitude of marginal utility depends on the magnitude of utility. Thus it depends on the particular way that we choose to measure utility. If we multiplied utility by 2, then marginal utility would also be multiplied by 2. We would still have a perfectly valid utility function in that it would represent the same preferences, but it would just be scaled differently.

This means that marginal utility itself has no behavioral content. How can we calculate marginal utility from a consumer's choice behavior? We can't. Choice behavior only reveals information about the way a consumer *ranks* different bundles of goods. Marginal utility depends on the particular utility function that we use to reflect the preference ordering and its magnitude has no particular significance. However, it turns out that marginal utility can be used to calculate something that does have behavioral content, as we will see in the next section.

4.5 Marginal Utility and MRS

A utility function $u(x_1, x_2)$ can be used to measure the marginal rate of substitution (MRS) defined in Chapter 3. Recall that the MRS measures the slope of the indifference curve at a given bundle of goods; it can be interpreted as the rate at which a consumer is just willing to substitute a small amount of good 2 for good 1.

This interpretation gives us a simple way to calculate the MRS. Consider a change in the consumption of each good, $(\Delta x_1, \Delta x_2)$, that keeps utility constant—that is, a change in consumption that moves us along the indifference curve. Then we must have

$$MU_1 \Delta x_1 + MU_2 \Delta x_2 = \Delta U = 0.$$

Solving for the slope of the indifference curve we have

$$\text{MRS} = \frac{\Delta x_2}{\Delta x_1} = -\frac{MU_1}{MU_2}. \tag{4.1}$$

(Note that we have 2 over 1 on the left-hand side of the equation and 1 over 2 on the right-hand side. Don't get confused!)

The algebraic sign of the MRS is negative: if you get more of good 1 you have to get *less* of good 2 in order to keep the same level of utility. However, it gets very tedious to keep track of that pesky minus sign, so economists often refer to the MRS by its absolute value—that is, as a positive number. We'll follow this convention as long as no confusion will result.

Now here is the interesting thing about the MRS calculation: the MRS can be measured by observing a person's actual behavior—we find that rate of exchange where he or she is just willing to stay put, as described in Chapter 3.

The utility function, and therefore the marginal utility function, is not uniquely determined. Any monotonic transformation of a utility function leaves you with another equally valid utility function. Thus, if we multiply utility by 2, for example, the marginal utility is multiplied by 2. Thus the magnitude of the marginal utility function depends on the choice of utility function, which is arbitrary. It doesn't depend on behavior alone; instead it depends on the utility function that we use to describe behavior.

But the *ratio* of marginal utilities gives us an observable magnitude—namely the marginal rate of substitution. The ratio of marginal utilities is independent of the particular transformation of the utility function you choose to use. Look at what happens if you multiply utility by 2. The MRS becomes

$$\text{MRS} = -\frac{2MU_1}{2MU_2}.$$

The 2s just cancel out, so the MRS remains the same.

The same sort of thing occurs when we take any monotonic transformation of a utility function. Taking a monotonic transformation is just relabeling the indifference curves, and the calculation for the MRS described above is concerned with moving along a given indifference curve. Even though the marginal utilities are changed by monotonic transformations, the *ratio* of marginal utilities is independent of the particular way chosen to represent the preferences.

4.6 Utility for Commuting

Utility functions are basically ways of describing choice behavior: if a bundle of goods X is chosen when a bundle of goods Y is available, then X must have a higher utility than Y. By examining choices consumers make we can estimate a utility function to describe their behavior.

This idea has been widely applied in the field of transportation economics to study consumers' commuting behavior. In most large cities commuters have a choice between taking public transit or driving to work. Each of these alternatives can be thought of as representing a bundle of different characteristics: travel time, waiting time, out-of-pocket costs, comfort, convenience, and so on. We could let x_1 be the amount of travel time involved in each kind of transportation, x_2 the amount of waiting time for each kind, and so on.

If $(x_1, x_2, \ldots, x_n)$ represents the values of n different characteristics of driving, say, and $(y_1, y_2, \ldots, y_n)$ represents the values of taking the bus, we can consider a model where the consumer decides to drive or take the bus depending on whether he prefers one bundle of characteristics to the other.

More specifically, let us suppose that the average consumer's preferences for characteristics can be represented by a utility function of the form

$$U(x_1, x_2, \ldots, x_n) = \beta_1 x_1 + \beta_2 x_2 + \cdots + \beta_n x_n,$$

where the coefficients β_1, β_2, and so on are unknown parameters. Any monotonic transformation of this utility function would describe the choice behavior equally well, of course, but the linear form is especially easy to work with from a statistical point of view.

Suppose now that we observe a number of similar consumers making choices between driving and taking the bus based on the particular pattern of commute times, costs, and so on that they face. There are statistical techniques that can be used to find the values of the coefficients β_i for $i = 1, \ldots, n$ that best fit the observed pattern of choices by a set of consumers. These statistical techniques give a way to estimate the utility function for different transportation modes.

One study reports a utility function that had the form[4]

$$U(TW, TT, C) = -0.147TW - 0.0411TT - 2.24C, \tag{4.2}$$

where

TW = total walking time to and from bus or car
TT = total time of trip in minutes
C = total cost of trip in dollars

The estimated utility function in the Domenich-McFadden book correctly described the choice between auto and bus transport for 93 percent of the households in their sample.

---

[4] See Thomas Domenich and Daniel McFadden, *Urban Travel Demand* (North-Holland Publishing Company, 1975). The estimation procedure in this book also incorporated various demographic characteristics of the households in addition to the purely economic variables described here.

The coefficients on the variables in Equation (4.2) describe the weight that an average household places on the various characteristics of their commuting trips; that is, the marginal utility of each characteristic. The *ratio* of one coefficient to another measures the marginal rate of substitution between one characteristic and another. For example, the ratio of the marginal utility of walking time to the marginal utility of total time indicates that walking time is viewed as being roughly 3 times as onerous as travel time by the average consumer. In other words, the consumer would be willing to substitute 3 minutes of additional travel time to save 1 minute of walking time.

Similarly, the ratio of cost to travel time indicates the average consumer's tradeoff between these two variables. In this study, the average commuter valued a minute of commute time at $0.0411/2.24 = 0.0183$ dollars per minute, which is $1.10 per hour. For comparison, the hourly wage for the average commuter in 1967, the year of the study, was about $2.85 an hour.

Such estimated utility functions can be very valuable for determining whether or not it is worthwhile to make some change in the public transportation system. For example, in the above utility function one of the significant factors explaining mode choice is the time involved in taking the trip. The city transit authority can, at some cost, add more buses to reduce this travel time. But will the number of extra riders warrant the increased expense?

Given a utility function and a sample of consumers we can forecast which consumers will drive and which consumers will choose to take the bus. This will give us some idea as to whether the revenue will be sufficient to cover the extra cost.

Furthermore, we can use the marginal rate of substitution to estimate the *value* that each consumer places on the reduced travel time. We saw above that in the Domenich-McFadden study the average commuter in 1967 valued commute time at a rate of $1.10 per hour. Thus the commuter should be willing to pay about $0.37 to cut 20 minutes from his or her trip. This number gives us a measure of the dollar benefit of providing more timely bus service. This benefit must be compared to the cost of providing more timely bus service in order to determine if such provision is worthwhile. Having a quantitative measure of benefit will certainly be helpful in making a rational decision about transport policy.

Summary

1. A utility function is simply a way to represent or summarize a preference ordering. The numerical magnitudes of utility levels have no intrinsic meaning.

2. Thus, given any one utility function, any monotonic transformation of it will represent the same preferences.

3. The marginal rate of substitution, MRS, can be calculated from the utility function via the formula $\text{MRS} = \Delta x_2/\Delta x_1 = -MU_1/MU_2$.

REVIEW QUESTIONS

1. The text said that raising a number to an odd power was a monotonic transformation. What about raising a number to an even power? Is this a monotonic transformation? (Hint: consider the case $f(u) = u^2$.)

2. Which of the following are monotonic transformations? (1) $u = 2v - 13$; (2) $u = -1/v^2$; (3) $u = 1/v^2$; (4) $u = \ln v$; (5) $u = -e^{-v}$; (6) $u = v^2$; (7) $u = v^2$ for $v > 0$; (8) $u = v^2$ for $v < 0$.

3. We claimed in the text that if preferences were monotonic, then a diagonal line through the origin would intersect each indifference curve exactly once. Can you prove this rigorously? (Hint: what would happen if it intersected some indifference curve twice?)

4. What kind of preferences are represented by a utility function of the form $u(x_1, x_2) = \sqrt{x_1 + x_2}$? What about the utility function $v(x_1, x_2) = 13x_1 + 13x_2$?

5. What kind of preferences are represented by a utility function of the form $u(x_1, x_2) = x_1 + \sqrt{x_2}$? Is the utility function $v(x_1, x_2) = x_1^2 + 2x_1\sqrt{x_2} + x_2$ a monotonic transformation of $u(x_1, x_2)$?

6. Consider the utility function $u(x_1, x_2) = \sqrt{x_1 x_2}$. What kind of preferences does it represent? Is the function $v(x_1, x_2) = x_1^2 x_2$ a monotonic transformation of $u(x_1, x_2)$? Is the function $w(x_1, x_2) = x_1^2 x_2^2$ a monotonic transformation of $u(x_1, x_2)$?

7. Can you explain why taking a monotonic transformation of a utility function doesn't change the marginal rate of substitution?

APPENDIX

First, let us clarify what is meant by "marginal utility." As elsewhere in economics, "marginal" just means a derivative. So the marginal utility of good 1 is just

$$MU_1 = \lim_{\Delta x_1 \to 0} \frac{u(x_1 + \Delta x_1, x_2) - u(x_1, x_2)}{\Delta x_1} = \frac{\partial u(x_1, x_2)}{\partial x_1}.$$

Note that we have used the *partial* derivative here, since the marginal utility of good 1 is computed holding good 2 fixed.

Now we can rephrase the derivation of the MRS given in the text using calculus. We'll do it two ways: first by using differentials, and second by using implicit functions.

For the first method, we consider making a change (dx_1, dx_2) that keeps utility constant. So we want

$$du = \frac{\partial u(x_1, x_2)}{\partial x_1} dx_1 + \frac{\partial u(x_1, x_2)}{\partial x_2} dx_2 = 0.$$

The first term measures the increase in utility from the small change dx_1, and the second term measures the increase in utility from the small change dx_2. We want to pick these changes so that the total change in utility, du, is zero. Solving for dx_2/dx_1 gives us

$$\frac{dx_2}{dx_1} = -\frac{\partial u(x_1, x_2)/\partial x_1}{\partial u(x_1, x_2)/\partial x_2},$$

which is just the calculus analog of equation (4.1) in the text.

As for the second method, we now think of the indifference curve as being described by a function $x_2(x_1)$. That is, for each value of x_1, the function $x_2(x_1)$ tells us how much x_2 we need to get on that specific indifference curve. Thus the function $x_2(x_1)$ has to satisfy the identity

$$u(x_1, x_2(x_1)) \equiv k,$$

where k is the utility label of the indifference curve in question.

We can differentiate both sides of this identity with respect to x_1 to get

$$\frac{\partial u(x_1, x_2)}{\partial x_1} + \frac{\partial u(x_1, x_2)}{\partial x_2} \frac{\partial x_2(x_1)}{\partial x_1} = 0.$$

Notice that x_1 occurs in two places in this identity, so changing x_1 will change the function in two ways, and we have to take the derivative at each place that x_1 appears.

We then solve this equation for $\partial x_2(x_1)/\partial x_1$ to find

$$\frac{\partial x_2(x_1)}{\partial x_1} = -\frac{\partial u(x_1, x_2)/\partial x_1}{\partial u(x_1, x_2)/\partial x_2},$$

just as we had before.

The implicit function method is a little more rigorous, but the differential method is more direct, as long as you don't do something silly.

Suppose that we take a monotonic transformation of a utility function, say, $v(x_1, x_2) = f(u(x_1, x_2))$. Let's calculate the MRS for this utility function. Using the chain rule

$$\text{MRS} = -\frac{\partial v/\partial x_1}{\partial v/\partial x_2} = -\frac{\partial f/\partial u}{\partial f/\partial u} \frac{\partial u/\partial x_1}{\partial u/\partial x_2}$$
$$= -\frac{\partial u/\partial x_1}{\partial u/\partial x_2}$$

since the $\partial f/\partial u$ term cancels out from both the numerator and denominator. This shows that the MRS is independent of the utility representation.

This gives a useful way to recognize preferences that are represented by different utility functions: given two utility functions, just compute the marginal rates of substitution and see if they are the same. If they are, then the two utility functions have the same indifference curves. If the direction of increasing preference is the same for each utility function, then the underlying preferences must be the same.

EXAMPLE: Cobb-Douglas Preferences

The MRS for Cobb-Douglas preferences is easy to calculate by using the formula derived above.

If we choose the log representation where

$$u(x_1, x_2) = c \ln x_1 + d \ln x_2,$$

then we have

$$\text{MRS} = -\frac{\partial u(x_1, x_2)/\partial x_1}{\partial u(x_1, x_2)/\partial x_2}$$

$$= -\frac{c/x_1}{d/x_2}$$

$$= -\frac{c}{d}\frac{x_2}{x_1}.$$

Note that the MRS only depends on the ratio of the two parameters and the quantity of the two goods in this case.

What if we choose the exponent representation where

$$u(x_1, x_2) = x_1^c x_2^d?$$

Then we have

$$\text{MRS} = -\frac{\partial u(x_1, x_2)/\partial x_1}{\partial u(x_1, x_2)/\partial x_2}$$

$$= -\frac{c x_1^{c-1} x_2^d}{d x_1^c x_2^{d-1}}$$

$$= -\frac{c x_2}{d x_1},$$

which is the same as we had before. Of course you knew all along that a monotonic transformation couldn't change the marginal rate of substitution!

CHAPTER **5**

CHOICE

In this chapter we will put together the budget set and the theory of preferences in order to examine the optimal choice of consumers. We said earlier that the economic model of consumer choice is that people choose the best bundle they can afford. We can now rephrase this in terms that sound more professional by saying that "consumers choose the most preferred bundle from their budget sets."

5.1 Optimal Choice

A typical case is illustrated in Figure 5.1. Here we have drawn the budget set and several of the consumer's indifference curves on the same diagram. We want to find the bundle in the budget set that is on the highest indifference curve. Since preferences are well-behaved, so that more is preferred to less, we can restrict our attention to bundles of goods that lie *on* the budget line and not worry about those *beneath* the budget line.

Now simply start at the right-hand corner of the budget line and move to the left. As we move along the budget line we note that we are moving to higher and higher indifference curves. We stop when we get to the highest indifference curve that just touches the budget line. In the diagram, the bundle of goods that is associated with the highest indifference curve that just touches the budget line is labeled (x_1^*, x_2^*).

The choice (x_1^*, x_2^*) is an **optimal choice** for the consumer. The set of bundles that she prefers to (x_1^*, x_2^*)—the set of bundles *above* her indifference curve—doesn't intersect the bundles she can afford—the bundles *beneath* her budget line. Thus the bundle (x_1^*, x_2^*) is the best bundle that the consumer can afford.

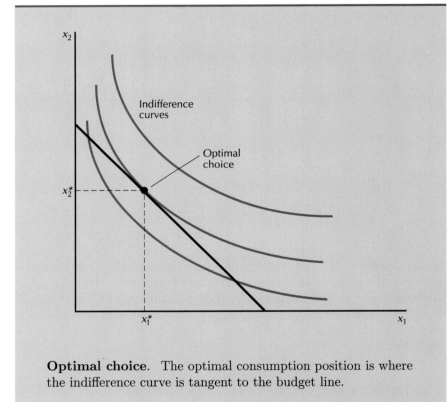

Figure
5.1

Optimal choice. The optimal consumption position is where the indifference curve is tangent to the budget line.

Note an important feature of this optimal bundle: at this choice, the indifference curve is *tangent* to the budget line. If you think about it a moment you'll see that this has to be the case: if the indifference curve weren't tangent, it would cross the budget line, and if it crossed the budget line, there would be some nearby point on the budget line that lies above the indifference curve—which means that we couldn't have started at an optimal bundle.

Does this tangency condition really *have* to hold at an optimal choice? Well, it doesn't hold in *all* cases, but it does hold for most interesting cases. What is always true is that at the optimal point the indifference curve can't cross the budget line. So when does "not crossing" imply tangent? Let's look at the exceptions first.

First, the indifference curve might not have a tangent line, as in Figure 5.2. Here the indifference curve has a kink at the optimal choice, and a tangent just isn't defined, since the mathematical definition of a tangent requires that there be a unique tangent line at each point. This case doesn't have much economic significance—it is more of a nuisance than anything else.

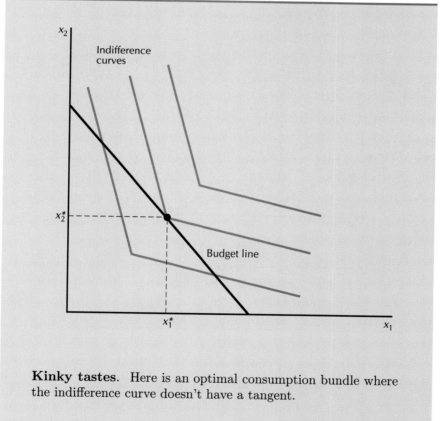

Kinky tastes. Here is an optimal consumption bundle where the indifference curve doesn't have a tangent.

Figure
5.2

The second exception is more interesting. Suppose that the optimal point occurs where the consumption of some good is zero as in Figure 5.3. Then the slope of the indifference curve and the slope of the budget line are different, but the indifference curve still doesn't *cross* the budget line.

We say that Figure 5.3 represents a **boundary optimum**, while a case like Figure 5.1 represents an **interior optimum**.

If we are willing to rule out "kinky tastes" we can forget about the example given in Figure 5.2.[1] And if we are willing to restrict ourselves only to *interior* optima, we can rule out the other example. If we have an interior optimum with smooth indifference curves, the slope of the indifference curve and the slope of the budget line must be the same ... because if they were different the indifference curve would cross the budget line, and we couldn't be at the optimal point.

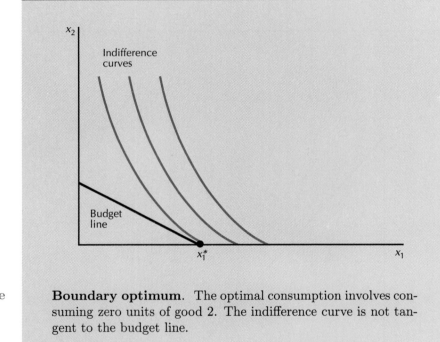

Figure 5.3

Boundary optimum. The optimal consumption involves consuming zero units of good 2. The indifference curve is not tangent to the budget line.

We've found a necessary condition that the optimal choice must satisfy. If the optimal choice involves consuming some of both goods—so that it is an interior optimum—then necessarily the indifference curve will be tangent to the budget line. But is the tangency condition a *sufficient* condition for a bundle to be optimal? If we find a bundle where the indifference curve is tangent to the budget line, can we be sure we have an optimal choice?

Look at Figure 5.4. Here we have three bundles where the tangency condition is satisfied, all of them interior, but only two of them are optimal.

[1] Otherwise, this book might get an R rating.

So in general, the tangency condition is only a necessary condition for optimality, not a sufficient condition.

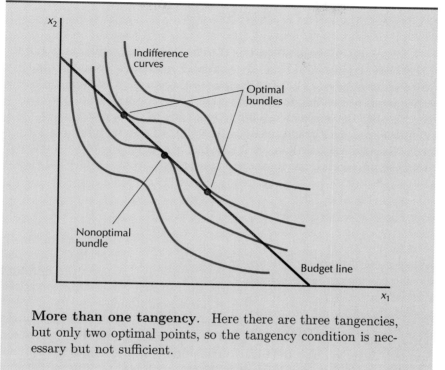

More than one tangency. Here there are three tangencies, but only two optimal points, so the tangency condition is necessary but not sufficient.

Figure
5.4

However, there is one important case where it is sufficient: the case of convex preferences. In the case of convex preferences, any point that satisfies the tangency condition must be an optimal point. This is clear geometrically: since convex indifference curves must curve away from the budget line, they can't bend back to touch it again.

Figure 5.4 also shows us that in general there may be more than one optimal bundle that satisfies the tangency condition. However, again convexity implies a restriction. If the indifference curves are *strictly* convex—they don't have any flat spots—then there will be only one optimal choice on each budget line. Although this can be shown mathematically, it is also quite plausible from looking at the figure.

The condition that the MRS must equal the slope of the budget line at an interior optimum is obvious graphically, but what does it mean economically? Recall that one of our interpretations of the MRS is that it is that rate of exchange at which the consumer is just willing to stay put. Well, the market is offering a rate of exchange to the consumer of $-p_1/p_2$—if you give up one unit of good 1, you can buy p_1/p_2 units of good 2. If the consumer is at a consumption bundle where he or she is willing to stay put, it must be one where the MRS is equal to this rate of exchange:

$$\text{MRS} = -\frac{p_1}{p_2}.$$

Another way to think about this is to imagine what would happen if the MRS were different from the price ratio. Suppose, for example, that the MRS is $\Delta x_2/\Delta x_1 = -1/2$ and the price ratio is $1/1$. Then this means the consumer is just willing to give up 2 units of good 1 in order to get 1 unit of good 2—but the market is willing to exchange them on a one-to-one basis. Thus the consumer would certainly be willing to give up some of good 1 in order to purchase a little more of good 2. Whenever the MRS is different from the price ratio, the consumer cannot be at his or her optimal choice.

5.2 Consumer Demand

The optimal choice of goods 1 and 2 at some set of prices and income is called the consumer's **demanded bundle**. In general when prices and income change, the consumer's optimal choice will change. The **demand function** is the function that relates the optimal choice—the quantities demanded—to the different values of prices and incomes.

We will write the demand functions as depending on both prices and income: $x_1(p_1, p_2, m)$ and $x_2(p_1, p_2, m)$. For each different set of prices and income, there will be a different combination of goods that is the optimal choice of the consumer. Different preferences will lead to different demand functions; we'll see some examples shortly. Our major goal in the next few chapters is to study the behavior of these demand functions—how the optimal choices change as prices and income change.

5.3 Some Examples

Let us apply the model of consumer choice we have developed to the examples of preferences described in Chapter 3. The basic procedure will be the same for each example: plot the indifference curves and budget line and find the point where the highest indifference curve touches the budget line.

Perfect Substitutes

The case of perfect substitutes is illustrated in Figure 5.5. We have three possible cases. If $p_2 > p_1$, then the slope of the budget line is flatter than the slope of the indifference curves. In this case, the optimal bundle is where the consumer spends all of his or her money on good 1. If $p_1 > p_2$, then the consumer purchases only good 2. Finally, if $p_1 = p_2$, there is a whole range of optimal choices—any amount of goods 1 and 2 that satisfies the budget constraint is optimal in this case. Thus the demand function for good 1 will be

$$x_1 = \begin{cases} m/p_1 & \text{when } p_1 < p_2; \\ \text{any number between 0 and } m/p_1 & \text{when } p_1 = p_2; \\ 0 & \text{when } p_1 > p_2. \end{cases}$$

Are these results consistent with common sense? All they say is that if two goods are perfect substitutes, then a consumer will purchase the cheaper one. If both goods have the same price, then the consumer doesn't care which one he or she purchases.

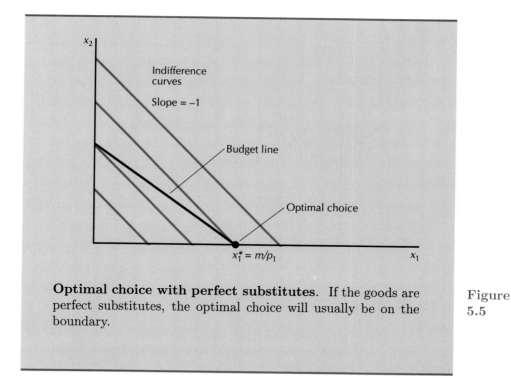

Optimal choice with perfect substitutes. If the goods are perfect substitutes, the optimal choice will usually be on the boundary.

Figure
5.5

Perfect Complements

The case of perfect complements is illustrated in Figure 5.6. Note that the optimal choice must always lie on the diagonal, where the consumer is purchasing equal amounts of both goods, no matter what the prices are.

In terms of our example, this says that people with two feet buy shoes in pairs.[2]

Let us solve for the optimal choice algebraically. We know that this consumer is purchasing the same amount of good 1 and good 2, no matter what the prices. Let this amount be denoted by x. Then we have to satisfy the budget constraint

$$p_1 x + p_2 x = m.$$

Solving for x gives us the optimal choices of goods 1 and 2:

$$x_1 = x_2 = x = \frac{m}{p_1 + p_2}.$$

The demand function for the optimal choice here is quite intuitive. Since the two goods are always consumed together, it is just as if the consumer were spending all of her money on a single good that had a price of $p_1 + p_2$.

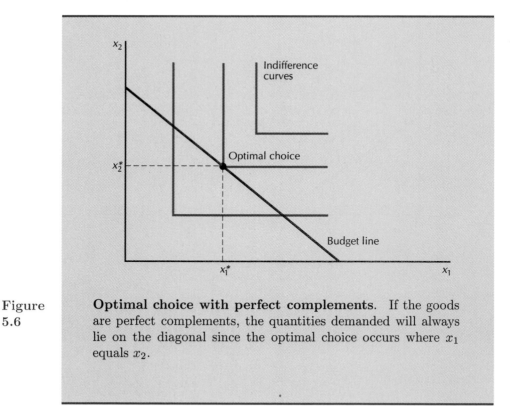

Figure 5.6

Optimal choice with perfect complements. If the goods are perfect complements, the quantities demanded will always lie on the diagonal since the optimal choice occurs where x_1 equals x_2.

---

[2] Don't worry, we'll get some more exciting results later on.

Discrete goods. In panel A the demand for good 1 is zero, while in panel B one unit will be demanded.

Figure
5.7

Neutrals and Bads

In the case of a neutral good the consumer spends all of her money on the good she likes and doesn't purchase any of the neutral good. The same thing happens if one commodity is a bad. Thus, if commodity 1 is a good and commodity 2 is a bad, then the demand functions will be

$$x_1 = \frac{m}{p_1}$$
$$x_2 = 0.$$

Discrete Goods

Suppose that good 1 is a discrete good that is available only in integer units, while good 2 is money to be spent on everything else. If the consumer chooses $1, 2, 3, \cdots$ units of good 1, she will implicitly choose the consumption bundles $(1, m - p_1)$, $(2, m - 2p_1)$, $(3, m - 3p_1)$, and so on. We can simply compare the utility of each of these bundles to see which has the highest utility.

Alternatively, we can use the indifference-curve analysis in Figure 5.7. As usual, the optimal bundle is the one on the highest indifference "curve." If the price of good 1 is very high, then the consumer will choose zero units of consumption; as the price decreases the consumer will find it optimal to consume 1 unit of the good. Typically, as the price decreases further the consumer will choose to consume more units of good 1.

Concave Preferences

Consider the situation illustrated in Figure 5.8. Is X the optimal choice? No! The optimal choice for these preferences is always going to be a boundary choice, like bundle Z. Think of what nonconvex preferences mean. If you have money to purchase ice cream and olives, and you don't like to consume them together, you'll spend all of your money on one or the other.

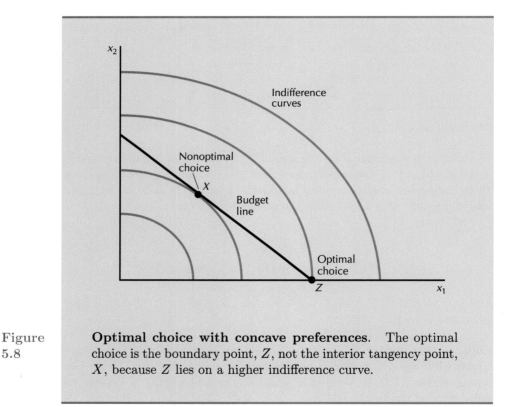

Figure 5.8

Optimal choice with concave preferences. The optimal choice is the boundary point, Z, not the interior tangency point, X, because Z lies on a higher indifference curve.

Cobb-Douglas Preferences

Suppose that the utility function is of the Cobb-Douglas form, $u(x_1, x_2) = x_1^c x_2^d$. In the Appendix to this chapter we use calculus to derive the optimal choices for this utility function. They turn out to be

$$x_1 = \frac{c}{c+d}\frac{m}{p_1}$$

$$x_2 = \frac{d}{c+d}\frac{m}{p_2}.$$

These demand functions are often useful in algebraic examples, so you should probably memorize them.

The Cobb-Douglas preferences have a convenient property. Consider the fraction of his income that a Cobb-Douglas consumer spends on good 1. If he consumes x_1 units of good 1, this costs him $p_1 x_1$, so this represents a fraction $p_1 x_1/m$ of total income. Substituting the demand function for x_1 we have

$$\frac{p_1 x_1}{m} = \frac{p_1}{m}\frac{c}{c+d}\frac{m}{p_1} = \frac{c}{c+d}.$$

Similarly the fraction of his income that the consumer spends on good 2 is $d/(c+d)$.

Thus the Cobb-Douglas consumer always spends a fixed fraction of his income on each good. The size of the fraction is determined by the exponent in the Cobb-Douglas function.

This is why it is often convenient to choose a representation of the Cobb-Douglas utility function in which the exponents sum to 1. If $u(x_1, x_2) = x_1^a x_2^{1-a}$, then we can immediately interpret a as the fraction of income spent on good 1. For this reason we will usually write Cobb-Douglas preferences in this form.

5.4 Estimating Utility Functions

We've now seen several different forms for preferences and utility functions and have examined the kinds of demand behavior generated by these preferences. But in real life we usually have to work the other way around: we observe demand behavior, but our problem is to determine what kind of preferences generated the observed behavior.

For example, suppose that we observe a consumer's choices at several different prices and income levels. An example is depicted in Table 5.1. This is a table of the demand for two goods at the different levels of prices and incomes that prevailed in different years. We have also computed the share of income spent on each good in each year using the formulas $s_1 = p_1 x_1/m$ and $s_2 = p_2 x_2/m$.

For these data, the expenditure shares are relatively constant. There are small variations from observation to observation, but they probably aren't large enough to worry about. The average expenditure share for good 1 is about 1/4, and the average income share for good 2 is about 3/4. It appears

Table
5.1

Some data describing consumption behavior.

Year	p_1	p_2	m	x_1	x_2	s_1	s_2	Utility
1	1	1	100	25	75	.25	.75	57.0
2	1	2	100	24	38	.24	.76	33.9
3	2	1	100	13	74	.26	.74	47.9
4	1	2	200	48	76	.24	.76	67.8
5	2	1	200	25	150	.25	.75	95.8
6	1	4	400	100	75	.25	.75	80.6
7	4	1	400	24	304	.24	.76	161.1

that a utility function of the form $u(x_1, x_2) = x_1^{\frac{1}{4}} x_2^{\frac{3}{4}}$ seems to fit these data pretty well. That is, a utility function of this form would generate choice behavior that is pretty close to the observed choice behavior. For convenience we have calculated the utility associated with each observation using this estimated Cobb-Douglas utility function.

As far as we can tell from the observed behavior it appears as though the consumer is maximizing the function $u(x_1, x_2) = x_1^{\frac{1}{4}} x_2^{\frac{3}{4}}$. It may well be that further observations on the consumer's behavior would lead us to reject this hypothesis. But based on the data we have, the fit to the optimizing model is pretty good.

This has very important implications, since we can now use this "fitted" utility function to evaluate the impact of proposed policy changes. Suppose, for example, that the government was contemplating imposing a system of taxes that would result in this consumer facing prices $(2, 3)$ and having an income of 200. According to our estimates, the demanded bundle at these prices would be

$$x_1 = \frac{1}{4}\frac{200}{2} = 25$$
$$x_2 = \frac{3}{4}\frac{200}{3} = 50.$$

The estimated utility of this bundle is

$$u(x_1, x_2) = 25^{\frac{1}{4}} 50^{\frac{3}{4}} \approx 42.$$

This means that the new tax policy would make the consumer better off than he was in year 2, but worse off than he was in year 3. Thus we can use the observed choice behavior to value the implications of proposed policy changes on this consumer.

Since this is such an important idea in economics, let us review the logic one more time. Given some observations on choice behavior, we try to determine what, if anything, is being maximized. Once we have an estimate of what it is that is being maximized, we can use this both to predict choice behavior in new situations and to evaluate proposed changes in the economic environment.

Of course we have described a very simple situation. In reality, we normally don't have detailed data on individual consumption choices. But we often have data on groups of individuals—teenagers, middle-class households, elderly people, and so on. These groups may have different preferences for different goods that are reflected in their patterns of consumption expenditure. We can estimate a utility function that describes their consumption patterns and then use this estimated utility function to forecast demand and evaluate policy proposals.

In the simple example described above, it was apparent that income shares were relatively constant so that the Cobb-Douglas utility function would give us a pretty good fit. In other cases, a more complicated form for the utility function would be appropriate. The calculations may then become messier, and we may need to use a computer for the estimation, but the essential idea of the procedure is the same.

5.5 Implications of the MRS Condition

In the last section we examined the important idea that observation of demand behavior tells us important things about the underlying preferences of the consumers that generated that behavior. Given sufficient observations on consumer choices it will often be possible to estimate the utility function that generated those choices.

But even observing *one* consumer choice at one set of prices will allow us to make some kinds of useful inferences about how consumer utility will change when consumption changes. Let us see how this works.

In well-organized markets, it is typical that everyone faces roughly the same prices for goods. Take, for example, two goods like butter and milk. If everyone faces the same prices for butter and milk, and everyone is optimizing, and everyone is at an interior solution ... then everyone must have the same marginal rate of substitution for butter and milk.

This follows directly from the analysis given above. The market is offering everyone the same rate of exchange for butter and milk, and everyone is adjusting their consumption of the goods until their own "internal" marginal valuation of the two goods equals the market's "external" valuation of the two goods.

Now the interesting thing about this statement is that it is independent of income and tastes. People may value their *total* consumption of the two goods very differently. Some people may be consuming a lot of butter and a little milk, and some may be doing the reverse. Some wealthy people may be consuming a lot of milk and a lot of butter while other people may be consuming just a little of each good. But everyone who is consuming the two goods must have the same marginal rate of substitution. Everyone who is consuming the goods must agree on how much one is worth in terms of the other: how much of one they would be willing to sacrifice to get some more of the other.

The fact that price ratios measure marginal rates of substitution is very important, for it means that we have a way to value possible changes in consumption bundles. Suppose, for example, that the price of milk is $1 a quart and the price of butter is $2 a pound. Then the marginal rate of substitution for all people who consume milk and butter must be 2: they have to have 2 quarts of milk to compensate them for giving up 1 pound of butter. Or conversely, they have to have 1 pound of butter to make it worth their while to give up 2 quarts of milk. Hence everyone who is consuming both goods will value a marginal change in consumption in the same way.

Now suppose that an inventor discovers a new way of turning milk into butter: for every 3 quarts of milk poured into this machine, you get out 1 pound of butter, and no other useful byproducts. Question: is there a market for this device? Answer: the venture capitalists won't beat a path to his door, that's for sure. For everyone is already operating at a point where they are just willing to trade 2 quarts of milk for 1 pound of butter; why would they be willing to substitute 3 quarts of milk for 1 pound of butter? The answer is they wouldn't; this invention isn't worth anything.

But what would happen if he got it to run in reverse so he could dump in a pound of butter get out 3 quarts of milk? Is there a market for this device? Answer: yes! The market prices of milk and butter tell us that people are just barely willing to trade one pound of butter for 2 quarts of milk. So getting 3 quarts of milk for a pound of butter is a better deal than is currently being offered in the marketplace. Sign me up for a thousand shares! (And several pounds of butter.)

The market prices show that the first machine is unprofitable: it produces $2 of butter by using $3 of milk. The fact that it is unprofitable is just another way of saying that people value the inputs more than the outputs. The second machine produces $3 worth of milk by using only $2 worth of butter. This machine is profitable because people value the outputs more than the inputs.

The point is that, since prices measure the rate at which people are just willing to substitute one good for another, they can be used to value policy proposals that involve making changes in consumption. The fact that prices are not arbitrary numbers but reflect how people value things on the margin is one of the most fundamental and important ideas in economics.

If we observe one choice at one set of prices we get the MRS at one consumption point. If the prices change and we observe another choice we get another MRS. As we observe more and more choices we learn more and more about the shape of the underlying preferences that may have generated the observed choice behavior.

5.6 Choosing Taxes

Even the small bit of consumer theory we have discussed so far can be used to derive interesting and important conclusions. Here is a nice example describing a choice between two types of taxes. We saw that a **quantity tax** is a tax on the amount consumed of a good, like a gasoline tax of 15 cents per gallon. An **income tax** is just a tax on income. If the government wants to raise a certain amount of revenue, is it better to raise it via a quantity tax or an income tax? Let's apply what we've learned to answer this question.

First we analyze the imposition of a quantity tax. Suppose that the original budget constraint is

$$p_1 x_1 + p_2 x_2 = m.$$

What is the budget constraint if we tax the consumption of good 1 at a rate of t? The answer is simple. From the viewpoint of the consumer it is just as if the price of good 1 has increased by an amount t. Thus the new budget constraint is

$$(p_1 + t)x_1 + p_2 x_2 = m. \tag{5.1}$$

Therefore a quantity tax on a good increases the price perceived by the consumer. Figure 5.9 gives an example of how that price change might affect demand. At this stage, we don't know for certain whether this tax will increase or decrease the consumption of good 1, although the presumption is that it will decrease it. Whichever is the case, we do know that the optimal choice, (x_1^*, x_2^*), must satisfy the budget constraint

$$(p_1 + t)x_1^* + p_2 x_2^* = m. \tag{5.2}$$

The revenue raised by this tax is $R^* = tx_1^*$.

Let's now consider an income tax that raises the same amount of revenue. The form of this budget constraint would be

$$p_1 x_1 + p_2 x_2 = m - R^*$$

or, substituting for R^*,

$$p_1 x_1 + p_2 x_2 = m - tx_1^*.$$

Where does this budget line go in Figure 5.9?

It is easy to see that it has the same slope as the original budget line, $-p_1/p_2$, but the problem is to determine its location. As it turns out, the budget line with the income tax must pass through the point (x_1^*, x_2^*). The way to check this is to plug (x_1^*, x_2^*) into the income-tax budget constraint and see if it is satisfied.

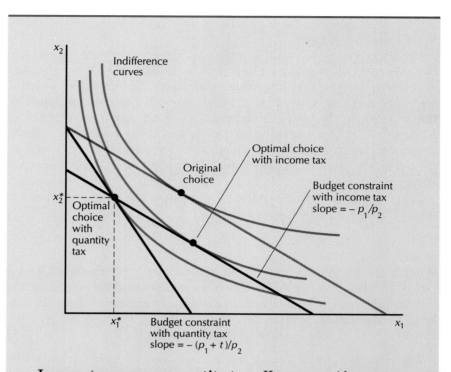

Figure
5.9

Income tax versus a quantity tax. Here we consider a quantity tax that raises revenue R^* and an income tax that raises the same revenue. The consumer will be better off under the income tax, since he can choose a point on a higher indifference curve.

Is it true that

$$p_1 x_1^* + p_2 x_2^* = m - t x_1^*?$$

Yes it is, since this is just a rearrangement of equation (5.2), which we know to be true.

This establishes that (x_1^*, x_2^*) lies on the income tax budget line: it is an *affordable* choice for the consumer. But is it an optimal choice? It is easy to see that the answer is no. At (x_1^*, x_2^*) the MRS is $-(p_1 + t)/p_2$. But the income tax allows us to trade at a rate of exchange of $-p_1/p_2$. Thus the budget line cuts the indifference curve at (x_1^*, x_2^*), which implies that there will be some point on the budget line that will be preferred to (x_1^*, x_2^*).

Therefore the income tax is definitely superior to the quantity tax in the sense that you can raise the same amount of revenue from a consumer and still leave him or her better off under the income tax than under the quantity tax.

This is a nice result, and worth remembering, but it is also worthwhile understanding its limitations. First, it only applies to one consumer. The argument shows that for any given consumer there is an income tax that will raise as much money from that consumer as a quantity tax and leave him or her better off. But the amount of that income tax will typically differ from person to person. So a *uniform* income tax for all consumers is not necessarily better than a *uniform* quantity tax for all consumers. (Think about a case where some consumer doesn't consume any of good 1—this person would certainly prefer the quantity tax to a uniform income tax.)

Second, we have assumed that when we impose the tax on income the consumer's income doesn't change. We have assumed that the income tax is basically a lump sum tax—one that just changes the amount of money a consumer has to spend but doesn't affect any choices he has to make. This is an unlikely assumption. If income is earned by the consumer, we might expect that taxing it will discourage earning income, so that after-tax income might fall by even more than the amount taken by the tax.

Third, we have totally left out the supply response to the tax. We've shown how demand responds to the tax change, but supply will respond too, and a complete analysis would take those changes into account as well.

Summary

1. The optimal choice of the consumer is that bundle in the consumer's budget set that lies on the highest indifference curve.

2. Typically the optimal bundle will be characterized by the condition that the slope of the indifference curve (the MRS) will equal the slope of the budget line.

3. If we observe several consumption choices it may be possible to estimate a utility function that would generate that sort of choice behavior. Such a utility function can be used to predict future choices and to estimate the utility to consumers of new economic policies.

4. If everyone faces the same prices for the two goods, then everyone will have the same marginal rate of substitution, and will thus be willing to trade off the two goods in the same way.

REVIEW QUESTIONS

1. If two goods are perfect substitutes, what is the demand function for good 2?

2. Suppose that indifference curves are described by straight lines with a slope of $-b$. Given arbitrary prices and money income p_1, p_2, and m, what will the consumer's optimal choices look like?

3. Suppose that a consumer always consumes 2 spoons of sugar with each cup of coffee. If the price of sugar is p_1 per spoonful and the price of coffee is p_2 per cup and the consumer has m dollars to spend on coffee and sugar, how much will he or she want to purchase?

4. Suppose that you have highly nonconvex preferences for ice cream and olives, like those given in the text, and that you face prices p_1, p_2 and have m dollars to spend. List the choices for the optimal consumption bundles.

5. If a consumer has a utility function $u(x_1, x_2) = x_1 x_2^4$, what fraction of her income will she spend on good 2?

6. For what kind of preferences will the consumer be just as well-off facing a quantity tax as an income tax?

APPENDIX

It is very useful to be able to solve the preference-maximization problem and get algebraic examples of actual demand functions. We did this in the body of the text for easy cases like perfect substitutes and perfect complements, and in this Appendix we'll see how to do it in more general cases.

First, we will generally want to represent the consumer's preferences by a utility function, $u(x_1, x_2)$. We've seen in Chapter 4 that this is not a very restrictive assumption; most well-behaved preferences can be described by a utility function.

The first thing to observe is that we already *know* how to solve the optimal-choice problem. We just have to put together the facts that we learned in the last three chapters. We know from this chapter that an optimal choice (x_1, x_2) must satisfy the condition

$$\text{MRS}(x_1, x_2) = -\frac{p_1}{p_2}, \tag{5.3}$$

and we saw in the Appendix to Chapter 4 that the MRS can be expressed as the negative of the ratio of derivatives of the utility function. Making this substitution and cancelling the minus signs, we have

$$\frac{\partial u(x_1, x_2)/\partial x_1}{\partial u(x_1, x_2)/\partial x_2} = \frac{p_1}{p_2}. \tag{5.4}$$

From Chapter 2 we know that the optimal choice must also satisfy the budget constraint

$$p_1 x_1 + p_2 x_2 = m. \tag{5.5}$$

This gives us two equations—the MRS condition and the budget constraint—and two unknowns, x_1 and x_2. All we have to do is to solve these two equations to find the optimal choices of x_1 and x_2 as a function of the prices and income. There are a number of ways to solve two equations in two unknowns. One way that always works, although it might not always be the simplest, is to solve the budget constraint for one of the choices, and then substitute that into the MRS condition.

Rewriting the budget constraint, we have

$$x_2 = \frac{m}{p_2} - \frac{p_1}{p_2}x_1 \qquad (5.6)$$

and substituting this into equation (5.4) we get

$$\frac{\partial u(x_1, m/p_2 - (p_1/p_2)x_1)/\partial x_1}{\partial u(x_1, m/p_2 - (p_1/p_2)x_1)/\partial x_2} = \frac{p_1}{p_2}.$$

This rather formidable looking expression has only one unknown variable, x_1, and it can typically be solved for x_1 in terms of (p_1, p_2, m). Then the budget constraint yields the solution for x_2 as a function of prices and income.

We can also derive the solution to the utility maximization problem in a more systematic way, using calculus conditions for maximization. To do this, we first pose the utility maximization problem as a constrained maximization problem:

$$\max_{x_1, x_2} u(x_1, x_2)$$

such that $p_1 x_1 + p_2 x_2 = m$.

This problem asks that we choose values of x_1 and x_2 that do two things: first, they have to satisfy the constraint, and second, they give a larger value for $u(x_1, x_2)$ than any other values of x_1 and x_2 that satisfy the constraint.

There are two useful ways to solve this kind of problem. The first way is simply to solve the constraint for one of the variables in terms of the other and then substitute it into the objective function.

For example, for any given value of x_1, the amount of x_2 that we need to satisfy the budget constraint is given by the linear function

$$x_2(x_1) = \frac{m}{p_2} - \frac{p_1}{p_2}x_1. \qquad (5.7)$$

Now substitute $x_2(x_1)$ for x_2 in the utility function to get the *unconstrained* maximization problem

$$\max_{x_1} u(x_1, m/p_2 - (p_1/p_2)x_1).$$

This is an unconstrained maximization problem in x_1 alone, since we have used the function $x_2(x_1)$ to ensure that the value of x_2 will always satisfy the budget constraint, whatever the value of x_1 is.

We can solve this kind of problem just by differentiating with respect to x_1 and setting the result equal to zero in the usual way. This procedure will give us a first-order condition of the form

$$\frac{\partial u(x_1, x_2(x_1))}{\partial x_1} + \frac{\partial u(x_1, x_2(x_1))}{\partial x_2}\frac{dx_2}{dx_1} = 0. \qquad (5.8)$$

Here the first term is the direct effect of how increasing x_1 increases utility. The second term consists of two parts: the rate of increase of utility as x_2 increases, $\partial u/\partial x_2$, times dx_2/dx_1, the rate of increase of x_2 as x_1 increases in order to continue to satisfy the budget equation. We can differentiate (5.7) to calculate this latter derivative

$$\frac{dx_2}{dx_1} = -\frac{p_1}{p_2}.$$

Substituting this into (5.8) gives us

$$\frac{\partial u(x_1^*, x_2^*)/\partial x_1}{\partial u(x_1^*, x_2^*)/\partial x_2} = \frac{p_1}{p_2},$$

which just says that the marginal rate of substitution between x_1 and x_2 must equal the price ratio at the optimal choice (x_1^*, x_2^*). This is exactly the condition we derived above: the slope of the indifference curve must equal the slope of the budget line. Of course the optimal choice must also satisfy the budget constraint $p_1 x_1^* + p_2 x_2^* = m$, which again gives us two equations in two unknowns.

The second way that these problems can be solved is through the use of **Lagrange multipliers**. This method starts by defining an auxiliary function known as the *Lagrangian*:

$$L = u(x_1, x_2) - \lambda(p_1 x_1 + p_2 x_2 - m).$$

The new variable λ is called a **Lagrange multiplier** since it is multiplied by the constraint.[3] Then Lagrange's theorem says that an optimal choice (x_1^*, x_2^*) must satisfy the three first-order conditions

$$\frac{\partial L}{\partial x_1} = \frac{\partial u(x_1^*, x_2^*)}{\partial x_1} - \lambda p_1 = 0$$

$$\frac{\partial L}{\partial x_2} = \frac{\partial u(x_1^*, x_2^*)}{\partial x_2} - \lambda p_2 = 0$$

$$\frac{\partial L}{\partial \lambda} = p_1 x_1^* + p_2 x_2^* - m = 0.$$

There are several interesting things about these three equations. First, note that they are simply the derivatives of the Lagrangian with respect to x_1, x_2, and λ, each set equal to zero. The last derivative, with respect to λ, is just the budget constraint. Second, we now have three equations for the three unknowns, x_1, x_2, and λ. We have a hope of solving for x_1 and x_2 in terms of p_1, p_2, and m.

Lagrange's theorem is proved in any advanced calculus book. It is used quite extensively in advanced economics courses, but for our purposes we only need to know the statement of the theorem and how to use it.

In our particular case, it is worthwhile noting that if we divide the first condition by the second one, we get

$$\frac{\partial u(x_1^*, x_2^*)/\partial x_1}{\partial u(x_1^*, x_2^*)/\partial x_2} = \frac{p_1}{p_2},$$

which simply says the MRS must equal the price ratio, just as before. The budget constraint gives us the other equation, so we are back to two equations in two unknowns.

---

[3] The Greek letter λ is pronounced "lamb-da."

EXAMPLE: Cobb-Douglas Demand Functions

In Chapter 4 we introduced the **Cobb-Douglas utility function**

$$u(x_1, x_2) = x_1^c x_2^d.$$

Since utility functions are only defined up to a monotonic transformation, it is convenient to take logs of this expression and work with

$$\ln u(x_1, x_2) = c \ln x_1 + d \ln x_2.$$

Let's find the demand functions for x_1 and x_2 for the Cobb-Douglas utility function. The problem we want to solve is

$$\max_{x_1, x_2} c \ln x_1 + d \ln x_2$$

such that $p_1 x_1 + p_2 x_2 = m.$

There are at least three ways to solve this problem. One way is just to write down the MRS condition and the budget constraint. Using the expression for the MRS derived in Chapter 4, we have

$$\frac{c x_2}{d x_1} = \frac{p_1}{p_2}$$

$$p_1 x_1 + p_2 x_2 = m.$$

These are two equations in two unknowns that can be solved for the optimal choice of x_1 and x_2. One way to solve them is to substitute the second into the first to get

$$\frac{c(m/p_2 - x_1 p_1/p_2)}{d x_1} = \frac{p_1}{p_2}.$$

Cross multiplying gives

$$c(m - x_1 p_1) = d p_1 x_1.$$

Rearranging this equation gives

$$cm = (c + d) p_1 x_1$$

or

$$x_1 = \frac{c}{c+d} \frac{m}{p_1}.$$

This is the demand function for x_1. To find the demand function for x_2, substitute into the budget constraint to get

$$x_2 = \frac{m}{p_2} - \frac{p_1}{p_2} \frac{c}{c+d} \frac{m}{p_1}$$

$$= \frac{d}{c+d} \frac{m}{p_2}.$$

The second way is to substitute the budget constraint into the maximization problem at the beginning. If we do this, our problem becomes

$$\max_{x_1} c \ln x_1 + d \ln(m/p_2 - x_1 p_1/p_2).$$

The first-order condition for this problem is

$$\frac{c}{x_1} - d \frac{p_2}{m - p_1 x_1} \frac{p_1}{p_2} = 0.$$

A little algebra—which you should do!—gives us the solution

$$x_1 = \frac{c}{c+d} \frac{m}{p_1}.$$

Substitute this back into the budget constraint $x_2 = m/p_2 - x_1 p_1/p_2$ to get

$$x_2 = \frac{d}{c+d} \frac{m}{p_2}.$$

These are the demand functions for the two goods, which, happily, are the same as those derived earlier by the other method.

Now for Lagrange's method. Set up the Lagrangian

$$L = c \ln x_1 + d \ln x_2 - \lambda(p_1 x_1 + p_2 x_2 - m)$$

and differentiate to get the three first-order conditions

$$\frac{\partial L}{\partial x_1} = \frac{c}{x_1} - \lambda p_1 = 0$$

$$\frac{\partial L}{\partial x_2} = \frac{d}{x_2} - \lambda p_2 = 0$$

$$\frac{\partial L}{\partial \lambda} = p_1 x_1 + p_2 x_2 - m = 0.$$

Now the trick is to solve them! The best way to proceed is to first solve for λ and then for x_1 and x_2. So we rearrange and cross multiply the first two equations to get

$$c = \lambda p_1 x_1$$

$$d = \lambda p_2 x_2.$$

These equations are just asking to be added together:

$$c + d = \lambda(p_1 x_1 + p_2 x_2) = \lambda m,$$

which gives us

$$\lambda = \frac{c+d}{m}.$$

Substitute this back into the first two equations and solve for x_1 and x_2 to get

$$x_1 = \frac{c}{c+d} \frac{m}{p_1}$$

$$x_2 = \frac{d}{c+d} \frac{m}{p_2},$$

just as before.

CHAPTER **6**

DEMAND

In the last chapter we presented the basic model of consumer choice: how maximizing utility subject to a budget constraint yields optimal choices. We saw that the optimal choices of the consumer depend on the consumer's income and the prices of the goods, and we worked a few examples to see what the optimal choices are for some simple kinds of preferences.

The consumer's **demand functions** give the optimal amounts of each of the goods as a function of the prices and income faced by the consumer. We write the demand functions as

$$x_1 = x_1(p_1, p_2, m)$$
$$x_2 = x_2(p_1, p_2, m).$$

The left-hand side of each equation stands for the quantity demanded. The right-hand side of each equation is the function that relates the prices and income to that quantity.

In this chapter we will examine how the demand for a good changes as prices and income change. Studying how a choice responds to changes in the economic environment is known as **comparative statics**, which we first described in Chapter 1. "Comparative" means that we want to compare two situations: before and after the change in the economic environment. "Statics" means that we are not concerned with any adjustment process that may be involved in moving from one choice to another; rather we will only examine the equilibrium choice.

In the case of the consumer, there are only two things in our model that affect the optimal choice: prices and income. The comparative statics questions in consumer theory therefore involve investigating how demand changes when prices and income change.

6.1 Normal and Inferior Goods

We start by considering how a consumer's demand for a good changes as his income changes. We want to know how the optimal choice at one income compares to the optimal choice at another level of income. During this exercise, we will hold the prices fixed and examine only the change in demand due to the income change.

We know how an increase in money income affects the budget line when prices are fixed—it shifts it outward in a parallel fashion. So how does this affect demand?

We would normally think that the demand for each good would increase when income increases, as shown in Figure 6.1. Economists, with a singular lack of imagination, call such goods **normal** goods. If good 1 is a normal good, then the demand for it increases when income increases, and decreases when income decreases. For a normal good the quantity demanded always changes in the same way as income changes:

$$\frac{\Delta x_1}{\Delta m} > 0.$$

If something is called normal, you can be sure that there must be a *possibility* of being abnormal. And indeed there is. Figure 6.2 presents an example of nice, well-behaved indifference curves where an increase of income results in a *reduction* in the consumption of one of the goods. Such a good is called an **inferior** good. This may be "abnormal," but when you think about it, inferior goods aren't all that unusual. There are many goods for which demand decreases as income increases; examples might include gruel, bologna, shacks, or nearly any kind of low-quality good.

Whether a good is inferior or not depends on the income level that we are examining. It might very well be that very poor people consume more bologna as their income increases. But after a point, the consumption of bologna would probably decline as income continued to increase. Since in real life the consumption of goods can increase or decrease when income increases, it is comforting to know that economic theory allows for both possibilities.

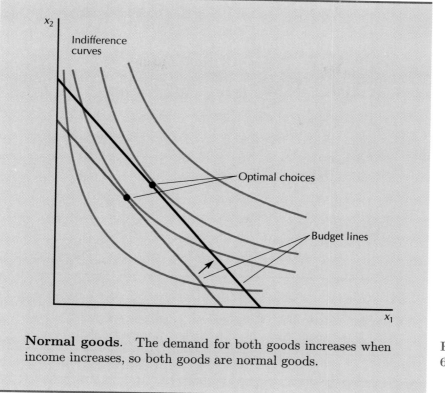

x_2

Indifference
curves

Optimal choices

Budget lines

x_1

Normal goods. The demand for both goods increases when
income increases, so both goods are normal goods.

Figure
6.1

6.2 Income Offer Curves and Engel Curves

We have seen that an increase in income corresponds to shifting the budget
line outward in a parallel manner. We can connect together the demanded
bundles that we get as we shift the budget line outward to construct the
income offer curve. This curve illustrates the bundles of goods that are
demanded at the different levels of income, as depicted in Figure 6.3A.
The income offer curve is also known as the **income expansion path**. If
both goods are normal goods, then the income expansion path will have a
positive slope, as depicted in Figure 6.3A.

For each level of income, m, there will be some optimal choice for each
of the goods. Let us focus on good 1 and consider the optimal choice at
each set of prices and income, $x_1(p_1, p_2, m)$. This is simply the demand
function for good 1. If we hold the prices of goods 1 and 2 fixed and look
at how demand changes as we change income, we generate a curve known
as the **Engel curve**. The Engel curve is a graph of the demand for one of
the goods as a function of income, with all prices being held constant. For
an example of an Engel curve, see Figure 6.3B.

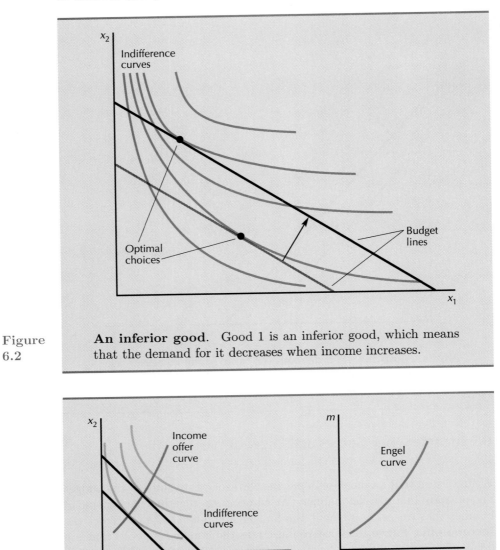

Figure
6.2

An inferior good. Good 1 is an inferior good, which means that the demand for it decreases when income increases.

A Income offer curve   **B** Engel curve

Figure
6.3

How demand changes as income changes. The income offer curve (or income expansion path) shown in panel A depicts the optimal choice at different levels of income and constant prices. When we plot the optimal choice of good 1 against income, m, we get the Engel curve, depicted in panel B.

6.3 Some Examples

Let's consider some of the preferences that we examined in Chapter 5 and see what their income offer curves and Engel curves look like.

Perfect Substitutes

The case of perfect substitutes is depicted in Figure 6.4. If $p_1 < p_2$, so that the consumer is specializing in consuming good 1, then if his income increases he will increase his consumption of good 1. Thus the income offer curve is the horizontal axis, as shown in Figure 6.4A.

Perfect substitutes. The income offer curve (A) and an Engel curve (B) in the case of perfect substitutes.

Figure
6.4

Since the demand for good 1 is $x_1 = m/p_1$ in this case, the Engel curve will be a straight line with a slope of p_1, as depicted in Figure 6.4B. (Since m is on the vertical axis, and x_1 on the horizontal axis, we can write $m = p_1 x_1$, which makes it clear that the slope is p_1.)

Perfect Complements

The demand behavior for perfect complements is shown in Figure 6.5. Since the consumer will always consume the same amount of each good, no matter what, the income offer curve is the diagonal line through the origin as depicted in Figure 6.5A. We have seen that the demand for good 1 is $x_1 = m/(p_1 + p_2)$, so the Engel curve is a straight line with a slope of $p_1 + p_2$ as shown in Figure 6.5B.

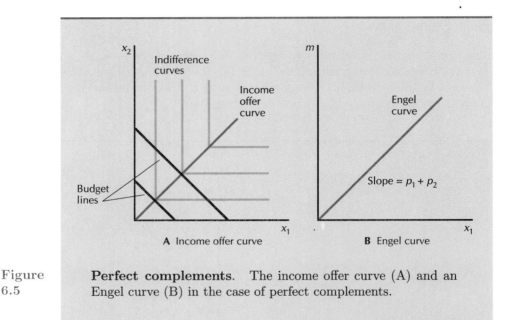

A Income offer curve
B Engel curve

Figure
6.5

Perfect complements. The income offer curve (A) and an Engel curve (B) in the case of perfect complements.

Cobb-Douglas Preferences

For the case of Cobb-Douglas preferences it is easier to look at the algebraic form of the demand functions to see what the graphs will look like. If $u(x_1, x_2) = x_1^a x_2^{1-a}$, the Cobb-Douglas demand for good 1 has the form $x_1 = am/p_1$. For a fixed value of p_1, this is a *linear* function of m. Thus doubling m will double demand, tripling m will triple demand, and so on. In fact, multiplying m by any positive number t will just multiply demand by the same amount.

The demand for good 2 is $x_2 = (1-a)m/p_2$, and this is also clearly linear. The fact that the demand functions for both goods are linear functions of income means that the income expansion paths will be straight lines through the origin, as depicted in Figure 6.6A. The Engel curve for good 1 will be a straight line with a slope of p_1/a, as depicted in Figure 6.6B.

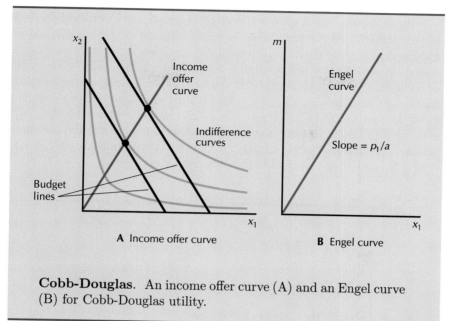

Cobb-Douglas. An income offer curve (A) and an Engel curve (B) for Cobb-Douglas utility.

Figure
6.6

Homothetic Preferences

All of the income offer curves and Engel curves that we have seen up to now have been straightforward—in fact they've been straight lines! This has happened because our examples have been so simple. Real Engel curves do not have to be straight lines. In general, when income goes up, the demand for a good could increase more or less rapidly than income increases. If the demand for a good goes up by a greater proportion than income, we say that it is a **luxury good**, and if it goes up by a lesser proportion than income we say that it is a **necessary good**.

The dividing line is the case where the demand for a good goes up by the same proportion as income. This is what happened in the three cases we examined above. What aspect of the consumer's preferences leads to this behavior?

Suppose that the consumer's preferences only depend on the *ratio* of good 1 to good 2. This means that if the consumer prefers (x_1, x_2) to (y_1, y_2), then she automatically prefers $(2x_1, 2x_2)$ to $(2y_1, 2y_2)$, $(3x_1, 3x_2)$ to $(3y_1, 3y_2)$, and so on, since the ratio of good 1 to good 2 is the same for all of these bundles. In fact, the consumer prefers (tx_1, tx_2) to (ty_1, ty_2) for any positive value of t. Preferences that have this property are known as **homothetic preferences**. It is not hard to show that the three examples of preferences given above—perfect substitutes, perfect complements, and Cobb-Douglas—are all homothetic preferences.

If the consumer has homothetic preferences, then the income offer curves are all straight lines through the origin, as shown in Figure 6.7. More specifically, if preferences are homothetic, it means that when income is scaled up or down by any amount $t > 0$, the demanded bundle scales up or down by the same amount. This can be established rigorously, but it is fairly clear from looking at the picture. If the indifference curve is tangent to the budget line at (x_1^*, x_2^*), then the indifference curve through (tx_1^*, tx_2^*) is tangent to the budget line that has t times as much income and the same prices. This implies that the Engel curves are straight lines as well. If you double income, you just double the demand for each good.

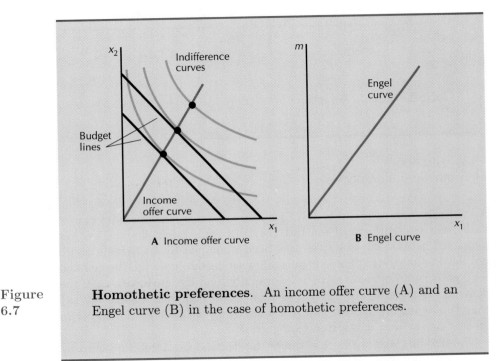

A Income offer curve   **B** Engel curve

Figure
6.7

Homothetic preferences. An income offer curve (A) and an Engel curve (B) in the case of homothetic preferences.

Homothetic preferences are very convenient since the income effects are so simple. Unfortunately, homothetic preferences aren't very realistic for the same reason! But they will often be of use in our examples.

Quasilinear Preferences

Another kind of preferences that generates a special form of income offer curves and Engel curves is the case of quasilinear preferences. Recall the definition of quasilinear preferences given in Chapter 4. This is the case where all indifference curves are "shifted" versions of one indifference curve as in Figure 6.8. Equivalently, the utility function for these preferences takes the form $u(x_1, x_2) = v(x_1) + x_2$. What happens if we shift the budget line outward? In this case, if an indifference curve is tangent to the budget line at a bundle (x_1^*, x_2^*), then another indifference curve must also be tangent at (x_1^*, x_2^*+k) for any constant k. Increasing income doesn't change the demand for good 1 at all, and all the extra income goes entirely to the consumption of good 2. If preferences are quasilinear, we sometimes say that there is a "zero income effect" for good 1. Thus the Engel curve for good 1 is a vertical line—as you change income, the demand for good 1 remains constant.

Quasilinear preferences. An income offer curve (A) and an Engel curve (B) with quasilinear preferences.

Figure
6.8

What would be a real-life situation where this kind of thing might occur? Suppose good 1 is pencils and good 2 is money to spend on other goods. Initially I may spend my income only on pencils, but when my income gets large enough, I stop buying additional pencils—all of my extra income is spent on other goods. Other examples of this sort might be salt or toothpaste. When we are examining a choice between all other goods and some single good that isn't a very large part of the consumer's budget, the quasilinear assumption may well be plausible, at least when the consumer's income is sufficiently large.

6.4 Ordinary Goods and Giffen Goods

Let us now consider price changes. Suppose that we decrease the price of good 1 and hold the price of good 2 and money income fixed. Then what can happen to the quantity demanded of good 1? Intuition tells us that the quantity demanded of good 1 should increase when its price decreases. Indeed this is the ordinary case, as depicted in Figure 6.9.

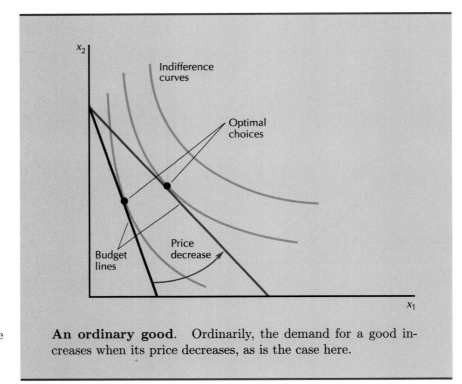

Figure
6.9

An ordinary good. Ordinarily, the demand for a good increases when its price decreases, as is the case here.

When the price of good 1 decreases, the budget line becomes flatter. Or said another way, the vertical intercept is fixed and the horizontal intercept moves to the right. In Figure 6.9, the optimal choice of good 1 moves to the right as well: the quantity demanded of good 1 has increased. But we might wonder whether this always happens this way. Is it always the case that, no matter what kind of preferences the consumer has, the demand for a good must increase when its price goes down?

As it turns out, the answer is no. It is logically possible to find well-behaved preferences for which a decrease in the price of good 1 leads to a reduction in the demand for good 1. Such a good is called a **Giffen good**,

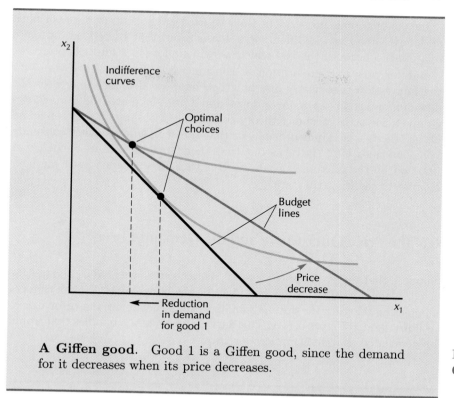

A Giffen good. Good 1 is a Giffen good, since the demand for it decreases when its price decreases.

Figure
6.10

after the nineteenth-century economist who first noted the possibility. An example is illustrated in Figure 6.10.

What is going on here in economic terms? What kind of preferences might give rise to the peculiar behavior depicted in Figure 6.10? Suppose that the two goods that you are consuming are gruel and milk and that you are currently consuming 7 bowls of gruel and 7 cups of milk a week. Now the price of gruel declines. If you consume the same 7 bowls of gruel a week, you will have money left over with which you can purchase more milk. In fact, with the extra money you have saved because of the lower price of gruel, you may decide to consume even more milk and reduce your consumption of gruel. The reduction in the price of gruel has freed up some extra money to be spent on other things—but one thing you might want to do with it is reduce your consumption of gruel! Thus the price change is to some extent *like* an income change. Even though *money* income remains constant, a change in the price of a good will change purchasing power, and thereby change demand.

So the Giffen good is not implausible purely on logical grounds, although Giffen goods are unlikely to be encountered in real-world behavior. Most goods are ordinary goods—when their price increases, the demand for them declines. We'll see why this is the ordinary situation a little later.

Incidentally, it is no accident that we used gruel as an example of both an inferior good and a Giffen good. It turns out that there is an intimate relationship between the two which we will explore in a later chapter.

But for now our exploration of consumer theory may leave you with the impression that nearly anything can happen: if income increases the demand for a good can go up or down, and if price increases the demand can go up or down. Is consumer theory compatible with *any* kind of behavior? Or are there some kinds of behavior that the economic model of consumer behavior rules out? It turns out that there *are* restrictions on behavior imposed by the maximizing model. But we'll have to wait until the next chapter to see what they are.

6.5 The Price Offer Curve and the Demand Curve

Suppose that we let the price of good 1 change while we hold p_2 and income fixed. Geometrically this involves pivoting the budget line. We can think of connecting together the optimal points to construct the **price offer curve** as illustrated in Figure 6.11A. This curve represents the bundles that would be demanded at different prices for good 1.

A Price offer curve   **B** Demand curve

Figure 6.11

The price offer curve and demand curve. Panel A contains a price offer curve, which depicts the optimal choices as the price of good 1 changes. Panel B contains the associated demand curve, which depicts a plot of the optimal choice of good 1 as a function of its price.

We can depict this same information in a different way. Again, hold the price of good 2 and money income fixed, and for each different value of p_1 plot the optimal level of consumption of good 1. The result is the **demand curve** depicted in Figure 6.11B. The demand curve is a plot of the demand function, $x_1(p_1, p_2, m)$, holding p_2 and m fixed at some predetermined values.

Ordinarily, when the price of a good increases, the demand for that good will decrease. Thus the price and quantity of a good will move in *opposite* directions, which means that the demand curve will typically have a negative slope. In terms of rates of change, we would normally have

$$\frac{\Delta x_1}{\Delta p_1} < 0,$$

which simply says that demand curves usually have a negative slope.

However, we have also seen that in the case of Giffen goods, the demand for a good may decrease when its price decreases. Thus it is possible, but not likely, to have a demand curve with a positive slope.

6.6 Some Examples

Let's look at a few examples of demand curves, using the preferences that we discussed in Chapter 3.

Perfect Substitutes

The offer curve and demand curve for perfect substitutes—the red and blue pencils example—are illustrated in Figure 6.12. As we saw in Chapter 5, the demand for good 1 is zero when $p_1 > p_2$, any amount on the budget line when $p_1 = p_2$, and m/p_1 when $p_1 < p_2$. The offer curve traces out these possibilities.

In order to find the demand curve, we fix the price of good 2 at some price p_2^* and graph the demand for good 1 versus the price of good 1 to get the shape depicted in Figure 6.12B.

Perfect Complements

The case of perfect complements—the right and left shoes example—is depicted in Figure 6.13. We know that whatever the prices are, a consumer will demand the same amount of goods 1 and 2. Thus his offer curve will be a diagonal line as depicted in Figure 6.13A.

We saw in Chapter 5 that the demand for good 1 is given by

$$x_1 = \frac{m}{p_1 + p_2}.$$

If we fix m and p_2 and plot the relationship between x_1 and p_1, we get the curve depicted in Figure 6.13B.

A Price offer curve

B Demand curve

Figure
6.12

Perfect substitutes. Price offer curve (A) and demand curve (B) in the case of perfect substitutes.

A Price offer curve

B Demand curve

Figure
6.13

Perfect complements. Price offer curve (A) and demand curve (B) in the case of perfect complements.

A Discrete Good

Suppose that good 1 is a discrete good. If p_1 is very high then the consumer will strictly prefer to consume zero units; if p_1 is low enough the consumer will strictly prefer to consume one unit. At some price r_1, the consumer will be indifferent between consuming good 1 or not consuming it. The price at which the consumer is just indifferent to consuming or not consuming the good is called the **reservation price**.[1] The indifference curves and demand curve are depicted in Figure 6.14.

A Optimal bundles at different prices   **B** Demand curve

A discrete good. As the price of good 1 decreases there will be some price, the reservation price, at which the consumer is just indifferent between consuming good 1 or not consuming it. As the price decreases further, more units of the discrete good will be demanded.

Figure 6.14

It is clear from the diagram that the demand behavior can be described by a sequence of reservation prices at which the consumer is just willing to purchase another unit of the good. At a price of r_1 the consumer is willing to buy 1 unit of the good; if the price falls to r_2, he is willing to buy another unit, and so on.

These prices can be described in terms of the original utility function. For example, r_1 is the price where the consumer is just indifferent between consuming 0 or 1 unit of good 1, so it must satisfy the equation

$$u(0, m) = u(1, m - r_1). \tag{6.1}$$

Similarly r_2 satisfies the equation

$$u(1, m - r_2) = u(2, m - 2r_2). \tag{6.2}$$

---

[1] The term reservation price comes from auction markets. When someone wanted to sell something in an auction he would typically state a minimum price at which he was willing to sell the good. If the best price offered was below this stated price, the seller reserved the right to purchase the item himself. This price became known as the seller's reservation price and eventually came to be used to describe the price at which someone was just willing to buy or sell some item.

The left-hand side of this equation is the utility from consuming one unit of the good at a price of r_2. The right-hand side is the utility from consuming two units of the good, each of which sells for r_2.

If the utility function is quasilinear, then the formulas describing the reservation prices become somewhat simpler. If $u(x_1, x_2) = v(x_1) + x_2$, and $v(0) = 0$, then we can write equation (6.1) as

$$v(0) + m = m = v(1) + m - r_1.$$

Since $v(0) = 0$, we can solve for r_1 to find

$$r_1 = v(1). \tag{6.3}$$

Similarly, we can write equation (6.2) as

$$v(1) + m - r_2 = v(2) + m - 2r_2.$$

Canceling terms and rearranging, this expression becomes

$$r_2 = v(2) - v(1).$$

Proceeding in this manner, the reservation price for the third unit of consumption is given by

$$r_3 = v(3) - v(2)$$

and so on.

In each case, the reservation price measures the increment in utility necessary to induce the consumer to choose an additional unit of the good. Loosely speaking, the reservation prices measure the marginal utilities associated with different levels of consumption of good 1. Our assumption of convex preferences implies that the sequence of reservation prices must decrease: $r_1 > r_2 > r_3 \cdots$.

Because of the special structure of the quasilinear utility function, the reservation prices do not depend on the amount of good 2 that the consumer has. This is certainly a special case, but it makes it very easy to describe demand behavior. Given any price p, we just find where it falls in the list of reservation prices. Suppose that p falls between r_6 and r_7, for example. The fact that $r_6 > p$ means that the consumer is willing to give up p dollars per unit bought to get 6 units of good 1, and the fact that $p > r_7$ means that the consumer is not willing to give up p dollars per unit to get the seventh unit of good 1.

This argument is quite intuitive, but let's look at the math just to make sure that it is clear. Suppose that the consumer demands 6 units of good 1. We want to show that we must have $r_6 \geq p \geq r_7$.

If the consumer is maximizing utility, then we must have

$$v(6) + m - 6p \geq v(x_1) + m - px_1$$

for all possible choices of x_1. In particular, we must have that

$$v(6) + m - 6p \geq v(5) + m - 5p.$$

Rearranging this equation we have

$$r_6 = v(6) - v(5) \geq p,$$

which is half of what we wanted to show.

By the same logic,

$$v(6) + m - 6p \geq v(7) + m - 7p.$$

Rearranging this gives us

$$p \geq v(7) - v(6) = r_7,$$

which is the other half of the inequality we wanted to establish.

6.7 Substitutes and Complements

We have already used the terms substitutes and complements, but it is now appropriate to give a formal definition. Since we have seen *perfect* substitutes and *perfect* complements several times already, it seems reasonable to look at the imperfect case.

Let's think about substitutes first. We said that red pencils and blue pencils might be thought of as perfect substitutes, at least for someone who didn't care about color. But what about pencils and pens? This is a case of "imperfect" substitutes. That is, pens and pencils are, to some degree, a substitute for each other, although they aren't as perfect a substitute for each other as red pencils and blue pencils.

Similarly, we said that right shoes and left shoes were perfect complements. But what about a pair of shoes and a pair of socks? Right shoes and left shoes are nearly always consumed together, and shoes and socks are *usually* consumed together. Complementary goods are those like shoes and socks that tend to be consumed together, albeit not always.

Now that we've discussed the basic idea of complements and substitutes, we can give a precise economic definition. Recall that the demand function for good 1, say, will typically be a function of the price of both good 1 and good 2, so we write $x_1(p_1, p_2, m)$. We can ask how the demand for good 1 changes as the price of good 2 changes: does it go up or down?

If the demand for good 1 goes up when the price of good 2 goes up, then we say that good 1 is a **substitute** for good 2. In terms of rates of change, good 1 is a substitute for good 2 if

$$\frac{\Delta x_1}{\Delta p_2} > 0.$$

The idea is that when good 2 gets more expensive the consumer switches to consuming good 1: the consumer *substitutes* away from the more expensive good to the less expensive good.

On the other hand, if the demand for good 1 goes down when the price of good 2 goes up, we say that good 1 is a **complement** to good 2. This means that

$$\frac{\Delta x_1}{\Delta p_2} < 0.$$

Complements are goods that are consumed together, like coffee and sugar, so when the price of one good rises, the consumption of both goods will tend to decrease.

The cases of perfect substitutes and perfect complements illustrate these points nicely. Note that $\Delta x_1/\Delta p_2$ is positive (or zero) in the case of perfect substitutes, and that $\Delta x_1/\Delta p_2$ is negative in the case of perfect complements.

A couple of warnings are in order about these concepts. First, the two-good case is rather special when it comes to complements and substitutes. Since income is being held fixed, if you spend more money on good 1, you'll have to spend less on good 2. This puts some restrictions on the kinds of behavior that are possible. When there are more than two goods, these restrictions are not so much of a problem.

Second, although the definition of substitutes and complements in terms of consumer demand behavior seems sensible, there are some difficulties with the definitions in more general environments. For example, if we use the above definitions in a situation involving more than two goods, it is perfectly possible that good 1 may be a substitute for good 3, but good 3 may be a complement for good 1. Because of this peculiar feature, more advanced treatments typically use a somewhat different definition of substitutes and complements. The definitions given above describe concepts known as **gross substitutes** and **gross complements**; they will be sufficient for our needs.

6.8 The Inverse Demand Function

If we hold p_2 and m fixed and plot p_1 against x_1 we get the **demand curve**. As suggested above, we typically think that the demand curve slopes downwards, so that higher prices lead to less demand, although the Giffen example shows that it could be otherwise.

As long as we do have a downward-sloping demand curve, as is usual, it is meaningful to speak of the **inverse demand function**. The inverse demand function is the demand function viewing price as a function of quantity. That is, for each level of demand for good 1, the inverse demand function measures what the price of good 1 would have to be in order for the consumer to choose that level of consumption. So the inverse demand function measures the same relationship as the direct demand function, but just from another point of view. Figure 6.15 depicts the inverse demand function—or the direct demand function, depending on your point of view.

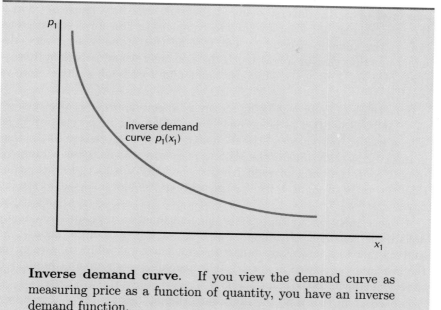

Inverse demand curve. If you view the demand curve as measuring price as a function of quantity, you have an inverse demand function.

Figure
6.15

Recall, for example, the Cobb-Douglas demand for good 1, $x_1 = am/p_1$. We could just as well write the relationship between price and quantity as $p_1 = am/x_1$. The first representation is the direct demand function; the second is the inverse demand function.

The inverse demand function has a useful economic interpretation. Recall that as long as both goods are being consumed in positive amounts, the optimal choice must satisfy the condition that the absolute value of the MRS equals the price ratio:

$$|\text{MRS}| = \frac{p_1}{p_2}.$$

This says that at the optimal level of demand for good 1, for example, we must have

$$p_1 = p_2|\text{MRS}|. \tag{6.4}$$

Thus, at the optimal level of demand for good 1, the price of good 1 is proportional to the absolute value of the MRS between good 1 and good 2.

Suppose for simplicity that the price of good 2 is one. Then equation (6.4) tells us that at the optimal level of demand, the price of good 1 measures how much the consumer is willing to give up of good 2 in order to get a little more of good 1. In this case the inverse demand function is simply measuring the absolute value of the MRS. For any optimal level of x_1 the inverse demand function tells how much of good 2 the consumer would want to have to compensate him for a small reduction in the amount of good 1. Or, turning this around, the inverse demand function measures how much the consumer would be willing to sacrifice of good 2 to make him just indifferent to having a little more of good 1.

If we think of good 2 as being money to spend on other goods, then we can think of the MRS as being how many dollars the individual would be willing to give up to have a little more of good 1. We suggested earlier that in this case, we can think of the MRS as measuring the marginal willingness to pay. Since the price of good 1 is just the MRS in this case, this means that the price of good 1 itself is measuring the marginal willingness to pay.

At each quantity x_1, the inverse demand function measures how many dollars the consumer is willing to give up for a little more of good 1; or, said another way, how many dollars the consumer was willing to give up for the last unit purchased of good 1. For a small enough amount of good 1, they come down to the same thing.

Looked at in this way, the downward-sloping demand curve has a new meaning. When x_1 is very small, the consumer is willing to give up a lot of money—that is, a lot of other goods, to acquire a little bit more of good 1. As x_1 is larger, the consumer is willing to give up less money, on the margin, to acquire a little more of good 1. Thus the marginal willingness to pay, in the sense of the marginal willingness to sacrifice good 2 for good 1, is decreasing as we increase the consumption of good 1.

Summary

1. The consumer's demand function for a good will in general depend on the prices of all goods and income.

2. A normal good is one for which the demand increases when income increases. An inferior good is one for which the demand decreases when income increases.

3. An ordinary good is one for which the demand decreases when its price increases. A Giffen good is one for which the demand increases when its price increases.

4. If the demand for good 1 increases when the price of good 2 increases, then good 1 is a substitute for good 2. If the demand for good 1 decreases in this situation, then it is a complement for good 2.

5. The inverse demand function measures the price at which a given quantity will be demanded. The height of the demand curve at a given level of consumption measures the marginal willingness to pay for an additional unit of the good at that consumption level.

REVIEW QUESTIONS

1. If the consumer is consuming exactly two goods, and she is always spending all of her money, can both of them be inferior goods?

2. Show that perfect substitutes are an example of homothetic preferences.

3. Show that Cobb-Douglas preferences are homothetic preferences.

4. The income offer curve is to the Engel curve as the price offer curve is to ...?

5. If the preferences are concave will the consumer ever consume both of the goods together?

6. What is the form of the inverse demand function for good 1 in the case of perfect complements?

APPENDIX

If preferences take a special form, this will mean that the demand functions that come from those preferences will take a special form. In Chapter 4 we described quasilinear preferences. These preferences involve indifference curves that are all parallel to one another and can be represented by a utility function of the form

$$u(x_1, x_2) = v(x_1) + x_2.$$

The maximization problem for a utility function like this is

$$\max_{x_1, x_2} v(x_1) + x_2$$

$$\text{s.t. } p_1 x_1 + p_2 x_2 = m.$$

Solving the budget constraint for x_2 as a function of x_1 and substituting into the objective function, we have

$$\max_{x_1} v(x_1) + m/p_2 - p_1 x_1/p_2.$$

Differentiating gives us the first-order condition

$$v'(x_1^*) = \frac{p_1}{p_2}.$$

This demand function has the interesting feature that the demand for good 1 must be independent of income—just as we saw by using indifference curves. The inverse demand curve is given by

$$p_1(x_1) = v'(x_1)p_2.$$

That is, the inverse demand function for good 1 is the derivative of the utility function times p_2. Once we have the demand function for good 1, the demand function for good 2 comes from the budget constraint.

For example, let us calculate the demand functions for the utility function

$$u(x_1, x_2) = \ln x_1 + x_2.$$

Applying the first-order condition gives

$$\frac{1}{x_1} = \frac{p_1}{p_2},$$

so the direct demand function for good 1 is

$$x_1 = \frac{p_2}{p_1},$$

and the inverse demand function is

$$p_1(x_1) = \frac{p_2}{x_1}.$$

The direct demand function for good 2 comes from substituting $x_1 = p_2/p_1$ into the budget constraint:

$$x_2 = \frac{m}{p_2} - 1.$$

A warning is in order concerning these demand functions. Note that the demand for good 1 is independent of income in this example. This is a general feature of a quasilinear utility function—the demand for good 1 remains constant as income changes. However, this is only true for some values of income. A demand function can't literally be independent of income for *all* values of income; after all, when income is zero, all demands are zero. The quasilinear demand function derived above is only relevant when a positive amount of each good is being consumed. For low levels of income, demands take a somewhat different form. See the discussion of quasilinear demand functions in Hal R. Varian, *Microeconomic Analysis,* 3rd ed. (New York: Norton, 1992).

CHAPTER 7

REVEALED PREFERENCE

In Chapter 6 we saw how we can use information about the consumer's preferences and budget constraint to determine his or her demand. In this chapter we reverse this process and show how we can use information about the consumer's demand to discover information about his or her preferences. Up until now, we were thinking about what preferences could tell us about people's behavior. But in real life, preferences are not directly observable: we have to discover people's preferences from observing their behavior. In this chapter we'll develop some tools to do this.

When we talk of determining people's preferences from observing their behavior, we have to assume that the preferences will remain unchanged while we observe the behavior. Over very long time spans, this is not very reasonable. But for the monthly or quarterly time spans that economists usually deal with, it seems unlikely that a particular consumer's tastes would change radically. Thus we will adopt a maintained hypothesis that the consumer's preferences are stable over the time period for which we observe his or her choice behavior.

7.1 The Idea of Revealed Preference

Before we begin this investigation, let's adopt the convention that in this chapter, the underlying preferences—whatever they may be—are known to be strictly convex. Thus there will be a *unique* demanded bundle at each budget. This assumption is not necessary for the theory of revealed preference, but the exposition will be simpler with it.

Consider Figure 7.1, where we have depicted a consumer's demanded bundle, (x_1, x_2), and another arbitrary bundle, (y_1, y_2), that is beneath the consumer's budget line. Suppose that we are willing to postulate that this consumer is an optimizing consumer of the sort we have been studying. What can we say about the consumer's preferences between these two bundles of goods?

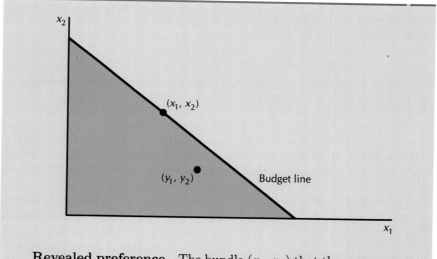

Revealed preference. The bundle (x_1, x_2) that the consumer chooses is revealed preferred to the bundle (y_1, y_2), a bundle that he could have chosen.

Figure 7.1

Well, the bundle (y_1, y_2) is certainly an affordable purchase at the given budget—the consumer could have bought it if he or she wanted to, and would even have had money left over. Since (x_1, x_2) is the *optimal* bundle, it must be better than anything else that the consumer could afford. Hence, in particular it must be better than (y_1, y_2).

The same argument holds for any bundle on or underneath the budget line other than the demanded bundle. Since it *could* have been bought at the given budget but wasn't, then what *was* bought must be better. Here is where we use the assumption that there is a *unique* demanded bundle for each budget. If preferences are not strictly convex, so that indifference curves have flat spots, it may be that some bundles that are *on* the budget line might be just as good as the demanded bundle. This complication can be handled without too much difficulty, but it is easier to just assume it away.

In Figure 7.1 all of the bundles in the shaded area underneath the budget line are revealed worse than the demanded bundle (x_1, x_2). This is because they could have been chosen, but were rejected in favor of (x_1, x_2). We will now translate this geometric discussion of revealed preference into algebra.

Let (x_1, x_2) be the bundle purchased at prices (p_1, p_2) when the consumer has income m. What does it mean to say that (y_1, y_2) is affordable at those prices and income? It simply means that (y_1, y_2) satisfies the budget constraint

$$p_1 y_1 + p_2 y_2 \leq m.$$

Since (x_1, x_2) is actually bought at the given budget, it must satisfy the budget constraint with equality

$$p_1 x_1 + p_2 x_2 = m.$$

Putting these two equations together, the fact that (y_1, y_2) is affordable at the budget (p_1, p_2, m) means that

$$p_1 x_1 + p_2 x_2 \geq p_1 y_1 + p_2 y_2.$$

If the above inequality is satisfied and (y_1, y_2) is actually a different bundle from (x_1, x_2), we say that (x_1, x_2) is **directly revealed preferred** to (y_1, y_2).

Note that the left-hand side of this inequality is the expenditure on the bundle that is *actually chosen* at prices (p_1, p_2). Thus revealed preference is a relation that holds between the bundle that is actually demanded at some budget and the bundles that *could have been* demanded at that budget.

The term "revealed preference" is actually a bit misleading. It does not inherently have anything to do with preferences, although we've seen above that if the consumer is making optimal choices, the two ideas are closely related. Instead of saying "X is revealed preferred to Y," it would be better to say "X is chosen over Y." When we say that X is revealed preferred to Y, all we are claiming is that X is chosen when Y could have been chosen; that is, that $p_1 x_1 + p_2 x_2 \geq p_1 y_1 + p_2 y_2$.

7.2 From Revealed Preference to Preference

We can summarize the above section very simply. It follows from our model of consumer behavior—that people are choosing the best things they can afford—that the choices they make are preferred to the choices that they could have made. Or, in the terminology of the last section, if (x_1, x_2) is *directly revealed preferred* to (y_1, y_2), then (x_1, x_2) is in fact *preferred* to (y_1, y_2). Let us state this principle more formally:

The Principle of Revealed Preference.   *Let (x_1, x_2) be the chosen bundle when prices are (p_1, p_2), and let (y_1, y_2) be some other bundle such that $p_1 x_1 + p_2 x_2 \geq p_1 y_1 + p_2 y_2$. Then if the consumer is choosing the most preferred bundle she can afford, we must have $(x_1, x_2) \succ (y_1, y_2)$.*

When you first encounter this principle, it may seem circular. If X is revealed preferred to Y, doesn't that automatically mean that X is preferred to Y? The answer is no. "Revealed preferred" just means that X was chosen when Y was affordable; "preference" means that the consumer ranks X ahead of Y. If the consumer chooses the best bundles she can afford, then "revealed preference" implies "preference," but that is a consequence of the model of behavior, not the definitions of the terms.

This is why it would be better to say that one bundle is "chosen over" another, as suggested above. Then we would state the principle of revealed preference by saying: "If a bundle X is chosen over a bundle Y, then X must be preferred to Y." In this statement it is clear how the model of behavior allows us to use observed choices to infer something about the underlying preferences.

Whatever terminology you use, the essential point is clear: if we observe that one bundle is chosen when another one is affordable, then we have learned something about the preferences between the two bundles: namely, that the first is preferred to the second.

Now suppose that we happen to know that (y_1, y_2) is a demanded bundle at prices (q_1, q_2) and that (y_1, y_2) is itself revealed preferred to some other bundle (z_1, z_2). That is,

$$q_1 y_1 + q_2 y_2 \geq q_1 z_1 + q_2 z_2.$$

Then we know that $(x_1, x_2) \succ (y_1, y_2)$ and that $(y_1, y_2) \succ (z_1, z_2)$. From the transitivity assumption we can conclude that $(x_1, x_2) \succ (z_1, z_2)$.

This argument is illustrated in Figure 7.2. Revealed preference and transitivity tell us that (x_1, x_2) must be better than (z_1, z_2) for the consumer who made the illustrated choices.

It is natural to say that in this case (x_1, x_2) is **indirectly revealed preferred** to (z_1, z_2). Of course the "chain" of observed choices may be longer than just three: if bundle A is directly revealed preferred to B, and B to C, and C to D, ... all the way to M, say, then bundle A is still indirectly revealed preferred to M. The chain of direct comparisons can be of any length.

If a bundle is either directly or indirectly revealed preferred to another bundle, we will say that the first bundle is **revealed preferred** to the

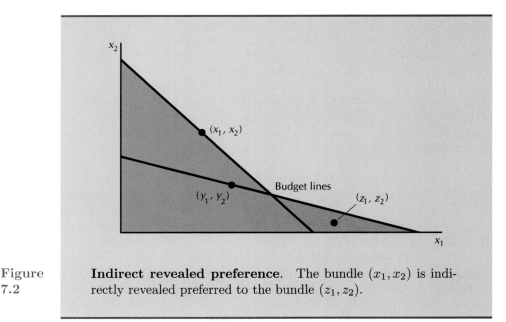

Figure
7.2
Indirect revealed preference. The bundle (x_1, x_2) is indirectly revealed preferred to the bundle (z_1, z_2).

second. The idea of revealed preference is simple, but it is surprisingly powerful. Just looking at a consumer's choices can give us a lot of information about the underlying preferences. Consider, for example, Figure 7.2. Here we have several observations on demanded bundles at different budgets. We can conclude from these observations that since (x_1, x_2) is revealed preferred, either directly or indirectly, to all of the bundles in the shaded area, (x_1, x_2) is in fact *preferred* to those bundles by the consumer who made these choices. Another way to say this is to note that the true indifference curve through (x_1, x_2), whatever it is, must lie above the shaded region.

7.3 Recovering Preferences

By observing choices made by the consumer, we can learn about his or her preferences. As we observe more and more choices, we can get a better and better estimate of what the consumer's preferences are like.

Such information about preferences can be very important in making policy decisions. Most economic policy involves trading off some goods for others: if we put a tax on shoes and subsidize clothing, we'll probably end up having more clothes and fewer shoes. In order to evaluate the desirability of such a policy, it is important to have some idea of what consumer preferences between clothes and shoes look like. By examining consumer choices, we can extract such information through the use of revealed preference and related techniques.

If we are willing to add more assumptions about consumer preferences, we can get more precise estimates about the shape of indifference curves. For example, suppose we observe two bundles Y and Z that are revealed preferred to X, as in Figure 7.3, and that we are willing to postulate preferences are convex. Then we know that all of the weighted averages of Y and Z are preferred to X as well. If we are willing to assume that preferences are monotonic, then all the bundles that have more of both goods than X, Y, and Z—or any of their weighted averages—are also preferred to X.

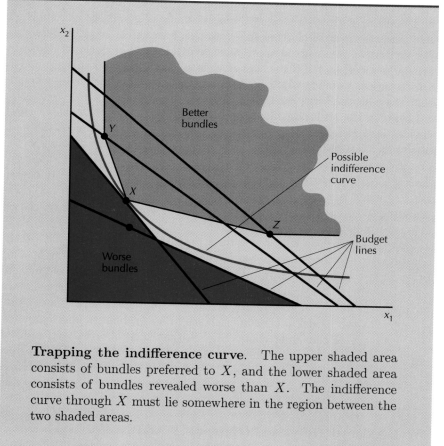

Trapping the indifference curve. The upper shaded area consists of bundles preferred to X, and the lower shaded area consists of bundles revealed worse than X. The indifference curve through X must lie somewhere in the region between the two shaded areas.

Figure 7.3

The region labeled "Worse bundles" in Figure 7.3 consists of all the bundles to which X is revealed preferred. That is, this region consists of all the bundles that cost less than X, along with all the bundles that cost less than bundles that cost less than X, and so on.

Thus, in Figure 7.3, we can conclude that all of the bundles in the upper shaded area are better than X, and that all of the bundles in the lower shaded area are worse than X, according to the preferences of the consumer who made the choices. The true indifference curve through X must lie somewhere between the two shaded sets. We've managed to trap the indifference curve quite tightly simply by an intelligent application of the idea of revealed preference and a few simple assumptions about preferences.

7.4 The Weak Axiom of Revealed Preference

All of the above relies on the assumption that the consumer *has* preferences and that she is always choosing the best bundle of goods she can afford. If the consumer is not behaving this way, the "estimates" of the indifference curves that we constructed above have no meaning. The question naturally arises: how can we tell if the consumer is following the maximizing model? Or, to turn it around: what kind of observation would lead us to conclude that the consumer was *not* maximizing?

Consider the situation illustrated in Figure 7.4. Could both of these choices be generated by a maximizing consumer? According to the logic of revealed preference, Figure 7.4 allows us to conclude two things: (1) (x_1, x_2) is preferred to (y_1, y_2); and (2) (y_1, y_2) is preferred to (x_1, x_2). This is clearly absurd. In Figure 7.4 the consumer has apparently chosen (x_1, x_2) when she could have chosen (y_1, y_2), indicating that (x_1, x_2) was preferred to (y_1, y_2), but then she chose (y_1, y_2) when she could have chosen (x_1, x_2)—indicating the opposite!

Clearly, this consumer cannot be a maximizing consumer. Either the consumer is not choosing the best bundle she can afford, or there is some other aspect of the choice problem that has changed that we have not observed. Perhaps the consumer's tastes or some other aspect of her economic environment have changed. In any event, a violation of this sort is not consistent with the model of consumer choice in an unchanged environment.

The theory of consumer choice implies that such observations will not occur. If the consumers are choosing the best things they can afford, then things that are affordable, but not chosen, must be worse than what is chosen. Economists have formulated this simple point in the following basic axiom of consumer theory

Weak Axiom of Revealed Preference (WARP). *If (x_1, x_2) is directly revealed preferred to (y_1, y_2), and the two bundles are not the same, then it cannot happen that (y_1, y_2) is directly revealed preferred to (x_1, x_2).*

In other words, if a bundle (x_1, x_2) is purchased at prices (p_1, p_2) and a different bundle (y_1, y_2) is purchased at prices (q_1, q_2), then if

$$p_1 x_1 + p_2 x_2 \geq p_1 y_1 + p_2 y_2,$$

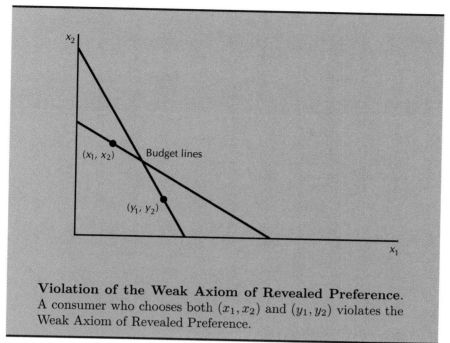

Violation of the Weak Axiom of Revealed Preference.
A consumer who chooses both (x_1, x_2) and (y_1, y_2) violates the
Weak Axiom of Revealed Preference.

**Figure
7.4**

it must *not* be the case that

$$q_1 y_1 + q_2 y_2 \geq q_1 x_1 + q_2 x_2.$$

In English: if the y-bundle is affordable when the x-bundle is purchased,
then when the y-bundle is purchased, the x-bundle must not be affordable.

The consumer in Figure 7.4 has *violated* WARP. Thus we know that this
consumer's behavior could not have been maximizing behavior.[1]

There is no set of indifference curves that could be drawn in Figure 7.4
that could make both bundles maximizing bundles. On the other hand,
the consumer in Figure 7.5 satisfies WARP. Here it is possible to find
indifference curves for which his behavior is optimal behavior. One possible
choice of indifference curves is illustrated.

Optional   ## 7.5 Checking WARP

It is important to understand that WARP is a condition that must be satisfied by a consumer who is always choosing the best things he or she can
afford. The Weak Axiom of Revealed Preference is a logical implication

---

[1] Could we say his behavior is WARPed? Well, we could, but not in polite company.

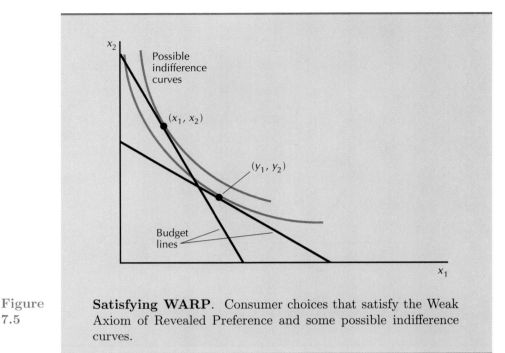

Figure
7.5

Satisfying WARP. Consumer choices that satisfy the Weak Axiom of Revealed Preference and some possible indifference curves.

of that model and can therefore be used to check whether or not a particular consumer, or an economic entity that we might want to model as a consumer, is consistent with our economic model.

Let's consider how we would go about systematically testing WARP in practice. Suppose that we observe several choices of bundles of goods at different prices. Let us use (p_1^t, p_2^t) to denote the tth observation of prices and (x_1^t, x_2^t) to denote the tth observation of choices. To use a specific example, let's take the data in Table 7.1.

Table
7.1

Some consumption data.

Observation	p_1	p_2	x_1	x_2
1	1	2	1	2
2	2	1	2	1
3	1	1	2	2

Given these data, we can compute how much it would cost the consumer to purchase each bundle of goods at each different set of prices, as we've done in Table 7.2. For example, the entry in row 3, column 1, measures how much money the consumer would have to spend at the third set of prices to purchase the first bundle of goods.

Cost of each bundle at each set of prices.

Table 7.2

		Bundles		
		1	2	3
Prices	1	5	4*	6
	2	4*	5	6
	3	3*	3*	4

The diagonal terms in Table 7.2 measure how much money the consumer is spending at each choice. The other entries in each row measure how much she would have spent if she had purchased a different bundle. Thus we can see whether bundle 3, say, is revealed preferred to bundle 1, by seeing if the entry in row 3, column 1 (how much the consumer would have to spend at the third set of prices to purchase the first bundle) is less than the entry in row 3, column 3 (how much the consumer actually spent at the third set of prices to purchase the third bundle). In this particular case, bundle 1 was affordable when bundle 3 was purchased, which means that bundle 3 is revealed preferred to bundle 1. Thus we put a star in row 3, column 1, of the table.

From a mathematical point of view, we simply put a star in the entry in row s, column t, if the number in that entry is less than the number in row s, column s.

We can use this table to check for violations of WARP. In this framework, a violation of WARP consists of two observations t and s such that row t, column s, contains a star *and* row s, column t, contains a star. For this would mean that the bundle purchased at s is revealed preferred to the bundle purchased at t and vice versa.

We can use a computer (or a research assistant) to check and see whether there are any pairs of observations like these in the observed choices. If there are, the choices are inconsistent with the economic theory of the consumer. Either the theory is wrong for this particular consumer, or something else has changed in the consumer's environment that we have not controlled for. Thus the Weak Axiom of Revealed Preference gives us an easily checkable condition for whether some observed choices are consistent with the economic theory of the consumer.

In Table 7.2, we observe that row 1, column 2, contains a star and row 2, column 1, contains a star. This means that observation 2 could have been chosen when the consumer actually chose observation 1 and vice versa. This is a violation of the Weak Axiom of Revealed Preference. We can conclude that the data depicted in Tables 7.1 and 7.2 could not be generated by a consumer with stable preferences who was always choosing the best things he or she could afford.

7.6 The Strong Axiom of Revealed Preference

The Weak Axiom of Revealed Preference described in the last section gives us an observable condition that must be satisfied by all optimizing consumers. But there is a stronger condition that is sometimes useful.

We have already noted that if a bundle of goods X is revealed preferred to a bundle Y, and Y is in turn revealed preferred to a bundle Z, then X must in fact be preferred to Z. If the consumer has consistent preferences, then we should never observe a sequence of choices that would reveal that Z was preferred to X.

The Weak Axiom of Revealed Preference requires that if X is *directly* revealed preferred to Y, then we should never observe Y being *directly* revealed preferred to X. The **Strong Axiom of Revealed Preference (SARP)** requires that the same sort of condition hold for *indirect* revealed preference. More formally, we have the following.

Strong Axiom of Revealed Preference (SARP). *If (x_1, x_2) is revealed preferred to (y_1, y_2) (either directly or indirectly) and (y_1, y_2) is different from (x_1, x_2), then (y_1, y_2) cannot be directly or indirectly revealed preferred to (x_1, x_2).*

It is clear that if the observed behavior is optimizing behavior then it must satisfy the SARP. For if the consumer is optimizing and (x_1, x_2) is revealed preferred to (y_1, y_2), either directly or indirectly, then we must have $(x_1, x_2) \succ (y_1, y_2)$. So having (x_1, x_2) revealed preferred to (y_1, y_2) *and* (y_1, y_2) revealed preferred to (x_1, x_2) would imply that $(x_1, x_2) \succ (y_1, y_2)$ *and* $(y_1, y_2) \succ (x_1, x_2)$, which is a contradiction. We can conclude that either the consumer must not be optimizing, or some other aspect of the consumer's environment—such as tastes, other prices, and so on—must have changed.

Roughly speaking, since the underlying preferences of the consumer must be transitive, it follows that the *revealed* preferences of the consumer must be transitive. Thus SARP is a *necessary* implication of optimizing behavior: if a consumer is always choosing the best things that he can afford, then his observed behavior must satisfy SARP. What is more surprising is that any behavior satisfying the Strong Axiom can be thought of as being generated by optimizing behavior in the following sense: if the observed choices satisfy SARP, we can always find nice, well-behaved preferences that *could have* generated the observed choices. In this sense SARP is a *sufficient* condition for optimizing behavior: if the observed choices satisfy SARP, then it is always possible to find preferences for which the observed behavior is optimizing behavior. The proof of this claim is unfortunately beyond the scope of this book, but appreciation of its importance is not.

What it means is that SARP gives us *all* of the restrictions on behavior imposed by the model of the optimizing consumer. For if the observed choices satisfy SARP, we can "construct" preferences that could have generated these choices. Thus SARP is both a necessary and a sufficient condition for observed choices to be compatible with the economic model of consumer choice.

Does this prove that the constructed preferences actually generated the observed choices? Of course not. As with any scientific statement, we can only show that observed behavior is not inconsistent with the statement. We can't prove that the economic model is correct; we can just determine the implications of that model and see if observed choices are consistent with those implications.

Optional   ## 7.7 How to Check SARP

Let us suppose that we have a table like Table 7.2 that has a star in row t and column s if observation t is directly revealed preferred to observation s. How can we use this table to check SARP?

The easiest way is first to transform the table. An example is given in Table 7.3. This is a table just like Table 7.2, but it uses a different set of numbers. Here the stars indicate direct revealed preference. The star in parentheses will be explained below.

How to check SARP.   Table
                                                        7.3

| | | \multicolumn{3}{c}{Bundles} |
		1	2	3
	1	20	10*	22$^{(*)}$
Prices	2	21	20	15*
	3	12	15	10

Now we systematically look through the entries of the table and see if there are any *chains* of observations that make some bundle indirectly revealed preferred to that one. For example, bundle 1 is directly revealed preferred to bundle 2 since there is a star in row 1, column 2. And bundle

2 is directly revealed preferred to bundle 3, since there is a star in row 2, column 3. Therefore bundle 1 is *indirectly* revealed preferred to bundle 3, and we indicate this by putting a star (in parentheses) in row 1, column 3.

In general, if we have many observations, we will have to look for chains of arbitrary length to see if one observation is indirectly revealed preferred to another. Although it may not be exactly obvious how to do this, it turns out that there are simple computer programs that can calculate the indirect revealed preference relation from the table describing the direct revealed preference relation. The computer can put a star in location st of the table if observation s is revealed preferred to observation t by any chain of other observations.

Once we have done this calculation, we can easily test for SARP. We just see if there is a situation where there is a star in row t, column s, *and* also a star in row s, column t. If so, we have found a situation where observation t is revealed preferred to observation s, either directly or indirectly, and, at the same time, observation s is revealed preferred to observation t. This is a violation of the Strong Axiom of Revealed Preference.

On the other hand, if we do not find such violations, then we know that the observations we have are consistent with the economic theory of the consumer. These observations could have been made by an optimizing consumer with well-behaved preferences. Thus we have a completely operational test for whether or not a particular consumer is acting in a way consistent with economic theory.

This is important, since we can model several kinds of economic units as behaving like consumers. Think, for example, of a household consisting of several people. Will its consumption choices maximize "household utility"? If we have some data on household consumption choices, we can use the Strong Axiom of Revealed Preference to see. Another economic unit that we might think of as acting like a consumer is a nonprofit organization like a hospital or a university. Do universities maximize a utility function in making their economic choices? If we have a list of the economic choices that a university makes when faced with different prices, we can, in principle, answer this kind of question.

7.8 Index Numbers

Suppose we examine the consumption bundles of a consumer at two different times and we want to compare how consumption has changed from one time to the other. Let b stand for the base period, and let t be some other time. How does "average" consumption in year t compare to consumption in the base period?

Suppose that at time t prices are (p_1^t, p_2^t) and that the consumer chooses (x_1^t, x_2^t). In the base period b, the prices are (p_1^b, p_2^b), and the consumer's choice is (x_1^b, x_2^b). We want to ask how the "average" consumption of the consumer has changed.

If we let w_1 and w_2 be some "weights" that go into making an average, then we can look at the following kind of quantity index:

$$I_q = \frac{w_1 x_1^t + w_2 x_2^t}{w_1 x_1^b + w_2 x_2^b}.$$

If I_q is greater than 1, we can say that the "average" consumption has gone up in the movement from b to t; if I_q is less than 1, we can say that the "average" consumption has gone down.

The question is, what do we use for the weights? A natural choice is to use the prices of the goods in question, since they measure in some sense the relative importance of the two goods. But there are two sets of prices here: which should we use?

If we use the base period prices for the weights, we have something called a **Laspeyres** index, and if we use the t period prices, we have something called a **Paasche** index. Both of these indices answer the question of what has happened to "average" consumption, but they just use different weights in the averaging process.

Substituting the t period prices for the weights, we see that the **Paasche quantity index** is given by

$$P_q = \frac{p_1^t x_1^t + p_2^t x_2^t}{p_1^t x_1^b + p_2^t x_2^b},$$

and substituting the b period prices shows that the **Laspeyres quantity index** is given by

$$L_q = \frac{p_1^b x_1^t + p_2^b x_2^t}{p_1^b x_1^b + p_2^b x_2^b}.$$

It turns out that the magnitude of the Laspeyres and Paasche indices can tell us something quite interesting about the consumer's welfare. Suppose that we have a situation where the Paasche quantity index is greater than 1:

$$P_q = \frac{p_1^t x_1^t + p_2^t x_2^t}{p_1^t x_1^b + p_2^t x_2^b} > 1.$$

What can we conclude about how well-off the consumer is at time t as compared to his situation at time b?

The answer is provided by revealed preference. Just cross multiply this inequality to give

$$p_1^t x_1^t + p_2^t x_2^t > p_1^t x_1^b + p_2^t x_2^b,$$

which immediately shows that the consumer must be better off at t than at b, since he could have consumed the b consumption bundle in the t situation but chose not to do so.

What if the Paasche index is *less* than 1? Then we would have

$$p_1^t x_1^t + p_2^t x_2^t < p_1^t x_1^b + p_2^t x_2^b,$$

which says that when the consumer chose bundle (x_1^t, x_2^t), bundle (x_1^b, x_2^b) was not affordable. But that doesn't say anything about the consumer's ranking of the bundles. Just because something costs more than you can afford doesn't mean that you prefer it to what you're consuming now.

What about the Laspeyres index? It works in a similar way. Suppose that the Laspeyres index is *less* than 1:

$$L_q = \frac{p_1^b x_1^t + p_2^b x_2^t}{p_1^b x_1^b + p_2^b x_2^b} < 1.$$

Cross multiplying yields

$$p_1^b x_1^b + p_2^b x_2^b > p_1^b x_1^t + p_2^b x_2^t,$$

which says that (x_1^b, x_2^b) is revealed preferred to (x_1^t, x_2^t). Thus the consumer is better off at time b than at time t.

7.9 Price Indices

Price indices work in much the same way. In general, a price index will be a weighted average of prices:

$$I_p = \frac{p_1^t w_1 + p_2^t w_2}{p_1^b w_1 + p_2^b w_2}.$$

In this case it is natural to choose the quantities as the weights for computing the averages. We get two different indices, depending on our choice of weights. If we choose the t period quantities for weights, we get the **Paasche price index**:

$$P_p = \frac{p_1^t x_1^t + p_2^t x_2^t}{p_1^b x_1^t + p_2^b x_2^t},$$

and if we choose the base period quantities we get the **Laspeyres price index**:

$$L_p = \frac{p_1^t x_1^b + p_2^t x_2^b}{p_1^b x_1^b + p_2^b x_2^b}.$$

Suppose that the Paasche price index is less than 1; what does revealed preference have to say about the welfare situation of the consumer in periods t and b?

Revealed preference doesn't say anything at all. The problem is that there are now different prices in the numerator and in the denominator of the fractions defining the indices, so the revealed preference comparison can't be made.

Let's define a new index of the change in total expenditure by

$$M = \frac{p_1^t x_1^t + p_2^t x_2^t}{p_1^b x_1^b + p_2^b x_2^b}.$$

This is the ratio of total expenditure in period t to the total expenditure in period b.

Now suppose that you are told that the Paasche price index was greater than M. This means that

$$P_p = \frac{p_1^t x_1^t + p_2^t x_2^t}{p_1^b x_1^t + p_2^b x_2^t} > \frac{p_1^t x_1^t + p_2^t x_2^t}{p_1^b x_1^b + p_2^b x_2^b}.$$

Canceling the numerators from each side of this expression and cross multiplying, we have

$$p_1^b x_1^b + p_2^b x_2^b > p_1^b x_1^t + p_2^b x_2^t.$$

This statement says that the bundle chosen at year b is revealed preferred to the bundle chosen at year t. This analysis implies that if the Paasche price index is greater than the expenditure index, then the consumer must be better off in year b than in year t.

This is quite intuitive. After all, if prices rise by more than income rises in the movement from b to t, we would expect that would tend to make the consumer worse off. The revealed preference analysis given above confirms this intuition.

A similar statement can be made for the Laspeyres price index. If the Laspeyres price index is less than M, then the consumer must be better off in year t than in year b. Again, this simply confirms the intuitive idea that if prices rise less than income, the consumer would become better off. In the case of price indices, what matters is not whether the index is greater or less than 1, but whether it is greater or less than the expenditure index.

EXAMPLE: Indexing Social Security Payments

Many elderly people have Social Security payments as their sole source of income. Because of this, there have been attempts to adjust Social Security payments in a way that will keep purchasing power constant even when prices change. Since the amount of payments will then depend on the movement of some price index or cost-of-living index, this kind of scheme is referred to as **indexing**.

One indexing proposal goes as follows. In some base year b, economists measure the average consumption bundle of senior citizens. In each
subsequent year the Social Security system adjusts payments so that the
"purchasing power" of the average senior citizen remains constant in the
sense that the average Social Security recipient is just able to afford the
consumption bundle available in year b, as depicted in Figure 7.6.

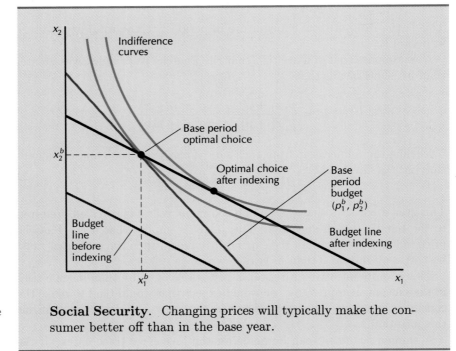

Figure
7.6

Social Security. Changing prices will typically make the consumer better off than in the base year.

One curious result of this indexing scheme is that the average senior
citizen will almost always be better off than he or she was in the base year
b. Suppose that year b is chosen as the base year for the price index. Then
the bundle (x_1^b, x_2^b) is the optimal bundle at the prices (p_1^b, p_2^b). This means
that the budget line at prices (p_1^b, p_2^b) must be tangent to the indifference
curve through (x_1^b, x_2^b).

Now suppose that prices change. To be specific, suppose that prices
increase so that the budget line, in the absence of Social Security, would
shift inward and tilt. The inward shift is due to the increase in prices; the
tilt is due to the change in relative prices. The indexing program would
then increase the Social Security payment so as to make the original bundle
(x_1^b, x_2^b) affordable at the new prices. But this means that the budget line
would cut the indifference curve, and there would be some other bundle

on the budget line that would be strictly preferred to (x_1^b, x_2^b). Thus the consumer would typically be able to choose a better bundle than he or she chose in the base year.

Summary

1. If one bundle is chosen when another could have been chosen, we say that the first bundle is revealed preferred to the second.

2. If the consumer is always choosing the most preferred bundles he or she can afford, this means that the chosen bundles must be preferred to the bundles that were affordable but weren't chosen.

3. Observing the choices of consumers can allow us to "recover" or estimate the preferences that lie behind those choices. The more choices we observe, the more precisely we can estimate the underlying preferences that generated those choices.

4. The Weak Axiom of Revealed Preference (WARP) and the Strong Axiom of Revealed Preference (SARP) are necessary conditions that consumer choices have to obey if they are to be consistent with the economic model of optimizing choice.

REVIEW QUESTIONS

1. When prices are $(p_1, p_2) = (1, 2)$ a consumer demands $(x_1, x_2) = (1, 2)$, and when prices are $(q_1, q_2) = (2, 1)$ the consumer demands $(y_1, y_2) = (2, 1)$. Is this behavior consistent with the model of maximizing behavior?

2. When prices are $(p_1, p_2) = (2, 1)$ a consumer demands $(x_1, x_2) = (1, 2)$, and when prices are $(q_1, q_2) = (1, 2)$ the consumer demands $(y_1, y_2) = (2, 1)$. Is this behavior consistent with the model of maximizing behavior?

3. In the preceding exercise, which bundle is preferred by the consumer, the x-bundle or the y-bundle?

4. We saw that the Social Security adjustment for changing prices would typically make recipients at least as well-off as they were at the base year. What kind of price changes would leave them just as well-off, no matter what kind of preferences they had?

5. In the same framework as the above question, what kind of preferences would leave the consumer just as well-off as he was in the base year, for *all* price changes?

CHAPTER 8

SLUTSKY EQUATION

Economists often are concerned with how a consumer's behavior changes in response to changes in the economic environment. The case we want to consider in this chapter is how a consumer's choice of a good responds to changes in its price. It is natural to think that when the price of a good rises the demand for it will fall. However, as we saw in Chapter 6 it is possible to construct examples where the optimal demand for a good *decreases* when its price falls. A good that has this property is called a **Giffen good**.

Giffen goods are pretty peculiar and are primarily a theoretical curiosity, but there are other situations where changes in prices might have "perverse" effects that, on reflection, turn out not to be so unreasonable. For example, we normally think that if people get a higher wage they will work more. But what if your wage went from $10 an hour to $1000 an hour? Would you really work more? Might you not decide to work fewer hours and use some of the money you've earned to do other things? What if your wage were $1,000,000 an hour? Wouldn't you work less?

For another example, think of what happens to your demand for apples when the price goes up. You would probably consume fewer apples. But how about a family who grew apples to sell? If the price of apples went up, their income might go up so much that they would feel that they could now afford to consume more of their own apples. For the consumers in this family, an increase in the price of apples might well lead to an increase in the consumption of apples.

What is going on here? How is it that changes in price can have these ambiguous effects on demand? In this chapter and the next we'll try to sort out these effects.

8.1 The Substitution Effect

When the price of a good changes, there are two sorts of effects: the rate at which you can exchange one good for another changes, and the total purchasing power of your income is altered. If, for example, good 1 becomes cheaper, it means that you have to give up less of good 2 to purchase good 1. The change in the price of good 1 has changed the rate at which the market allows you to "substitute" good 2 for good 1. The trade-off between the two goods that the market presents the consumer has changed.

At the same time, if good 1 becomes cheaper it means that your money income will buy more of good 1. The purchasing power of your money has gone up; although the number of dollars you have is the same, the amount that they will buy has increased.

The first part—the change in demand due to the change in the rate of exchange between the two goods—is called the **substitution effect**. The second effect—the change in demand due to having more purchasing power—is called the **income effect**. These are only rough definitions of the two effects. In order to give a more precise definition we have to consider the two effects in greater detail.

The way that we will do this is to break the price movement into two steps: first we will let the *relative* prices change and adjust money income so as to hold purchasing power constant, then we will let purchasing power adjust while holding the relative prices constant.

This is best explained by referring to Figure 8.1. Here we have a situation where the price of good 1 has declined. This means that the budget line rotates around the vertical intercept m/p_2 and becomes flatter. We can break this movement of the budget line up into two steps: first *pivot* the budget line around the *original* demanded bundle and then *shift* the pivoted line out to the *new* demanded bundle.

This "pivot-shift" operation gives us a convenient way to decompose the change in demand into two pieces. The first step—the pivot—is a movement where the slope of the budget line changes while its purchasing power stays constant, while the second step is a movement where the slope stays constant and the purchasing power changes. This decomposition is only a hypothetical construction—the consumer simply observes a change

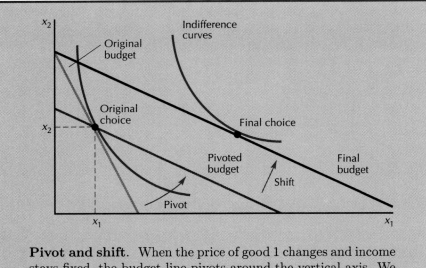

Figure 8.1

Pivot and shift. When the price of good 1 changes and income stays fixed, the budget line pivots around the vertical axis. We will view this adjustment as occurring in two stages: first pivot the budget line around the *original* choice, and then shift this line outward to the new demanded bundle.

in price and chooses a new bundle of goods in response. But in analyzing how the consumer's choice changes, it is useful to think of the budget line changing in two stages—first the pivot, then the shift.

What are the economic meanings of the pivoted and the shifted budget lines? Let us first consider the pivoted line. Here we have a budget line with the same slope and thus the same relative prices as the final budget line. However, the money income associated with this budget line is different, since the vertical intercept is different. Since the original consumption bundle (x_1, x_2) lies on the pivoted budget line, that consumption bundle is just affordable. The purchasing power of the consumer has remained constant in the sense that the original bundle of goods is just affordable at the new pivoted line.

Let us calculate how much we have to adjust money income in order to keep the old bundle just affordable. Let m' be the amount of money income that will just make the original consumption bundle affordable; this will be the amount of money income associated with the pivoted budget line. Since (x_1, x_2) is affordable at both (p_1, p_2, m) and (p_1', p_2, m'), we have

$$m' = p_1' x_1 + p_2 x_2$$
$$m = p_1 x_1 + p_2 x_2.$$

Subtracting the second equation from the first gives

$$m' - m = x_1[p_1' - p_1].$$

This equation says that the change in money income necessary to make the old bundle affordable at the new prices is just the original amount of consumption of good 1 times the change in prices.

Letting $\Delta p_1 = p_1' - p_1$ represent the change in price 1, and $\Delta m = m' - m$ represent the change in income necessary to make the old bundle just affordable, we have

$$\Delta m = x_1 \Delta p_1. \tag{8.1}$$

Note that the change in income and the change in price will always move in the same direction: if the price goes up, then we have to raise income to keep the same bundle affordable.

Let's use some actual numbers. Suppose that the consumer is originally consuming 20 candy bars a week, and that candy bars cost 50 cents a piece. If the price of candy bars goes up by 10 cents—so that $\Delta p_1 = .60 - .50 = .10$—how much would income have to change to make the old consumption bundle affordable?

We can apply the formula given above. If the consumer had $2.00 more income, he would just be able to consume the same number of candy bars, namely, 20. In terms of the formula:

$$\Delta m = \Delta p_1 \times x_1 = .10 \times 20 = \$2.00.$$

Now we have a formula for the pivoted budget line: it is just the budget line at the new price with income changed by Δm. Note that if the price of good 1 goes down, then the adjustment in income will be negative. When a price goes down, a consumer's purchasing power goes up, so we will have to decrease the consumer's income in order to keep purchasing power fixed. Similarly, when a price goes up, purchasing power goes down, so the change in income necessary to keep purchasing power constant must be positive.

Although (x_1, x_2) is still affordable, it is not generally the optimal purchase at the pivoted budget line. In Figure 8.2 we have denoted the optimal purchase on the pivoted budget line by Y. This bundle of goods is the optimal bundle of goods when we change the price and then adjust dollar income so as to keep the old bundle of goods just affordable. The movement from X to Y is known as the **substitution effect**. It indicates how the consumer "substitutes" one good for the other when a price changes but purchasing power remains constant.

More precisely, the substitution effect, Δx_1^s, is the change in the demand for good 1 when the price of good 1 changes to p_1' and, at the same time, money income changes to m':

$$\Delta x_1^s = x_1(p_1', m') - x_1(p_1, m).$$

In order to determine the substitution effect, we must use the consumer's demand function to calculate the optimal choices at (p_1', m') and (p_1, m). The change in the demand for good 1 may be large or small, depending

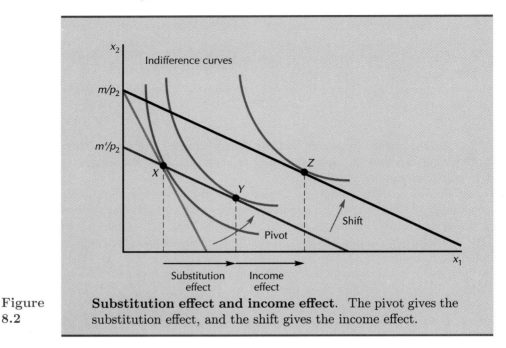

Figure
8.2
Substitution effect and income effect. The pivot gives the substitution effect, and the shift gives the income effect.

on the shape of the consumer's indifference curves. But given the demand function, it is easy to just plug in the numbers to calculate the substitution effect. (Of course the demand for good 1 may well depend on the price of good 2; but the price of good 2 is being held constant during this exercise, so we've left it out of the demand function so as not to clutter the notation.)

The substitution effect is sometimes called the change in **compensated demand**. The idea is that the consumer is being compensated for a price rise by having enough income given back to him to purchase his old bundle. Of course if the price goes down he is "compensated" by having money taken away from him. We'll generally stick with the "substitution" terminology, for consistency, but the "compensation" terminology is also widely used.

EXAMPLE: Calculating the Substitution Effect

Suppose that the consumer has a demand function for milk of the form

$$x_1 = 10 + \frac{m}{10p_1}.$$

Originally his income is $120 per week and the price of milk is $3 per quart. Thus his demand for milk will be $10 + 120/(10 \times 3) = 14$ quarts per week.

Now suppose that the price of milk falls to \$2 per quart. Then his demand at this new price will be $10 + 120/(10 \times 2) = 16$ quarts of milk per week. The *total* change in demand is $+2$ quarts a week.

In order to calculate the substitution effect, we must first calculate how much income would have to change in order to make the original consumption of milk just affordable when the price of milk is \$2 a quart. We apply the formula (8.1):

$$\Delta m = x_1 \Delta p_1 = 14 \times (2 - 3) = -\$14.$$

Thus the level of income necessary to keep purchasing power constant is $m' = m + \Delta m = 120 - 14 = 106$. What is the consumer's demand for milk at the new price, \$2 per quart, and this level of income? Just plug the numbers into the demand function to find

$$x_1(p_1', m') = x_1(2, 106) = 10 + \frac{106}{10 \times 2} = 15.3.$$

Thus the substitution effect is

$$\Delta x_1^s = x_1(2, 106) - x_1(3, 120) = 15.3 - 14 = 1.3.$$

8.2 The Income Effect

We turn now to the second stage of the price adjustment—the shift movement. This is also easy to interpret economically. We know that a parallel shift of the budget line is the movement that occurs when income changes while relative prices remain constant. Thus the second stage of the price adjustment is called the **income effect**. We simply change the consumer's income from m' to m, keeping the prices constant at (p_1', p_2). In Figure 8.2 this change moves us from the point (y_1, y_2) to (z_1, z_2). It is natural to call this last movement the income effect since all we are doing is changing income while keeping the prices fixed at the new prices.

More precisely, the income effect, Δx_1^n, is the change in the demand for good 1 when we change income from m' to m, holding the price of good 1 fixed at p_1':

$$\Delta x_1^n = x_1(p_1', m) - x_1(p_1', m').$$

We have already considered the income effect earlier in section 6.1. There we saw that the income effect can operate either way: it will tend to increase or decrease the demand for good 1 depending on whether we have a normal good or an inferior good.

When the price of a good decreases, we need to decrease income in order to keep purchasing power constant. If the good is a normal good, then this decrease in income will lead to a decrease in demand. If the good is an inferior good, then the decrease in income will lead to an increase in demand.

EXAMPLE: Calculating the Income Effect

In the example given earlier in this chapter we saw that

$$x_1(p_1', m) = x_1(2, 120) = 16$$
$$x_1(p_1', m') = x_1(2, 106) = 15.3.$$

Thus the income effect for this problem is

$$\Delta x_1^n = x_1(2, 120) - x_1(2, 106) = 16 - 15.3 = 0.7.$$

Since milk is a normal good for this consumer, the demand for milk increases when income increases.

8.3 Sign of the Substitution Effect

We have seen above that the income effect can be positive or negative, depending on whether the good is a normal good or an inferior good. What about the substitution effect? If the price of a good goes down, as in Figure 8.2, then the change in the demand for the good due to the substitution effect *must* be nonnegative. That is, if $p_1 > p_1'$, then we *must* have $x_1(p_1', m') \geq x_1(p_1, m)$, so that $\Delta x_1^s \geq 0$.

The proof of this goes as follows. Consider the points on the pivoted budget line in Figure 8.2 where the amount of good 1 consumed is less than at the bundle X. These bundles were all affordable at the old prices (p_1, p_2) but they weren't purchased. Instead the bundle X was purchased. If the consumer is always choosing the best bundle he can afford, then X must be preferred to all of the bundles on the part of the pivoted line that lies inside the original budget set.

This means that the optimal choice on the pivoted budget line must not be one of the bundles that lies underneath the original budget line. The optimal choice on the pivoted line would have to be either X or some point to the right of X. But this means that the new optimal choice must involve consuming at least as much of good 1 as originally, just as we wanted to show. In the case illustrated in Figure 8.2, the optimal choice at the pivoted budget line is the bundle Y, which certainly involves consuming more of good 1 than at the original consumption point, X.

The substitution effect always moves opposite to the price movement. We say that *the substitution effect is negative*, since the change in demand due to the substitution effect is opposite to the change in price: if the price increases, the demand for the good due to the substitution effect decreases.

8.4 The Total Change in Demand

The total change in demand, Δx_1, is the change in demand due to the change in price, holding income constant:

$$\Delta x_1 = x_1(p_1', m) - x_1(p_1, m).$$

We have seen above how this change can be broken up into two changes: the substitution effect and the income effect. In terms of the symbols defined above,

$$\Delta x_1 = \Delta x_1^s + \Delta x_1^n$$
$$x_1(p_1', m) - x_1(p_1, m) = [x_1(p_1', m') - x_1(p_1, m)]$$
$$+ [x_1(p_1', m) - x_1(p_1', m')].$$

In words this equation says that the total change in demand equals the substitution effect plus the income effect. This equation is called the **Slutsky identity**.[1] Note that it is an identity: it is true for all values of p_1, p_1', m, and m'. The first and fourth terms on the right-hand side cancel out, so the right-hand side is *identically* equal to the left-hand side.

The content of the Slutsky identity is not just the algebraic identity—that is a mathematical triviality. The content comes in the interpretation of the two terms on the right-hand side: the substitution effect and the income effect. In particular, we can use what we know about the signs of the income and substitution effects to determine the sign of the total effect.

While the substitution effect must always be negative—opposite the change in the price—the income effect can go either way. Thus the total effect may be positive or negative. However, if we have a normal good, then the substitution effect and the income effect work in the same direction. An increase in price means that demand will go down due to the substitution effect. If the price goes up, it is like a decrease in income, which, for a normal good, means a decrease in demand. Both effects reinforce each other. In terms of our notation, the change in demand due to a price increase for a normal good means that

$$\Delta x_1 = \Delta x_1^s + \Delta x_1^n.$$
$$(-) \quad (-) \quad (-)$$

(The minus signs beneath each term indicate that each term in this expression is negative.)

---

[1] Named for Eugen Slutsky (1880–1948), a Russian economist who investigated demand theory.

Note carefully the sign on the income effect. Since we are considering a situation where the price rises, this implies a decrease in purchasing power—for a normal good this will imply a decrease in demand.

On the other hand, if we have an inferior good, it might happen that the income effect outweighs the substitution effect, so that the total change in demand associated with a price increase is actually positive. This would be a case where

$$\Delta x_1 = \Delta x_1^s + \Delta x_1^n.$$
$$(?) \quad (-) \quad (+)$$

If the second term on the right-hand side—the income effect—is large enough, the total change in demand could be positive. This would mean that an increase in price could result in an *increase* in demand. This is the perverse Giffen case described earlier: the increase in price has reduced the consumer's purchasing power so much that he has increased his consumption of the inferior good.

But the Slutsky identity shows that this kind of perverse effect can only occur for inferior goods: if a good is a normal good, then the income and substitution effects reinforce each other, so that the total change in demand is always in the "right" direction.

Thus a Giffen good must be an inferior good. But an inferior good is not necessarily a Giffen good: the income effect not only has to be of the "wrong" sign, it also has to be large enough to outweigh the "right" sign of the substitution effect. This is why Giffen goods are so rarely observed in real life: they would not only have to be inferior goods, but they would have to be *very* inferior.

This is illustrated graphically in Figure 8.3. Here we illustrate the usual pivot-shift operation to find the substitution effect and the income effect. In both cases, good 1 is an inferior good, and the income effect is therefore negative. In Figure 8.3A, the income effect is large enough to outweigh the substitution effect and produce a Giffen good. In Figure 8.3B, the income effect is smaller, and thus good 1 responds in the ordinary way to the change in its price.

8.5 Rates of Change

We have seen that the income and substitution effects can be described graphically as a combination of pivots and shifts, or they can be described algebraically in the Slutsky identity

$$\Delta x_1 = \Delta x_1^s + \Delta x_1^n,$$

which simply says that the total change in demand is the substitution effect plus the income effect. The Slutsky identity here is stated in terms

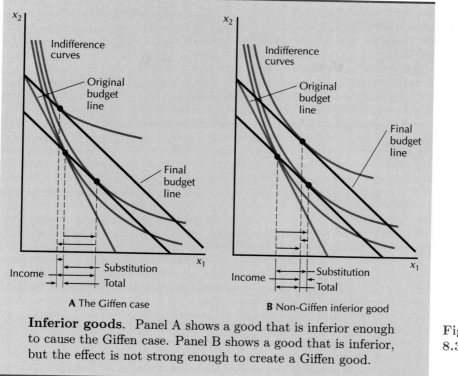

A The Giffen case

B Non-Giffen inferior good

Inferior goods. Panel A shows a good that is inferior enough to cause the Giffen case. Panel B shows a good that is inferior, but the effect is not strong enough to create a Giffen good.

Figure
8.3

of absolute changes, but it is more common to express it in terms of *rates* of change.

When we express the Slutsky identity in terms of rates of change it turns out to be convenient to define Δx_1^m to be the *negative* of the income effect:

$$\Delta x_1^m = x_1(p_1', m') - x_1(p_1', m) = -\Delta x_1^n.$$

Given this definition, the Slutsky identity becomes

$$\Delta x_1 = \Delta x_1^s - \Delta x_1^m.$$

If we divide each side of the identity by Δp_1, we have

$$\frac{\Delta x_1}{\Delta p_1} = \frac{\Delta x_1^s}{\Delta p_1} - \frac{\Delta x_1^m}{\Delta p_1}. \tag{8.2}$$

The first term on the right-hand side is the rate of change of demand when price changes and income is adjusted so as to keep the old bundle affordable—the substitution effect. Let's work on the second term. Since we have an income change in the numerator, it would be nice to get an income change in the denominator.

Remember that the income change, Δm, and the price change, Δp_1, are related by the formula

$$\Delta m = x_1 \Delta p_1.$$

Solving for Δp_1 we find

$$\Delta p_1 = \frac{\Delta m}{x_1}.$$

Now substitute this expression into the last term in (8.2) to get our final formula:

$$\frac{\Delta x_1}{\Delta p_1} = \frac{\Delta x_1^s}{\Delta p_1} - \frac{\Delta x_1^m}{\Delta m} x_1.$$

This is the Slutsky identity in terms of rates of change. We can interpret each term as follows:

$$\frac{\Delta x_1}{\Delta p_1} = \frac{x_1(p_1', m) - x_1(p_1, m)}{\Delta p_1}$$

is the rate of change in demand as price changes, holding income fixed;

$$\frac{\Delta x_1^s}{\Delta p_1} = \frac{x_1(p_1', m') - x_1(p_1, m)}{\Delta p_1}$$

is the rate of change in demand as the price changes, adjusting income so as to keep the old bundle just affordable, that is, the substitution effect; and

$$\frac{\Delta x_1^m}{\Delta m} x_1 = \frac{x_1(p_1', m') - x_1(p_1', m)}{m' - m} x_1 \tag{8.3}$$

is the rate of change of demand holding prices fixed and adjusting income, that is, the income effect.

The income effect is itself composed of two pieces: how demand changes as income changes, times the original level of demand. When the price changes by Δp_1, the change in demand due to the income effect is

$$\Delta x_1^m = \frac{x_1(p_1', m') - x_1(p_1', m)}{\Delta m} x_1 \Delta p_1.$$

But this last term, $x_1 \Delta p_1$, is just the change in income necessary to keep the old bundle feasible. That is, $x_1 \Delta p_1 = \Delta m$, so the change in demand due to the income effect reduces to

$$\Delta x_1^m = \frac{x_1(p_1', m') - x_1(p_1', m)}{\Delta m} \Delta m,$$

just as we had before.

8.6 The Law of Demand

In Chapter 5 we voiced some concerns over the fact that consumer theory seemed to have no particular content: demand could go up or down when a price increased, and demand could go up or down when income increased. If a theory doesn't restrict observed behavior in *some* fashion it isn't much of a theory. A model that is consistent with all behavior has no real content.

However, we know that consumer theory does have some content—we've seen that choices generated by an optimizing consumer must satisfy the Strong Axiom of Revealed Preference. Furthermore, we've seen that any price change can be decomposed into two changes: a substitution effect that is sure to be negative—opposite the direction of the price change— and an income effect whose sign depends on whether the good is a normal good or an inferior good.

Although consumer theory doesn't restrict how demand changes when price changes or how demand changes when income changes, it does restrict how these two kinds of changes interact. In particular, we have the following.

The Law of Demand.   *If the demand for a good increases when income increases, then the demand for that good must decrease when its price increases.*

This follows directly from the Slutsky equation: if the demand increases when income increases, we have a normal good. And if we have a normal good, then the substitution effect and the income effect reinforce each other, and an increase in price will unambiguously reduce demand.

8.7 Examples of Income and Substitution Effects

Let's now consider some examples of price changes for particular kinds of preferences and decompose the demand changes into the income and the substitution effects.

We start with the case of perfect complements. The Slutsky decomposition is illustrated in Figure 8.4. When we pivot the budget line around the chosen point, the optimal choice at the new budget line is the same as at the old one—this means that the substitution effect is zero. The change in demand is due entirely to the income effect.

What about the case of perfect substitutes, illustrated in Figure 8.5? Here when we tilt the budget line, the demand bundle jumps from the vertical axis to the horizontal axis. There is no shifting left to do! The entire change in demand is due to the substitution effect.

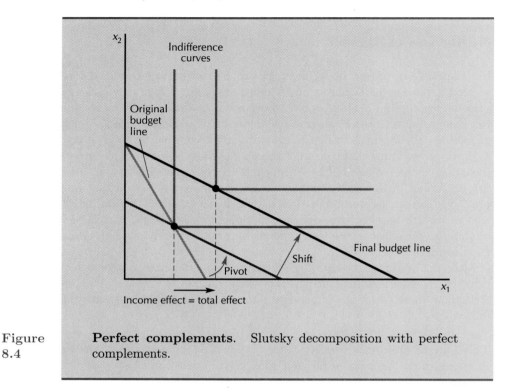

Figure
8.4

Perfect complements. Slutsky decomposition with perfect complements.

As a third example, let us consider the case of quasilinear preferences. This situation is somewhat peculiar. We have already seen that a shift in income causes no change in demand for good 1 when preferences are quasilinear. This means that the entire change in demand for good 1 is due to the substitution effect, and that the income effect is zero, as illustrated in Figure 8.6.

EXAMPLE: Rebating a Tax

In 1974 the Organization of Petroleum Exporting Countries (OPEC) instituted an oil embargo against the United States. OPEC was able to stop oil shipments to U.S. ports for several weeks. The vulnerability of the United States to such disruptions was very disturbing to Congress and the president, and there were many plans proposed to reduce the United States's dependence on foreign oil.

One such plan involved increasing the gasoline tax. Increasing the cost of gasoline to the consumers would make them reduce their consumption of gasoline, and the reduced demand for gasoline would in turn reduce the demand for foreign oil.

But a straight increase in the tax on gasoline would hit consumers where it hurts—in the pocketbook—and by itself such a plan would be politically

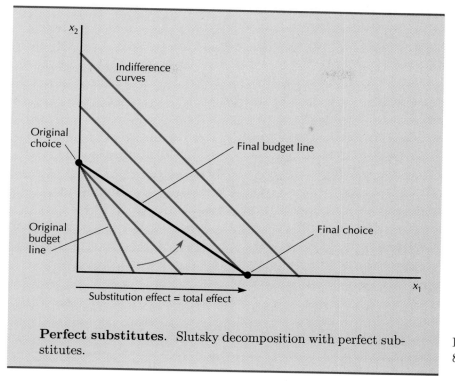

Perfect substitutes. Slutsky decomposition with perfect substitutes.

Figure
8.5

infeasible. So it was suggested that the revenues raised from consumers by this tax would be returned to the consumers in the form of direct money payments, or via the reduction of some other tax.

Critics of this proposal argued that paying the revenue raised by the tax back to the consumers would have no effect on demand since they could just use the rebated money to purchase more gasoline. What does economic analysis say about this plan?

Let us suppose, for simplicity, that the tax on gasoline would end up being passed along entirely to the consumers of gasoline so that the price of gasoline will go up by exactly the amount of the tax. (In general, only part of the tax would be passed along, but we will ignore that complication here.) Suppose that the tax would raise the price of gasoline from p to $p' = p + t$, and that the average consumer would respond by reducing his demand from x to x'. The average consumer is paying t dollars more for gasoline, and he is consuming x' gallons of gasoline after the tax is imposed, so the amount of revenue raised by the tax from the average consumer would be

$$R = tx' = (p' - p)x'.$$

Note that the revenue raised by the tax will depend on how much gasoline the consumer *ends up* consuming, x', not how much he was initially

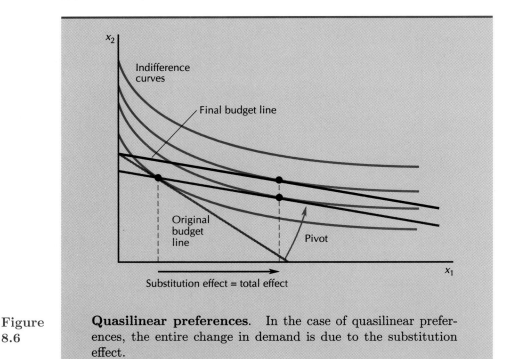

Figure
8.6

Quasilinear preferences. In the case of quasilinear preferences, the entire change in demand is due to the substitution
effect.

consuming, x.

If we let y be the expenditure on all other goods and set its price to be
1, then the original budget constraint is

$$px + y = m, \tag{8.4}$$

and the budget constraint in the presence of the tax-rebate plan is

$$(p + t)x' + y' = m + tx'. \tag{8.5}$$

In budget constraint (8.5) the average consumer is choosing the left-hand
side variables—the consumption of each good—but the right-hand side—
his income and the rebate from the government—are taken as fixed. The
rebate depends on what all consumers do, not what the average consumer
does. In this case, the rebate turns out to be the taxes collected from the
average consumer—but that's because he is average, not because of any
causal connection.

If we cancel tx' from each side of equation (8.5), we have

$$px' + y' = m.$$

Thus (x', y') is a bundle that was affordable under the original budget
constraint and rejected in favor of (x, y). Thus it must be that (x, y)

is preferred to (x', y'): the consumers are made worse off by this plan. Perhaps that is why it was never put into effect!

The equilibrium with a rebated tax is depicted in Figure 8.7. The tax makes good 1 more expensive, and the rebate increases money income. The original bundle is no longer affordable, and the consumer is definitely made worse off. The consumer's choice under the tax-rebate plan involves consuming less gasoline and more of "all other goods."

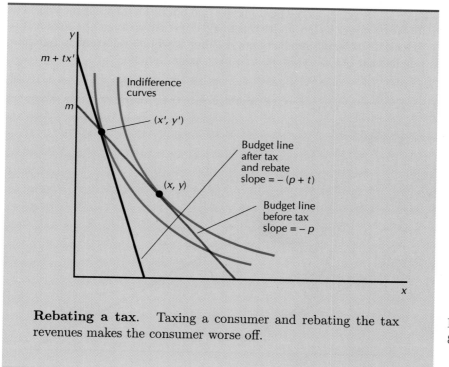

Rebating a tax.   Taxing a consumer and rebating the tax revenues makes the consumer worse off.

Figure
8.7

What can we say about the amount of consumption of gasoline? The average consumer could afford his old consumption of gasoline, but because of the tax, gasoline is now more expensive. In general, the consumer would choose to consume less of it.

8.8 Another Substitution Effect

The substitution effect is the name that economists give to the change in demand when prices change but a consumer's purchasing power is held constant, so that the original bundle remains affordable. At least this is *one* definition of the substitution effect. There is another definition that is also useful.

The definition we have studied above is called the **Slutsky substitution effect**. The definition we will describe in this section is called the **Hicks substitution effect**.[2]

Suppose that instead of pivoting the budget line around the original consumption bundle, we now *roll* the budget line around the indifference curve through the original consumption bundle, as depicted in Figure 8.8. In this way we present the consumer with a new budget line that has the same relative prices as the final budget line but has a different income. The purchasing power he has under this budget line will no longer be sufficient to purchase his original bundle of goods—but it will be sufficient to purchase a bundle that is just *indifferent* to his original bundle.

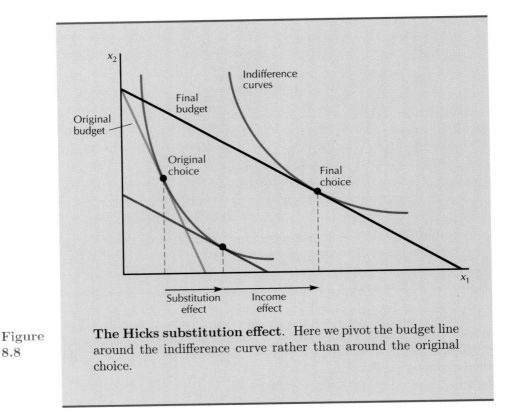

Figure 8.8

The Hicks substitution effect. Here we pivot the budget line around the indifference curve rather than around the original choice.

Thus the Hicks substitution effect keeps *utility* constant rather than keeping purchasing power constant. The Slutsky substitution effect gives the

---

[2] The concept is named for Sir John Hicks, an English recipient of the Nobel Prize in Economics.

consumer just enough money to get back to his old level of consumption, while the Hicks substitution effect gives the consumer just enough money to get back to his old indifference curve. Despite this difference in definition, it turns out that the Hicks substitution effect must be negative—in the sense that it is in a direction opposite that of the price change—just like the Slutsky substitution effect.

The proof is again by revealed preference. Let (x_1, x_2) be a demanded bundle at some prices (p_1, p_2), and let (y_1, y_2) be a demanded bundle at some other prices (q_1, q_2). Suppose that income is such that the consumer is indifferent between (x_1, x_2) and (y_1, y_2). Since the consumer is indifferent between (x_1, x_2) and (y_1, y_2), neither bundle can be revealed preferred to the other.

Using the definition of revealed preference, this means that the following two inequalities are *not* true:

$$p_1 x_1 + p_2 x_2 > p_1 y_1 + p_2 y_2$$

$$q_1 y_1 + q_2 y_2 > q_1 x_1 + q_2 x_2.$$

It follows that these inequalities *are* true:

$$p_1 x_1 + p_2 x_2 \le p_1 y_1 + p_2 y_2$$

$$q_1 y_1 + q_2 y_2 \le q_1 x_1 + q_2 x_2.$$

Adding these inequalities together and rearranging them we have

$$(q_1 - p_1)(y_1 - x_1) + (q_2 - p_2)(y_2 - x_2) \le 0.$$

This is a general statement about how demands change when prices change if income is adjusted so as to keep the consumer on the same indifference curve. In the particular case we are concerned with, we are only changing the first price. Therefore $q_2 = p_2$, and we are left with

$$(q_1 - p_1)(y_1 - x_1) \le 0.$$

This equation says that the change in the quantity demanded must have the opposite sign from that of the price change, which is what we wanted to show.

The total change in demand is still equal to the substitution effect plus the income effect—but now it is the Hicks substitution effect. Since the Hicks substitution effect is also negative, the Slutsky equation takes exactly the same form as we had earlier and has exactly the same interpretation. Both the Slutsky and Hicks definitions of the substitution effect have their place, and which is more useful depends on the problem at hand. It can be shown that for small changes in price, the two substitution effects are virtually identical.

8.9 Compensated Demand Curves

We have seen how the quantity demanded changes as a price changes in three different contexts: holding income fixed (the standard case), holding purchasing power fixed (the Slutsky substitution effect), and holding utility fixed (the Hicks substitution effect). We can draw the relationship between price and quantity demanded holding any of these three variables fixed. This gives rise to three different demand curves: the standard demand curve, the Slutsky demand curve, and the Hicks demand curve.

The analysis of this chapter shows that the Slutsky and Hicks demand curves are always downward sloping curves. Furthermore the ordinary demand curve is a downward sloping curve for normal goods. However, the Giffen analysis shows that it is theoretically possible that the ordinary demand curve may slope upwards for an inferior good.

The Hicksian demand curve—the one with utility held constant—is sometimes called the **compensated demand curve.** This terminology arises naturally if you think of constructing the Hicksian demand curve by adjusting income as the price changes so as to keep the consumer's utility constant. Hence the consumer is "compensated" for the price changes, and his utility is the same at every point on the Hicksian demand curve. This is in contrast to the situation with an ordinary demand curve. In this case the consumer is worse off facing higher prices than lower prices since his income is constant.

The compensated demand curve turns out to be very useful in advanced courses, especially in treatments of benefit-cost analysis. In this sort of analysis it is natural to ask what size payments are necessary to compensate consumers for some policy change. The magnitude of such payments gives a useful estimate of the cost of the policy change. However, actual calculation of compensated demand curves requires more mathematical machinery than we have developed in this text.

Summary

1. When the price of a good decreases, there will be two effects on consumption. The change in relative prices makes the consumer want to consume more of the cheaper good. The increase in purchasing power due to the lower price may increase or decrease consumption, depending on whether the good is a normal good or an inferior good.

2. The change in demand due to the change in relative prices is called the substitution effect; the change due to the change in purchasing power is called the income effect.

3. The substitution effect is how demand changes when prices change and purchasing power is held constant, in the sense that the original bundle remains affordable. To hold real purchasing power constant, money income will have to change. The necessary change in money income is given by $\Delta m = x_1 \Delta p_1$.

4. The Slutsky equation says that the total change in demand is the sum of the substitution effect and the income effect.

5. The Law of Demand says that normal goods must have downward-sloping demand curves.

REVIEW QUESTIONS

1. Suppose a consumer has preferences between two goods that are perfect substitutes. Can you change prices in such a way that the entire demand response is due to the income effect?

2. Suppose that preferences are concave. Is it still the case that the substitution effect is negative?

3. In the case of the gasoline tax, what would happen if the rebate to the consumers were based on their original consumption of gasoline, x, rather than on their final consumption of gasoline, x'?

4. In the case described in the preceding question, would the government be paying out more or less than it received in tax revenues?

5. In this case would the consumers be better off or worse off if the tax with rebate based on original consumption were in effect?

APPENDIX

Let us derive the Slutsky equation using calculus. Consider the Slutsky definition of the substitution effect, in which the income is adjusted so as to give the consumer just enough to buy the original consumption bundle, which we will now denote by $(\overline{x}_1, \overline{x}_2)$. If the prices are (p_1, p_2), then the consumer's actual choice with this adjustment will depend on (p_1, p_2) and $(\overline{x}_1, \overline{x}_2)$. Let's call this relationship the **Slutsky demand function** for good 1, and write it as $x_1^s(p_1, p_2, \overline{x}_1, \overline{x}_2)$.

Suppose the original demanded bundle is $(\overline{x}_1, \overline{x}_2)$ at prices $(\overline{p}_1, \overline{p}_2)$ and income $\overline{m}$. The Slutsky demand function tells us what the consumer would demand facing some different prices (p_1, p_2) and having income $p_1\overline{x}_1 + p_2\overline{x}_2$. Thus the Slutsky demand function at $(p_1, p_2, \overline{x}_1, \overline{x}_2)$ is the ordinary demand at (p_1, p_2) and income $p_1\overline{x}_1 + p_2\overline{x}_2$. That is,

$$x_1^s(p_1, p_2, \overline{x}_1, \overline{x}_2) \equiv x_1(p_1, p_2, p_1\overline{x}_1 + p_2\overline{x}_2).$$

This equation says that the Slutsky demand at prices (p_1, p_2) is that amount which the consumer would demand if he had enough income to purchase his original bundle of goods $(\bar{x}_1, \bar{x}_2)$. This is just the definition of the Slutsky demand function.

Differentiating this identity with respect to p_1, we have

$$\frac{\partial x_1^s(p_1, p_2, \bar{x}_1, \bar{x}_2)}{\partial p_1} = \frac{\partial x_1(p_1, p_2, \overline{m})}{\partial p_1} + \frac{\partial x_1(p_1, p_2, \overline{m})}{\partial m}\bar{x}_1.$$

Rearranging we have

$$\frac{\partial x_1(p_1, p_2, \overline{m})}{\partial p_1} = \frac{\partial x_1^s(p_1, p_2, \bar{x}_1, \bar{x}_2)}{\partial p_1} - \frac{\partial x_1(p_1, p_2, \overline{m})}{\partial m}\bar{x}_1.$$

Note the use of the chain rule in this calculation.

This is a derivative form of the Slutsky equation. It says that the total effect of a price change is composed of a substitution effect (where income is adjusted to keep the bundle $(\bar{x}_1, \bar{x}_2)$ feasible) and an income effect. We know from the text that the substitution effect is negative and that the sign of the income effect depends on whether the good in question is inferior or not. As you can see, this is just the form of the Slutsky equation considered in the text, except that we have replaced the Δ's with derivative signs.

What about the Hicks substitution effect? It is also possible to define a Slutsky equation for it. We let $x_1^h(p_1, p_2, \bar{u})$ be the Hicksian demand function, which measures how much the consumer demands of good 1 at prices (p_1, p_2) if income is adjusted to keep the level of *utility* constant at the original level $\bar{u}$. It turns out that in this case the Slutsky equation takes the form

$$\frac{\partial x_1(p_1, p_2, m)}{\partial p_1} = \frac{\partial x_1^h(p_1, p_2, \bar{u})}{\partial p_1} - \frac{\partial x_1(p_1, p_2, m)}{\partial m}\bar{x}_1.$$

The proof of this equation hinges on the fact that

$$\frac{\partial x_1^h(p_1, p_2, \bar{u})}{\partial p_1} = \frac{\partial x_1^s(p_1, p_2, \bar{x}_1, \bar{x}_2)}{\partial p_1}$$

for infinitesimal changes in price. That is, for derivative size changes in price, the Slutsky substitution and the Hicks substitution effect are the same. The proof of this is not terribly difficult, but it involves some concepts that are beyond the scope of this book. A relatively simple proof is given in Hal R. Varian, *Microeconomic Analysis,* 3rd ed. (New York: Norton, 1992).

EXAMPLE: Rebating a Small Tax

We can use the calculus version of the Slutsky equation to see how consumption choices would react to a small change in a tax when the tax revenues are rebated to the consumers.

Assume, as before, that the tax causes the price to rise by the full amount of the tax. Let x be the amount of gasoline, p its original price, and t the amount of the tax. Then the change in consumption will be given by

$$dx = \frac{\partial x}{\partial p} t + \frac{\partial x}{\partial m} tx.$$

The first term measures how demand responds to the price change times the amount of the price change—which gives us the price effect of the tax. The second terms tells us how demand responds to a change in income times the amount that income has changed—income has gone up by the amount of the tax revenues rebated to the consumer.

Now use Slutsky's equation to expand the first term on the right-hand side to get the substitution and income effects of the price change itself:

$$dx = \frac{\partial x^s}{\partial p} t - \frac{\partial x}{\partial m} tx + \frac{\partial x}{\partial m} tx = \frac{\partial x^s}{\partial p} t.$$

The income effect cancels out, and all that is left is the pure substitution effect. Imposing a small tax and rebating the revenues of the tax is just like imposing a price change and adjusting income so that the old consumption bundle is feasible—as long as the tax is small enough so that the derivative approximation is valid.

CHAPTER **9**

BUYING AND SELLING

In the simple model of the consumer that we considered in the preceding chapters, the income of the consumer was given. In reality people earn their income by selling things that they own: items that they have produced, assets that they have accumulated, or, most commonly, their own labor. In this chapter we will examine how the earlier model must be modified so as to describe this kind of behavior.

9.1 Net and Gross Demands

As before, we will limit ourselves to the two-good model. We now suppose that the consumer starts off with an **endowment** of the two goods, which we will denote by (ω_1, ω_2).[1] This is how much of the two goods the consumer has *before* he enters the market. Think of a farmer who goes to market with ω_1 units of carrots and ω_2 units of potatoes. The farmer inspects the prices available at the market and decides how much he wants to buy and sell of the two goods.

---

[1] The Greek letter ω, omega, is pronounced "o–may–gah."

Let us make a distinction here between the consumer's **gross demands** and his **net demands**. The gross demand for a good is the amount of the good that the consumer actually ends up consuming: how much of each of the goods he or she takes home from the market. The net demand for a good is the *difference* between what the consumer ends up with (the gross demand) and the initial endowment of goods. The net demand for a good is simply the amount that is bought or sold of the good.

If we let (x_1, x_2) be the gross demands, then $(x_1 - \omega_1, x_2 - \omega_2)$ are the net demands. Note that while the gross demands are typically positive numbers, the net demands may be positive or negative. If the net demand for good 1 is negative, it means that the consumer wants to consume less of good 1 than she has; that is, she wants to *supply* good 1 to the market. A negative net demand is simply an amount supplied.

For purposes of economic analysis, the gross demands are the more important, since that is what the consumer is ultimately concerned with. But the net demands are what are actually exhibited in the market and thus are closer to what the layman means by demand or supply.

9.2 The Budget Constraint

The first thing we should do is to consider the form of the budget constraint. What constrains the consumer's final consumption? It must be that the value of the bundle of goods that she goes home with must be equal to the value of the bundle of goods that she came with. Or, algebraically:

$$p_1 x_1 + p_2 x_2 = p_1 \omega_1 + p_2 \omega_2.$$

We could just as well express this budget line in terms of net demands as

$$p_1(x_1 - \omega_1) + p_2(x_2 - \omega_2) = 0.$$

If $(x_1 - \omega_1)$ is positive we say that the consumer is a **net buyer** or **net demander** of good 1; if it is negative we say that she is a **net seller** or **net supplier**. Then the above equation says that the value of what the consumer buys must equal the value of what she sells, which seems sensible enough.

We could also express the budget line when the endowment is present in a form similar to the way we described it before. Now it takes two equations:

$$p_1 x_1 + p_2 x_2 = m$$
$$m = p_1 \omega_1 + p_2 \omega_2.$$

Once the prices are fixed, the value of the endowment, and hence the consumer's money income, is fixed.

What does the budget line look like graphically? When we fix the prices, money income is fixed, and we have a budget equation just like we had before. Thus the slope must be given by $-p_1/p_2$, just as before, so the only problem is to determine the location of the line.

The location of the line can be determined by the following simple observation: the endowment bundle is always on the budget line. That is, one value of (x_1, x_2) that satisfies the budget line is $x_1 = \omega_1$ and $x_2 = \omega_2$. The endowment is always just affordable, since the amount you have to spend is precisely the value of the endowment.

Putting these facts together shows that the budget line has a slope of $-p_1/p_2$ and passes through the endowment point. This is depicted in Figure 9.1.

 Figure 9.1

The budget line. The budget line passes through the endowment and has a slope of $-p_1/p_2$.

Given this budget constraint, the consumer can choose the optimal consumption bundle just as before. In Figure 9.1 we have shown an example of an optimal consumption bundle (x_1^*, x_2^*). Just as before, it will satisfy the optimality condition that the marginal rate of substitution is equal to the price ratio.

In this particular case, $x_1^* > \omega_1$ and $x_2^* < \omega_2$, so the consumer is a net buyer of good 1 and a net seller of good 2. The net demands are simply the net amounts that the consumer buys or sells of the two goods. In general the consumer may decide to be either a buyer or a seller depending on the relative prices of the two goods.

9.3 Changing the Endowment

In our previous analysis of choice we examined how the optimal consumption changed as the money income changed while the prices remained fixed. We can do a similar analysis here by asking how the optimal consumption changes as the *endowment* changes while the prices remain fixed.

For example, suppose that the endowment changes from (ω_1, ω_2) to some other value (ω_1', ω_2') such that

$$p_1\omega_1 + p_2\omega_2 > p_1\omega_1' + p_2\omega_2'.$$

This inequality means that the new endowment (ω_1', ω_2') is worth less than the old endowment—the money income that the consumer could achieve by selling her endowment is less.

This is depicted graphically in Figure 9.2A: the budget line shifts inward. Since this is exactly the same as a reduction in money income, we can conclude the same two things that we concluded in our examination of that case. First, the consumer is definitely worse off with the endowment (ω_1', ω_2') than she was with the old endowment, since her consumption possibilities have been reduced. Second, her demand for each good will change according to whether that good is a normal good or an inferior good.

For example, if good 1 is a normal good and the consumer's endowment changes in a way that reduces its value, we can conclude that the consumer's demand for good 1 will decrease.

The case where the value of the endowment increases is depicted in Figure 9.2B. Following the above argument we conclude that if the budget line shifts outward in a parallel way, the consumer must be made better off. Algebraically, if the endowment changes from (ω_1, ω_2) to (ω_1', ω_2') and $p_1\omega_1 + p_2\omega_2 < p_1\omega_1' + p_2\omega_2'$, then the consumer's new budget set must contain her old budget set. This in turn implies that the optimal choice of the consumer with the new budget set must be preferred to the optimal choice given the old endowment.

It is worthwhile pondering this point a moment. In Chapter 7 we argued that just because a consumption bundle had a higher cost than another didn't mean that it would be preferred to the other bundle. But that only holds for a bundle that must be *consumed*. If a consumer can sell a bundle of goods on a free market at constant prices, then she will always prefer a higher-valued bundle to a lower-valued bundle, simply because a

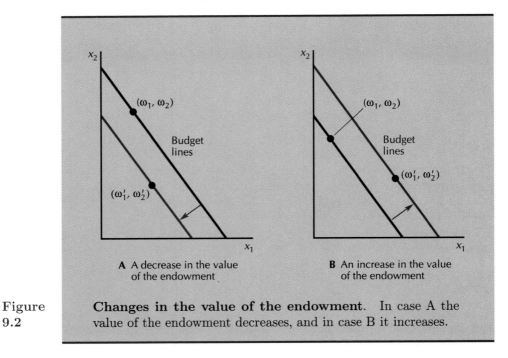

A A decrease in the value
of the endowment

B An increase in the value
of the endowment

Figure
9.2

Changes in the value of the endowment. In case A the value of the endowment decreases, and in case B it increases.

higher-valued bundle gives her more income, and thus more consumption possibilities. Therefore, an *endowment* that has a higher value will always be preferred to an endowment with a lower value. This simple observation will turn out to have some important implications later on.

There's one more case to consider: what happens if $p_1\omega_1 + p_2\omega_2 = p_1\omega_1' + p_2\omega_2'$? Then the budget set doesn't change at all: the consumer is just as well-off with (ω_1, ω_2) as with (ω_1', ω_2'), and her optimal choice should be exactly the same. The endowment has just shifted along the original budget line.

9.4 Price Changes

Earlier, when we examined how demand changed when price changed, we conducted our investigation under the hypothesis that money income remained constant. Now, when money income is determined by the value of the endowment, such a hypothesis is unreasonable: if the value of a good you are selling changes, your money income will certainly change. Thus in the case where the consumer has an endowment, changing prices automatically implies changing income.

Let us first think about this geometrically. If the price of good 1 decreases, we know that the budget line becomes flatter. Since the endowment bundle is always affordable, this means that the budget line must pivot around the endowment, as depicted in Figure 9.3.

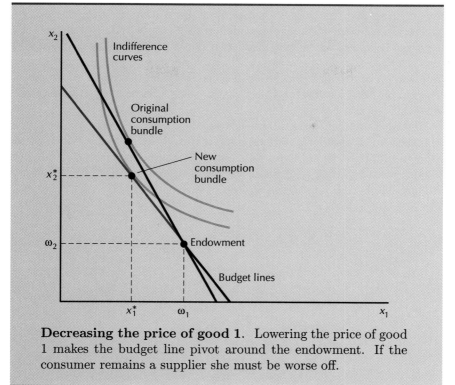

Decreasing the price of good 1. Lowering the price of good 1 makes the budget line pivot around the endowment. If the consumer remains a supplier she must be worse off.

Figure 9.3

In this case, the consumer is initially a seller of good 1 and remains a seller of good 1 even after the price has *declined*. What can we say about this consumer's welfare? In the case depicted, the consumer is on a lower indifference curve after the price change than before, but will this be true in general? The answer comes from applying the principle of revealed preference.

If the consumer remains a supplier, then her new consumption bundle must be on the colored part of the new budget line. But this part of the new budget line is inside the original budget set: all of these choices were open to the consumer before the price changed. Therefore, by revealed preference, all of these choices are worse than the original consumption bundle. We can therefore conclude that if the price of a good that a consumer is selling goes down, and the consumer decides to remain a seller, then the consumer's welfare must have declined.

What if the price of a good that the consumer is selling decreases and the consumer decides to switch to being a buyer of that good? In this case, the consumer may be better off or she may be worse off—there is no way to tell.

Let us now turn to the situation where the consumer is a net buyer of a good. In this case everything neatly turns around: if the consumer is a net buyer of a good, its price *increases*, and the consumer optimally decides to remain a buyer, then she must definitely be worse off. But if the price increase leads her to become a seller, it could go either way—she may be better off, or she may be worse off. These observations follow from a simple application of revealed preference just like the cases described above, but it is good practice for you to draw a graph just to make sure you understand how this works.

Revealed preference also allows us to make some interesting points about the decision of whether to remain a buyer or to become a seller when prices change. Suppose, as in Figure 9.4, that the consumer is a net buyer of good 1, and consider what happens if the price of good 1 *decreases*. Then the budget line becomes flatter as in Figure 9.4.

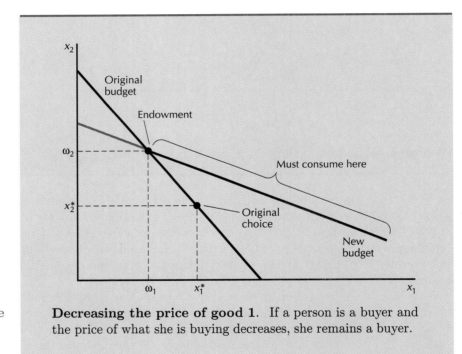

Figure
9.4
Decreasing the price of good 1. If a person is a buyer and the price of what she is buying decreases, she remains a buyer.

As usual we don't know for certain whether the consumer will buy more or less of good 1—it depends on her tastes. However, we can say something for sure: *the consumer will continue to be a net buyer of good 1—she will not switch to being a seller.*

How do we know this? Well, consider what would happen if the consumer did switch. Then she would be consuming somewhere on the colored part of the new budget line in Figure 9.4. But those consumption bundles were feasible for her when she faced the original budget line, and she rejected them in favor of (x_1^*, x_2^*). So (x_1^*, x_2^*) must be better than any of those points. And under the *new* budget line, (x_1^*, x_2^*) is a feasible consumption bundle. So whatever she consumes under the new budget line, it must be better than (x_1^*, x_2^*)—and thus better than any points on the colored part of the new budget line. This implies that her consumption of x_1 must be to the right of her endowment point—that is, she must remain a net demander of good 1.

Again, this kind of observation applies equally well to a person who is a net seller of a good: if the price of what she is selling goes *up*, she will not switch to being a net buyer. We can't tell for sure if the consumer will consume more or less of the good she is selling—but we know that she will keep selling it if the price goes up.

9.5 Offer Curves and Demand Curves

Recall from Chapter 6 that price offer curves depict those combinations of both goods that may be demanded by a consumer and that demand curves depict the relationship between the price and the quantity demanded of some good. Exactly the same constructions work when the consumer has an endowment of both goods.

Consider, for example, Figure 9.5, which illustrates the price offer curve and the demand curve for a consumer. The offer curve will always pass through the endowment, because at some price the endowment will be a demanded bundle; that is, at some prices the consumer will optimally choose not to trade.

As we've seen, the consumer may decide to be a buyer of good 1 for some prices and a seller of good 1 for other prices. Thus the offer curve will generally pass to the left and to the right of the endowment point.

The demand curve illustrated in Figure 9.5B is the gross demand curve—it measures the total amount the consumer chooses to consume of good 1. We have illustrated the net demand curve in Figure 9.6.

Note that the net demand for good 1 will typically be negative for some prices. This will be when the price of good 1 becomes so high that the consumer chooses to become a seller of good 1. At some price the consumer switches between being a net demander to being a net supplier of good 1.

It is conventional to plot the supply curve in the positive orthant, although it actually makes more sense to think of supply as just a negative demand. We'll bow to tradition here and plot the net supply curve in the normal way—as a positive amount, as in Figure 9.6.

Algebraically the net demand for good 1, $d_1(p_1, p_2)$, is the difference between the gross demand $x_1(p_1, p_2)$ and the endowment of good 1, when this difference is positive; that is, when the consumer wants more of the good than he or she has:

$$d_1(p_1, p_2) = \begin{cases} x_1(p_1, p_2) - \omega_1 & \text{if this is positive;} \\ 0 & \text{otherwise.} \end{cases}$$

Figure
9.5   **The offer curve and the demand curve.** These are two
ways of depicting the relationship between the demanded bundle
and the prices when an endowment is present.

The net supply curve is the difference between how much the consumer
has of good 1 and how much he or she wants when *this* difference is positive:

$$s_1(p_1, p_2) = \begin{cases} \omega_1 - x_1(p_1, p_2) & \text{if this is positive;} \\ 0 & \text{otherwise.} \end{cases}$$

Everything that we've established about the properties of demand behavior applies directly to the supply behavior of a consumer—because supply
is just negative demand. If the *gross* demand curve is always downward
sloping, then the net demand curve will be downward sloping and the supply curve will be upward sloping. Think about it: if an increase in the
price makes the net demand more negative, then the net supply will be
more positive.

9.6 The Slutsky Equation Revisited

The above applications of revealed preference are handy, but they don't
really answer the main question: how does the demand for a good react to
a change in its price? We saw in Chapter 8 that if money income was held
constant, and the good was a normal good, then a reduction in its price
must lead to an increase in demand.

The catch is the phrase "money income was held constant." The case we
are examining here necessarily involves a change in money income, since
the value of the endowment will necessarily change when a price changes.

Gross demand, net demand, and net supply. Using the gross demand and net demand to depict the demand and supply behavior.

Figure
9.6

In Chapter 8 we described the Slutsky equation that decomposed the change in demand due to a price change into a substitution effect and an income effect. The income effect was due to the change in purchasing power when prices change. But now, purchasing power has two reasons to change when a price changes. The first is the one involved in the definition of the Slutsky equation: when a price falls, for example, you can buy just as much of a good as you were consuming before and have some extra money left over. Let us refer to this as the **ordinary income effect**. But the second effect is new. When the price of a good changes, it changes the value of your endowment and thus changes your money income. For example, if you are a net supplier of a good, then a fall in its price will reduce your money income directly since you won't be able to sell your endowment for as much money as you could before. We will have the same effects that we had before, plus an extra income effect from the influence of the prices on the value of the endowment bundle. We'll call this the **endowment income effect**.

In the earlier form of the Slutsky equation, the amount of money income you had was fixed. Now we have to worry about how your money income changes as the value of your endowment changes. Thus, when we calculate the effect of a change in price on demand, the Slutsky equation will take the form:

total change in demand = change due to substitution effect + change in demand due to ordinary income effect + change in demand due to endowment income effect.

The first two effects are familiar. As before, let us use Δx_1 to stand for the total change in demand, Δx_1^s to stand for the change in demand due to the substitution effect, and Δx_1^m to stand for the change in demand due to the ordinary income effect. Then we can substitute these terms into the above "verbal equation" to get the Slutsky equation in terms of rates of change:

$$\frac{\Delta x_1}{\Delta p_1} = \frac{\Delta x_1^s}{\Delta p_1} - x_1 \frac{\Delta x_1^m}{\Delta m} + \text{endowment income effect.} \qquad (9.1)$$

What will the last term look like? We'll derive an explicit expression below, but let us first think about what is involved. When the price of the endowment changes, money income will change, and this change in money income will induce a change in demand. Thus the endowment income effect will consist of two terms:

endowment income effect = change in demand when income changes
× the change in income when price changes. $\qquad$ (9.2)

Let's look at the second effect first. Since income is defined to be

$$m = p_1 \omega_1 + p_2 \omega_2,$$

we have

$$\frac{\Delta m}{\Delta p_1} = \omega_1.$$

This tells us how money income changes when the price of good 1 changes: if you have 10 units of good 1 to sell, and its price goes up by $1, your money income will go up by $10.

The first term in equation (9.2) is just how demand changes when income changes. We already have an expression for this: it is $\Delta x_1^m / \Delta m$: the change in demand divided by the change in income. Thus the endowment income effect is given by

$$\text{endowment income effect} = \frac{\Delta x_1^m}{\Delta m} \frac{\Delta m}{\Delta p_1} = \frac{\Delta x_1^m}{\Delta m} \omega_1. \qquad (9.3)$$

Inserting equation (9.3) into equation (9.1) we get the final form of the Slutsky equation:

$$\frac{\Delta x_1}{\Delta p_1} = \frac{\Delta x_1^s}{\Delta p_1} + (\omega_1 - x_1) \frac{\Delta x_1^m}{\Delta m}.$$

This equation can be used to answer the question posed above. We know that the sign of the substitution effect is always negative—opposite the direction of the change in price. Let us suppose that the good is a normal good, so that $\Delta x_1^m / \Delta m > 0$. Then the sign of the combined income effect depends on whether the person is a net demander or a net supplier of the good in question. If the person is a net demander of a normal good, and its price increases, then the consumer will necessarily buy less of it. If the consumer is a net supplier of a normal good, then the sign of the total effect is ambiguous: it depends on the magnitude of the (positive) combined income effect as compared to the magnitude of the (negative) substitution effect.

As before, each of these changes can be depicted graphically, although the graph gets rather messy. Refer to Figure 9.7, which depicts the Slutsky decomposition of a price change. The total change in the demand for good 1 is indicated by the movement from A to C. This is the sum of three separate movements: the substitution effect, which is the movement from A to B, and two income effects. The ordinary income effect, which is the movement from B to D, is the change in demand *holding money income fixed*—that is, the same income effect that we examined in Chapter 8. But since the value of the endowment changes when prices change, there is now an extra income effect: because of the change in the value of the endowment, money income changes. This change in money income shifts the budget line back inward so that it passes through the endowment bundle. The change in demand from D to C measures this endowment income effect.

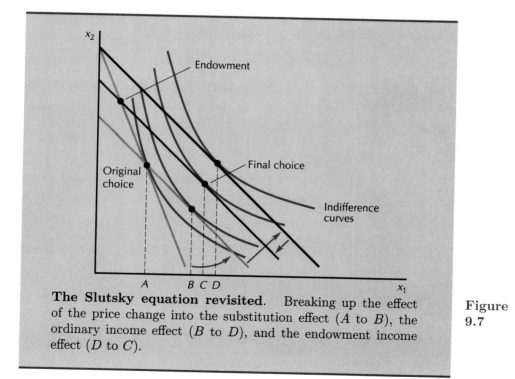

The Slutsky equation revisited.   Breaking up the effect of the price change into the substitution effect (A to B), the ordinary income effect (B to D), and the endowment income effect (D to C).

Figure
9.7

9.7 Use of the Slutsky Equation

Suppose that we have a consumer who sells apples and oranges that he grows on a few trees in his backyard, like the consumer we described at the beginning of Chapter 8. We said there that if the price of apples increased, then this consumer might actually consume more apples. Using the Slutsky equation derived in this chapter, it is not hard to see why. If we let x_a stand for the consumer's demand for apples, and let p_a be the price of apples, then we know that

$$\underset{(-)}{\frac{\Delta x_a}{\Delta p_a}} = \underset{(+)}{\frac{\Delta x_a^s}{\Delta p_a}} + (w_a - x_a) \underset{(+)}{\frac{\Delta x_a^m}{\Delta m}}.$$

This says that the total change in the demand for apples when the price of apples changes is the substitution effect plus the income effect. The substitution effect works in the right direction—increasing the price decreases the demand for apples. But if apples are a normal good for this consumer, the income effect works in the wrong direction. Since the consumer is a net supplier of apples, the increase in the price of apples increases his money income so much that he wants to consume more apples due to the income effect. If the latter term is strong enough to outweigh the substitution effect, we can easily get the "perverse" result.

EXAMPLE: Calculating the Endowment Income Effect

Let's try a little numerical example. Suppose that a dairy farmer produces 40 quarts of milk a week. Initially the price of milk is $3 a quart. His demand function for milk, for his own consumption, is

$$x_1 = 10 + \frac{m}{10p_1}.$$

Since he is producing 40 quarts at $3 a quart, his income is $120 a week. His initial demand for milk is therefore $x_1 = 14$. Now suppose that the price of milk changes to $2 a quart. His money income will then change to $m' = 2 \times 40 = \$80$, and his demand will be $x_1' = 10 + 80/20 = 14$.

If his money income had remained fixed at $m = \$120$, he would have purchased $x_1 = 10 + 120/10 \times 2 = 16$ quarts of milk at this price. Thus the endowment income effect—the change in his demand due to the change in the value of his endowment—is -2. The substitution effect and the ordinary income effect for this problem were calculated in Chapter 8.

9.8 Labor Supply

Let us apply the idea of an endowment to analyzing a consumer's labor supply decision. The consumer can choose to work a lot and have relatively high consumption, or can choose to work a little and have a small consumption. The amount of consumption and labor will be determined by the interaction of the consumer's preferences and the budget constraint.

The Budget Constraint

Let us suppose that the consumer initially has some money income M that she receives whether she works or not. This might be income from investments or from relatives, for example. We call this amount the consumer's **nonlabor income**. (The consumer could have zero nonlabor income, but we want to allow for the possibility that it is positive.)

Let us use C to indicate the amount of consumption the consumer has, and use p to denote the price of consumption. Then letting w be the wage rate, and L the amount of labor supplied, we have the budget constraint:

$$pC = M + wL.$$

This says that the value of what the consumer consumes must be equal to her nonlabor income plus her labor income.

Let us try to compare the above formulation to the previous examples of budget constraints. The major difference is that we have something that the consumer is choosing—labor supply—on the right-hand side of the equation. We can easily transpose it to the left-hand side to get

$$pC - wL = M.$$

This is better, but we have a minus sign where we normally have a plus sign. How can we remedy this? Let us suppose that there is some maximum amount of labor supply possible—24 hours a day, 7 days a week, or whatever is compatible with the units of measurement we are using. Let $\overline{L}$ denote this amount of labor time. Then adding $w\overline{L}$ to each side and rearranging we have

$$pC + w(\overline{L} - L) = M + w\overline{L}.$$

Let us define $\overline{C} = M/p$, the amount of consumption that the consumer would have if she didn't work at all. That is, $\overline{C}$ is her endowment of consumption, so we write

$$pC + w(\overline{L} - L) = p\overline{C} + w\overline{L}.$$

Now we have an equation very much like those we've seen before. We have two choice variables on the left-hand side and two endowment variables on the right-hand side. The variable $\overline{L} - L$ can be interpreted as the amount of "leisure"—that is, time that isn't labor time. Let us use the variable R (for relaxation!) to denote leisure, so that $R = \overline{L} - L$. Then the total amount of time you have available for leisure is $\overline{R} = \overline{L}$ and the budget constraint becomes

$$pC + wR = p\overline{C} + w\overline{R}.$$

The above equation is formally identical to the very first budget constraint that we wrote in this chapter. However, it has a much more interesting interpretation. It says that the value of a consumer's consumption plus her leisure has to equal the value of her endowment of consumption and her endowment of time, where her endowment of time is valued at her wage rate. The wage rate is not only the price of labor, it is also the price of *leisure*.

After all, if your wage rate is $10 an hour and you decide to consume an extra hour's leisure, how much does it cost you? The answer is that it costs you $10 in forgone income—that's the price of that extra hour's consumption of leisure. Economists sometimes say that the wage rate is the **opportunity cost** of leisure.

The right-hand side of this budget constraint is sometimes called the consumer's **full income** or **implicit income**. It measures the value of what the consumer owns—her endowment of consumption goods, if any, and her endowment of her own time. This is to be distinguished from the consumer's **measured income**, which is simply the income she receives from selling off some of her time.

The nice thing about this budget constraint is that it is just like the ones we've seen before. It passes through the endowment point $(\overline{L}, \overline{C})$ and has a slope of $-w/p$. The endowment would be what the consumer would get if she did not engage in market trade at all, and the slope of the budget line tells us the rate at which the market will exchange one good for another.

The optimal choice occurs where the marginal rate of substitution—the tradeoff between consumption and leisure—equals w/p, the **real wage**, as depicted in Figure 9.8. The value of the extra consumption to the consumer from working a little more has to be just equal to the value of the lost leisure that it takes to generate that consumption. The real wage is the amount of consumption that the consumer can purchase if she gives up an hour of leisure.

9.9 Comparative Statics of Labor Supply

First let us consider how a consumer's labor supply changes as money income changes with the price and wage held fixed. If you won the state

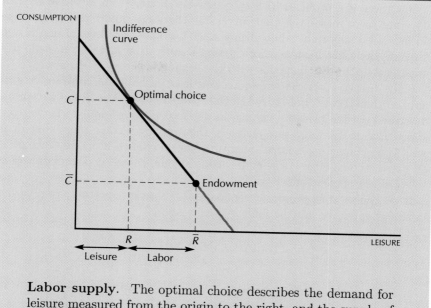

Labor supply. The optimal choice describes the demand for leisure measured from the origin to the right, and the supply of labor measured from the endowment to the left.

Figure
9.8

lottery and got a big increase in nonlabor income, what would happen to your supply of labor? What would happen to your demand for leisure?

For most people, the supply of labor would drop when their money income increased. In other words, leisure is probably a normal good for most people: when their money income rises, people choose to consume more leisure. There seems to be a fair amount of evidence for this observation, so we will adopt it as a maintained hypothesis: we will assume that leisure is a normal good.

What does this imply about the response of the consumer's labor supply to changes in the wage rate? When the wage rate increases there are two effects: the return to working more increase and the cost of consuming leisure increases. By using the ideas of income and substitution effects and the Slutsky equation we can isolate these individual effects and analyze them.

When the wage rate increases, leisure becomes more expensive, which by itself leads people to want less of it (the substitution effect). Since leisure is a normal good, we would then predict that an increase in the wage rate would necessarily lead to a decrease in the demand for leisure—that is, an increase in the supply of labor. This follows from the Slutsky equation given in Chapter 8. A normal good must have a negatively sloped demand curve. If leisure is a normal good, then the supply curve of labor must be positively sloped.

But there is a problem with this analysis. First, at an intuitive level, it does not seem reasonable that increasing the wage would *always* result in an increased supply of labor. If my wage becomes very high, I might well "spend" the extra income in consuming leisure. How can we reconcile this apparently plausible behavior with the economic theory given above?

If the theory gives the wrong answer, it is probably because we've misapplied the theory. And indeed in this case we have. The Slutsky example described earlier gave the change in demand *holding money income constant*. But if the wage rate changes, then money income must change as well. The change in demand resulting from a change in money income is an extra income effect—the endowment income effect. It occurs on top of the ordinary income effect.

If we apply the *appropriate* version of the Slutsky equation given earlier in this chapter, we get the following expression:

$$\frac{\Delta R}{\Delta w} = \text{substitution effect} + (\overline{R} - R) \frac{\Delta R}{\Delta m}.$$
$$(-) \qquad\qquad (+) \quad (+)$$

(9.4)

In this expression the substitution effect is definitely negative, as it always is, and $\Delta R/\Delta m$ is positive since we are assuming that leisure is a normal good. But $(\overline{R} - R)$ is positive as well, so the sign of the whole expression is ambiguous. Unlike the usual case of consumer demand, the demand for leisure will have an ambiguous sign, even if leisure is a normal good. As the wage rate increases, people may work more or less.

Why does this ambiguity arise? When the wage rate increases, the substitution effect says work more in order to substitute consumption for leisure. But when the wage rate increases, the value of the endowment goes up as well. This is just like extra income, which may very well be consumed in taking extra leisure. Which is the larger effect is an empirical matter and cannot be decided by theory alone. We have to look at people's actual labor supply decisions to determine which effect dominates.

The case where an increase in the wage rate results in a decrease in the supply of labor is represented by a **backward-bending labor supply curve**. The Slutsky equation tells us that this effect is more likely to occur the larger is $(\overline{R} - R)$, that is, the larger is the supply of labor. When $\overline{R} = R$, the consumer is consuming only leisure, so an increase in the wage will result in a pure substitution effect and thus an increase in the supply of labor. But as the labor supply increases, each increase in the wage gives the consumer additional income for all the hours he is working, so that after some point he may well decide to use this extra income to "purchase" additional leisure—that is, to *reduce* his supply of labor.

A backward-bending labor supply curve is depicted in Figure 9.9. When the wage rate is small, the substitution effect is larger than the income effect, and an increase in the wage will decrease the demand for leisure and hence increase the supply of labor. But for larger wage rates the income

effect may outweigh the substitution effect, and an increase in the wage
will *reduce* the supply of labor.

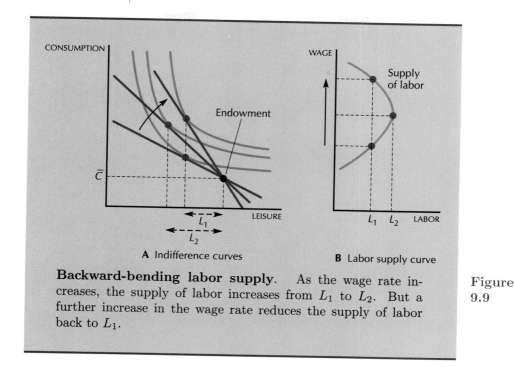

Backward-bending labor supply.   As the wage rate increases, the supply of labor increases from L_1 to L_2. But a
further increase in the wage rate reduces the supply of labor
back to L_1.

Figure
9.9

EXAMPLE: Overtime and the Supply of Labor

Consider a worker who has chosen to supply a certain amount of labor
$L^* = \overline{R} - R^*$ when faced with the wage rate w as depicted in Figure 9.10.
Now suppose that the firm offers him a higher wage, $w' > w$, for extra time
that he chooses to work. Such a payment is known as an **overtime wage**.

In terms of Figure 9.10, this means that the slope of the budget line will
be steeper for labor supplied in excess of L^*. But then we know that the
worker will optimally choose to supply more labor, by the usual sort of
revealed preference argument: the choices involving working less than L^*
were available before the overtime was offered and were rejected.

Note that we get an unambiguous increase in labor supply with an overtime wage, whereas just offering a higher wage for all hours worked has an
ambiguous effect—as discussed above, labor supply may increase or it may
decrease. The reason is that the response to an overtime wage is essentially
a pure substitution effect—the change in the optimal choice resulting from

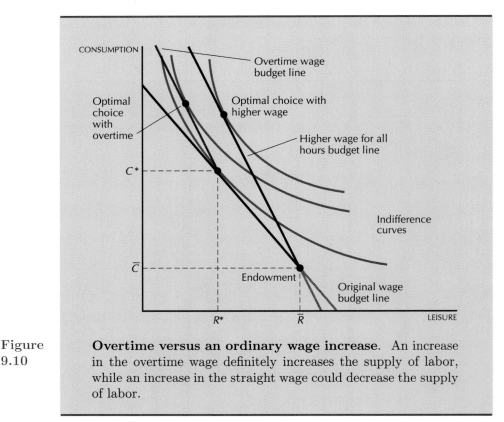

Figure 9.10

Overtime versus an ordinary wage increase. An increase in the overtime wage definitely increases the supply of labor, while an increase in the straight wage could decrease the supply of labor.

pivoting the budget line around the chosen point. Overtime gives a higher payment for the *extra* hours worked, whereas a straight increase in the wage gives a higher payment for *all* hours worked. Thus a straight-wage increase involves both a substitution and an income effect while an overtime-wage increase results in a pure substitution effect. An example of this is shown in Figure 9.10. There an increase in the straight wage results in a *decrease* in labor supply, while an increase in the overtime wage results in an increase in labor supply.

Summary

1. Consumers earn income by selling their endowment of goods.

2. The gross demand for a good is the amount that the consumer ends up consuming. The net demand for a good is the amount the consumer buys. Thus the net demand is the difference between the gross demand and the endowment.

3. The budget constraint has a slope of $-p_1/p_2$ and passes through the endowment bundle.

4. When a price changes, the value of what the consumer has to sell will change and thereby generate an additional income effect in the Slutsky equation.

5. Labor supply is an interesting example of the interaction of income and substitution effects. Due to the interaction of these two effects, the response of labor supply to a change in the wage rate is ambiguous.

REVIEW QUESTIONS

1. If a consumer's net demands are $(5, -3)$ and her endowment is $(4, 4)$, what are her gross demands?

2. The prices are $(p_1, p_2) = (2, 3)$, and the consumer is currently consuming $(x_1, x_2) = (4, 4)$. There is a perfect market for the two goods in which they can be bought and sold costlessly. Will the consumer necessarily prefer consuming the bundle $(y_1, y_2) = (3, 5)$? Will she necessarily prefer having the bundle (y_1, y_2)?

3. The prices are $(p_1, p_2) = (2, 3)$, and the consumer is currently consuming $(x_1, x_2) = (4, 4)$. Now the prices change to $(q_1, q_2) = (2, 4)$. Could the consumer be better off under these new prices?

4. The U.S. currently imports about half of the petroleum that it uses. The rest of its needs are met by domestic production. Could the price of oil rise so much that the U.S. would be made better off?

5. Suppose that by some miracle the number of hours in the day increased from 24 to 30 hours (with luck this would happen shortly before exam week). How would this affect the budget constraint?

6. If leisure is an inferior good, what can you say about the slope of the labor supply curve?

APPENDIX

The derivation of the Slutsky equation in the text contained one bit of hand waving. When we considered how changing the monetary value of the endowment affects demand, we said that it was equal to $\Delta x_1^m / \Delta m$. In our old version of the Slutsky equation this was the rate of change in demand when income changed so as to keep the original consumption bundle affordable. But that will not necessarily be equal to the rate of change of demand when the value of the endowment changes. Let's examine this point in a little more detail.

Let the price of good 1 change from p_1 to p'_1, and use m'' to denote the new money income at the price p'_1 due to the change in the value of the endowment. Suppose that the price of good 2 remains fixed so we can omit it as an argument of the demand function.

By definition of m'', we know that

$$m'' - m = \Delta p_1 \omega_1.$$

Note that it is identically true that

$$\frac{x_1(p'_1, m'') - x_1(p_1, m)}{\Delta p_1} =$$

$$+ \frac{x_1(p'_1, m') - x_1(p_1, m)}{\Delta p_1} \quad \text{(substitution effect)}$$

$$- \frac{x_1(p'_1, m') - x_1(p'_1, m)}{\Delta p_1} \quad \text{(ordinary income effect)}$$

$$+ \frac{x_1(p'_1, m'') - x_1(p'_1, m)}{\Delta p_1} \quad \text{(endowment income effect)}.$$

(Just cancel out identical terms with opposite signs on the right-hand side.)

By definition of the ordinary income effect,

$$\Delta p_1 = \frac{m' - m}{x_1}$$

and by definition of the endowment income effect,

$$\Delta p_1 = \frac{m'' - m}{\omega_1}.$$

Making these replacements gives us a Slutsky equation of the form

$$\frac{x_1(p'_1, m'') - x_1(p_1, m)}{\Delta p_1} =$$

$$+ \frac{x_1(p'_1, m') - x_1(p_1, m)}{\Delta p_1} \quad \text{(substitution effect)}$$

$$- \frac{x_1(p'_1, m') - x_1(p'_1, m)}{m' - m} x_1 \quad \text{(ordinary income effect)}$$

$$+ \frac{x_1(p'_1, m'') - x_1(p'_1, m)}{m'' - m} \omega_1 \quad \text{(endowment income effect)}.$$

Writing this in terms of Δs, we have

$$\frac{\Delta x_1}{\Delta p_1} = \frac{\Delta x_1^s}{\Delta p_1} - \frac{\Delta x_1^m}{\Delta m} x_1 + \frac{\Delta x_1^w}{\Delta m} \omega_1.$$

The only new term here is the last one. It tells how the demand for good 1 changes as income changes, times the *endowment* of good 1. This is precisely the endowment income effect.

Suppose that we are considering a very small price change, and thus a small associated income change. Then the fractions in the two income effects will be virtually the same, since the *rate* of change of good 1 when income changes from m to m' should be about the same as when income changes from m to m''. For such small changes we can collect terms and write the last two terms—the income effects—as

$$\frac{\Delta x_1^m}{\Delta m}(\omega_1 - x_1),$$

which yields a Slutsky equation of the same form as that derived earlier:

$$\frac{\Delta x_1}{\Delta p_1} = \frac{\Delta x_1^s}{\Delta p_1} + (\omega_1 - x_1)\frac{\Delta x_1^m}{\Delta m}.$$

If we want to express the Slutsky equation in calculus terms, we can just take limits in this expression. Or, if you prefer, we can calculate the correct equation directly, just by taking partial derivatives. Let $x_1(p_1, m(p_1))$ be the demand function for good 1 where we hold price 2 fixed and recognize that money income depends on the price of good 1 via the relationship $m(p_1) = p_1\omega_1 + p_2\omega_2$. Then we can write

$$\frac{dx_1(p_1, m(p_1))}{dp_1} = \frac{\partial x_1(p_1, m)}{\partial p_1} + \frac{\partial x_1(p_1, m)}{\partial m}\frac{dm(p_1)}{dp_1}.$$

By the definition of $m(p_1)$ we know how income changes when price changes:

$$\frac{\partial m(p_1)}{\partial p_1} = \omega_1, \tag{9.5}$$

and by the Slutsky equation we know how demand changes when price changes, holding money income fixed:

$$\frac{\partial x_1(p_1, m)}{\partial p_1} = \frac{\partial x_1^s(p_1)}{\partial p_1} - \frac{\partial x(p_1, m)}{\partial m}x_1. \tag{9.6}$$

Inserting equation (9.6) into equation (9.5) we have

$$\frac{dx_1(p_1, m(p_1))}{dp_1} = \frac{\partial x_1^s(p_1)}{\partial p_1} + \frac{\partial x(p_1, m)}{\partial m}(\omega_1 - x_1),$$

which is the form of the Slutsky equation that we want.

CHAPTER 10

INTERTEMPORAL CHOICE

In this chapter we continue our examination of consumer behavior by considering the choices involved in saving and consuming over time. Choices of consumption over time are known as **intertemporal choices**.

10.1 The Budget Constraint

Let us imagine a consumer who chooses how much of some good to consume in each of two time periods. We will usually want to think of this good as being a composite good, as described in Chapter 2, but you can think of it as being a specific commodity if you wish. We denote the amount of consumption in each period by (c_1, c_2) and suppose that the prices of consumption in each period are constant at 1. The amount of money the consumer will have in each period is denoted by (m_1, m_2).

Suppose initially that the only way the consumer has of transferring money from period 1 to period 2 is by saving it without earning interest. Furthermore let us assume for the moment that he has no possibility of

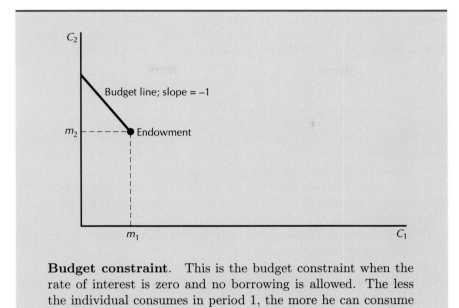

Budget constraint. This is the budget constraint when the
rate of interest is zero and no borrowing is allowed. The less
the individual consumes in period 1, the more he can consume
in period 2.

Figure
10.1

borrowing money, so that the most he can spend in period 1 is m_1. His
budget constraint will then look like the one depicted in Figure 10.1.

We see that there will be two possible kinds of choices. The consumer
could choose to consume at (m_1, m_2), which means that he just consumes
his income each period, or he can choose to consume less than his income
during the first period. In this latter case, the consumer is saving some of
his first-period consumption for a later date.

Now, let us allow the consumer to borrow and lend money at some
interest rate r. Keeping the prices of consumption in each period at 1 for
convenience, let us derive the budget constraint. Suppose first that the
consumer decides to be a saver so his first period consumption, c_1, is less
than his first-period income, m_1. In this case he will earn interest on the
amount he saves, $m_1 - c_1$, at the interest rate r. The amount that he can
consume next period is given by

$$c_2 = m_2 + (m_1 - c_1) + r(m_1 - c_1)$$
$$= m_2 + (1 + r)(m_1 - c_1). \qquad (10.1)$$

This says that the amount that the consumer can consume in period 2 is
his income plus the amount he saved from period 1, plus the interest that
he earned on his savings.

Now suppose that the consumer is a borrower so that his first-period
consumption is greater than his first-period income. The consumer is a

borrower if $c_1 > m_1$, and the interest he has to *pay* in the second period will be $r(c_1 - m_1)$. Of course, he also has to pay back the amount that he borrowed, $c_1 - m_1$. This means his budget constraint is given by

$$c_2 = m_2 - r(c_1 - m_1) - (c_1 - m_1)$$
$$= m_2 + (1+r)(m_1 - c_1),$$

which is just what we had before. If $m_1 - c_1$ is positive, then the consumer earns interest on this savings; if $m_1 - c_1$ is negative, then the consumer pays interest on his borrowings.

If $c_1 = m_1$, then necessarily $c_2 = m_2$, and the consumer is neither a borrower nor a lender. We might say that this consumption position is the "Polonius point."[1]

We can rearrange the budget constraint for the consumer to get two alternative forms that are useful:

$$(1+r)c_1 + c_2 = (1+r)m_1 + m_2 \tag{10.2}$$

and

$$c_1 + \frac{c_2}{1+r} = m_1 + \frac{m_2}{1+r}. \tag{10.3}$$

Note that both equations have the form

$$p_1 x_1 + p_2 x_2 = p_1 m_1 + p_2 m_2.$$

In equation (10.2), $p_1 = 1 + r$ and $p_2 = 1$. In equation (10.3), $p_1 = 1$ and $p_2 = 1/(1+r)$.

We say that equation (10.2) expresses the budget constraint in terms of **future value** and that equation (10.3) expresses the budget constraint in terms of **present value**. The reason for this terminology is that the first budget constraint makes the price of future consumption equal to 1, while the second budget constraint makes the price of present consumption equal to 1. The first budget constraint measures the period-1 price *relative* to the period-2 price, while the second equation does the reverse.

The geometric interpretation of present value and future value is given in Figure 10.2. The present value of an endowment of money in two periods is the amount of money in period 1 that would generate the same budget set as the endowment. This is just the horizontal intercept of the budget line, which gives the maximum amount of first-period consumption possible.

---

[1] "Neither a borrower, nor a lender be; For loan oft loses both itself and friend, And borrowing dulls the edge of husbandry." *Hamlet*, Act I, scene *iii*; Polonius giving advice to his son.

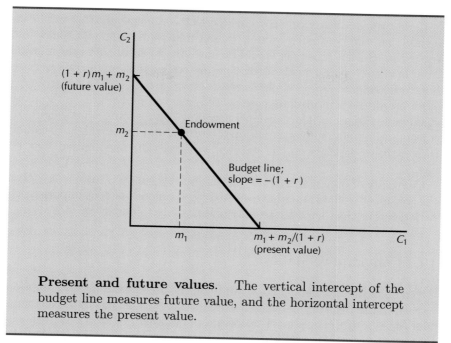

Present and future values. The vertical intercept of the budget line measures future value, and the horizontal intercept measures the present value.

Figure
10.2

Examining the budget constraint, this amount is $\bar{c}_1 = m_1 + m_2/(1 + r)$, which is the present value of the endowment.

Similarly, the vertical intercept is the maximum amount of second-period consumption, which occurs when $c_1 = 0$. Again, from the budget constraint, we can solve for this amount $\bar{c}_2 = (1 + r)m_1 + m_2$, the future value of the endowment.

The present-value form is the more important way to express the intertemporal budget constraint since it measures the future relative to the present, which is the way we naturally look at it.

It is easy from any of these equations to see the form of this budget constraint. The budget line passes through (m_1, m_2), since that is always an *affordable* consumption pattern, and the budget line has a slope of $-(1 + r)$.

10.2 Preferences for Consumption

Let us now consider the consumer's preferences, as represented by his indifference curves. The shape of the indifference curves indicates the consumer's tastes for consumption at different times. If we drew indifference curves with a constant slope of -1, for example, they would represent tastes of a consumer who didn't care whether he consumed today or tomorrow. His marginal rate of substitution between today and tomorrow is -1.

If we drew indifference curves for perfect complements, this would indicate that the consumer wanted to consume equal amounts today and tomorrow. Such a consumer would be unwilling to substitute consumption from one time period to the other, no matter what it might be worth to him to do so.

As usual, the intermediate case of well-behaved preferences is the more reasonable situation. The consumer is willing to substitute some amount of consumption today for consumption tomorrow, and how much he is willing to substitute depends on the particular pattern of consumption that he has.

Convexity of preferences is very natural in this context, since it says that the consumer would rather have an "average" amount of consumption each period rather than have a lot today and nothing tomorrow or vice versa.

10.3 Comparative Statics

Given a consumer's budget constraint and his preferences for consumption in each of the two periods, we can examine the optimal choice of consumption (c_1, c_2). If the consumer chooses a point where $c_1 < m_1$, we will say that she is a **lender**, and if $c_1 > m_1$, we say that she is a **borrower**. In Figure 10.3A we have depicted a case where the consumer is a borrower, and in Figure 10.3B we have depicted a lender.

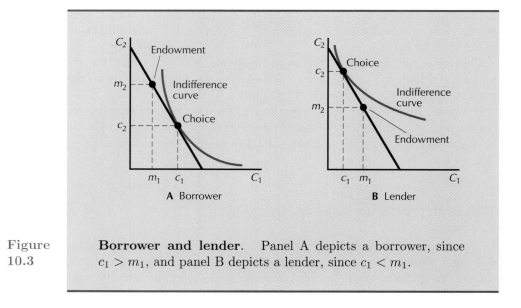

Figure
10.3   **Borrower and lender.**   Panel A depicts a borrower, since $c_1 > m_1$, and panel B depicts a lender, since $c_1 < m_1$.

Let us now consider how the consumer would react to a change in the interest rate. From equation (10.1) we see that increasing the rate of interest must tilt the budget line to a steeper position: for a given reduction in c_1 you will get more consumption in the second period if the interest rate is higher. Of course the endowment always remains affordable, so the tilt is really a pivot around the endowment.

We can also say something about how the choice of being a borrower or a lender changes as the interest rate changes. There are two cases, depending on whether the consumer is initially a borrower or initially a lender. Suppose first that he is a lender. Then it turns out that if the interest rate increases, the consumer must remain a lender.

This argument is illustrated in Figure 10.4. If the consumer is initially a lender, then his consumption bundle is to the left of the endowment point. Now let the interest rate increase. Is it possible that the consumer shifts to a new consumption point to the *right* of the endowment?

No, because that would violate the principle of revealed preference: choices to the right of the endowment point were available to the consumer when he faced the original budget set and were rejected in favor of the chosen point. Since the original optimal bundle is still available at the new budget line, the new optimal bundle must be a point *outside* the old budget set—which means it must be to the left of the endowment. The consumer must remain a lender when the interest rate increases.

There is a similar effect for borrowers: if the consumer is initially a borrower, and the interest rate declines, he or she will remain a borrower. (You might sketch a diagram similar to Figure 10.4 and see if you can spell out the argument.)

Thus if a person is a lender and the interest rate increases, he will remain a lender. If a person is a borrower and the interest rate decreases, he will remain a borrower. On the other hand, if a person is a lender and the interest rate decreases, he may well decide to switch to being a borrower; similarly, an increase in the interest rate may induce a borrower to become a lender. Revealed preference tells us nothing about these last two cases.

Revealed preference can also be used to make judgments about how the consumer's welfare changes as the interest rate changes. If the consumer is initially a borrower, and the interest rate rises, but he decides to remain a borrower, then he must be worse off at the new interest rate. This argument is illustrated in Figure 10.5; if the consumer remains a borrower, he must be operating at a point that was affordable under the old budget set but was rejected, which implies that he must be worse off.

10.4 The Slutsky Equation and Intertemporal Choice

The Slutsky equation can be used to decompose the change in demand due to an interest rate change into income effects and substitution effects, just

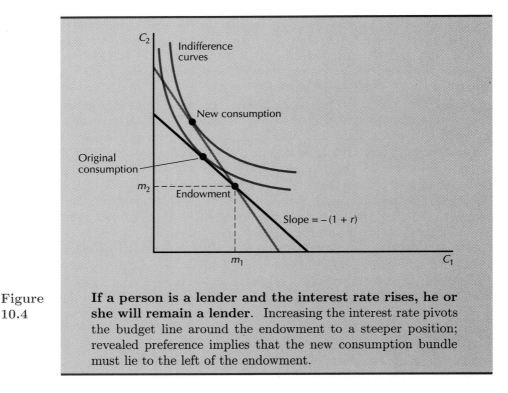

Figure 10.4

If a person is a lender and the interest rate rises, he or she will remain a lender. Increasing the interest rate pivots the budget line around the endowment to a steeper position; revealed preference implies that the new consumption bundle must lie to the left of the endowment.

as in Chapter 9. Suppose that the interest rate rises. What will be the effect on consumption in each period?

This is a case that is easier to analyze by using the future-value budget constraint, rather than the present-value constraint. In terms of the future-value budget constraint, raising the interest rate is just like raising the price of consumption today as compared to consumption tomorrow. Writing out the Slutsky equation we have

$$\frac{\Delta c_1^t}{\Delta p_1} = \frac{\Delta c_1^s}{\Delta p_1} + (m_1 - c_1) \frac{\Delta c_1^m}{\Delta m}.$$
$$(?) \qquad (-) \qquad (?) \qquad (+)$$

The substitution effect, as always, works opposite the direction of price. In this case the price of period-1 consumption goes up, so the substitution effect says the consumer should consume less first period. This is the meaning of the minus sign under the substitution effect. Let's assume that consumption this period is a normal good, so that the very last term—how consumption changes as income changes—will be positive. So we put a plus sign under the last term. Now the sign of the whole expression will depend on the sign of $(m_1 - c_1)$. If the person is a borrower, this term will be negative and the whole expression will therefore unambiguously be

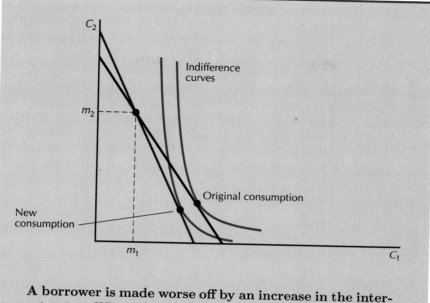

A borrower is made worse off by an increase in the interest rate. When the interest rate facing a borrower increases and the consumer chooses to remain a borrower, he or she is certainly worse off.

Figure
10.5

negative—for a borrower, an increase in the interest rate must lower today's consumption.

Why does this happen? When the interest rate rises, there is always a substitution effect towards consuming less today. For a borrower, an increase in the interest rate means that he will have to pay more interest tomorrow. This effect induces him to borrow less, and thus consume less, in the first period.

For a lender the effect is ambiguous. The total effect is the sum of a negative substitution effect and a positive income effect. From the viewpoint of a lender an increase in the interest rate may give him so much extra income that he will want to consume even more first period.

The effects of changing interest rates are not terribly mysterious. There is an income effect and a substitution effect as in any other price change. But without a tool like the Slutsky equation to separate out the various effects, the changes may be hard to disentangle. With such a tool, the sorting out of the effects is quite straightforward.

10.5 Inflation

The above analysis has all been conducted in terms of a general "consumption" good. Giving up Δc units of consumption today buys you $(1+r)\Delta c$ units of consumption tomorrow. Implicit in this analysis is the assumption that the "price" of consumption doesn't change—there is no inflation or deflation.

However, the analysis is not hard to modify to deal with the case of inflation. Let us suppose that the consumption good now has a different price in each period. It is convenient to choose today's price of consumption as 1 and to let p_2 be the price of consumption tomorrow. It is also convenient to think of the endowment as being measured in units of the consumption goods as well, so that the monetary value of the endowment in period 2 is $p_2 m_2$. Then the amount of money the consumer can spend in the second period is given by

$$p_2 c_2 = p_2 m_2 + (1+r)(m_1 - c_1),$$

and the amount of consumption available second period is

$$c_2 = m_2 + \frac{1+r}{p_2}(m_1 - c_1).$$

Note that this equation is very similar to the equation given earlier—we just use $(1+r)/p_2$ rather than $1+r$.

Let us express this budget constraint in terms of the rate of inflation. The inflation rate, π, is just the rate at which prices grow. Recalling that $p_1 = 1$, we have

$$p_2 = 1 + \pi,$$

which gives us

$$c_2 = m_2 + \frac{1+r}{1+\pi}(m_1 - c_1).$$

Let's create a new variable ρ, the **real interest rate**, and define it by[2]

$$1 + \rho = \frac{1+r}{1+\pi}$$

so that the budget constraint becomes

$$c_2 = m_2 + (1+\rho)(m_1 - c_1).$$

One plus the real interest rate measures how much extra *consumption* you can get in period 2 if you give up some *consumption* in period 1. That is why it is called the *real* rate of interest: it tells you how much extra consumption you can get, not how many extra dollars you can get.

---

[2] The Greek letter ρ, rho, is pronounced "row."

The interest rate on dollars is called the **nominal** rate of interest. As we've seen above, the relationship between the two is given by

$$1 + \rho = \frac{1 + r}{1 + \pi}.$$

In order to get an explicit expression for ρ, we write this equation as

$$\rho = \frac{1 + r}{1 + \pi} - 1 = \frac{1 + r}{1 + \pi} - \frac{1 + \pi}{1 + \pi}$$
$$= \frac{r - \pi}{1 + \pi}.$$

This is an exact expression for the real interest rate, but it is common to use an approximation. If the inflation rate isn't too large, the denominator of the fraction will be only slightly larger than 1. Thus the real rate of interest will be approximately given by

$$\rho \approx r - \pi,$$

which says that the real rate of interest is just the nominal rate minus the rate of inflation. (The symbol $\approx$ means "approximately equal to.") This makes perfectly good sense: if the interest rate is 18 percent, but prices are rising at 10 percent, then the real interest rate—the extra consumption you can buy next period if you give up some consumption now—will be roughly 8 percent.

Of course, we are always looking into the future when making consumption plans. Typically, we know the nominal rate of interest for the next period, but the rate of inflation for next period is unknown. The real interest rate is usually taken to be the current interest rate minus the *expected* rate of inflation. To the extent that people have different estimates about what the next year's rate of inflation will be, they will have different estimates of the real interest rate. If inflation can be reasonably well forecast, these differences may not be too large.

10.6 Present Value: A Closer Look

Let us return now to the two forms of the budget constraint described earlier in section 10.1 in equations (10.2) and (10.3):

$$(1 + r)c_1 + c_2 = (1 + r)m_1 + m_2$$

and

$$c_1 + \frac{c_2}{1 + r} = m_1 + \frac{m_2}{1 + r}.$$

Consider just the right-hand sides of these two equations. We said that the first one expresses the value of the endowment in terms of future value and that the second one expresses it in terms of present value.

Let us examine the concept of future value first. If we can borrow and lend at an interest rate of r, what is the future equivalent of \$1 today? The answer is $(1 + r)$ dollars. That is, \$1 today can be turned into $(1 + r)$ dollars next period simply by lending it to the bank at an interest rate r. In other words, $(1 + r)$ dollars next period is equivalent to \$1 today since that is how much you would have to pay next period to purchase—that is, borrow—\$1 today. The value $(1 + r)$ is just the price of \$1 today, relative to \$1 next period. This can be easily seen from the first budget constraint: it is expressed in terms of future dollars—the second-period dollars have a price of 1, and first-period dollars are measured relative to them.

What about present value? This is just the reverse: everything is measured in terms of today's dollars. How much is a dollar next period worth in terms of a dollar today? The answer is $1/(1 + r)$ dollars. This is because $1/(1 + r)$ dollars can be turned into a dollar next period simply by saving it at the rate of interest r. The *present value* of a dollar to be delivered next period is $1/(1 + r)$.

The concept of present value gives us another way to express the budget for a two-period consumption problem: a consumption plan is affordable if *the present value of consumption equals the present value of income.*

The idea of present value has an important implication that is closely related to a point made in Chapter 9: if the consumer can freely buy and sell goods at constant prices, then the consumer would always prefer a higher-valued endowment to a lower-valued one. In the case of intertemporal decisions, this principle implies that *if a consumer can freely borrow and lend at a constant interest rate, then the consumer would always prefer a pattern of income with a higher present value to a pattern with a lower present value.*

This is true for the same reason that the statement in Chapter 9 was true: an endowment with a higher value gives rise to a budget line that is farther out. The new budget set contains the old budget set, which means that the consumer would have all the consumption opportunities she had with the old budget set plus some more. Economists sometimes say that an endowment with a higher present value **dominates** one with a lower present value in the sense that the consumer can have larger consumption in *every* period by selling the endowment with the higher present value that she could get by selling the endowment with the lower present value.

Of course, if the present value of one endowment is higher than another, then the future value will be higher as well. However, it turns out that the present value is a more convenient way to measure the purchasing power of an endowment of money over time, and it is the measure to which we will devote the most attention.

10.7 Analyzing Present Value for Several Periods

Let us consider a three-period model. We suppose that we can borrow or lend money at an interest rate r each period and that this interest rate will remain constant over the three periods. Thus the price of consumption in period 2 in terms of period-1 consumption will be $1/(1+r)$, just as before.

What will the price of period-3 consumption be? Well, if I invest \$1 today, it will grow into $(1+r)$ dollars next period; and if I leave this money invested, it will grow into $(1+r)^2$ dollars by the third period. Thus if I start with $1/(1+r)^2$ dollars today, I can turn this into \$1 in period 3. The price of period-3 consumption relative to period-1 consumption is therefore $1/(1+r)^2$. Each extra dollar's worth of consumption in period 3 costs me $1/(1+r)^2$ dollars today. This implies that the budget constraint will have the form

$$c_1 + \frac{c_2}{1+r} + \frac{c_3}{(1+r)^2} = m_1 + \frac{m_2}{1+r} + \frac{m_3}{(1+r)^2}.$$

This is just like the budget constraints we've seen before, where the price of period-t consumption in terms of today's consumption is given by

$$p_t = \frac{1}{(1+r)^{t-1}}.$$

As before, moving to an endowment that has a higher present value at these prices will be preferred by any consumer, since such a change will necessarily shift the budget set farther out.

We have derived this budget constraint under the assumption of constant interest rates, but it is easy to generalize to the case of changing interest rates. Suppose, for example, that the interest earned on savings from period 1 to 2 is r_1, while savings from period 2 to 3 earn r_2. Then \$1 in period 1 will grow to $(1+r_1)(1+r_2)$ dollars in period 3. The present value of \$1 in period 3 is therefore $1/(1+r_1)(1+r_2)$. This implies that the correct form of the budget constraint is

$$c_1 + \frac{c_2}{1+r_1} + \frac{c_3}{(1+r_1)(1+r_2)} = m_1 + \frac{m_2}{1+r_1} + \frac{m_3}{(1+r_1)(1+r_2)}.$$

This expression is not so hard to deal with, but we will typically be content to examine the case of constant interest rates.

Table 10.1 contains some examples of the present value of \$1 T years in the future at different interest rates. The notable fact about this table is how quickly the present value goes down for "reasonable" interest rates. For example, at an interest rate of 10 percent, the value of \$1 20 years from now is only 15 cents.

Table
10.1

The present value of \$1 t years in the future.

Rate	1	2	5	10	15	20	25	30
.05	.95	.91	.78	.61	.48	.37	.30	.23
.10	.91	.83	.62	.39	.24	.15	.09	.06
.15	.87	.76	.50	.25	.12	.06	.03	.02
.20	.83	.69	.40	.16	.06	.03	.01	.00

10.8 Use of Present Value

Let us start by stating an important general principle: *present value is the only correct way to convert a stream of payments into today's dollars.* This principle follows directly from the definition of present value: the present value measures the value of a consumer's endowment of money. As long as the consumer can borrow and lend freely at a constant interest rate, an endowment with higher present value can always generate *more* consumption in every period than an endowment with lower present value. Regardless of your own tastes for consumption in different periods, you should always prefer a stream of money that has a higher present value to one with lower present value—since that always gives you more consumption possibilities in every period.

This argument is illustrated in Figure 10.6. In this figure, (m'_1, m'_2) is a worse consumption bundle than the consumer's original endowment, (m_1, m_2), since it lies beneath the indifference curve through her endowment. Nevertheless, the consumer would prefer (m'_1, m'_2) to (m_1, m_2) if she is able to borrow and lend at the interest rate r. This is true because with the endowment (m'_1, m'_2) she can afford to consume a bundle such as (c_1, c_2), which is unambiguously better than her current consumption bundle.

One very useful application of present value is in valuing the income streams offered by different kinds of investments. If you want to compare two different investments that yield different streams of payments to see which is better, you simply compute the two present values and choose the larger one. The investment with the larger present value always gives you more consumption possibilities.

Sometimes it is necessary to purchase an income stream by making a stream of payments over time. For example, one could purchase an apartment building by borrowing money from a bank and making mortgage payments over a number of years. Suppose that the income stream (M_1, M_2) can be purchased by making a stream of payments (P_1, P_2).

In this case we can evaluate the investment by comparing the present

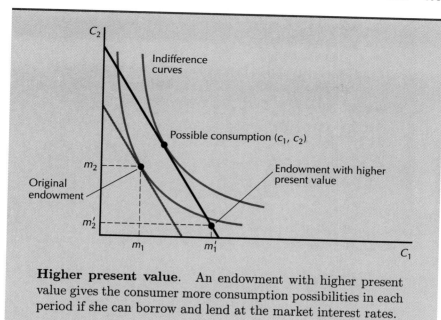

Higher present value. An endowment with higher present value gives the consumer more consumption possibilities in each period if she can borrow and lend at the market interest rates.

Figure
10.6

value of the income stream to the present value of the payment stream. If

$$M_1 + \frac{M_2}{1+r} > P_1 + \frac{P_2}{1+r}, \tag{10.4}$$

the present value of the income stream exceeds the present value of its cost, so this is a good investment—it will increase the present value of our endowment.

An equivalent way to value the investment is to use the idea of **net present value**. In order to calculate this number we calculate at the *net* cash flow in each period and then discount this stream back to the present. In this example, the net cash flow is $(M_1 - P_1, M_2 - P_2)$, and the net present value is

$$NPV = M_1 - P_1 + \frac{M_2 - P_2}{1+r}.$$

Comparing this to equation (10.4) we see that the investment should be purchased if and only if the net present value is positive.

The net present value calculation is very convenient since it allows us to add all of the positive and negative cash flows together in each period and then discount the resulting stream of cash flows.

EXAMPLE: Valuing a Stream of Payments

Suppose that we are considering two investments, A and B. Investment A pays $100 now and will also pay $200 next year. Investment B pays $0 now, and will generate $310 next year. Which is the better investment?

The answer depends on the interest rate. If the interest rate is zero, the answer is clear—just add up the payments. For if the interest rate is zero, then the present-value calculation boils down to summing up the payments.

If the interest rate is zero, the present value of investment A is

$$PV_A = 100 + 200 = 300,$$

and the present value of investment B is

$$PV_B = 0 + 310 = 310,$$

so B is the preferred investment.

But we get the opposite answer if the interest rate is high enough. Suppose, for example, that the interest rate is 20 percent. Then the present-value calculation becomes

$$PV_A = 100 + \frac{200}{1.20} = 266.67$$

$$PV_B = 0 + \frac{310}{1.20} = 258.33.$$

Now A is the better investment. The fact that A pays back more money earlier means that it will have a higher present value when the interest rate is large enough.

EXAMPLE: The True Cost of a Credit Card

Borrowing money on a credit card is expensive: many companies quote yearly interest charges of 15 to 21 percent. However, because of the way these finance charges are computed, the true interest rate on credit card debt are much higher than this.

Suppose that a credit card owner charges a $2000 purchase on the first day of the month and that the finance charge is 1.5 percent a month. If the consumer pays the entire balance by the end of the month, he does not have to pay the finance charge. If the consumer pays none of the $2,000, he has to pay a finance charge of $2000 × .015 = $30 at the beginning of the next month.

What happens if the consumer pays $1,800 towards the $2000 balance on the last day of the month? In this case, the consumer has borrowed only $200, so the finance charge should be $3. However, many credit card companies charge the consumers much more than this. The reason is that many companies base their charges on the "average monthly balance," even if part of that balance is paid by the end of the month. In this example, the average monthly balance would be about $2000 (30 days of the $2000 balance and 1 day of the $200 balance). The finance charge would therefore be slightly less than $30, even though the consumer has only borrowed $200. Based on the actual amount of money borrowed, this is an interest rate of 15 percent a month!

10.9 Bonds

Securities are financial instruments that promise certain patterns of payment schedules. There are many kinds of financial instruments because there are many kinds of payment schedules that people want. Financial markets give people the opportunity to trade different patterns of cash flows over time. These cash flows are typically used to finance consumption at some time or other.

The particular kind of security that we will examine here is a **bond**. Bonds are issued by governments and corporations. They are basically a way to borrow money. The borrower—the agent who issues the bond—promises to pay a fixed number of dollars x (the **coupon**) each period until a certain date T (the **maturity date**), at which point the borrower will pay an amount F (the **face value**) to the holder of the bond.

Thus the payment stream of a bond looks like $(x, x, x, \ldots, F)$. If the interest rate is constant, the present discounted value of such a bond is easy to compute. It is given by

$$PV = \frac{x}{(1+r)} + \frac{x}{(1+r)^2} + \cdots + \frac{F}{(1+r)^T}.$$

Note that the present value of a bond will decline if the interest rate increases. Why is this? When the interest rate goes up the price now for $1 delivered in the future goes down. So the future payments of the bond will be worth less now.

There is a large and developed market for bonds. The market value of outstanding bonds will fluctuate as the interest rate fluctuates since the present value of the stream of payments represented by the bond will change.

An interesting special kind of a bond is a bond that makes payments forever. These are called **consols** or **perpetuities**. Suppose that we consider a consol that promises to pay x dollars a year forever. To compute the value of this consol we have to compute the infinite sum:

$$PV = \frac{x}{1+r} + \frac{x}{(1+r)^2} + \cdots.$$

The trick to computing this is to factor out $1/(1+r)$ to get

$$PV = \frac{1}{1+r} \left[x + \frac{x}{(1+r)} + \frac{x}{(1+r)^2} + \cdots \right].$$

But the term in the brackets is just x plus the present value! Substituting and solving for PV:

$$PV = \frac{1}{(1+r)}[x + PV]$$
$$= \frac{x}{r}.$$

This wasn't hard to do, but there is an easy way to get the answer right off. How much money, V, would you need at an interest rate r to get x dollars forever? Just write down the equation

$$Vr = x,$$

which says that the interest on V must equal x. But then the value of such an investment is given by

$$V = \frac{x}{r}.$$

Thus it must be that the present value of a consol that promises to pay x dollars forever must be given by x/r.

For a consol it is easy to see directly how increasing the interest rate reduces the value of a bond. Suppose, for example, that a consol is issued when the interest rate is 10 percent. Then if it promises to pay $10 a year forever, it will be worth $100 now—since $100 would generate $10 a year in interest income.

Now suppose that the interest rate goes up to 20 percent. The value of the consol must fall to $50, since it only takes $50 to earn $10 a year at a 20 percent interest rate.

The formula for the consol can be used to calculate an approximate value of a long-term bond. If the interest rate is 10 percent, for example, the value of $1 30 years from now is only 6 cents. For the size of interest rates we usually encounter, 30 years might as well be infinity.

EXAMPLE: Installment Loans

Suppose that you borrow $1000 that you promise to pay back in 12 monthly installments of $100 each. What rate of interest are you paying?

At first glance it seems that your interest rate is 20 percent: you have borrowed $1000, and you are paying back $1200. But this analysis is incorrect. For you haven't really borrowed $1000 for an entire year. You have borrowed $1000 for a month, and then you pay back $100. Then you only have borrowed $900, and you owe only a month's interest on the $900. You borrow that for a month and then pay back another $100. And so on.

The stream of payments that we want to value is

$$(1000, -100, -100, \ldots, -100).$$

We can find the interest rate that makes the present value of this stream equal to zero by using a calculator or a computer. The actual interest rate that you are paying on the installment loan is about 35 percent!

10.10 Taxes

In the United States, interest payments are taxed as ordinary income. This means that you pay the same tax on interest income as on labor income. Suppose that your marginal tax bracket is t, so that each *extra* dollar of income, Δm, increases your tax liability by $t\Delta m$. Then if you invest X dollars in an asset, you'll receive an interest payment of rX. But you'll also have to pay taxes of trX on this income, which will leave you with only $(1-t)rX$ dollars of after-tax income. We call the rate $(1-t)r$ the **after-tax interest rate**.

What if you decide to borrow X dollars, rather than lend them? Then you'll have to make an interest payment of rX. In the United States, some interest payments are tax deductible and some are not. For example, the interest payments for a mortgage are tax deductable, but interest payments on ordinary consumer loans are not. On the other hand, businesses can deduct most kinds of the interest payments that they make.

If a particular interest payment is tax deductible, you can subtract your interest payment from your other income and only pay taxes on what's left. Thus the rX dollars you pay in interest will reduce your tax payments by trX. The total cost of the X dollars you borrowed will be $rX - trX = (1-t)rX$.

Thus the after-tax interest rate is the same whether you are borrowing or lending, for people in the same tax bracket. The tax on saving will reduce the amount of money that people want to save, but the subsidy on borrowing will increase the amount of money that people want to borrow.

EXAMPLE: Scholarships and Savings

Many students in the United States receive some form of financial aid to help defray college costs. The amount of financial aid a student receives depends on many factors, but one important factor is the family's ability to pay for college expenses. Most U.S. colleges and universities use a standard measure of ability to pay calculated by the College Entrance Examination Board (CEEB).

If a student wishes to apply for financial aid, his or her family must fill out a questionnaire describing their financial circumstances. The CEEB uses the information on the income and assets of the parents to construct a measure of "adjusted available income." The fraction of their adjusted available income that parents are expected to contribute varies between 22 and 47 percent, depending on income. In 1985, parents with a total before-tax income of around $35,000 dollars were expected to contribute about $7000 toward college expenses.

Each additional dollar of assets that the parents accumulate increases their expected contribution and decreases the amount of financial aid that their child can hope to receive. The formula used by the CEEB effectively imposes a tax on parents who save for their children's college education. Martin Feldstein, President of the National Bureau of Economic Research (NBER) and Professor of Economics at Harvard University, calculated the magnitude of this tax.[3]

Consider the situation of some parents contemplating saving an additional dollar just as their daughter enters college. At a 6 percent rate of interest, the future value of a dollar 4 years from now is $1.26. Since federal and state taxes must be paid on interest income, the dollar yields $1.19 in after-tax income in 4 years. However, since this additional dollar of savings increases the total assets of the parents, the amount of aid received by the daughter goes down during *each* of her four college years. The effect of this "education tax" is to reduce the future value of the dollar to only 87 cents after 4 years. This is equivalent to an income tax of 150 percent!

Feldstein also examined the savings behavior of a sample of middle-class households with pre-college children. He estimates that a household with income of $40,000 a year and two college-age children saves about 50 percent less than they would otherwise due to the combination of federal, state, and "education" taxes that they face.

10.11 Choice of the Interest Rate

In the above discussion, we've talked about "the interest rate." In real life there are many interest rates: there are nominal rates, real rates, before-tax rates, after-tax rates, short-term rates, long-term rates, and so on. Which is the "right" rate to use in doing present-value analysis?

The way to answer this question is to think about the fundamentals. The idea of present discounted value arose because we wanted to be able to convert money at one point in time to an equivalent amount at another point in time. "The interest rate" is the return on an investment that allows us to transfer funds in this way.

If we want to apply this analysis when there are a variety of interest rates available, we need to ask which one has the properties most like the stream of payments we are trying to value. If the stream of payments is not taxed, we should use an after-tax interest rate. If the stream of payments will continue for 30 years, we should use a long-term interest rate. If the stream of payments is risky, we should use the interest rate on an investment with similar risk characteristics. (We'll have more to say later about what this last statement actually means.)

---

[3] Martin Feldstein, "College Scholarship Rules and Private Savings," NBER Working Paper 4032, March 1992.

The interest rate measures the **opportunity cost** of funds—the value of alternative uses of your money. So every stream of payments should be compared to your best alternative that has similar characteristics in terms of tax treatment, risk, and liquidity.

Summary

1. The budget constraint for intertemporal consumption can be expressed in terms of present value or future value.

2. The comparative statics results derived earlier for general choice problems can be applied to intertemporal consumption as well.

3. The real rate of interest measures the extra consumption that you can get in the future by giving up some consumption today.

4. A consumer who can borrow and lend at a constant interest rate should always prefer an endowment with a higher present value to one with a lower present value.

REVIEW QUESTIONS

1. How much is $1 million to be delivered 20 years in the future worth today if the interest rate is 20 percent?

2. As the interest rate rises, does the intertemporal budget constraint become steeper or flatter?

3. Would the assumption that goods are perfect substitutes be valid in a study of intertemporal food purchases?

4. A consumer, who is initially a lender, remains a lender even after a decline in interest rates. Is this consumer better off or worse off after the change in interest rates? If the consumer becomes a borrower after the change is he better off or worse off?

5. What is the present value of $100 one year from now if the interest rate is 10%? What is the present value if the interest rate is 5%?

CHAPTER **11**

ASSET MARKETS

Assets are goods that provide a flow of services over time. Assets can provide a flow of consumption services, like housing services, or can provide a flow of money that can be used to purchase consumption. Assets that provide a monetary flow are called **financial assets**.

The bonds that we discussed in the last chapter are examples of financial assets. The flow of services they provide is the flow of interest payments. Other sorts of financial assets such as corporate stock provide different patterns of cash flows. In this chapter we will examine the functioning of asset markets under conditions of complete certainty about the future flow of services provided by the asset.

11.1 Rates of Return

Under this admittedly extreme hypothesis, we have a simple principle relating asset rates of return: if there is no uncertainty about the cash flow provided by assets, then all assets have to have the same rate of return. The reason is obvious: if one asset had a higher rate of return than another, and both assets were otherwise identical, then no one would want to buy the asset with the lower rate of return. So in equilibrium, all assets that are actually held must pay the same rate of return.

Let us consider the process by which these rates of return adjust. Consider an asset A that has current price p_0 and is expected to have a price of p_1 tomorrow. Everyone is certain about what today's price of the asset is, and everyone is certain about what tomorrow's price will be. We suppose for simplicity that there are no dividends or other cash payments between periods 0 and 1. Suppose furthermore that there is another investment, B, that one can hold between periods 0 and 1 that will pay an interest rate of r. Now consider two possible investment plans: either invest one dollar in asset A and cash it in next period, or invest one dollar in asset B and earn interest of r dollars over the period.

What are the values of these two investment plans at the end of the first period? We first ask how many units of the asset we must purchase to make a one dollar investment in it. Letting x be this amount we have the equation

$$p_0 x = 1$$

or

$$x = \frac{1}{p_0}.$$

It follows that the future value of one dollar's worth of this asset next period will be

$$FV = p_1 x = \frac{p_1}{p_0}.$$

On the other hand, if we invest one dollar in asset B, we will have $1 + r$ dollars next period. If assets A and B are both held in equilibrium, then a dollar invested in either one of them must be worth the same amount second period. Thus we have an equilibrium condition:

$$1 + r = \frac{p_1}{p_0}.$$

What happens if this equality is not satisfied? Then there is a sure way to make money. For example, if

$$1 + r > \frac{p_1}{p_0},$$

people who own asset A can sell one unit for p_0 dollars in the first period and invest the money in asset B. Next period their investment in asset B will be worth $p_0(1 + r)$, which is greater than p_1 by the above equation. This will guarantee that second period they will have enough money to repurchase asset A, and be back where they started from, but now with extra money.

This kind of operation—buying some of one asset and selling some of another to realize a sure return—is known as **riskless arbitrage**, or **arbitrage** for short. As long as there are people around looking for "sure things" we would expect that well-functioning markets should quickly eliminate any opportunities for arbitrage. Therefore, another way to state our equilibrium condition is to say that in equilibrium *there should be no opportunities for arbitrage*. We'll refer to this as the **no arbitrage condition**.

But how does arbitrage actually work to eliminate the inequality? In the example given above, we argued that if $1 + r > p_1/p_0$, then anyone who held asset A would want to sell it first period, since they were guaranteed enough money to repurchase it second period. But who would they sell it to? Who would want to buy it? There would be plenty of people willing to supply asset A at p_0, but there wouldn't be anyone foolish enough to demand it at that price.

This means that supply would exceed demand and therefore the price will fall. How far will it fall? Just enough to satisfy the arbitrage condition: until $1 + r = p_1/p_0$.

11.2 Arbitrage and Present Value

We can rewrite the arbitrage condition in a useful way by cross multiplying to get

$$p_0 = \frac{p_1}{1 + r}.$$

This says that the current price of an asset must be its present value. Essentially we have converted the future-value comparison in the arbitrage condition to a present-value comparison. So if the no arbitrage condition is satisfied, then we are assured that assets must sell for their present values. Any deviation from present-value pricing leaves a sure way to make money.

11.3 Adjustments for Differences among Assets

The no arbitrage rule assumes that the asset services provided by the two assets are identical, except for the purely monetary difference. If the services provided by the assets have different characteristics, then we would want to adjust for those differences before we blandly assert that the two assets must have the same equilibrium rate of return.

For example, one asset might be easier to sell than the other. We sometimes express this by saying that one asset is more **liquid** than another. In this case, we might want to adjust the rate of return to take account of the difficulty involved in finding a buyer for the asset. Thus a house that is worth $100,000 is probably a less liquid asset than $100,000 in Treasury bills.

Similarly, one asset might be riskier than another. The rate of return on one asset may be guaranteed, while the rate of return on another asset may be highly risky. We'll examine ways to adjust for risk differences in Chapter 13.

Here we want to consider two other types of adjustment we might make. One is adjustment for assets that have some return in consumption value, and the other is for assets that have different tax characteristics.

11.4 Assets with Consumption Returns

Many assets pay off only in money. But there are other assets that pay off in terms of consumption as well. The prime example of this is housing. If you own a house that you live in, then you don't have to rent living quarters; thus part of the "return" to owning the house is the fact that you get to live in the house without paying rent. Or, put another way, you get to pay the rent for your house to yourself. This latter way of putting it sounds peculiar, but it contains an important insight.

It is true that you don't make an *explicit* rental payment to yourself for the privilege of living in your house, but it turns out to be fruitful to think of a homeowner as *implicitly* making such a payment. The **implicit rental rate** on your house is the rate at which you could rent a similar house. Or, equivalently, it is the rate at which you could rent your house to someone else on the open market. By choosing to "rent your house to yourself" you are forgoing the opportunity of earning rental payments from someone else, and thus incurring an opportunity cost.

Suppose that the implicit rental payment on your house would work out to T dollars per year. Then part of the return to owning your house is the fact that it generates for you an implicit income of T dollars per year—the money that you would otherwise have to pay to live in the same circumstances as you do now.

But that is not the entire return on your house. As real estate agents never tire of telling us, a house is also an *investment*. When you buy a house you pay a significant amount of money for it, and you might reasonably expect to earn a monetary return on this investment as well, through an increase in the value of your house. This increase in the value of an asset is known as **appreciation**.

Let us use A to represent the expected appreciation in the dollar value of your house over a year. The total return to owning your house is the sum of the rental return, T, and the investment return, A. If your house initially cost P, then the *total* rate of return on your initial investment in housing is

$$h = \frac{T + A}{P}.$$

This total rate of return is composed of the consumption rate of return, T/P, and the investment rate of return, A/P.

Let us use r to represent the rate of return on other financial assets. Then the total rate of return on housing should, in equilibrium, be equal to r:

$$r = \frac{T + A}{P}.$$

Think about it this way. At the beginning of the year, you can invest P in a bank and earn rP dollars, or you can invest P dollars in a house and save T dollars of rent and earn A dollars by the end of the year. The total return from these two investments has to be the same. If $T + A < rP$ you would be better off investing your money in the bank and paying T dollars in rent. You would then have $rP - T > A$ dollars at the end of the year. If $T + A > rP$, then housing would be the better choice. (Of course, this is ignoring the real estate agent's commission and other transactions costs associated with the purchase and sale.)

Since the total return should rise at the rate of interest, the financial rate of return A/P will generally be less than the rate of interest. Thus in general, assets that pay off in consumption will in equilibrium have a lower financial rate of return than purely financial assets. This means that buying consumption goods such as houses, or paintings, or jewelry *solely* as a financial investment is probably not a good idea since the rate of return on these assets will probably be lower than the rate of return on purely financial assets, because part of the price of the asset reflects the consumption return that people receive from owning such assets. On the other hand, if you place a sufficiently high value on the consumption return on such assets, or you can generate rental income from the assets, it may well make sense to buy them. The *total* return on such assets may well make this a sensible choice.

11.5 Taxation of Asset Returns

The Internal Revenue Service distinguishes two kinds of asset returns for purposes of taxation. The first kind is the **dividend** or **interest** return. These are returns that are paid periodically—each year or each month— over the life of the asset. You pay taxes on interest and dividend income at your ordinary tax rate, the same rate that you pay on your labor income.

The second kind of returns are called **capital gains**. Capital gains occur when you sell an asset at a price higher than the price at which you bought it. Capital gains are taxed only when you actually sell the asset. Under the current tax law, capital gains are taxed at the same rate as ordinary income, but there are some proposals to tax them at a more favorable rate.

It is sometimes argued that taxing capital gains at the same rate as ordinary income is a "neutral" policy. However, this claim can be disputed for at least two reasons. The first reason is that the capital gains taxes are only paid when the asset is sold, while taxes on dividends or interest are paid every year. The fact that the capital gains taxes are deferred until time of sale makes the effective tax rate on capital gains *lower* than the tax rate on ordinary income.

A second reason that equal taxation of capital gains and ordinary income is not neutral is that the capital gains tax is based on the increase in the *dollar* value of an asset. If asset values are increasing just because of inflation, then a consumer may owe taxes on an asset whose *real* value hasn't changed. For example, suppose that a person buys an asset for $100 and 10 years later it is worth $200. Suppose that the general price level also doubles in this same ten-year period. Then the person would owe taxes on a $100 capital gain even though the purchasing power of his asset hadn't changed at all. This tends to make the tax on capital gains *higher* than that on ordinary income. Which of the two effects dominates is a controversial question.

In addition to the differential taxation of dividends and capital gains there are many other aspects of the tax law that treat asset returns differently. For example, in the United States, **municipal bonds**, bonds issued by cities or states, are not taxed by the Federal government. As we indicated earlier, the consumption returns from owner-occupied housing is not taxed. Furthermore, in the United States even part of the capital gains from owner-occupied housing is not taxed.

The fact that different assets are taxed differently means that the arbitrage rule must adjust for the tax differences in comparing rates of return. Suppose that one asset pays a before-tax interest rate, r_b, and another asset pays a return that is tax exempt, r_e. Then if both assets are held by individuals who pay taxes on income at rate t, we must have

$$(1 - t)r_b = r_e.$$

That is, the after-tax return on each asset must be the same. Otherwise, individuals would not want to hold both assets—it would always pay them to switch exclusively to holding the asset that gave them the higher after-tax return. Of course, this discussion ignores other differences in the assets such as liquidity, risk, and so on.

11.6 Applications

The fact that all riskless assets must earn the same return is obvious, but very important. It has surprisingly powerful implications for the functioning of asset markets.

Depletable Resources

Let us study the market equilibrium for a depletable resource like oil. Consider a competitive oil market, with many suppliers, and suppose for simplicity that there are zero costs to extract oil from the ground. Then how will the price of oil change over time?

It turns out that the price of oil must rise at the rate of interest. To see this, simply note that oil in the ground is an asset like any other asset. If it is worthwhile for a producer to hold it from one period to the next, it must provide a return to him equivalent to the financial return he could get elsewhere. If we let p_{t+1} and p_t be the prices at times $t+1$ and t, then we have

$$p_{t+1} = (1+r)p_t$$

as our no arbitrage condition in the oil market.

The argument boils down to this simple idea: oil in the ground is like money in the bank. If money in the bank earns a rate of return of r, then oil in the ground must earn the same rate of return. If oil in the ground earned a higher return than money in the bank, then no one would take oil out of the ground, preferring to wait till later to extract it, thus pushing the current price of oil up. If oil in the ground earned a lower return than money in the bank, then the owners of oil wells would try to pump their oil out immediately in order to put the money in the bank, thereby depressing the current price of oil.

This argument tells us how the price of oil changes. But what determines the price level itself? The price level turns out to be determined by the demand for oil. Let us consider a very simple model of the demand side of the market.

Suppose that the demand for oil is constant at D barrels a year and that there is a total world supply of S barrels. Thus we have a total of $T = S/D$ years of oil left. When the oil has been depleted we will have to use an alternative technology, say liquefied coal, which can be produced at a constant cost of C dollars per barrel. We suppose that liquefied coal is a perfect substitute for oil in all applications.

Now, T years from now, when the oil is just being exhausted, how much must it sell for? Clearly it must sell for C dollars a barrel, the price of its perfect substitute, liquefied coal. This means that the price today of a barrel of oil, p_0, must grow at the rate of interest r over the next T years to be equal to C. This gives us the equation

$$p_0(1+r)^T = C$$

or

$$p_0 = \frac{C}{(1+r)^T}.$$

This expression gives us the current price of oil as a function of the other variables in the problem. We can now ask interesting comparative statics questions. For example, what happens if there is an unforeseen new discovery of oil? This means that T, the number of years remaining of oil, will increase, and thus $(1+r)^T$ will increase, thereby decreasing p_0. So an increase in the supply of oil will, not surprisingly, decrease its current price.

What if there is a technological breakthrough that decreases the value of C? Then the above equation shows that p_0 must decrease. The price of oil has to be equal to the price of its perfect substitute, liquefied coal, when liquefied coal is the only alternative.

When to Cut a Forest

Suppose that the size of a forest—measured in terms of the lumber that you can get from it—is some function of time, $F(t)$. Suppose further that the price of lumber is constant and that the rate of growth of the tree starts high and gradually declines. If there is a competitive market for lumber, when should the forest be cut for timber?

Answer: when the rate of growth of the forest equals the interest rate. Before that, the forest is earning a higher rate of return than money in the bank, and after that point it is earning less than money in the bank. The optimal time to cut a forest is when its growth rate just equals the interest rate.

We can express this more formally by looking at the present value of cutting the forest at time T. This will be

$$PV = \frac{F(T)}{(1+r)^T}.$$

We want to find the choice of T that maximizes the present value—that is, that makes the value of the forest as large as possible. If we choose a very small value of T, the rate of growth of the forest will exceed the interest rate, which means that the PV would be increasing so it would pay to wait a little longer. On the other hand, if we consider a very large value of T, the forest would be growing more slowly than the interest rate, so the PV would be decreasing. The choice of T that maximizes present value occurs when the rate of growth of the forest just equals the interest rate.

This argument is illustrated in Figure 11.1. In Figure 11.1A we have plotted the *rate* of growth of the forest and the *rate* of growth of a dollar invested in a bank. If we want to have the largest amount of money at some unspecified point in the future, we should always invest our money in the asset with the highest return available at each point in time. When the forest is young, it is the asset with the highest return. As it matures, its rate of growth declines, and eventually the bank offers a higher return.

The effect on total wealth is illustrated in Figure 11.1B. Before T wealth grows most rapidly when invested in the forest. After T it grows most

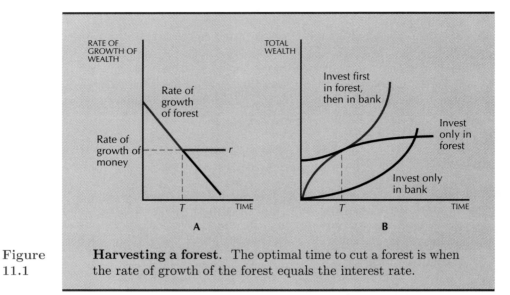

Figure 11.1

Harvesting a forest. The optimal time to cut a forest is when the rate of growth of the forest equals the interest rate.

rapidly when invested in the bank. Therefore, the optimal strategy is to invest in the forest up until time T, then harvest the forest, and invest the proceeds in the bank.

EXAMPLE: Gasoline Prices during the Gulf War

In the Summer of 1990 Iraq invaded Kuwait. As a response to this, the United Nations imposed a blockade on oil imports from Iraq. Immediately after the blockade was announced the price of oil jumped up on world markets. At the same time price of gasoline at U.S. pumps increased significantly. This in turn led to cries of "war profiteering" and several segments about the oil industry on the evening news broadcasts.

Those who felt the price increase was unjustified argued that it would take at least 6 weeks for the new, higher-priced oil to wend its way across to the Atlantic and to be refined into gasoline. The oil companies, they argued, were making "excessive" profits by raising the price of gasoline that had already been produced using cheap oil.

Let's think about this argument as economists. Suppose that you own an asset—say gasoline in a storage tank—that is currently worth $1 a gallon. Six weeks from now, you know that it will be worth $1.50 a gallon. What price will you sell it for now? Certainly you would be foolish to sell it for much less than $1.50 a gallon—at any price much lower than that you would be better off letting the gasoline sit in the storage tank for 6 weeks. The same intertemporal arbitrage reasoning about extracting oil from the ground applies to gasoline in a storage tank. The (appropriate discounted) price of gasoline tomorrow has to equal the price of gasoline today if you want firms to supply gasoline today.

This makes perfect sense from a welfare point of view as well: if gasoline is going to be more expensive in the near future, doesn't it make sense to consume less of it today? The increased price of gasoline encourages immediate conservation measures and reflects the true scarcity price of gasoline.

Ironically, the same phenomenon occured two years later in Russia. During the transition to a market economy, Russian oil sold for about $3 a barrel at a time when the world price was about $19 a barrel. The oil producers anticipated that the price of oil would soon be allowed to rise—so they tried to hold back as much oil as possible from current production. As one Russian producer put it, "Have you seen anyone in New York selling one dollar for 10 cents?" The result was long lines in front of the gasoline pumps for Russian consumers.[1]

11.7 Financial Institutions

Asset markets allow people to change their pattern of consumption over time. Consider, for example, two people A and B who have different endowments of wealth. A might have $100 today and nothing tomorrow, while B might have $100 tomorrow and nothing today. It might well happen that each would rather have $50 today and $50 tomorrow. But they can reach this pattern of consumption simply by trading: A gives B $50 today, and B gives A $50 tomorrow.

In this particular case, the interest rate is zero: A lends B $50 and only gets $50 in return the next day. If people have convex preferences over consumption today and tomorrow, they would like to smooth their consumption over time, rather than consume everything in one period, even if the interest rate were zero.

We can repeat the same kind of story for other patterns of asset endowments. One individual might have an endowment that provides a steady stream of payments and prefer to have a lump sum, while another might have a lump sum and prefer a steady stream. For example, a twenty-year-old individual might want to have a lump sum of money now to buy a house, while a sixty-year-old might want to have a steady stream of money to finance his retirement. It is clear that both of these individuals could gain by trading their endowments with each other.

In a modern economy financial institutions exist to facilitate these trades. In the case described above, the sixty-year-old can put his lump sum of money in the bank, and the bank can then lend it to the twenty-year-old.

---

[1] See Louis Uchitelle, "Russians Line Up for Gas as Refineries Sit on Cheap Oil," *New York Times,* July 12, 1992, page 4.

The twenty-year-old then makes mortgage payments to the bank, which are, in turn, transferred to the sixty-year-old as interest payments. Of course, the bank takes its cut for arranging the trade, but if the banking industry is sufficiently competitive, this cut should end up pretty close to the actual costs of doing business.

Banks aren't the only kind of financial institution that allow one to reallocate consumption over time. Another important example is the stock market. Suppose that an entrepreneur starts a company that becomes successful. In order to start the company, the entrepreneur probably had some financial backers who put up money to help him get started—to pay the bills until the revenues started rolling in. Once the company has been established, the owners of the company have a claim to the profits that the company will generate in the future: they have a claim to a stream of payments.

But it may well be that they prefer a lump-sum reward for their efforts now. In this case, the owners can decide to sell the firm to other people via the stock market. They issue shares in the company that entitle the shareholders to a cut of the future profits of the firm in exchange for a lump-sum payment now. People who want to purchase part of the stream of profits of the firm pay the original owners for these shares. In this way, both sides of the market can reallocate their wealth over time.

There are a variety of other institutions and markets that help facilitate intertemporal trade. But what happens when the buyers and sellers aren't evenly matched? What happens if more people want to sell consumption tomorrow than want to buy it? Just as in any market, if the supply of something exceeds the demand, the price will fall. In this case, the price of consumption tomorrow will fall. We saw earlier that the price of consumption tomorrow was given by

$$p = \frac{1}{1+r},$$

so this means that the interest rate must rise. The increase in the interest rate induces people to save more and to demand less consumption now, and thus tends to equate demand and supply.

Summary

1. In equilibrium, all assets with certain payoffs must earn the same rate of return. Otherwise there would be a riskless arbitrage opportunity.

2. The fact that all assets must earn the same return implies that all assets will sell for their present value.

3. If assets are taxed differently, or have different risk characteristics, then we must compare their after-tax rates of return or their risk-adjusted rates of return.

REVIEW QUESTIONS

1. Suppose asset A can be sold for $11 next period. If assets similar to A are paying a rate of return of 10%, what must be asset A's current price?

2. A house, which you could rent for $10,000 a year and sell for $110,000 a year from now, can be purchased for $100,000. What is the rate of return on this house?

3. The payments of certain types of bonds (e.g., municipal bonds) are not taxable. If similar taxable bonds are paying 10% and everyone faces a marginal tax rate of 40%, what rate of return must the nontaxable bonds pay?

4. Suppose that a scarce resource, facing a constant demand, will be exhausted in 10 years. If an alternative resource will be available at a price of $40 and if the interest rate is 10%, what must the price of the scarce resource be today?

APPENDIX

Suppose that you invest $1 in an asset yielding an interest rate r where the interest is paid once a year. Then after T years you will have $(1 + r)^T$ dollars. Suppose now that the interest is paid monthly. This means that the monthly interest rate will be $r/12$, and there will be $12T$ payments, so that after T years you will have $(1+r/12)^{12T}$ dollars. If the interest rate is paid daily, you will have $(1 + r/365)^{365T}$ and so on.

In general, if the interest is paid n times a year, you will have $(1 + r/n)^{nT}$ dollars after T years. It is natural to ask how much money you will have if the interest is paid *continuously*. That is, we ask what is the limit of this expression as n goes to infinity. It turns out that this is given by the following expression:

$$e^{rT} = \lim_{n \to \infty} (1 + r/n)^{nT},$$

where e is $2.7183\ldots$, the base of natural logarithms.

This expression for continuous compounding is very convenient for calculations. For example, let us verify the claim in the text that the optimal time to harvest the forest is when the rate of growth of the forest equals the interest rate. Since the forest will be worth $F(T)$ at time T, the present value of the forest harvested at time T is

$$V(T) = \frac{F(T)}{e^{rT}} = e^{-rT} F(T).$$

In order to maximize the present value, we differentiate this with respect to T and set the resulting expression equal to zero. This yields

$$V'(T) = e^{-rT} F'(T) - re^{-rT} F(T) = 0$$

or

$$F'(T) - rF(T) = 0.$$

This can be rearranged to establish the result:

$$r = \frac{F'(T)}{F(T)}.$$

This equation says that the optimal value of T satisfies the condition that the rate of interest equals the rate of growth of the value of the forest.

CHAPTER **12**

UNCERTAINTY

Uncertainty is a fact of life. People face risks every time they take a shower, walk across the street, or make an investment. But there are financial institutions such as insurance markets and the stock market that can mitigate at least some of these risks. We will study the functioning of these markets in the next chapter, but first we must study individual behavior with respect to choices involving uncertainty.

12.1 Contingent Consumption

Since we now know all about the standard theory of consumer choice, let's try to use what we know to understand choice under uncertainty. The first question to ask is what is the basic "thing" that is being chosen?

The consumer is presumably concerned with the **probability distribution** of getting different consumption bundles of goods. A probability distribution consists of a list of different outcomes—in this case, consumption bundles—and the probability associated with each outcome. When a consumer decides how much automobile insurance to buy or how much to invest in the stock market, he is in effect deciding on a pattern of probability distribution across different amounts of consumption.

For example, suppose that you have $100 now and that you are contemplating buying lottery ticket number 13. If number 13 is drawn in the lottery, the holder will be paid $200. This ticket costs, say, $5. The two outcomes that are of interest are the event that the ticket is drawn and the event that it isn't.

Your original endowment of wealth—the amount that you would have if you did not purchase the lottery ticket—is $100 if 13 is drawn, and $100 if it isn't drawn. But if you buy the lottery ticket for $5, you will have a wealth distribution consisting of $295 if the ticket is a winner, and $95 if it is not a winner. The original endowment of probabilities of wealth in different circumstances has been changed by the purchase of the lottery ticket. Let us examine this point in more detail.

In this discussion we'll restrict ourselves to examining monetary gambles for convenience of exposition. Of course, it is not money alone that matters; it is the consumption that money can buy that is the ultimate "good" being chosen. The same principles apply to gambles over goods, but restricting ourselves to monetary outcomes makes things simpler. Second, we will restrict ourselves to very simple situations where there are only a few possible outcomes. Again, this is only for reasons of simplicity.

Above we described the case of gambling in a lottery; here we'll consider the case of insurance. Suppose that an individual initially has $35,000 worth of assets, but there is a possibility that he may lose $10,000. For example, his car may be stolen, or a storm may damage his house. Suppose that the probability of this event happening is $p = .01$. Then the probability distribution the person is facing is a 1 percent probability of having $25,000 of assets, and a 99 percent probability of having $35,000.

Insurance offers a way to change this probability distribution. Suppose that there is an insurance contract that will pay the person $100 if the loss occurs in exchange for a $1 premium. Of course the premium must be paid whether or not the loss occurs. If the person decides to purchase $10,000 dollars of insurance, it will cost him $100. In this case he will have a 1 percent chance of having $34,900 ($35,000 of other assets − $10,000 loss + $10,000 payment from the insurance payment − $100 insurance premium) and a 99 percent chance of having $34,900 ($35,000 of assets − $100 insurance premium). Thus the consumer ends up with the same wealth no matter what happens. He is now fully insured against loss.

In general, if this person purchases K dollars of insurance and has to pay a premium γK, then he will face the gamble:[1]

probability .01 of getting $\$25,000 + K - \gamma K$

---

[1] The Greek letter γ, gamma, is pronounced "gam-ma."

and

probability .99 of getting $\$35,000 - \gamma K$.

What kind of insurance will this person choose? Well, that depends on his preferences. He might be very conservative and choose to purchase a lot of insurance, or he might like to take risks and not purchase any insurance at all. People have different preferences over probability distributions in the same way that they have different preferences over the consumption of ordinary goods.

In fact, one very fruitful way to look at decision making under uncertainty is just to think of the money available under different circumstances as different goods. A thousand dollars after a large loss has occurred may mean a very different thing from a thousand dollars when it hasn't. Of course, we don't have to apply this idea just to money: an ice cream cone if it happens to be hot and sunny tomorrow is a very different good from an ice cream cone if it is rainy and cold. In general, consumption goods will be of different value to a person depending upon the circumstances under which they become available.

Let us think of the different outcomes of some random event as being different **states of nature**. In the insurance example given above there were two states of nature: the loss occurs or it doesn't. But in general there could be many different states of nature. We can then think of a **contingent consumption plan** as being a specification of what will be consumed in each different state of nature—each different outcome of the random process. *Contingent* means depending on something not yet certain, so a contingent consumption plan means a plan that depends on the outcome of some event. In the case of insurance purchases, the contingent consumption was described by the terms of the insurance contract: how much money you would have if a loss occurred and how much you would have if it didn't. In the case of the rainy and sunny days, the contingent consumption would just be the *plan* of what would be consumed given the various outcomes of the weather.

People have preferences over different plans of consumption, just like they have preferences over actual consumption. It certainly might make you feel better now to know that you are fully insured. People make choices that reflect their preferences over consumption in different circumstances, and we can use the theory of choice that we have developed to analyze those choices.

If we think about a contingent consumption plan as being just an ordinary consumption bundle, we are right back in the framework described in the previous chapters. We can think of preferences as being defined over different consumption plans, with the "terms of trade" being given by the budget constraint. We can then model the consumer as choosing the best consumption plan he or she can afford, just as we have done all along.

Let's describe the insurance purchase in terms of the indifference-curve analysis we've been using. The two states of nature are the event that the loss occurs and the event that it doesn't. The contingent consumptions are the values of how much money you would have in each circumstance. We can plot this on a graph as in Figure 12.1.

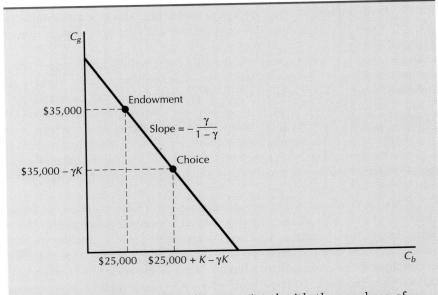

Figure 12.1

Insurance. The budget line associated with the purchase of insurance. The insurance premium γ allows us to give up some consumption in the good outcome (C_g) in order to have more consumption in the bad outcome (C_b).

Your endowment of contingent consumption is \$25,000 in the "bad" state—if the loss occurs—and \$35,000 in the "good" state—if it doesn't occur. Insurance offers you a way to move away from this endowment point. If you purchase K dollars' worth of insurance, you give up γK dollars of consumption possibilities in the good state in exchange for $K - \gamma K$ dollars of consumption possibilities in the bad state. Thus the consumption you lose in the good state, divided by the extra consumption you gain in the bad state, is

$$\frac{\Delta C_g}{\Delta C_b} = -\frac{\gamma K}{K - \gamma K} = -\frac{\gamma}{1 - \gamma}.$$

This is the slope of the budget line through your endowment. It is just as if the price of consumption in the good state is $1 - \gamma$ and the price in the bad state is γ.

We can draw in the indifference curves that a person might have for contingent consumption. Here again it is very natural for indifference curves to have a convex shape: this means that the person would rather have a constant amount of consumption in each state than a large amount in one state and a low amount in the other.

Given the indifference curves for consumption in each state of nature, we can look at the choice of how much insurance to purchase. As usual, this will be characterized by a tangency condition: the marginal rate of substitution between consumption in each state of nature should be equal to the price at which you can trade off consumption in those states.

Of course, once we have a model of optimal choice, we can apply all of the machinery developed in early chapters to its analysis. We can examine how the demand for insurance changes as the price of insurance changes, as the wealth of the consumer changes, and so on. The theory of consumer behavior is perfectly adequate to model behavior under uncertainty as well as certainty.

12.2 Utility Functions and Probabilities

If the consumer has reasonable preferences about consumption in different circumstances, then we will be able to use a utility function to describe these preferences, just as we have done in other contexts. However, the fact that we are considering choice under uncertainty does add a special structure to the choice problem. In general, how a person values consumption in one state as compared to another will depend on the *probability* that the state in question will actually occur. In other words, the rate at which I am willing to substitute consumption if it rains for consumption if it doesn't should have something to do with how likely I think it is to rain. The preferences for consumption in different states of nature will depend on the beliefs of the individual about how likely those states are.

For this reason, we will write the utility function as depending on the probabilities as well as on the consumption levels. Suppose that we are considering two mutually exclusive states such as rain and shine, loss or no loss, or whatever. Let c_1 and c_2 represent consumption in states 1 and 2, and let π_1 and π_2 be the probabilities that state 1 or state 2 actually occurs.

If the two states are mutually exclusive, so that only one of them can happen, then $\pi_2 = 1 - \pi_1$. But we'll generally write out both probabilities just to keep things looking symmetric.

Given this notation, we can write the utility function for consumption in states 1 and 2 as $u(c_1, c_2, \pi_1, \pi_2)$. This is the function that represents the individual's preference over consumption in each state.

EXAMPLE: Some Examples of Utility Functions

We can use nearly any of the examples of utility functions that we've seen up until now in the context of choice under uncertainty. One nice example is the case of perfect substitutes. Here it is natural to weight each consumption by the probability that it will occur. This gives us a utility function of the form

$$u(c_1, c_2, \pi_1, \pi_2) = \pi_1 c_1 + \pi_2 c_2.$$

In the context of uncertainty, this kind of expression is known as the **expected value**. It is just the average level of consumption that you would get.

Another example of a utility function that might be used to examine choice under uncertainty is the Cobb–Douglas utility function:

$$u(c_1, c_2, \pi, 1 - \pi) = c_1^\pi c_2^{1-\pi}.$$

Here the utility attached to any combination of consumption bundles depends on the pattern of consumption in a nonlinear way.

As usual, we can take a monotonic transformation of utility and still represent the same preferences. It turns out that the logarithm of the Cobb-Douglas utility will be very convenient in what follows. This will give us a utility function of the form

$$\ln u(c_1, c_2, \pi_1, \pi_2) = \pi_1 \ln c_1 + \pi_2 \ln c_2.$$

12.3 Expected Utility

One particularly convenient form that the utility function might take is the following:

$$u(c_1, c_2, \pi_1, \pi_2) = \pi_1 v(c_1) + \pi_2 v(c_2).$$

This says that utility can be written as a weighted sum of some function of consumption in each state, $v(c_1)$ and $v(c_2)$, where the weights are given by the probabilities π_1 and π_2.

Two examples of this were given above. The perfect substitutes, or expected value utility function, had this form where $v(c) = c$. The Cobb-Douglas didn't have this form originally, but when we expressed it in terms of logs, it had the linear form with $v(c) = \ln c$.

If one of the states is certain, so that $\pi_1 = 1$, say, then $v(c_1)$ is the utility of certain consumption in state 1. Similarly, if $\pi_2 = 1$, $v(c_2)$ is the utility of consumption in state 2. Thus the expression

$$\pi_1 v(c_1) + \pi_2 v(c_2)$$

represents the average utility, or the expected utility, of the pattern of consumption (c_1, c_2).

For this reason, we refer to a utility function with the particular form described here as an **expected utility function**, or, sometimes, a **von Neumann-Morgenstern utility function**.[2]

When we say that a consumer's preferences can be represented by an expected utility function, or that the consumer's preferences have the expected utility property, we mean that we can choose a utility function that has the additive form described above. Of course we could also choose a different form; any monotonic transformation of an expected utility function is a utility function that describes the same preferences. But the additive form representation turns out to be especially convenient. If the consumer's preferences are described by $\pi_1 \ln c_1 + \pi_2 \ln c_2$ they will also be described by $c_1^{\pi_1} c_2^{\pi_2}$. But the latter representation does not have the expected utility property, while the former does.

On the other hand, the expected utility function can be subjected to some kinds of monotonic transformation and still have the expected utility property. We say that a function $v(u)$ is a **positive affine transformation** if it can be written in the form: $v(u) = au + b$ where $a > 0$. A positive affine transformation simply means multiplying by a positive number and adding a constant. It turns out that if you subject an expected utility function to a positive affine transformation, it not only represents the same preferences (this is obvious since an affine transformation is just a special kind of monotonic transformation) but it also still has the expected utility property.

Economists say that an expected utility function is "unique up to an affine transformation." This just means that you can apply an affine transformation to it and get another expected utility function that represents the same preferences. But any other kind of transformation will destroy the expected utility property.

12.4 Why Expected Utility Is Reasonable

The expected utility representation is a convenient one, but is it a reasonable one? Why would we think that preferences over uncertain choices would have the particular structure implied by the expected utility function? As it turns out there are compelling reasons why expected utility is a reasonable objective for choice problems in the face of uncertainty.

The fact that outcomes of the random choice are consumption goods that will be consumed in different circumstances means that ultimately

[2] John von Neumann was one of the major figures in mathematics in the twentieth century. He also contributed several important insights to physics, computer science, and economic theory. Oscar Morgenstern was an economist at Princeton who, along with von Neumann, helped to develop mathematical game theory.

only one of those outcomes is actually going to occur. Either your house will burn down or it won't; either it will be a rainy day or a sunny day. The way we have set up the choice problem means that only one of the many possible outcomes is going to occur, and hence only one of the contingent consumption plans will actually be realized.

This turns out to have a very interesting implication. Suppose you are considering purchasing fire insurance on your house for the coming year. In making this choice you will be concerned about wealth in three situations: your wealth now (c_0), your wealth if your house burns down (c_1), and your wealth if it doesn't (c_2). (Of course, what you really care about are your consumption possibilities in each outcome, but we are simply using wealth as a proxy for consumption here.) If π_1 is the probability that your house burns down and π_2 is the probability that it doesn't, then your preferences over these three different consumptions can generally be represented by a utility function $u(\pi_1, \pi_2, c_0, c_1, c_2)$.

Suppose that we are considering the tradeoff between wealth now and one of the possible outcomes—say, how much money we would be willing to sacrifice now to get a little more money if the house burns down. *Then this decision should be independent of how much consumption you will have in the other state of nature—how much wealth you will have if the house is not destroyed.* For the house will either burn down or it won't. If it happens to burn down, then the value of extra wealth shouldn't depend on how much wealth you would have if it *didn't* burn down. Bygones are bygones—so what *doesn't* happen shouldn't affect the value of consumption in the outcome that *does* happen.

Note that this is an *assumption* about an individual's preferences. It may be violated. When people are considering a choice between two things, the amount of a third thing they have typically matters. The choice between coffee and tea may well depend on how much cream you have. But this is because you consume coffee together with cream. If you considered a choice where you rolled a die and got either coffee, *or* tea, *or* cream, then the amount of cream that you might get shouldn't affect your preferences between coffee and tea. Why? Because you are either getting one thing or the other: if you end up with cream, the fact that you might have gotten either coffee or tea is irrelevant.

Thus in choice under uncertainty there is a natural kind of "independence" between the different outcomes because they must be consumed separately—in different states of nature. The choices that people plan to make in one state of nature should be independent from the choices that they plan to make in other states of nature. This assumption is known as the **independence assumption**. It turns out that this implies that the utility function for contingent consumption will take a very special structure: it has to be additive across the different contingent consumption bundles.

That is, if c_1, c_2, and c_3 are the consumptions in different states of nature, and π_1, π_2, and π_3 are the probabilities that these three different states of nature materialize, then if the independence assumption alluded to above is satisfied, the utility function must take the form

$$U(c_1, c_2, c_3) = \pi_1 u(c_1) + \pi_2 u(c_2) + \pi_3 u(c_3).$$

This is what we have called an expected utility function. Note that the expected utility function does indeed satisfy the property that the marginal rate of substitution between two goods is independent of how much there is of the third good. The marginal rate of substitution between goods 1 and 2, say, takes the form

$$\begin{aligned}
\text{MRS}_{12} &= \frac{\Delta U(c_1, c_2, c_3)/\Delta c_1}{\Delta U(c_1, c_2, c_3)/\Delta c_2} \\
&= \frac{\pi_1 \Delta u(c_1)/\Delta c_1}{\pi_2 \Delta u(c_2)/\Delta c_2}.
\end{aligned}$$

This MRS depends only on how much you have of goods 1 and 2, not how much you have of good 3.

12.5 Risk Aversion

We claimed above that the expected utility function had some very convenient properties for analyzing choice under uncertainty. In this section we'll give an example of this.

Let's apply the expected utility framework to a simple choice problem. Suppose that a consumer currently has $10 of wealth and is contemplating a gamble that gives him a 50 percent probability of winning $5 and a 50 percent probability of losing $5. His wealth will therefore be random: he has a 50 percent probability of ending up with $5 and a 50 percent probability of ending up with $15. The *expected value* of his wealth is $10, and the expected utility is

$$\frac{1}{2}u(\$15) + \frac{1}{2}u(\$5).$$

This is depicted in Figure 12.2. The expected utility of wealth is the average of the two numbers $u(\$15)$ and $u(\$5)$, labeled $.5u(5) + .5u(15)$ in the graph. We have also depicted the utility of the expected value of wealth, which is labeled $u(\$10)$. Note that in this diagram the expected utility of wealth is less than the utility of the expected wealth. That is,

$$u\left(\frac{1}{2}15 + \frac{1}{2}5\right) = u(10) > \frac{1}{2}u(15) + \frac{1}{2}u(5).$$

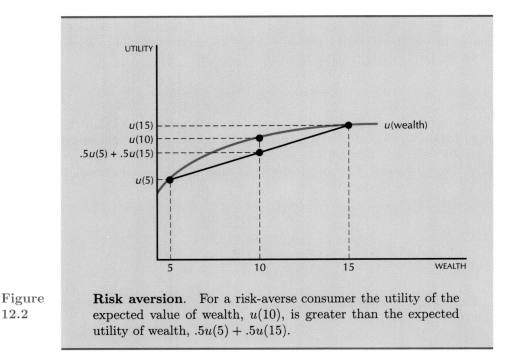

Figure
12.2
Risk aversion. For a risk-averse consumer the utility of the expected value of wealth, $u(10)$, is greater than the expected utility of wealth, $.5u(5) + .5u(15)$.

In this case we say that the consumer is **risk averse** since he prefers to have the expected value of his wealth rather than face the gamble. Of course, it could happen that the preferences of the consumer were such that he prefers a a random distribution of wealth to its expected value, in which case we say that the consumer is a **risk lover**. An example is given in Figure 12.3.

Note the difference between Figures 12.2 and 12.3. The risk-averse consumer has a *concave* utility function—its slope gets flatter as wealth is increased. The risk-loving consumer has a *convex* utility function—its slope gets steeper as wealth increases. Thus the curvature of the utility function measures the consumer's attitude toward risk. In general, the more concave the utility function, the more risk averse the consumer will be, and the more convex the utility function, the more risk loving the consumer will be.

The intermediate case is that of a linear utility function. Here the consumer is **risk neutral**: the expected utility of wealth is the utility of its expected value. In this case the consumer doesn't care about the riskiness of his wealth at all—only about its expected value.

EXAMPLE: The Demand for Insurance

Let's apply the expected utility structure to the demand for insurance that we considered earlier. Recall that in that example the person had a wealth

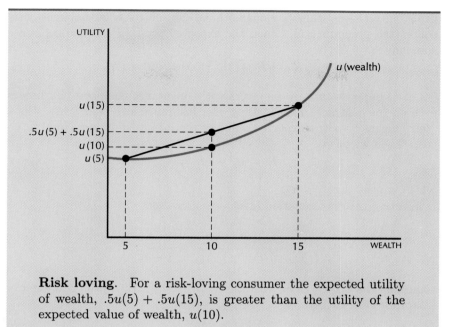

Risk loving. For a risk-loving consumer the expected utility of wealth, $.5u(5) + .5u(15)$, is greater than the utility of the expected value of wealth, $u(10)$.

Figure
12.3

of $35,000 and that he might incur a loss of $10,000. The probability of the loss was 1 percent, and it cost him γK to purchase K dollars of insurance. By examining this choice problem using indifference curves we saw that the optimal choice of insurance was determined by the condition that the MRS between consumption in the two outcomes—loss or no loss—must be equal to $-\gamma/(1 - \gamma)$. Let π be the probability that the loss will occur, and $1 - \pi$ be the probability that it won't occur.

Let state 1 be the situation involving no loss, so that the person's wealth in that state is

$$c_1 = \$35,000 - \gamma K,$$

and let state 2 be the loss situation with wealth

$$c_2 = \$35,000 - \$10,000 + K - \gamma K.$$

Then the consumer's optimal choice of insurance is determined by the condition that his MRS between consumption in the two outcomes be equal to the price ratio:

$$\text{MRS} = -\frac{\pi \Delta u(c_2)/\Delta c_2}{(1 - \pi)\Delta u(c_1)/\Delta c_1} = -\frac{\gamma}{1 - \gamma}. \tag{12.1}$$

Now let us look at the insurance contract from the viewpoint of the insurance company. With probability π they must pay out K, and with probability $(1 - \pi)$ they pay out nothing. No matter what happens, they collect the premium γK. Then the expected profit, P, of the insurance company is

$$P = \gamma K - \pi K - (1 - \pi) \cdot 0 = \gamma K - \pi K.$$

Let us suppose that on the average the insurance company just breaks even on the contract. That is, they offer insurance at a "fair" rate, where "fair" means that the expected value of the insurance is just equal to its cost. Then we have

$$P = \gamma K - \pi K = 0,$$

which implies that $\gamma = \pi$.

Inserting this into equation (12.1) we have

$$\frac{\pi \Delta u(c_2)/\Delta c_2}{(1 - \pi)\Delta u(c_1)/\Delta c_1} = \frac{\pi}{1 - \pi}.$$

Canceling the π's leaves us with the condition that the optimal amount of insurance must satisfy

$$\frac{\Delta u(c_1)}{\Delta c_1} = \frac{\Delta u(c_2)}{\Delta c_2}. \tag{12.2}$$

This equation says that the *marginal utility of an extra dollar of income if the loss occurs should be equal to the marginal utility of an extra dollar of income if the loss doesn't occur.*

Let us suppose that the consumer is risk averse, so that his marginal utility of money is declining as the amount of money he has increases. Then if $c_1 > c_2$, the marginal utility at c_1 would be less than the marginal utility at c_2, and vice versa. Furthermore, if the marginal utilities of income are equal at c_1 and c_2, as they are in equation (12.2), then we must have $c_1 = c_2$. Applying the formulas for c_1 and c_2, we find

$$35,000 - \gamma K = 25,000 + K - \gamma K,$$

which implies that $K = \$10,000$. This means that when given a chance to buy insurance at a "fair" premium, a risk-averse consumer will always choose to fully insure.

This happens because the utility of wealth in each state depends only on the total amount of wealth the consumer has in that state—and not what he *might* have in some other state—so that if the total amounts of wealth the consumer has in each state are equal, the marginal utilities of wealth must be equal as well.

To sum up: if the consumer is a risk-averse, expected utility maximizer and if he is offered fair insurance against a loss, then he will optimally choose to fully insure.

12.6 Diversification

Let us turn now to a different topic involving uncertainty—the benefits of diversification. Suppose that you are considering investing $100 in two different companies, one that makes sunglasses and one that makes raincoats. The long-range weather forecasters have told you that next summer is equally likely to be rainy or sunny. How should you invest your money?

Wouldn't it make sense to hedge your bets and put some money in each? By diversifying your holdings of the two investments, you can get a return on your investment that is more certain, and therefore more desirable if you are a risk-averse person.

Suppose, for example, that shares of the raincoat company and the sunglasses company currently sell for $10 apiece. If it is a rainy summer, the raincoat company will be worth $20 and the sunglasses company will be worth $5. If it is a sunny summer, the payoffs are reversed: the sunglasses company will be worth $20 and the raincoat company will be worth $5. If you invest your entire $100 in the sunglasses company, you are taking a gamble that has a 50 percent chance of giving you $200 and a 50 percent chance of giving you $50. The same magnitude of payoffs results if you invest all your money in the sunglasses company: in either case you have an expected payoff of $125.

But look what happens if you put half of your money in each. Then, if it is sunny you get $100 from the sunglasses investment and $25 from the raincoat investment. But if it is rainy, you get $100 from the raincoat investment and $25 from the sunglasses investment. Either way, you end up with $125 for sure. By diversifying your investment in the two companies, you have managed to reduce the overall risk of your investment, while keeping the expected payoff the same.

Diversification was quite easy in this example: the two assets were perfectly negatively correlated—when one went up, the other went down. Pairs of assets like this can be extremely valuable because they can reduce risk so dramatically. But, alas, they are also very hard to find. Most asset values move together: when GM stock is high, so is Ford stock, and so is Goodrich stock. But as long as asset price movements are not *perfectly* positively correlated, there will be some gains from diversification.

12.7 Risk Spreading

Let us return now to the example of insurance. There we considered the situation of an individual who had $35,000 and faced a .01 probability of a $10,000 loss. Suppose that there were 1000 such individuals. Then, on average, there would be 10 losses incurred, and thus $100,000 lost each year. Each of the 1000 people would face an *expected loss* of .01 times $10,000, or

$100 a year. Let us suppose that the probability that any person incurs a loss doesn't affect the probability that any of the others incur losses. That is, let us suppose that the risks are *independent.*

Then each individual will have an expected wealth of $.99 \times \$35,000 + .01 \times \$25,000 = \$34,900$. But each individual also bears a large amount of risk: each person has a 1 percent probability of losing $10,000.

Suppose that each consumer decides to *diversify* the risk that he or she faces. How can they do this? Answer: by selling some of their risk to other individuals. Suppose that the 1000 consumers decide to insure one another. If anybody incurs the $10,000 loss, each of the 1000 consumers will contribute $10 to that person. This way, the poor person whose house burns down is compensated for his loss, and the other consumers have the peace of mind that they will be compensated if that poor soul happens to be themselves! This is an example of **risk spreading**: each consumer spreads his risk over all of the other consumers and thereby reduces the amount of risk he bears.

Now on the average, 10 houses will burn down a year, so on the average, each of the 1000 individuals will be paying out $100 a year. But this is just on the average. Some years there might be 12 losses, and other years there might be 8 losses. The probability is very small that an individual would actually have to pay out more than $200, say, in any one year, but even so, the risk is there.

But there is even a way to diversify this risk. Suppose that the homeowners agree to pay $100 a year for certain, whether or not there are any losses. Then they can build up a cash reserve fund that can be used in those years when there are multiple fires. They are paying $100 a year for certain, and on average that money will be sufficient to compensate homeowners for fires.

As you can see, we now have something very much like a cooperative insurance company. We could add a few more features: the insurance company gets to invest its cash reserve fund and earn interest on its assets, and so on, but the essence of the insurance company is clearly present.

12.8 Role of the Stock Market

The stock market plays a role similar to that of the insurance market in that it allows for risk spreading. Recall from Chapter 11 that we argued that the stock market allowed the original owners of firms to convert their stream of returns over time to a lump sum. Well, the stock market also allows them to convert their risky position of having all their wealth tied up in one enterprise to a situation where they have a lump sum that they can invest in a variety of assets. The original owners of the firm have an incentive to issue shares in their company so that they can spread the risk of that single company over a large number of shareholders.

Similarly, the later shareholders of a company can use the stock market to reallocate their risks. If a company you hold shares in is adopting a policy that is too risky for your taste—or too conservative—you can sell those shares and purchase others.

In the case of insurance, an individual was able to reduce his risk to zero by purchasing insurance. For a flat fee of $100, the individual could purchase full insurance against the $10,000 loss. This was true because there was basically no risk in the aggregate: if the probability of the loss occurring was 1 percent, then on average 10 of the 1000 people would face a loss—we just didn't know which ones.

In the case of the stock market, there is risk in the aggregate. One year the stock market as a whole might do well, and another year it might do poorly. Somebody has to bear that kind of risk. The stock market offers a way to transfer risky investments from people who don't want to bear risk to people who are willing to bear risk.

Of course, few people outside of Las Vegas *like* to bear risk: most people are risk averse. Thus the stock market allows people to transfer risk from people who don't want to bear it to people who are willing to bear it if they are sufficiently compensated for it. We'll explore this idea further in the next chapter.

Summary

1. Consumption in different states of nature can be viewed as consumption goods, and all the analysis of previous chapters can be applied to choice under uncertainty.

2. However, the utility function that summarizes choice behavior under uncertainty may have a special structure. In particular, if the utility function is linear in the probabilities, then the utility assigned to a gamble will just be the expected utility of the various outcomes.

3. The curvature of the expected utility function describes the consumer's attitudes toward risk. If it is concave, the consumer is a risk averter; and if it is convex, the consumer is a risk lover.

4. Financial institutions such as insurance markets and the stock market provide ways for consumers to diversify and spread risks.

REVIEW QUESTIONS

1. How can one reach the consumption points to the left of the endowment in Figure 12.1?

2. Which of the following utility functions have the expected utility property? (a) $u(c_1, c_2, \pi_1, \pi_2) = a(\pi_1 c_1 + \pi_2 c_2)$, (b) $u(c_1, c_2, \pi_1, \pi_2) = \pi_1 c_1 + \pi_2 c_2^2$, (c) $u(c_1, c_2, \pi_1, \pi_2) = \pi_1 \ln c_1 + \pi_2 \ln c_2 + 17$.

3. A risk-averse individual is offered a choice between a gamble that pays $1000 with a probability of 25% and $100 with a probability of 75%, or a payment of $325. Which would he choose?

4. What if the payment was $320?

5. Draw a utility function that exhibits risk-loving behavior for small gambles and risk-averse behavior for larger gambles.

6. Why might a neighborhood group have a harder time self insuring for flood damage versus fire damage?

APPENDIX

Let us examine a simple problem to demonstrate the principles of expected utility maximization. Suppose that the consumer has some wealth w and is considering investing some amount x in a risky asset. This asset could earn a return of r_g in the "good" outcome, or it could earn a return of r_b in the "bad" outcome. You should think of r_g as being a positive return—the asset increases in value, and r_b being a negative return—a decrease in asset value.

Thus the consumer's wealth in the good and bad outcomes will be

$$W_g = (w - x) + x(1 + r_g) = w + xr_g$$
$$W_b = (w - x) + x(1 + r_b) = w + xr_b.$$

Suppose that the good outcome occurs with probability π and the bad outcome with probability $(1 - \pi)$. Then the expected utility if the consumer decides to invest x dollars is

$$EU(x) = \pi u(w + xr_g) + (1 - \pi)u(w + xr_b).$$

The consumer wants to choose x so as to maximize this expression.

Differentiating with respect to x, we find the way in which utility changes as x changes:

$$EU'(x) = \pi u'(w + xr_g)r_g + (1 - \pi)u'(w + xr_b)r_b. \tag{12.3}$$

The second derivative of utility with respect to x is

$$EU''(x) = \pi u''(w + xr_g)r_g^2 + (1 - \pi)u''(w + xr_b)r_b^2. \tag{12.4}$$

If the consumer is risk averse his utility function will be concave, which implies that $u''(w) < 0$ for every level of wealth. Thus the second derivative of expected utility is unambiguously negative. Expected utility will be a concave function of x.

Consider the change in expected utility for the first dollar invested in the risky asset. This is just equation (12.3) with the derivative evaluated at $x = 0$:

$$EU'(0) = \pi u'(w)r_g + (1 - \pi)u'(w)r_b$$
$$= u'(w)[\pi r_g + (1 - \pi)r_b].$$

The expression inside the brackets is the **expected return** on the asset. If the expected return on the asset is negative, then expected utility must decrease when the first dollar is invested in the asset. But since the second derivative of expected utility is negative due to concavity, then utility must continue to decrease as additional dollars are invested.

Hence we have found that if the *expected value* of a gamble is negative, a risk averter will have the highest *expected utility* at $x^* = 0$: he will want no part of a losing proposition.

On the other hand, if the expected return on the asset is positive, then increasing x from zero will increase expected utility. Thus he will always want to invest a little bit in the risky asset, no matter how risk averse he is.

Expected utility as a function of x is illustrated in Figure 12.4. In Figure 12.4A the expected return is negative, and the optimal choice is $x^* = 0$. In Figure 12.4B the expected return is positive over some range, so the consumer wants to invest some positive amount x^* in the risky asset.

How much to invest in the risky asset. In panel A, the optimal investment is zero, but in panel B the consumer wants to invest a positive amount.

Figure 12.4

The optimal amount for the consumer to invest will be determined by the condition that the derivative of expected utility with respect to x be equal to zero. Since the second derivative of utility is automatically negative due to concavity, this will be a global maximum.

Setting (12.3) equal to zero we have

$$EU'(x) = \pi u'(w + xr_g)r_g + (1 - \pi)u'(w + xr_b)r_b = 0. \qquad (12.5)$$

This equation determines the optimal choice of x for the consumer in question.

EXAMPLE: The Effect of Taxation on Investment in Risky Assets

How does the level of investment in a risky asset behave when you tax its return? If the individual pays taxes at rate t, then the after-tax returns will be $(1 - t)r_g$ and $(1 - t)r_b$. Thus the first-order condition determining his optimal investment, x, will be

$$EU'(x) = \pi u'(w + x(1 - t)r_g)(1 - t)r_g + (1 - \pi)u'(w + x(1 - t)r_b)(1 - t)r_b = 0.$$

Canceling the $(1 - t)$ terms, we have

$$EU'(x) = \pi u'(w + x(1 - t)r_g)r_g + (1 - \pi)u'(w + x(1 - t)r_b)r_b = 0. \quad (12.6)$$

Let us denote the solution to the maximization problem without taxes—when $t = 0$—by x^* and denote the solution to the maximization problem with taxes by $\hat{x}$. What is the relationship between x^* and $\hat{x}$?

Your first impulse is probably to think that $x^* > \hat{x}$—that taxation of a risky asset will tend to discourage investment in it. But that turns out to be exactly wrong! Taxing a risky asset in the way we described will actually *encourage* investment in it!

In fact, there is an exact relation between x^* and $\hat{x}$. It must be the case that

$$\hat{x} = \frac{x^*}{1 - t}.$$

The proof is simply to note that this value of $\hat{x}$ satisfies the first-order condition for the optimal choice in the presence of the tax. Substituting this choice into equation (12.6) we have

$$EU'(\hat{x}) = \pi u'(w + \frac{x^*}{1 - t}(1 - t)r_g)r_g$$
$$+ (1 - \pi)u'(w + \frac{x^*}{1 - t}(1 - t)r_b)r_b$$
$$= \pi u'(w + x^* r_g)r_g + (1 - \pi)u'(w + x^* r_b)r_b = 0,$$

where the last equality follows from the fact that x^* is the optimal solution when there is no tax.

What is going on here? How can imposing a tax increase the amount of investment in the risky asset? Here is what is happening. When the tax is imposed, the individual will have less of a gain in the good state, but he will also have *less of a loss in the bad state*. By scaling his original investment up by $1/(1 - t)$ the consumer can reproduce the same *after-tax* returns that he had before the tax was put in place. The tax reduces his expected return, but it also reduces his risk: by increasing his investment the consumer can get exactly the same pattern of returns he had before and thus completely offset the effect of the tax. A tax on a risky investment represents a tax on the gain when the return is positive—but it represents a subsidy on the loss when the return is negative.

CHAPTER **13**

RISKY ASSETS

In the last chapter we examined a model of individual behavior under uncertainty and the role of two economic institutions for dealing with uncertainty: insurance markets and stock markets. In this chapter we will further explore how stock markets serve to allocate risk. In order to do this, it is convenient to consider a simplified model of behavior under uncertainty.

13.1 Mean-Variance Utility

In the last chapter we examined the expected utility model of choice under uncertainty. Another approach to choice under uncertainty is to describe the probability distributions that are the objects of choice by a few parameters and think of the utility function as being defined over those parameters. The most popular example of this approach is the **mean-variance model**. Instead of thinking that a consumer's preferences depend on the entire probability distribution of his wealth over every possible outcome, we suppose that his preferences can be well described by considering just a few summary statistics about the probability distribution of his wealth.

Let us suppose that a random variable w takes on the values w_s for $s = 1, \ldots, S$ with probability π_s. The **mean** of a probability distribution is simply its average value:

$$\mu_w = \sum_{s=1}^{S} \pi_s w_s.$$

This is the formula for an average: take each outcome w_s, weight it by the probability that it occurs, and sum it up over all outcomes.[1]

The **variance** of a probability distribution is the average value of $(w - \mu_w)^2$:

$$\sigma_w^2 = \sum_{s=1}^{S} \pi_s (w_s - \mu_w)^2.$$

The variance measures the "spread" of the distribution and is a reasonable measure of the riskiness involved. A closely related measure is the **standard deviation**, denoted by σ_w, which is the square root of the variance: $\sigma_w = \sqrt{\sigma_w^2}$.

The mean of a probability distribution measures its average value—what the distribution is centered around. The variance of the distribution measures the "spread" of the distribution—how spread out it is around the mean. See Figure 13.1 for a graphical depiction of probability distributions with different means and variances.

The mean-variance model assumes that the utility of a probability distribution that gives the investor wealth w_s with a probability of π_s can be expressed as a function of the mean and variance of that distribution, $u(\mu_w, \sigma_w^2)$. Or, if it is more convenient, the utility can be expressed as a function of the mean and standard deviation, $u(\mu_w, \sigma_w)$. Since both variance and standard deviation are measures of the riskiness of the wealth distribution, we can think of utility as depending on either one.

This model can be thought of as a simplification of the expected utility model described in the preceding chapter. If the choices that are being made can be completely characterized in terms of their mean and variance, then a utility function for mean and variance will be able to rank choices in the same way that an expected utility function will rank them. Furthermore, even if the probability distributions cannot be completely characterized by their means and variances, the mean-variance model may well serve as a reasonable approximation to the expected utility model.

We will make the natural assumption that a higher expected return is good, other things being equal, and that a higher variance is bad. This is simply another way to state the assumption that people are typically averse to risk.

---

[1] The Greek letter μ, mu, is pronounced "mew." The Greek letter σ, sigma, is pronounced "sig-ma."

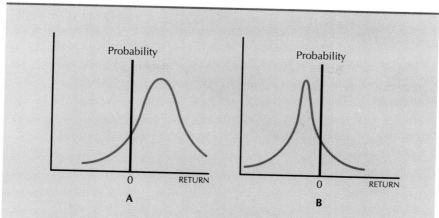

Mean and variance. The probability distribution depicted in panel A has a positive mean, while that depicted in panel B has a negative mean. The distribution in panel A is more "spread out" than the one in panel B, which means that it has a larger variance.

Figure
13.1

Let us use the mean-variance model to analyze a simple portfolio problem. Suppose that you can invest in two different assets. One of them, the **risk-free asset**, always pays a fixed rate of return, r_f. This would be something like a Treasury bill that pays a fixed rate of interest regardless of what happens.

The other asset is a **risky asset**. Think of this asset as being an investment in a large mutual fund that buys stocks. If the stock market does well, then your investment will do well. If the stock market does poorly, your investment will do poorly. Let m_s be the return on this asset if state s occurs, and let π_s be the probability that state s will occur. We'll use r_m to denote the expected return of the risky asset and σ_m to denote the standard deviation of its return.

Of course you don't have to choose one or the other of these assets; typically you'll be able to divide your wealth between the two. If you hold a fraction of your wealth x in the risky asset, and a fraction $(1-x)$ in the risk-free asset, the expected return on your portfolio will be given by

$$r_x = \sum_{s=1}^{S}(xm_s + (1-x)r_f)\pi_s$$

$$= x\sum_{s=1}^{S}m_s\pi_s + (1-x)r_f\sum_{s=1}^{S}\pi_s.$$

Since $\sum \pi_s = 1$, we have

$$r_x = xr_m + (1-x)r_f.$$

Figure 13.2

Risk and return. The budget line measures the cost of achieving a larger expected return in terms of the increased standard deviation of the return. At the optimal choice the indifference curve must be tangent to this budget line.

Thus the expected return on the portfolio is a weighted average of the two expected returns.

The variance of your portfolio return will be given by

$$\sigma_x^2 = \sum_{s=1}^{S}(xm_s + (1-x)r_f - r_x)^2\pi_s.$$

Substituting for r_x, this becomes

$$\sigma_x^2 = \sum_{s=1}^{S}(xm_s - xr_m)^2\pi_s$$

$$= \sum_{s=1}^{S}x^2(m_s - r_m)^2\pi_s$$

$$= x^2\sigma_m^2.$$

Thus the standard deviation of the portfolio return is given by

$$\sigma_x = \sqrt{x^2\sigma_m^2} = x\sigma_m.$$

It is natural to assume that $r_m > r_f$, since a risk-averse investor would never hold the risky asset if it had a lower expected return than the risk-free asset. It follows that if you choose to devote a higher fraction of your wealth to the risky asset, you will get a higher expected return, but you will also incur higher risk. This is depicted in Figure 13.2.

If you set $x = 1$ you will put all of your money in the risky asset and you will have an expected return and standard deviation of (r_m, σ_m). If you set $x = 0$ you will put all of your wealth in the sure asset and you have an expected return and standard deviation of $(r_f, 0)$. If you set x somewhere between 0 and 1, you will end up somewhere in the middle of the line connecting these two points. This line gives us a budget line describing the market tradeoff between risk and return.

Since we are assuming that people's preferences depend only on the mean and variance of their wealth, we can draw indifference curves that illustrate an individual's preferences for risk and return. If people are risk averse, then a higher expected return makes them better off and a higher standard deviation makes them worse off. This means that standard deviation is a "bad." It follows that the indifference curves will have a positive slope, as shown in Figure 13.2.

At the optimal choice of risk and return the slope of the indifference curve has to equal the slope of the budget line in Figure 13.2. We might call this slope the **price of risk** since it measures how risk and return can be traded off in making portfolio choices. From inspection of Figure 13.2 the price of risk is given by

$$p = \frac{r_m - r_f}{\sigma_m}. \tag{13.1}$$

So our optimal portfolio choice between the sure and the risky asset could be characterized by saying that the marginal rate of substitution between risk and return must be equal to the price of risk:

$$\text{MRS} = -\frac{\Delta U / \Delta \sigma}{\Delta U / \Delta \mu} = \frac{r_m - r_f}{\sigma_m}. \tag{13.2}$$

Now suppose that there are many individuals who are choosing between these two assets. Each one of them has to have his marginal rate of substitution equal to the price of risk. Thus in equilibrium all of the individuals' MRSs will be equal: when people are given sufficient opportunities to trade risks, the equilibrium price of risk will be equal across individuals. Risk is like any other good in this respect.

We can use the ideas that we have developed in earlier chapters to examine how choices change as the parameters of the problem change. All of the framework of normal goods, inferior goods, revealed preference, and so on can be brought to bear on this model. For example, suppose that an individual is offered a choice of a new risky asset y that has a mean return of r_y, say, and a standard deviation of σ_y, as illustrated in Figure 13.3.

If offered the choice between investing in x and investing in y, which will the consumer choose? The original budget set and the new budget set are both depicted in Figure 13.3. Note that every choice of risk and return that was possible in the original budget set is possible with the new budget

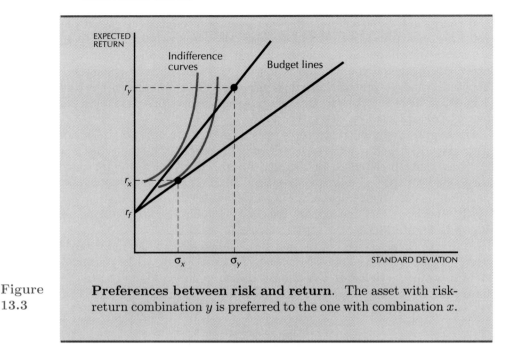

EXPECTED RETURN

Indifference curves

Budget lines

r_y

r_x

r_f

σ_x σ_y

STANDARD DEVIATION

Figure
13.3

Preferences between risk and return. The asset with risk-return combination y is preferred to the one with combination x.

set since the new budget set contains the old one. Thus investing in the asset y and the risk-free asset is definitely better than investing in x and the risk-free asset, since the consumer can choose a better final portfolio.

The fact that the consumer can choose how much of the risky asset he wants to hold is very important for this argument. If this were an "all or nothing" choice where the consumer was compelled to invest all of his money in either x or y, we would get a very different outcome. In the example depicted in Figure 13.3, the consumer would prefer investing all of his money in x to investing all of his money in y, since x lies on a higher indifference curve than y. But if he can mix the risky asset with the risk-free asset, he would always prefer to mix with y rather than to mix with x.

13.2 Measuring Risk

We have a model above that describes the price of risk . . . but how do we measure the *amount* of risk in an asset? The first thing that you would probably think of is the standard deviation of an asset's return. After all, we are assuming that utility depends on the mean and variance of wealth, aren't we?

In the above example, where there is only one risky asset, that is exactly right: the amount of risk in the risky asset is its standard deviation. But if there are many risky assets, the standard deviation is not an appropriate measure for the amount of risk in an asset.

This is because a consumer's utility depends on the mean and variance of total wealth—not the mean and variance of any single asset that he might hold. What matters is how the returns of the various assets a consumer holds *interact* to create a mean and variance of his wealth. As in the rest of economics, it is the marginal impact of a given asset on total utility that determines its value, not the value of that asset held alone. Just as the value of an extra cup of coffee may depend on how much cream is available, the amount that someone would be willing to pay for an extra share of a risky asset will depend on how it interacts with other assets in his portfolio.

Suppose, for example, that you are considering purchasing two assets, and you know that there are only two possible outcomes that can happen. Asset A will be worth either $10 or −$5, and asset B will be worth either −$5 or $10. But when asset A is worth $10, asset B will be worth −$5 and vice versa. In other words the values of the two assets will be *negatively correlated:* when one has a large value, the other will have a small value.

Suppose that the two outcomes are equally likely, so that the average value of each asset will be $2.50. Then if you don't care about risk at all and you must hold one asset or the other, the most that you would be willing to pay for either one would be $2.50—the expected value of each asset. If you are averse to risk, you would be willing to pay even less than $2.50.

But what if you can hold both assets? Then if you hold one share of each asset, you will get $5 whichever outcome arises. Whenever one asset is worth $10, the other is worth −$5. Thus, if you can hold both assets, the amount that you would be willing to pay to purchase *both* assets would be $5.

This example shows in a vivid way that the value of an asset will depend in general on how it is correlated with other assets. Assets that move in opposite directions—that are negatively correlated with each other—are very valuable because they reduce overall risk. In general the value of an asset tends to depend much more on the correlation of its return with other assets than with its own variation. Thus the amount of risk in an asset depends on its correlation with other assets.

It is convenient to measure the risk in an asset relative to the risk in the stock market as a whole. We call the riskiness of a stock relative to the risk of the market the **beta** of a stock, and denote it by the Greek letter β. Thus, if i represents some particular stock, we write β_i for its riskiness relative to the market as a whole. Roughly speaking:

$$\beta_i = \frac{\text{how risky asset } i \text{ is}}{\text{how risky the stock market is}}.$$

If a stock has a beta of 1, then it is just as risky as the market as a whole;

when the market moves up by 10 percent, this stock will, on the average, move up by 10 percent. If a stock has a beta of less than 1, then when the market moves up by 10 percent, the stock will move up by less than 10 percent. The beta of a stock can be estimated by statistical methods to determine how sensitive the movements of one variable are relative to another, and there are many investment advisory services that can provide you with estimates of the beta of a stock.[2]

13.3 Equilibrium in a Market for Risky Assets

We are now in a position to state the equilibrium condition for a market with risky assets. Recall that in a market with only certain returns, we saw that all assets had to earn the same rate of return. Here we have a similar principle: all assets, after adjusting for risk, have to earn the same rate of return.

The catch is about adjusting for risk. How do we do that? The answer comes from the analysis of optimal choice given earlier. Recall that we considered the choice of an optimal portfolio that contained a riskless asset and a risky asset. The risky asset was interpreted as being a mutual fund— a diversified portfolio including many risky assets. In this section we'll suppose that this portfolio consists of *all* risky assets.

Then we can identify the expected return on this market portfolio of risky assets with the market expected return, r_m, and identify the standard deviation of the market return with the market risk, σ_m. The return on the safe asset is r_f, the risk-free return.

We saw in equation (13.1) that the price of risk, p, is given by

$$p = \frac{r_m - r_f}{\sigma_m}.$$

We said above that the amount of risk in a given asset i relative to the total risk in the market is denoted by β_i. This means that to measure the *total* amount of risk in asset i, we have to multiply by the market risk, σ_m. Thus the total risk in asset i is given by $\beta_i \sigma_m$.

What is the cost of this risk? Just multiply the total amount of risk, $\beta_i \sigma_m$, by the price of risk. This gives us the *risk adjustment:*

$$\text{risk adjustment} = \beta_i \sigma_m p$$
$$= \beta_i \sigma_m \frac{r_m - r_f}{\sigma_m}$$
$$= \beta_i (r_m - r_f).$$

---

[2] The Greek letter β, beta, is pronounced "bait-uh." For those of you who know some statistics, the beta of a stock is defined to be $\beta_i = \text{cov}(\tilde{r}_i, \tilde{r}_m)/\text{var}(\tilde{r}_m)$. That is, β_i is the covariance of the return on the stock with the market return divided by the variance of the market return.

Now we can state the equilibrium condition in markets for risky assets: in equilibrium all assets should have the same risk-adjusted rate of return. The logic is just like the logic used in Chapter 12: if one asset had a higher risk-adjusted rate of return than another, everyone would want to hold the asset with the higher risk-adjusted rate. Thus in equilibrium the risk-adjusted rates of return must be equalized.

If there are two assets i and j that have expected returns r_i and r_j and betas of β_i and β_j, we must have the following equation satisfied in equilibrium:

$$r_i - \beta_i(r_m - r_f) = r_j - \beta_j(r_m - r_f).$$

This equation says that in equilibrium the risk-adjusted returns on the two assets must be the same—where the risk adjustment comes from multiplying the total risk of the asset by the price of risk.

Another way to express this condition is to note the following. The risk-free asset, by definition, must have $\beta_f = 0$. This is because it has zero risk, and β measures the amount of risk in an asset. Thus for any asset i we must have

$$r_i - \beta_i(r_m - r_f) = r_f - \beta_f(r_m - r_f) = r_f.$$

Rearranging, this equation says

$$r_i = r_f + \beta_i(r_m - r_f)$$

or that the expected return on any asset must be the risk-free return plus the risk adjustment. This latter term reflects the extra return that people demand in order to bear the risk that the asset embodies. This equation is the main result of the **Capital Asset Pricing Model (CAPM)**, which has many uses in the study of financial markets.

13.4 How Returns Adjust

In studying asset markets under certainty, we showed how prices of assets adjust to equalize returns. Let's look at the same adjustment process here.

According to the model sketched out above, the expected return on any asset should be the risk-free return plus the risk premium:

$$r_i = r_f + \beta_i(r_m - r_f).$$

In Figure 13.4 we have illustrated this line in a graph with the different values of beta plotted along the horizontal axis and different expected returns on the vertical axis. According to our model, all assets that are held

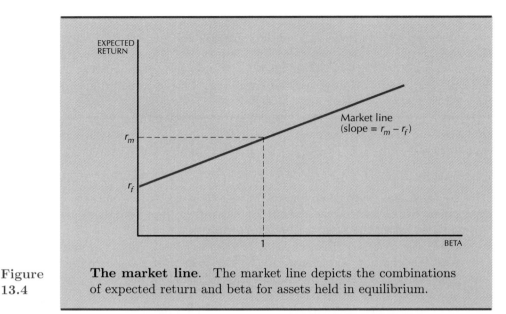

Figure
13.4

The market line. The market line depicts the combinations
of expected return and beta for assets held in equilibrium.

in equilibrium have to lie along this line. This line is called the **market
line**.

What if some asset's expected return and beta didn't lie on the market
line? What would happen?

The expected return on the asset is the expected change in its price
divided by its current price:

$$r_i = \text{ expected value of } \frac{p_1 - p_0}{p_0}.$$

This is just like the definition we had before, with the addition of the word
"expected." We have to include "expected" now since the price of the asset
tomorrow is uncertain.

Suppose that you found an asset whose expected return, adjusted for
risk, was higher than the risk-free rate:

$$r_i - \beta_i(r_m - r_f) > r_f.$$

Then this asset is a very good deal. It is giving a higher risk-adjusted
return than the risk-free rate.

When people discover that this asset exists, they will want to buy it.
They might want to keep it for themselves, or they might want to buy it
and sell it to others, but since it is offering a better tradeoff between risk
and return than existing assets, there is certainly a market for it.

But as people attempt to buy this asset they will bid up today's price:
p_0 will rise. This means that the expected return $r_i = (p_1 - p_0)/p_0$ will

fall. How far will it fall? Just enough to lower the expected rate of return back down to the market line.

Thus it is a good deal to buy an asset that lies above the market line. For when people discover that it has a higher return given its risk than assets they currently hold, they will bid up the price of that asset.

This is all dependent on the hypothesis that people agree about the amount of risk in various assets. If they disagree about the expected returns or the betas of different assets, the model becomes much more complicated.

EXAMPLE: Ranking Mutual Funds

The Capital Asset Pricing Model can be used to compare different investments with respect to their risk and their return. One popular kind of investment is a mutual fund. These are large organizations that accept money from individual investors and use this money to buy and sell stocks of companies. The profits made by such investments are then paid out to the individual investors.

The advantage of a mutual fund is that you have professionals managing your money. The disadvantage is they charge you for managing it. These fees are usually not terribly large, however, and most small investors are probably well advised to use a mutual fund.

But how do you choose a mutual fund in which to invest? You want one with a high expected return of course, but you also probably want one with a minimum amount of risk. The question is, how much risk are you willing to tolerate to get that high expected return?

One thing that you might do is to look at the historical performance of various mutual funds and calculate the average yearly return and the beta—the amount of risk—of each mutual fund you are considering. Since we haven't discussed the precise definition of beta, you might find it hard to calculate. But there are books where you can look up the historical betas of mutual funds.

If you plotted the expected returns versus the betas, you would get a diagram similar to that depicted in Figure 13.5.[3] Note that the mutual funds with high expected returns will generally have high risk. The high expected returns are there to compensate people for bearing risk.

One interesting thing you can do with the mutual fund diagram is to compare investing with professional managers to a very simple strategy like investing part of your money in an **index fund**. There are several

---

[3] See Michael Jensen, "The Performance of Mutual Funds in the Period 1945–1964," *Journal of Finance*, 23 (May 1968), 389–416, for a more detailed discussion of how to examine mutual fund performance using the tools we have sketched out in this chapter. Mark Grinblatt and Sheridan Titman have examined more recent data in "Mutual Fund Performance: An Analysis of Quarterly Portfolio Holdings," *The Journal of Business*, 62 (July 1989), 393–416.

indices of stock market activity like the Dow-Jones Industrial Average, or the Standard and Poor's Index, and so on. The indices are typically the average returns on a given day of a certain group of stocks. The Standard and Poor's Index, for example, is based on the average performance of 500 large stocks in the United States.

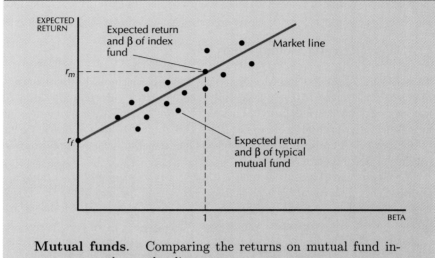

Figure 13.5

Mutual funds. Comparing the returns on mutual fund investment to the market line.

An **index fund** is a mutual fund that holds the stocks that make up such an index. This means that you are guaranteed to get the average performance of the stocks in the index, virtually by definition. Since holding the average is not a very difficult thing to do—at least compared to trying to beat the average—index funds typically have low management fees. Since an index fund holds a very broad base of risky assets, it will have a beta that is very close to 1—it will be just as risky as the market as a whole, because the index fund holds nearly all the stocks in the market as a whole.

How does an index fund do as compared to the typical mutual fund? Remember the comparison has to be made with respect to both risk and return of the investment. One way to do this is to plot the expected return and beta of a Standard and Poor's Index fund, and draw the line connecting it to the risk-free rate, as in Figure 13.5. You can get any combination of risk and return on this line that you want just by deciding how much money you want to invest in the risk-free asset and how much you want to invest in the index fund.

Now let's count the number of mutual funds that plot below this line. These are mutual funds that offer risk and return combinations that are dominated by those available by the index fund/risk-free asset combinations. When this is done, it turns out that the vast majority of the risk-return combinations offered by mutual funds are below the line. The number of funds that plot above the line is no more than could be expected by chance alone.

But seen another way, this finding might not be too surprising. The stock market is an incredibly competitive environment. People are always trying to find undervalued stocks in order to purchase them. This means that on average, stocks are usually trading for what they're really worth. If that is the case, then betting the averages is a pretty reasonable strategy—since beating the averages is almost impossible.

Summary

1. We can use the budget set and indifference curve apparatus developed earlier to examine the choice of how much money to invest in risky and riskless assets.

2. The marginal rate of substitution between risk and return will have to equal the slope of the budget line. This slope is known as the price of risk.

3. The amount of risk present in an asset depends to a large extent on its correlation with other assets. An asset that moves opposite the direction of other assets helps to reduce the overall risk of your portfolio.

4. The amount of risk in an asset relative to that of the market as a whole is called the **beta** of the asset.

5. The fundamental equilibrium condition in asset markets is that risk-adjusted returns have to be the same.

REVIEW QUESTIONS

1. If the risk-free rate of return is 6%, and if a risky asset is available with a return of 9% and a standard deviation of 3%, what is the maximum rate of return you can achieve if you are willing to accept a standard deviation of 2%? What percentage of your wealth would have to be invested in the risky asset?

2. What is the price of risk in the above exercise?

3. If a stock has a β of 1.5, the return on the market is 10%, and the risk-free rate of return is 5%, what expected rate of return should this stock offer according to the Capital Asset Pricing Model? If the expected value of the stock is $100, what price should the stock be selling for today?

CHAPTER 14

CONSUMER'S SURPLUS

In the preceding chapters we have seen how to derive a consumer's demand function from the underlying preferences or utility function. But in practice we are usually concerned with the reverse problem—how to estimate preferences or utility from observed demand behavior.

We have already examined this problem in two other contexts. In Chapter 5 we showed how one could estimate the parameters of a utility function from observing demand behavior. In the Cobb-Douglas example used in that chapter, we were able to estimate a utility function that described the observed choice behavior simply by calculating the average expenditure share of each good. The resulting utility function could then be used to evaluate changes in consumption.

In Chapter 7 we described how to use revealed preference analysis to recover estimates of the underlying preferences that may have generated some observed choices. These estimated indifference curves can also be used to evaluate changes in consumption.

In this chapter we will consider some more approaches to the problem of estimating utility from observing demand behavior. Although some of the methods we will examine are less general than the two methods we examined previously, they will turn out to be useful in several applications that we will discuss later in the book.

We will start by reviewing a special case of demand behavior for which it is very easy to recover an estimate of utility. Later we will consider more general cases of preferences and demand behavior.

14.1 Demand for a Discrete Good

Let us start by reviewing demand for a discrete good with quasilinear utility, as described in Chapter 6. Suppose that the utility function takes the form $v(x) + y$ and that the x-good is only available in integer amounts. Let us think of the y-good as money to be spent on other goods and set its price to 1. Let p be the price of the x-good.

We saw in Chapter 6 that in this case consumer behavior can be described in terms of the reservation prices, $r_1 = v(1) - v(0)$, $r_2 = v(2) - v(1)$, and so on. The relationship between reservation prices and demand was very simple: if n units of the discrete good are demanded, then $r_n \geq p \geq r_{n+1}$.

To verify this, let's look at an example. Suppose that the consumer chooses to consume 6 units of the x-good when its price is p. Then the utility of consuming $(6, m - 6p)$ must be at least as large as the utility of consuming any other bundle $(x, m - px)$:

$$v(6) + m - 6p \geq v(x) + m - px. \tag{14.1}$$

In particular this inequality must hold for $x = 5$, which gives us

$$v(6) + m - 6p \geq v(5) + m - 5p.$$

Rearranging, we have $v(6) - v(5) = r_6 \geq p$.

Equation (14.1) must also hold for $x = 7$. This gives us

$$v(6) + m - 6p \geq v(7) + m - 7p,$$

which can be rearranged to yield

$$p \geq v(7) - v(6) = r_7.$$

This argument shows that if 6 units of the x-good is demanded, then the price of the x-good must lie between r_6 and r_7. In general, if n units of the x-good are demanded at price p, then $r_n \geq p \geq r_{n+1}$, as we wanted to show. The list of reservation prices contains all the information necessary to describe the demand behavior. The graph of the reservation prices forms a "staircase" as shown in Figure 14.1. This staircase is precisely the demand curve for the discrete good.

14.2 Constructing Utility from Demand

We have just seen how to construct the demand curve given the reservation prices or the utility function. But we can also do the same operation in reverse. If we are given the demand curve, we can construct the utility function—at least in the special case of quasilinear utility.

At one level, this is just a trivial operation of arithmetic. The reservation prices are defined to be the difference in utility:

$$r_1 = v(1) - v(0)$$
$$r_2 = v(2) - v(1)$$
$$r_3 = v(3) - v(2)$$
$$\vdots$$

If we want to calculate $v(3)$, for example, we simply add up both sides of this list of equations to find

$$r_1 + r_2 + r_3 = v(3) - v(0).$$

It is convenient to set the utility from consuming zero units of the good equal to zero, so that $v(0) = 0$, and therefore $v(n)$ is just the sum of the first n reservation prices.

This construction has a nice geometrical interpretation that is illustrated in Figure 14.1A. The utility from consuming n units of the discrete good is just the area of the first n bars which make up the demand function. This is true because the height of each bar is the reservation price associated with that level of demand and the width of each bar is 1. This area is sometimes called the **gross benefit** or the **gross consumer's surplus** associated with the consumption of the good.

Note that this is only the utility associated with the consumption of good 1. The final utility of consumption depends on the how much the consumer consumes of good 1 *and* good 2. If the consumer chooses n units of the discrete good, then he will have $m - pn$ dollars left over to purchase other things. This leaves him with a total utility of

$$v(n) + m - pn.$$

This utility also has an interpretation as an area: we just take the area depicted in Figure 14.1A, subtract off the expenditure on the discrete good, and add m.

The term $v(n) - pn$ is called **consumer's surplus** or the **net consumer's surplus**. It measures the net benefits from consuming n units of the discrete good: the utility $v(n)$ minus the reduction in the expenditure on consumption of the other good. The consumer's surplus is depicted in Figure 14.1B.

Reservation prices and consumer's surplus. The gross benefit in panel A is the area under the demand curve. This measures the utility from consuming the x-good. The consumer's surplus is depicted in panel B. It measures the utility from consuming both goods when the first good has to be purchased at a constant price p.

Figure
14.1

14.3 Other Interpretations of Consumer's Surplus

There are some other ways to think about consumer's surplus. Suppose that the price of the discrete good is p. Then the value that the consumer places on the first unit of consumption of that good is r_1, but he only has to pay p for it. This gives him a "surplus" of $r_1 - p$ on the first unit of consumption. He values the second unit of consumption at r_2, but again he only has to pay p for it. This gives him a surplus of $r_2 - p$ on that unit. If we add this up over all n units the consumer chooses, we get his total consumer's surplus:

$$CS = r_1 - p + r_2 - p + \cdots + r_n - p = r_1 + \cdots + r_n - np.$$

Since the sum of the reservation prices just gives us the utility of consumption of good 1, we can also write this as

$$CS = v(n) - pn.$$

We can interpret consumer's surplus in yet another way. Suppose that a consumer is consuming n units of the discrete good and paying pn dollars to do so. How much money would he need to induce him to give up his entire consumption of this good? Let R be the required amount of money. Then R must satisfy the equation

$$v(0) + m + R = v(n) + m - pn.$$

Since $v(0) = 0$ by definition, this equation reduces to

$$R = v(n) - pn,$$

which is just consumer's surplus. Hence the consumer's surplus measures how much a consumer would need to be paid to give up his entire consumption of some good.

14.4 From Consumer's Surplus to Consumers' Surplus

Up until now we have been considering the case of a single consumer. If several consumers are involved we can add up each consumer's surplus across all the consumers to create an aggregate measure of the **consumers' surplus**. Note carefully the distinction between the two concepts: consumer's surplus refers to the surplus of a single consumer; consumers' surplus refers to the sum of the surpluses across a number of consumers.

Consumers' surplus serves as a convenient measure of the aggregate gains from trade, just as consumer's surplus serves as a measure of the individual gains from trade.

14.5 Approximating a Continuous Demand

We have seen that the area underneath the demand curve for a discrete good measures the utility of consumption of that good. We can extend this to the case of a good available in continuous quantities by approximating the continuous demand curve by a staircase demand curve. The area under the continuous demand curve is then approximately equal to the area under the staircase demand.

See Figure 14.2 for an example. In the Appendix to this chapter we show how to use calculus to calculate the exact area under a demand curve.

14.6 Quasilinear Utility

It is worth thinking about the role that quasilinear utility plays in this analysis. In general the price at which a consumer is willing to purchase

A Approximation to gross surplus   **B** Approximation to net surplus

Approximating a continuous demand. The consumer's surplus associated with a continuous demand curve can be approximated by the consumer's surplus associated with a discrete approximation to it.

Figure
14.2

some amount of good 1 will depend on how much money he has for consuming other goods. This means that in general the reservation prices for good 1 will depend on how much good 2 is being consumed.

But in the special case of quasilinear utility the reservation prices are independent of the amount of money the consumer has to spend on other goods. Economists say that with quasilinear utility there is "no income effect" since changes in income don't affect demand. This is what allows us to calculate utility in such a simple way. Using the area under the demand curve to measure utility will only be *exactly* correct when the utility function is quasilinear.

But it may often be a good approximation. If the demand for a good doesn't change very much when income changes, then the income effects won't matter very much, and the change in consumer's surplus will be a reasonable approximation to the change in the consumer's utility.[1]

14.7 Interpreting the Change in Consumer's Surplus

We are usually not terribly interested in the absolute level of consumer's surplus. We are generally more interested in the change in consumer's

---

[1] Of course, the change in consumer's surplus is only one way to represent a change in utility—the change in the square root of consumer's surplus would be just as good. But it is standard to use consumer's surplus as a standard measure of utility.

surplus that results from some policy change. For example, suppose the price of a good changes from p' to p''. How does the consumer's surplus change?

In Figure 14.3 we have illustrated the change in consumer's surplus associated with a change in price. The change in consumer's surplus is the difference between two roughly triangular regions and will therefore have a roughly trapezoidal shape. The trapezoid is further composed of two subregions, the rectangle indicated by R and the roughly triangular region indicated by T.

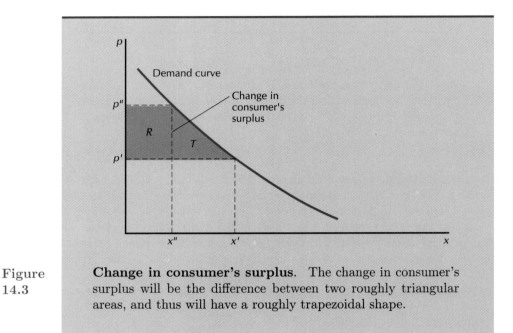

Figure
14.3

Change in consumer's surplus. The change in consumer's surplus will be the difference between two roughly triangular areas, and thus will have a roughly trapezoidal shape.

The rectangle measures the loss in surplus due to the fact that the consumer is now paying more for all the units he continues to consume. After the price increases the consumer continues to consume x'' units of the good, and each unit of the good is now more expensive by $p'' - p'$. This means he has to spend $(p'' - p')x''$ more money than he did before just to consume x'' units of the good.

But this is not the entire welfare loss. Due to the increase in the price of the x-good, the consumer has decided to consume less of it than he was before. The triangle T measures the value of the *lost* consumption of the x-good. The total loss to the consumer is the sum of these two effects: R measures the loss from having to pay more for the units he continues to consume, and T measures the loss from the reduced consumption.

EXAMPLE: The Change in Consumer's Surplus

Question: Consider the linear demand curve $D(p) = 20 - 2p$. When the price changes from 2 to 3 what is the associated change in consumer's surplus?

Answer: When $p = 2$, $D(2) = 16$, and when $p = 3$, $D(3) = 14$. Thus we want to compute the area of a trapezoid with a height of 1 and bases of 14 and 16. This is equivalent to a rectangle with height 1 and base 14 (having an area of 14), plus a triangle of height 1 and base 2 (having an area of 1). The total area will therefore be 15.

14.8 Compensating and Equivalent Variation

The theory of consumer's surplus is very tidy in the case of quasilinear utility. Even if utility is not quasilinear, consumer's surplus may still be a reasonable measure of consumer's welfare in many applications. Usually the errors in measuring demand curves outweigh the approximation errors from using consumer's surplus.

But it may be that for some applications an approximation may not be good enough. In this section we'll outline a way to measure "utility changes" without using consumer's surplus. There are really two separate issues involved. The first has to do with how to estimate utility when we can observe a number of consumer choices. The second has to do with how we can measure utility in monetary units.

We've already investigated the estimation problem. We gave an example of how to estimate a Cobb-Douglas utility function in Chapter 6. In that example we noticed that expenditure shares were relatively constant and that we could use the average expenditure share as estimates of the Cobb-Douglas parameters. If the demand behavior didn't exhibit this particular feature, we would have to choose a more complicated utility function, but the principle would be just the same: if we have enough observations on demand behavior and that behavior is consistent with maximizing something, then we will generally be able to estimate the function that is being maximized.

Once we have an estimate of the utility function that describes some observed choice behavior we can use this function to evaluate the impact of proposed changes in prices and consumption levels. At the most fundamental level of analysis, this is the best we can hope for. All that matters are the consumer's preferences; any utility function that describes the consumer's preferences is as good as any other.

However, in some applications it may be convenient to use certain monetary measures of utility. For example, we could ask how much money we would have to give a consumer to compensate him for a change in his consumption patterns. A measure of this type essentially measures a change in utility, but it measures it in monetary units. What are convenient ways to do this?

Suppose that we consider the situation depicted in Figure 14.4. Here the consumer initially faces some prices $(p_1^*, 1)$ and consumes some bundle (x_1^*, x_2^*). The price of good 1 then increases from p_1^* to $\hat{p}_1$, and the consumer changes his consumption to $(\hat{x}_1, \hat{x}_2)$. How much does this price change hurt the consumer?

Figure
14.4

The compensating and the equivalent variations. Panel A shows the compensating variation (CV), and panel B shows the equivalent variation (EV).

One way to answer this question is to ask how much money we would have to give the consumer *after* the price change to make him just as well off as he was *before* the price change. In terms of the diagram, we ask how far up we would have to shift the new budget line to make it tangent to the indifference curve that passes through the original consumption point (x_1^*, x_2^*). The change in income necessary to restore the consumer to his original indifference curve is called the **compensating variation** in income, since it is the change in income that will just compensate the consumer for the price change. The compensating variation measures how much extra money the government would have to give the consumer if it wanted to exactly compensate the consumer for the price change.

Another way to measure the impact of a price change in monetary terms is to ask how much money would have to be taken away from the consumer *before* the price change to leave him as well off as he would be *after* the price change. This is called the **equivalent variation** in income since it is the income change that is equivalent to the price change in terms of the change in utility. In Figure 14.4 we ask how far down we must shift the original budget line to just touch the indifference curve that passes through the new consumption bundle. The equivalent variation measures the maximum amount of income that the consumer would be willing to pay to avoid the price change.

In general the amount of money that the consumer would be willing to pay to avoid a price change would be different from the amount of money that the consumer would have to be paid to compensate him for a price change. After all, at different sets of prices a dollar is worth a different amount to a consumer since it will purchase different amounts of consumption.

In geometric terms, the compensating and equivalent variations are just two different ways to measure "how far apart" two indifference curves are. In each case we are measuring the distance between two indifference curves by seeing how far apart their tangent lines are. In general this measure of distance will depend on the slope of the tangent lines—that is, on the prices that we choose to determine the budget lines.

However, the compensating and equivalent variation are the same in one important case—the case of quasilinear utility. In this case the indifference curves are parallel, so the distance between any two indifference curves is the same no matter where it is measured, as depicted in Figure 14.5. In the case of quasilinear utility the compensating variation, the equivalent variation, and the change in consumer's surplus all give the same measure of the monetary value of a price change.

EXAMPLE: Compensating and Equivalent Variations

Suppose that a consumer has a utility function $u(x_1, x_2) = x_1^{\frac{1}{2}} x_2^{\frac{1}{2}}$. He originally faces prices $(1, 1)$ and has income 100. Then the price of good 1 increases to 2. What are the compensating and equivalent variations?

We know that the demand functions for this Cobb-Douglas utility function are given by

$$x_1 = \frac{m}{2p_1}$$

$$x_2 = \frac{m}{2p_2}.$$

Using this formula, we see that the consumer's demands change from $(x_1^*, x_2^*) = (50, 50)$ to $(\hat{x}_1, \hat{x}_2) = (25, 50)$.

To calculate the compensating variation we ask how much money would be necessary at prices $(2,1)$ to make the consumer as well off as he was consuming the bundle $(50,50)$? If the prices were $(2,1)$ and the consumer

Figure
14.5
Quasilinear preferences. With quasilinear preferences, the distance between two indifference curves is independent of the slope of the budget lines.

had income m, we can substitute into the demand functions to find that the consumer would optimally choose the bundle $(m/4, m/2)$. Setting the utility of this bundle equal to the utility of the bundle $(50, 50)$ we have

$$\left(\frac{m}{4}\right)^{\frac{1}{2}} \left(\frac{m}{2}\right)^{\frac{1}{2}} = 50^{\frac{1}{2}} 50^{\frac{1}{2}}.$$

Solving for m gives us
$$m = 100\sqrt{2} \approx 141.$$

Hence the consumer would need about $141 - 100 = \$41$ of additional money after the price change to make him as well off as he was before the price change.

In order to calculate the equivalent variation we ask how much money would be necessary at the prices $(1,1)$ to make the consumer as well off as he would be consuming the bundle $(25,50)$. Letting m stand for this amount of money and following the same logic as before,

$$\left(\frac{m}{2}\right)^{\frac{1}{2}} \left(\frac{m}{2}\right)^{\frac{1}{2}} = 25^{\frac{1}{2}} 50^{\frac{1}{2}}.$$

Solving for m gives us
$$m = 50\sqrt{2} \approx 70.$$

Thus if the consumer had an income of \$70 at the original prices, he would be just as well off as he would be facing the new prices and having an income of \$100. The equivalent variation in income is therefore about $100 - 70 = \$30$.

EXAMPLE: Compensating and Equivalent Variation for Quasilinear Preferences

Suppose that the consumer has a quasilinear utility function $v(x_1) + x_2$. We know that in this case the demand for good 1 will depend only on the price of good 1, so we write it as $x_1(p_1)$. Suppose that the price changes from p_1^* to $\hat{p}_1$. What are the compensating and equivalent variations?

At the price p_1^*, the consumer chooses $x_1^* = x_1(p_1^*)$ and has a utility of $v(x_1^*) + m - p_1^* x_1^*$. At the price $\hat{p}_1$, the consumer choose $\hat{x}_1 = x_1(\hat{p}_1)$ and has a utility of $v(\hat{x}_1) + m - \hat{p}_1 \hat{x}_1$.

Let C be the compensating variation. This is the amount of extra money the consumer would need after the price change to make him as well off as he would be before the price change. Setting these utilities equal we have

$$v(\hat{x}_1) + m + C - \hat{p}_1 \hat{x}_1 = v(x_1^*) + m - p_1^* x_1^*.$$

Solving for C we have

$$C = v(x_1^*) - v(\hat{x}_1) + \hat{p}_1 \hat{x}_1 - p_1^* x_1^*.$$

Let E be the equivalent variation. This is the amount of money that you could take away from the consumer before the price change that would leave him with the same utility that he would have after the price change. Thus it satisfies the equation

$$v(x_1^*) + m - E - p_1^* x_1^* = v(\hat{x}_1) + m - \hat{p}_1 \hat{x}_1.$$

Solving for E, we have

$$E = v(x_1^*) - v(\hat{x}_1) + \hat{p}_1 \hat{x}_1 - p_1^* x_1^*.$$

Note that for the case of quasilinear utility the compensating and equivalent variation are the same. Furthermore, they are both equal to the change in (net) consumer's surplus:

$$\Delta CS = [v(x_1^*) - p_1^* x_1^*] - [v(\hat{x}_1) - \hat{p}_1 \hat{x}_1].$$

14.9 Producer's Surplus

The demand curve measures the amount that will be demanded at each price; the **supply curve** measures the amount that will be supplied at each price. Just as the area *under* the demand curve measures the surplus enjoyed by the demanders of a good, the area *above* the supply curve measures the surplus enjoyed by the suppliers of a good.

We've referred to the area under the demand curve as consumer's surplus. By analogy, the area above the supply curve is known as **producer's surplus**. The terms consumer's surplus and producer's surplus are somewhat misleading, since who is doing the consuming and who is doing the producing really doesn't matter. It would be better to use the terms "demander's surplus" and "supplier's surplus," but we'll bow to tradition and use the standard terminology.

Suppose that we have a supply curve for a good. This simply measures the amount of a good that will be supplied at each possible price. The good could be supplied by an individual who owns the good in question, or it could be supplied by a firm that produces the good. We'll take the latter interpretation so as to stick with the traditional terminology and depict the producer's supply curve in Figure 14.6. If the producer is able to sell x^* units of her product in a market at a price p^*, what is the surplus she enjoys?

It is most convenient to conduct the analysis in terms of the producer's *inverse* supply curve, $p_s(x)$. This function measures what the price would have to be to get the producer to supply x units of the good.

Figure
14.6

Producer's surplus. The net producer's surplus is the triangular area to the left of the supply curve in panel A, and the change in producer's surplus is the trapezoidal area in panel B.

Think about the inverse supply function for a discrete good. In this case the producer is willing to sell the first unit of the good at price $p_s(1)$, but she actually gets the market price p^* for it. Similarly, she is willing to sell the second unit for $p_s(2)$, but she gets p^* for it. Continuing in this way we see that the producer will be just willing to sell the last unit for $p_s(x^*) = p^*$.

The difference between the minimum amount she would be willing to sell the x^* units for and the amount she actually sells the units for is the **net producer's surplus**. It is the triangular area depicted in Figure 14.6A.

Just as in the case of consumer's surplus, we can ask how producer's surplus changes when the price increases from p' to p''. In general, the change in producer's surplus will be the difference between two triangular regions and will therefore generally have the roughly trapezoidal shape depicted in Figure 14.6B. As in the case of consumer's surplus, the roughly trapezoidal region will be composed of a rectangular region R and a roughly triangular region T. The rectangle measures the gain from selling the units previously sold anyway at p' at the higher price p''. The roughly triangular region measures the gain from selling the extra units at the price p''. This is analogous to the change in consumer's surplus considered earlier.

Although it is common to refer to this kind of change as an increase in producer's surplus, in a deeper sense it really represents an increase in consumer's surplus that accrues to the consumers who own the firm that generated the supply curve. Producer's surplus is closely related to the idea of profit, but we'll have to wait until we study firm behavior in more detail to spell out the relationship.

14.10 Calculating Gains and Losses

If we have estimates of the market demand and supply curves for a good, it is not difficult in principle to calculate the loss in consumers' surplus due to changes in government policies. For example, suppose the government decides to change its tax treatment of some good. This will result in a change in the prices that consumers face and therefore a change in the amount of the good that they will choose to consume. We can calculate the consumers' surplus associated with different tax proposals and see which tax reforms generate the smallest loss.

This is often useful information for judging various methods of taxation, but it suffers from two defects. First, as we've indicated earlier, the consumer's surplus calculation is only valid for special forms of preferences—namely, preferences representable by a quasilinear utility function. We argued earlier that this kind of utility function may be a reasonable approximation for goods for which changes in income lead to small changes in demand, but for goods whose consumption is closely related to income, the use of consumer surplus may be inappropriate.

Second, the calculation of this loss effectively lumps together all the consumers and producers and generates an estimate of the "cost" of a social policy only for some mythical "representative consumer." In many cases it is desirable to know not only the average cost across the population, but who bears the costs. The political success or failure of policies often depends more on the *distribution* of gains and losses than on the average gain or loss.

Consumer's surplus may be easy to calculate, but we've seen that it is not that much more difficult to calculate the true compensating or equivalent variation associated with a price change. If we have estimates of the demand functions of each household—or at least the demand functions for a sample of representative households—we can calculate the impact of a policy change on each household in terms of the compensating or equivalent variation. Thus we will have a measure of the "benefits" or "costs" imposed on each household by the proposed policy change.

Mervyn King, an economist at the London School of Economics, has described a nice example of this approach to analyzing the implications of reforming the tax treatment of housing in Britain in his paper "Welfare Analysis of Tax Reforms Using Household Data," *Journal of Public Economics*, 21 (1983), 183–214.

King first examined the housing expenditures of 5,895 households and estimated a demand function that best described their purchases of housing services. Next, he used this demand function to determine a utility function for each household. Finally, he used the estimated utility function to calculate how much each household would gain or lose under certain changes in the taxation of housing in Britain. The measure that he used was similar to the equivalent variation described earlier in this chapter. The basic nature of the tax reform he studied was to eliminate tax concessions to owner-occupied housing and to raise rents in public housing. The revenues generated by these changes would be handed back to the households in the form of transfers proportional to household income.

King found that 4,888 of the 5,895 households would benefit from this kind of reform. More importantly he could identify explicitly those households that would have significant losses from the tax reform. King found, for example, that 94 percent of the highest income households gained from the reform, while only 58 percent of the lowest income households gained. This kind of information would allow special measures to be undertaken which might help in designing the tax reform in a way that could satisfy distributional objectives.

Summary

1. In the case of a discrete good and quasilinear utility, the utility associated with the consumption of n units of the discrete good is just the sum of the first n reservation prices.

2. This sum is the gross benefit of consuming the good. If we subtract the amount spent on the purchase of the good, we get the consumer's surplus.

3. The change in consumer's surplus associated with a price change has a roughly trapezoidal shape. It can be interpreted as the change in utility associated with the price change.

4. In general, we can use the compensating variation and the equivalent variation in income to measure the monetary impact of a price change.

5. If utility is quasilinear, the compensating variation, the equivalent variation, and the change in consumer's surplus are all equal. Even if utility is not quasilinear, the change in consumer's surplus may serve as a good approximation of the impact of the price change on a consumer's utility.

6. In the case of supply behavior we can define a producer's surplus that measures the net benefits to the supplier from producing a given amount of output.

REVIEW QUESTIONS

1. Suppose that the demand curve is given by $D(p) = 10 - p$. What is the gross benefit from consuming 6 units of the good?

2. In the above example, if the price changes from 4 to 6, what is the change in consumer's surplus?

3. Suppose that a consumer is consuming 10 units of a discrete good and the price increases from $5 per unit to $6. However, after the price change the consumer continues to consume 10 units of the discrete good. What is the loss in the consumer's surplus from this price change?

APPENDIX

Let's use some calculus to treat consumer's surplus rigorously. Start with the problem of maximizing quasilinear utility:

$$\max_{x,y} v(x) + y$$

$$\text{such that } px + y = m.$$

Substituting from the budget constraint we have

$$\max_x v(x) + m - px.$$

The first-order condition for this problem is

$$v'(x) = p.$$

This means that the inverse demand function $p(x)$ is defined by

$$p(x) = v'(x). \tag{14.2}$$

Note the analogy with the discrete-good framework described in the text: the price at which the consumer is just willing to consume x units is equal to the marginal utility.

But since the inverse demand curve measures the derivative of utility, we can simply integrate under the inverse demand function to find the utility function.

Carrying out the integration we have:

$$v(x) = v(x) - v(0) = \int_0^x v'(t)\,dt = \int_0^x p(t)\,dt.$$

Hence utility associated with the consumption of the x-good is just the area under the demand curve.

EXAMPLE: A Few Demand Functions

Suppose that the demand function is linear, so that $x(p) = a - bp$. Then the change in consumer's surplus when the price moves from p to q is given by

$$\int_p^q (a - bt)\,dt = at - b\frac{t^2}{2}\Big]_p^q = a(q - p) - b\frac{q^2 - p^2}{2}.$$

Another commonly used demand function, which we examine in more detail in the next chapter, has the form $x(p) = Ap^\epsilon$, where $\epsilon < 0$ and A is some positive constant. When the price changes from p to q, the associated change in consumer's surplus is

$$\int_p^q At^\epsilon\,dt = A\frac{t^{\epsilon+1}}{\epsilon+1}\Big]_p^q = A\frac{q^{\epsilon+1} - p^{\epsilon+1}}{\epsilon+1},$$

for $\epsilon \neq -1$.

When $\epsilon = -1$, this demand function is $x(p) = A/p$, which is closely related to our old friend the Cobb-Douglas demand, $x(p) = am/p$. The change in consumer's surplus for the Cobb-Douglas demand is

$$\int_p^q \frac{am}{t}\,dt = am \ln t\Big]_p^q = am(\ln q - \ln p).$$

Comparison of CV, CS, and EV.

Table
14.1

p_1	CV	CS	EV
1	0.00	0.00	0.00
2	7.18	6.93	6.70
3	11.61	10.99	10.40
4	14.87	13.86	12.94
5	17.46	16.09	14.87

EXAMPLE: CV, EV, and Consumer's Surplus

In the text we calculated the compensating and equivalent variations for the Cobb-Douglas utility function. In the preceding example we calculated the change in consumer's surplus for the Cobb-Douglas utility function. Here we compare these three monetary measures of the impact on utility of a price change.

Suppose that the price of good 1 changes from 1 to $2, 3 \ldots$ while the price of good 2 stays fixed at 1 and income stays fixed at 100. Table 14.1 shows the equivalent variation (EV), compensating variation (CV), and the change in consumer's surplus (CS) for the Cobb-Douglas utility function $u(x_1, x_2) = x_1^{\frac{1}{10}} x_2^{\frac{9}{10}}$.

Note that the change in consumer's surplus always lies between the CV and the EV and that the difference between the three numbers is relatively small. It is possible to show that both of these facts are true in reasonably general circumstances. See Robert Willig, "Consumer's Surplus without Apology," *American Economic Review*, 66 (1976), 589–597.

CHAPTER 15

MARKET DEMAND

We have seen in earlier chapters how to model individual consumer choice. Here we see how to add up individual choices to get total **market demand**. Once we have derived the market demand curve, we will examine some of its properties, such as the relationship between demand and revenue.

15.1 From Individual to Market Demand

Let us use $x_i^1(p_1, p_2, m_i)$ to represent consumer i's demand function for good 1 and $x_i^2(p_1, p_2, m_i)$ for consumer i's demand function for good 2. Suppose that there are n consumers. Then the **market demand** for good 1, also called the **aggregate demand** for good 1, is the sum of these individual demands over all consumers:

$$X^1(p_1, p_2, m_1, \ldots, m_n) = \sum_{i=1}^{n} x_i^1(p_1, p_2, m_i).$$

The analogous equation holds for good 2.

Since each individual's demand for each good depends on prices and his or her money income, the aggregate demand will generally depend on prices and the *distribution* of incomes. However, it is sometimes convenient to think of the aggregate demand as the demand of some "representative consumer" who has an income that is just the sum of all individual incomes. The conditions under which this can be done are rather restrictive, and a complete discussion of this issue is beyond the scope of this book.

If we do make the representative consumer assumption, the aggregate demand function will have the form $X^1(p_1, p_2, M)$, where M is the sum of the incomes of the individual consumers. Under this assumption, the aggregate demand in the economy is just like the demand of some individual who faces prices (p_1, p_2) and has income M.

If we fix all the money incomes and the price of good 2, we can illustrate the relation between the aggregate demand for good 1 and its price, as in Figure 15.1. Note that this curve is drawn holding all other prices and incomes fixed. If these other prices and incomes change, the aggregate demand curve will shift.

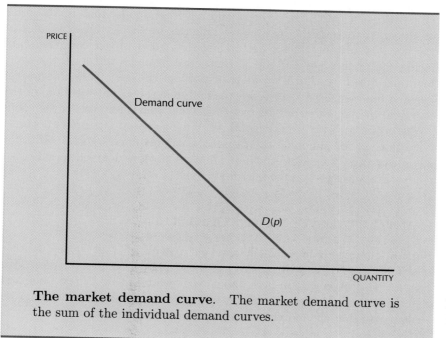

The market demand curve. The market demand curve is the sum of the individual demand curves.

Figure
15.1

For example, if goods 1 and 2 are substitutes, then we know that increasing the price of good 2 will tend to increase the demand for good 1 whatever its price. This means that increasing the price of good 2 will tend to shift the aggregate demand curve for good 1 outward. Similarly, if goods 1 and 2 are complements, increasing the price of good 2 will shift the aggregate demand curve for good 1 inward.

If good 1 is a normal good for an individual, then increasing that individual's money income, holding everything else fixed, would tend to increase that individual's demand, and therefore shift the aggregate demand curve outward. If we adopt the representative consumer model, and suppose that good 1 is a normal good for the representative consumer, then any economic change that increases aggregate income will increase the demand for good 1.

15.2 The Inverse Demand Function

We can look at the aggregate demand curve as giving us quantity as a function of price or as giving us price as a function of quantity. When we want to emphasize this latter view, we will sometimes refer to the **inverse demand function**, $P(X)$. This function measures what the market price for good 1 would have to be for X units of it to be demanded.

We've seen earlier that the price of a good measures the marginal rate of substitution (MRS) between it and all other goods; that is, the price of a good represents the marginal willingness to pay for an extra unit of the good by anyone who is demanding that good. If all consumers are facing the same prices for goods, then all consumers will have the same marginal rate of substitution at their optimal choices. Thus the inverse demand function, $P(X)$, measures the marginal rate of substitution, or the marginal willingness to pay, of *every* consumer who is purchasing the good.

The geometric interpretation of this summing operation is pretty obvious. Note that we are summing the demand or supply curves *horizontally*: for any given price, we add up the individuals' quantities demanded, which, of course, are measured on the horizontal axis.

EXAMPLE: Adding Up "Linear" Demand Curves

Suppose that one individual's demand curve is $D_1(p) = 20 - p$ and another individual's is $D_2(p) = 10 - 2p$. What is the market demand function? We have to be a little careful here about what we mean by "linear" demand functions. Since a negative amount of a good usually has no meaning, we *really* mean that the individual demand functions have the form

$$D_1(p) = \max\{20 - p, 0\}$$
$$D_2(p) = \max\{10 - 2p, 0\}.$$

What economists call "linear" demand curves actually aren't linear functions! The sum of the two demand curves looks like the curve depicted in Figure 15.2. Note the kink at $p = 5$.

The sum of two "linear" demand curves. Since the demand curves are only linear for positive quantities, there will typically be a kink in the market demand curve.

Figure
15.2

15.3 Discrete Goods

If a good is available only in discrete amounts, then we have seen that the demand for that good for a single consumer can be described in terms of the consumer's reservation prices. Here we examine the market demand for this kind of good. For simplicity, we will restrict ourselves to the case where the good will be available in units of zero or one.

In this case the demand of a consumer is completely described by his reservation price—the price at which he is just willing to purchase one unit. In Figure 15.3 we have depicted the demand curves for two consumers, A and B, and the market demand, which is the sum of these two demand curves. Note that the market demand curve in this case must "slope downward," since a decrease in the market price must increase the number of consumers who are willing to pay at least that price.

15.4 The Extensive and the Intensive Margin

In preceding chapters we have concentrated on consumer choice in which the consumer was consuming positive amounts of each good. When the price changes, the consumer decides to consume more or less of one good or the other, but still ends up consuming some of both goods. Economists sometimes say that this is an adjustment on the **intensive margin**.

In the reservation-price model, the consumers are deciding whether or not to enter the market for one of the goods. This is sometimes called an adjustment on the **extensive margin**. The slope of the aggregate demand curve will be affected by both sorts of decisions.

Figure
15.3

Market demand for a discrete good. The market demand
curve is the sum of the demand curves of all the consumers in
the market, here represented by the two consumers A and B.

We saw earlier that the adjustment on the intensive margin was in the
"right" direction for normal goods: when the price went up, the quantity
demanded went down. The adjustment on the extensive margin also works
in the "right" direction. Thus aggregate demand curves can generally be
expected to slope downward.

15.5 Elasticity

In Chapter 6 we saw how to derive a demand function from a consumer's
underlying preferences. It is often of interest to have a measure of how
"responsive" demand is to some change in price or income. Now the first
idea that springs to mind is to use the slope of a demand function as a
measure of responsiveness. After all, the definition of the slope of a demand
function is the change in quantity demanded divided by the change in price:

$$\text{slope of demand function} = \frac{\Delta q}{\Delta p},$$

and that certainly looks like a measure of responsiveness.

Well, it is a measure of responsiveness—but it presents some problems.
The most important one is that the slope of a demand function depends on
the units in which you measure price and quantity. If you measure demand
in gallons rather than in quarts, the slope becomes four times smaller.
Rather than specify units all the time, it is convenient to consider a unit-
free measure of responsiveness. Economists have chosen to use a measure
known as **elasticity**.

The **price elasticity of demand**, ϵ, is defined to be the percent change
in quantity divided by the percent change in price.[1] A 10 percent increase

---

[1] The Greek letter ϵ, epsilon, is pronounced "eps-i-lon."

in price is the same percentage increase whether the price is measured in American dollars or English pounds; thus measuring increases in percentage terms keeps the definition of elasticity unit-free.

In symbols the definition of elasticity is

$$\epsilon = \frac{\Delta q/q}{\Delta p/p}.$$

Rearranging this definition we have the more common expression:

$$\epsilon = \frac{p}{q}\frac{\Delta q}{\Delta p}.$$

Hence elasticity can be expressed as the ratio of price to quantity multiplied by the slope of the demand function. In the Appendix to this chapter we describe elasticity in terms of the derivative of the demand function. If you know calculus, the derivative formulation is the most convenient way to think about elasticity.

The sign of the elasticity of demand is generally negative, since demand curves invariably have a negative slope. However, it is tedious to keep referring to an elasticity of *minus* something-or-other, so it is common in verbal discussion to refer to elasticities of 2 or 3, rather than -2 or -3. We will try to keep the signs straight in the text by referring to the absolute value of elasticity, but you should be aware that verbal treatments tend to drop the minus sign.

Another problem with negative numbers arises when we compare magnitudes. Is an elasticity of -3 greater or less than an elasticity of -2? From an algebraic point of view -3 is smaller than -2, but economists tend to say that the demand with the elasticity of -3 is "more elastic" than the one with -2. In this book we will make comparisons in terms of absolute value so as to avoid this kind of ambiguity.

EXAMPLE: The Elasticity of a Linear Demand Curve

Consider the linear demand curve, $q = a - bp$, depicted in Figure 15.4. The slope of this demand curve is a constant, $-b$. Plugging this into the formula for elasticity we have

$$\epsilon = \frac{-bp}{q} = \frac{-bp}{a - bp}.$$

When $p = 0$, the elasticity of demand is zero. When $q = 0$, the elasticity of demand is (negative) infinity. At what value of price is the elasticity of demand equal to -1?

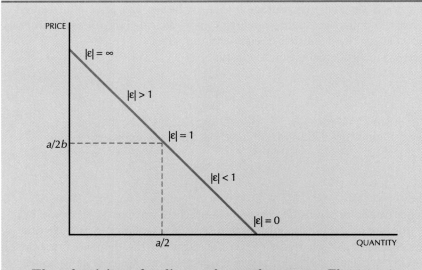

Figure
15.4
The elasticity of a linear demand curve. Elasticity is infinite at the vertical intercept, one halfway down the curve, and zero at the horizontal intercept.

To find such a price, we write down the equation

$$\frac{-bp}{a - bp} = -1$$

and solve it for p. This gives

$$p = \frac{a}{2b},$$

which, as we see in Figure 15.4, is just halfway down the demand curve.

15.6 Elasticity and Demand

If a good has an elasticity of demand greater than 1 in absolute value we say that it has an **elastic demand**. If the elasticity is less than 1 in absolute value we say that it has an **inelastic demand**. And if it has an elasticity of exactly -1, we say it has **unit elastic demand**.

An elastic demand curve is one for which the quantity demanded is very responsive to price: if you increase the price by 1 percent, the quantity demanded decreases by more than 1 percent. So think of elasticity as the responsiveness of the quantity demanded to price, and it will be easy to remember what elastic and inelastic mean.

In general the elasticity of demand for a good depends to a large extent on how many close substitutes it has. Take an extreme case—our old friend, the red pencils and blue pencils example. Suppose that everyone regards these goods as perfect substitutes. Then if some of each of them are bought, they must sell for the same price. Now think what would happen to the demand for red pencils if their price rose, and the price of blue pencils stayed constant. Clearly it would drop to zero—the demand for red pencils is very elastic since it has a perfect substitute.

If a good has many close substitutes, we would expect that its demand curve would be very responsive to its price changes. On the other hand, if there are few close substitutes for a good, it can exhibit a quite inelastic demand.

15.7 Elasticity and Revenue

Revenue is just the price of a good times the quantity sold of that good. If the price of a good increases, then the quantity sold decreases, so revenue may increase or decrease. Which way it goes obviously depends on how responsive demand is to the price change. If demand drops a lot when the price increases, then revenue will fall. If demand drops only a little when the price increases, then revenue will increase. This suggests that the direction of the change in revenue has something to do with the elasticity of demand.

Indeed, there is a very useful relationship between price elasticity and revenue change. The definition of revenue is

$$R = pq.$$

If we let the price change to $p + \Delta p$ and the quantity change to $q + \Delta q$, we have a new revenue of

$$R' = (p + \Delta p)(q + \Delta q)$$
$$= pq + q\Delta p + p\Delta q + \Delta p\Delta q.$$

Subtracting R from R' we have

$$\Delta R = q\Delta p + p\Delta q + \Delta p\Delta q.$$

For small values of Δp and Δq, the last term can safely be neglected, leaving us with an expression for the change in revenue of the form

$$\Delta R = q\Delta p + p\Delta q.$$

That is, the change in revenue is roughly equal to the quantity times the change in price plus the original price times the change in quantity. If we want an expression for the rate of change of revenue per change in price, we just divide this expression by Δp to get

$$\frac{\Delta R}{\Delta p} = q + p\frac{\Delta q}{\Delta p}.$$

This is treated geometrically in Figure 15.5. The revenue is just the area of the box: price times quantity. When the price increases, we add a rectangular area on the top of the box, which is approximately $q\Delta p$, but we subtract an area on the side of the box, which is approximately $p\Delta q$. For small changes, this is exactly the expression given above. (The leftover part, $\Delta p\Delta q$, is the little square in the corner of the box, which will be very small relative to the other magnitudes.)

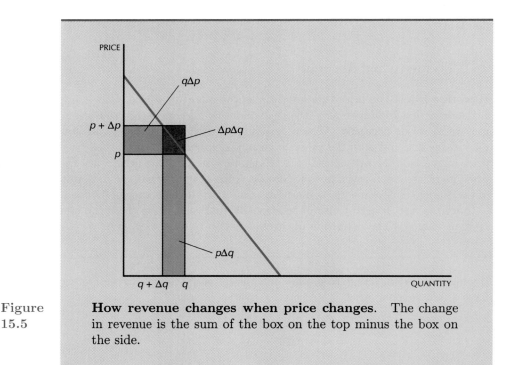

Figure 15.5

How revenue changes when price changes. The change in revenue is the sum of the box on the top minus the box on the side.

When will the net result of these two effects be positive? That is, when do we satisfy the following inequality:

$$\frac{\Delta R}{\Delta p} = p\frac{\Delta q}{\Delta p} + q(p) > 0?$$

Rearranging we have

$$\frac{p}{q}\frac{\Delta q}{\Delta p} > -1.$$

The left-hand side of this expression is $\epsilon(p)$, which is a negative number. Multiplying through by -1 reverses the direction of the inequality to give us:

$$|\epsilon(p)| < 1.$$

Thus revenue increases when price increases if the elasticity of demand is less than 1 in absolute value. Similarly, revenue decreases when price increases if the elasticity of demand is greater than 1 in absolute value.

Another way to see this is to write the revenue change as we did above:

$$\Delta R = p\Delta q + q\Delta p > 0$$

and rearrange this to get

$$-\frac{p}{q}\frac{\Delta q}{\Delta p} = |\epsilon(p)| < 1.$$

Yet a third way to see this is to take the formula for $\Delta R/\Delta p$ and rearrange it as follows:

$$\frac{\Delta R}{\Delta p} = q + p\frac{\Delta q}{\Delta p}$$

$$= q\left[1 + \frac{p}{q}\frac{\Delta q}{\Delta p}\right]$$

$$= q\left[1 + \epsilon(p)\right].$$

Since demand elasticity is naturally negative, we can also write this expression as

$$\frac{\Delta R}{\Delta p} = q\left[1 - |\epsilon(p)|\right].$$

In this formula it is easy to see how revenue responds to a change in price: if the absolute value of elasticity is greater than 1, then $\Delta R/\Delta p$ must be negative and vice versa.

The intuitive content of these mathematical facts is not hard to remember. If demand is very responsive to price—that is, it is very elastic—then an increase in price will reduce demand so much that revenue will fall. If demand is very unresponsive to price—it is very inelastic—then an increase in price will not change demand very much, and overall revenue will increase. The dividing line happens to be an elasticity of -1. At this point if the price increases by 1 percent, the quantity will decrease by 1 percent, so overall revenue doesn't change at all.

EXAMPLE: Strikes and Profits

In 1979 the United Farm Workers called for a strike against lettuce growers in California. The strike was highly effective: the production of lettuce was cut almost in half. But the reduction in the supply of lettuce inevitably caused an increase in the price of lettuce. In fact, during the strike the price of lettuce rose by nearly 400 percent. Since production halved and prices quadrupled, the net result of was almost a *doubling* producer profits![2]

One might well ask why the producers eventually settled the strike. The answer involves short-run and long-run supply responses. Most of the lettuce consumed in U.S. during the winter months is grown in the Imperial Valley. When the supply of this lettuce was drastically reduced in one season, there wasn't time to replace it with lettuce from elsewhere so the market price of lettuce skyrocketed. If the strike had held for several seasons, lettuce could be planted in other regions. This increase in supply from other sources would tend reduce the price of lettuce back to its normal level, thereby reducing the profits of the Imperial Valley growers.

15.8 Constant Elasticity Demands

What kind of demand curve gives us a constant elasticity of demand? In a linear demand curve the elasticity of demand goes from zero to infinity, which is not exactly what you would call constant, so that's not the answer.

We can use the revenue calculation described above to get an example. We know that if the elasticity is 1 at price p, then the revenue will not change when the price changes by a small amount. So if the revenue remains constant for all changes in price, we must have a demand curve that has an elasticity of -1 everywhere.

But this is easy. We just want price and quantity to be related by the formula

$$pq = \overline{R},$$

which means that

$$q = \frac{\overline{R}}{p}$$

is the formula for a demand function with constant elasticity of -1. The graph of the function $q = \overline{R}/p$ is given in Figure 15.6. Note that price times quantity is constant along the demand curve.

The general formula for a demand with a constant elasticity of ϵ turns out to be

$$q = Ap^{\epsilon},$$

where A is an arbitrary positive constant and ϵ, being an elasticity, will typically be negative. This formula will be useful in some examples later on.

A convenient way to express a constant elasticity demand curve is to take logarithms and write

$$\ln q = \ln A + \epsilon \ln p.$$

---

[2] See Colin Carter, et. al., "Agricultural Labor Strikes and Farmers' Incomes," *Economic Inquiry*, 25, 1987,121–133.

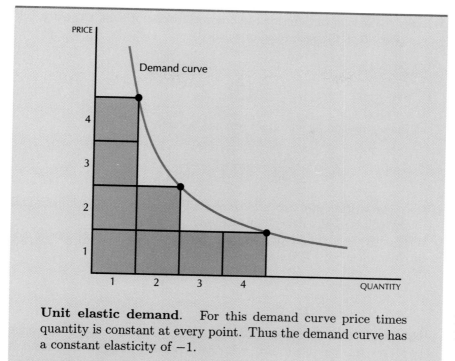

PRICE

4

3

2

1

Demand curve

1   2   3   4   QUANTITY

Unit elastic demand.   For this demand curve price times
quantity is constant at every point. Thus the demand curve has
a constant elasticity of -1.

Figure
15.6

In this expression, the logarithm of q depends in a linear way on the logarithm of p.

15.9 Elasticity and Marginal Revenue

In section 15.7 we examined how revenue changes when you change the
price of a good, but it is often of interest to consider how revenue changes
when you change the quantity of a good. This is especially useful when we
are considering production decisions by firms.

We saw earlier that for small changes in price and quantity, the change
in revenue is given by

$$\Delta R = p\Delta q + q\Delta p.$$

If we divide both sides of this expression by Δq, we get the expression for
marginal revenue:

$$\text{MR} = \frac{\Delta R}{\Delta q} = p + q\frac{\Delta p}{\Delta q}.$$

There is a useful way to rearrange this formula. Note that we can also
write this as

$$\frac{\Delta R}{\Delta q} = p\left[1 + \frac{q\Delta p}{p\Delta q}\right].$$

What is the second term inside the brackets? Nope, it's not elasticity, but you're close. It is the reciprocal of elasticity:

$$\frac{1}{\epsilon} = \frac{1}{\frac{p\Delta q}{q\Delta p}} = \frac{q\Delta p}{p\Delta q}.$$

Thus the expression for marginal revenue becomes

$$\frac{\Delta R}{\Delta q} = p(q)\left[1 + \frac{1}{\epsilon(q)}\right].$$

(Here we've written $p(q)$ and $\epsilon(q)$ to remind ourselves that both price and elasticity will typically depend on the level of output.)

When there is a danger of confusion due to the fact that elasticity is a negative number we will sometimes write this expression as

$$\frac{\Delta R}{\Delta q} = p(q)\left[1 - \frac{1}{|\epsilon(q)|}\right].$$

This means that if elasticity of demand is -1, then marginal revenue is zero—revenue doesn't change when you increase output. If demand is inelastic, then $|\epsilon|$ is less than 1, which means $1/|\epsilon|$ is greater than 1. Thus $1-1/|\epsilon|$ is negative, so that revenue will decrease when you increase output.

This is quite intuitive. If demand isn't very responsive to price, then you have to cut prices a lot to increase output: so revenue goes down. This is all completely consistent with the earlier discussion about how revenue changes as we change price, since an increase in quantity means a decrease in price and vice versa.

EXAMPLE: Setting a Price

Suppose that you were in charge of setting a price for some product that you were producing and that you had a good estimate of the demand curve for that product. Let us suppose that your goal is to set a price that maximizes profits—revenue minus costs. Then you would never want to set it where the elasticity of demand was less than 1—you would never want to set a price where demand was inelastic.

Why? Consider what would happen if you raised your price. Then your revenues would increase—since demand was inelastic—and the quantity you were selling would decrease. But if the quantity sold decreases, then your production costs must also decrease, or at least, they can't increase. So your overall profit must rise, which shows that operating at an inelastic part of the demand curve cannot yield maximal profits.

15.10 Marginal Revenue Curves

We saw in the last section that marginal revenue is given by

$$\frac{\Delta R}{\Delta q} = p(q) + \frac{\Delta p(q)}{\Delta q}q$$

or

$$\frac{\Delta R}{\Delta q} = p(q)\left[1 - \frac{1}{|\epsilon(q)|}\right].$$

We will find it useful to plot these marginal revenue curves. First, note that when quantity is zero, marginal revenue is just equal to the price. For the first unit of the good sold, the extra revenue you get is just the price. But after that, the marginal revenue will be less than the price, since $\Delta p/\Delta q$ is negative.

Think about it. If you decide to sell one more unit of output, you will have to decrease the price. But this reduction in price reduces the revenue you receive on all the units of output that you were selling already. Thus the extra revenue you receive will be less than the price that you get for selling the extra unit.

Let's consider the special case of the linear (inverse) demand curve:

$$p(q) = a - bq.$$

Here it is easy to see that the slope of the inverse demand curve is constant:

$$\frac{\Delta p}{\Delta q} = -b.$$

Thus the formula for marginal revenue becomes

$$\frac{\Delta R}{\Delta q} = p(q) + \frac{\Delta p(q)}{\Delta q}q$$
$$= p(q) - bq$$
$$= a - bq - bq$$
$$= a - 2bq.$$

This marginal revenue curve is depicted in Figure 15.7A. The marginal revenue curve has the same vertical intercept as the demand curve, but has twice the slope. Marginal revenue is negative when $q > a/2b$. The quantity $a/2b$ is the quantity at which the elasticity is equal to -1. At any larger

Figure
15.7

Marginal revenue. (A) Marginal revenue for a linear demand curve. (B) Marginal revenue for a constant elasticity demand curve.

quantity demand will be inelastic, which implies that marginal revenue is negative.

The constant elasticity demand curve provides another special case of the marginal revenue curve. (See Figure 15.7B.) If the elasticity of demand is constant at $\epsilon(q) = \epsilon$, then the marginal revenue curve will have the form

$$MR = p(q)\left[1 - \frac{1}{|\epsilon|}\right].$$

Since the term in brackets is constant, the marginal revenue curve is some constant fraction of the inverse demand curve. When $|\epsilon| = 1$, the marginal revenue curve is constant at zero. When $|\epsilon| > 1$, the marginal revenue curve lies below the inverse demand curve, as depicted. When $|\epsilon| < 1$, marginal revenue is negative.

15.11 Income Elasticity

Recall that the price elasticity of demand is defined as

$$\text{price elasticity of demand} = \frac{\%\ \text{change in quantity demanded}}{\%\ \text{change in price}}.$$

This gives us a unit-free measure of how the amount demanded responds to a change in price.

The **income elasticity of demand** is used to describe how the quantity demanded responds to a change in income; its definition is

$$\text{income elasticity of demand} = \frac{\%\ \text{change in quantity}}{\%\ \text{change in income}}.$$

Recall that a **normal good** is one for which an increase in income leads to an increase in demand; so for this sort of good the income elasticity of demand is positive. An **inferior good** is one for which an increase in income leads to a decrease in demand; for this sort of good, the income elasticity of demand is negative. Economists sometimes use the term **luxury goods**. These are goods that have an income elasticity of demand that is greater than 1: a 1 percent increase in income leads to *more* than a 1 percent increase in demand for a luxury good.

As a general rule of thumb, however, income elasticities tend to cluster around 1. We can see the reason for this by examining the budget constraint. Write the budget constraints for two different levels of income:

$$p_1 x_1' + p_2 x_2' = m'$$
$$p_1 x_1^0 + p_2 x_2^0 = m^0.$$

Subtract the second equation from the first and let Δ denote differences, as usual:

$$p_1\,\Delta x_1 + p_2\,\Delta x_2 = \Delta m.$$

Now multiply and divide price i by x_i/x_i and divide both sides by m:

$$\frac{p_1 x_1}{m}\frac{\Delta x_1}{x_1} + \frac{p_2 x_2}{m}\frac{\Delta x_2}{x_2} = \frac{\Delta m}{m}.$$

Finally, divide both sides by $\Delta m/m$, and use $s_i = p_i x_i/m$ to denote the **expenditure share** of good i. This gives us our final equation,

$$s_1\frac{\Delta x_1/x_1}{\Delta m/m} + s_2\frac{\Delta x_2/x_2}{\Delta m/m} = 1.$$

This equation says that the *weighted average of the income elasticities is 1*, where the weights are the expenditure shares. Luxury goods that have an income elasticity greater than 1 must be counterbalanced by goods that have an income elasticity less than 1, so that "on average" income elasticities are about 1.

Summary

1. The market demand curve is simply the sum of the individual demand curves.

2. The reservation price measures the price at which a consumer is just indifferent between purchasing or not purchasing a good.

3. The demand function measures quantity demanded as a function of price. The inverse demand function measures price as a function of quantity. A given demand curve can be described in either way.

4. The elasticity of demand measures the responsiveness of the quantity demanded to price. It is formally defined as the percent change in quantity divided by the percent change in price.

5. If the absolute value of the elasticity of demand is less than 1 at some point, we say that demand is *inelastic* at that point. If the absolute value of elasticity is greater than 1 at some point, we say demand is *elastic* at that point. If the absolute value of the elasticity of demand at some point is exactly 1, we say that the demand has *unitary* elasticity at that point.

6. If demand is inelastic at some point, then an increase in quantity will result in a reduction in revenue. If demand is elastic, then an increase in quantity will result in an increase in revenue.

7. The marginal revenue is the extra revenue one gets from increasing the quantity sold. The formula relating marginal revenue and elasticity is $\mathrm{MR} = p[1 + 1/\epsilon] = p[1 - 1/|\epsilon|]$.

8. If the inverse demand curve is a linear function $p(q) = a - bq$, then the marginal revenue is given by $\mathrm{MR} = a - 2bq$.

9. Income elasticity measures the responsiveness of the quantity demanded to income. It is formally defined as the percent change in quantity divided by the percent change in income.

REVIEW QUESTIONS

1. If the market demand curve is $D(p) = 100 - .5p$, what is the inverse demand curve?

2. An addict's demand function for a drug may be very inelastic, but the market demand function might be quite elastic. How can this be?

3. If $D(p) = 12 - 2p$, what price will maximize revenue?

4. Suppose that the demand curve for a good is given by $D(p) = 100/p$. What price will maximize revenue?

5. True or false? In a two good model if one good is an inferior good the other good must be a luxury good.

APPENDIX

In terms of derivatives the price elasticity of demand is defined by

$$\epsilon = \frac{p}{q}\frac{dq}{dp}.$$

In the text we claimed that the formula for a constant elasticity demand curve was $q = Ap^{\epsilon}$. To verify that this is correct, we can just differentiate it with respect to price:

$$\frac{dq}{dp} = \epsilon A p^{\epsilon - 1}$$

and multiply by price over quantity:

$$\frac{p}{q}\frac{dq}{dp} = \frac{p}{Ap^{\epsilon}}\epsilon A p^{\epsilon - 1} = \epsilon.$$

Everything conveniently cancels, leaving us with ϵ as required.

A linear demand curve has the formula $q(p) = a - bp$. The elasticity of demand at a point p is given by

$$\epsilon = \frac{p}{q}\frac{dq}{dp} = \frac{-bp}{a - bp}.$$

When p is zero, the elasticity is zero. When q is zero, the elasticity is infinite.

Revenue is given by $R(p) = pq(p)$. To see how revenue changes as p changes we differentiate revenue with respect to p to get

$$R'(p) = pq'(p) + q(p).$$

Suppose that revenue increases when p increases. Then we have

$$R'(p) = p\frac{dq}{dp} + q(p) > 0.$$

Rearranging, we have

$$\epsilon = \frac{p}{q}\frac{dq}{dp} > -1.$$

Recalling that dq/dp is negative and multiplying through by -1, we find

$$|\epsilon| < 1.$$

Hence if revenue increases when price increases, we must be at an inelastic part of the demand curve.

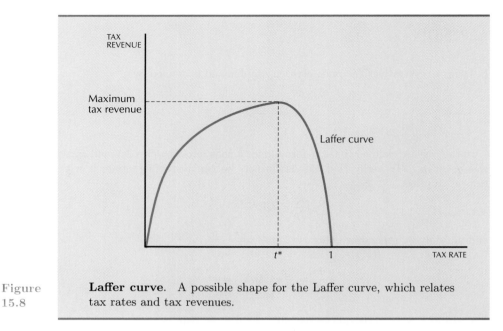

Figure
15.8
Laffer curve. A possible shape for the Laffer curve, which relates
tax rates and tax revenues.

EXAMPLE: The Laffer Curve

In this section we'll consider some simple elasticity calculations that can be used
to examine an issue of considerable policy interest, namely, how tax revenue
changes when the tax rate changes.

Suppose that we graph tax revenue versus the tax rate. If the tax rate is zero,
then tax revenues are zero; if the tax rate is 1, nobody will want to demand
or supply the good in question, so the tax revenue is also zero. Thus revenue
as a function of the tax rate must first increase and eventually decrease. (Of
course, it can go up and down several times between zero and 1, but we'll ignore
this possibility to keep things simple.) The curve that relates tax rates and tax
revenues is known as the **Laffer curve**, depicted in Figure 15.8.

The interesting feature of the Laffer curve is that it suggests that when the tax
rate is high enough, an increase in the tax rate will end up *reducing* the revenues
collected. The reduction in the supply of the good due to the increase in the tax
rate can be so large that tax revenue actually decreases. This is called the Laffer
effect, after the economist who popularized this diagram in the early eighties. It
has been said that the virtue of the Laffer curve is that you can explain it to a
congressman in half an hour and he can talk about it for six months. Indeed,
the Laffer curve figured prominently in the debate over the effect of the 1980 tax
cuts. The catch in the above argument is the phrase "high enough." Just how
high does the tax rate have to be for the Laffer effect to work?

To answer this question let's consider the following simple model of the labor
market. Suppose that firms will demand zero labor if the wage is greater than
$\overline{w}$ and an arbitrarily large amount of labor if the wage is exactly $\overline{w}$. This means
that the demand curve for labor is flat at some wage $\overline{w}$. Suppose that the supply

curve of labor, $S(p)$, has a conventional upward slope. The equilibrium in the labor market is depicted in Figure 15.9.

Labor market. Equilibrium in the labor market with a horizontal demand curve for labor. When labor income is taxed, less will be supplied at each wage rate.

Figure 15.9

If we put a tax on labor at the rate t, then if the firm pays $\overline{w}$, the worker only gets $w = (1 - t)\overline{w}$. Thus the supply curve of labor tilts to the left, and the amount of labor sold drops, as in Figure 15.9. The after-tax wage has gone down and this has discouraged the sale of labor. So far so good.

Tax revenue, T, is therefore given by the formula

$$T = t\overline{w}S(w),$$

where $w = (1 - t)\overline{w}$ and $S(w)$ is the supply of labor.

In order to see how tax revenue changes as we change the tax rate we differentiate this formula with respect to t to find

$$\frac{dT}{dt} = \left[-t\frac{dS(w)}{dw}\overline{w} + S(w) \right] \overline{w}. \tag{15.1}$$

(Note the use of the chain rule and the fact that $dw/dt = -\overline{w}$.)

The Laffer effect occurs when revenues decline when t increases—that is, when this expression is negative. Now this clearly means that the supply of labor is going to have to be quite elastic—it has to drop a lot when the tax increases. So let's try to see what values of elasticity will make this expression negative.

In order for equation (15.1) to be negative, we must have

$$-t\frac{dS(w)}{dw}\overline{w} + S(w) < 0.$$

Transposing yields

$$t\frac{dS(w)}{dw}\overline{w} > S(w),$$

and dividing both sides by $tS(w)$ gives

$$\frac{dS(w)}{dw}\frac{\overline{w}}{S(w)} > \frac{1}{t}.$$

Multiplying both sides by $(1-t)$ and using the fact that $w = (1-t)\overline{w}$ gives us

$$\frac{dS}{dw}\frac{w}{S} > \frac{1-t}{t}.$$

The left-hand side of this expression is the elasticity of labor supply. We have shown that the Laffer effect can only occur if the elasticity of labor supply is greater than $(1-t)/t$.

Let us take an extreme case and suppose that the tax rate on labor income is 50 percent. Then the Laffer effect can occur only when the elasticity of labor supply is greater than 1. This means that a 1 percent reduction in the wage would lead to more than a 1 percent reduction in the labor supply. This is a very large response.

Econometricians have often estimated labor-supply elasticities, and about the largest value anyone has ever found has been around 0.2. So the Laffer effect seems pretty unlikely for the kinds of tax rates that we have in the United States. However, in other countries, such as Sweden, tax rates go much higher, and there is some evidence that the Laffer phenomenon may have occurred.[3]

EXAMPLE: Another Expression for Elasticity

Here is another expression for elasticity that is sometimes useful. It turns out that elasticity can also be expressed as

$$\frac{d\ln Q}{d\ln P}.$$

The proof involves repeated application of the chain rule. We start by noting that

$$\frac{d\ln Q}{d\ln P} = \frac{d\ln Q}{dQ}\frac{dQ}{d\ln P}$$

$$= \frac{1}{Q}\frac{dQ}{d\ln P}. \tag{15.2}$$

---

[3] See Charles E. Stuart, "Swedish Tax Rates, Labor Supply, and Tax Revenues," *Journal of Political Economy*, 89, 5 (October 1981), 1020–38.

We also note that

$$\frac{dQ}{dP} = \frac{dQ}{d\ln P}\frac{d\ln P}{dP}$$
$$= \frac{dQ}{d\ln P}\frac{1}{P},$$

which implies that

$$\frac{dQ}{d\ln P} = P\frac{dQ}{dP}.$$

Substituting this into equation (15.2), we have

$$\frac{d\ln Q}{d\ln P} = \frac{1}{Q}\frac{dQ}{dP}P = \epsilon,$$

which is what we wanted to establish.

Thus elasticity measures the slope of the demand curve plotted on log-log paper: how the log of the quantity changes as the log of the price changes.

CHAPTER **16**

EQUILIBRIUM

In preceding chapters we have seen how to construct individual demand curves by using information about preferences and prices. In Chapter 15 we added up these individual demand curves to construct market demand curves. In this chapter we will describe how to use these market demand curves to determine the equilibrium market price.

In Chapter 1 we said that there were two fundamental principles of micro-economic analysis. These were the optimization principle and the equilib-rium principle. Up until now we have been studying examples of the opti-mization principle: what follows from the assumption that people choose their consumption optimally from their budget sets. In later chapters we will continue to use optimization analysis to study the profit-maximization behavior of firms. Finally, we combine the behavior of consumers and firms to study the equilibrium outcomes of their interaction in the market.

But before undertaking that study in detail it seems worthwhile at this point to give some examples of equilibrium analysis—how the prices adjust so as to make the demand and supply decisions of economic agents com-patible. In order to do so, we will have to briefly consider the other side of the market—the supply side.

16.1 Supply

We have already seen a few examples of supply curves. In Chapter 1 we looked at a vertical supply curve for apartments. In Chapter 9 we considered situations where consumers would choose to be net suppliers or demanders of goods that they owned, and we analyzed labor-supply decisions.

In all of these cases the supply curve simply measured how much the consumer was willing to supply of a good at each possible market price. Indeed, this is the definition of the supply curve: for each p, we determine how much of the good will be supplied, $S(p)$. In the next few chapters we will discuss the supply behavior of firms. However, for many purposes, it is not really necessary to know where the supply curve or the demand curve comes from in terms of the optimizing behavior that generates the curves. For many problems the fact that there is a functional relationship between the price and the quantity that consumers want to demand or supply at that price is enough to highlight important insights.

16.2 Market Equilibrium

Suppose that we have a number of consumers of a good. Given their individual demand curves we can add them up to get a market demand curve. Similarly, if we have a number of independent suppliers of this good, we can add up their individual supply curves to get the **market supply curve**.

The individual demanders and suppliers are assumed to take prices as given—outside of their control—and simply determine their best response given those market prices. A market where each economic agent takes the market price as outside of his or her control is called a **competitive market.**

The usual justification for the competitive-market assumption is that each consumer or producer is a small part of the market as a whole and thus has a negligible effect on the market price. For example, each supplier of wheat takes the market price to be more or less independent of his actions when he determines how much wheat he wants to produce and supply to the market.

Although the market price may be independent of any *one* agent's actions in a competitive market, it is the actions of all the agents together that determine the market price. The **equilibrium price** of a good is that price where the supply of the good equals the demand. Geometrically, this is the price where the demand and the supply curves cross.

If we let $D(p)$ be the market demand curve and $S(p)$ the market supply curve, the equilibrium price is the price p^* that solves the equation

$$D(p^*) = S(p^*).$$

The solution to this equation, p^*, is the price where market demand equals market supply.

Why should this be an equilibrium price? An economic equilibrium is a situation where all agents are choosing the best possible action for themselves and each person's behavior is consistent with that of the others. At any price other than an equilibrium price, some agents' behaviors would be infeasible, and there would therefore be a reason for their behavior to change. Thus a price that is not an equilibrium price cannot be expected to persist since at least some agents would have an incentive to change their behavior.

The demand and supply curves represent the optimal choices of the agents involved, and the fact that they are equal at some price p^* indicates that the behaviors of the demanders and suppliers are compatible. At any price *other* than the price where demand equals supply these two conditions will *not* be met.

For example, suppose that we consider some price $p' < p^*$ where demand is greater than supply. Then some suppliers will realize that they can sell their goods at more than the going price p' to the disappointed demanders. As more and more suppliers realize this, the market price will be pushed up to the point where demand and supply are equal.

Similarly if $p' > p^*$, so that demand is less than supply, then some suppliers will not be able to sell the amount that they expected to sell. The only way in which they will be able to sell more output will be to offer it at a lower price. But if all suppliers are selling the identical goods, and if some supplier offers to sell at a lower price, the other suppliers must match that price. Thus excess supply exerts a downward pressure on the market price. Only when the amount that people want to buy at a given price equals the amount that people want to sell at that price will the market be in equilibrium.

16.3 Two Special Cases

There are two special cases of market equilibrium that are worth mentioning since they come up fairly often. The first is the case of fixed supply. Here the amount supplied is some given number and is independent of price; that is, the supply curve is vertical. In this case the equilibrium *quantity* is determined entirely by the supply conditions and the equilibrium *price* is determined entirely by demand conditions.

The opposite case is the case where the supply curve is completely horizontal. If an industry has a perfectly horizontal supply curve, it means that the industry will supply any amount of a good at a constant price. In this situation the equilibrium *price* is determined by the supply conditions, while the equilibrium *quantity* is determined by the demand curve.

The two cases are depicted in Figure 16.1. In these two special cases the determination of price and quantity can be separated; but in the general case the equilibrium price and the equilibrium quantity are jointly determined by the demand and supply curves.

Special cases of equilibrium. Case A shows a vertical supply curve where the equilibrium price is determined solely by the demand curve. Case B depicts a horizontal supply curve where the equilibrium price is determined solely by the supply curve.

Figure
16.1

16.4 Inverse Demand and Supply Curves

We can look at market equilibrium in a slightly different way that is often useful. As indicated earlier, individual demand curves are normally viewed as giving the optimal quantities demanded as a function of the price charged. But we can also view them as inverse demand functions that measure the *price* that someone is willing to pay in order to acquire some given amount of a good. The same thing holds for supply curves. They can be viewed as measuring the quantity supplied as a function of the price. But we can also view them as measuring the *price* that must prevail in order to generate a given amount of supply.

These same constructions can be used with *market* demand and *market* supply curves, and the interpretations are just those given above. In this framework an equilibrium price is determined by finding that quantity at which the amount the demanders are willing to pay to consume that quantity is the same as the price that suppliers must receive in order to supply that quantity.

Thus, if we let $P_S(q)$ be the inverse supply function and $P_D(q)$ be the inverse demand function, equilibrium is determined by the condition

$$P_S(q^*) = P_D(q^*).$$

EXAMPLE: Equilibrium with Linear Curves

Suppose that both the demand and the supply curves are linear:

$$D(p) = a - bp$$

$$S(p) = c + dp.$$

The coefficients (a, b, c, d) are the parameters that determine the intercepts and slopes of these linear curves. The equilibrium price can be found by solving the following equation:

$$D(p) = a - bp = c + dp = S(p).$$

The answer is

$$p^* = \frac{a - c}{d + b}.$$

The equilibrium quantity demanded (and supplied) is

$$D(p^*) = a - bp^*$$
$$= a - b\frac{a - c}{b + d}$$
$$= \frac{ad + bc}{b + d}.$$

We can also solve this problem by using the inverse demand and supply curves. First we need to find the inverse demand curve. At what price is some quantity q demanded? Simply substitute q for $D(p)$ and solve for p. We have

$$q = a - bp,$$

so

$$P_D(q) = \frac{a - q}{b}.$$

In the same manner we find

$$P_S(q) = \frac{q - c}{d}.$$

Setting the demand price equal to the supply price and solving for the equilibrium quantity we have

$$P_D(q) = \frac{a - q}{b} = \frac{q - c}{d} = P_S(q)$$

$$q^* = \frac{ad + bc}{b + d}.$$

Note that this gives the same answer as in the original problem for both the equilibrium price and the equilibrium quantity.

16.5 Comparative Statics

After we have found an equilibrium by using the demand equals supply condition (or the demand price equals the supply price condition), we can see how it will change as the demand and supply curves change. For example, it is easy to see that if the demand curve shifts to the right in a parallel way—some fixed amount more is demanded at every price—the equilibrium price and quantity must both rise. On the other hand, if the supply curve shifts to the right, the equilibrium quantity rises, but the equilibrium price must fall.

What if both curves shift to the right? Then the quantity will definitely increase while the change in price is ambiguous—it could increase or it could decrease.

EXAMPLE: Shifting Both Curves

Question: Consider the competitive market for apartments described in Chapter 1. Let the equilibrium price in that market be p^* and the equilibrium quantity be q^*. Suppose that a developer converts m of the apartments to condominiums, which are bought by the people who are currently living in the apartments. What happens to the equilibrium price?

Answer: The situation is depicted in Figure 16.2. The demand and supply curves both shift to the left by the *same* amount. Hence the price is unchanged and the quantity sold simply drops by m.

Algebraically the new equilibrium price is determined by

$$D(p) - m = S(p) - m,$$

which clearly has the same solution as the original demand equals supply condition.

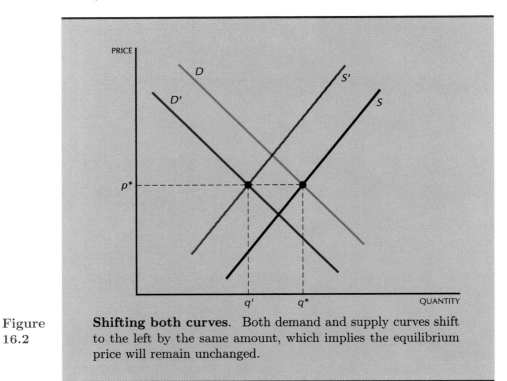

Figure
16.2

Shifting both curves. Both demand and supply curves shift to the left by the same amount, which implies the equilibrium price will remain unchanged.

16.6 Taxes

Describing a market before and after taxes are imposed presents a very nice exercise in comparative statics, as well as being of considerable interest in the conduct of economic policy. Let us see how it is done.

The fundamental thing to understand about taxes is that when a tax is present in a market, there are *two* prices of interest: the price the demander pays and the price the supplier gets. These two prices—the demand price and the supply price—differ by the amount of the tax.

There are several different kinds of taxes that one might impose. Two examples we will consider here are **quantity taxes** and **value** taxes (also called **ad valorem** taxes).

A quantity tax is a tax levied per unit of quantity bought or sold. Gasoline taxes are a good example of this. The gasoline tax is roughly 12 cents a gallon. If the demander is paying $P_D = \$1.50$ per gallon of gasoline, the supplier is getting $P_S = \$1.50 - .12 = \$1.38$ per gallon. In general, if t is the amount of the quantity tax per unit sold, then

$$P_D = P_S + t.$$

A value tax is a tax expressed in percentage units. State sales taxes are the most common example of value taxes. If your state has a 5 percent sales tax, then when you pay $1.05 for something (including the tax), the supplier gets $1.00. In general, if the tax rate is given by τ, then

$$P_D = (1 + \tau)P_S.$$

Let us consider what happens in a market when a quantity tax is imposed. For our first case we suppose that the supplier is required to pay the tax, as in the case of the gasoline tax. Then the amount supplied will depend on the supply price—the amount the supplier actually gets after paying the tax—and the amount demanded will depend on the demand price—the amount that the demander pays. The amount that the supplier gets will be the amount the demander pays minus the amount of the tax. This gives us two equations:

$$D(P_D) = S(P_S)$$

$$P_S = P_D - t.$$

Substituting the second equation into the first, we have the equilibrium condition:

$$D(P_D) = S(P_D - t).$$

Alternatively we could also rearrange the second equation to get $P_D = P_S + t$ and then substitute to find

$$D(P_S + t) = S(P_S).$$

Either way is equally valid; which one you use will depends on convenience in a particular case.

Now suppose that instead of the supplier paying the tax, the demander has to pay the tax. Then we write

$$P_D - t = P_S,$$

which says that the amount paid by the demander minus the tax equals the price received by the supplier. Substituting this into the demand equals supply condition we find

$$D(P_D) = S(P_D - t).$$

Note that this is the same equation as in the case where the supplier pays the tax. As far as the equilibrium price facing the demanders and the suppliers is concerned, it really doesn't matter who is responsible for paying the tax—it just matters that the tax must be paid by someone.

This really isn't so mysterious. Think of the gasoline tax. There the tax is included in the posted price. But if the price were instead listed as the before-tax price and the gasoline tax were added on as a separate item to be paid by the demanders, then do you think that the amount of gasoline demanded would change? After all, the final price to the consumers would be the same whichever way the tax was charged. Insofar as the consumers can recognize the net cost to them of goods they purchase, it really doesn't matter which way the tax is levied.

There is an even simpler way to show this using the inverse demand and supply functions. The equilibrium quantity traded is that quantity q^* such that the demand price at q^* *minus the tax being paid* is just equal to the supply price at q^*. In symbols:

$$P_D(q^*) - t = P_S(q^*).$$

If the tax is being imposed on the suppliers, then the condition is that the supply price *plus the amount of the tax* must equal the demand price:

$$P_D(q^*) = P_S(q^*) + t.$$

But these are the same equations, so the same equilibrium prices and quantities must result.

Finally, we consider the geometry of the situation. This is most easily seen by using the inverse demand and supply curves discussed above. We want to find the quantity where the curve $P_D(q) - t$ crosses the curve $P_S(q)$. In order to locate this point we simply shift the demand curve down by t and see where this shifted demand curve intersects the original supply curve. Alternatively we can find the quantity where $P_D(q)$ equals $P_S(q) + t$. To do this, we simply shift the supply curve up by the amount of the tax. Either way gives us the correct answer for the equilibrium quantity. The picture is given in Figure 16.3.

From this diagram we can easily see the qualitative effects of the tax. The quantity sold must decrease, the price paid by the demanders must go up, and the price received by the suppliers must go down.

Figure 16.4 depicts another way to determine the impact of a tax. Think about the definition of equilibrium in this market. We want to find a quantity q^* such that when the supplier faces the price p_s and the demander faces the price $p_d = p_s + t$, the quantity q^* is demanded by the demander and supplied by the supplier. Let us represent the tax t by a vertical line segment and slide it along the supply curve until it just touches the demand curve. That point is our equilibrium quantity!

EXAMPLE: Taxation with Linear Demand and Supply

Suppose that the demand and supply curves are both linear. Then if we impose a tax in this market, the equilibrium is determined by the equations

$$a - b p_D = c + d p_S$$

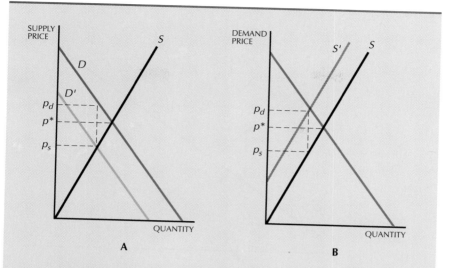

The imposition of a tax.   In order to study the impact of
a tax, we can either shift the demand curve down, as in panel
A, or shift the supply curve up, as in panel B. The equilibrium
prices paid by the demanders and received by the suppliers will
be the same either way.

Figure
16.3

and

$$p_D = p_S + t.$$

Substituting from the second equation into the first, we have

$$a - b(p_S + t) = c + dp_S.$$

Solving for the equilibrium supply price, p_S^*, gives

$$p_S^* = \frac{a - c - bt}{d + b}.$$

The equilibrium demand price, p_D^*, is then given by $p_S^* + t$:

$$p_D^* = \frac{a - c - bt}{d + b} + t$$

$$= \frac{a - c + dt}{d + b}.$$

Note that the price paid by the demander increases and the price received
by the supplier decreases. The amount of the price change depends on the
slope of the demand and supply curves.

Figure
16.4

Another way to determine the impact of a tax. Slide
the line segment along the supply curve until it hits the demand
curve.

16.7 Passing Along a Tax

One often hears about how a tax on producers doesn't hurt profits, since
firms can simply pass along a tax to consumers. As we've seen above, a tax
really shouldn't be regarded as a tax on firms or on consumers. Rather,
taxes are on transactions *between* firms and consumers. In general, a tax
will both raise the price paid by consumers and lower the price received by
firms. How much of a tax gets passed along will therefore depend on the
characteristics of demand and supply.

  This is easiest to see in the extreme cases: when we have a perfectly
horizontal supply curve or a perfectly vertical supply curve. These are also
known as the case of **perfectly elastic** and **perfectly inelastic** supply.

  We've already encountered these two special cases earlier in this chapter.
If an industry has a horizontal supply curve, it means that the industry will
supply any amount desired of the good at some given price, and zero units
of the good at any lower price. In this case the price is entirely determined
by the supply curve and the quantity sold is determined by demand. If
an industry has a vertical supply curve, it means that the quantity of the
good is fixed. The equilibrium price of the good is determined entirely by
demand.

  Let's consider the imposition of a tax in a market with a perfectly elastic
supply curve. As we've seen above, imposing a tax is just like shifting the

Special cases of taxation.   (A) In the case of a perfectly
elastic supply curve the tax gets completely passed along to the
consumers. (B) In the case of a perfectly inelastic supply none
of the tax gets passed along.

Figure
16.5

supply curve up by the amount of the tax, as illustrated in Figure 16.5A.

In the case of a perfectly elastic supply curve it is easy to see that the
price to the consumers goes up by exactly the amount of the tax. The
supply price is exactly the same as it was before the tax, and the demanders
end up paying the entire tax. When you think about the meaning of the
horizontal supply curve, this is not hard to understand. The horizontal
supply curve means that the industry is willing to supply any amount of
the good at some particular price, p^*, and zero amount at any lower price.
Thus, if any amount of the good is going to be sold at all in equilibrium,
the suppliers must receive p^* for selling it. This effectively determines the
equilibrium supply price, and the demand price is $p^* + t$.

The opposite case is illustrated in Figure 16.5B. If the supply curve is
vertical and we "shift the supply curve up," we don't change anything in
the diagram. The supply curve just slides along itself, and we still have
the same amount of the good supplied, with or without the tax. In this
case, the demanders determine the equilibrium price of the good, and they
are willing to pay a certain amount, p^*, for the supply of the good that is
available, tax or no tax. Thus they end up paying p^*, and the suppliers
end up receiving $p^* - t$. The entire amount of the tax is paid by the
suppliers.

This case often strikes people as paradoxical, but it really isn't. If the
suppliers could raise their prices after the tax is imposed and still sell their
entire fixed supply, they would have raised their prices before the tax was
imposed and made more money! If the demand curve doesn't move, then

the only way the price can increase is if the supply is reduced. If a policy doesn't change either supply or demand, it certainly can't affect price.

Now that we understand the special cases, we can examine the in-between case where the supply curve has an upward slope but is not perfectly vertical. In this situation, the amount of the tax that gets passed along will depend on the steepness of the supply curve relative to the demand curve. If the supply curve is nearly horizontal, nearly all of the tax gets passed along to the consumers, while if the supply curve is nearly vertical, almost none of the tax gets passed along. See Figure 16.6 for some examples.

Passing along a tax. (A) If the supply curve is nearly horizontal, much of the tax can be passed along. (B) If it is nearly vertical, very little of the tax can be passed along.

16.8 The Deadweight Loss of a Tax

We've seen that taxing a good will typically increase the price paid by the demanders and decrease the price received by the suppliers. This certainly represents a cost to the demanders and suppliers, but from the economist's viewpoint, the real cost of the tax is that the output has been reduced.

The lost output is the social cost of the tax. Let us explore the social cost of a tax using the consumers' and producers' surplus tools developed in Chapter 14. We start with the diagram given in Figure 16.7. This depicts the equilibrium demand price and supply price after a tax, t, has been imposed.

Output has been decreased by this tax, and we can use the tools of consumers' and producers' surplus to value the social loss. The loss in consumers' surplus is given by the areas $A + B$, and the loss in producers' surplus is given in areas $C + D$. These are the same kind of losses that we examined in Chapter 14.

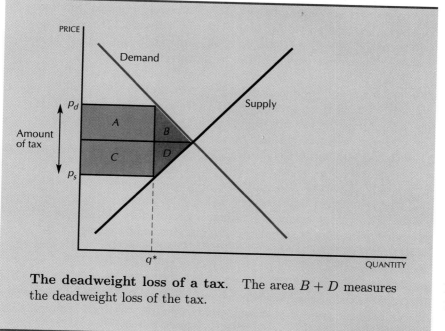

The deadweight loss of a tax.   The area $B + D$ measures the deadweight loss of the tax.

Figure 16.7

Since we're after an expression for the social cost of the tax, it seems sensible to add the areas $A + B$ and $C + D$ to each other to get the total loss to the consumers and to the producers of the good in question. However, we've still left out one party—namely, the government.

The government *gains* revenue from the tax. And, of course, the consumers who benefit from the government services provided with these tax revenues also gain from the tax. We can't really say how much they gain until we know what the tax revenues will be spent on.

Let us make the assumption that the tax revenues will just be handed back to the consumers and the producers, or equivalently that the services provided by the government revenues will be just equal in value to the revenues spent on them.

Then the net benefit to the government is the area $A + C$—the total revenue from the tax. Since the loss of producers' and consumers' surpluses are net costs, and the tax revenue to the government is a net benefit, the total net cost of the tax is the algebraic sum of these areas: the loss in consumers' surplus, $-(A + B)$, the loss in producers' surplus, $-(C + D)$, and the gain in government revenue, $+(A + C)$.

The net result is the area $-(B + D)$. This area is known as the **deadweight loss** of the tax or the **excess burden** of the tax. This latter phrase is especially descriptive.

Recall the interpretation of the loss of consumers' surplus. It is how much the consumers would pay to avoid the tax. In terms of this diagram the consumers are willing to pay $A + B$ to avoid the tax. Similarly, the producers are willing to pay $C + D$ to avoid the tax. Together they are willing to pay $A + B + C + D$ to avoid a tax that raises $A + C$ dollars of revenue. The *excess burden* of the tax is therefore $B + D$.

What is the source of this excess burden? Basically it is the lost value to the consumers and producers due to the reduction in the sales of the good. You can't tax what isn't there.[1] So the government doesn't get any revenue on the reduction in sales of the good. From the viewpoint of society, it is a pure loss—a deadweight loss.

We could also derive the deadweight loss directly from its definition, by just measuring the social value of the lost output. Suppose that we start at the old equilibrium and start moving to the left. The first unit lost was one where the price that someone was willing to pay for it was just equal to the price that someone was willing to sell it for. Here there is hardly any social loss since this unit was the marginal unit that was sold.

Now move a little farther to the left. The demand price measures how much someone was willing to pay to receive the good, and the supply price measures the price at which someone was willing to supply the good. The difference is the lost value on that unit of the good. If we add this up over the units of the good that are not produced and consumed because of the presence of the tax, we get the deadweight loss.

EXAMPLE: The Market for Loans

The amount of borrowing or lending in an economy is influenced to a large degree by the interest rate charged. The interest rate serves as a price in the market for loans.

We can let $D(r)$ be the demand for loans by borrowers and $S(r)$ be the supply of loans by lenders. The equilibrium interest rate, r^*, is then determined by the condition that demand equal supply:

$$D(r^*) = S(r^*). \tag{16.1}$$

Suppose we consider adding taxes to this model. What will happen to the equilibrium interest rate?

---

[1] At least the government hasn't figured out how to do this yet. But they're working on it.

In the U.S. economy individuals have to pay income tax on the interest they earn from lending money. If everyone is in the same tax bracket, t, the after-tax interest rate facing lenders will be $(1 - t)r$. Thus the supply of loans, which depends on the after-tax interest rate, will be $S((1 - t)r)$.

On the other hand, the Internal Revenue Service code allows many borrowers to deduct their interest charges, so if the borrowers are in the same tax bracket as the lenders, the after-tax interest rate they pay will be $(1 - t)r$. Hence the demand for loans will be $D((1 - t)r)$. The equation for interest rate determination with taxes present is then

$$D((1 - t)r') = S((1 - t)r'). \tag{16.2}$$

Now observe that if r^* solves equation (16.1), then $r^* = (1 - t)r'$ must solve equation (16.2) so that

$$r^* = (1 - t)r',$$

or

$$r' = \frac{r^*}{(1 - t)}.$$

Thus the interest rate in the presence of the tax will be higher by $1/(1-t)$. The *after-tax* interest rate $(1 - t)r'$ will be r^*, just as it was before the tax was imposed!

Figure 16.8 may make things clearer. Making interest income taxable will tilt the supply curve for loans up by a factor of $1/(1 - t)$; but making interest payments tax deductible will also tilt the demand curve for loans up by $1/(1 - t)$. The net result is that the market interest rate rises by precisely $1/(1 - t)$.

Inverse demand and supply functions provide another way to look at this problem. Let $r_b(q)$ be the inverse demand function for borrowers. This tells us what the after-tax interest rate would have to be to induce people to borrow q. Similarly, let $r_l(q)$ be the inverse supply function for lenders. The equilibrium amount lent will then be determined by the condition

$$r_b(q^*) = r_l(q^*). \tag{16.3}$$

Now introduce taxes into the situation. To make things more interesting, we'll allow borrowers and lenders to be in different tax brackets, denoted by t_b and t_l. If the market interest rate is r, then the after-tax rate facing borrowers will be $(1 - t_b)r$, and the quantity they choose to borrow will be determined by the equation

$$(1 - t_b)r = r_b(q)$$

or

$$r = \frac{r_b(q)}{1 - t_b}. \tag{16.4}$$

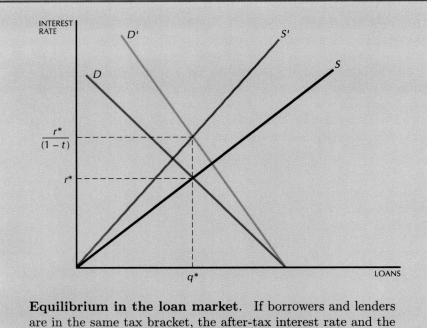

Figure
16.8 **Equilibrium in the loan market.** If borrowers and lenders
are in the same tax bracket, the after-tax interest rate and the
amount borrowed are unchanged.

Similarly, the after-tax rate facing lenders will be $(1-t_l)r$, and the amount
they choose to lend will be determined by the equation

$$(1 - t_l)r = r_l(q)$$

or

$$r = \frac{r_l(q)}{1 - t_l}. \tag{16.5}$$

Combining equations (16.4) and (16.5) gives the equilibrium condition:

$$r = \frac{r_b(\hat{q})}{1 - t_b} = \frac{r_l(\hat{q})}{1 - t_l}. \tag{16.6}$$

From this equation it is easy to see that if borrowers and lenders are in the
same tax bracket, so that $t_b = t_l$, then $\hat{q} = q^*$. What if they are in different
tax brackets? It is not hard to see that the tax law is subsidizing borrowers
and taxing lenders, but what is the net effect? If the borrowers face a
higher price than the lenders, then the system is a net tax on borrowing,
but if the borrowers face a lower price than the lenders, then it is a net
subsidy. Rewriting the equilibrium condition, equation (16.6), we have

$$r_b(\hat{q}) = \frac{1 - t_b}{1 - t_l} r_l(\hat{q}).$$

Thus borrowers will face a higher price than lenders if

$$\frac{1 - t_b}{1 - t_l} > 1,$$

which means that $t_l > t_b$. So if the tax bracket of lenders is greater than the tax bracket of borrowers, the system is a net tax on borrowing, but if $t_l < t_b$, it is a net subsidy.

EXAMPLE: Food Subsidies

In years when there were bad harvests in nineteenth-century England the rich would provide charitable assistance to the poor by buying up the harvest, consuming a fixed amount of the grain, and selling the remainder to the poor at half the price they paid for it. At first thought this seems like it would provide significant benefits to the poor, but on second thought, doubts begin to arise.

The only way that the poor can be made better off is if they end up consuming more grain. But there is a fixed amount of grain available after the harvest. So how can the poor be better off because of this policy?

As a matter of fact they are not; the poor end up paying exactly the same price for the grain with or without the policy. To see why, we will model the equilibrium with and without this program. Let $D(p)$ be the demand curve for the poor, K the amount demanded by the rich, and S the fixed amount supplied in a year with a bad harvest. By assumption the supply of grain and the demand by the rich are fixed. Without the charity provided by the rich, the equilibrium price is determined by total demand equals total supply:

$$D(p^*) + K = S.$$

With the program in place, the equilibrium price is determined by

$$D(\hat{p}/2) + K = S.$$

But now observe: if p^* solves the first equation, then $\hat{p} = 2p^*$ solves the second equation. So when the rich offer to buy the grain and distribute it to the poor, the market price is simply bid up to twice the original price—and the poor pay the same price they did before!

When you think about it this isn't too surprising. If the demand of the rich is fixed and the supply of grain is fixed, then the amount that the poor can consume is fixed. Thus the equilibrium price facing the poor is determined entirely by their own demand curve; the equilibrium price will be the same, regardless of how the grain is provided to the poor.

16.9 Pareto Efficiency

An economic situation is **Pareto efficient** if there is no way to make
any person better off without hurting anybody else. Pareto efficiency is a
desirable thing—if there is some way to make some group of people better
off, why not do it?—but efficiency is not the only goal of economic policy.
For example, efficiency has almost nothing to say about income distribution
or economic justice.

However, efficiency is an important goal, and it is worth asking how well
a competitive market does in achieving Pareto efficiency. A competitive
market, or any economic mechanism, has to determine two things. First,
how much is produced, and second, who gets it. A competitive market
determines how much is produced based on how much people are willing to
pay to purchase the good as compared to how much people must be paid
to supply the good.

Consider Figure 16.9. At any amount of output less than the competitive
amount q^*, there is someone who is willing to supply an extra unit of the
good at a price that is less than the price that someone is willing to pay
for an extra unit of the good.

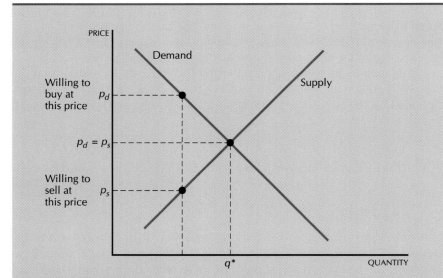

Figure
16.9

Pareto efficiency. The competitive market determines a
Pareto efficient amount of output because at q^* the price that
someone is willing to pay to buy an extra unit of the good is
equal to the price that someone must be paid to sell an extra
unit of the good.

If the good were produced and exchanged between these two people at any price between the demand price and the supply price, they would both be made better off. Thus any amount less than the equilibrium amount cannot be Pareto efficient, since there will be at least two people who could be made better off.

Similarly, at any output larger than q^*, the amount someone would be willing to pay for an extra unit of the good is less than the price that it would take to get it supplied. Only at the market equilibrium q^* would we have a Pareto efficient amount of output supplied—an amount such that the willingness to pay for an extra unit is just equal to the willingness to be paid to supply an extra unit.

Thus the competitive market produces a Pareto efficient amount of output. What about the way in which the good is allocated among the consumers? In a competitive market everyone pays the same price for a good—the marginal rate of substitution between the good and "all other goods" is equal to the price of the good. Everyone who is willing to pay this price is able to purchase the good, and everyone who is not willing to pay this price cannot purchase the good.

What would happen if there were an allocation of the good where the marginal rates of substitution between the good and "all other goods" were not the same? Then there must be at least two people who value a marginal unit of the good differently. Maybe one values a marginal unit at $5 and one values it at $4. Then if the one with the lower value sells a bit of the good to the one with the higher value at any price between $4 and $5, both people would be made better off. Thus any allocation with different marginal rates of substitution cannot be Pareto efficient.

EXAMPLE: Waiting in Line

One commonly used way to allocate resources is by making people wait in line. We can analyze this mechanism for resource allocation using the same tools that we have developed for analyzing the market mechanism. Let us look at a concrete example: suppose that your university is going to distribute tickets to the championship basketball game. Each person who waits in line can get one ticket for free.

The cost of a ticket will then simply be the cost of waiting in line. People who want to see the basketball game very much will camp out outside the ticket office so as to be sure to get a ticket. People who don't care very much about the game may drop by a few minutes before the ticket window opens on the off chance that some tickets will be left. The willingness to pay for a ticket should no longer be measured in dollars but rather in waiting time, since tickets will be allocated according to willingness to wait.

Will waiting in line result in a Pareto efficient allocation of tickets? Ask yourself whether it is possible that someone who waited for a ticket might be willing to sell it to someone who didn't wait in line. Often this will be the case, simply because willingness to wait and willingness to pay differ across the population. If someone is willing to wait in line to buy a ticket and then sell it to someone else, allocating tickets by willingness to wait does not exhaust all the gains to trade—some people would generally still be willing to trade the tickets after the tickets have been allocated. Since waiting in line does not exhaust all of the gains from trade, it does not in general result in a Pareto efficient outcome.

If you allocate a good using a price set in dollars, then the dollars paid by the demanders provide benefits to the suppliers of the good. If you allocate a good using waiting time, the hours spent in line don't benefit anybody. The waiting time imposes a cost on the buyers of the good and provide no benefits at all to the suppliers. Waiting in line is a form of **deadweight loss**—the people who wait in line pay a "price" but no one else receives any benefits from the price they pay.

Summary

1. The supply curve measures how much people will be willing to supply of some good at each price.

2. An equilibrium price is one where the quantity that people are willing to supply equals the quantity that people are willing to demand.

3. The study of how the equilibrium price and quantity change when the underlying demand and supply curves change is another example of comparative statics.

4. When a good is taxed, there will always be two prices: the price paid by the demanders and the price received by the suppliers. The difference between the two represents the amount of the tax.

5. How much of a tax gets passed along to consumers depends on the relative steepness of the demand and supply curves. If the supply curve is horizontal, all of the tax gets passed along to consumers; if the supply curve is vertical, none of the tax gets passed along.

6. The deadweight loss of a tax is the net loss in consumers' surplus plus producers' surplus that arises from imposing the tax. It measures the value of the output that is not sold due to the presence of the tax.

7. A situation is Pareto efficient if there is no way to make some group of people better off without making some other group worse off.

8. The Pareto efficient amount of output to supply in a single market is that amount where the demand and supply curves cross, since this is the

only point where the amount that demanders are willing to pay for an extra unit of output equals the price at which suppliers are willing to supply an extra unit of output.

REVIEW QUESTIONS

1. What is the effect of a subsidy in a market with a horizontal supply curve? With a vertical supply curve?

2. Suppose that the demand curve is vertical while the supply curve slopes upward. If a tax is imposed in this market who ends up paying it?

3. Suppose that all consumers view red pencils and blue pencils as perfect substitutes. Suppose that the supply curve for red pencils is upward sloping. Let the price of red pencils and blue pencils be p_r and p_b. What would happen if the government put a tax only on red pencils?

4. The United States imports about half of its petroleum needs. Suppose that the rest of the oil producers are willing to supply as much oil as the United States wants at a constant price of $25 a barrel. What would happen to the price of domestic oil if a tax of $5 a barrel were placed on foreign oil?

5. Suppose that the supply curve is vertical. What is the deadweight loss of a tax in this market?

6. Consider the tax treatment of borrowing and lending described in the text. How much revenue does this tax system raise if borrowers and lenders are in the same tax bracket?

7. Does such a tax system raise a positive or negative amount of revenue when $t_l < t_b$?

CHAPTER 17

AUCTIONS

Auctions are one of the oldest form of markets, dating back to at least 500 BC. Today, all sorts of commodities, from used computers to fresh flowers, are sold using auctions.

Economists became interested in auctions in the early 1970s when the OPEC oil cartel raised the price of oil. The U.S. Department of the Interior decided to hold auctions to sell the right to drill in coastal areas that were expected to contain vast amounts of oil. The government asked economists how to design these auctions, and private firms hired economists as consultants to help them design a bidding strategy. This effort prompted considerable research in auction design and strategy.

More recently, the Federal Communications Commission (FCC) decided to auction off parts of the radio spectrum for use by cellular phones, personal digital assistants, and other communication devices. Again, economists played a major role in the design of both the auctions and the strategies used by the bidders. These auctions were hailed as very successful public policy, resulting in revenues to the U.S. government of over twenty-three billion dollars to date.

Other countries have also used auctions for privatization projects. For example, Australia sold off several government-owned electricity plants, and New Zealand auctioned off parts of its state-owned telephone system.

Consumer-oriented auctions have also experienced something of a renaissance on the Internet. There are hundreds of auctions on the Internet, selling collectibles, computer equipment, travel services, and other items. OnSale claims to be the largest, reporting over forty-one million dollars worth of merchandise sold in 1997.

17.1 Classification of Auctions

The economic classification of auctions involves two considerations: first, what is the nature of the good that is being auctioned, and second, what are the rules of bidding? With respect to the nature of the good, economists distinguish between **private-value auctions** and **common-value auctions**.

In a private-value auction, each participant has a potentially different value for the good in question. A particular piece of art may be worth $500 to one collector, $200 to another, and $50 to yet another, depending on their taste. In a common-value auction, the good in question is worth essentially the same amount to every bidder, although the bidders may have different estimates of that common value. The auction for off-shore drilling rights described above had this characteristic: a given tract either had a certain amount of oil or not. Different oil companies may have had different estimates about how much oil was there, based on the outcomes of their geological surveys, but the oil had the same market value regardless of who won the auction.

We will spend most of the time in this chapter discussing private-value auctions, since they are the most familiar case. At the end of the chapter, we will describe some of the features of common-value auctions.

Bidding Rules

The most prevalent form of bidding structure for an auction is the **English auction**. The auctioneer starts with a **reserve price**, which is the lowest price at which the seller of the good will part with it.[1] Bidders successively offer higher prices; generally each bid must exceed the previous bid by some minimal **bid increment**. When no participant is willing to increase the bid further, the item is awarded to the highest bidder.

Another form of auction is known as a **Dutch auction**, due to its use in the Netherlands for selling cheese and fresh flowers. In this case the auctioneer starts with a high price and gradually lowers it by steps until someone is willing to buy the item. In practice, the "auctioneer" is often a mechanical device like a dial with a pointer which rotates to lower and

---

[1] See the footnote about "reservation price" in Chapter 6.

lower values as the auction progresses. Dutch auctions can proceed very rapidly, which is one of their chief virtues.

Yet a third form of auctions is a **sealed-bid auction**. In this type of auction, each bidder writes down a bid on a slip of paper and seals it in an envelope. The envelopes are collected and opened, and the good is awarded to the person with the highest bid who then pays the auctioneer the amount that he or she bid. If there is a reserve price, and all bids are lower than the reserve price, then no one may receive the item.

Sealed-bid auctions are commonly used for construction work. The person who wants the construction work done requests bids from several contractors with the understanding that the job will be awarded to the contractor with the lowest bid.

Finally, we consider a variant on the sealed bid-auction that is known as the **philatelist auction** or **Vickrey auction**. The first name is due to the fact that this auction form was originally used by stamp collectors; the second name is in honor of William Vickrey, who received the 1996 Nobel prize for his pioneering work in analyzing auctions. The Vickrey auction is like the sealed-bid auction, with one critical difference: the good is awarded to the highest bidder, but at the *second-highest* price. In other words, the person who bids the most gets the good, but he or she only has to pay the bid made by the second-highest bidder. Though at first this sounds like a rather strange auction form, we will see below that it has some very nice properties.

17.2 Auction Design

Let us suppose that we have a single item to auction off and that there are n bidders with (private) values $v_1, \ldots, v_n$. For simplicity, we assume that the values are all positive and that the seller has a zero value. Our goal is to choose an auction form to sell this item.

This is a special case of an **economic mechanism design** problem. In the case of the auction there are two natural goals that we might have in mind:

- **Pareto efficiency.** Design an auction that results in a Pareto efficient outcome.
- **Profit maximization.** Design an auction that yields the highest expected profit to the seller.

Profit maximization seems pretty straightforward, but what does Pareto efficiency mean in this context? It is not hard to see that Pareto efficiency requires that the good be assigned to the person with the highest value. To see this, suppose that person 1 has the highest value and person 2 has some lower value for the good. If person 2 receives the good, then there is an easy way to make both 1 and 2 better off: transfer the good from person 2 to person 1 and have person 1 pay person 2 some price p that lies between v_1 and v_2. This shows that assigning the good to anyone but the person who has the highest value cannot be Pareto efficient.

If the seller knows the values $v_1, \ldots, v_n$ the auction design problem is pretty trivial. In the case of profit maximization, the seller should just award the item to the person with the highest value and charge him or her that value. If the desired goal is Pareto efficiency, the person with the highest value should still get the good, but the price paid could be any amount between that person's value and zero, since the distribution of the surplus does not matter for Pareto efficiency.

The more interesting case is when the seller does not know the buyers' values. How can one achieve efficiency or profit maximization in this case?

First consider Pareto efficiency. It is not hard to see that an English auction achieves the desired outcome: the person with the highest value will end up with the good. It requires only a little more thought to determine the price that this person will pay: it will be the value of the *second-highest* bidder plus, perhaps, the minimal bid increment.

Think of a specific case where the highest value is, say $100, the second-highest value is $80, and the bid increment is, say, $5. Then the person with the $100 valuation would be willing to bid $85, while the person with the $80 value would not. Just as we claimed, the person with the highest valuation gets the good, at the second highest price (plus, perhaps, the bid increment). (We keep saying "perhaps" since if both players bid $80 there would be a tie and the exact outcome would depend on the rule used for tie-breaking.)

What about profit maximization? This case turns out to be more difficult to analyze since it depends on the *beliefs* that the seller has about the buyers' valuations. To see how this works, suppose that there are just two bidders either of whom could have a value of $10 or $100 for the item in question. Assume these two cases are equally likely, so that there are four equally probable arrangements for the values of bidders 1 and 2: (10,10), (10,100), (100,10), (100,100). Finally, suppose that the minimal bid increment is $1 and that ties are resolved by flipping a coin.

In this example, the winning bids in the four cases described above will be (10,11,11,100) and the bidder with the highest value will always get the good. The expected revenue to the seller is $33 $= \frac{1}{4}(10 + 11 + 11 + 100)$.

Can the seller do better than this? Yes, if he sets an appropriate reservation price. In this case, the profit-maximizing reservation price is $100. Three-quarters of the time, the seller will sell the item for this price, and one-quarter of the time there will be no winning bid. This yields an expected revenue of $75, much higher than the expected revenue yielded by the English auction with no reservation price.

Note that this policy is *not* Pareto efficient, since one-quarter of the time no one gets the good. This is analogous to the deadweight loss of monopoly and arises for exactly the same reason.

The addition of the reservation price is very important if you are interested in profit maximization. In 1990, the New Zealand government auctioned off some of the spectrum for use by radio, television, and cellular telephones, using a Vickrey auction. In one case, the winning bid was NZ\$100,000, but the second-highest bid was only NZ\$6! This auction may have led to a Pareto efficient outcome, but it was certainly not revenue maximizing!

We have seen that the English auction with a zero reservation price guarantees Pareto efficiency. What about the Dutch auction? The answer here is not necessarily. To see this, consider a case with two bidders who have values of \$100 and \$80. If the high-value person believes (erroneously!) that the second-highest value is \$70, he or she would plan to wait until the auctioneer reached, say, \$75 before bidding. But, by then, it would be too late—the person with the second-highest value would have already bought the good at \$80. In general, there is no guarantee that the good will be awarded to the person with the highest valuation.

The same holds for the case of a sealed-bid auction. The optimal bid for each of the agents depends on their *beliefs* about the values of the other agents. If those beliefs are inaccurate, the good may easily end up being awarded to someone who does not have the highest valuation.[2]

Finally, we consider the Vickrey auction—the variant on the sealed-bid auction where the highest bidder gets the item, but only has to pay the second-highest price.

First we observe that *if* everyone bids their true value for the good in question, the item will end up being awarded to the person with the highest value, who will pay a price equal to that of the person with the second-highest value. This is essentially the same as the outcome of the English auction (up to the bid increment, which can be arbitrarily small).

But is it optimal to state your true value in a Vickrey auction? We saw that for the standard sealed-bid auction, this is not generally the case. But the Vickrey auction is different: the surprising answer is that it is always in each player's interest to write down their true value.

To see why, let us look at the special case of two bidders, who have values v_1 and v_2 and write down bids of b_1 and b_2. The expected payoff to bidder 1 is:

$$\text{Prob}(b_1 \geq b_2)[v_1 - b_2],$$

---

[2] On the other hand, if all players' beliefs are accurate, on average, and all bidders play optimally, the various auction forms described above turn out to yield the same allocation and the same expected price in equilibrium. For a detailed analysis, see P. Milgrom, "Auctions and Bidding: a Primer," *Journal of Economic Perspectives*, **3**(3), 1989, 3–22, and P. Klemperer, "Auction Theory: A Guide to the Literature," *Economic Surveys*, **13**(3), 1999, 227–286.

where "Prob" stands for "probability."

The first term in this expression is the probability that bidder 1 has the highest bid; the second term is the consumer surplus that bidder 1 enjoys if he wins. (If $b_1 < b_2$, then bidder 1 gets a surplus of 0, so there is no need to consider the term containing $\text{Prob}(b_1 \leq b_2)$.)

Suppose that $v_1 > b_2$. Then bidder 1 wants to make the probability of winning as large as possible, which he can do by setting $b_1 = v_1$. Suppose, on the other hand, that $v_1 < b_2$. Then bidder 1 wants to make the probability of winning as small as possible, which he can do by setting $b_1 = v_1$. In either case, an optimal strategy for bidder 1 is to set his bid equal to his true value! Honesty is the best policy ... at least in a Vickrey auction!

The interesting feature of the Vickrey auction is that it achieves essentially the same outcome as an English auction, but without the iteration. This is apparently why it was used by stamp collectors. They sold stamps at their conventions using English auctions and via their newsletters using sealed-bid auctions. Someone noticed that the sealed-bid auction would mimic the outcome of the English auctions if they used the second-highest bid rule. But it was left to Vickrey to conduct the full-fledged analysis of the philatelist auction and show that truth-telling was the optimal strategy and that the philatelist auction was equivalent to the English auction.

17.3 Problems with Auctions

We've seen above that English auctions (or Vickrey auctions) have the desirable property of achieving Pareto efficient outcomes. This makes them attractive candidates for resource allocation mechanisms. In fact, most of the airwave auctions used by the FCC were variants on the English auction.

But English auctions are not perfect. They are still susceptible to collusion. The example of pooling in auction markets, described in Chapter 24, shows how antique dealers in Philadelphia colluded on their bidding strategies in auctions.

There are also various ways to manipulate the outcome of auctions. In the analysis described earlier, we assumed that a bid *committed* the bidder to pay. However, some auction designs allow bidders to drop out once the winning bids are revealed. Such an option allows for manipulation. For example, in 1993 the Australian government auctioned off licenses for satellite-television services using a standard sealed-bid auction. The winning bid for one of the licenses, A\$212 million, was made by a company called Ucom. Once the government announced Ucom had won, they proceeded to default on their bid, leaving the government to award the license to the second-highest bidder—which was also Ucom! They defaulted on this bid as well; four months later, after several more defaults, they paid A\$117 million for the license, which was A\$95 million less than their initial winning bid! The license ended up being awarded to the highest bidder at the second-highest price—but the poorly designed auction caused at least a year delay in bringing pay-TV to Australia.[3]

17.4 The Winner's Curse

We turn now to the examination of **common-value auctions**, where the good that is being awarded has the *same* value to all bidders. However, each of the bidders may have different estimates of that value. To emphasize this, let us write the (estimated) value of bidder i as $v + \epsilon_i$ where v is the true, common value and ϵ_i is the "error term" associated with bidder i's estimate.

Let's examine a sealed-bid auction in this framework. What bid should bidder i place? To develop some intuition, let's see what happens if each bidder bids their estimated value. In this case, the person with the highest value of ϵ_i, ϵ_{max}, gets the good. But as long as $\epsilon_{max} > 0$, this person is paying more than v, the true value of the good. This is the so-called **Winner's Curse**. If you win the auction, it is because you have overestimated the value of the good being sold. In other words, you have won only because you were too optimistic!

The *optimal* strategy in a common-value auction like this is to bid less than your estimated value—and the more bidders there are, the lower you want your own bid to be. Think about it: if you are the highest bidder out of five bidders you may be overly optimistic, but if you are the highest bidder out of twenty bidders you must be *super* optimistic. The more bidders there are, the more humble you should be about your own estimates of the "true value" of the good in question.

The Winner's Curse seemed to be operating in the FCC's May 1996 spectrum auction for personal communications services. The largest bidder in that auction, NextWave Personal Communications Inc., bid $4.2 billion for sixty-three licenses, winning them all. However, in January 1998 the company filed for Chapter Eleven bankruptcy protection, after finding itself unable to pay its bills.

Summary

1. Auctions have been used for thousands of years to sell things.

2. If each bidder's value is independent of the other bidders, the auction is said to be a private-value auction. If the value of the item being sold is

---

[3] See John McMillan, "Selling Spectrum Rights," *Journal of Economic Perspectives*, **8**(3), 145–152, for details of this story and how its lessons were incorporated into the design of the U.S. spectrum auction. This article also describes the New Zealand example mentioned earlier.

essentially the same for everyone, the auction is said to be a common-value auction.

3. Common auction forms are the English auction, the Dutch auction, the sealed-bid auction, and the Vickrey auction.

4. English auctions and Vickrey auctions have the desirable property that their outcomes are Pareto efficient.

5. Profit-maximizing auctions typically require a strategic choice of the reservation price.

6. Despite their advantages as market mechanisms, auctions are vulnerable to collusion and other forms of strategic behavior.

REVIEW QUESTIONS

1. Consider an auction of antique quilts to collectors. Is this a private-value or a common-value auction?

2. Suppose that there are only two bidders with values of $8 and $10 for an item with a bid increment of $1. What should the reservation price be in a profit-maximizing English auction?

3. Suppose that we have two copies of *Intermediate Microeconomics* to sell to three (enthusiastic) students. How can we use a sealed-bid auction that will guarantee that the bidders with the two highest values get the books?

4. Consider the Ucom example in the text. Was the auction design efficient? Did it maximize profits?

5. A game theorist fills a jar with pennies and auctions it off on the first day of class using an English auction. Is this a private-value or a common-value auction? Do you think the winning bidder usually makes a profit?

CHAPTER **18**

TECHNOLOGY

In this chapter we begin our study of firm behavior. The first thing to do is to examine the constraints on a firm's behavior. When a firm makes choices it faces many constraints. These constraints are imposed by its customers, by its competitors, and by nature. In this chapter we're going to consider the latter source of constraints: nature. Nature imposes the constraint that there are only certain feasible ways to produce outputs from inputs: there are only certain kinds of technological choices that are possible. Here we will study how economists describe these technological constraints.

If you understand consumer theory, production theory will be very easy since the same tools are used. In fact, production theory is much simpler than consumption theory because the output of a production process is generally observable, whereas the "output" of consumption (utility) is not directly observable.

18.1 Inputs and Outputs

Inputs to production are called **factors of production**. Factors of production are often classified into broad categories such as land, labor, capital, and raw materials. It is pretty apparent what labor, land, and raw materials mean, but capital may be a new concept. **Capital goods** are those inputs to production that are themselves produced goods. Basically capital goods are machines of one sort or another: tractors, buildings, computers, or whatever.

Sometimes capital is used to describe the money used to start up or maintain a business. We will always use the term **financial capital** for this concept and use the term capital goods, or **physical capital**, for produced factors of production.

We will usually want to think of inputs and outputs as being measured in *flow* units: a certain amount of labor per week and a certain number of machine hours per week will produce a certain amount of output a week.

We won't find it necessary to use the classifications given above very often. Most of what we want to describe about technology can be done without reference to the *kind* of inputs and outputs involved—just with the amounts of inputs and outputs.

18.2 Describing Technological Constraints

Nature imposes **technological constraints** on firms: only certain combinations of inputs are feasible ways to produce a given amount of output, and the firm must limit itself to technologically feasible production plans.

The easiest way to describe feasible production plans is to list them. That is, we can list all combinations of inputs and outputs that are technologically feasible. The set of all combinations of inputs and outputs that comprise a technologically feasible way to produce is called a **production set.**

Suppose, for example, that we have only one input, measured by x, and one output, measured by y. Then a production set might have the shape indicated in Figure 18.1. To say that some point (x, y) is in the production set is just to say that it is technologically possible to produce y amount of output if you have x amount of input. The production set shows the *possible* technological choices facing a firm.

As long as the inputs to the firm are costly it makes sense to limit ourselves to examining the *maximum possible output* for a given level of input. This is the boundary of the production set depicted in Figure 18.1. The function describing the boundary of this set is known as the **production function.** It measures the maximum possible output that you can get from a given amount of input.

Of course, the concept of a production function applies equally well if there are several inputs. If, for example, we consider the case of two inputs, the production function $f(x_1, x_2)$ would measure the maximum amount of output y that we could get if we had x_1 units of factor 1 and x_2 units of factor 2.

$y = $ OUTPUT

$y = f(x) = $ production function

Production set

$x = $ INPUT

Figure 18.1

A production set. Here is a possible shape for a production set.

In the two-input case there is a convenient way to depict production relations known as the **isoquant**. An isoquant is the set of all possible combinations of inputs 1 and 2 that are just sufficient to produce a given amount of output.

Isoquants are similar to indifference curves. As we've seen earlier, an indifference curve depicts the different consumption bundles that are just sufficient to produce a certain level of utility. But there is one important difference between indifference curves and isoquants. Isoquants are labeled with the amount of output they can produce, not with a utility level. Thus the labeling of isoquants is fixed by the technology and doesn't have the kind of arbitrary nature that the utility labeling has.

18.3 Examples of Technology

Since we already know a lot about indifference curves, it is easy to understand how isoquants work. Let's consider a few examples of technologies and their isoquants.

Fixed Proportions

Suppose that we are producing holes and that the only way to get a hole is to use one man and one shovel. Extra shovels aren't worth anything, and neither are extra men. Thus the total number of holes that you can produce will be the minimum of the number of men and the number of shovels that you have. We write the production function as $f(x_1, x_2) = \min\{x_1, x_2\}$.

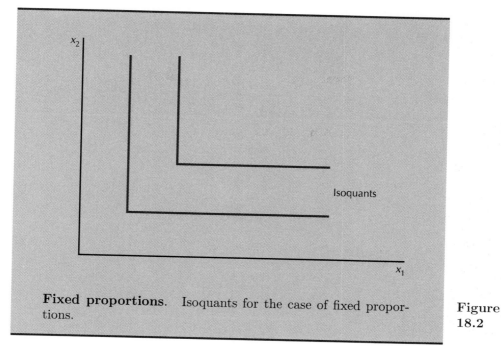

Fixed proportions. Isoquants for the case of fixed proportions.

Figure
18.2

The isoquants look like those depicted in Figure 18.2. Note that these isoquants are just like the case of perfect complements in consumer theory.

Perfect Substitutes

Suppose now that we are producing homework and the inputs are red pencils and blue pencils. The amount of homework produced depends only on the total number of pencils, so we write the production function as $f(x_1, x_2) = x_1 + x_2$. The resulting isoquants are just like the case of perfect substitutes in consumer theory, as depicted in Figure 18.3.

Cobb-Douglas

If the production function has the form $f(x_1, x_2) = Ax_1^a x_2^b$, then we say that it is a **Cobb-Douglas production function**. This is just like the functional form for Cobb-Douglas preferences that we studied earlier. The numerical magnitude of the utility function was not important, so we set $A = 1$ and usually set $a + b = 1$. But the magnitude of the production function does matter so we have to allow these parameters to take arbitrary values. The parameter A measures, roughly speaking, the scale of production: how much output we would get if we used one unit of each input. The parameters a and b measure how the amount of output responds to

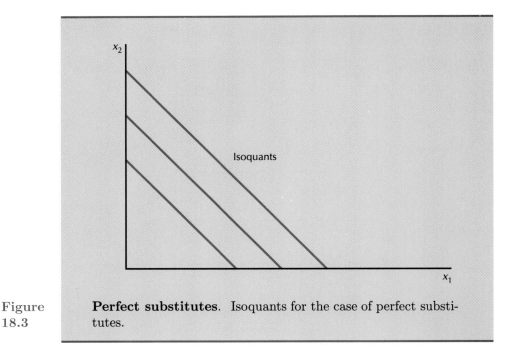

Figure
18.3
Perfect substitutes. Isoquants for the case of perfect substitutes.

changes in the inputs. We'll examine their impact in more detail later on. In some of the examples, we will choose to set $A = 1$ in order to simplify the calculations.

The Cobb-Douglas isoquants have the same nice, well-behaved shape that the Cobb-Douglas indifference curves have; as in the case of utility functions, the Cobb-Douglas production function is about the simplest example of well-behaved isoquants.

18.4 Properties of Technology

As in the case of consumers, it is common to assume certain properties about technology. First we will generally assume that technologies are **monotonic**: if you increase the amount of at least one of the inputs, it should be possible to produce at least as much output as you were producing originally. This is sometimes referred to as the property of **free disposal**: if the firm can costlessly dispose of any inputs, having extra inputs around can't hurt it.

Second, we will often assume that the technology is **convex**. This means that if you have two ways to produce y units of output, (x_1, x_2) and (z_1, z_2), then their weighted average will produce *at least* y units of output.

One argument for convex technologies goes as follows. Suppose that you have a way to produce 1 unit of output using a_1 units of factor 1 and a_2

units of factor 2 and that you have another way to produce 1 unit of output using b_1 units of factor 1 and b_2 units of factor 2. We call these two ways to produce output **production techniques**.

Furthermore, let us suppose that you are free to scale the output up by arbitrary amounts so that $(100a_1, 100a_2)$ and $(100b_1, 100b_2)$ will produce 100 units of output. But now note that if you have $25a_1 + 75b_1$ units of factor 1 and $25a_2 + 75b_2$ units of factor 2 you can still produce 100 units of output: just produce 25 units of the output using the "a" technique and 75 units of the output using the "b" technique.

This is depicted in Figure 18.4. By choosing the level at which you operate each of the two activities, you can produce a given amount of output in a variety of different ways. In particular, every input combination along the line connecting $(100a_1, 100a_2)$ and $(100b_1, 100b_2)$ will be a feasible way to produce 100 units of output.

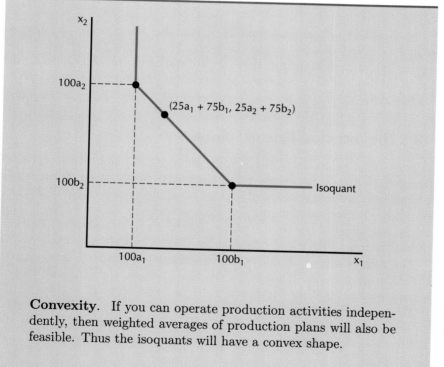

Convexity. If you can operate production activities independently, then weighted averages of production plans will also be feasible. Thus the isoquants will have a convex shape.

Figure 18.4

In this kind of technology, where you can scale the production process up and down easily and where separate production processes don't interfere with each other, convexity is a very natural assumption.

18.5 The Marginal Product

Suppose that we are operating at some point, (x_1, x_2), and that we consider using a little bit more of factor 1 while keeping factor 2 fixed at the level x_2. How much more output will we get per additional unit of factor 1? We have to look at the change in output per unit change of factor 1:

$$\frac{\Delta y}{\Delta x_1} = \frac{f(x_1 + \Delta x_1, x_2) - f(x_1, x_2)}{\Delta x_1}.$$

We call this the **marginal product of factor 1**. The marginal product of factor 2 is defined in a similar way, and we denote them by $MP_1(x_1, x_2)$ and $MP_2(x_1, x_2)$, respectively.

Sometimes we will be a bit sloppy about the concept of marginal product and describe it as the extra output we get from having "one" more unit of factor 1. As long as "one" is small relative to the total amount of factor 1 that we are using, this will be satisfactory. But we should remember that a marginal product is a *rate*: the extra amount of output per unit of extra input.

The concept of marginal product is just like the concept of marginal utility that we described in our discussion of consumer theory, except for the ordinal nature of utility. Here, we are discussing physical output: the marginal product of a factor is a specific number, which can, in principle, be observed.

18.6 The Technical Rate of Substitution

Suppose that we are operating at some point (x_1, x_2) and that we consider giving up a little bit of factor 1 and using just enough more of factor 2 to produce the same amount of output y. How much extra of factor 2, Δx_2, do we need if we are going to give up a little bit of factor 1, Δx_1? This is just the slope of the isoquant; we refer to it as the **technical rate of substitution (TRS)**, and denote it by $\mathrm{TRS}(x_1, x_2)$.

The technical rate of substitution measures the tradeoff between two inputs in production. It measures the rate at which the firm will have to substitute one input for another in order to keep output constant.

To derive a formula for the TRS, we can use the same idea that we used to determine the slope of the indifference curve. Consider a change in our use of factors 1 and 2 that keeps output fixed. Then we have

$$\Delta y = MP_1(x_1, x_2)\Delta x_1 + MP_2(x_1, x_2)\Delta x_2 = 0,$$

which we can solve to get

$$\mathrm{TRS}(x_1, x_2) = \frac{\Delta x_2}{\Delta x_1} = -\frac{MP_1(x_1, x_2)}{MP_2(x_1, x_2)}.$$

Note the similarity with the definition of the marginal rate of substitution.

18.7 Diminishing Marginal Product

Suppose that we have certain amounts of factors 1 and 2 and we consider adding more of factor 1 while holding factor 2 fixed at a given level. What might happen to the marginal product of factor 1?

As long as we have a monotonic technology, we know that the total output will go up as we increase the amount of factor 1. But it is natural to expect that it will go up at a decreasing rate. Let's consider a specific example, the case of farming.

One man on one acre of land might produce 100 bushels of corn. If we add another man and keep the same amount of land, we might get 200 bushels of corn, so in this case the marginal product of an extra worker is 100. Now keep adding workers to this acre of land. Each worker may produce more output, but eventually the extra amount of corn produced by an extra worker will be less than 100 bushels. After 4 or 5 people are added the additional output per worker will drop to 90, 80, 70 ... or even fewer bushels of corn. If we get hundreds of workers crowded together on this one acre of land, an extra worker may even cause output to go down! As in the making of broth, extra cooks *can* make things worse.

Thus we would typically expect that the marginal product of a factor will diminish as we get more and more of that factor. This is called the **law of diminishing marginal product**. It isn't really a "law"; it's just a common feature of most kinds of production processes.

It is important to emphasize that the law of diminishing marginal product applies only when all *other* inputs are being held fixed. In the farming example, we considered changing only the labor input, holding the land and raw materials fixed.

18.8 Diminishing Technical Rate of Substitution

Another closely related assumption about technology is that of **diminishing technical rate of substitution**. This says that as we increase the amount of factor 1, and adjust factor 2 so as to stay on the same isoquant, the technical rate of substitution declines. Roughly speaking, the assumption of diminishing TRS means that the slope of an isoquant must decrease in absolute value as we move along the isoquant in the direction of increasing x_1, and it must increase as we move in the direction of increasing x_2. This means that the isoquants will have the same sort of convex shape that well-behaved indifference curves have.

The assumptions of a diminishing technical rate of substitution and diminishing marginal product are closely related but are not exactly the same. Diminishing marginal product is an assumption about how the marginal product changes as we increase the amount of one factor, *holding the other factor fixed.* Diminishing TRS is about how the *ratio* of the marginal products—the slope of the isoquant—changes as we increase the amount of one factor and *reduce the amount of the other factor so as to stay on the same isoquant.*

18.9 The Long Run and the Short Run

Let us return now to the original idea of a technology as being just a list of the feasible production plans. We may want to distinguish between the production plans that are *immediately* feasible and those that are *eventually* feasible.

In the **short run**, there will be some factors of production that are fixed at predetermined levels. Our farmer described above might only consider production plans that involve a fixed amount of land, if that is all he has access to. It may be true that if he had more land, he could produce more corn, but in the short run he is stuck with the amount of land that he has.

On the other hand, in the long run the farmer is free to purchase more land, or to sell some of the land he now owns. He can adjust the level of the land input so as to maximize his profits.

The economist's distinction between the long run and the short run is this: in the short run there is at least one factor of production that is fixed: a fixed amount of land, a fixed plant size, a fixed number of machines, or whatever. In the **long run**, *all* the factors of production can be varied.

There is no specific time interval implied here. What is the long run and what is the short run depends on what kinds of choices we are examining. In the short run at least some factors are fixed at given levels, but in the long run the amount used of these factors can be changed.

Let's suppose that factor 2, say, is fixed at $\overline{x}_2$ in the short run. Then the relevant production function for the short run is $f(x_1, \overline{x}_2)$. We can plot the functional relation between output and x_1 in a diagram like Figure 18.5.

Note that we have drawn the short-run production function as getting flatter and flatter as the amount of factor 1 increases. This is just the law of diminishing marginal product in action again. Of course, it can easily happen that there is an initial region of increasing marginal returns where the marginal product of factor 1 increases as we add more of it. In the case of the farmer adding labor, it might be that the first few workers added increase output more and more because they would be able to divide up jobs efficiently, and so on. But given the fixed amount of land, eventually the marginal product of labor will decline.

18.10 Returns to Scale

Now let's consider a different kind of experiment. Instead of increasing the amount of one input while holding the other input fixed, let's increase the

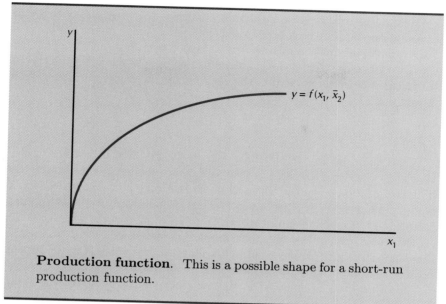

$y = f(x_1, \bar{x}_2)$

Production function. This is a possible shape for a short-run production function.

Figure
18.5

amount of *all* inputs to the production function. In other words, let's scale the amount of all inputs up by some constant factor: for example, use twice as much of both factor 1 and factor 2.

If we use twice as much of each input, how much output will we get? The most likely outcome is that we will get twice as much output. This is called the case of **constant returns to scale**. In terms of the production function, this means that two times as much of each input gives two times as much output. In the case of two inputs we can express this mathematically by

$$2f(x_1, x_2) = f(2x_1, 2x_2).$$

In general, if we scale all of the inputs up by some amount t, constant returns to scale implies that we should get t times as much output:

$$tf(x_1, x_2) = f(tx_1, tx_2).$$

We say that this is the likely outcome for the following reason: it should typically be possible for the firm to *replicate* what it was doing before. If the firm has twice as much of each input, it can just set up two plants side by side and thereby get twice as much output. With three times as much of each input, it can set up three plants, and so on.

Note that it is perfectly possible for a technology to exhibit constant returns to scale and diminishing marginal product to each factor. **Returns to scale** describes what happens when you increase *all* inputs, while diminishing marginal product describes what happens when you increase *one* of the inputs and hold the others fixed.

Constant returns to scale is the most "natural" case because of the replication argument, but that isn't to say that other things might not happen. For example, it could happen that if we scale up both inputs by some factor t, we get *more* than t times as much output. This is called the case of **increasing returns to scale**. Mathematically, increasing returns to scale means that

$$f(tx_1, tx_2) > tf(x_1, x_2).$$

for all $t > 1$.

What would be an example of a technology that had increasing returns to scale? One nice example is that of an oil pipeline. If we double the diameter of a pipe, we use twice as much materials, but the cross section of the pipe goes up by a factor of 4. Thus we will likely be able to pump more than twice as much oil through it.

(Of course, we can't push this example too far. If we keep doubling the diameter of the pipe, it will eventually collapse of its own weight. Increasing returns to scale usually just applies over some range of output.)

The other case to consider is that of **decreasing returns to scale**, where

$$f(tx_1, tx_2) < tf(x_1, x_2)$$

for all $t > 1$.

This case is somewhat peculiar. If we get less than twice as much output from having twice as much of each input, we must be doing something wrong. After all, we could just replicate what we were doing before!

The usual way in which diminishing returns to scale arises is because we forgot to account for some input. If we have twice as much of every input but one, we won't be able to exactly replicate what we were doing before, so there is no reason that we have to get twice as much output. Diminishing returns to scale is really a short-run phenomenon, with something being held fixed.

Of course, a technology can exhibit different kinds of returns to scale at different levels of production. It may well happen that for low levels of production, the technology exhibits increasing returns to scale—as you scale all the inputs by some small amount t, the output increases by *more* than t. Later on, for larger levels of output, increasing scale by t may just increase output by the same factor t.

Summary

1. The technological constraints of the firm are described by the production set, which depicts all the technologically feasible combinations of inputs and outputs, and by the production function, which gives the maximum amount of output associated with a given amount of the inputs.

2. Another way to describe the technological constraints facing a firm is through the use of isoquants—curves that indicate all the combinations of inputs capable of producing a given level of output.

3. We generally assume that isoquants are convex and monotonic, just like well–behaved preferences.

4. The marginal product measures the extra output per extra unit of an input, holding all other inputs fixed. We typically assume that the marginal product of an input diminishes as we use more and more of that input.

5. The technical rate of substitution (TRS) measures the slope of an isoquant. We generally assume that the TRS diminishes as we move out along an isoquant—which is another way of saying that the isoquant has a convex shape.

6. In the short run some inputs are fixed, while in the long run all inputs are variable.

7. Returns to scale refers to the way that output changes as we change the *scale* of production. If we scale all inputs up by some amount t and output goes up by the same factor, then we have constant returns to scale. If output scales up by more that t, we have increasing returns to scale; and if it scales up by less than t, we have decreasing returns to scale.

REVIEW QUESTIONS

1. Consider the production function $f(x_1, x_2) = x_1^2 x_2^2$. Does this exhibit constant, increasing, or decreasing returns to scale?

2. Consider the production function $f(x_1, x_2) = 4x_1^{\frac{1}{2}} x_2^{\frac{1}{3}}$. Does this exhibit constant, increasing, or decreasing returns to scale?

3. The Cobb-Douglas production function is given by $f(x_1, x_2) = Ax_1^a x_2^b$. It turns out that the type of returns to scale of this function will depend on the magnitude of $a + b$. Which values of $a + b$ will be associated with the different kinds of returns to scale?

4. The technical rate of substitution between factors x_2 and x_1 is -4. If you desire to produce the same amount of output but cut your use of x_1 by 3 units, how many more units of x_2 will you need?

5. True or false? If the law of diminishing marginal product did not hold, the world's food supply could be grown in a flowerpot.

6. In a production process is it possible to have decreasing marginal product in an input and yet increasing returns to scale?

CHAPTER 19

PROFIT
MAXIMIZATION

In the last chapter we discussed ways to describe the technological choices facing the firm. In this chapter we describe a model of how the firm chooses the amount to produce and the method of production to employ. The model we will use is the model of profit maximization: the firm chooses a production plan so as to maximize its profits.

In this chapter we will assume that the firm faces fixed prices for its inputs and outputs. We said earlier that economists call a market where the individual producers take the prices as outside their control a **competitive market**. So in this chapter we want to study the profit-maximization problem of a firm that faces competitive markets for the factors of production it uses and the output goods it produces.

19.1 Profits

Profits are defined as revenues minus cost. Suppose that the firm produces n outputs $(y_1, \ldots, y_n)$ and uses m inputs $(x_1, \ldots, x_m)$. Let the prices of the output goods be $(p_1, \ldots, p_n)$ and the prices of the inputs be $(w_1, \ldots, w_m)$.

The profits the firm receives, π, can be expressed as

$$\pi = \sum_{i=1}^{n} p_i y_i - \sum_{i=1}^{m} w_i x_i.$$

The first term is revenue, and the second term is cost.

In the expression for cost we should be sure to include *all* of the factors of production used by the firm, valued at their market price. Usually this is pretty obvious, but in cases where the firm is owned and operated by the same individual, it is possible to forget about some of the factors.

For example, if an individual works in his own firm, then his labor is an input and it should be counted as part of the costs. His wage rate is simply the market price of his labor—what he *would* be getting if he sold his labor on the open market. Similarly, if a farmer owns some land and uses it in his production, that land should be valued at its market value for purposes of computing the economic costs.

We have seen that economic costs like these are often referred to as **opportunity costs**. The name comes from the idea that if you are using your labor, for example, in one application, you forgo the opportunity of employing it elsewhere. Therefore those lost wages are part of the cost of production. Similarly with the land example: the farmer has the opportunity of renting his land to someone else, but he chooses to forgo that rental income in favor of renting it to himself. The lost rents are part of the opportunity cost of his production.

The economic definition of profit requires that we value all inputs and outputs at their opportunity cost. Profits as determined by accountants do not necessarily accurately measure economic profits, as they typically use historical costs—what a factor was purchased for originally—rather than economic costs—what a factor would cost if purchased now. There are many variations on the use of the term "profit," but we will always stick to the economic definition.

Another confusion that sometimes arises is due to getting time scales mixed up. We usually think of the factor inputs as being measured in terms of *flows*. So many labor hours per week and so many machine hours per week will produce so much output per week. Then the factor prices will be measured in units appropriate for the purchase of such flows. Wages are naturally expressed in terms of dollars per hour. The analog for machines would be the **rental rate**—the rate at which you can rent a machine for the given time period.

In many cases there isn't a very well-developed market for the rental of machines, since firms will typically buy their capital equipment. In this case, we have to compute the implicit rental rate by seeing how much it would cost to buy a machine at the beginning of the period and sell it at the end of the period.

19.2 The Organization of Firms

In a capitalist economy, firms are owned by individuals. Firms are only legal entities; ultimately it is the owners of firms who are responsible for the behavior of the firm, and it is the owners who reap the rewards or pay the costs of that behavior.

Generally speaking, firms can be organized as proprietorships, partnerships, or corporations. A **proprietorship** is a firm that is owned by a single individual. A **partnership** is owned by two or more individuals. A **corporation** is usually owned by several individuals as well, but under the law has an existence separate from that of its owners. Thus a partnership will last only as long as both partners are alive and agree to maintain its existence. A corporation can last longer than the lifetimes of any of its owners. For this reason, most large firms are organized as corporations.

The owners of each of these different types of firms may have different goals with respect to managing the operation of the firm. In a proprietorship or a partnership the owners of the firm usually take a direct role in actually managing the day-to-day operations of the firm, so they are in a position to carry out whatever objectives they have in operating the firm. Typically, the owners would be interested in maximizing the profits of their firm, but, if they have nonprofit goals, they can certainly indulge in these goals instead.

In a corporation, the owners of the corporation are often distinct from the managers of the corporation. Thus there is a separation of ownership and control. The owners of the corporation must define an objective for the managers to follow in their running of the firm, and then do their best to see that they actually pursue the goals the owners have in mind. Again, profit maximization is a common goal. As we'll see below, this goal, properly interpreted, is likely to lead the managers of the firm to choose actions that are in the interests of the owners of the firm.

19.3 Profits and Stock Market Value

Often the production process that a firm uses goes on for many periods. Inputs put in place at time t pay off with a whole flow of services at later times. For example, a factory building erected by a firm could last for 50 or 100 years. In this case an input at one point in time helps to produce output at other times in the future.

In this case we have to value a flow of costs and a flow of revenues over time. As we've seen in Chapter 10, the appropriate way to do this is to use the concept of present value. When people can borrow and lend in financial markets, the interest rate can be used to define a natural price of consumption at different times. Firms have access to the same sorts of financial markets, and the interest rate can be used to value investment decisions in exactly the same way.

Consider a world of perfect certainty where a firm's flow of future profits is publicly known. Then the present value of those profits would be the **present value of the firm**. It would be how much someone would be willing to pay to purchase the firm.

As we indicated above, most large firms are organized as corporations, which means that they are jointly owned by a number of individuals. The corporation issues stock certificates to represent ownership of shares in the corporation. At certain times the corporation issues dividends on these shares, which represent a share of the profits of the firm. The shares of ownership in the corporation are bought and sold in the **stock market**. The price of a share represents the present value of the stream of dividends that people expect to receive from the corporation. The total stock market value of a firm represents the present value of the stream of profits that the firm is expected to generate. Thus the objective of the firm—maximizing the present value of the stream of profits the firm generates—could also be described as the goal of maximizing stock market value. In a world of certainty, these two goals are the same thing.

The owners of the firm will generally want the firm to choose production plans that maximize the stock market value of the firm, since that will make the value of the shares they hold as large as possible. We saw in Chapter 10 that whatever an individual's tastes for consumption at different times, he or she will always prefer an endowment with a higher present value to one with a lower present value. By maximizing stock market value, a firm makes its shareholders' budget sets as large as possible, and thereby acts in the best interests of all of its shareholders.

If there is uncertainty about a firm's stream of profits, then instructing managers to maximize profits has no meaning. Should they maximize expected profits? Should they maximize the expected utility of profits? What attitude toward risky investments should the managers have? It is difficult to assign a meaning to profit maximization when there is uncertainty present. However, in a world of uncertainty, maximizing *stock market value* still has meaning. If the managers of a firm attempt to make the value of the firm's shares as large as possible then they make the firm's owners—the shareholders—as well-off as possible. Thus maximizing stock market value gives a well-defined objective function to the firm in nearly all economic environments.

Despite these remarks about time and uncertainty, we will generally limit ourselves to the examination of much simpler profit-maximization problems, namely, those in which there is a single, certain output and a single period of time. This simple story still generates significant insights and builds the proper intuition to study more general models of firm behavior. Most of the ideas that we will examine carry over in a natural way to these more general models.

19.4 Fixed and Variable Factors

In a given time period, it may be very difficult to adjust some of the inputs. Typically a firm may have contractual obligations to employ certain inputs at certain levels. An example of this would be a lease on a building, where the firm is legally obligated to purchase a certain amount of space over the period under examination. We refer to a factor of production that is in a fixed amount for the firm as a **fixed factor**. If a factor can be used in different amounts, we refer to it as a **variable factor**.

As we saw in Chapter 18, the short run is defined as that period of time in which there are some fixed factors—factors that can only be used in fixed amounts. In the long run, on the other hand, the firm is free to vary all of the factors of production: all factors are variable factors.

There is no rigid boundary between the short run and the long run. The exact time period involved depends on the problem under examination. The important thing is that some of the factors of production are fixed in the short run and variable in the long run. Since all factors are variable in the long run, a firm is always free to decide to use zero inputs and produce zero output—that is, to go out of business. Thus the least profits a firm can make in the long run are zero profits.

In the short run, the firm is obligated to employ some factors, even if it decides to produce zero output. Therefore it is perfectly possible that the firm could make *negative* profits in the short run.

By definition, fixed factors are factors of production that must be paid for even if the firm decides to produce zero output: if a firm has a long-term lease on a building, it must make its lease payments each period whether or not it decides to produce anything that period. But there is another category of factors that only need to be paid for if the firm decides to produce a positive amount of output. One example is electricity used for lighting. If the firm produces zero output, it doesn't have to provide any lighting; but if it produces any positive amount of output, it has to purchase a fixed amount of electricity to use for lighting.

Factors such as these are called **quasi-fixed factors**. They are factors of production that must be used in a fixed amount, independent of the output of the firm, as long as the output is positive. The distinction between fixed factors and quasi-fixed factors is sometimes useful in analyzing the economic behavior of the firm.

19.5 Short-Run Profit Maximization

Let's consider the short-run profit-maximization problem when input 2 is fixed at some level $\bar{x}_2$. Let $f(x_1, x_2)$ be the production function for the firm, let p be the price of output, and let w_1 and w_2 be the prices of the two inputs. Then the profit-maximization problem facing the firm can be written as

$$\max_{x_1} \ pf(x_1, \overline{x}_2) - w_1 x_1 - w_2 \overline{x}_2.$$

The condition for the optimal choice of factor 1 is not difficult to determine.

If x_1^* is the profit-maximizing choice of factor 1, then the output price times the marginal product of factor 1 should equal the price of factor 1. In symbols,

$$pMP_1(x_1^*, \overline{x}_2) = w_1.$$

In other words, the *value of the marginal product of a factor should equal its price*.

In order to understand this rule, think about the decision to employ a little more of factor 1. As you add a little more of it, Δx_1, you produce $\Delta y = MP_1 \Delta x_1$ more output that is worth $pMP_1 \Delta x_1$. But this marginal output costs $w_1 \Delta x_1$ to produce. If the value of marginal product exceeds its cost, then profits can be increased by *increasing* input 1. If the value of marginal product is less than its cost, then profits can be increased by *decreasing* the level of input 1.

If the profits of the firm are as large as possible, then profits should not increase when we increase or decrease input 1. This means that at a profit-maximizing choice of inputs and outputs, the value of the marginal product, $pMP_1(x_1^*, \overline{x}_2)$, should equal the factor price, w_1.

We can derive the same condition graphically. Consider Figure 19.1. The curved line represents the production function holding factor 2 fixed at $\overline{x}_2$. Using y to denote the output of the firm, profits are given by

$$\pi = py - w_1 x_1 - w_2 \overline{x}_2.$$

This expression can be solved for y to express output as a function of x_1:

$$y = \frac{\pi}{p} + \frac{w_2}{p} \overline{x}_2 + \frac{w_1}{p} x_1. \tag{19.1}$$

This equation describes **isoprofit lines**. These are just all combinations of the input goods and the output good that give a constant level of profit, π. As π varies we get a family of parallel straight lines each with a slope of w_1/p and each having a vertical intercept of $\pi/p + w_2 \overline{x}_2/p$, which measures the profits plus the fixed costs of the firm.

The fixed costs are fixed, so the only thing that really varies as we move from one isoprofit line to another is the level of profits. Thus higher levels of profit will be associated with isoprofit lines with higher vertical intercepts.

The profit-maximization problem is then to find the point on the production function that has the highest associated isoprofit line. Such a point is illustrated in Figure 19.1. As usual it is characterized by a tangency condition: the slope of the production function should equal the slope of

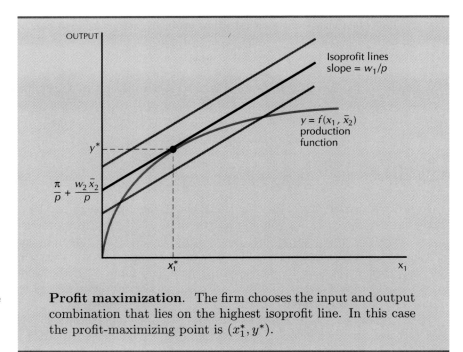

OUTPUT

Isoprofit lines
slope = w_1/p

$y = f(x_1, \bar{x}_2)$
production
function

y^*

$\dfrac{\pi}{p} + \dfrac{w_2\,\bar{x}_2}{p}$

x_1^*

x_1

Figure
19.1

Profit maximization. The firm chooses the input and output combination that lies on the highest isoprofit line. In this case the profit-maximizing point is (x_1^*, y^*).

the isoprofit line. Since the slope of the production function is the marginal product, and the slope of the isoprofit line is w_1/p, this condition can also be written as

$$MP_1 = \frac{w_1}{p},$$

which is equivalent to the condition we derived above.

19.6 Comparative Statics

We can use the geometry depicted in Figure 19.1 to analyze how a firm's choice of inputs and outputs varies as the prices of inputs and outputs vary. This gives us one way to analyze the **comparative statics** of firm behavior.

For example: how does the optimal choice of factor 1 vary as we vary its factor price w_1? Referring to equation (19.1), which defines the isoprofit line, we see that increasing w_1 will make the isoprofit line steeper, as shown in Figure 19.2A. When the isoprofit line is steeper, the tangency must occur further to the left. Thus the optimal level of factor 1 must decrease. This simply means that as the price of factor 1 increases, the demand for factor 1 must decrease: factor demand curves must slope downward.

Similarly, if the output price decreases the isoprofit line must become steeper, as shown in Figure 19.2B. By the same argument as given in the

Comparative statics. Panel A shows that increasing w_1 will reduce the demand for factor 1. Panel B shows that increasing the price of output will increase the demand for factor 1 and therefore increase the supply of output.

Figure
19.2

last paragraph the profit-maximizing choice of factor 1 will decrease. If the amount of factor 1 decreases and the level of factor 2 is fixed in the short run by assumption, then the supply of output must decrease. This gives us another comparative statics result: a reduction in the output price must decrease the supply of output. In other words, the supply function must slope upwards.

Finally, we can ask what will happen if the price of factor 2 changes? Because this is a short-run analysis, changing the price of factor 2 will not change the firm's choice of factor 2—in the short run, the level of factor 2 is fixed at $\overline{x}_2$. Changing the price of factor 2 has no effect on the *slope* of the isoprofit line. Thus the optimal choice of factor 1 will not change, nor will the supply of output. All that changes are the profits that the firm makes.

19.7 Profit Maximization in the Long Run

In the long run the firm is free to choose the level of all inputs. Thus the long-run profit-maximization problem can be posed as

$$\max_{x_1, x_2} \; pf(x_1, x_2) - w_1 x_1 - w_2 x_2.$$

This is basically the same as the short-run problem described above, but now both factors are free to vary.

The condition describing the optimal choices is essentially the same as before, but now we have to apply it to *each* factor. Before we saw that the value of the marginal product of factor 1 must be equal to its price, whatever the level of factor 2. The same sort of condition must now hold for *each* factor choice:

$$pMP_1(x_1^*, x_2^*) = w_1$$

$$pMP_2(x_1^*, x_2^*) = w_2.$$

If the firm has made the optimal choices of factors 1 and 2, the value of the marginal product of each factor should equal its price. At the optimal choice, the firm's profits cannot increase by changing the level of either input.

The argument is the same as used for the short-run profit-maximizing decisions. If the value of the marginal product of factor 1, for example, exceeded the price of factor 1, then using a little more of factor 1 would produce MP_1 more output, which would sell for pMP_1 dollars. If the value of this output exceeds the cost of the factor used to produce it, it clearly pays to expand the use of this factor.

These two conditions give us two equations in two unknowns, x_1^* and x_2^*. If we know how the marginal products behave as a function of x_1 and x_2, we will be able to solve for the optimal choice of each factor as a function of the prices. The resulting equations are known as the **factor demand curves**.

19.8 Inverse Factor Demand Curves

The **factor demand curves** of a firm measure the relationship between the price of a factor and the profit-maximizing choice of that factor. We saw above how to find the profit-maximizing choices: for any prices, (p, w_1, w_2), we just find those factor demands, (x_1^*, x_2^*), such that the value of the marginal product of each factor equals its price.

The **inverse factor demand curve** measures the same relationship, but from a different point of view. It measures what the factor prices must be for some given quantity of inputs to be demanded. Given the optimal choice of factor 2, we can draw the relationship between the optimal choice of factor 1 and its price in a diagram like that depicted in Figure 19.3. This is simply a graph of the equation

$$pMP_1(x_1, x_2^*) = w_1.$$

This curve will be downward sloping by the assumption of diminishing marginal product. For any level of x_1, this curve depicts what the factor price must be in order to induce the firm to demand that level of x_1, holding factor 2 fixed at x_2^*.

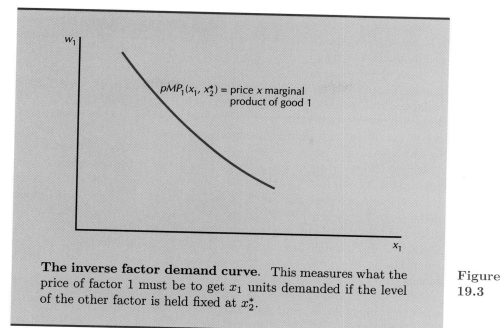

The inverse factor demand curve. This measures what the price of factor 1 must be to get x_1 units demanded if the level of the other factor is held fixed at x_2^*.

Figure
19.3

19.9 Profit Maximization and Returns to Scale

There is an important relationship between competitive profit maximization and returns to scale. Suppose that a firm has chosen a long-run profit-maximizing output $y^* = f(x_1^*, x_2^*)$, which it is producing using input levels (x_1^*, x_2^*).

Then its profits are given by

$$\pi^* = py^* - w_1 x_1^* - w_2 x_2^*.$$

Suppose that this firm's production function exhibits constant returns to scale and that it is making positive profits in equilibrium. Then consider what would happen if it doubled the level of its input usage. According to the constant returns to scale hypothesis, it would double its output level. What would happen to profits?

It is not hard to see that its profits would also double. But this contradicts the assumption that its original choice was profit maximizing! We derived this contradiction by assuming that the original profit level was positive; if the original level of profits were zero there would be no problem: two times zero is still zero.

This argument shows that the only reasonable long-run level of profits for a competitive firm that has constant returns to scale at all levels of output is a zero level of profits. (Of course if a firm has negative profits in the long run, it should go out of business.)

Most people find this to be a surprising statement. Firms are out to maximize profits aren't they? How can it be that they can only get zero profits in the long run?

Think about what would happen to a firm that did try to expand indefinitely. Three things might occur. First, the firm could get so large that it could not really operate effectively. This is just saying that the firm *really* doesn't have constant returns to scale at all levels of output. Eventually, due to coordination problems, it might enter a region of decreasing returns to scale.

Second, the firm might get so large that it would totally dominate the market for its product. In this case there is no reason for it to behave competitively—to take the price of output as given. Instead, it would make sense for such a firm to try to use its size to influence the market price. The model of competitive profit maximization would no longer be a sensible way for the firm to behave, since it would effectively have no competitors. We'll investigate more appropriate models of firm behavior in this situation when we discuss monopoly.

Third, if one firm can make positive profits with a constant returns to scale technology, so can any other firm with access to the same technology. If one firm wants to expand its output, so would other firms. But if all firms expand their outputs, this will certainly push down the price of output and lower the profits of all the firms in the industry.

19.10 Revealed Profitability

When a profit-maximizing firm makes its choice of inputs and outputs it reveals two things: first, that the inputs and outputs used represent a *feasible* production plan, and second, that these choices are more profitable than other feasible choices that the firm could have made. Let us examine these points in more detail.

Suppose that we observe two choices that the firm makes at two different sets of prices. At time t, it faces prices (p^t, w_1^t, w_2^t) and makes choices (y^t, x_1^t, x_2^t). At time s, it faces prices (p^s, w_1^s, w_2^s) and makes choices (y^s, x_1^s, x_2^s). If the production function of the firm hasn't changed between times s and t and if the firm is a profit maximizer, then we must have

$$p^t y^t - w_1^t x_1^t - w_2^t x_2^t \geq p^t y^s - w_1^t x_1^s - w_2^t x_2^s \qquad (19.2)$$

and

$$p^s y^s - w_1^s x_1^s - w_2^s x_2^s \geq p^s y^t - w_1^s x_1^t - w_2^s x_2^t. \qquad (19.3)$$

That is, the profits that the firm achieved facing the t period prices must be larger than if they used the s period plan and vice versa. If either of these inequalities were violated, the firm could not have been a profit-maximizing firm (with an unchanging technology).

Thus if we ever observe two time periods where these inequalities are violated we would know that the firm was not maximizing profits in at least one of the two periods. The satisfaction of these inequalities is virtually an axiom of profit-maximizing behavior, so it might be referred to as the **Weak Axiom of Profit Maximization (WAPM)**.

If the firm's choices satisfy WAPM, we can derive a useful comparative statics statement about the behavior of factor demands and output supplies when prices change. Transpose the two sides of equation (19.3) to get

$$-p^s y^t + w_1^s x_1^t + w_2^s x_1^t \geq -p^s y^s + w_1^s x_1^s + w_2^s x_2^s \qquad (19.4)$$

and add equation (19.4) to equation (19.2) to get

$$(p^t - p^s)y^t - (w_1^t - w_1^s)x_1^t - (w_2^t - w_2^s)x_2^t$$
$$\geq (p^t - p^s)y^s - (w_1^t - w_1^s)x_1^s - (w_2^t - w_2^s)x_2^s. \qquad (19.5)$$

Now rearrange this equation to yield

$$(p^t - p^s)(y^t - y^s) - (w_1^t - w_1^s)(x_1^t - x_1^s) - (w_2^t - w_2^s)(x_2^t - x_2^s) \geq 0. \quad (19.6)$$

Finally define the change in prices, $\Delta p = (p^t - p^s)$, the change in output, $\Delta y = (y^t - y^s)$, and so on to find

$$\Delta p \Delta y - \Delta w_1 \Delta x_1 - \Delta w_2 \Delta x_2 \geq 0. \qquad (19.7)$$

This equation is our final result. It says that the change in the price of output times the change in output minus the change in each factor price times the change in that factor must be nonnegative. This equation comes solely from the definition of profit maximization. Yet it contains all of the comparative statics results about profit-maximizing choices!

For example, suppose that we consider a situation where the price of output changes, but the price of each factor stays constant. If $\Delta w_1 = \Delta w_2 = 0$, then equation (19.7) reduces to

$$\Delta p \Delta y \geq 0.$$

Thus if the price of output goes up, so that $\Delta p > 0$, then the change in output must be nonnegative as well, $\Delta y \geq 0$. This says that the profit-maximizing supply curve of a competitive firm must have a positive (or at least a zero) slope.

Similarly, if the price of output and of factor 2 remain constant, equation (19.7) becomes

$$-\Delta w_1 \Delta x_1 \geq 0,$$

which is to say

$$\Delta w_1 \Delta x_1 \leq 0.$$

Thus if the price of factor 1 goes up, so that $\Delta w_1 > 0$, then equation (19.7) implies that the demand for factor 1 will go down (or at worst stay the same), so that $\Delta x_1 \leq 0$. This means that the factor demand curve must be a decreasing function of the factor price: factor demand curves have a negative slope.

The simple inequality in WAPM, and its implication in equation (19.7), give us strong observable restrictions about how a firm will behave. It is natural to ask whether these are all of the restrictions that the model of profit maximization imposes on firm behavior. Said another way, if we observe a firm's choices, and these choices satisfy WAPM, can we construct an estimate of the technology for which the observed choices are profit-maximizing choices? It turns out that the answer is yes. Figure 19.4 shows how to construct such a technology.

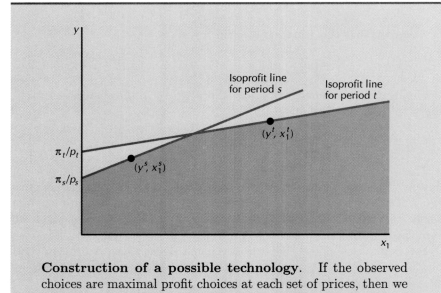

Figure 19.4

Construction of a possible technology. If the observed choices are maximal profit choices at each set of prices, then we can estimate the shape of the technology that generated those choices by using the isoprofit lines.

In order to illustrate the argument graphically, we suppose that there is one input and one output. Suppose that we are given an observed choice in period t and in period s, which we indicate by (p^t, w_1^t, y^t, x_1^t) and (p^s, w_1^s, y^s, x_1^s). In each period we can calculate the profits π_s and π_t and plot all the combinations of y and x_1 that yield these profits.

That is, we plot the two isoprofit lines

$$\pi_t = p^t y - w_1^t x_1$$

and

$$\pi_s = p^s y - w_1^s x_1.$$

The points above the isoprofit line for period t have higher profits than π_t at period t prices, and the points above the isoprofit line for period s have higher profits than π_s at period s prices. WAPM requires that the choice in period t must lie below the period s isoprofit line and that the choice in period s must lie below the period t isoprofit line.

If this condition is satisfied, it is not hard to generate a technology for which (y^t, x_1^t) and (y^s, x_1^s) are profit-maximizing choices. Just take the shaded area beneath the two lines. These are all of the choices that yield lower profits than the observed choices at both sets of prices.

The proof that this technology will generate the observed choices as profit-maximizing choices is clear geometrically. At the prices (p^t, w_1^t), the choice (y^t, x_1^t) is on the highest isoprofit line possible, and the same goes for the period s choice.

Thus, when the observed choices satisfy WAPM, we can "reconstruct" an estimate of a technology that might have generated the observations. In this sense, any observed choices consistent with WAPM could be profit-maximizing choices. As we observe more choices that the firm makes, we get a tighter estimate of the production function, as illustrated in Figure 19.5.

This estimate of the production function can be used to forecast firm behavior in other environments or for other uses in economic analysis.

Estimating the technology. As we observe more choices we get a tighter estimate of the production function.

Figure 19.5

EXAMPLE: How Do Farmers React to Price Supports?

The U.S. government currently spends between \$40 and \$60 billion a year in aid to farmers. A large fraction of this amount is used to subsidize the production of various products including milk, wheat, corn, soybeans, and cotton. Occasionally, attempts are made to reduce or eliminate these subsidies. The effect of elimination of these subsidies would be to reduce the price of the product received by the farmers.

Farmers sometimes argue that eliminating the subsidies to milk, for example, would not reduce the total supply of milk, since dairy farmers would choose to *increase* their herds and their supply of milk so as to keep their standard of living constant.

If farmers are behaving so as to maximize profits, this is impossible. As we've seen above, the logic of profit maximization *requires* that a decrease in the price of an output leads to a reduction in its supply: if Δp is negative, then Δy must be negative as well.

It is certainly possible that small family farms have goals other than simple maximization of profits, but larger "agribusiness" farms are more likely to be profit maximizers. Thus the perverse response to the elimination of subsidies alluded to above could only occur on a limited scale, if at all.

19.11 Cost Minimization

If a firm is maximizing profits and if it chooses to supply some output y, then it must be minimizing the cost of producing y. If this were not so, then there would be some cheaper way of producing y units of output, which would mean that the firm was not maximizing profits in the first place.

This simple observation turns out to be quite useful in examining firm behavior. It turns out to be convenient to break the profit-maximization problem into two stages: first we figure out how to minimize the costs of producing any desired level of output y, then we figure out which level of output is indeed a profit-maximizing level of output. We begin this task in the next chapter.

Summary

1. Profits are the difference between revenues and costs. In this definition it is important that all costs be measured using the appropriate market prices.

2. Fixed factors are factors whose amount is independent of the level of output; variable factors are factors whose amount used changes as the level of output changes.

3. In the short run, some factors must be used in predetermined amounts. In the long run, all factors are free to vary.

4. If the firm is maximizing profits, then the value of the marginal product of each factor that it is free to vary must equal its factor price.

5. The logic of profit maximization implies that the supply function of a competitive firm must be an increasing function of the price of output and that each factor demand function must be a decreasing function of its price.

6. If a competitive firm exhibits constant returns to scale, then its long-run maximum profits must be zero.

REVIEW QUESTIONS

1. In the short run, if the price of the fixed factor is increased, what will happen to profits?

2. If a firm had everywhere increasing returns to scale, what would happen to its profits if prices remained fixed and if it doubled its scale of operation?

3. If a firm had decreasing returns to scale at all levels of output and it divided up into two equal-size smaller firms, what would happen to its overall profits?

4. A gardener exclaims: "For only $1 in seeds I've grown over $20 in produce!" Besides the fact that most of the produce is in the form of zucchini, what other observations would a cynical economist make about this situation?

5. Is maximizing a firm's profits always identical to maximizing the firm's stock market value?

6. If $pMP_1 > w_1$, then should the firm increase or decrease the amount of factor 1 in order to increase profits?

7. Suppose a firm is maximizing profits in the short run with variable factor x_1 and fixed factor x_2. If the price of x_2 goes down, what happens to the firm's use of x_1? What happens to the firm's level of profits?

8. A profit-maximizing competitive firm that is making positive profits in long-run equilibrium (may/may not) have a technology with constant returns to scale.

APPENDIX

The profit-maximization problem of the firm is

$$\max_{x_1, x_2} p f(x_1, x_2) - w_1 x_1 - w_2 x_2,$$

which has first-order conditions

$$p \frac{\partial f(x_1^*, x_2^*)}{\partial x_1} - w_1 = 0$$

$$p \frac{\partial f(x_1^*, x_2^*)}{\partial x_2} - w_2 = 0.$$

These are just the same as the marginal product conditions given in the text. Let's see how profit-maximizing behavior looks using the Cobb-Douglas production function.

Suppose the Cobb-Douglas function is given by $f(x_1, x_2) = x_1^a x_2^b$. Then the two first-order conditions become

$$pa x_1^{a-1} x_2^b - w_1 = 0$$

$$pb x_1^a x_2^{b-1} - w_2 = 0.$$

Multiply the first equation by x_1 and the second equation by x_2 to get

$$pa x_1^a x_2^b - w_1 x_1 = 0$$

$$pb x_1^a x_2^b - w_2 x_2 = 0.$$

Using $y = x_1^a x_2^b$ to denote the level of output of this firm we can rewrite these expressions as

$$pay = w_1 x_1$$

$$pby = w_2 x_2.$$

Solving for x_1 and x_2 we have

$$x_1^* = \frac{apy}{w_1}$$

$$x_2^* = \frac{bpy}{w_2}.$$

This gives us the demands for the two factors as a function of the optimal output choice. But we still have to solve for the optimal choice of output. Inserting the optimal factor demands into the Cobb-Douglas production function, we have the expression

$$\left(\frac{pay}{w_1} \right)^a \left(\frac{pby}{w_2} \right)^b = y.$$

Factoring out the y gives

$$\left(\frac{pa}{w_1} \right)^a \left(\frac{pb}{w_2} \right)^b y^{a+b} = y.$$

Or

$$y = \left(\frac{pa}{w_1}\right)^{\frac{a}{1-a-b}} \left(\frac{pb}{w_2}\right)^{\frac{b}{1-a-b}}.$$

This gives us the supply function of the Cobb-Douglas firm. Along with the factor demand functions derived above it gives us a complete solution to the profit-maximization problem.

Note that when the firm exhibits constant returns to scale—when $a + b = 1$—this supply function is not well defined. As long as the output and input prices are consistent with zero profits, a firm with a Cobb-Douglas technology is indifferent about its level of supply.

CHAPTER **20**

COST
MINIMIZATION

Our goal is to study the behavior of profit-maximizing firms in both competitive and noncompetitive market environments. In the last chapter we began our investigation of profit-maximizing behavior in a competitive environment by examining the profit-maximization problem directly.

However, some important insights can be gained through a more indirect approach. Our strategy will be to break up the profit-maximization problem into two pieces. First, we will look at the problem of how to minimize the costs of producing any given level of output, and then we will look at how to choose the most profitable level of output. In this chapter we'll look at the first step—minimizing the costs of producing a given level of output.

20.1 Cost Minimization

Suppose that we have two factors of production that have prices w_1 and w_2, and that we want to figure out the cheapest way to produce a given level of output, y. If we let x_1 and x_2 measure the amounts used of the two factors and let $f(x_1, x_2)$ be the production function for the firm, we can write this problem as

$$\min_{x_1, x_2} w_1 x_1 + w_2 x_2$$

$$\text{such that } f(x_1, x_2) = y.$$

The same warnings apply as in the preceding chapter concerning this sort of analysis: make sure that you have included *all* costs of production in the calculation of costs, and make sure that everything is being measured on a compatible time scale.

The solution to this cost-minimization problem—the minimum costs necessary to achieve the desired level of output—will depend on w_1, w_2, and y, so we write it as $c(w_1, w_2, y)$. This function is known as the **cost function** and will be of considerable interest to us. The cost function $c(w_1, w_2, y)$ measures the minimal costs of producing y units of output when factor prices are (w_1, w_2).

In order to understand the solution to this problem, let us depict the costs and the technological constraints facing the firm on the same diagram. The isoquants give us the technological constraints—all the combinations of x_1 and x_2 that can produce y.

Suppose that we want to plot all the combinations of inputs that have some given level of cost, C. We can write this as

$$w_1 x_1 + w_2 x_2 = C,$$

which can be rearranged to give

$$x_2 = \frac{C}{w_2} - \frac{w_1}{w_2} x_1.$$

It is easy to see that this is a straight line with a slope of $-w_1/w_2$ and a vertical intercept of C/w_2. As we let the number C vary we get a whole family of **isocost lines**. Every point on an isocost curve has the same cost, C, and higher isocost lines are associated with higher costs.

Thus our cost-minimization problem can be rephrased as: find the point on the isoquant that has the lowest possible isocost line associated with it. Such a point is illustrated in Figure 20.1.

Note that if the optimal solution involves using some of each factor, and if the isoquant is a nice smooth curve, then the cost-minimizing point will be characterized by a tangency condition: the slope of the isoquant must be equal to the slope of the isocost curve. Or, using the terminology of Chapter 18, the *technical rate of substitution must equal the factor price ratio*:

$$-\frac{MP_1(x_1^*, x_2^*)}{MP_2(x_1^*, x_2^*)} = \text{TRS}(x_1^*, x_2^*) = -\frac{w_1}{w_2}. \tag{20.1}$$

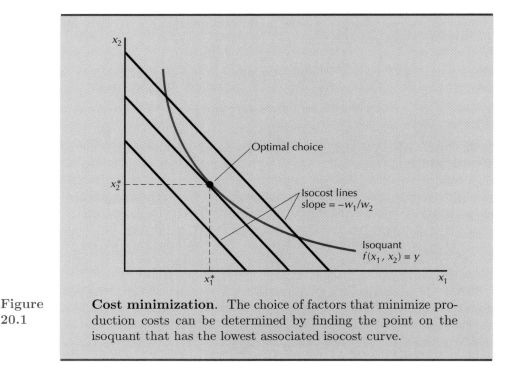

Figure
20.1

Cost minimization. The choice of factors that minimize production costs can be determined by finding the point on the isoquant that has the lowest associated isocost curve.

(If we have a boundary solution where one of the two factors isn't used, this tangency condition need not be met. Similarly, if the production function has "kinks," the tangency condition has no meaning. These exceptions are just like the situation with the consumer, so we won't emphasize these cases in this chapter.)

The algebra that lies behind equation (20.1) is not difficult. Consider any change in the pattern of production $(\Delta x_1, \Delta x_2)$ that keeps output constant. Such a change must satisfy

$$MP_1(x_1^*, x_2^*)\Delta x_1 + MP_2(x_1^*, x_2^*)\Delta x_2 = 0. \qquad (20.2)$$

Note that Δx_1 and Δx_2 must be of opposite signs; if you increase the amount used of factor 1 you must decrease the amount used of factor 2 in order to keep output constant.

If we are at the cost minimum, then this change cannot lower costs, so we have

$$w_1 \Delta x_1 + w_2 \Delta x_2 \geq 0. \qquad (20.3)$$

Now consider the change $(-\Delta x_1, -\Delta x_2)$. This also produces a constant level of output, and it too cannot lower costs. This implies that

$$-w_1 \Delta x_1 - w_2 \Delta x_2 \geq 0. \qquad (20.4)$$

Putting expressions (20.3) and (20.4) together gives us

$$w_1 \Delta x_1 + w_2 \Delta x_2 = 0. \tag{20.5}$$

Solving equations (20.2) and (20.5) for $\Delta x_2 / \Delta x_1$ gives

$$\frac{\Delta x_2}{\Delta x_1} = -\frac{w_1}{w_2} = -\frac{MP_1(x_1^*, x_2^*)}{MP_2(x_1^*, x_2^*)},$$

which is just the condition for cost minimization derived above by a geo-metric argument.

Note that Figure 20.1 bears a certain resemblance to the solution to the consumer-choice problem depicted earlier. Although the solutions look the same, they really aren't the same kind of problem. In the consumer problem, the straight line was the budget constraint, and the consumer moved along the budget constraint to find the most-preferred position. In the producer problem, the isoquant is the technological constraint and the producer moves along the isoquant to find the optimal position.

The choices of inputs that yield minimal costs for the firm will in general depend on the input prices and the level of output that the firm wants to produce, so we write these choices as $x_1(w_1, w_2, y)$ and $x_2(w_1, w_2, y)$. These are called the **conditional factor demand functions**, or **derived factor demands**. They measure the relationship between the prices and output and the optimal factor choice of the firm, *conditional* on the firm producing a given level of output, y.

Note carefully the difference between the *conditional* factor demands and the profit-maximizing factor demands discussed in the last chapter. The conditional factor demands give the cost-minimizing choices for a given *level* of output; the profit-maximizing factor demands give the profit-maximizing choices for a given *price* of output.

Conditional factor demands are usually not directly observed; they are a hypothetical construct. They answer the question of how much of each factor *would* the firm use if it wanted to produce a given level of output in the cheapest way. However, the conditional factor demands are useful as a way of separating the problem of determining the optimal level of output from the problem of determining the most cost-effective method of production.

EXAMPLE: Minimizing Costs for Specific Technologies

Suppose that we consider a technology where the factors are perfect com-plements, so that $f(x_1, x_2) = \min\{x_1, x_2\}$. Then if we want to produce y units of output, we clearly need y units of x_1 and y units of x_2. Thus the minimal costs of production will be

$$c(w_1, w_2, y) = w_1 y + w_2 y = (w_1 + w_2)y.$$

What about the perfect substitutes technology, $f(x_1, x_2) = x_1 + x_2$? Since goods 1 and 2 are perfect substitutes in production it is clear that the firm will use whichever is cheaper. Thus the minimum cost of producing y units of output will be $w_1 y$ or $w_2 y$, whichever is less. In other words:

$$c(w_1, w_2, y) = \min\{w_1 y, w_2 y\} = \min\{w_1, w_2\} y.$$

Finally, we consider the Cobb-Douglas technology, which is described by the formula $f(x_1, x_2) = x_1^a x_2^b$. In this case we can use calculus techniques to show that the cost function will have the form

$$c(w_1, w_2, y) = K w_1^{\frac{a}{a+b}} w_2^{\frac{b}{a+b}} y^{\frac{1}{a+b}},$$

where K is a constant that depends on a and b. The details of the calculation are presented in the Appendix.

20.2 Revealed Cost Minimization

The assumption that the firm chooses factors to minimize the cost of producing output will have implications for how the observed choices change as factor prices change.

Suppose that we observe two sets of prices, (w_1^t, w_2^t) and (w_1^s, w_2^s), and the associated choices of the firm, (x_1^t, x_2^t) and (x_1^s, x_2^s). Suppose that each of these choices produces the same output level y. Then if each choice is a cost-minimizing choice at its associated prices, we must have

$$w_1^t x_1^t + w_2^t x_2^t \leq w_1^t x_1^s + w_2^t x_2^s$$

and

$$w_1^s x_1^s + w_2^s x_2^s \leq w_1^s x_1^t + w_2^s x_2^t.$$

If the firm is always choosing the cost-minimizing way to produce y units of output, then its choices at times t and s must satisfy these inequalities. We will refer to these inequalities as the **Weak Axiom of Cost Minimization (WACM)**.

Write the second equation as

$$-w_1^s x_1^t - w_2^s x_2^t \leq -w_1^s x_1^s - w_2^s x_2^s$$

and add it to the first equation to get

$$(w_1^t - w_1^s) x_1^t + (w_2^t - w_2^s) x_2^t \leq (w_1^t - w_1^s) x_1^s + (w_2^t - w_2^s) x_2^s,$$

which can be rearranged to give us

$$(w_1^t - w_1^s)(x_1^t - x_1^s) + (w_2^t - w_2^s)(x_2^t - x_2^s) \leq 0.$$

Using the delta notation to depict the *changes* in the factor demands and factor prices, we have

$$\Delta w_1 \Delta x_1 + \Delta w_2 \Delta x_2 \leq 0.$$

This equation follows solely from the assumption of cost-minimizing behavior. It implies restrictions on how the firm's behavior can change when input prices change and output remains constant.

For example, if the price of the first factor increases and the price of the second factor stays constant, then $\Delta w_2 = 0$, so the inequality becomes

$$\Delta w_1 \Delta x_1 \leq 0.$$

If the price of factor 1 increases, then this inequality implies that the demand for factor 1 must decrease; thus the conditional factor demand functions must slope down.

What can we say about how the minimal costs change as we change the parameters of the problem? It is easy to see that costs must increase if either factor price increases: if one good becomes more expensive and the other stays the same, the minimal costs cannot go down and in general will increase. Similarly, if the firm chooses to produce more output and factor prices remain constant, the firm's costs will have to increase.

Returns to Scale and the Cost Function

In Chapter 18 we discussed the idea of returns to scale for the production function. Recall that a technology is said to have increasing, decreasing, or constant returns to scale as $f(tx_1, tx_2)$ is greater, less than, or equal to $tf(x_1, x_2)$ for all $t > 1$. It turns out that there is a nice relation between the kind of returns to scale exhibited by the production function and the behavior of the cost function.

Suppose first that we have the natural case of constant returns to scale. Imagine that we have solved the cost-minimization problem to produce 1 unit of output, so that we know the **unit cost function**, $c(w_1, w_2, 1)$. Now what is the cheapest way to produce y units of output? Simple: we just use y times as much of every input as we were using to produce 1 unit of output. This would mean that the minimal cost to produce y units of output would just be $c(w_1, w_2, 1)y$. In the case of constant returns to scale, the cost function is linear in output.

What if we have increasing returns to scale? In this case it turns out that costs increase less than linearly in output. If the firm decides to produce twice as much output, it can do so at *less* than twice the cost, as long as the factor prices remain fixed. This is a natural implication of the idea of increasing returns to scale: if the firm doubles its inputs, it will more than double its output. Thus if it wants to produce double the output, it will be able to do so by using less than twice as much of every input.

But using twice as much of every input will exactly double costs. So using less than twice as much of every input will make costs go up by less than twice as much: this is just saying that the cost function will increase less than linearly with respect to output.

Similarly, if the technology exhibits decreasing returns to scale, the cost function will increase more than linearly with respect to output. If output doubles, costs will more than double.

These facts can be expressed in terms of the behavior of the **average cost function**. The average cost function is simply the cost *per unit* to produce y units of output:

$$AC(y) = \frac{c(w_1, w_2, y)}{y}.$$

If the technology exhibits constant returns to scale, then we saw above that the cost function had the form $c(w_1, w_2, y) = c(w_1, w_2, 1)y$. This means that the average cost function will be

$$AC(w_1, w_2, y) = \frac{c(w_1, w_2, 1)y}{y} = c(w_1, w_2, 1).$$

That is, the cost per unit of output will be constant no matter what level of output the firm wants to produce.

If the technology exhibits increasing returns to scale, then the costs will increase less than linearly with respect to output, so the average costs will be declining in output: as output increases, the average costs of production will tend to fall.

Similarly, if the technology exhibits decreasing returns to scale, then average costs will rise as output increases.

As we saw earlier, a given technology can have *regions* of increasing, constant, or decreasing returns to scale—output can increase more rapidly, equally rapidly, or less rapidly than the scale of operation of the firm at different levels of production. Similarly, the cost function can increase less rapidly, equally rapidly, or more rapidly than output at different levels of production. This implies that the average cost function may decrease, remain constant, or increase over different levels of output. In the next chapter we will explore these possibilities in more detail.

From now on we will be most concerned with the behavior of the cost function with respect to the output variable. For the most part we will regard the factor prices as being fixed at some predetermined levels and only think of costs as depending on the output choice of the firm. Thus for the remainder of the book we will write the cost function as a function of output alone: $c(y)$.

20.4 Long-Run and Short-Run Costs

The cost function is defined as the minimum cost of achieving a given level of output. Often it is important to distinguish the minimum costs if the firm is allowed to adjust all of its factors of production from the minimum costs if the firm is only allowed to adjust some of its factors.

We have defined the short run to be a time period where some of the factors of production must be used in a fixed amount. In the long run, all factors are free to vary. The **short-run cost function** is defined as the minimum cost to produce a given level of output, only adjusting the variable factors of production. The **long-run cost function** gives the minimum cost of producing a given level of output, adjusting *all* of the factors of production.

Suppose that in the short run factor 2 is fixed at some predetermined level $\bar{x}_2$, but in the long run it is free to vary. Then the short-run cost function is defined by

$$c_s(y, \bar{x}_2) = \min_{x_1} w_1 x_1 + w_2 \bar{x}_2$$

such that $f(x_1, \bar{x}_2) = y$.

Note that in general the minimum cost to produce y units of output in the short run will depend on the amount and cost of the fixed factor that is available.

In the case of two factors, this minimization problem is easy to solve: we just find the smallest amount of x_1 such that $f(x_1, \bar{x}_2) = y$. However, if there are many factors of production that are variable in the short run the cost-minimization problem will involve more elaborate calculation.

The short-run factor demand function for factor 1 is the amount of factor 1 that minimizes costs. In general it will depend on the factor prices and on the levels of the fixed factors as well, so we write the short-run factor demands as

$$x_1 = x_1^s(w_1, w_2, \bar{x}_2, y)$$
$$x_2 = \bar{x}_2.$$

These equations just say, for example, that if the building size is fixed in the short run, then the number of workers that a firm wants to hire at any given set of prices and output choice will typically depend on the size of the building.

Note that by definition of the short-run cost function

$$c_s(y, \bar{x}_2) = w_1 x_1^s(w_1, w_2, \bar{x}_2, y) + w_2 \bar{x}_2.$$

This just says that the minimum cost of producing output y is the cost associated with using the cost-minimizing choice of inputs. This is true by definition but turns out to be useful nevertheless.

The long-run cost function in this example is defined by

$$c(y) = \min_{x_1,x_2} w_1 x_1 + w_2 x_2$$

such that $f(x_1, x_2) = y$.

Here both factors are free to vary. Long-run costs depend only on the level of output that the firm wants to produce along with factor prices. We write the long-run cost function as $c(y)$, and write the long-run factor demands as

$$x_1 = x_1(w_1, w_2, y)$$
$$x_2 = x_2(w_1, w_2, y).$$

We can also write the long-run cost function as

$$c(y) = w_1 x_1(w_1, w_2, y) + w_2 x_2(w_1, w_2, y).$$

Just as before, this simply says that the minimum costs are the costs that the firm gets by using the cost-minimizing choice of factors.

There is an interesting relation between the short-run and the long-run cost functions that we will use in the next chapter. For simplicity, let us suppose that factor prices are fixed at some predetermined levels and write the long-run factor demands as

$$x_1 = x_1(y)$$
$$x_2 = x_2(y).$$

Then the long-run cost function can also be written as

$$c(y) = c_s(y, x_2(y)).$$

To see why this is true, just think about what it means. The equation says that the minimum costs when all factors are variable is just the minimum cost when factor 2 is fixed *at the level that minimizes long-run costs*. It follows that the long-run demand for the variable factor—the cost-minimizing choice—is given by

$$x_1(w_1, w_2, y) = x_1^s(w_1, w_2, x_2(y), y).$$

This equation says that the cost-minimizing amount of the variable factor in the long run is that amount that the firm would choose in the short run—if it happened to have the long-run cost-minimizing amount of the fixed factor.

20.5 Fixed and Quasi-Fixed Costs

In Chapter 19 we made the distinction between fixed factors and quasi-fixed factors. Fixed factors are factors that must receive payment whether or not any output is produced. Quasi-fixed factors must be paid only if the firm decides to produce a positive amount of output.

It is natural to define fixed costs and quasi-fixed costs in a similar manner. **Fixed costs** are costs associated with the fixed factors: they are independent of the level of output, and, in particular, they must be paid whether or not the firm produces output. **Quasi-fixed costs** are costs that are also independent of the level of output, but only need to be paid if the firm produces a positive amount of output.

There are no fixed costs in the long run, by definition. However, there may easily be quasi-fixed costs in the long run. If it is necessary to spend a fixed amount of money before any output at all can be produced, then quasi-fixed costs will be present.

20.6 Sunk Costs

Sunk costs are another kind of fixed costs. The concept is best explained by example. Suppose that you have decided to lease an office for a year. The monthly rent that you have committed to pay is a fixed cost, since you are obligated to pay it regardless of the amount of output you produce. Now suppose that you decide to refurbish the office by painting it and buying furniture. The cost for paint is a fixed cost, but it is also a **sunk cost** since it is a payment that is made and cannot be recovered. The cost of buying the furniture, on the other hand, is not entirely sunk, since you can resell the furniture when you are done with it. It's only the *difference* between the cost of new and used furniture that is sunk.

To spell this out in more detail, suppose that you borrow $20,000 at the beginning of the year at, say, 10 percent interest. You sign a lease to rent an office and pay $12,000 in advance rent for next year. You spend $6,000 on office furniture and $2,000 to paint the office. At the end of the year you pay back the $20,000 loan plus the $2,000 interest payment and sell the used office furniture for $5,000.

Your total sunk costs consist of the $12,000 rent, the $2,000 of interest, the $2,000 of paint, but only $1,000 for the furniture, since $5,000 of the orginal furniture expenditure is recoverable.

The difference between sunk costs and recoverable costs can be quite significant. A $100,000 expenditure to purchase five light trucks sounds like a lot of money, but if they can later be sold on the used truck market for $80,000, the actual sunk cost is only $20,000. A $100,000 expenditure on a custom-made press for stamping out gizmos that has a zero resale value is quite different; in this case the entire expenditure is sunk.

The best way to keep these issues straight is to make sure to treat all expenditures on a flow basis: how much does it cost to do business for a year? That way, one is less likely to forget the resale value of capital equipment and more likely to keep the distinction between sunk costs and recoverable costs clear.

Summary

1. The cost function, $c(w_1, w_2, y)$, measures the minimum costs of producing a given level of output at given factor prices.

2. Cost-minimizing behavior imposes observable restrictions on choices that firms make. In particular, conditional factor demand functions will be negatively sloped.

3. There is an intimate relationship between the returns to scale exhibited by the technology and the behavior of the cost function. *Increasing* returns to scale implies *decreasing* average cost, *decreasing* returns to scale implies *increasing* average cost, and *constant* returns to scale implies *constant* average cost.

4. Sunk costs are costs that are not recoverable.

REVIEW QUESTIONS

1. Prove that a profit-maximizing firm will always minimize costs.

2. If a firm is producing where $MP_1/w_1 > MP_2/w_2$, what can it do to reduce costs but maintain the same output?

3. Suppose that a cost-minimizing firm uses two inputs that are perfect substitutes. If the two inputs are priced the same, what do the conditional factor demands look like for the inputs?

4. The price of paper used by a cost-minimizing firm increases. The firm responds to this price change by changing its demand for certain inputs, but it keeps its output constant. What happens to the firm's use of paper?

5. If a firm uses n inputs $(n > 2)$, what inequality does the theory of revealed cost minimization imply about changes in factor prices (Δw_i) and the changes in factor demands (Δx_i) for a given level of output?

APPENDIX

Let us study the cost-minimization problem posed in the text using the optimization techniques introduced in Chapter 5. The problem is a constrained-minimization problem of the form

$$\min_{x_1, x_2} w_1 x_1 + w_2 x_2$$

$$\text{such that } f(x_1, x_2) = y.$$

Recall that we had several techniques to solve this kind of problem. One way was to substitute the constraint into the objective function. This can still be used when we have a specific functional form for $f(x_1, x_2)$, but isn't much use in the general case.

The second method was the method of Lagrange multipliers and that works fine. To apply this method we set up the Lagrangian

$$L = w_1 x_1 + w_2 x_2 - \lambda (f(x_1, x_2) - y)$$

and differentiate with respect to x_1, x_2 and λ. This gives us the first-order conditions:

$$w_1 - \lambda \frac{\partial f(x_1, x_2)}{\partial x_1} = 0$$

$$w_2 - \lambda \frac{\partial f(x_1, x_2)}{\partial x_2} = 0$$

$$f(x_1, x_2) - y = 0.$$

The last condition is simply the constraint. We can rearrange the first two equations and divide the first equation by the second equation to get

$$\frac{w_1}{w_2} = \frac{\partial f(x_1, x_2)/\partial x_1}{\partial f(x_1, x_2)/\partial x_2}.$$

Note that this is the same first-order condition that we derived in the text: the technical rate of substitution must equal the factor price ratio.

Let's apply this method to the Cobb-Douglas production function:

$$f(x_1, x_2) = x_1^a x_2^b.$$

The cost-minimization problem is then

$$\min_{x_1, x_2} w_1 x_1 + w_2 x_2$$

$$\text{such that } x_1^a x_2^b = y.$$

Here we have a specific functional form, and we can solve it using either the substitution method or the Lagrangian method. The substitution method would involve first solving the constraint for x_2 as a function of x_1:

$$x_2 = \left(y x_1^{-a} \right)^{1/b}$$

and then substituting this into the objective function to get the unconstrained minimization problem

$$\min_{x_1} w_1 x_1 + w_2 \left(y x_1^{-a} \right)^{1/b}.$$

We could now differentiate with respect to x_1 and set resulting derivative equal to zero, as usual. The resulting equation can be solved to get x_1 as a function of w_1, w_2, and y, to get the conditional factor demand for x_1. This isn't hard to do, but the algebra is messy, so we won't write down the details.

We will, however, solve the Lagrangian problem. The three first-order conditions are

$$w_1 = \lambda a x_1^{a-1} x_2^{b}$$
$$w_2 = \lambda b x_1^{a} x_2^{b-1}$$
$$y = x_1^{a} x_2^{b}.$$

Multiply the first equation by x_1 and the second equation by x_2 to get

$$w_1 x_1 = \lambda a x_1^{a} x_2^{b} = \lambda a y$$

$$w_2 x_2 = \lambda b x_1^{a} x_2^{b} = \lambda b y,$$

so that

$$x_1 = \lambda \frac{ay}{w_1} \tag{20.6}$$

$$x_2 = \lambda \frac{by}{w_2}. \tag{20.7}$$

Now we use the third equation to solve for λ. Substituting the solutions for x_1 and x_2 into the third first-order condition, we have

$$\left(\frac{\lambda a y}{w_1} \right)^{a} \left(\frac{\lambda b y}{w_2} \right)^{b} = y.$$

We can solve this equation for λ to get the rather formidable expression

$$\lambda = \left(a^{-a} b^{-b} w_1^{a} w_2^{b} y^{1-a-b} \right)^{\frac{1}{a+b}},$$

which, along with equations (20.6) and (20.7), gives us our final solutions for x_1 and x_2. These factor demand functions will take the form

$$x_1(w_1, w_2, y) = \left(\frac{a}{b} \right)^{\frac{b}{a+b}} w_1^{\frac{-b}{a+b}} w_2^{\frac{b}{a+b}} y^{\frac{1}{a+b}}$$

$$x_2(w_1, w_2, y) = \left(\frac{a}{b} \right)^{-\frac{a}{a+b}} w_1^{\frac{a}{a+b}} w_2^{\frac{-a}{a+b}} y^{\frac{1}{a+b}}.$$

The cost function can be found by writing down the costs when the firm makes the cost-minimizing choices. That is,

$$c(w_1, w_2, y) = w_1 x_1(w_1, w_2, y) + w_2 x_2(w_1, w_2, y).$$

Some tedious algebra shows that

$$c(w_1, w_2, y) = \left[\left(\frac{a}{b}\right)^{\frac{b}{a+b}} + \left(\frac{a}{b}\right)^{\frac{-a}{a+b}}\right] w_1^{\frac{a}{a+b}} w_2^{\frac{b}{a+b}} y^{\frac{1}{a+b}}.$$

(Don't worry, this formula won't be on the final exam. It is presented only to demonstrate how to get an explicit solution to the cost-minimization problem by applying the method of Lagrange multipliers.)

Note that costs will increase more than, equal to, or less than linearly with output as $a + b$ is less than, equal to, or greater than 1. This makes sense since the Cobb-Douglas technology exhibits decreasing, constant, or increasing returns to scale depending on the value of $a + b$.

CHAPTER 21

COST
CURVES

In the last chapter we described the cost-minimizing behavior of a firm. Here we continue that investigation through the use of an important geometric construction, the **cost curve**. Cost curves can be used to depict graphically the cost function of a firm and are important in studying the determination of optimal output choices.

21.1 Average Costs

Consider the cost function described in the last chapter. This is the function $c(w_1, w_2, y)$ that gives the minimum cost of producing output level y when factor prices are (w_1, w_2). In the rest of this chapter we will take the factor prices to be fixed so that we can write cost as a function of y alone, $c(y)$.

Some of the costs of the firm are independent of the level of output of the firm. As we've seen in Chapter 20, these are the fixed costs. Fixed costs are the costs that must be paid regardless of what level of output the firm produces. For example, the firm might have mortgage payments that are required no matter what its level of output.

Other costs change when output changes: these are the variable costs. The total costs of the firm can always be written as the sum of the variable costs, $c_v(y)$, and the fixed costs, F:

$$c(y) = c_v(y) + F.$$

The **average cost function** measures the cost per unit of output. The **average variable cost function** measures the variable costs per unit of output, and the **average fixed cost function** measures the fixed costs per unit output. By the above equation:

$$AC(y) = \frac{c(y)}{y} = \frac{c_v(y)}{y} + \frac{F}{y} = AVC(y) + AFC(y)$$

where $AVC(y)$ stands for average variable costs and $AFC(y)$ stands for average fixed costs. What do these functions look like? The easiest one is certainly the average fixed cost function: when $y = 0$ it is infinite, and as y increases the average fixed cost decreases toward zero. This is depicted in Figure 21.1A.

Construction of the average cost curve. (A) The average fixed costs decrease as output is increased. (B) The average variable costs eventually increase as output is increased. (C) The combination of these two effects produces a U-shaped average cost curve.

Figure 21.1

Consider the variable cost function. Start at a zero level of output and consider producing one unit. Then the average variable costs at $y = 1$ is just the variable cost of producing this one unit. Now increase the level of production to 2 units. We would expect that, at worst, variable costs would double, so that average variable costs would remain constant. If we can organize production in a more efficient way as the scale of output is increased, the average variable costs might even decrease initially. But eventually we would expect the average variable costs to rise. Why? If fixed factors are present, they will eventually constrain the production process.

For example, suppose that the fixed costs are due to the rent or mortgage payments on a building of fixed size. Then as production increases, average variable costs—the per-unit production costs—may remain constant for a while. But as the capacity of the building is reached, these costs will rise sharply, producing an average variable cost curve of the form depicted in Figure 21.1B.

The average cost curve is the sum of these two curves; thus it will have the U-shape indicated in Figure 21.1C. The initial decline in average costs is due to the decline in average fixed costs; the eventual increase in average costs is due to the increase in average variable costs. The combination of these two effects yields the U-shape depicted in the diagram.

21.2 Marginal Costs

There is one more cost curve of interest: the **marginal cost curve**. The marginal cost curve measures the *change* in costs for a given change in output. That is, at any given level of output y, we can ask how costs will change if we change output by some amount Δy:

$$MC(y) = \frac{\Delta c(y)}{\Delta y} = \frac{c(y + \Delta y) - c(y)}{\Delta y}.$$

We could just as well write the definition of marginal costs in terms of the variable cost function:

$$MC(y) = \frac{\Delta c_v(y)}{\Delta y} = \frac{c_v(y + \Delta y) - c_v(y)}{\Delta y}.$$

This is equivalent to the first definition, since $c(y) = c_v(y) + F$ and the fixed costs, F, don't change as y changes.

Often we think of Δy as being one unit of output, so that marginal cost indicates the change in our costs if we consider producing one more discrete unit of output. If we are thinking of the production of a discrete good, then marginal cost of producing y units of output is just $c(y) - c(y - 1)$. This is often a convenient way to think about marginal cost, but is sometimes misleading. Remember, marginal cost measures a *rate of change*: the change in costs divided by a change in output. If the change in output is a single unit, then marginal cost looks like a simple change in costs, but it is really a rate of change as we increase the output by one unit.

How can we put this marginal cost curve on the diagram presented above? First we note the following. The variable costs are zero when zero units of output are produced, by definition. Thus for the first unit of output produced

$$MC(1) = \frac{c_v(1) + F - c_v(0) - F}{1} = \frac{c_v(1)}{1} = AVC(1).$$

Thus the marginal cost for the first small unit of amount equals the average variable cost for a single unit of output.

Now suppose that we are producing in a range of output where *average* variable costs are decreasing. Then it must be that the *marginal* costs are less than the average variable costs in this range. For the way that you push an average down is to add in numbers that are less than the average.

Think about a sequence of numbers representing average costs at different levels of output. If the average is decreasing, it must be that the cost of each additional unit produced is less than average up to that point. To make the average go down, you have to be adding additional units that are less than the average.

Similarly, if we are in a region where average variable costs are rising, then it must be the case that the marginal costs are greater than the average variable costs—it is the higher marginal costs that are pushing the average up.

Thus we know that the marginal cost curve must lie below the average variable cost curve to the left of its minimum point and above it to the right. This implies that the marginal cost curve must intersect the average variable cost curve at its minimum point.

Exactly the same kind of argument applies for the average cost curve. If average costs are falling, then marginal costs must be less than the average costs and if average costs are rising the marginal costs must be larger than the average costs. These observations allow us to draw in the marginal cost curve as in Figure 21.2.

To review the important points:

- The average variable cost curve may initially slope down but need not. However, it will eventually rise, as long as there are fixed factors that constrain production.

- The average cost curve will initially fall due to declining fixed costs but then rise due to the increasing average variable costs.

- The marginal cost and average variable cost are the same at the first unit of output.

- The marginal cost curve passes through the minimum point of both the average variable cost and the average cost curves.

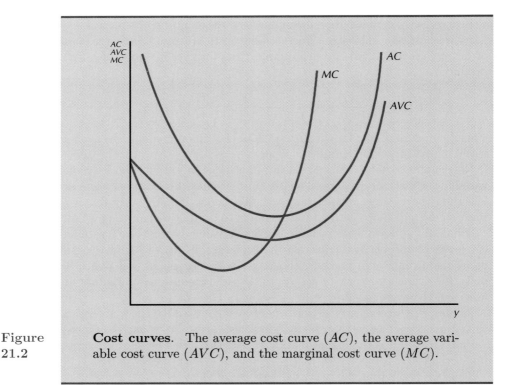

Figure
21.2

Cost curves. The average cost curve (AC), the average variable cost curve (AVC), and the marginal cost curve (MC).

21.3 Marginal Costs and Variable Costs

There are also some other relationships between the various curves. Here is
one that is not so obvious: it turns out that the area beneath the marginal
cost curve up to y gives us the variable cost of producing y units of output.
Why is that?

The marginal cost curve measures the cost of producing each additional
unit of output. If we add up the cost of producing each unit of output we
will get the total costs of production—except for fixed costs.

This argument can be made rigorous in the case where the output good
is produced in discrete amounts. First, we note that

$$c_v(y) = [c_v(y) - c_v(y-1)] + [c_v(y-1) - c_v(y-2] + \\ \cdots + [c_v(1) - c_v(0)].$$

This is true since $c_v(0) = 0$ and all the middle terms cancel out; that is, the
second term cancels the third term, the fourth term cancels the fifth term,
and so on. But each term in this sum is the marginal cost at a different
level of output:

$$c_v(y) = MC(y-1) + MC(y-2) + \cdots + MC(0).$$

Thus each term in the sum represents the area of a rectangle with height $MC(y)$ and base of 1. Summing up all these rectangles gives us the area under the marginal cost curve as depicted in Figure 21.3.

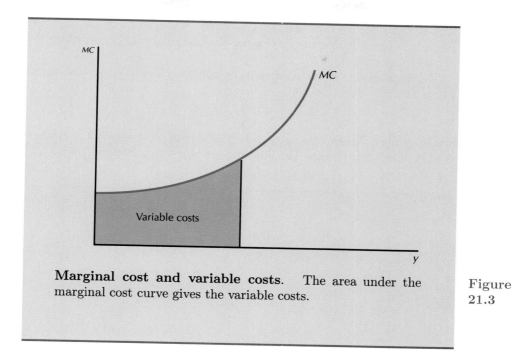

Marginal cost and variable costs.   The area under the marginal cost curve gives the variable costs.

Figure
21.3

EXAMPLE: Specific Cost Curves

Let's consider the cost function $c(y) = y^2 + 1$. We have the following derived cost curves:

- variable costs: $c_v(y) = y^2$

- fixed costs: $c_f(y) = 1$

- average variable costs: $AVC(y) = y^2/y = y$

- average fixed costs: $AFC(y) = 1/y$

- average costs: $AC(y) = \dfrac{y^2 + 1}{y} = y + \dfrac{1}{y}$

- marginal costs: $MC(y) = 2y$

These are all obvious except for the last one, which is also obvious if you know calculus. If the cost function is $c(y) = y^2 + F$, then the marginal cost function is given by $MC(y) = 2y$. If you don't know this fact already, memorize it, because you'll use it in the exercises.

What do these cost curves look like? The easiest way to draw them is first to draw the average variable cost curve, which is a straight line with slope 1. Then it is also simple to draw the marginal cost curve, which is a straight line with slope 2.

The average cost curve reaches its minimum where average cost equals marginal cost, which says

$$y + \frac{1}{y} = 2y,$$

which can be solved to give $y_{\min} = 1$. The average cost at $y = 1$ is 2, which is also the marginal cost. The final picture is given in Figure 21.4.

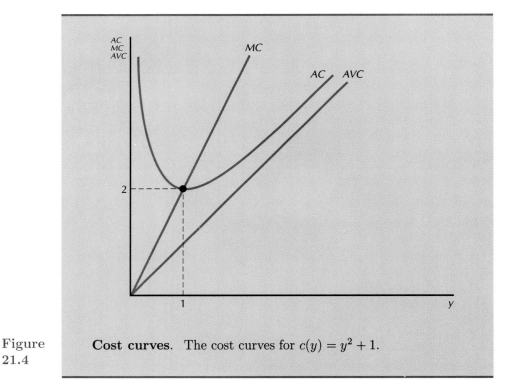

Figure 21.4

Cost curves. The cost curves for $c(y) = y^2 + 1$.

EXAMPLE: Marginal Cost Curves for Two Plants

Suppose that you have two plants that have two different cost functions, $c_1(y_1)$ and $c_2(y_2)$. You want to produce y units of output in the cheapest way. In general, you will want to produce some amount of output in each plant. The question is, how much should you produce in each plant?

Set up the minimization problem:

$$\min_{y_1, y_2} c_1(y_1) + c_2(y_2)$$

such that $y_1 + y_2 = y$.

Now how do you solve it? It turns out that at the optimal division of output between the two plants we must have the marginal cost of producing output at plant 1 equal to the marginal cost of producing output at plant 2. In order to prove this, suppose the marginal costs were not equal; then it would pay to shift a small amount of output from the plant with higher marginal costs to the plant with lower marginal costs. If the output division is optimal, then switching output from one plant to the other can't lower costs.

Let $c(y)$ be the cost function that gives the cheapest way to produce y units of output—that is, the cost of producing y units of output given that you have divided output in the best way between the two plants. The marginal cost of producing an extra unit of output must be the same no matter which plant you produce it in.

We depict the two marginal cost curves, $MC_1(y_1)$ and $MC_2(y_2)$, in Figure 21.5. The marginal cost curve for the two plants taken together is just the horizontal sum of the two marginal cost curves, as depicted in Figure 21.5C.

Marginal costs for a firm with two plants. The overall marginal cost curve on the right is the horizontal sum of the marginal cost curves for the two plants shown on the left.

Figure
21.5

For any fixed level of marginal costs, say c, we will produce y_1^* and y_2^* such that $MC_1(y_1^*) = MC(y_2^*) = c$, and we will thus have $y_1^* + y_2^*$ units of output produced. Thus the amount of output produced at any marginal cost c is just the sum of the outputs where the marginal cost of plant 1 equals c and the marginal cost of plant 2 equals c: the horizontal sum of the marginal cost curves.

21.4 Long-Run Costs

In the above analysis, we have regarded the firm's fixed costs as being the costs that involve payments to factors that it is unable to adjust in the short run. In the long run a firm can choose the level of its "fixed" factors—they are no longer fixed.

Of course, there may still be quasi-fixed factors in the long run. That is, it may be a feature of the technology that some costs have to be paid to produce any positive level of output. But in the long run there are no fixed costs, in the sense that it is always possible to produce zero units of output at zero costs—that is, it is always possible to go out of business. If quasi-fixed factors are present in the long run, then the average cost curve will tend to have a U-shape, just as in the short run. But in the long run it will always be possible to produce zero units of output at a zero cost, by definition of the long run.

Of course, what constitutes the long run depends on the problem we are analyzing. If we are considering the fixed factor to be the size of the plant, then the long run will be how long it would take the firm to change the size of its plant. If we are considering the fixed factor to be the contractual obligations to pay salaries, then the long run would be how long it would take the firm to change the size of its work force.

Just to be specific, let's think of the fixed factor as being plant size and denote it by k. The firm's short-run cost function, given that it has a plant of k square feet, will be denoted by $c_s(y, k)$, where the s subscript stands for "short run." (Here k is playing the role of $\overline{x}_2$ in Chapter 20.)

For any given level of output, there will be some plant size that is the optimal size to produce that level of output. Let us denote this plant size by $k(y)$. This is the firm's conditional factor demand for plant size as a function of output. (Of course, it also depends on the prices of plant size and other factors of production, but we have suppressed these arguments.) Then, as we've seen in Chapter 20, the long-run cost function of the firm will be given by $c_s(y, k(y))$. This is the total cost of producing an output level y, given that the firm is allowed to adjust its plant size optimally. The long-run cost function of the firm is just the short-run cost function evaluated at the optimal choice of the fixed factors:

$$c(y) = c_s(y, k(y)).$$

Let us see how this looks graphically. Pick some level of output y^*, and let $k^* = k(y^*)$ be the optimal plant size for that level of output. The short-run cost function for a plant of size k^* will be given by $c_s(y, k^*)$, and the long-run cost function will be given by $c(y) = c_s(y, k(y))$, just as above.

Now, note the important fact that the short-run cost to produce output y must always be at least as large as the long-run cost to produce y. Why? In the short run the firm has a fixed plant size, while in the long run the firm is free to adjust its plant size. Since one of its long-run choices is always to choose the plant size k^*, its optimal choice to produce y units of output must have costs at least as small as $c(y, k^*)$. This means that the firm must be able to do at least as well by adjusting plant size as by having it fixed. Thus

$$c(y) \le c_s(y, k^*)$$

for all levels of y.

In fact, at one particular level of y, namely y^*, we know that

$$c(y^*) = c_s(y^*, k^*).$$

Why? Because at y^* the *optimal* choice of plant size is k^*. So at y^*, the long-run costs and the short-run costs are the same.

Short-run and long-run average costs. The short-run average cost curve must be tangent to the long-run average cost curve.

Figure
21.6

If the short-run cost is always greater than the long-run cost and they are equal at one level of output, then this means that the short-run and the long-run average costs have the same property: $AC(y) \leq AC_s(y, k^*)$ and $AC(y^*) = AC_s(y^*, k^*)$. This implies that the short-run average cost curve always lies above the long-run average cost curve and that they touch at one point, y^*. Thus the long-run average cost curve (LAC) and the short-run average cost curve (SAC) must be tangent at that point, as depicted in Figure 21.6.

We can do the same sort of construction for levels of output other than y^*. Suppose we pick outputs $y_1, y_2, \ldots, y_n$ and accompanying plant sizes $k_1 = k(y_1), k_2 = k(y_2), \ldots, k_n = k(y_n)$. Then we get a picture like that in Figure 21.7. We summarize Figure 21.7 by saying that the long-run average cost curve is the **lower envelope** of the short-run average cost curves.

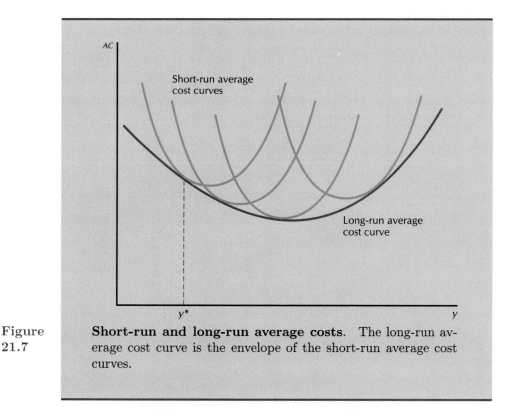

Figure 21.7

Short-run and long-run average costs. The long-run average cost curve is the envelope of the short-run average cost curves.

21.5 Discrete Levels of Plant Size

In the above discussion we have implicitly assumed that we can choose a continuous number of different plant sizes. Thus each different level of output has a unique optimal plant size associated with it. But we can also consider what happens if there are only a few different levels of plant size to choose from.

Suppose, for example, that we have four different choices, k_1, k_2, k_3, and k_4. We have depicted the four different average cost curves associated with these plant sizes in Figure 21.8.

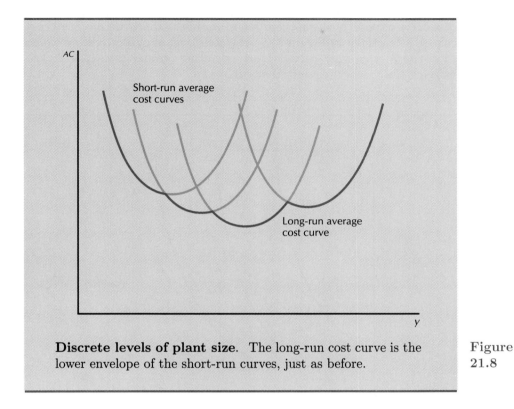

Discrete levels of plant size. The long-run cost curve is the lower envelope of the short-run curves, just as before.

Figure 21.8

How can we construct the long-run average cost curve? Well, remember the long-run average cost curve is the cost curve you get by adjusting k optimally. In this case that isn't hard to do: since there are only four different plant sizes, we just see which one has the lowest costs associated with it and pick that plant size. That is, for any level of output y, we just choose the plant size that gives us the minimum cost of producing that output level.

Thus the long-run average cost curve will be the lower envelope of the short-run average costs, as depicted in Figure 21.8. Note that this figure has qualitatively the same implications as Figure 21.7: the short-run average costs always are at least as large as the long-run average costs, and they are the same at the level of output where the long-run demand for the fixed factor equals the amount of the fixed factor that you have.

21.6 Long-Run Marginal Costs

We've seen in the last section that the long-run average cost curve is the lower envelope of the short-run average cost curves. What are the implications of this for marginal costs? Let's first consider the case where there are discrete levels of plant size. In this situation the long-run marginal cost curve consists of the appropriate pieces of the short-run marginal cost curves, as depicted in Figure 21.9. For each level of output, we see which short-run average cost curve we are operating on and then look at the marginal cost associated with that curve.

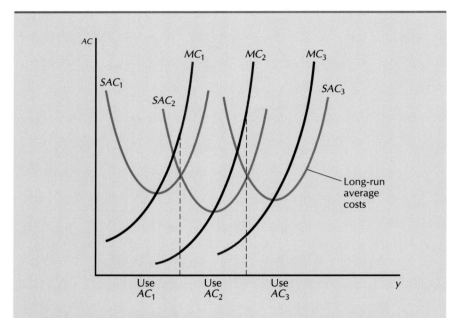

Long-run marginal costs. When there are discrete levels of the fixed factor, the firm will choose the amount of the fixed factor to minimize average costs. Thus the long-run marginal cost curve will consist of the various segments of the short-run marginal cost curves associated with each different level of the fixed factor.

Figure
21.9

This has to hold true no matter how many different plant sizes there are, so the picture for the continuous case looks like Figure 21.10. The long-run marginal cost at any output level y has to equal the short-run marginal cost associated with the optimal level of plant size to produce y.

Long-run marginal costs.   The relationship between the long-run and the short-run marginal costs with continuous levels of the fixed factor.

Figure
21.10

Summary

1. Average costs are composed of average variable costs plus average fixed costs. Average fixed costs always decline with output, while average variable costs tend to increase. The net result is a U-shaped average cost curve.

2. The marginal cost curve lies below the average cost curve when average costs are decreasing, and above when they are increasing. Thus marginal costs must equal average costs at the point of minimum average costs.

3. The area under the marginal cost curve measures the variable costs.

4. The long-run average cost curve is the lower envelope of the short-run average cost curves.

REVIEW QUESTIONS

1. Which of the following are true? (1) Average fixed costs never increase with output; (2) average total costs are always greater than or equal to average variable costs; (3) average cost can never rise while marginal costs are declining.

2. A firm produces identical outputs at two different plants. If the marginal cost at the first plant exceeds the marginal cost at the second plant, how can the firm reduce costs and maintain the same level of output?

3. True or false? In the long run a firm always operates at the minimum level of average costs for the optimally sized plant to produce a given amount of output.

APPENDIX

In the text we claimed that average variable cost equals marginal cost for the first unit of output. In calculus terms this becomes

$$\lim_{y \to 0} \frac{c_v(y)}{y} = \lim_{y \to 0} c'(y).$$

The left-hand side of this expression is not defined at $y = 0$. But its limit is defined, and we can compute it using l'Hôpital's rule, which states that the limit of a fraction whose numerator and denominator both approach zero is given by the limit of the derivatives of the numerator and the denominator. Applying this rule, we have

$$\lim_{y \to 0} \frac{c_v(y)}{y} = \frac{\lim_{y \to 0} dc_v(y)/dy}{\lim_{y \to 0} dy/dy} = \frac{c'(0)}{1},$$

which establishes the claim.

We also claimed that the area under the marginal cost curve gave us variable cost. This is easy to show using the fundamental theorem of calculus. Since

$$MC(y) = \frac{dc_v(y)}{dy},$$

we know that the area under the marginal cost curve is

$$c_v(y) = \int_0^y \frac{dc_v(x)}{dx}\, dx = c_v(y) - c_v(0) = c_v(y).$$

The discussion of long-run and short-run marginal cost curves is all pretty clear geometrically, but what does it mean economically? It turns out that the calculus argument gives the nicest intuition. The argument is simple. The marginal cost of production is just the change in cost that arises from changing output. In the short run we have to keep plant size (or whatever) fixed, while in the long run we are free to adjust it. So the long-run marginal cost will consist of two pieces: how costs change holding plant size fixed plus how costs change when plant size adjusts. But if the plant size is chosen optimally, this last term has to be zero! Thus the long-run and the short-run marginal costs have to be the same.

The mathematical proof involves the chain rule. Using the definition from the text:

$$c(y) \equiv c_s(y, k(y)).$$

Differentiating with respect to y gives

$$\frac{dc(y)}{dy} = \frac{\partial c_s(y, k)}{\partial y} + \frac{\partial c_s(y, k)}{\partial k}\frac{\partial k(y)}{\partial y}.$$

If we evaluate this at a specific level of output y^* and its associated optimal plant size $k^* = k(y^*)$, we know that

$$\frac{\partial c_s(y^*, k^*)}{\partial k} = 0$$

because that is the necessary first-order condition for k^* to be the cost-minimizing plant size at y^*. Thus the second term in the expression cancels out and all that we have left is the short-run marginal cost:

$$\frac{dc(y^*)}{dy} = \frac{\partial c_s(y^*, k^*)}{\partial y}.$$

CHAPTER 22

FIRM SUPPLY

In this chapter we will see how to derive the supply curve of a competitive firm from its cost function using the model of profit maximization. The first thing we have to do is to describe the market environment in which the firm operates.

22.1 Market Environments

Every firm faces two important decisions: choosing how much it should produce and choosing what price it should set. If there were no constraints on a profit-maximizing firm, it would set an arbitrarily high price and produce an arbitrarily large amount of output. But no firm exists in such an unconstrained environment. In general, the firm faces two sorts of constraints on its actions.

First, it faces the **technological constraints** summarized by the production function. There are only certain feasible combinations of inputs and outputs, and even the most profit-hungry firm has to respect the realities of the physical world. We have already discussed how we can summarize the technological constraints, and we've seen how the technological constraints lead to the **economic constraints** summarized by the cost function.

But now we bring in a new constraint—or at least an old constraint from a different perspective. This is the **market constraint**. A firm can produce whatever is physically feasible, and it can set whatever price it wants ... but it can only sell as much as people are willing to buy.

If it sets a certain price p it will sell a certain amount of output x. We call the relationship between the price a firm sets and the amount that it sells the **demand curve facing the firm**.

If there were only one firm in the market, the demand curve facing the firm would be very simple to describe: it is just the market demand curve described in earlier chapters on consumer behavior. For the market demand curve measures how much of the good people want to buy at each price. Thus the demand curve summarizes the market constraints facing a firm that has a market all to itself.

But if there are other firms in the market, the constraints facing an individual firm will be different. In this case, the firm has to guess how the *other* firms in the market will behave when it chooses its price and output.

This is not an easy problem to solve, either for firms or for economists. There are a lot of different possibilities, and we will try to examine them in a systematic way. We'll use the term **market environment** to describe the ways that firms respond to each other when they make their pricing and output decisions.

In this chapter we'll examine the simplest market environment, that of **pure competition**. This is a good comparison point for many other environments, and it is of considerable interest in its own right. First let's give the economist's definition of pure competition, and then we'll try to justify it.

22.2 Pure Competition

To a lay person, "competition" has the connotation of intense rivalry. That's why students are often surprised that the economist's definition of competition seems so passive: we say that a market is **purely competitive** if each firm assumes that the market price is independent of its own level of output. Thus, in a competitive market, each firm only has to worry about how much output it wants to produce. Whatever it produces can only be sold at one price: the going market price.

In what sort of environment might this be a reasonable assumption for a firm to make? Well, suppose that we have an industry composed of many firms that produce an identical product, and that each firm is a small part of the market. A good example would be the market for wheat. There are thousands of wheat farmers in the United States, and even the largest of them produces only an infinitesimal fraction of the total supply. It is reasonable in this case for any one firm in the industry to take the market price as being predetermined. A wheat farmer doesn't have to worry about what price to set for his wheat—if he wants to sell any at all, he has to sell it at the market price. He is a **price taker**: the price is given as far as he is concerned; all he has to worry about is how much to produce.

This kind of situation—an identical product and many small firms—is a classic example of a situation where price-taking behavior is sensible. But it is not the only case where price-taking behavior is possible. Even if there are only a few firms in the market, they may still treat the market price as being outside their control.

Think of a case where there is a fixed supply of a perishable good: say fresh fish or cut flowers in a marketplace. Even if there are only 3 or 4 firms in the market, each firm may have to take the *other* firms' prices as given. If the customers in the market only buy at the lowest price, then the lowest price being offered is the market price. If one of the other firms wants to sell anything at all, it will have to sell at the market price. So in this sort of situation competitive behavior—taking the market price as outside of your control—seems plausible as well.

We can describe the relationship between price and quantity perceived by a competitive firm in terms of a diagram as in Figure 22.1. As you can see, this demand curve is very simple. A competitive firm believes that it will sell nothing if it charges a price higher than the market price. If it sells at the market price, it can sell whatever amount it wants, and if it sells below the market price, it will get the entire market demand at that price.

As usual we can think of this kind of demand curve in two ways. If we think of quantity as a function of price, this curve says that you can sell any amount you want at or below the market price. If we think of price as a function of quantity, it says that no matter how much you sell, the market price will be independent of your sales.

(Of course, this doesn't have to be true for literally *any* amount. Price has to be independent of your output for any amount you might consider selling. In the case of the cut-flower seller, the price has to be independent of how much she sells for any amount up to her stock on hand—the maximum that she could consider selling.)

It is important to understand the difference between the "demand curve facing a firm" and the "market demand curve." The market demand curve measures the relationship between the market price and the total amount of output sold. The demand curve facing a firm measures the relationship between the market price and the output of *that particular firm.*

The market demand curve depends on consumers' behavior. The demand curve facing a firm not only depends on consumers' behavior but it also depends on the behavior of the other firms. The usual justification for the competitive model is that when there are many small firms in the market, each one faces a demand curve that is essentially flat. But even if there are only two firms in the market, and one insists on charging a fixed price no matter what, then the other firm in the market will face a competitive demand curve like the one depicted in Figure 22.1. Thus the competitive model may hold in a wider variety of circumstances than is apparent at first glance.

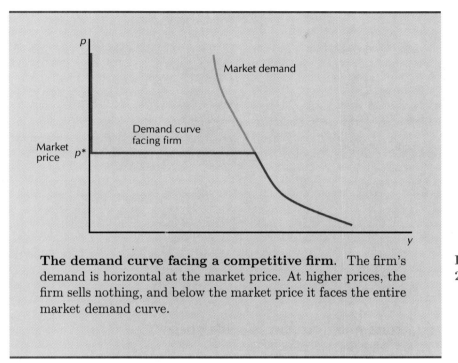

The demand curve facing a competitive firm. The firm's demand is horizontal at the market price. At higher prices, the firm sells nothing, and below the market price it faces the entire market demand curve.

Figure
22.1

22.3 The Supply Decision of a Competitive Firm

Let us use the facts we have discovered about cost curves to figure out the supply curve of a competitive firm. By definition a competitive firm ignores its influence on the market price. Thus the maximization problem facing a competitive firm is

$$\max_{y} py - c(y).$$

This just says that the competitive firm wants to maximize its profits: the difference between its revenue, py, and its costs, $c(y)$.

What level of output will a competitive firm choose to produce? Answer: it will operate where marginal revenue equals marginal cost—where the extra revenue gained by one more unit of output just equals the extra cost of producing another unit. If this condition did not hold, the firm could always increase its profits by changing its level of output.

In the case of a competitive firm, marginal revenue is simply the price. To see this, ask how much extra revenue a competitive firm gets when it increases its output by Δy. We have

$$\Delta R = p\Delta y$$

since by hypothesis p doesn't change. Thus the extra revenue per unit of output is given by

$$\frac{\Delta R}{\Delta y} = p,$$

which is the expression for marginal revenue.

Thus a competitive firm will choose a level of output y where the marginal cost that it faces at y is just equal to the market price. In symbols:

$$p = MC(y).$$

For a given market price, p, we want to find the level of output where profits are maximal. If price is greater than marginal cost at some level of output y, then the firm can increase its profits by producing a little more output. For price greater than marginal costs means

$$p - \frac{\Delta c}{\Delta y} > 0.$$

So increasing output by Δy means that

$$p\Delta y - \frac{\Delta c}{\Delta y}\Delta y > 0.$$

Simplifying we find that

$$p\Delta y - \Delta c > 0,$$

which means that the increase in revenues from the extra output exceeds the increase in costs. Thus profits must increase.

A similar argument can be made when price is less than marginal cost. Then reducing output will increase profits, since the lost revenues are more than compensated for by the reduced costs.

So at the optimal level of output, a firm must be producing where price equals marginal costs. Whatever the level of the market price p, the firm will choose a level of output y where $p = MC(y)$. Thus the marginal cost curve of a competitive firm is precisely its supply curve. Or put another way, the market price is precisely marginal cost—as long as each firm is producing at its profit-maximizing level.

Marginal cost and supply. Although there are two levels of output where price equals marginal cost, the profit-maximizing quantity supplied can lie only on the upward-sloping part of the marginal cost curve.

Figure
22.2

22.4 An Exception

Well ... maybe not *precisely*. There are two troublesome cases. The first case is when there are several levels of output where price equals marginal cost, such as the case depicted in Figure 22.2. Here there are two levels of output where price equals marginal cost. Which one will the firm choose?

It is not hard to see the answer. Consider the first intersection, where the marginal cost curve is sloping down. Now if we increase output a little bit here, the costs of each additional unit of output will decrease. That's what it means to say that the marginal cost curve is decreasing. But the market price will stay the same. Thus profits must definitely go up.

So we can rule out levels of output where the marginal cost curve slopes downward. At those points an increase in output must always increase profits. The supply curve of a competitive firm must lie along the upward-sloping part of the marginal cost curve. This means that the supply curve itself must always be upward sloping. The "Giffen good" phenomenon cannot arise for supply curves.

Price equals marginal cost is a *necessary* condition for profit maximization. It is not in general a *sufficient* condition. Just because we find a point where price equals marginal cost doesn't mean that we've found the maximum profit point. But if we find the maximum profit point, we know that price must equal marginal cost.

22.5 Another Exception

This discussion is assuming that it is profitable to produce something. After all it could be that the best thing for a firm to do is to produce zero output. Since it is always possible to produce a zero level of output, we have to compare our candidate for profit maximization with the choice of doing nothing at all.

If a firm produces zero output it still has to pay its fixed costs, F. Thus the profits from producing zero units of output are just $-F$. The profits from producing a level of output y are $py - c_v(y) - F$. The firm is better off going out of business when

$$-F > py - c_v(y) - F,$$

that is, when the "profits" from producing nothing, and just paying the fixed costs, exceed the profits from producing where price equals marginal cost. Rearranging this equation gives us the **shutdown condition**:

$$AVC(y) = \frac{c_v(y)}{y} > p.$$

If average variable costs are greater than p, the firm would be better off producing zero units of output. This makes good sense, since it says that the revenues from selling the output y don't even cover the *variable* costs of production, $c_v(y)$. In this case the firm might as well go out of business. If it produces nothing it will lose its fixed costs, but it would lose even more if it continued to produce.

This discussion indicates that only the portions of the marginal cost curve that lie above the average variable cost curve are possible points on the supply curve. If a point where price equals marginal cost is beneath the average variable cost curve, the firm would optimally choose to produce zero units of output.

We now have a picture for the supply curve like that in Figure 22.3. The competitive firm produces along the part of the marginal cost curve that is upward sloping and lies above the average variable cost curve.

EXAMPLE: Pricing Operating Systems

A computer requires an operating system in order to run, and most hardware manufacturers sell their computers with the operating systems already

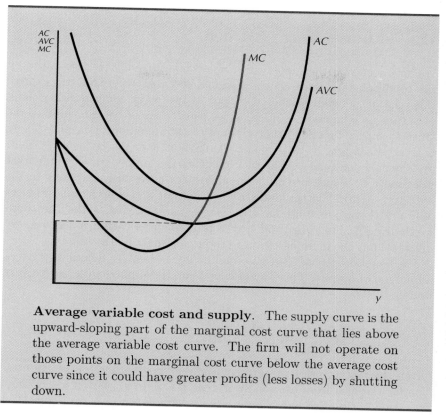

Average variable cost and supply. The supply curve is the upward-sloping part of the marginal cost curve that lies above the average variable cost curve. The firm will not operate on those points on the marginal cost curve below the average cost curve since it could have greater profits (less losses) by shutting down.

Figure 22.3

installed. In the early 1980s several operating system producers were fighting for supremacy in the IBM-PC-compatible microcomputer market. The common practice at that time was for the producer of the operating system to charge the computer manufacturer for each copy of the operating system that was *installed* on a microcomputer that it sold.

Microsoft Corporation offered an alternative plan in which the charge to the manufacturer was based on the number of microcomputers that were *built* by the manufacturer. Microsoft set their licensing fee low enough that this plan was attractive to the producers.

Note the clever nature of Microsoft's pricing strategy: once the contract with a manufacturer was signed, the marginal cost of installing MS-DOS on an already-built computer was zero. Installing a competing operating system, on the other hand, could cost $50 to $100. The hardware manufacturer (and ultimately the user) paid Microsoft for the operating system, but the structure of the pricing contract made MS-DOS very attractive relative to the competition. As a result, Microsoft ended up being the default operating system installed on microcomputers and achieved a market penetration of over 90 percent.

22.6 The Inverse Supply Function

We have seen that the supply curve of a competitive firm is determined by the condition that price equals marginal cost. As before we can express this relation between price and output in two ways: we can either think of output as a function of price, as we usually do, or we can think of the "inverse supply function" that gives price as a function of output. There is a certain insight to be gained by looking at it in the latter way. Since price equals marginal cost at each point on the supply curve, the market price must be a measure of marginal cost for every firm operating in the industry. A firm that produces a lot of output and a firm that produces only a little output must have the *same marginal cost,* if they are both maximizing profits. The total cost of production of each firm can be very different, but the marginal cost of production must be the same.

The equation $p = MC(y)$ gives us the inverse supply function: price as a function of output. This way of expressing the supply curve can be very useful.

22.7 Profits and Producer's Surplus

Given the market price we can now compute the optimal operating position for the firm from the condition that $p = MC(y)$. Given the optimal operating position we can compute the profits of the firm. In Figure 22.4 the area of the box is just p^*y^*, or total revenue. The area $y^* AC(y^*)$ is total costs since

$$yAC(y) = y\frac{c(y)}{y} = c(y).$$

Profits are simply the difference between these two areas.

Recall our discussion of **producer's surplus** in Chapter 14. We defined producer's surplus to be the area to the left of the supply curve, in analogy to consumer's surplus, which was the area to the left of the demand curve. It turns out that producer's surplus is closely related to the profits of a firm. More precisely, producer's surplus is equal to revenues minus variable costs, or equivalently, profits plus the fixed costs:

profits $= py - c_v(y) - F$

producer's surplus $= py - c_v(y)$.

The most direct way to measure producer's surplus is to look at the difference between the revenue box and the box $y^* AVC(y^*)$, as in Figure 22.5A. But there are other ways to measure producer's surplus by using the marginal cost curve itself.

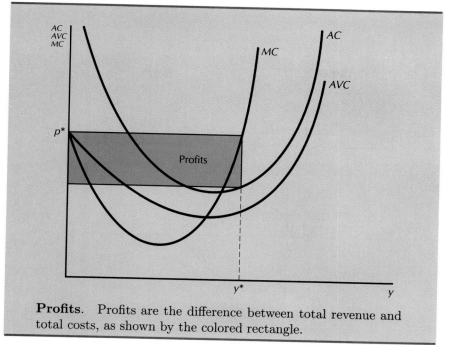

Profits.   Profits are the difference between total revenue and total costs, as shown by the colored rectangle.

Figure
22.4

We know from Chapter 21 that the area under the marginal cost curve measures the total variable costs. This is true because the area under the marginal cost curve is the cost of producing the first unit plus the cost of producing the second unit, and so on. So to get producer's surplus, we can subtract the area under the marginal cost curve from the revenue box and get the area depicted in Figure 22.5B.

Finally, we can combine the two ways of measuring producer's surplus. Use the "box" definition up to the point where marginal cost equals average variable cost, and then use the area above the marginal cost curve, as shown in Figure 22.5C. This latter way is the most convenient for most applications since it is just the area to the left of the supply curve. Note that this is consistent with definition of producer's surplus given in Chapter 14.

We are seldom interested in the *total* amount of producer's surplus; more often it is the *change* in producer's surplus that is of interest. The change in producer's surplus when the firm moves from output y^* to output y' will generally be a trapezoidal shaped region like that depicted in Figure 22.6.

Note that the change in producer's surplus in moving from y^* to y' is just the change in profits in moving from y^* to y', since by definition the fixed costs don't change. Thus we can measure the impact on profits of a change in output from the information contained in the marginal cost curve, without having to refer to the average cost curve at all.

Figure
22.5

Producer's surplus. Three equivalent ways to measure producer's surplus. Panel A depicts a box measuring revenue minus variable cost. Panel B depicts the area above the marginal cost curve. Panel C uses the box up until output z (area R) and then uses the area above the marginal cost curve (area T).

EXAMPLE: The Supply Curve for a Specific Cost Function

What does the supply curve look like for the example given in the last chapter where $c(y) = y^2 + 1$? In that example the marginal cost curve was always above the average variable cost curve, and it always sloped upward. So "price equals marginal costs" gives us the supply curve directly. Substituting $2y$ for marginal cost we get the formula

$$p = 2y.$$

This gives us the inverse supply curve, or price as a function of output. Solving for output as a function of price we have

$$S(p) = y = \frac{p}{2}$$

as our formula for the supply curve. This is depicted in Figure 22.7.

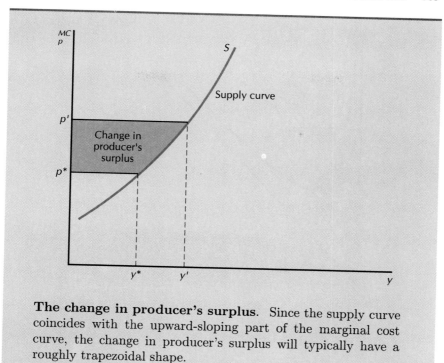

The change in producer's surplus. Since the supply curve coincides with the upward-sloping part of the marginal cost curve, the change in producer's surplus will typically have a roughly trapezoidal shape.

Figure
22.6

If we substitute this supply function into the definition of profits, we can calculate the maximum profits for each price p. Performing the calculation we have:

$$\pi(p) = py - c(y)$$

$$= p\frac{p}{2} - \left(\frac{p}{2}\right)^2 - 1$$

$$= \frac{p^2}{4} - 1.$$

How do the maximum profits relate to producer's surplus? In Figure 22.7 we see that producer's surplus—the area to the left of the supply curve between a price of zero and a price of p—will be a triangle with a base of $y = p/2$ and a height of p. The area of this triangle is

$$A = \left(\frac{1}{2}\right)\left(\frac{p}{2}\right)p = \frac{p^2}{4}.$$

Comparing this with the profits expression, we see that producer's surplus equals profits plus fixed costs, as claimed.

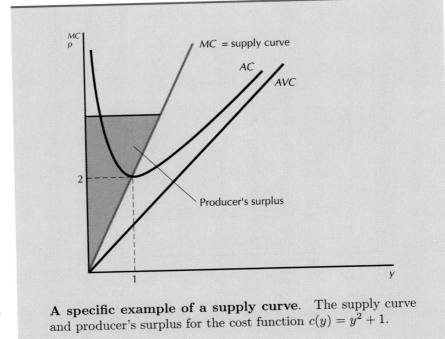

Figure
22.7

A specific example of a supply curve. The supply curve and producer's surplus for the cost function $c(y) = y^2 + 1$.

22.8 The Long-Run Supply Curve of a Firm

The long-run supply function for the firm measures how much the firm would optimally produce when it is allowed to adjust plant size (or whatever factors are fixed in the short run). That is, the long-run supply curve will be given by

$$p = MC_l(y) = MC(y, k(y)).$$

The short-run supply curve is given by price equals marginal cost at some fixed level of k:

$$p = MC(y, k).$$

Note the difference between the two expressions. The short-run supply curve involves the marginal cost of output holding k fixed at a given level of output, while the long-run supply curve involves the marginal cost of output when you adjust k optimally.

Now, we know something about the relationship between short-run and long-run marginal costs: the short-run and the long-run marginal costs coincide at the level of output y^* where the fixed factor choice associated with the short-run marginal cost is the optimal choice, k^*. Thus the short-run and the long-run supply curves of the firm coincide at y^*, as in Figure 22.8.

In the short run the firm has some factors in fixed supply; in the long run these factors are variable. Thus, when the price of output changes, the

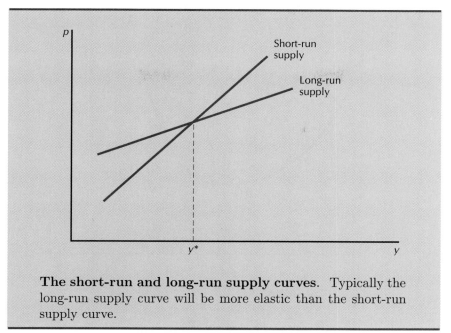

The short-run and long-run supply curves. Typically the long-run supply curve will be more elastic than the short-run supply curve.

Figure
22.8

firm has more choices to adjust in the long run than in the short run. This suggests that the long-run supply curve will be more responsive to price—more elastic—than the short-run supply curve, as illustrated in Figure 22.8.

What else can we say about the long-run supply curve? The long run is defined to be that time period in which the firm is free to adjust all of its inputs. One choice that the firm has is the choice of whether to remain in business. Since in the long run the firm can always get zero profits by going out of business, the profits that the firm makes in long-run equilibrium have to be at least zero:

$$py - c(y) \geq 0,$$

which means

$$p \geq \frac{c(y)}{y}.$$

This says that in the long run price has to be at least as large as average cost. Thus the relevant part of the long-run supply curve is the upward-sloping part of the marginal cost curve that lies above the long-run average cost curve, as depicted in Figure 22.9.

This is completely consistent with the short-run story. In the long run all costs are variable costs, so the short-run condition of having price above average variable cost is equivalent to the long-run condition of having price above average cost.

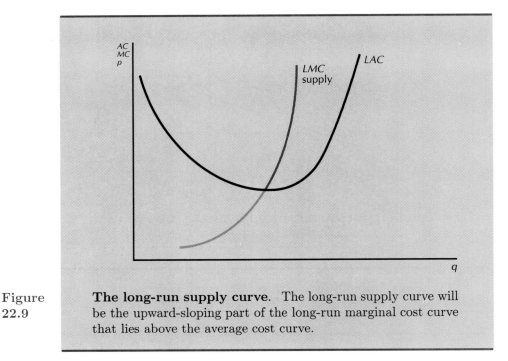

Figure
22.9

The long-run supply curve. The long-run supply curve will be the upward-sloping part of the long-run marginal cost curve that lies above the average cost curve.

22.9 Long-Run Constant Average Costs

One particular case of interest occurs when the long-run technology of the firm exhibits constant returns to scale. Here the long-run supply curve will be the long-run marginal cost curve, which, in the case of constant average cost, coincides with the long-run average cost curve. Thus we have the situation depicted in Figure 22.10, where the long-run supply curve is a horizontal line at c_{min}, the level of constant average cost.

This supply curve means that the firm is willing to supply any amount of output at $p = c_{min}$, an arbitrarily large amount of output at $p > c_{min}$, and zero output at $p < c_{min}$. When we think about the replication argument for constant returns to scale this makes perfect sense. Constant returns to scale implies that if you can produce 1 unit for c_{min} dollars, you can produce n units for nc_{min} dollars. Therefore you will be willing to supply any amount of output at a price equal to c_{min}, and an arbitrarily large amount of output at any price greater than c_{min}.

On the other hand, if $p < c_{min}$, so that you cannot break even supplying even one unit of output, you will certainly not be able to break even supplying n units of output. Hence, for any price less than c_{min}, you will want to supply zero units of output.

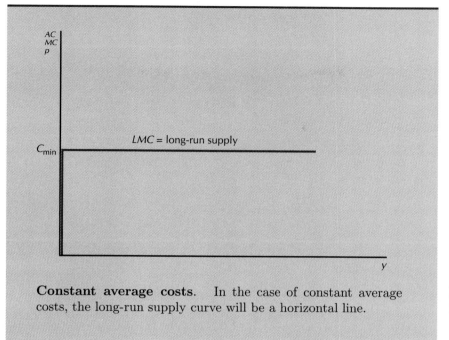

Constant average costs.   In the case of constant average costs, the long-run supply curve will be a horizontal line.

Figure
22.10

Summary

1. The relationship between the price a firm charges and the output that it sells is known as the demand curve facing the firm. By definition, a competitive firm faces a horizontal demand curve whose height is determined by the market price—the price charged by the other firms in the market.

2. The (short-run) supply curve of a competitive firm is that portion of its (short-run) marginal cost curve that is upward sloping and lies above the average variable cost curve.

3. The change in producer's surplus when the market price changes from p_1 to p_2 is the area to the left of the marginal cost curve between p_1 and p_2. It also measures the firm's change in profits.

4. The long-run supply curve of a firm is that portion of its long-run marginal cost curve that is upward sloping and that lies above its long-run average cost curve.

REVIEW QUESTIONS

1. A firm has a cost function given by $c(y) = 10y^2 + 1000$. What is its supply curve?

2. A firm has a cost function given by $c(y) = 10y^2 + 1000$. At what output is average cost minimized?

3. If the supply curve is given by $S(p) = 100 + 20p$, what is the formula for the inverse supply curve?

4. A firm has a supply function given by $S(p) = 4p$. Its fixed costs are 100. If the price changes from 10 to 20, what is the change in its profits?

5. If the long-run cost function is $c(y) = y^2 + 1$, what is the long-run supply curve of the firm?

6. Classify each of the following as either technological or market constraints: the price of inputs, the number of other firms in the market, the quantity of output produced, and the ability to produce more given the current input levels.

7. What is the major assumption that characterizes a purely competitive market?

8. In a purely competitive market a firm's marginal revenue is always equal to what? A profit-maximizing firm in such a market will operate at what level of output?

9. If average variable costs exceed the market price, what level of output should the firm produce? What if there are no fixed costs?

10. Is it ever better for a perfectly competitive firm to produce output even though it is losing money? If so, when?

11. In a perfectly competitive market what is the relationship between the market price and the cost of production for all firms in the industry?

APPENDIX

The discussion in this chapter is very simple if you speak calculus. The profit-maximization problem is

$$\max_{y} \ py - c(y)$$

such that $y \geq 0$.

The necessary conditions for the optimal supply, y^*, are the first-order condition

$$p - c'(y^*) = 0$$

and the second-order condition

$$-c''(y^*) \le 0.$$

The first-order condition says price equals marginal cost, and the second-order condition says that the marginal cost must be increasing. Of course this is presuming that $y^* > 0$. If price is less than average variable cost at y^*, it will pay the firm to produce a zero level of output. To determine the supply curve of a competitive firm, we must find all the points where the first- and second-order conditions are satisfied and compare them to each other—and to $y = 0$—and pick the one with the largest profits. That's the profit-maximizing supply.

CHAPTER 23

INDUSTRY SUPPLY

We have seen how to derive a firm's supply curve from its marginal cost curve. But in a competitive market there will typically be many firms, so the supply curve the industry presents to the market will be the sum of the supplies of all the individual firms. In this chapter we will investigate the **industry supply curve**.

23.1 Short-Run Industry Supply

We begin by studying an industry with a fixed number of firms, n. We let $S_i(p)$ be the supply curve of firm i, so that the **industry supply curve**, or the **market supply curve** is

$$S(p) = \sum_{i=1}^{n} S_i(p),$$

which is the sum of the individual supply curves. Geometrically we take the sum of the quantities supplied by each firm at each price, which gives us a *horizontal* sum of supply curves, as in Figure 23.1.

The industry supply curve. The industry supply curve $(S_1 + S_2)$ is the sum of the individual supply curves (S_1 and S_2).

Figure 23.1

23.2 Industry Equilibrium in the Short Run

In order to find the industry equilibrium we take this market supply curve and find the intersection with the market demand curve. This gives us an equilibrium price, p^*.

Given this equilibrium price, we can go back to look at the individual firms and examine their output levels and profits. A typical configuration with three firms, A, B, and C, is illustrated in Figure 23.2. In this example, firm A is operating at a price and output combination that lies on its average cost curve. This means that

$$p = \frac{c(y)}{y}.$$

Cross multiplying and rearranging, we have

$$py - c(y) = 0.$$

Thus firm A is making zero profits.

Firm B is operating at a point where price is greater than average cost: $p > c(y)/y$, which means it is making a profit in this short-run equilibrium.

Figure 23.2

Short-run equilibrium. An example of a short-run equilibrium with three firms. Firm A is making zero profits, firm B is making positive profits, and firm C is making negative profits, that is, making a loss.

Firm C is operating where price is less than average cost, so it is making negative profits, that is, making a loss.

In general, combinations of price and output that lie above the average cost curve represent positive profits, and combinations that lie below represent negative profits. Even if a firm is making negative profits, it will still be better for it to stay in business in the short run if the price and output combination lie above the average *variable* cost curve. For in this case, it will make less of a loss by remaining in business than by producing a zero level of output.

23.3 Industry Equilibrium in the Long Run

In the long run, firms are able to adjust their fixed factors. They can choose the plant size, or the capital equipment, or whatever to maximize their long-run profits. This just means that they will move from their short-run to their long-run cost curves, and this adds no new analytical difficulties: we simply use the long-run supply curves as determined by the long-run marginal cost curve.

However, there is an additional long-run effect that may occur. If a firm is making losses in the long run, there is no reason to stay in the industry, so we would expect to see such a firm *exit* the industry, since by exiting from the industry, the firm could reduce its losses to zero. This is just another way of saying that the only relevant part of a firm's supply curve in the long run is that part that lies *on or above* the average cost curve—since these are locations that correspond to nonnegative profits.

Similarly, if a firm is making profits we would expect *entry* to occur. After all, the cost curve is supposed to include the cost of all factors necessary to produce output, measured at their market price (i.e., their opportunity cost). If a firm is making profits in the long run it means that *anybody* can go to market, acquire those factors, and produce the same amount of output at the same cost.

In most competitive industries there are no restrictions against new firms entering the industry; in this case we say the industry exhibits **free entry**. However, in some industries there are **barriers to entry**, such as licenses or legal restrictions on how many firms can be in the industry. For example, regulations on the sales of alcohol in many states prevent free entry to the retail liquor industry.

The two long-run effects—acquiring different fixed factors and the entry and exit phenomena—are closely related. An existing firm in an industry can decide to acquire a new plant or store and produce more output. Or a new firm may enter the industry by acquiring a new plant and producing output. The only difference is in who owns the new production facilities.

Of course as more firms enter the industry—and firms that are losing money exit the industry—the total amount produced will change and lead to a change in the market price. This in turn will affect profits and the incentives to exit and enter. What will the final equilibrium look like in an industry with free entry?

Let's examine a case where all firms have identical long-run cost functions, say, $c(y)$. Given the cost function we can compute the level of output where average costs are minimized, which we denote by y^*. We let $p^* = c(y^*)/y^*$ be the minimum value of average cost. This cost is significant because it is the lowest price that could be charged in the market and still allow firms to break even.

We can now graph the industry supply curves for each different number of firms that can be in the market. Figure 23.3 illustrates the industry supply curves if there are $1, \ldots, 4$ firms in the market. (We are using 4 firms only for purposes of an example; in reality, one would expect there to be many more firms in a competitive industry.) Note that since all firms have the same supply curve, the total amount supplied if 2 firms are in the market is just twice as much as when 1 firm is the market, the supply when 3 firms are in the market is just three times as much, and so on.

Now add two more lines to the diagram: a horizontal line at p^*, the minimum price consistent with nonnegative profits, and the market demand curve. Consider the intersections of the demand curve and the supply curves for $n = 1, 2, \ldots$ firms. If firms enter the industry when positive profits are being made, then the relevant intersection is the *lowest price consistent with nonnegative profits*. This is denoted by p' in Figure 23.3, and it happens to occur when there are three firms in the market. If one

Figure
23.3
Industry supply curves with free entry. Supply curves for
$1, \ldots, 4$ firms. The equilibrium price, p', occurs at the lowest
possible intersection of demand and supply such that $p' \geq p^*$.

more firm enters the market, profits are pushed to be negative. In this
case, the maximum number of competitive firms this industry can support
is three.

23.4 The Long-Run Supply Curve

The construction given in the last section—draw the industry supply curves
for each possible number of firms that could be in the market and then look
for the largest number of firms consistent with nonnegative profits—is perfectly rigorous and easy to apply. However, there is a useful approximation
that usually gives something very close to the right answer.

Let's see if there is some way to construct *one* industry supply curve out
of the n curves we have above. The first thing to note is that we can rule
out all of the points on the supply curve that are below p^*, since those can
never be long-run operating positions. But we can also rule out some of
the points on the supply curves *above* p^*.

We typically assume that the market demand curve is downward sloping. The steepest possible demand curve is therefore a vertical line. This
implies that points like A in Figure 23.3 would never be observed—for any
downward-sloping demand curve that passed through A would also have
to intersect a supply curve associated with a larger number of firms, as

shown by the hypothetical demand curve D'' passing through the point A in Figure 23.3.

Thus we can eliminate a portion of each supply curve from being a possible long-run equilibrium position. Every point on the one-firm supply curve that lies to the right of the intersection of the two-firm supply curve and the line determined by p^* cannot be consistent with long-run equilibrium. Similarly, every point on the two-firm supply curve that lies to the right of the intersection of the three-firm supply curve with the p^* line cannot be consistent with long-run equilibrium ... and every point on the n-firm supply curve that lies to the right of the intersection of the $n + 1$-firm supply curve with the p^* line cannot be consistent with equilibrium.

The parts of the supply curves on which the long-run equilibrium can actually occur are indicated by the colored lines in Figure 23.4. The nth colored line segment shows all the combinations of prices and industry output that are consistent with having n firms in long-run equilibrium. Note that these line segments get flatter and flatter as we consider larger and larger levels of industry output, involving more and more firms in the industry.

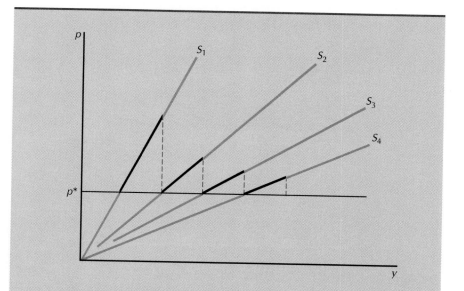

The long-run supply curve.   We can eliminate portions of the supply curves that can never be intersections with a downward-sloping market demand curve in the long run, such as the points on each supply curve to the right of the dotted lines.

Figure 23.4

Why do these curves get flatter? Think about it. If there is one firm in the market and the price goes up by Δp, it will produce, say, Δy more output. If there are n firms in the market and the price goes up by Δp, *each* firm will produce Δy more output, so we will get $n\Delta y$ more output in total. This means that the supply curve will be getting flatter and flatter as there are more and more firms in the market, since the supply of output will be more and more sensitive to price.

By the time we get a reasonable number of firms in the market, the slope of the supply curve will be very flat indeed. Flat enough so that it is reasonable to take it as having a slope of zero—that is, as taking the long-run industry supply curve to be a flat line at price equals minimum average cost. This will be a poor approximation if there are only a few firms in the industry in the long run. But the assumption that a small number of firms behave competitively will also probably be a poor approximation! If there are a reasonable number of firms in the long run, the equilibrium price cannot get far from minimum average cost. This is depicted in Figure 23.5.

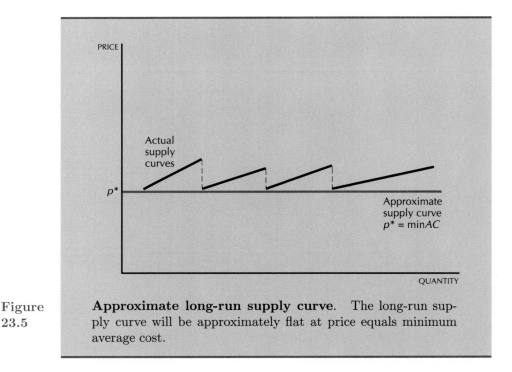

Figure
23.5

Approximate long-run supply curve. The long-run supply curve will be approximately flat at price equals minimum average cost.

This result has the important implication that in a competitive industry with free entry, profits cannot get very far from zero. If there are significant levels of profits in an industry with free entry, it will induce other firms to enter that industry and thereby push profits toward zero.

Remember, the correct calculation of economic costs involves measuring all factors of production at their market prices. As long as *all* factors are being measured and properly priced, a firm earning positive profits can be exactly duplicated by anyone. Anyone can go to the open market and purchase the factors of production necessary to produce the same output in the same way as the firm in question.

In an industry with free entry and exit, the long-run average cost curve should be essentially flat at a price equal to the minimum average cost. This is just the kind of long-run supply curve that a single firm with constant returns to scale would have. This is no accident. We argued that constant returns to scale was a reasonable assumption since a firm could always replicate what it was doing before. But another firm could replicate it as well! Expanding output by building a duplicate plant is just like a new firm entering the market with duplicate production facilities. Thus the long-run supply curve of a competitive industry with free entry will look like the long-run supply curve of a firm with constant returns to scale: a flat line at price equals minimum average cost.

EXAMPLE: Taxation in the Long Run and in the Short Run

Consider an industry that has free entry and exit. Suppose that initially it is in a long-run equilibrium with a fixed number of firms, and zero profits, as depicted in Figure 23.6. In the short run, with a fixed number of firms, the supply curve of the industry is upward sloping, while in the long run, with a variable number of firms, the supply curve is flat at price equals minimum average cost.

What happens when we put a tax on this industry? We use the geometric analysis discussed in Chapter 16: in order to find the new price paid by the demanders, we shift the supply curve up by the amount of the tax.

In general, the consumers will face a higher price and the producers will receive a lower price after the tax is imposed. But the producers were just breaking even before the tax was imposed; thus they must be losing money at any lower price. These economic losses will encourage some firms to leave the industry. Thus the supply of output will be reduced, and the price to the consumers will rise even further.

In the long run, the industry will supply along the horizontal long-run supply curve. In order to supply along this curve, the firms will have to receive a price equal to the minimum average cost—just what they were receiving before the tax was imposed. Thus the price to the consumers will have to rise by the entire amount of the tax.

In Figure 23.6, the equilibrium is initially at $P_D = P_S$. Then the tax is imposed, shifting the short-run supply curve up by the amount of the tax, and the equilibrium price paid by the demanders increases to P'_D. The

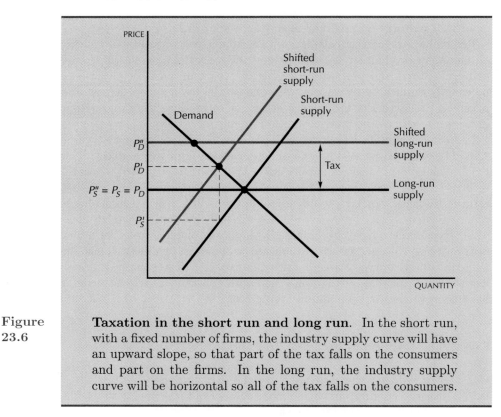

Figure
23.6

Taxation in the short run and long run. In the short run, with a fixed number of firms, the industry supply curve will have an upward slope, so that part of the tax falls on the consumers and part on the firms. In the long run, the industry supply curve will be horizontal so all of the tax falls on the consumers.

equilibrium price received by the suppliers falls to $P_S' = P_D' - t$. But this is only in the short run—when there are a fixed number of firms in the industry. Because of free entry and exit, the *long-run* supply curve in the industry is horizontal at $P_D = P_S$ = minimum average cost. Hence, in the long run, shifting up the supply curve implies that the entire amount of the tax gets passed along to the consumers.

To sum up: in an industry with free entry, a tax will initially raise the price to the consumers by less than the amount of the tax, since some of the incidence of the tax will fall on the producers. But in the long run the tax will induce firms to exit from the industry, thereby reducing supply, so that consumers will eventually end up paying the entire burden of the tax.

23.5 The Meaning of Zero Profits

In an industry with free entry, profits will be driven to zero by new entrants: whenever profits are positive, there will be an incentive for a new firm to come in to acquire some of those profits. When profits are zero it doesn't mean that the industry disappears; it just means that it stops growing, since there is no longer an inducement to enter.

In a long-run equilibrium with zero profits, all of the factors of production are being paid their market price—the same market price that these factors could earn elsewhere. The owner of the firm, for example, is still collecting a payment for her labor time, or for the amount of money she invested in the firm, or for whatever she contributes to the operation of the firm. The same goes for all other factors of production. The firm is still making money—it is just that all the money that it makes is being paid out to purchase the inputs that it uses. Each factor of production is earning the same amount in this industry that it could earn elsewhere, so there are no extra rewards—no pure profits—to attract new factors of production to this industry. But there is nothing to cause them to leave either. Industries in long-run equilibrium with zero profits are mature industries; they're not likely to appear as the cover story in *Business Week*, but they form the backbone of the economy.

Remember, economic profits are defined using the market prices of all factors of production. The market prices measure the opportunity cost of those factors—what they could earn elsewhere. Any amount of money earned in excess of the payments to the factors of production is a pure economic profit. But whenever someone finds a pure economic profit, other people will try to enter the industry and acquire some of that profit for themselves. It is this attempt to capture economic profits that eventually drives them to zero in a competitive industry with free entry.

In some quarters, the profit motive is regarded with some disdain. But when you think about it purely on economic grounds, profits are providing exactly the right signals as far as resource allocation is concerned. If a firm is making positive profits, it means that people value the output of the firm more highly than they value the inputs. Doesn't it make sense to have more firms producing that kind of output?

23.6 Fixed Factors and Economic Rent

If there is free entry, profits are driven to zero in the long run. But not every industry has free entry. In some industries the number of firms in the industry is fixed.

A common reason for this is that there are some factors of production that are available in fixed supply. We said that in the long run the fixed factors could be bought or sold by an individual firm. But there are some factors that are fixed for the *economy as a whole* even in the long run.

The most obvious example of this is in resource-extraction industries: oil in the ground is a necessary input to the oil-extraction industry, and there is only so much oil around to be extracted. A similar statement could be made for coal, gas, precious metals, or any other such resource.

Agriculture gives another example. There is only a certain amount of land that is suitable for agriculture.

A more exotic example of such a fixed factor is talent. There are only a certain number of people who possess the necessary level of talent to be professional athletes or entertainers. There may be "free entry" into such fields—but only for those who are good enough to get in!

There are other cases where the fixed factor is fixed not by nature, but by law. In many industries it is necessary to have a license or permit, and the number of these permits may be fixed by law. The taxicab industry in many cities is regulated in this way. Liquor licenses are another example.

If there are restrictions such as the above on the number of firms in the industry, so that firms cannot enter the industry freely, it may appear that it is possible to have an industry with positive profits in the long run, with no economic forces to drive those profits to zero.

This appearance is wrong. There is an economic force that pushes profits to zero. If a firm is operating at a point where its profits appear to be positive in the long run, it is probably because we are not appropriately measuring the market value of whatever it is that is preventing entry.

Here it is important to remember the economic definition of costs: we should value each factor of production at its *market price*—its opportunity cost. If it appears that a farmer is making positive profits after we have subtracted his costs of production, it is probably because we have forgotten to subtract the cost of his land.

Suppose that we manage to value all of the inputs to farming except for the land cost, and we end up with π dollars per year for profits. How much would the land be worth on a free market? How much would someone pay to rent that land for a year?

The answer is: they would be willing to rent it for π dollars per year, the "profits" that it brings in. You wouldn't even have to know anything about farming to rent this land and earn π dollars—after all, we valued the farmer's labor at its market price as well, and that means that you can hire a farmer and still make π dollars of profit. So the market value of that land—its competitive rent—is just π. The economic profits to farming are zero.

Note that the rental rate determined by this procedure may have nothing whatsoever to do with the historical cost of the farm. What matters is not what you bought it for, but what you can sell it for—that's what determines opportunity cost.

Whenever there is some fixed factor that is preventing entry into an industry, there will be an equilibrium rental rate for that factor. Even with fixed factors, you can always enter an industry by buying out the position of a firm that is currently in the industry. Every firm in the industry has the option of selling out—and the opportunity cost of not doing so is a cost of production that it has to consider.

Thus in one sense it is always the *possibility* of entry that drives profits to zero. After all, there are two ways to enter an industry: you can form a new firm, or you can buy out an existing firm that is currently in the industry. If a new firm can buy everything necessary to produce in an industry and still make a profit, it will do so. But if there are some factors that are in fixed supply, then competition for those factors among potential entrants will bid the prices of these factors up to a point where the profit disappears.

EXAMPLE: Taxi Licenses in New York City

Earlier we said that licenses to operate New York City taxicabs sell for about $100,000. Yet in 1986 taxicab drivers made only about $400 for a 50-hour week; this translated into less than an $8 hourly wage. The New York Taxi and Limosine Commission argued that this wage was too low to attract skilled drivers and that taxi fares should be raised in order to attract better drivers.

An economist would argue that allowing the fares to increase would have virtually no effect on the take-home pay of the drivers; all that would happen is that the value of the taxicab license would increase. We can see why by examining the commission's figures for the costs of operating a taxi. In 1986, the lease rate was $55 for a day shift and $65 for a night shift. The driver who leased the taxi paid for the gasoline and netted about $80 a day in income.

But note how much the owner of the taxicab license made. Assuming that the cab could be rented for two shifts for 320 days a year, the lease income comes to $38,400. Insurance, depreciation, maintenance, and so on amounted to about $21,100 a year; this leaves a net profit of $17,300 per year. Since the license cost about $100,000, this indicates a total return of about 17 percent.

An increase in the rate that taxis were allowed to charge would be reflected directly in the value of the license. A fare increase that brought in an extra $10,000 a year would result in a license's value increasing by about $60,000. The wage rate for the cab drivers—which is set in the labor market—would not be affected by such a change.[1]

23.7 Economic Rent

The examples in the last section are instances of **economic rent**. Economic rent is defined as those payments to a factor of production that are in excess of the minimum payment necessary to have that factor supplied.

---

[1] Figures are taken from an unsigned editorial in the *New York Times,* August 17, 1986.

Consider, for example, the case of oil discussed earlier. In order to produce oil you need some labor, some machinery, and, most importantly, some oil in the ground! Suppose that it costs $1 a barrel to pump oil out of the ground from an existing well. Then any price in excess of $1 a barrel will induce firms to supply oil from existing wells. But the actual price of oil is much higher than $1 a barrel. People want oil for various reasons, and they are willing to pay more than its cost of production to get it. The excess of the price of oil over its cost of production is economic rent.

Why don't firms enter this industry? Well, they try. But there is only a certain amount of oil available. Oil will sell for more than its cost of production because of the limited supply.

Now consider taxicab licenses. Viewed as pieces of paper, these cost almost nothing to produce. But in New York City a taxicab license can sell for $100,000! Why don't people enter this industry and produce more taxicab licenses? The reason is that entry is illegal—the supply of taxicab licenses is controlled by the city.

Farmland is yet another example of economic rent. In the aggregate, the total amount of land is fixed. There would be just as much land supplied at zero dollars an acre as at $1000 an acre. Thus in the aggregate, the payments to land constitute economic rent.

From the viewpoint of the economy as a whole, it is the price of agricultural products that determines the value of agricultural land. But from the viewpoint of the individual farmer, the value of his land is a cost of production that enters into the pricing of his product.

This is depicted in Figure 23.7. Here AVC represents the average cost curve for all factors of production *excluding* land costs. (We are assuming that land is the only fixed factor.) If the price of the crop grown on this land is p^*, then the "profits" attributable to the land are measured by the area of the box: these are the economic rents. This is how much the land would rent for in a competitive market—whatever it took to drive the profits to zero.

The average cost curve *including* the value of the land is labeled AC. If we measure the value of the land correctly, the economic profits to operating the farm will be exactly zero. Since the equilibrium rent for the land will be whatever it takes to drive profits to zero, we have

$$p^*y^* - c_v(y^*) - \text{rent} = 0$$

or

$$\text{rent} = p^*y^* - c_v(y^*). \tag{23.1}$$

This is precisely what we referred to as producer's surplus earlier. Indeed, it is the same concept, simply viewed in a different light. Thus we can also measure rent by taking the area to the left of the marginal cost curve, as we saw earlier.

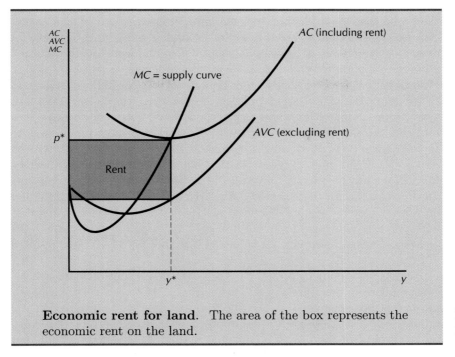

Economic rent for land. The area of the box represents the economic rent on the land.

Figure
23.7

Given the definition of rent in equation (23.1), it is now easy to see the truth of what we said earlier: it is the equilibrium price that determines rent, not the reverse. The firm supplies along its marginal cost curve— which is independent of the expenditures on the fixed factors. The rent will adjust to drive profits to zero.

23.8 Rental Rates and Prices

Since we are measuring output in flow units—so much output per unit of time, we should be careful to measure profits and rents in dollars per unit of time. Thus in the above discussion we talked about the rent per year for land or for a taxicab license.

If the land or the license is to be sold outright rather than rented, the equilibrium price would be the present value of the stream of rental payments. This is a simple consequence of the usual argument that assets generating a stream of payments should sell for their present values in a competitive market.

EXAMPLE: Liquor Licenses

In the United States, each state sets its own policy with respect to sales of alcohol. Some states have a liquor monopoly; other states issue licenses to those who wish to sell alcohol. In some cases, licenses are issued on payment of a fee; in other cases, the number of licenses is fixed. In Michigan, for example, the number of licenses for sales of beer and wine for consumption on premises is limited to one for every 1,500 residents.

After each Federal census, a state liquor control board allocates licenses to communities whose populations have grown. (Licenses are not taken away from communities whose populations have fallen, however.) This artificial scarcity of licenses has created a vibrant market for licenses to serve liquor in many fast-growing communities. For example, in 1983 Ann Arbor, Michigan, had sixty-six existing liquor licenses. Six new licenses were allowed to be issued as a result of the 1980 census, and 33 applicants lined up to lobby for these licenses. At the time, the market value of a liquor license was about $80,000. The local newspaper ran a story asserting that "demand exceeds supply for liquor licenses." It was hardly surprising to the local economists that giving away an $80,000 asset for a zero price resulted in excess demand!

There have been many proposals to relax the liquor control laws in Michigan by allowing the state to issue new licenses. However, these proposals have never been enacted into law due to the opposition of various political groups. Some of these groups are opposed to the consumption of alcohol on grounds of public health or religion. Others have somewhat different motives. For example, one of the most vociferous opponents of relaxed liquor laws is the Michigan Licensed Beverage Association, a group that represents the sellers of alcoholic beverages in Michigan. Though at first glance it appears paradoxical that this group would oppose liberalization of the liquor laws, a little reflection indicates a possible reason: issuing more liquor licenses would undoubtably lower the resale value of *existing* licenses—imposing significant capital losses on current holders of such licenses.

23.9 The Politics of Rent

Often economic rent exists because of legal restrictions on entry into the industry. We mentioned two examples above: taxicab licenses and liquor licenses. In each of these cases the number of licenses is fixed by law, thus restricting entry to the industry and creating economic rents.

Suppose that the New York City government wants to increase the number of operating taxicabs. What will happen to the market value of the existing taxicab licenses? Obviously they will fall in value. This reduction in value hits the industry right in the pocketbook, and it is sure to create a lobbying force to oppose any such move.

The federal government also artificially restricts output of some products in such a way as to create a rent. For example, the federal government has declared that tobacco can only be grown on certain lands. The value of this land is then determined by the demand for tobacco products. Any attempt to eliminate this licensing system has to contend with a serious lobby. Once the government creates artificial scarcity, it is very hard to eliminate it. The beneficiaries of the artificial scarcity—the people who have acquired the right to operate in the industry—will vigorously oppose any attempts to enlarge the industry.

The incumbents in an industry in which entry is legally restricted may well devote considerable resources to maintaining their favored position. Lobbying expenses, lawyers' fees, public relations costs, and so on can be substantial. From the viewpoint of society these kinds of expenses represent pure social waste. They aren't true costs of production; they don't lead to any *more* output being produced. Lobbying and public relations efforts just determine who gets the money associated with existing output.

Efforts directed at keeping or acquiring claims to factors in fixed supplies are sometimes referred to as **rent seeking**. From the viewpoint of society they represent a pure deadweight loss since they don't create any more output, they just change the market value of existing factors of production.

EXAMPLE: Farming the Government

There is only one good thing to say about the U.S. program of farm subsidies: it produces a never-ending source of examples for economics textbooks. Every new reform of the farm program brings new problems. "If you want to find the holes in a program, just toss them out to farmers. No one is more innovative in finding ways to use them," says Terry Bar, the vice president of the National Council of Farm Cooperatives.[2]

Up until 1996 the basic structure of farm subsidies in the U.S. involved price supports: the Federal government guaranteed a support price for a crop and would make up the difference if the price fell below the support price. In order to qualify for this program, a farmer had to agree not to farm a certain fraction of his land.

By the very nature of this plan, most of the benefits accrued to the large farmers. According to one calculation, 13 percent of the direct Federal subsidies were going to the 1 percent of the farmers who had sales over $500,000 a year. The Food Security Act of 1985 significantly restricted the payments to large farmers. As a result, the farmers broke up their holdings by leasing the land to local investors. The investors would acquire parcels large enough to take advantage of the subsidies, but too small to run into the restrictions aimed at large farmers. Once the land was acquired the investor would register it with a government program that would pay the

---

[2] Quoted in William Robbins, "Limits on Subsidies to Big Farms Go Awry, Sending Costs Climbing," *New York Times*, June 15, 1987, A1.

investor *not* to plant the land. This practice became known as "farming the government."

According to one study, the restriction on payments to the large farmers in the 1985 farm act resulted in the creation of 31,000 new applicants for farm subsidies. The cost of these subsidies was in the neighborhood of $2.3 billion.

Note that the ostensible goal of the program—restricting the amount of government subsidies paid to large farmers—has not been achieved. When the large farmers rent their land to small farmers, the market price of the rents depends on the generosity of the Federal subsidies. The higher the subsidies, the higher the equilibrium rent the large farmers receive. The benefits from the subsidy program still falls on those who initially own the land, since it is ultimately the value of what the land can earn—either from growing crops or farming the government—that determines its market value.

The Farm Act of 1996 promised a phaseout of most agricultural subsidies by 2002. However, the 1998 federal budget restored over 6 billion dollars of federal farm subsidies, illustrating once again how hard it is to reconcile politics and economics.

23.10 Energy Policy

We end this chapter with an extended example that uses some of the concepts we have developed.

In 1974 the Organization of Petroleum Exporting Countries (OPEC) levied a significant increase in the price of oil. Countries that had no domestically produced petroleum had little choice about energy policy— the price of oil and goods produced using oil had to rise.

At that time the United States produced about half of its domestic oil consumption, and Congress felt that it was unfair that the domestic producers should receive "windfall profits" from an uncontrolled increase in price. (The term windfall profits refers to an increase in profits due to some outside event, as opposed to an increase in profits due to production decisions.) Consequently, Congress devised a bizarre plan to attempt to hold down the price of products that used oil. The most prominent of these products is gasoline, so we will analyze the effect of the program for that market.

Two-Tiered Oil Pricing

The policy adopted by Congress was known as "two-tiered" oil pricing, and it went something like this. Imported oil would sell for whatever its market price was, but domestic oil—oil produced from wells that were in place before 1974—would sell for its old price: the price that it sold for before OPEC. Roughly speaking, we'll say that imported oil sold for about $15 a barrel, while domestic oil sold for around $5. The idea was that the average price of oil would then be about $10 a barrel and this would help hold down the price of gasoline.

Could such a scheme work? Let's think about it from the viewpoint of the gasoline producers. What would the supply curve of gasoline look like? In order to answer this question we have to ask what the marginal cost curve for gasoline looked like.

What would you do if you were a gasoline refiner? Obviously you would try to use the cheap domestic oil first. Only after you had exhausted your supplies of domestic oil would you turn to the more expensive imported oil. Thus the aggregate marginal cost curve—the industry supply curve—for gasoline would have to look something like that depicted in Figure 23.8. The curve takes a jump at the point where the U.S. production of domestic oil is exhausted and the imported oil begins to be used. Before that point, the domestic price of oil measures the relevant factor price for producing gasoline. After that point, it is the price of foreign oil that is the relevant factor price.

Figure 23.8 depicts the supply curve for gasoline if all oil were to sell for the world price of $15 a barrel, and if all oil were to sell for the domestic price of $5 a barrel. If domestic oil actually sells for $5 a barrel and foreign oil sells for $15 a barrel, then the supply curve for gasoline will coincide with the $5-a-barrel supply curve until the cheaper domestic oil is used up, and then coincide with the $15-a-barrel supply curve.

Now let's find the intersection of this supply curve with the market demand curve to find the equilibrium price in Figure 23.8. The diagram reveals an interesting fact: the price of gasoline is exactly the same in the two-tiered system as it would be if all oil sold at the price of foreign oil! The price of gasoline is determined by the *marginal* cost of production, and the *marginal* cost is determined by the cost of the imported oil.

If you think about it a minute, this makes perfectly good sense. The gasoline companies will sell their product at the price the market will bear. Just because you were lucky enough to get some cheap oil doesn't mean you won't sell your gasoline for the same price that other firms are selling theirs for.

Suppose for the moment that all oil did sell for one price, and that equilibrium was reached at the price p^*. Then the government comes along and lowers the price of the first 100 barrels of oil that each refiner used. Will this affect their supply decision? No way—in order to affect supply you have to change the incentives at the margin. The only way to get a lower price of gasoline is to increase the supply, which means that you have to make the marginal cost of oil cheaper.

The two-tiered oil pricing policy was simply a transfer from the domestic oil producers to the domestic oil refiners. The domestic producers got $10

Figure
23.8

The supply curve for gasoline. Under the two-tiered oil pricing policy, the supply curve of gasoline would be discontinuous, jumping from the lower supply curve to the upper supply curve when the cheaper oil was exhausted.

less for their oil than they would have otherwise, and the profits they would have gotten went to the gasoline refiners. It had no effect on the supply of gasoline, and thus it could have no effect on the price of gasoline.

Price Controls

The economic forces inherent in this argument didn't take long to make themselves felt. The Department of Energy soon realized that it couldn't allow market forces to determine the price of gasoline under the two-tiered system—since market forces alone would imply one price of gasoline, which would be the same price that would prevail in the absence of the two-tiered system.

So they instituted price controls on gasoline. Each refiner was required to charge a price for gasoline that was based on the costs of producing the gasoline—which in turn was primarily determined by the cost of the oil that the refiner was able to purchase.

The availability of cheap domestic oil varied with location. In Texas the refiners were close to the major source of production and thus were able to purchase large supplies of cheap oil. Due to the price controls, the price of Texas gasoline was relatively cheap. In New England, virtually all oil had to be imported, and thus the price of gasoline in New England was quite high.

When you have different prices for the same product, it is natural for firms to try to sell at the higher price. Again, the Department of Energy had to intervene to prevent the uncontrolled shipping of gasoline from low-price regions to high-price regions. The result of this intervention was the famous gasoline shortages of the mid-seventies. Periodically, the supply of gasoline in a region of the country would dry up, and there would be little available at any price. The free market system of supplying petroleum products had never exhibited such behavior; the shortages were entirely due to the two-tiered oil pricing system coupled with price controls.

Economists pointed this out at the time, but it didn't have much effect on policy. What did have an effect was lobbying by the gasoline refiners. Much of the domestic oil was sold on long-term contracts, and some refiners were able to buy a lot of it, while others could only buy the expensive foreign oil. Naturally they objected that this was unfair, so Congress figured out another scheme to allocate the cheap domestic oil more equitably.

The Entitlement Program

This program was known as the "entitlement program," and it went something like this. Each time a refiner bought a barrel of expensive foreign oil he got a coupon that allowed him to buy a certain amount of cheap domestic oil. The amount that the refiner was allowed to buy depended on supply conditions, but let's say that it was one for one: each barrel of foreign oil that he bought for $15 allowed him to buy one barrel of domestic oil for $5.

What did this do to the marginal price of oil? Now the marginal price of oil was just a weighted average of the domestic price and the foreign price of oil; in the one-for-one case described above, the price would be $10. The effect on the supply curve of gasoline is depicted in Figure 23.9.

The marginal cost of oil was reduced all right, and that meant that the price of gasoline was reduced as well. But look who is paying for it: the domestic oil producers! The United States was buying foreign oil that cost $15 a barrel in real dollars and pretending that it only cost $10. The domestic oil producers were required to sell their oil for less than the market price on the world oil market. We were subsidizing the importation of foreign oil and forcing the domestic oil producers to pay the subsidy!

Eventually this program was abandoned as well, and the U.S. imposed a tax on the domestic production of oil so that the U.S. oil producers wouldn't reap windfall profits due to OPEC's action. Of course, such a tax

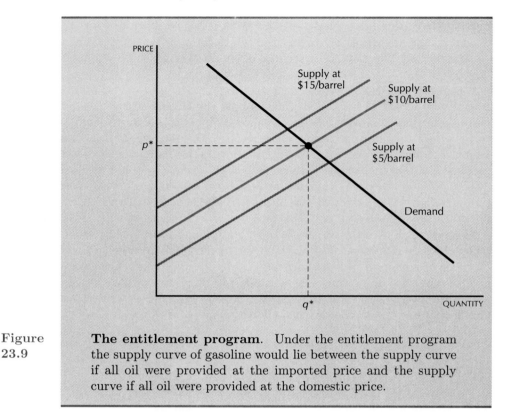

Figure 23.9

The entitlement program. Under the entitlement program the supply curve of gasoline would lie between the supply curve if all oil were provided at the imported price and the supply curve if all oil were provided at the domestic price.

discouraged production of domestic oil, and thereby increases the price of gasoline, but this was apparently acceptable to Congress at the time.

Summary

1. The short-run supply curve of an industry is just the horizontal sum of the supply curves of the individual firms in that industry.

2. The long-run supply curve of an industry must take into account the exit and entry of firms in the industry.

3. If there is free entry and exit, then the long-run equilibrium will involve the maximum number of firms consistent with nonnegative profits. This means that the long-run supply curve will be essentially horizontal at a price equal to the minimum average cost.

4. If there are forces preventing the entry of firms into a profitable industry, the factors that prevent entry will earn economic rents. The rent earned is determined by the price of the output of the industry.

REVIEW QUESTIONS

1. If $S_1(p) = p-10$ and $S_2(p) = p-15$, then at what price does the industry supply curve have a kink in it?

2. In the short run the demand for cigarettes is totally inelastic. In the long run, suppose that it is perfectly elastic. What is the impact of a cigarette tax on the price that consumers pay in the short run and in the long run?

3. True or false? Convenience stores near the campus have high prices because they have to pay high rents.

4. True or false? In long-run industry equilibrium no firm will be losing money.

5. According to the model presented in this chapter, what determines the amount of entry or exit a given industry experiences?

6. The model of entry presented in this chapter implies that the more firms in a given industry, the (steeper, flatter) is the long-run industry supply curve.

7. A New York City cab operator appears to be making positive profits in the long run after carefully accounting for the operating and labor costs. Does this violate the competitive model? Why or why not?

CHAPTER **24**

MONOPOLY

In the preceding chapters we have analyzed the behavior of a competitive industry, a market structure that is most likely when there are a large number of small firms. In this chapter we turn to the opposite extreme and consider an industry structure when there is only *one* firm in the industry—a **monopoly**.

When there is only one firm in a market, that firm is very unlikely to take the market price as given. Instead, a monopoly would recognize its influence over the market price and choose that level of price and output that maximized its overall profits.

Of course, it can't choose price and output independently; for any given price, the monopoly will be able to sell only what the market will bear. If it chooses a high price, it will be able to sell only a small quantity. The demand behavior of the consumers will constrain the monopolist's choice of price and quantity.

We can view the monopolist as choosing the price and letting the consumers choose how much they wish to buy at that price, or we can think of the monopolist as choosing the quantity, and letting the consumers decide what price they will pay for that quantity. The first approach is probably more natural, but the second turns out to be analytically more convenient. Of course, both approaches are equivalent when done correctly.

24.1 Maximizing Profits

We begin by studying the monopolist's profit-maximization problem. Let us use $p(y)$ to denote the market inverse demand curve and $c(y)$ to denote the cost function. Let $r(y) = p(y)y$ denote the revenue function of the monopolist. The monopolist's profit-maximization problem then takes the form

$$\max_{y} \ r(y) - c(y).$$

The optimality condition for this problem is straightforward: at the optimal choice of output we must have marginal revenue equal to marginal cost. If marginal revenue were less than marginal cost it would pay the firm to decrease output, since the savings in cost would more than make up for the loss in revenue. If the marginal revenue were greater than the marginal cost, it would pay the firm to increase output. The only point where the firm has no incentive to change output is where marginal revenue equals marginal cost.

In terms of algebra, we can write the optimization condition as

$$MR = MC$$

or

$$\frac{\Delta r}{\Delta y} = \frac{\Delta c}{\Delta y}.$$

The same $MR = MC$ condition has to hold in the case of a competitive firm; in that case, marginal revenue is equal to the price and the condition reduces to price equals marginal cost.

In the case of a monopolist, the marginal revenue term is slightly more complicated. If the monopolist decides to increase its output by Δy, there are two effects on revenues. First it sells more output and receives a revenue of $p\Delta y$ from that. But second, the monopolist pushes the price down by Δp and it gets this lower price on *all* the output it has been selling.

Thus the total effect on revenues of changing output by Δy will be

$$\Delta r = p\Delta y + y\Delta p,$$

so that the change in revenue divided by the change in output—the marginal revenue—is

$$\frac{\Delta r}{\Delta y} = p + \frac{\Delta p}{\Delta y}y.$$

(This is exactly the same derivation we went through in our discussion of marginal revenue in Chapter 15. You might want to review that material before proceeding.)

Another way to think about this is to think of the monopolist as choosing its output and price simultaneously—recognizing, of course, the constraint imposed by the demand curve. If the monopolist wants to sell more output it has to lower its price. But this lower price will mean a lower price for all of the units it is selling, not just the new units. Hence the term $y\Delta p$.

In the competitive case, a firm that could lower its price below the price charged by other firms would immediately capture the entire market from its competitors. But in the monopolistic case, the monopoly already has the entire market; when it lowers its price, it has to take into account the effect of the price reduction on all the units it sells.

Following the discussion in Chapter 15, we can also express marginal revenue in terms of elasticity via the formula

$$MR(y) = p(y)\left[1 + \frac{1}{\epsilon(y)}\right]$$

and write the "marginal revenue equals marginal costs" optimality condition as

$$p(y)\left[1 + \frac{1}{\epsilon(y)}\right] = MC(y). \tag{24.1}$$

Since elasticity is naturally negative, we could also write this expression as

$$p(y)\left[1 - \frac{1}{|\epsilon(y)|}\right] = MC(y).$$

From these equations it is easy to see the connection with the competitive case: in the competitive case, the firm faces a flat demand curve—an infinitely elastic demand curve. This means that $1/|\epsilon| = 1/\infty = 0$, so the appropriate version of this equation for a competitive firm is simply price equals marginal cost.

Note that a monopolist will never choose to operate where the demand curve is *inelastic*. For if $|\epsilon| < 1$, then $1/|\epsilon| > 1$, and the marginal revenue is negative, so it can't possibly equal marginal cost. The meaning of this becomes clear when we think of what is implied by an inelastic demand curve: if $|\epsilon| < 1$, then reducing output will increase revenues, and reducing output must reduce total cost, so profits will necessarily increase. Thus any point where $|\epsilon| < 1$ cannot be a profit maximum for a monopolist, since it could increase its profits by producing less output. It follows that a point that yields maximum profits can only occur where $|\epsilon| \geq 1$.

24.2 Linear Demand Curve and Monopoly

Suppose that the monopolist faces a linear demand curve

$$p(y) = a - by.$$

Then the revenue function is

$$r(y) = p(y)y = ay - by^2,$$

and the marginal revenue function is

$$MR(y) = a - 2by.$$

(This follows from the formula given at the end of Chapter 15. It is easy to derive using simple calculus. If you don't know calculus, just memorize the formula, since we will use it quite a bit.)

Note that the marginal revenue function has the same vertical intercept, a, as the demand curve, but it is twice as steep. This gives us an easy way to draw the marginal revenue curve. We know that the vertical intercept is a. To get the horizontal intercept, just take half of the horizontal intercept of the demand curve. Then connect the two intercepts with a straight line. We have illustrated the demand curve and the marginal revenue curve in Figure 24.1.

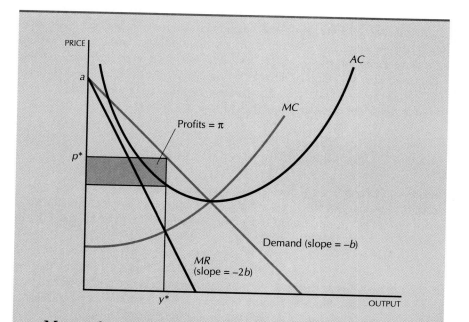

Monopoly with a linear demand curve. The monopolist's profit-maximizing output occurs where marginal revenue equals marginal cost.

Figure
24.1

The optimal output, y^*, is where the marginal revenue curve intersects the marginal cost curve. The monopolist will then charge the maximum price it can get at this output, $p(y^*)$. This gives the monopolist a revenue of $p(y^*)y^*$ from which we subtract the total cost $c(y^*) = AC(y^*)y^*$, leaving a profit area as illustrated.

24.3 Markup Pricing

We can use the elasticity formula for the monopolist to express its optimal pricing policy in another way. Rearranging equation (24.1) we have

$$p(y) = \frac{MC(y^*)}{1 - 1/|\epsilon(y)|}. \tag{24.2}$$

This formulation indicates that the market price is a markup over marginal cost, where the amount of the markup depends on the elasticity of demand. The markup is given by

$$\frac{1}{1 - 1/|\epsilon(y)|}.$$

Since the monopolist always operates where the demand curve is elastic, we are assured that $|\epsilon| > 1$, and thus the markup is greater than 1.

In the case of a constant-elasticity demand curve, this formula is especially simple since $\epsilon(y)$ is a constant. A monopolist who faces a constant-elasticity demand curve will charge a price that is a *constant* markup on marginal cost. This is illustrated in Figure 24.2. The curve labeled $MC/(1 - 1/|\epsilon|)$ is a constant fraction higher than the marginal cost curve; the optimal level of output occurs where $p = MC/(1 - 1/|\epsilon|)$.

EXAMPLE: The Impact of Taxes on a Monopolist

Let us consider a firm with constant marginal costs and ask what happens to the price charged when a quantity tax is imposed. Clearly the marginal costs go up by the amount of the tax, but what happens to the market price?

Let's first consider the case of a linear demand curve, as depicted in Figure 24.3. When the marginal cost curve, MC, shifts up by the amount of the tax to $MC+t$, the intersection of marginal revenue and marginal cost moves to the left. Since the demand curve is half as steep as the marginal revenue curve, the price goes up by half the amount of the tax.

This is easy to see algebraically. The marginal revenue equals marginal cost plus the tax condition is

$$a - 2by = c + t.$$

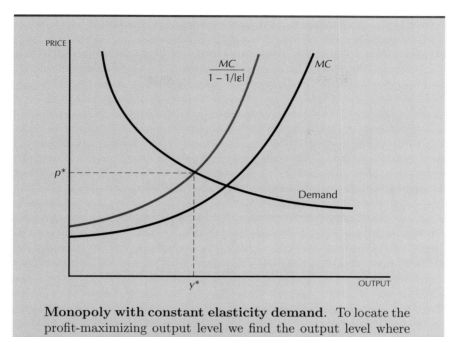

Monopoly with constant elasticity demand. To locate the profit-maximizing output level we find the output level where the curve $MC/(1 - 1/|\epsilon|)$ crosses the demand curve.

Figure
24.2

Solving for y yields

$$y = \frac{a - c - t}{2b}.$$

Thus the change in output is given by

$$\frac{\Delta y}{\Delta t} = -\frac{1}{2b}.$$

The demand curve is

$$p(y) = a - by,$$

so price will change by $-b$ times the change in output:

$$\frac{\Delta p}{\Delta t} = -b \times -\frac{1}{2b} = \frac{1}{2}.$$

In this calculation the factor $1/2$ occurs because of the assumptions of the linear demand curve and constant marginal costs. Together these assumptions imply that the price rises by less than the tax increase. Is this likely to be true in general?

The answer is no—in general a tax may increase the price by more or less than the amount of the tax. For an easy example, consider the case of a monopolist facing a constant-elasticity demand curve. Then we have

$$p = \frac{c + t}{1 - 1/|\epsilon|},$$

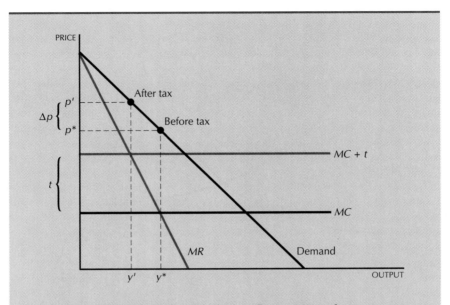

PRICE

p'

$\Delta p \{$

p^*

After tax

Before tax

$t \{$

MC + t

MC

MR

Demand

y' y^*

OUTPUT

Figure
24.3

Linear demand and taxation. Imposition of a tax on a
monopolist facing a linear demand. Note that the price will rise
by half the amount of the tax.

so that

$$\frac{\Delta p}{\Delta t} = \frac{1}{1 - 1/|\epsilon|},$$

which is certainly bigger than 1. In this case, the monopolist passes on
more than the amount of the tax.

Another kind of tax that we might consider is the case of a profits tax.
In this case the monopolist is required to pay some fraction τ of its profits
to the government. The maximization problem that it faces is then

$$\max_{y} (1 - \tau)[p(y)y - c(y)].$$

But the value of y that maximizes profits will also maximize $(1 - \tau)$ times
profits. Thus a pure profits tax will have no effect on a monopolist's choice
of output.

24.4 Inefficiency of Monopoly

A competitive industry operates at a point where price equals marginal
cost. A monopolized industry operates where price is greater than marginal cost. Thus in general the price will be higher and the output lower

if a firm behaves monopolistically rather than competitively. For this reason, consumers will typically be worse off in an industry organized as a monopoly than in one organized competitively.

But, by the same token, the firm will be better off! Counting both the firm and the consumer, it is not clear whether competition or monopoly will be a "better" arrangement. It appears that one must make a value judgment about the relative welfare of consumers and the owners of firms. However, we will see that one can argue against monopoly on grounds of efficiency alone.

Consider a monopoly situation, as depicted in Figure 24.4. Suppose that we could somehow costlessly force this firm to behave as a competitor and take the market price as being set exogenously. Then we would have (p_c, y_c) for the competitive price and output. Alternatively, if the firm recognized its influence on the market price and chose its level of output so as to maximize profits, we would see the monopoly price and output (p_m, y_m).

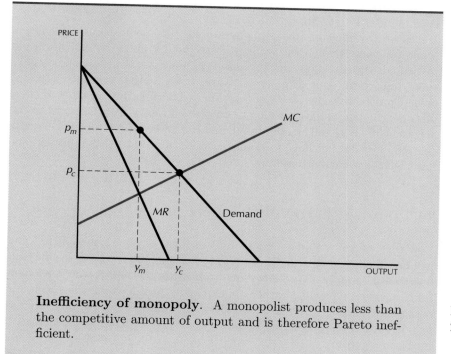

Inefficiency of monopoly. A monopolist produces less than the competitive amount of output and is therefore Pareto inefficient.

Figure 24.4

Recall that an economic arrangement is Pareto efficient if there is no way to make anyone better off without making somebody else worse off. Is the monopoly level of output Pareto efficient?

Remember the definition of the inverse demand curve. At each level of output, $p(y)$ measures how much people are willing to pay for an additional unit of the good. Since $p(y)$ is greater than $MC(y)$ for all the output levels between y_m and y_c, there is a whole range of output where people are willing to pay more for a unit of output than it costs to produce it. Clearly there is a potential for Pareto improvement here!

For example, consider the situation at the monopoly level of output y_m. Since $p(y_m) > MC(y_m)$ we know that there is someone who is willing to pay more for an extra unit of output than it costs to produce that extra unit. Suppose that the firm produces this extra output and sells it to this person at any price p where $p(y_m) > p > MC(y_m)$. Then this consumer is made better off because he or she was just willing to pay $p(y_m)$ for that unit of consumption, and it was sold for $p < p(y_m)$. Similarly, it cost the monopolist $MC(y_m)$ to produce that extra unit of output and it sold it for $p > MC(y_m)$. All the other units of output are being sold for the same price as before, so nothing has changed there. But in the sale of the extra unit of output, each side of the market gets some extra surplus—each side of the market is made better off and no one else is made worse off. We have found a Pareto improvement.

It is worthwhile considering the reason for this inefficiency. The efficient level of output is when the willingness to pay for an extra unit of output just equals the cost of producing this extra unit. A competitive firm makes this comparison. But a monopolist also looks at the effect of increasing output on the revenue received from the **inframarginal** units, and these inframarginal units have nothing to do with efficiency. A monopolist would always be ready to sell an additional unit at a lower price than it is currently charging if it did not have to lower the price of all the other inframarginal units that it is currently selling.

24.5 Deadweight Loss of Monopoly

Now that we know that a monopoly is inefficient, we might want to know just how inefficient it is. Is there a way to measure the total loss in efficiency due to a monopoly? We know how to measure the loss to the consumers from having to pay p_m rather than p_c—we just look at the change in consumers' surplus. Similarly, for the firm we know how to measure the gain in profits from charging p_m rather than p_c—we just use the change in producer's surplus.

The most natural way to combine these two numbers is to treat the firm—or, more properly, the owners of the firm—and the consumers of the firm's output symmetrically and add together the profits of the firm and the consumers' surplus. The change in the profits of the firm—the change in producer's surplus—measures how much the owners would be willing to pay to get the higher price under monopoly, and the change in consumers' surplus measures how much the consumers would have to be paid to compensate them for the higher price. Thus the difference between these two numbers should give a sensible measure of the net benefit or cost of the monopoly.

The changes in the producer's and consumers' surplus from a movement from monopolistic to competitive output are illustrated in Figure 24.5. The monopolist's surplus goes down by A due to the lower price on the units he was already selling. It goes up by C due to the profits on the extra units it is now selling.

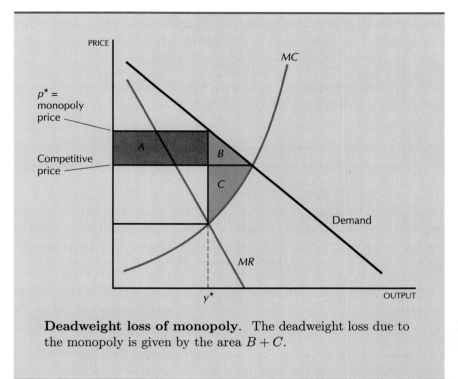

Deadweight loss of monopoly. The deadweight loss due to the monopoly is given by the area $B + C$.

Figure
24.5

The consumers' surplus goes up by A, since the consumers are now getting all the units they were buying before at a cheaper price; and it goes up by B, since they get some surplus on the extra units that are being sold. The area A is just a transfer from the monopolist to the consumer; one side of the market is made better off and one side is made worse off, but the total surplus doesn't change. The area $B + C$ represents a true increase in surplus—this area measures the value that the consumers and the producers place on the extra output that has been produced.

The area $B + C$ is known as the **deadweight loss** due to the monopoly. It provides a measure of how much worse off people are paying the monopoly price than paying the competitive price. The deadweight loss due to monopoly, like the deadweight loss due to a tax, measures the value of the lost output by valuing each unit of lost output at the price that people are willing to pay for that unit.

To see that the deadweight loss measures the value of the lost output, think about starting at the monopoly point and providing one additinal unit of output. The value of that marginal unit of output is the market price. The cost of producing the additional unit of output is the marginal cost. Thus the "social value" of producing an extra unit will be simply the price minus the marginal cost. Now consider the value of the next unit of output; again its social value will be the gap between price and marginal cost at that level of output. And so it goes. As we move from the monopoly level of output to the competitive level of output, we "sum up" the distances between the demand curve and the marginal cost curve to generate the value of the lost output due to the monopoly behavior. The total area between the two curves from the monopoly output to the competitive output is the deadweight loss.

EXAMPLE: The Optimal Life of a Patent

A **patent** offers inventors the exclusive right to benefit from their inventions for a limited period of time. Thus a patent offers a kind of limited monopoly. The reason for offering such patent protection is to encourage innovation. In the absence of a patent system, it is likely that individuals and firms would be unwilling to invest much in research and development, since any new discoveries that they would make could be copied by competitors.

In the United States the life of a patent is 17 years. During that period, the holders of the patent have a monopoly on the invention; after the patent expires, anyone is free to utilize the technology described in the patent. The longer the life of a patent, the more gains can be accrued by the inventors, and thus the more incentive they have to invest in research and development. However, the longer the monopoly is allowed to exist, the more deadweight loss will be generated. The benefit from a long patent life is that it encourages innovation; the cost is that it encourages monopoly. The "optimal" patent life is the period that balances these two conflicting effects.

The problem of determining the optimal patent life has been examined by William Nordhaus of Yale University.[1] As Nordhaus indicates, the problem is very complex and there are many unknown relationships involved. Nevertheless, some simple calculations can give some insight as to whether

---

[1] William Nordhaus, *Invention, Growth, and Welfare* (Cambridge, Mass.: M.I.T. Press, 1969).

the current patent life is wildly out of line with the estimated benefits and costs described above.

Nordhaus found that for "run-of-the-mill" inventions, a patent life of 17 years was roughly 90 percent efficient—meaning that it achieved 90 percent of the maximum possible consumers' surplus. On the basis of these figures, it does not seem like there is a compelling reason to make drastic changes in the patent system.

24.6 Natural Monopoly

We have seen earlier that the Pareto efficient amount of output in an industry occurs where price equals marginal cost. A monopolist produces where marginal revenue equals marginal cost and thus produces too little output. It would seem that regulating a monopoly to eliminate the inefficiency is pretty easy—all the regulator has to do is to set price equal to marginal cost, and profit maximization will do the rest. Unfortunately, this analysis leaves out one important aspect of the problem: it may be that the monopolist would make negative profits at such a price.

An example of this is shown in Figure 24.6. Here the minimum point of the average cost curve is to the right of the demand curve, and the intersection of demand and marginal cost lies underneath the average cost curve. Even though the level of output y_{MC} is efficient, it is not profitable. If a regulator set this level of output, the monopolist would prefer to go out of business.

This kind of situation often arises with public utilities. Think of a gas company, for example. Here the technology involves very large fixed costs— creating and maintaining the gas delivery pipes—and a very small marginal cost to providing extra units of gas—once the pipe is laid, it costs very little to pump more gas down the pipe. Similarly, a local telephone company involves very large fixed costs for providing the wires and switching network, while the marginal costs of an extra unit of telephone service is very low. When there are large fixed costs and small marginal costs, you can easily get the kind of situation described in Figure 24.6. Such a situation is referred to as a **natural monopoly**.

If allowing a natural monopolist to set the monopoly price is undesirable due to the Pareto inefficiency, and forcing the natural monopoly to produce at the competitive price is infeasible due to negative profits, what is left? For the most part natural monopolies are regulated or operated by governments. Different countries have adopted different approaches. In some countries the telephone service is provided by the government and in others it is provided by private firms that are regulated by the government. Both of these approaches have their advantages and disadvantages.

For example, let us consider the case of government regulation of a natural monopoly. If the regulated firm is to require no subsidy, it must make

Figure
24.6

A natural monopoly. If a natural monopolist operates where price equals marginal cost, then it will produce an efficient level of output, y_{MC}, but it will be unable to cover its costs. If it is required to produce an output where price equals average cost, y_{AC}, then it will cover its costs, but will produce too little output relative to the efficient amount.

nonnegative profits, which means it must operate on or above the average cost curve. If it is to provide service to all who are willing to pay for it, it must also operate on the demand curve. Thus the natural operating position for a regulated firm is a point like (p_{AC}, y_{AC}) in Figure 24.6. Here the firm is selling its product at the average cost of production, so it covers its costs, but it is producing too little output relative to the efficient level of output.

This solution is often adopted as a reasonable pricing policy for a natural monopolist. Government regulators set the prices that the public utility is allowed to charge. Ideally these prices are supposed to be prices that just allow the firm to break even—produce at a point where price equals average costs.

The problem facing the regulators is to determine just what the true costs of the firm are. Usually there is a public utility commission that investigates the costs of the monopoly in an attempt to determine the true average cost and then sets a price that will cover costs. (Of course, one of these costs is the payment that the firm has to make to its shareholders and other creditors in exchange for the money they have loaned to the firm.)

In the United States these regulatory boards operate at the state and local level. Typically electricity, natural gas, and telephone service operate in this way. Other natural monopolies like cable TV are usually regulated at the local level.

The other solution to the problem of natural monopoly is to let the government operate it. The ideal solution here in this case is to operate the service at price equals marginal cost and provide a lump-sum subsidy to keep the firm in operation. This is often the practice for local public transportation systems such as buses and subways. The lump-sum subsidies may not reflect inefficient operation *per se* but rather, simply reflect the large fixed costs associated with such public utilities.

Then again, the subsidies may just represent inefficiency! The problem with government-run monopolies is that it is almost as difficult to measure their costs as it is to measure the costs of regulated public utilities. Government regulatory commissions that oversee the operations of public utilities often subject them to probing hearings to require them to justify cost data whereas an internal government bureaucracy may escape such intense scrutiny. The government bureaucrats who run such government monopolies may turn out to be less accountable to the public than those who run the regulated monopolies.

24.7 What Causes Monopolies?

Given information on costs and demand, when would we predict that an industry would be competitive and when would we predict that it would be monopolized? In general the answer depends on the relationship between the average cost curve and the demand curve. The crucial factor is the size of the **minimum efficient scale (MES)**, the level of output that minimizes average cost, relative to the size of demand.

Consider Figure 24.7 where we have illustrated the average cost curves and the market demand curves for two goods. In the first case there is room in the market for many firms, each charging a price close to p^* and each operating at a relatively small scale. In the second market, only one firm can make positive profits. We would expect that the first market might well operate as a competitive market and that the second would operate as a monopolist.

Thus the shape of the average cost curve, which in turn is determined by the underlying technology, is one important aspect that determines whether a market will operate competitively or monopolistically. If the minimum efficient scale of production—the level of output that minimizes average costs—is small relative to the size of the market, we might expect that competitive conditions will prevail.

Note that this is a *relative* statement: what matters is the scale relative to the market size. We can't do too much about the minimum efficient scale—

Figure
24.7

Demand relative to minimum efficient scale. (A) If demand is large relative to the minimum efficient scale, a competitive market is likely to result. (B) If it is small, a monopolistic industry structure is possible.

that is determined by the technology. But economic policy can influence the size of the market. If a country chooses nonrestrictive foreign-trade policies, so that domestic firms face foreign competition, then the domestic firms' ability to influence prices will be much less. Conversely, if a country adopts restrictive trade policies, so that the size of the market is limited only to that country, then monopolistic practices are more likely to take hold.

If monopolies arise because the minimum efficient scale is large relative to the size of the market, and it is infeasible to increase the size of the market, then the industry is a candidate for regulation or other sorts of government intervention. Of course such regulation and intervention are costly too. Regulatory boards cost money, and the efforts of the firm to satisfy the regulatory boards can be quite expensive. From society's point of view, the question should be whether the deadweight loss of the monopoly exceeds the costs of regulation.

A second reason why monopoly might occur is that several different firms in an industry might be able to collude and restrict output in order to raise prices and thereby increase their profits. When firms collude in this way and attempt to reduce output and increase price, we say the industry is organized as a **cartel**.

Cartels are illegal. The Antitrust Division of the Justice Department is charged with searching for evidence of noncompetitive behavior on the part of firms. If the government can establish that a group of firms attempted to restrict output or engaged in certain other anticompetitive practices, the firms in question can be forced to pay heavy fines.

On the other hand, an industry may have one dominant firm purely by historical accident. If one firm is first to enter some market, it may have enough of a cost advantage to be able to discourage other firms from entering the industry. Suppose, for example, that there are very large "tooling-up" costs to entering an industry. Then the incumbent—the firm already in the industry—may under certain conditions be able to convince potential entrants that it will cut its prices drastically if they attempt to enter the industry. By preventing entry in this manner, a firm can eventually dominate a market. We will study an example of pricing to prevent entry in Chapter 28.

EXAMPLE: Diamonds Are Forever

The De Beers diamond cartel was formed by Sir Ernest Oppenheimer, a South African mine operator, in 1930. It has since grown into one of the world's most successful cartels. De Beers handles over 80% of the world's yearly production of diamonds and has managed to maintain this near-monopoly for several decades. Over the years, De Beers has developed several mechanism to maintain control of the diamond market.

First, it maintains considerable stocks of diamonds of all types. If a producer attempts to sell outside the cartel, De Beers can quickly flood the market with the same type of diamond, thereby punishing the defector from the cartel. Second, large producers' quotas are based on the *proportion* of total sales. When the market is weak, everyone's production quota is reduced proportionally, thereby automatically increasing scarcity and raising prices.

Third, De Beers is involved at both the mining and wholesaling levels of diamond production. In the wholesale market diamonds are sold to cutters in boxes of assorted diamonds: buyers take a whole box or nothing—they cannot choose individual stones. If the market is weak for a certain size of diamond, De Beers can reduce the number of those diamonds offered in the boxes, thereby making them more scarce.

Finally, De Beers can influence the direction of final demand for diamonds by the $110 million a year it spends on advertising. Again, this advertising can be adjusted to encourage demand for the types and sizes of diamonds that are in relatively scarce supply.[2]

EXAMPLE: Pooling in Auction Markets

Adam Smith once said "People of the same trade seldom meet together, even for merriment and diversion, but the conversation ends in a conspiracy against the public, or in some contrivance to raise prices." Bidding

---

[2] A short description of the diamond market can be found in "The cartel lives to face another threat," *The Economist,* January 10, 1987, 58–60. A more detailed description can be found in Edward J. Epstein, *Cartel* (New York: Putnam, 1978).

pools in auctions provide an illustrative example of Smith's observation. In 1988 the Justice Department charged 12 Philadelphia antique dealers with antitrust violations for their participation in this particular kind of "conspiracy against the public."[3]

The dealers were accused of participating in "bidding rings," or "pools," at antique furniture auctions. The members of a pool would appoint one member to bid on certain items. If this bidder succeeded in acquiring an item, the participating dealers would then hold a subsequent private auction, called a "knockout," in which the members of the pool bid among themselves for the item. This practice allowed the members of the pool to acquire the items at much lower prices than would have prevailed if they had bid separately; in many cases the prices in the knockout auctions were 50 to 100 percent greater than the prices paid to the original sellers of the goods.

The dealers were surprised by the Justice Department suit; they considered pooling a common business practice in their trade and did not think it was illegal. They thought of the pools as a tradition of cooperation among themselves; being invited to join a pool was considered a "mark of distinction." According to one dealer, "The day I was allowed to go into the pool was a banner day. If you weren't in the pool, you weren't considered much of a dealer." The dealers were so naive that they kept careful records of their payments in the knockout auctions, which were later used by the Justice Department in the suits against the dealers.

The Justice Department argued "if they are joining together to hold down the price [received by the seller] that is illegal." The Justice Department view prevailed over that of the dealers: 11 of the 12 dealers pleaded guilty and settled the matter with fines of $1,000 to $50,000 and probation. The dealer who held out for a jury trial was found guilty and sentenced to 30 days of house arrest and a fine of $30,000.

Summary

1. When there is only a single firm in an industry, we say that it is a monopoly.

2. A monopolist operates at a point where marginal revenue equals marginal cost. Hence a monopolist charges a price that is a markup on marginal cost, where the size of the markup depends on the elasticity of demand.

3. Since a monopolist charges a price in excess of marginal cost, it will produce an inefficient amount of output. The size of the inefficiency can

[3] See Meg Cox, "At Many Auctions, Illegal Bidding Thrives As a Longtime Practice Among Dealers," *Wall Street Journal*, February 19, 1988, which served as the source for this example.

be measured by the deadweight loss—the net loss of consumers' and the producer's surplus.

4. A natural monopoly occurs when a firm cannot operate at an efficient level of output without losing money. Many public utilities are natural monopolies of this sort and are therefore regulated by the government.

5. Whether an industry is competitive or monopolized depends in part on the nature of technology. If the minimum efficient scale is large relative to demand, then the market is likely to be monopolized. But if the minimum efficient scale is small relative to demand, there is room for many firms in the industry, and there is a hope for a competitive market structure.

REVIEW QUESTIONS

1. The market demand curve for heroin is said to be highly inelastic. Heroin supply is also said to be monopolized by the Mafia, which we assume to be interested in maximizing profits. Are these two statements consistent?

2. The monopolist faces a demand curve given by $D(p) = 100 - 2p$. Its cost function is $c(y) = 2y$. What is its optimal level of output and price?

3. The monopolist faces a demand curve given by $D(p) = 10p^{-3}$. Its cost function is $c(y) = 2y$. What is its optimal level of output and price?

4. If $D(p) = 100/p$ and $c(y) = y^2$, what is the optimal level of output of the monopolist? (Be careful.)

5. A monopolist is operating at an output level where $|\epsilon| = 3$. The government imposes a quantity tax of \$6 per unit of output. If the demand curve facing the monopolist is linear, how much does the price rise?

6. What is the answer to the above question if the demand curve facing the monopolist has constant elasticity?

7. If the demand curve facing the monopolist has a constant elasticity of 2, then what will be the monopolist's markup on marginal cost?

8. The government is considering subsidizing the marginal costs of the monopolist described in the question above. What level of subsidy should the government choose if it wants the monopolist to produce the socially optimal amount of output?

9. Show mathematically that a monopolist always sets its price above marginal cost.

10. True or false? Imposing a quantity tax on a monopolist will always cause the market price to increase by the amount of the tax.

11. What problems face a regulatory agency attempting to force a monopolist to charge the perfectly competitive price?

12. What kinds of economic and technological conditions are conducive to the formation of monopolies?

APPENDIX

Define the revenue function by $r(y) = p(y)y$. Then the monopolist's profit-maximization problem is

$$\max \ r(y) - c(y).$$

The first-order condition for this problem is simply

$$r'(y) - c'(y) = 0,$$

which implies that marginal revenue should equal marginal cost at the optimal choice of output.

Differentiating the definition of the revenue function gives $r'(y) = p(y) + p'(y)y$, and substituting this into the monopolist's first-order condition yields the alternative form

$$p(y) + p'(y)y = c'(y).$$

The second-order condition for the monopolist's profit-maximization problem is

$$r''(y) - c''(y) \leq 0.$$

This implies that

$$c''(y) \geq r''(y)$$

or that the slope of the marginal cost curve exceeds the slope of the marginal revenue curve.

CHAPTER 25

MONOPOLY BEHAVIOR

In a competitive market there are typically several firms selling an identical product. Any attempt by one of the firms to sell its product at more than the market price leads consumers to desert the high-priced firm in favor of its competitors. In a monopolized market there is only one firm selling a given product. When a monopolist raises its price it loses some, but not all, of its customers.

In reality most industries are somewhere in between these two extremes. If a gas station in a small town raises the price at which it sells gasoline and it loses most of its customers, it is reasonable to think that this firm must behave as a competitive firm. If a restaurant in the same town raises its price and loses only a few of its customers, then it is reasonable to think that this restaurant has some degree of monopoly power.

If a firm has some degree of monopoly power it has more options open to it than a firm in a perfectly competitive industry. For example, it can use more complicated pricing and marketing strategies than a firm in a competitive industry. Or it can try to differentiate its product from the products sold by its competitors to enhance its market power even further. In this chapter we will examine how firms can enhance and exploit their market power.

25.1 Price Discrimination

We have argued earlier that a monopoly operates at an inefficient level of output since it restricts output to a point where people are willing to pay more for extra output than it costs to produce it. The monopolist doesn't want to produce this *extra* output, because it would force down the price that it would be able to get for *all* of its output.

But if the monopolist could sell different units of output at different prices, then we have another story. Selling different units of output at different prices is called **price discrimination**. Economists generally consider the following three kinds of price discrimination:

First-degree price discrimination means that the monopolist sells different units of output for different prices *and* these prices may differ from person to person. This is sometimes known as the case of **perfect price discrimination**.

Second-degree price discrimination means that the monopolist sells different units of output for different prices, but every individual who buys the same amount of the good pays the same price. Thus prices differ across the units of the good, but not across people. The most common example of this is bulk discounts.

Third-degree price discrimination occurs when the monopolist sells output to different people for different prices, but every unit of output sold to a given person sells for the same price. This is the most common form of price discrimination, and examples include senior citizens' discounts, student discounts, and so on.

Let us look at each of these to see what economics can say about how price discrimination works.

25.2 First-Degree Price Discrimination

Under **first-degree price discrimination**, or **perfect price discrimination**, each unit of the good is sold to the individual who values it most highly, at the maximum price that this individual is willing to pay for it.

Consider Figure 25.1, which illustrates two consumers' demand curves for a good. Think of a reservation price model for demand where the individuals choose integer amounts of the goods and each step in the demand curve represents a change in the willingness to pay for additional units of the good. We have also illustrated (constant) marginal cost curves for the good.

A producer who is able to perfectly price discriminate will sell each unit of the good at the highest price it will command, that is, at each consumer's reservation price. Since each unit is sold to each consumer at his or her reservation price for that unit, there is no consumers' surplus generated in

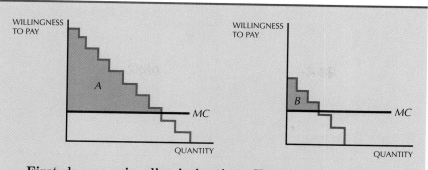

First-degree price discrimination. Here are two consumers' demand curves for a good along with the constant marginal cost curve. The producer sells each unit of the good at the maximum price it will command, which yields it the maximum possible profit.

Figure
25.1

this market; all the surplus goes to the producer. In Figure 25.1 the colored areas indicate the *producer's surplus* accruing to the monopolist. In an ordinary competitive market setting these areas would represent *consumers' surplus*, but in the case of perfect price discrimination, the monopolist is able to appropriate this surplus for itself.

Since the producer gets all the surplus in the market, it wants to make sure that the surplus is as large as possible. Put another way, the producer's goal is to maximize its profits (producer's surplus) subject to the constraint that the consumers are just willing to purchase the good. This means that the outcome will be Pareto efficient, since there will be no way to make both the consumers and the producer better off: the producer's profit can't be increased, since it is already the maximal possible profit, and the consumers' surplus can't be increased without reducing the profit of the producer.

If we move to the smooth demand curve approximation, as in Figure 25.2, we see that a perfectly price-discriminating monopolist must produce at an output level where price equals marginal cost: if price were greater than marginal cost, that would mean that there is someone who is willing to pay more than it costs to produce an extra unit of output. So why not produce that extra unit and sell it to that person at his or her reservation price, and thus increase profits?

Just as in the case of a competitive market, the sum of producer's and consumers' surpluses is maximized. However, in the case of perfect price discrimination the producer ends up getting *all* the surplus generated in the market!

We have interpreted first-degree price discrimination as selling each unit at the maximum price it will command. But we could also think of it as selling a fixed amount of the good at a "take it or leave it" price. In the

Figure
25.2

**First-degree price discrimination with smooth demand
curves.** Here are two consumers' smoothed demand curves
for a good along with the constant marginal cost curve. Here
the producer maximizes profits by producing where price equals
marginal cost, just as in the case of a competitive market.

case illustrated in Figure 25.2, the monopolist would offer to sell x_1^0 units of
the good to person 1 at a price equal to the area under person 1's demand
curve and offer to sell x_2^0 units of the good to person 2 at a price equal to
the area under person 2's demand curve B. As before, each person would
end up with zero consumer's surplus, and the entire surplus of $A+B$ would
end up in the hands of the monopolist.

Perfect price discrimination is an idealized concept—as the word "perfect" might suggest—but it is interesting theoretically since it gives us an
example of a resource allocation mechanism other than a competitive market that achieves Pareto efficiency. There are very few real-life examples
of perfect price discrimination. The closest example would be something
like a small-town doctor who charges his patients different prices, based on
their ability to pay.

25.3 Second-Degree Price Discrimination

Second-degree price discrimination is also known as the case of **nonlinear pricing**, since it means that the price per unit of output is not
constant but depends on how much you buy. This form of price discrimination is commonly used by public utilities; for example, the price per unit
of electricity often depends on how much is bought. In other industries
bulk discounts for large purchases are sometimes available.

Let us consider the case depicted earlier in Figure 25.2. We saw that
the monopolist would *like* to sell an amount x_1^0 to person 1 at price A
and an amount x_2^0 to person 2 at price B. To set the right prices, the

monopolist has to *know* the demand curves of the consumers; that is, the monopolist has to know the exact willingness to pay of each person. Even if the monopolist knows something about the statistical distribution of willingness to pay—for example, that college students are willing to pay less than yuppies for movie tickets—it might be hard to tell a yuppie from a college student when they are standing in line at the ticket booth.

Similarly, an airline ticket agent may know that business travelers are willing to pay more than tourists for their airplane tickets, but it is often difficult to tell whether a particular person is a business traveler or a tourist. If switching from a grey flannel suit to Bermuda shorts would save $500 on travel expenses, corporate dress codes could change quickly!

The problem with the first-degree price discrimination example depicted in Figure 25.2 is that person 1—the high-willingess-to-pay person—can *pretend* to be person 2, the low-willingess-to-pay person. The seller may have no effective way to tell them apart.

One way to get around this problem is to offer two different price-quantity packages in the market. One package will be targeted toward the high-demand person, the other package toward the low-demand person. It can often happen that the monopolist can construct price-quantity packages that will induce the consumers to choose the package meant for them; in economics jargon, the monopolist constructs price-quantity packages that give the consumers an incentive to **self select**.

In order to see how this works, Figure 25.3 illustrates the same kind of demand curves used in Figure 25.2, but now laid on top of each other. We've also set marginal cost equal to zero in this diagram to keep the argument simple.

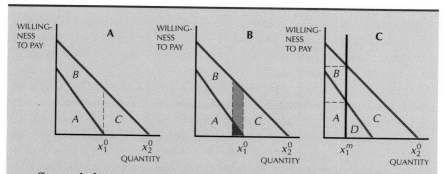

Second-degree price discrimination. These are the demand curves of two consumers; the producer has zero marginal cost by assumption. Panel A illustrates the self-selection problem. Panel B shows what happens if the monpolist reduces the output targeted for consumer 1, and panel C illustrates the profit-maximizing solution.

Figure
25.3

As before, the monopolist would like to offer x_1^0 at price A and to offer x_2^0 at price $A + B + C$. This would capture all the surplus for the monopolist and generate the most possible profit. Unfortunately for the monopolist, these price-quantity combinations are not compatible with self-selection. The high-demand consumer would find it optimal to choose the quantity x_1^0 and pay price A; this would leave him with a surplus equal to area B, which is better than the zero surplus he would get if he chose x_2^0.

One thing the monopolist can do is to offer x_2^0 at a price of $A + C$. In this case the high-demand consumer finds it optimal to choose x_2^0 and receive a gross surplus of $A + B + C$. He pays the monopolist $A + C$, which yields a net surplus of B for consumer 2—just what he would get if he chose x_1^0. This generally yields more profit to the monopolist than it would get by offering only one price-quantity combination.

But the story doesn't end here. There's yet a further thing the monopolist can do to increase profits. Suppose that instead of offering x_1^0 at price A to the low-demand consumer, the monopolist offers a bit less than that at a price slightly less than A. This reduces the monopolist's profits on person 1 by the small colored triangle illustrated in Figure 25.3B. But note that since person 1's package is now less attractive to person 2, the monopolist can now charge *more* to person 2 for x_2^0! By reducing x_1^0, the monopolist makes area A a little smaller (by the dark triangle) but makes area C bigger (by the triangle plus the light trapezoid area). The net result is that the monopolist's profits increase.

Continuing in this way, the monopolist will want to reduce the amount offered to person 1 up to the point where the profit lost on person 1 due to a further reduction in output just equals the profit gained on person 2. At this point, illustrated in Figure 25.3C, the marginal benefits and costs of quantity reduction just balance. Person 1 chooses x_1^m and is charged A; person 2 chooses x_2^0 and is charged $A + C + D$. Person 1 ends up with a zero surplus and person 2 ends up with a surplus of B—just what he would get if he chose to consume x_1^m.

In practice, the monopolist often encourages this self-selection not by adjusting the *quantity* of the good, as in this example, but rather by adjusting the *quality* of the good. The quantities in the model just examined can be re-interpreted as qualities, and everything works as before. In general, the monopolist will want to reduce the quality offered to the low end of its market so as not to cannibalize sales at the high end. Without the high-end consumers, the low-end consumers would be offered higher quality, but they would still end up with zero surplus. Without the low-end consumers, the high-end consumers would have zero surplus, so it is beneficial to the high-end consumers to have the low-end consumers present. This is because the monopolist has to cut the price to the high-end consumers to discourage them from choosing the product targeted to the low-end consumers.

EXAMPLE: Price Discrimination in Airfares

The airline industry has been very successful at price discrimination (although industry representatives prefer to use the term "yield management.") The model described above applies reasonably well to the problem faced by airlines: there are essentially two types of consumers, business travelers and individual travelers, who generally have quite different willingnesses to pay. Although there are several competing airlines in the U.S. market, it is quite common to see only one or two airlines serving specific city pairs. This gives the airlines considerable freedom in setting prices.

We have seen that the optimal pricing policy for a monopolist dealing with two groups of consumers is to sell to the high-willingness-to-pay market at a high price and offer a reduced-quality product to the market with the lower willingness to pay. The point of the reduced-quality product is to dissuade those with a high willingness to pay from purchasing the lower priced good.

The way the airlines implement this is to offer an "unrestricted fare" for business travel and a "restricted fare" for non-business travel. The restricted fare often requires advanced purchase, a Saturday-night stayover, or other such impositions. The point of these impositions, of course, is to be able to discriminate between the high-demand business travelers and the more price sensitive individual travelers. By offering a "degraded" product—the restricted fares—the airlines can charge the customers who require flexible travel arrangements considerably more for their tickets.

Such arrangements may well be socially useful; without the ability to price discriminate, a firm may decide that it is optimal to sell *only* to the high-demand markets.

Another way that airlines price discriminate is with first-class and coach-class travel. First-class travelers pay substantially more for their tickets, but they receive an enhanced level of service: more space, better food, and more attention. Coach-class travelers, on the other hand, receive a lower level of service on all these dimensions. This sort of quality discrimination has been a feature of transportation services for hundreds of years. Witness, for example, this commentary on railroad pricing by Emile Dupuit, a nineteenth century French economist:

It is not because of the few thousand francs which would have to be spent to put a roof over the third-class carriage or to upholster the third-class seats that some company or other has open carriages with wooden benches ... What the company is trying to do is prevent the passengers who can pay the second-class fare from traveling third class; it hits the poor, not because it wants to hurt them, but to frighten the rich ... And it is again for the same reason that the companies, having proved almost cruel to the third-class passengers and mean to the second-class ones, become lavish in dealing with first-class customers. Having refused the poor what is necessary, they give the rich what is superfluous.[1]

The next time you fly coach class, perhaps it will be of some solace to know that rail travel in nineteenth century France was even more uncomfortable!

25.4 Third-Degree Price Discrimination

Recall that this means that the monopolist sells to different people at different prices, but every unit of the good sold to a given group is sold at the same price. Third-degree price discrimination is the most common form of price discrimination. Examples of this might be student discounts at the movies, or senior citizens' discounts at the drugstore. How does the monopolist determine the optimal prices to charge in each market?

Let us suppose that the monopolist is able to identify two groups of people and can sell an item to each group at a different price. We suppose that the consumers in each market are not able to resell the good. Let us use $p_1(y_1)$ and $p_2(y_2)$ to denote the inverse demand curves of groups 1 and 2, respectively, and let $c(y_1 + y_2)$ be the cost of producing output. Then the profit-maximization problem facing the monopolist is

$$\max_{y_1, y_2} \; p_1(y_1)y_1 + p_2(y_2)y_2 - c(y_1 + y_2).$$

The optimal solution must have

$$MR_1(y_1) = MC(y_1 + y_2)$$

$$MR_2(y_2) = MC(y_1 + y_2).$$

That is, the marginal cost of producing an extra unit of output must be equal to the marginal revenue in *each* market. If the marginal revenue in market 1 exceeded marginal cost, it would pay to expand output in market 1, and similarly for market 2. Since marginal cost is the same in each market, this means of course that marginal revenue in each market must also be the same. Thus a good should bring the same increase in revenue whether it is sold in market 1 or in market 2.

We can use the standard elasticity formula for marginal revenue and write the profit-maximization conditions as

$$p_1(y_1) \left[1 - \frac{1}{|\epsilon_1(y_1)|}\right] = MC(y_1 + y_2)$$

---

[1] Translation by R. B. Ekelund in "Price Discrimination and Product Differentiation in Economic Theory: An Early Analysis," *Quarterly Journal of Economics*, 84 (1970), 268–78.

$$p_2(y_2) \left[1 - \frac{1}{|\epsilon_2(y_2)|} \right] = MC(y_1 + y_2),$$

where $\epsilon_1(y_1)$ and $\epsilon_2(y_2)$ represent the elasticities of demand in the respective markets, evaluated at the profit-maximizing choices of output.

Now note the following. If $p_1 > p_2$, then we must have

$$1 - \frac{1}{|\epsilon_1(y_1)|} < 1 - \frac{1}{|\epsilon_2(y_2)|},$$

which in turn implies that

$$\frac{1}{|\epsilon_1(y_1)|} > \frac{1}{|\epsilon_2(y_2)|}.$$

This means that

$$|\epsilon_2(y_2)| > |\epsilon_1(y_1)|.$$

Thus the market with the higher price must have the lower elasticity of demand. Upon reflection, this is quite sensible. An elastic demand is a price-sensitive demand. A firm that price discriminates will therefore set a low price for the price-sensitive group and a high price for the group that is relatively price insensitive. In this way it maximizes its overall profits.

We suggested that senior citizens' discounts and student discounts were good examples of third-degree price discrimination. Now we can see why they have discounts. It is likely that students and senior citizens are more sensitive to price than the average consumer and thus have more elastic demands for the relevant region of prices. Therefore a profit-maximizing firm will price discriminate in their favor.

EXAMPLE: Linear Demand Curves

Let's consider a problem where the firm faces two markets with linear demand curves, $x_1 = a - bp_1$ and $x_2 = c - dp_2$. Suppose for simplicity that marginal costs are zero. If the firm is allowed to price discriminate, it will produce where marginal revenue equals zero in each market—at a price and output combination that is halfway down each demand curve, with outputs $x_1^* = a/2$ and $x_2^* = c/2$ and prices $p_1^* = a/2b$ and $p_2^* = c/2d$.

Suppose that the firm were forced to sell in both markets at the same price. Then it would face a demand curve of $x = (a + c) - (b + d)p$ and would produce halfway down this demand curve, resulting in an output of $x^* = (a + c)/2$ and price of $p^* = (a + c)/2(b + d)$. Note that the total output is the same whether or not price discrimination is allowed. (This is a special feature of the linear demand curve and does not hold in general.)

However, there is an important exception to this statement. We have assumed that when the monopolist chooses the optimal single price it will sell a positive amount of output in each market. It may very well happen that at the profit-maximizing price, the monopolist will sell output to only one of the markets, as illustrated in Figure 25.4.

Here we have two linear demand curves; since marginal cost is assumed to be zero, the monopolist will want to operate at a point where the elasticity of demand is -1, which we know to be halfway down the market demand curve. Thus the price p_1^* is a profit-maximizing price—lowering the price any further would reduce revenues in market 1. If the demand in market 2 is very small, the monopolist may not want to lower its price any further in order to sell to this market: it will end up selling only to the larger market.

In this case, allowing price discrimination will unambiguously increase total output, since the monopolist will find it in its interest to sell to both markets if it can charge a different price in each one.

Figure
25.4

Price discrimination with linear demands. If the monopolist can charge only one price, it will charge p_1^*, and sell only to market 1. But if price discrimination is allowed, it will also sell at price p_2^* to market 2.

EXAMPLE: Calculating Optimal Price Discrimination

Suppose that a monopolist faces two markets with demand curves given by

$$D_1(p_1) = 100 - p_1$$
$$D_2(p_2) = 100 - 2p_2.$$

Assume that the monopolist's marginal cost is constant at $20 a unit. If it can price discriminate, what price should it charge in each market in order to maximize profits? What if it can't price discriminate? Then what price should it charge?

To solve the price-discrimination problem, we first calculate the inverse demand functions:

$$p_1(y_1) = 100 - y_1$$
$$p_2(y_2) = 50 - y_2/2.$$

Marginal revenue equals marginal cost in each market yields the two equations:

$$100 - 2y_1 = 20$$
$$50 - y_2 = 20.$$

Solving we have $y_1^* = 40$ and $y_2^* = 30$. Substituting back into the inverse demand functions gives us the prices $p_1^* = 60$ and $p_2^* = 35$.

If the monopolist must charge the same price in each market, we first calculate the total demand:

$$D(p) = D_1(p_1) + D_2(p_2) = 200 - 3p.$$

The inverse demand curve is

$$p(y) = \frac{200}{3} - \frac{y}{3}.$$

Marginal revenue equals marginal cost gives us

$$\frac{200}{3} - \frac{2}{3}y = 20,$$

which can be solved to give $y^* = 70$ and $p^* = 43\frac{1}{3}$.

In accord with the discussion in the previous section, it is important to check that this price generates non-negative demands in each market. However, it is easily checked that this is the case.

EXAMPLE: Price Discrimination in Academic Journals

Most written scholarly communication takes place in academic journals. These journals are sold by subscription to libraries and to individual scholars. It is very common to see different subscription prices being charged to libraries and individuals. In general, we would expect that the demand by libraries would be much more inelastic than demand by individuals, and, just as economic analysis would predict, the prices for library subscriptions are typically much higher than the prices for individual subscriptions. Often library subscriptions are 2 to 3 times more expensive than subscriptions to individuals.

More recently, some publishers have begun to price discriminate by geography. During 1984, when the U.S. dollar was at an all-time high as compared to the English pound, many British publishers began to charge different prices to U.S. subscribers than to European subscribers. It would be expected that the U.S. demand would be more inelastic. Since the dollar price of British journals was rather low due to the exchange rate, a 10 percent increase in the U.S. price would result in a smaller percentage drop in demand than a similar increase in the British price. Thus, on grounds of profit maximization, it made sense for the British publishers to raise the prices of their journals to the group with the lower elasticity of demand—the U.S. subscribers. According to a 1984 study, North American libraries were charged an average of 67 percent more for their journals than U.K. libraries, and 34 percent more than anyone else in the world.[2]

Further evidence for price discrimination can be found by examining the pattern of price increases. According to a study by the University of Michigan Library, "... publishers have carefully considered their new pricing strategy. There seems to be a direct correlation ... between patterns of library usage and the magnitude of the pricing differential. The greater the use, the larger the differential."[3]

By 1986 the exchange rate had turned in favor of the pound, and the dollar prices of the British journals had increased significantly. Along with the price increase came some serious resistance to the higher prices. The concluding sentences of the Michigan report are illustrative: "One expects that a vendor with a monopoly on a product will charge according to demand. What the campus as a customer must determine is whether it will continue to pay up to 114% more than its British counterparts for the identical product."

25.5 Bundling

Firms often choose to sell goods in **bundles**: packages of related goods offered for sale together. A noteworthy example is a bundle of software, sometimes known as a "software suite." Such a bundle might consist of several different software tools—a word processor, a spreadsheet, and a presentation tool—that are sold together in one set. Another example is a magazine: this consists of a bundle of articles that could, in principle, be sold separately. Similarly, magazines are often sold via subscription—which is just a way of bundling separate issues together.

---

[2] Hamaker, C. and Astle, D., "Recent Pricing Patterns in British Journal Publishing," *Library Acquisitions: Practice and Theory*, 8, 4 (Spring 1984), 225–32.

[3] The study was conducted by Robert Houbeck for the University of Michigan Library, and published in Vol. 2, No. 1 of the *University Library Update*, April 1986.

Bundling can be due to cost savings: it is often less expensive to sell several articles stapled together than it is to sell each of them separately. Or it may be due to complementarities among the goods involved: software programs sold in bundles often work together more effectively than off-the-shelf programs.

But there can also be reasons involving consumer behavior. Let's consider a simple example. Suppose that there are two classes of consumers and two different software programs, a word processor and a spreadsheet. Type A consumers are willing to pay $120 for the word processor and $100 for the spreadsheet. Type B consumers have the opposite preferences: they are willing to pay $120 for the spreadsheet and $100 for the word processor. This information is summarized in Table 25.1.

Willingness to pay for software components.

Table 25.1

Type of consumer	Word processor	Spreadsheet
Type A consumers	120	100
Type B consumers	100	120

Suppose that you are selling these products. For simplicity, let us assume that the marginal cost is negligible so that you only want to maximize revenue. Furthermore, make the conservative assumption that the willingess to pay for the bundle consisting of the word processor and the spreadsheet is just the sum of the willingesses to pay for each component.

Now consider the profits from two different marketing policies. First, suppose that you sell each item separately. The revenue maximizing policy is to set a price of $100 for each piece of software. If you do this, you will sell two copies of the word processor and two copies of the spreadsheet, and receive a total revenue of $400.

But what if you bundle the items together? In this case, you could sell *each* bundle for $220, and receive a net revenue of $440. The bundling strategy is clearly more attractive!

What is going on in this example? Recall that when you sell an item to several different people, the price is determined by the purchaser who has the *lowest* willingess to pay. The more diverse the valuations of the individuals, the lower the price you have to charge to sell a given number of items. In this case bundling the word processor and the spreadsheet reduces the dispersion of willingess to pay—allowing the monopolist to set a higher price for the bundle of goods.

EXAMPLE: Software Suites

Microsoft, Lotus, and other software manufacturers have taken to bundling much of their applications software. For example, in 1993 Microsoft offered a spreadsheet, word processor, presentation tool, and database as the "Microsoft Office" package at a suggested retail price of $750. (The discounted "street price" was about $450.) If bought separately, the individual software applications would total $1,565! Lotus offered its "Smart Suite" at essentially the same price; its separate components sold for a total of $1,730.

According to an article by Steve Lohr in the October 15, 1993, *New York Times*, 50 percent of Microsoft's applications software was sold in bundles, and generated revenue of over $1 billion a year.

These software suites fit the bundling model well. Tastes for software are often very heterogeneous. Some people use a word processor every day and use a spreadsheet only occasionally. Other people have the reverse pattern of software use. If you wish to sell a spreadsheet to a large number of users, you have to sell it at a price that will be attractive to an occasional user. Similarly with the word processor: it is the willingness to pay of the *marginal* user that sets the market price. By bundling the two products together, the dispersion of willingnesses to pay is reduced and total profits can increase.

This is not to say that bundling is the whole story in software suites; other phenomena are also at work. The individual components of the suites are guaranteed to work well together; they are complementary goods in this respect. Furthermore, the success of a piece of software tends to depend strongly on how many people use it, and bundling software helps to build market share. We will investigate this phenomenon of **network externalities** in a subsequent chapter.

25.6 Two-Part Tariffs

Consider the pricing problem facing the owners of an amusement park. They can set one price for tickets to get into the park and another price for the rides. How should they set these two prices if they want to maximize profits? Note that the demand for access and the demand for rides are interrelated: the price that people are willing to pay to get into the park will depend on the price that they have to pay for the rides. This kind of two-part pricing scheme is known as a **two-part tariff**.[4]

Other applications of two-part tariffs abound: Polaroid sells its camera for one price and its film for another. People who are deciding whether

---

[4] See the classic article by Walter Oi, "A Disneyland Dilemma: Two-Part Tariffs for a Mickey Mouse Monopoly," *Quarterly Journal of Economics*, 85 (1971), 77–96.

or not to purchase the camera presumably consider the price of the film. A company that makes razor blades sells the razor for one price and the blades for another—again the price they set for the blades influences the demand for razors and vice versa.

Let us consider how to solve this pricing problem in the context of the original example: the so-called Disneyland Dilemma. As usual we will make some simplifying assumptions. First, we assume that there is only one kind of ride in Disneyland. Second, we assume that people only desire to go to Disneyland for the rides. Finally, we assume that everyone has the same tastes for rides.

In Figure 25.5 we have depicted the demand curve and the (constant) marginal cost curve for rides. As usual the demand curve slopes down—if Disney sets a high price for each ride, fewer rides will be taken. Suppose that they set a price of p^*, as in Figure 25.5, that leads to a demand for x^* rides. How much will they be able to charge for admission to the park, given that the rides cost p^*?

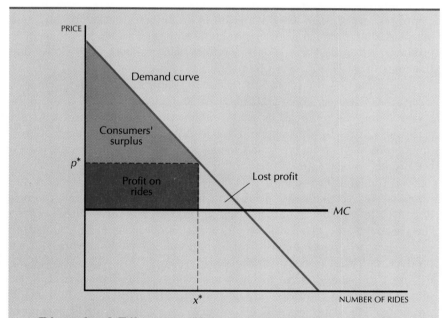

Disneyland Dilemma. If the owners of the park set a price of p^*, then x^* rides will be demanded. The consumers' surplus measures the price that they can charge for admission to the park. The total profits of the firm are maximized when the owners set price equal to marginal cost.

Figure
25.5

The total willingness to pay for x^* rides is measured by the consumers' surplus. Hence the most that the owners of the park can charge for admission is the area labeled "consumer's surplus" in Figure 25.5. The total profits to the monopolist is this area plus the profit on the rides, $(p^* - MC)x^*$.

It is not hard to see that total profits are maximized when price equals marginal cost: we've seen before that this price gives the largest possible consumer plus producer surplus. Since the monopolist gets to charge people their consumers' surplus, setting price equal to marginal cost and the entry fee to the resulting consumer's surplus is the profit-maximizing policy.

Indeed, this is the policy that Disneyland, and most other amusement parks follow. There is one price for admission, but then the attractions inside are free. It appears that the marginal cost of the rides is less than the transactions cost of collecting a separate payment for them.

25.7 Monopolistic Competition

We have described a monopolistic industry as being one in which there is a single large producer. But we've been somewhat vague about exactly what comprises an industry. One definition of an industry is that it consists of all firms that produce a given product. But then what do we mean by product? After all, there is only one firm that produces Coca-Cola—does that mean that this firm is a monopolist?

Clearly the answer is no. The Coca-Cola firm still has to compete with other producers of soft drinks. We should really think of an industry as being the set of firms that produce products that are viewed as close substitutes by consumers. Each firm in the industry can produce a unique product—a unique brand name, say—but consumers view each of the brands as being substitutes to some degree.

Even though a firm may have a legal monopoly on its trademarks, and brand names, so that other firms can't produce *exactly* the same product, it is usually possible for other firms to produce *similar* products. From the viewpoint of a given firm, the production decisions of its competitors will be a very important consideration in deciding exactly how much it will produce and what price it can charge.

Thus the demand curve facing a firm will usually depend on the output decisions and the prices charged by other firms that produce similar products. The slope of the demand curve facing the firm will depend on how similar the other firms' products are. If a large number of the firms in the industry produce *identical* products, then the demand curve facing any one of them will be essentially flat. Each firm must sell its product for whatever price the other firms are charging. Any firm that tried to raise its price above the prices of the other firms selling identical products would soon lose all of its customers.

On the other hand, if one firm has the exclusive rights to sell a particular product, then it may be able to raise its price without losing all of its customers. Some, but not all, of its customers may switch to competitors' products. Just how many customers switch depends on how similar the customers think the products are—that is, on the elasticity of the demand curve facing the firm.

If a firm is making a profit selling a product in an industry, and other firms are not allowed to perfectly reproduce that product, they still may find it profitable to enter that industry and produce a similar but distinctive product. Economists refer to this phenomenon as **product differentiation**—each firm attempts to differentiate its product from the other firms in the industry. The more successful it is at differentiating its product from other firms selling similar products, the more monopoly power it has—that is, the less elastic is the demand curve for the product. For example, consider the soft drink industry. In this industry there are a number of firms producing similar, but not identical products. Each product has its following of consumers, and so has some degree of market power.

An industry structure such as that described above shares elements of both competition and monopoly; it is therefore referred to as **monopolistic competition**. The industry structure is monopolistic in that each firm faces a downward-sloping demand curve for its product. It therefore has some market power in the sense that it can set its own price, rather than passively accept the market price as does a competitive firm. On the other hand the firms must compete for customers in terms of both price and the kinds of products they sell. Furthermore, there are no restrictions against new firms entering into a monopolistically competitive industry. In these aspects the industry is like a competitive industry.

Monopolistic competition is probably the most prevalent form of industry structure. Unfortunately, it is also the most difficult form to analyze. The extreme cases of pure monopoly and pure competition are much simpler and can often be used as first approximations to more elaborate models of monopolistic competition. In a detailed model of a monopolistically competitive industry, much depends on the specific details of the products and technology, as well as on the nature of the strategic choices available to firms. It is unreasonable to model a monopolistically competitive industry in the abstract, as we have done with the simpler cases of pure competition and pure monopoly. Rather, the institutional details of the particular industry under consideration must be examined. We will describe some methods that economists use to analyze strategic choice in the next two chapters, but a detailed study of monopolistic competition will have to wait for more advanced courses.

We can, however, describe an interesting feature of the free entry aspect of monopolistic competition. As more and more firms enter the industry for a particular kind of product, how would we expect the demand curve of an incumbent firm to change? First, we would expect the demand curve to shift inward since we would expect that at each price, it would sell fewer units of output as more firms enter the industry. Second, we would expect that the demand curve facing a given firm would become more elastic as more firms produced more and more similar products. Thus entry into an industry by new firms with similar products will tend to shift the demand curves facing existing firms to the left and make them flatter.

If firms continue to enter the industry as long as they expect to make a profit, equilibrium must satisfy the following three conditions:

1. Each firm is selling at a price and output combination on its demand curve.

2. Each firm is maximizing its profits, given the demand curve facing it.

3. Entry has forced the profits of each firm down to zero.

These facts imply a very particular geometrical relationship between the demand curve and the average cost curve: the demand curve and the average cost curve must be tangent to each other.

The argument is illustrated in Figure 25.6. Fact 1 says that the output and price combination must be somewhere on the demand curve, and fact 3 says that the output and price combination must also be on the average cost curve. Thus the operating position of the firm must be at a point that lies on both curves. Could the demand curve cross the average cost curve? No, because then there would be some point on the demand curve above the average cost curve—but this would be a point yielding *positive* profits.[5] And by fact 2, the zero profit point is a profit maximum.

Another way to see this is to examine what would happen if the firm depicted in Figure 25.6 charged any price other than the break-even price. At any other price, higher or lower, the firm would lose money, while at the break-even price, the firm makes zero profits. Thus the break-even price is the profit-maximizing price.

There are two worthwhile observations about the monopolistically competitive equilibrium. First, although profits are zero, the situation is still Pareto inefficient. Profits have nothing to do with the efficiency question: when price is greater than marginal cost, there is an efficiency argument for expanding output.

Second, it is clear that firms will typically be operating to the left of the level of output where average cost is minimized. This has sometimes been interpreted as saying that in monopolistic competition there is "excess capacity." If there were fewer firms, each could operate at a more efficient scale of operation, which would be better for consumers. However, if there were fewer firms there would also be less product variety, and this would

---

[5] If $p > c(y)/y$, then simple algebra shows that $py - c(y) > 0$.

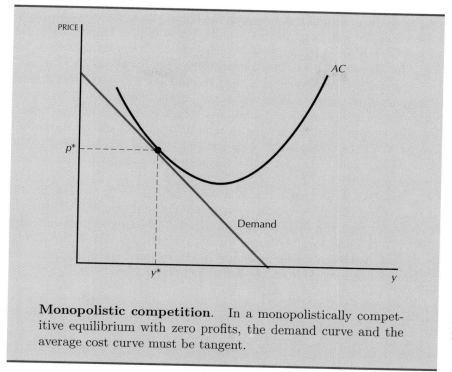

Monopolistic competition. In a monopolistically competitive equilibrium with zero profits, the demand curve and the
average cost curve must be tangent.

Figure
25.6

tend to make consumers worse off. Which of these effects dominates is a
difficult question to answer.

25.8 A Location Model of Product Differentiation

In Atlantic City there is a boardwalk that stretches along the beach. Some
ice cream vendors with pushcarts want to sell ice cream on the boardwalk.
If one vendor is going to be given the concession to sell ice cream on the
boardwalk, where should he locate?[6]

Suppose that consumers are distributed evenly along the beach. From a
social point of view, it makes sense to locate the ice cream vendor so that
the total distance walked by all the consumers is minimized. It is not hard
to see that this optimal location is halfway along the boardwalk.

Now suppose that two ice cream vendors are allowed. Suppose that we
fix the price that they are able to charge for their ice cream and just ask
where they should locate in order to minimize the total distance walked. If
each consumer walks to the ice cream vendor nearest him, we should put

---

[6] The discussion here is based on the classic model of Harold Hotelling, "Stability in
Competition," *Economic Journal*, March 1929.

one vendor a quarter of the way along the boardwalk and one vendor three-quarters of the way along the boardwalk. The consumer halfway along the boardwalk will be indifferent between the two ice cream vendors; each has a market share of one-half of the consumers. (See Figure 25.7A.)

But do the ice cream vendors have an incentive to stay in these locations? Put yourself in the position of vendor L. If you move a little bit to the right, you will steal some of the other vendor's customers and you won't lose any of your own. By moving to the right, you will still be the closest vendor to all the customers to your left and you will still be closer to the customers on your right. You will therefore increase your market share and your profits.

But vendor R can reason the same way—by moving to the left, he will steal some of the other vendor's customers and not lose any of his own! This shows that the socially optimal location patterns are not an equilibrium. The only equilibrium is for both vendors to sell in the middle of the boardwalk, as shown in Figure 25.7B. In this case, competition for customers has resulted in an *inefficient* location pattern.

Figure 25.7

Competition in location. Panel A shows the socially optimal location pattern; L locates one-quarter of the way along the line and R locates three-quarters of the way along. But each vendor will find it in its private interest to move toward the middle. The only equilibrium location is for both vendors to be in the middle, as shown in Panel B.

The boardwalk model can serve as a metaphor for other sorts of product-differentiation problems. Instead of the boardwalk, think of the choice of music varieties by two radio stations. At one extreme we have classical music and at the other we have heavy metal rock. Each listener chooses the station that appeals more to his tastes. If the classical station plays music that is a bit more toward the middle of the taste spectrum, it won't lose the classical clients, but it will gain a few of the middlebrow listeners. If the rock station moves a bit toward the middle, it won't lose any of its rock lovers but will get a few of the middlebrow listeners. In equilibrium, both stations play the same sort of music and the people with more extreme tastes are unhappy with both of them!

25.9 Product Differentiation

The boardwalk model suggest that monopolistic competition will result in too little product differentiation: each firm will want to make its product similar to that of the other firm in order to steal the other firm's customers. Indeed, we can think of markets in which there is too much imitation relative to what seems to be optimal.

However, it doesn't always work this way. Suppose that the boardwalk is *very* long. Then each ice cream vendor would be perfectly happy sitting near each end of the boardwalk. If their market areas don't overlap, nothing is to be gained from moving closer to the middle of the boardwalk. In this case, neither monopolist has an incentive to imitate the other, and the products are about as different as they can get.

It is possible to produce models of monopolistic competition where there is *excessive* product differentiation. In such models, each firm attempts to make consumers think that its product is different from the products of its competitors so as to create some degree of market power. If the firms succeed in convincing the consumers that their product has no close substitutes, they will be able to charge a higher price for it than they would otherwise be able to do.

This leads each producer to invest heavily in creating a distinctive brand identity. Laundry soap, for example, is a pretty standardized commodity. Yet manufacturers invest huge amounts of money in advertisements that claim cleaner clothes, better smell, and a generally happier existence if you choose their brand rather than a competitor's. This "product positioning" is much like the ice cream vendors locating far away from each other in order to avoid head-to-head competition.

25.10 More Vendors

We have shown that if there are two vendors whose market areas overlap, and each seller sells the same price, they will both end up located at the "middle" of the boardwalk. What happens if there are more than two vendors who compete in their location?

The next easiest case is that of three vendors. This case gives rise to a rather peculiar outcome: there may be *no* equilibrium location pattern! To see this, look at Figure 25.8. If there are three vendors located on the boardwalk, there must be one located between the other two. As before, it pays each of the "outside" vendors to move towards the middle vendor since they can steal some of its customers without losing any of their own. But if they get *too* close to the other vendor, it pays it to jump immediately to the right of its right-hand competitor or immediately to the left of its left-hand competitor to steal *its* market. No matter what the location pattern, it pays someone to move!

Figure 25.8

No equilibrium. There is no pure strategy equilibrium in the Hotelling model with 3 firms since for any configuration, at least one firm wants to change location.

Luckily, this "perverse" result only holds in the case of three competitors. If there are four or more competitors, an equilibrium location pattern will generally emerge.

Summary

1. There will typically be an incentive for a monopolist to engage in price discrimination of some sort.

2. Perfect price discrimination involves charging each customer a different take-it-or-leave-it price. This will result in an efficient level of output.

3. If a firm can charge different prices in two different markets, it will tend to charge the lower price in the market with the more elastic demand.

4. If a firm can set a two-part tariff, and consumers are identical, then it will generally want to set price equal to marginal cost and make all of its profits from the entry fee.

5. The industry structure known as monopolistic competition refers to a situation in which there is product differentiation, so each firm has some degree of monopoly power, but there is also free entry so that profits are driven to zero.

6. Monopolistic competition can result in too much or too little product differentiation in general.

REVIEW QUESTIONS

1. Will a monopoly ever provide a Pareto efficient level of output on its own?

2. Suppose that a monopolist sells to two groups that have constant elasticity demand curves, with elasticity ϵ_1 and ϵ_2. The marginal cost of production is constant at c. What price is charged to each group?

3. Suppose that the amusement park owner can practice perfect first-degree price discrimination by charging a different price for each ride. Assume that all rides have zero marginal cost and all consumers have the same tastes. Will the monopolist do better charging for rides and setting a zero price for admission, or better by charging for admission and setting a zero price for rides?

4. Disneyland also offers a discount on admissions to residents of Southern California. (You show them your zip code at the gate.) What kind of price discrimination is this? What does this imply about the elasticity of demand for Disney attractions by Southern Californians?

CHAPTER 26

FACTOR MARKETS

In our examination of factor demands in Chapter 19 we only considered the case of a firm that faced a competitive output market and a competitive factor market. Now that we have studied monopoly behavior, we can examine some alternative specifications of factor demand behavior. For example, what happens to factor demands if a firm behaves as a monopolist in its output market? Or what happens to factor demands if a firm is the sole demander for the use of some factors? We investigate these questions and some related questions in this chapter.

26.1 Monopoly in the Output Market

When a firm determines its profit-maximizing demand for a factor, it will always want to choose a quantity such that the marginal revenue from hiring a little more of that factor just equals the marginal cost of doing so. This follows from the standard logic: if the marginal revenue of some action didn't equal the marginal cost of that action, then it would pay for the firm to change the action.

This general rule takes various special forms depending on our assumptions about the environment in which the firm operates. For example, suppose that the firm has a monopoly for its output. For simplicity we will suppose that there is only one factor of production and write the production function as $y = f(x)$. The revenue that the firm receives depends on its production of output so we write $R(y) = p(y)y$, where $p(y)$ is the inverse demand function. Let us see how a marginal increase in the amount of the input affects the revenues of the firm.

Suppose that we increase the amount of the input a little bit, Δx. This will result in a small increase in output, Δy. The ratio of the increase in output to the increase in the input is the **marginal product** of the factor:

$$MP_x = \frac{\Delta y}{\Delta x} = \frac{f(x + \Delta x) - f(x)}{\Delta x}. \qquad (26.1)$$

This increase in output will cause revenue to change. The change in revenue is called the **marginal revenue**.

$$MR_y = \frac{\Delta R}{\Delta y} = \frac{R(y + \Delta y) - R(y)}{\Delta y}. \qquad (26.2)$$

The effect on revenue due to the marginal increase in the input is called the **marginal revenue product**. Examining equations (26.1) and (26.2) we see that it is given by

$$MRP_x = \frac{\Delta R}{\Delta x} = \frac{\Delta R}{\Delta y}\frac{\Delta y}{\Delta x}$$
$$= MR_y \times MP_x.$$

We can use our standard expression for marginal revenue to write this as

$$MRP_x = \left[p(y) + \frac{\Delta p}{\Delta y}y \right] MP_x$$
$$= p(y) \left[1 + \frac{1}{\epsilon} \right] MP_x$$
$$= p(y) \left[1 - \frac{1}{|\epsilon|} \right] MP_x.$$

The first expression is the usual expression for marginal revenue. The second and third expressions use the elasticity form of marginal revenue, which was discussed in Chapter 15.

Now it is easy to see how this generalizes the competitive case we examined earlier in Chapter 19. The elasticity of the demand curve facing an individual firm in a competitive market is infinite; consequently the marginal revenue for a competitive firm is just equal to price. Hence the "marginal revenue product" of an input for a firm in a competitive market is just the **value of the marginal product** of that input, pMP_x.

How does the marginal revenue product (in the case of a monopoly) compare to the value of the marginal product? Since the demand curve has a negative slope, we see that the marginal revenue product will always be less than the value of the marginal product:

$$MRP_x = p\left[1 - \frac{1}{|\epsilon|}\right] MP_x \leq pMP_x.$$

As long as the demand function is not perfectly elastic, the MRP_x will be strictly less than pMP_x. This means that at any level of employment of the factor, the marginal value of an additional unit is less for a monopolist than for a competitive firm. In the rest of this section we will assume that we are dealing with this case—the case where the monopolist actually has some monopoly power.

At first encounter this statement seems paradoxical since a monopolist makes higher profits than a competitive firm. In this sense the total factor input is "worth more" to a monopolist than to a competitive firm.

The resolution of this "paradox" is to note the difference between total value and marginal value. The total amount employed of the factor is indeed worth more to the monopolist than to the competitive firm since the monopolist will make more profits from the factor than the competitive firm. However, at a *given* level of output an increase in the employment of the factor will increase output and *reduce* the price that a monopolist is able to charge. But an increase in a competitive firm's output will not change the price it can charge. Thus on the margin, a small *increase* in the employment of the factor is worth less to the monopolist than to the competitive firm.

Since increases in the factor employment are worth less to a monopolist than to a competitive firm on the margin in the short run, it makes sense that the monopolist would usually want to employ less of the input. Indeed this is generally true: the monopolist increases its profits by reducing its output, and so it will usually hire lower amounts of inputs than a competitive firm.

In order to determine how much of the factor a firm employs, we have to compare the marginal revenue of an additional unit of the factor to the marginal cost of hiring that factor. Let us assume that the firm operates in a competitive factor market, so that it can hire as much of the factor as it wants at a constant price of w. In this case, the competitive firm wants to hire x_c units of the factor, where

$$pMP(x_c) = w.$$

The monopolist, on the other hand, wants to hire x_m units of the factor, where

$$MRP(x_m) = w.$$

We have illustrated this in Figure 26.1. Since $MRP(x) < pMP(x)$, the point where $MRP(x_m) = w$ will always be to the left of the point where $pMP(x_c) = w$. Hence the monopolist will hire less than the competitive firm.

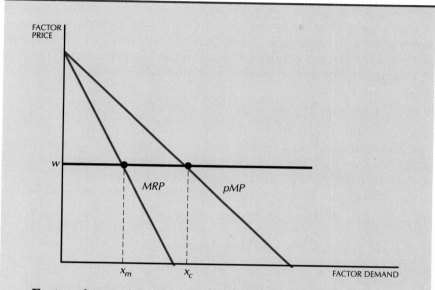

Factor demand by a monopolist. Since the marginal revenue product curve (MRP) lies beneath the curve measuring the value of the marginal product (pMP), the factor demand by a monopolist must be less than the factor demand by the same firm if it behaves competitively.

Figure 26.1

26.2 Monopsony

In a monopoly there is a single seller of a commodity. In a **monopsony** there is a single buyer. The analysis of a monopsonist is similar to that of a monopolist. For simplicity, we suppose that the buyer produces output that will be sold in a competitive market.

As above, we will suppose that the firm produces output using a single factor according to the production function $y = f(x)$. However, unlike the discussion above, we suppose that the firm dominates the factor market in which it operates and recognizes the amount of the factor that it demands will influence the price that it has to pay for this factor.

We summarize this relationship by the (inverse) supply curve $w(x)$. The interpretation of this function is that if the firm wants to hire x units of the factor it must pay a price of $w(x)$. We assume that $w(x)$ is an increasing function: the more of the x-factor the firm wants to employ, the higher must be the factor price it offers.

A firm in a competitive factor market by definition faces a flat factor supply curve: it can hire as much as it wants at the going factor price. A monopsonist faces an upward-sloping factor supply curve: the more it wants to hire, the higher a factor price it must offer. A firm in a competitive factor market is a **price taker**. A monopsonist is a **price maker**.

The profit-maximization problem facing the monopsonist is

$$\max_{x} \; pf(x) - w(x)x.$$

The condition for profit maximization is that the marginal revenue from hiring an extra unit of the factor should equal the marginal cost of that unit. Since we have assumed a competitive output market the marginal revenue is simply pMP_x. What about the marginal cost?

The total change in costs from hiring Δx more of the factor will be

$$\Delta c = w\Delta x + x\Delta w,$$

so that the change in costs per unit change in Δx is

$$\frac{\Delta c}{\Delta x} = MC_x = w + \frac{\Delta w}{\Delta x}x.$$

The interpretation of this expression is similar to the interpretation of the marginal revenue expression: when the firm increases its employment of the factor it has to pay $w\Delta x$ more in payment to the factor. But the increased demand for the factor will push the factor price up by Δw, and the firm has to pay this higher price on all of the units it was previously employing.

We can also write the marginal cost of hiring additional units of the factor as

$$MC_x = w \left[1 + \frac{x}{w}\frac{\Delta w}{\Delta x} \right]$$
$$= w \left[1 + \frac{1}{\eta} \right]$$

where η is the *supply* elasticity of the factor. Since supply curves typically slope upward, η will be a positive number. If the supply curve is *perfectly elastic*, so that η is infinite, this reduces to the case of a firm facing a competitive factor market. Note the similarity of these observations with the analogous case of a monopolist.

Let's analyze the case of a monopsonist facing a linear supply curve for the factor. The inverse supply curve has the form

$$w(x) = a + bx,$$

so that total costs have the form

$$C(x) = w(x)x = ax + bx^2,$$

and thus the marginal cost of an additional unit of the input is

$$MC_x(x) = a + 2bx.$$

The construction of the monopsony solution is given in Figure 26.2. We find the position where the value of the marginal product equals marginal cost to determine x^* and then see what the factor price must be at that point.

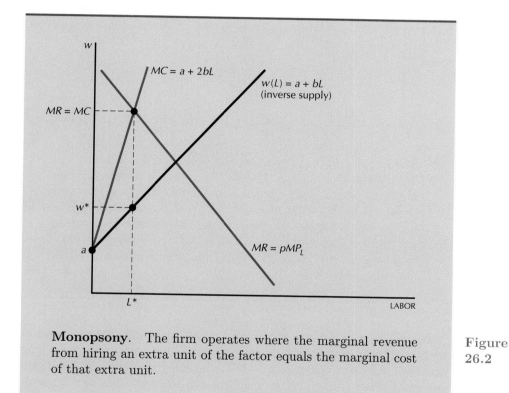

Monopsony. The firm operates where the marginal revenue from hiring an extra unit of the factor equals the marginal cost of that extra unit.

Figure 26.2

Since the marginal cost of hiring an extra unit of the factor exceeds the factor price, the factor price will be lower than if the firm had faced a competitive factor market. Too little of the factor will be hired relative to the competitive market. Just as in the case of the monopoly, a monopsonist operates at a Pareto inefficient point. But the inefficiency now lies in the factor market rather than in the output market.

EXAMPLE: The Minimum Wage

Suppose that the labor market is competitive and that the government
sets a minimum wage that is higher than the prevailing equilibrium wage.
Since demand equals supply at the equilibrium wage, the supply of labor
will exceed the demand for labor at the higher minimum wage. This is
depicted in Figure 26.3A.

Figure
26.3

Minimum wage. Panel A shows the effect of a minimum wage
in a competitive labor market. At the competitive wage, w_c, employment would be L_c. At the minimum wage, $\overline{w}$, employment
is only L_{mw}. Panel B shows the effect of a minimum wage in
a monopsonized labor market. Under monopsony, the wage is
w_m and employment is L_m, which is less than the employment
in the competitive labor market. If the minimum wage is set to
w_c, employment will increase to L_c.

Things are very different if the labor market is dominated by a monopsonist. In this case, it is possible that imposing a minimum wage may
actually *increase* employment. This is depicted in Figure 26.3B. If the
government sets the minimum wage equal to the wage that would prevail
in a competitive market, the "monopsonist" now perceives that it can hire
workers at a constant wage of w_c. Since the wage rate it faces is now independent of how many workers it hires, it will hire until the value of the
marginal product equals w_c. That is, it will hire just as many workers as
if it faced a competitive labor market.

Setting a wage floor for a monopsonist is just like setting a price ceiling
for a monopolist; each policy makes the firm behave as though it faced a
competitive market.

26.3 Upstream and Downstream Monopolies

We have now examined two cases involving imperfect competition and factor markets: the case of a firm with a monopoly in the output market but facing a competitive factor market, and the case of a firm with a competitive output market that faces a monopolized factor market. Other variations are possible. The firm could face a monopoly seller in its factor market for example. Or it could face a monopsony buyer in its output market. It doesn't make much sense to plod through each possible case; they quickly become repetitive. However, we will examine one interesting market structure in which a monopoly produces output that is used as a factor of production by another monopolist.

Suppose then that one monopolist produces output x at a constant marginal cost of c. We call this monopolist the **upstream monopolist**. It sells the x-factor to another monopolist, the **downstream monopolist** at a price of k. The downstream monopolist uses the x-factor to produce output y according to the production function $y = f(x)$. This output is then sold in a monopolist market in which the inverse demand curve is $p(y)$. For purposes of this example, we consider a linear inverse demand curve $p(y) = a - by$.

To make things simple, think of the production function as just being $y = x$, so that for each unit of the x-input, the monopolist can produce one unit of the y-output. We further suppose that the downstream monopolist has no costs of production other than the unit price k that it must pay to the upstream monopolist.

In order to see how this market works, start with the downstream monopolist. Its profit-maximization problem is

$$\max_{y} p(y)y - ky = [a - by]y - ky.$$

Setting marginal revenue equal to marginal cost, we have

$$a - 2by = k,$$

which implies that

$$y = \frac{a - k}{2b}.$$

Since the monopolist demands one unit of the x-input for each y-output that it produces, this expression also determines the factor demand function

$$x = \frac{a - k}{2b}. \tag{26.3}$$

This function tells us the relationship between the factor price k and the amount of the factor that the downstream monopolist will demand.

Turn now to the problem of the upstream monopolist. Presumably it understands this process and can determine how much of the x-good it will sell if it sets various prices k; this is simply the factor demand function given in equation (26.3). The upstream monopolist wants to choose x to maximize its profit.

We can determine this level easily enough. Solving equation (26.3) for k as a function of x we have

$$k = a - 2bx.$$

The marginal revenue associated with this factor demand function is

$$MR = a - 4bx.$$

Setting marginal revenue equal to marginal cost we have

$$a - 4bx = c,$$

or

$$x = \frac{a - c}{4b}.$$

Since the production function is simply $y = x$, this also gives us the total amount of the final product that is produced:

$$y = \frac{a - c}{4b}. \tag{26.4}$$

It is of interest to compare this to the amount that would be produced by a single integrated monopolist. Suppose that the upstream and the downstream firm merged so that we had one monopolist who faced an output inverse demand function $p = a - by$ and faced a constant marginal cost of c per unit produced. The marginal revenue equals marginal cost equation is

$$a - 2by = c,$$

which implies that the profit-maximizing output is

$$y = \frac{a - c}{2b}. \tag{26.5}$$

Comparing equation (26.4) to equation (26.5) we see that the integrated monopolist produces *twice* as much output as the nonintegrated monopolists.

This is depicted in Figure 26.4. The final demand curve facing the downstream monopolist $p(y)$, and the marginal revenue curve associated with this demand function is itself the demand function facing the upstream monopolist. The marginal revenue curve associated with this demand function

Upstream and downstream monopoly. The downstream monopolist faces the (inverse) demand curve $p(y)$. The marginal revenue associated with this demand curve is $MR_D(y)$. This in turn is the demand curve facing the upstream monopolist, and the associated marginal revenue curve is $MR_U(y)$. The integrated monopolist produces at y_i^*; the nonintegrated monopolist produces at y_m^*.

Figure
26.4

is therefore *four* times as steep as the final demand curve—which is why the output in this market is half what it would be in the integrated market.

Of course the fact that the final marginal revenue curve is exactly four times as steep is particular to the linear demand case. However, it is not hard to see that an integrated monopolist will always produce more than an upstream-downstream pair of monopolists. In the latter case the upstream monopolist raises its price above its marginal cost and then the downstream monopolist raises its price above this already marked-up cost. There is a **double markup**. The price is not only too high from a social point of view, it is too high from the viewpoint of maximizing total monopoly profits! If the two monopolists merged, price would go down and profits would go up.

Summary

1. A profit-maximizing firm always wants to set the marginal revenue of each action it takes equal to the marginal cost of that action.

2. In the case of a monopolist, the marginal revenue associated with an

increase in the employment of a factor is called the marginal revenue product.

3. For a monopolist, the marginal revenue product will always be smaller than the value of the marginal product due to the fact that the marginal revenue from increasing output is always less than price.

4. Just as a monopoly consists of a market with a single seller, a monopsony consists of a market with a single buyer.

5. For a monopsonist the marginal cost curve associated with a factor will be steeper than the supply curve of that factor.

6. Hence a monopsonist will hire an inefficiently small amount of the factor of production.

7. If an upstream monopolist sells a factor to a downstream monopolist, then the final price of output will be too high due to the double markup phenomenon.

REVIEW QUESTIONS

1. We saw that a monopolist never produced where the demand for output was inelastic. Will a monopsonist produce where a factor is inelastically supplied?

2. In our example of the minimum wage, what would happen if the labor market was dominated by a monopsonist and the government set a wage that was above the competitive wage?

3. In our examination of the upstream and downstream monopolists we derived expressions for the total output produced. What are the appropriate expressions for the equilibrium prices, p and k?

APPENDIX

We can calculate marginal revenue product by using the chain rule. Let $y = f(x)$ be the production function and $p(y)$ be the inverse demand function. Revenue as a function of the factor employment is just

$$R(x) = p(f(x))f(x).$$

Differentiating this expression with respect to x we have

$$\frac{dR(x)}{dx} = p(y)f'(x) + f(x)p'(y)f'(x)$$
$$= [p(y) + p'(y)y]f'(x)$$
$$= MR \times MP.$$

Let us examine the behavior of a firm that is a competitor in its output market and a monopsonist in its factor market. Letting $w(x)$ be the inverse factor supply function, the profit-maximization problem is

$$\max_{x} pf(x) - w(x)x.$$

Differentiating with respect to x, we have

$$pf'(x) = w(x) + w'(x)x = w(x)\left[1 + \frac{x}{w}\frac{dw}{dx}\right] = w(x)\left[1 + \frac{1}{\eta}\right].$$

Since the factor supply curve slopes upward, the right-hand side of this expression will be larger than w. Hence the monopsonist will choose to employ less of the factor than would a firm that behaves competitively in the factor market.

CHAPTER **27**

OLIGOPOLY

We have now investigated two important forms of market structure: pure competition, where there are typically many small competitors, and pure monopoly, where there is only one large firm in the market. However, much of the world lies between these two extremes. Often there are a number of competitors in the market, but not so many as to regard each of them as having a negligible effect on price. This is the situation known as **oligopoly**.

The model of monopolistic competition described in Chapter 24 is a special form of oligopoly that emphasizes issues of product differentiation and entry. However, the models of oligopoly that we will study in this chapter are more concerned with the strategic interactions that arise in an industry with a small number of firms.

There are several models that are relevant since there are several different ways for firms to behave in an oligopolistic environment. It is unreasonable to expect one grand model since many different behavior patterns can be observed in the real world. What we want is a guide to some of the possible patterns of behavior and some indication of what factors might be important in deciding when the various models are applicable.

For simplicity, we will usually restrict ourselves to the case of two firms; this is called a situation of **duopoly**. The duopoly case allows us to capture many of the important features of firms engaged in strategic interaction without the notational complications involved in models with a larger number of firms. Also, we will limit ourselves to investigation of cases in which each firm is producing an identical product. This allows us to avoid the problems of product differentiation and focus only on strategic interactions.

27.1 Choosing a Strategy

If there are two firms in the market and they are producing a homogeneous product, then there are four variables of interest: the price that each firm charges and the quantities that each firm produces.

When one firm decides about its choices for prices and quantities it may already know the choices made by the other firm. If one firm gets to set its price before the other firm, we call it the **price leader** and the other firm the **price follower**. Similarly, one firm may get to choose its quantity first, in which case it is a **quantity leader** and the other is a **quantity follower**. The strategic interactions in these cases form a **sequential game**.[1]

On the other hand, it may be that when one firm makes its choices it doesn't know the choices made by the other firm. In this case, it has to guess about the other firm's choice in order to make a sensible decision itself. This is a **simultaneous game**. Again there are two possibilities: the firms could each simultaneously choose prices or each simultaneously choose quantities.

This classification scheme gives us four possibilities: quantity leadership, price leadership, simultaneous quantity setting, and simultaneous price setting. Each of these types of interaction gives rise to a different set of strategic issues.

There is also another possible form of interaction that we will examine. Instead of the firms competing against each other in one form or another they may be able to **collude**. In this case the two firms can jointly agree to set prices and quantities that maximize the sum of their profits. This sort of collusion is called a **cooperative game**.

27.2 Quantity Leadership

In the case of quantity leadership, one firm makes a choice before the other firm. This is sometimes called the **Stackelberg model** in honor of the

---

[1] We will examine game theory in more detail in the next chapter, but it seems appropriate to introduce these specific examples here.

first economist who systematically studied leader-follower interactions.[2]

The Stackelberg model is often used to describe industries in which there is a dominant firm, or a natural leader. For example, IBM is often considered to be a dominant firm in the computer industry. A commonly observed pattern of behavior is for smaller firms in the computer industry to wait for IBM's announcements of new products and then adjust their own product decisions accordingly. In this case we might want to model the computer industry with IBM playing the role of a Stackelberg leader, and the other firms in the industry being Stackelberg followers.

Let us turn now to the details of the theoretical model. Suppose that firm 1 is the leader and that it chooses to produce a quantity y_1. Firm 2 responds by choosing a quantity y_2. Each firm knows that the equilibrium price in the market depends on the total output produced. We use the inverse demand function $p(Y)$ to indicate the equilibrium price as a function of industry output, $Y = y_1 + y_2$.

What output should the leader choose to maximize its profits? The answer depends on how the leader thinks that the follower will react to its choice. Presumably the leader should expect that the follower will attempt to maximize profits as well, given the choice made by the leader. In order for the leader to make a sensible decision about its own production, it has to consider the follower's profit-maximization problem.

The Follower's Problem

We assume that the follower wants to maximize its profits

$$\max_{y_2} \ p(y_1 + y_2)y_2 - c_2(y_2).$$

The follower's profit depends on the output choice of the leader, but from the viewpoint of the follower the leader's output is predetermined—the production by the leader has already been made, and the follower simply views it as a constant.

The follower wants to choose an output level such that marginal revenue equals marginal cost:

$$MR_2 = p(y_1 + y_2) + \frac{\Delta p}{\Delta y_2}y_2 = MC_2.$$

The marginal revenue has the usual interpretation. When the follower increases its output, it increases its revenue by selling more output at the

---

[2] Heinrich von Stackelberg was a German economist who published his influential work on market organization, *Marktform und Gleichgewicht*, in 1934.

market price. But it also pushes the price down by Δp, and this lowers its profits on all the units that were previously sold at the higher price.

The important thing to observe is that the profit-maximizing choice of the follower will depend on the choice made by the leader. We write this relationship as

$$y_2 = f_2(y_1).$$

The function $f_2(y_1)$ tells us the profit-maximizing output of the follower as a function of the leader's choice. This function is called the **reaction function** since it tells us how the follower will react to the leader's choice of output.

Let's derive a reaction curve in the simple case of linear demand. In this case the (inverse) demand function takes the form $p(y_1+y_2) = a-b(y_1+y_2)$. For convenience we'll take costs to be zero.

Then the profit function for firm 2 is

$$\pi_2(y_1, y_2) = [a - b(y_1 + y_2)]y_2$$

or

$$\pi_2(y_1, y_2) = ay_2 - by_1y_2 - by_2^2.$$

We can use this expression to draw the **isoprofit lines** in Figure 27.1. These are lines depicting those combinations of y_1 and y_2 that yield a constant level of profit to firm 2. That is, the isoprofit lines are comprised of all points (y_1, y_2) that satisfy equations of the form

$$ay_2 - by_1y_2 - by_2^2 = \overline{\pi}_2.$$

Note that profits to firm 2 will increase as we move to isoprofit lines that are further to the left. This is true since if we fix the output of firm 2 at some level, firm 2's profits will increase as firm 1's output decreases. Firm 2 will make its maximum possible profits when it is a monopolist; that is, when firm 1 chooses to produce zero units of output.

For each possible choice of firm 1's output, firm 2 wants to choose its own output to make its profits as large as possible. This means that for each choice of y_1, firm 2 will pick the value of y_2 that puts it on the isoprofit line furthest to the left, as illustrated in Figure 27.1. This point will satisfy the usual sort of tangency condition: the slope of the isoprofit line must be vertical at the optimal choice. The locus of these tangencies describes firm 2's reaction curve, $f_2(y_1)$.

To see this result algebraically, we need an expression for the marginal revenue associated with the profit function for firm 2. It turns out that this expression is given by

$$MR_2(y_1, y_2) = a - by_1 - 2by_2.$$

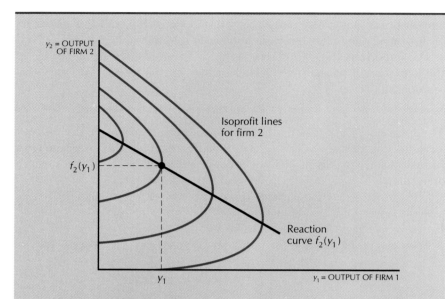

Figure
27.1

Derivation of a reaction curve. This reaction curve gives the profit-maximizing output for the follower, firm 2, for each output choice of the leader, firm 1. For each choice of y_1 the follower chooses the output level $f_2(y_1)$ associated with the isoprofit line farthest to the left.

(This is easy to derive using calculus. If you don't know calculus, you'll just have to take this statement on faith.) Setting the marginal revenue equal to marginal cost, which is zero in this example, we have

$$a - by_1 - 2by_2 = 0,$$

which we can solve to derive firm 2's reaction curve:

$$y_2 = \frac{a - by_1}{2b}.$$

This reaction curve is the straight line depicted in Figure 27.1.

The Leader's Problem

We have now examined how the follower will choose its output *given* the choice of the leader. We turn now to the leader's profit-maximization problem.

Presumably, the leader is also aware that its actions influence the output choice of the follower. This relationship is summarized by the reaction function $f_2(y_1)$. Hence when making its output choice it should recognize the influence that it exerts on the follower.

The profit-maximization problem for the leader therefore becomes

$$\max_{y_1} p(y_1 + y_2)y_1 - c_1(y_1)$$

such that $y_2 = f_2(y_1)$.

Substituting the second equation into the first gives us

$$\max_{y_1} p[y_1 + f_2(y_1)]y_1 - c_1(y_1).$$

Note that the leader recognizes that when it chooses output y_1, the total output produced will be $y_1 + f_2(y_1)$: its own output *plus* the output produced by the follower.

When the leader contemplates changing its output it has to recognize the influence it exerts on the follower. Let's examine this in the context of the linear demand curve described above. There we saw that the reaction function was given by

$$f_2(y_1) = y_2 = \frac{a - by_1}{2b}. \tag{27.1}$$

Since we've assumed that marginal costs are zero, the leader's profits are

$$\pi_1(y_1, y_2) = p(y_1 + y_2)y_1 = ay_1 - by_1^2 - by_1y_2. \tag{27.2}$$

But the output of the follower, y_2, will depend on the leader's choice via the reaction function $y_2 = f_2(y_1)$.

Substituting from equation (27.1) into equation (27.2) we have

$$\pi_1(y_1, y_2) = ay_1 - by_1^2 - by_1 f_2(y_1)$$
$$= ay_1 - by_1^2 - by_1 \frac{a - by_1}{2b}.$$

Simplifying this expression gives us

$$\pi_1(y_1, y_2) = \frac{a}{2}y_1 - \frac{b}{2}y_1^2.$$

The marginal revenue for this function is

$$MR = \frac{a}{2} - by_1.$$

Setting this equal to marginal cost, which is zero in this example, and solving for y_1 gives us

$$y_1^* = \frac{a}{2b}.$$

In order to find the follower's output, we simply substitute y_1^* into the reaction function,

$$y_2^* = \frac{a - by_1^*}{2b}$$
$$= \frac{a}{4b}.$$

These two equations give a total industry output of $y_1^* + y_2^* = 3a/4b$.

The Stackelberg solution can also be illustrated graphically using the isoprofit curves depicted in Figure 27.2. (This figure also illustrates the Cournot equilibrium which will be described in section 27.5.) Here we have illustrated the reaction curves for both firms and the isoprofit curves for firm 1. The isoprofit curves for firm 1 have the same general shape as the isoprofit curves for firm 2; they are simply rotated 90 degrees. Higher profits for firm 1 are associated with isoprofit curves that are lower down since firm 1's profits will increase as firm 2's output decreases.

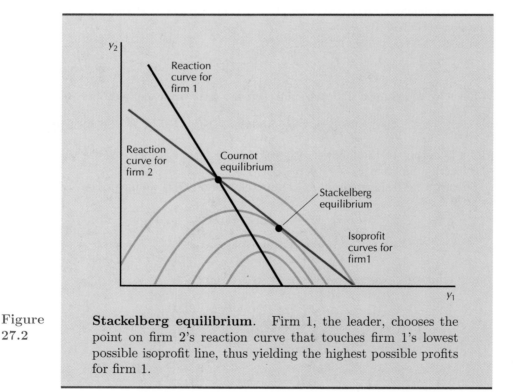

Figure
27.2

Stackelberg equilibrium. Firm 1, the leader, chooses the point on firm 2's reaction curve that touches firm 1's lowest possible isoprofit line, thus yielding the highest possible profits for firm 1.

Firm 2 is behaving as a follower, which means that it will choose an output along its reaction curve, $f_2(y_1)$. Thus firm 1 wants to choose an output combination on the reaction curve that gives it the highest possible profits. But the highest possible profits means picking that point on the reaction curve that touches the *lowest* isoprofit line, as illustrated in Figure 27.2. It follows by the usual logic of maximization that the reaction curve must be tangent to the isoprofit curve at this point.

27.3 Price Leadership

Instead of setting quantity, the leader may instead set price. In order to make a sensible decision about how to set its price, the leader must forecast how the follower will behave. Accordingly, we must first investigate the profit-maximization problem facing the follower.

The first thing we observe is that in equilibrium the follower must always set the same price as the leader. This follows from our assumption that the two firms are selling identical products. If one charged a different price from the other, all of the consumers would prefer the producer with the lower price, and we couldn't have an equilibrium with both firms producing.

Suppose that the leader has set a price p. We will suppose that the follower takes this price as given and chooses its profit-maximizing output. This is essentially the same as the competitive behavior we investigated earlier. In the competitive model, each firm takes the price as being outside of its control because it is such a small part of the market; in the price-leadership model, the follower takes the price as being outside of its control since it has already been set by the leader.

The follower wants to maximize profits:

$$\max_{y_2} \ py_2 - c_2(y_2).$$

This leads to the familiar condition that the follower will want to choose an output level where price equals marginal cost. This determines a supply curve for the follower, $S(p)$, which we have illustrated in Figure 27.3.

Turn now to the problem facing the leader. It realizes that if it sets a price p, the follower will supply $S(p)$. That means that the amount of output the leader will sell will be $R(p) = D(p) - S(p)$. This is called the **residual demand curve** facing the leader.

Suppose that the leader has a constant marginal cost of production c. Then the profits that it achieves for any price p are given by:

$$\pi_1(p) = (p - c)[D(p) - S(p)] = (p - c)R(p).$$

In order to maximize profits the leader wants to choose a price and output combination where marginal revenue equals marginal cost. However, the marginal revenue should be the marginal revenue for the *residual* demand curve—the curve that actually measures how much output it will be able to

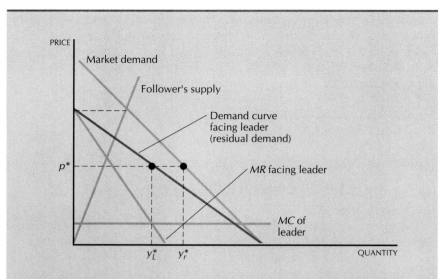

PRICE

Market demand

Follower's supply

Demand curve
facing leader
(residual demand)

p^*

MR facing leader

MC of
leader

y_L^* y_r^* QUANTITY

Figure
27.3

Price leader. The demand curve facing the leader is the market demand curve minus the follower's supply curve. The leader equates marginal revenue and marginal cost to find the optimal quantity to supply, y_L^*. The total amount supplied to the market is y_T^* and the equilibrium price is p^*.

sell at each given price. In Figure 27.3 the residual demand curve is linear; therefore the marginal revenue curve associated with it will have the same vertical intercept and be twice as steep.

Let's look at a simple algebraic example. Suppose that the inverse demand curve is $D(p) = a - bp$. The follower has a cost function $c_2(y_2) = y_2^2/2$, and the leader has a cost function $c_1(y_1) = cy_1$.

For any price p the follower wants to operate where price equals marginal cost. If the cost function is $c_2(y_2) = y_2^2/2$, it can be shown that the marginal cost curve is $MC_2(y_2) = y_2$. Setting price equal to marginal cost gives us

$$p = y_2.$$

Solving for the follower's supply curve gives $y_2 = S(p) = p$.

The demand curve facing the leader—the residual demand curve—is

$$R(p) = D(p) - S(p) = a - bp - p = a - (b+1)p.$$

From now on this is just like an ordinary monopoly problem. Solving for p as a function of the leader's output y_1, we have

$$p = \frac{a}{b+1} - \frac{1}{b+1}y_1. \tag{27.3}$$

This is the inverse demand function facing the leader. The associated marginal revenue curve has the same intercept and is twice as steep. This means that it is given by

$$MR_1 = \frac{a}{b+1} - \frac{2}{b+1}y_1.$$

Setting marginal revenue equal to marginal cost gives us the equation

$$MR_1 = \frac{a}{b+1} - \frac{2}{b+1}y_1 = c = MC_1.$$

Solving for the leader's profit-maximizing output, we have

$$y_1^* = \frac{a - c(b+1)}{2}.$$

We could go on and substitute this into equation (27.3) to get the equilibrium price, but the equation is not particularly interesting.

27.4 Comparing Price Leadership and Quantity Leadership

We've seen how to calculate the equilibrium price and output in the case of quantity leadership and price leadership. Each model determines a different equilibrium price and output combination; each model is appropriate in different circumstances.

One way to think about quantity setting is to think of the firm as making a capacity choice. When a firm sets a quantity it is in effect determining how much it is able to supply to the market. If one firm is able to make an investment in capacity first, then it is naturally modeled as a quantity leader.

On the other hand, suppose that we look at a market where capacity choices are not important but one of the firms distributes a catalog of prices. It is natural to think of this firm as a price setter. It's rivals may then take the catalog price as given and make their own pricing and supply decision accordingly.

Whether the price-leadership or the quantity-leadership model is appropriate is not a question that can be answered on the basis of pure theory. We have to look at how the firms actually make their decisions in order to choose the most appropriate model.

27.5 Simultaneous Quantity Setting

One difficulty with the leader-follower model is that it is necessarily asymmetric: one firm is able to make its decision before the other firm. In some situations this is unreasonable. For example, suppose that two firms are *simultaneously* trying to decide what quantity to produce. Here each firm has to forecast what the other firm's output will be in order to make a sensible decision itself.

In this section we will examine a one-period model in which each firm has to forecast the other firm's output choice. Given its forecast, each firm then chooses a profit-maximizing output for itself. We then seek an equilibrium in forecasts—a situation where each firm finds its beliefs about the other firm to be confirmed. This model is known as the **Cournot model**, after the nineteenth-century French mathematician who first examined its implications.[3]

We begin by assuming that firm 1 expects that firm 2 will produce y_2^e units of output. (The e stands for *expected* output.) If firm 1 decides to produce y_1 units of output, it expects that the total output produced will be $Y = y_1 + y_2^e$, and output will yield a market price of $p(Y) = p(y_1 + y_2^e)$. The profit-maximization problem of firm 1 is then

$$\max_{y_1} p(y_1 + y_2^e)y_1 - c(y_1).$$

For any given belief about the output of firm 2, y_2^e, there will be some optimal choice of output for firm 1, y_1. Let us write this functional relationship between the *expected output* of firm 2 and the *optimal choice* of firm 1 as

$$y_1 = f_1(y_2^e).$$

This function is simply the reaction function that we investigated earlier in this chapter. In our original treatment the reaction function gave the follower's output as a function of the leader's choice. Here the reaction function gives one firm's optimal choice as a function of its *beliefs* about the other firm's choice. Although the interpretation of the reaction function is different in the two cases, the mathematical definition is exactly the same.

Similarly, we can derive firm 2's reaction curve:

$$y_2 = f_2(y_1^e),$$

which gives firm 2's optimal choice of output for a given expectation about firm 1's output, y_1^e.

Now, recall that each firm is choosing its output level *assuming* that the other firm's output will be at y_1^e or y_2^e. For arbitrary values of y_1^e and y_2^e this won't happen—in general firm 1's *optimal* level of output, y_1, will be different from what firm 2 *expects* the output to be, y_1^e.

Let us seek an output combination (y_1^*, y_2^*) such that the optimal output level for firm 1, assuming firm 2 produces y_2^*, is y_1^* and the optimal output

---

[3] Augustin Cournot (pronounced "core-no") was born in 1801. His book, *Researches into the Mathematical Principles of the Theory of Wealth*, was published in 1838.

level for firm 2, assuming that firm 1 stays at y_1^*, is y_2^*. In other words, the output choices (y_1^*, y_2^*) satisfy

$$y_1^* = f_1(y_2^*)$$

$$y_2^* = f_2(y_1^*).$$

Such a combination of output levels is known as a **Cournot equilibrium**. In a Cournot equilibrium, each firm is maximizing its profits, given its beliefs about the other firm's output choice, and, furthermore, those beliefs are confirmed in equilibrium: each firm optimally chooses to produce the amount of output that the other firm expects it to produce. In a Cournot equilibrium neither firm will find it profitable to change its output once it discovers the choice actually made by the other firm.

An example of a Cournot equilibrium is given in Figure 27.2. The Cournot equilibrium is simply the pair of outputs at which the two reaction curves cross. At such a point, each firm is producing a profit-maximizing level of output given the output choice of the other firm.

27.6 An Example of Cournot Equilibrium

Recall the case of the linear demand function and zero marginal costs that we investigated earlier. We saw that in this case the reaction function for firm 2 took the form

$$y_2 = \frac{a - by_1^e}{2b}.$$

Since in this example firm 1 is exactly the same as firm 2, its reaction curve has the same form:

$$y_1 = \frac{a - by_2^e}{2b}.$$

Figure 27.4 depicts this pair of reaction curves. The intersection of the two lines gives us the Cournot equilibrium. At this point each firm's choice is the profit-maximizing choice, given its beliefs about the other firm's behavior, and each firm's beliefs about the other firm's behavior are confirmed by its *actual* behavior.

In order to calculate the Cournot equilibrium algebraically, we look for the point (y_1, y_2) where each firm is doing what the other firm expects it to do. We set $y_1 = y_1^e$ and $y_2 = y_2^e$, which gives us the following two equations in two unknowns:

$$y_1 = \frac{a - by_2}{2b}$$

$$y_2 = \frac{a - by_1}{2b}.$$

Figure
27.4

Cournot equilibrium. Each firm is maximizing its profits, given its beliefs about the other firm's output decision. The Cournot equilibrium is at (y_1^*, y_2^*), where the two reaction curves cross.

In this example, both firms are identical, so each will produce the same level of output in equilibrium. Hence we can substitute $y_1 = y_2$ into one of the above equations to get

$$y_1 = \frac{a - by_1}{2b}.$$

Solving for y_1^*, we get

$$y_1^* = \frac{a}{3b}.$$

Since the two firms are identical, this implies that

$$y_2^* = \frac{a}{3b}$$

as well, and the total industry output is

$$y_1^* + y_2^* = \frac{2a}{3b}.$$

27.7 Adjustment to Equilibrium

We can use Figure 27.4 to describe a process of adjustment to equilibrium. Suppose that at time t the firms are producing outputs (y_1^t, y_2^t), which are not necessarily equilibrium outputs. If firm 1 expects that firm 2 is going to continue to keep its output at y_2^t, then next period firm 1 would want to choose the profit-maximizing output given that expectation, namely $f_1(y_2^t)$. Thus firm 1's choice in period $t+1$ will be given by

$$y_1^{t+1} = f_1(y_2^t).$$

Firm 2 can reason the same way, so firm 2's choice next period will be

$$y_2^{t+1} = f_2(y_1^t).$$

These equations describe how each firm adjusts its output in the face of the other firm's choice. Figure 27.4 illustrates the movement of the outputs of the firms implied by this behavior. Here is the way to interpret the diagram. Start with some operating point (y_1^t, y_2^t). Given firm 2's level of output, firm 1 optimally chooses to produce $y_1^{t+1} = f_1(y_2^t)$ next period. We find this point in the diagram by moving horizontally to the left until we hit firm 1's reaction curve.

If firm 2 expects firm 1 to continue to produce y_1^{t+1}, its optimal response is to produce y_2^{t+1}. We find this point by moving vertically upward until we hit firm 2's reaction function. We continue to move along the "staircase" to determine the sequence of output choices of the two firms. In the example illustrated, this adjustment process converges to the Cournot equilibrium. We say that in this case the Cournot equilibrium is a **stable equilibrium**.

Despite the intuitive appeal of this adjustment process, it does present some difficulties. Each firm is assuming that the other's output will be fixed from one period to the next, but as it turns out, both firms keep changing their output. Only in equilibrium is one firm's expectation about the other firm's output choice actually satisfied. For this reason, we will generally ignore the question of how the equilibrium is reached and focus only on the issue of how the firms behave in the equilibrium.

27.8 Many Firms in Cournot Equilibrium

Suppose now that we have several firms involved in a Cournot equilibrium, not just two. In this case we suppose that each firm has an expectation about the output choices of the other firms in the industry and seek to describe the equilibrium output.

Suppose that there are n firms and let $Y = y_1 + \cdots + y_n$ be the total industry output. Then the "marginal revenue equals marginal cost condition" for firm i is

$$p(Y) + \frac{\Delta p}{\Delta Y} y_i = MC(y_i).$$

If we factor out $P(Y)$ and multiply the second term by Y/Y, we can write this equation as

$$p(Y) \left[1 + \frac{\Delta p}{\Delta Y} \frac{Y}{p(Y)} \frac{y_i}{Y} \right] = MC(y_i).$$

Using the definition of elasticity of the aggregate demand curve and letting $s_i = y_i/Y$ be firm i's share of total market output, this reduces to

$$p(Y) \left[1 - \frac{s_i}{|\epsilon(Y)|} \right] = MC(y_i). \qquad (27.4)$$

We can also write this expression as

$$p(Y) \left[1 - \frac{1}{|\epsilon(Y)|/s_i} \right] = MC(y_i).$$

This looks just like the expression for the monopolist except for the s_i term. We can think of $\epsilon(Y)/s_i$ as being the elasticity of the demand curve facing the firm: the smaller the market share of the firm, the more elastic the demand curve it faces.

If its market share is 1—the firm is a monopolist—the demand curve facing the firm is the market demand curve, so the condition just reduces to that of the monopolist. If the firm is a very small part of a large market, its market share is effectively zero, and the demand curve facing the firm is effectively flat. Thus the condition reduces to that of the pure competitor: price equals marginal cost.

This is one justification for the competitive model described in Chapter 22. If there are a large number of firms, then each firm's influence on the market price is negligible, and the Cournot equilibrium is effectively the same as pure competition.

27.9 Simultaneous Price Setting

In the Cournot model described above we have assumed that firms were choosing their quantities and letting the market determine the price. Another approach is to think of firms as setting their prices and letting the market determine the quantity sold. This model is known as **Bertrand competition**.[4]

---

[4] Joseph Bertrand, also a French mathematician, presented his model in a review of Cournot's work.

When a firm chooses its price, it has to forecast the price set by the other firm in the industry. Just as in the case of Cournot equilibrium we want to find a pair of prices such that each price is a profit-maximizing choice given the choice made by the other firm.

What does a Bertrand equilibrium look like? When firms are selling identical products, as we have been assuming, the Bertrand equilibrium has a very simple structure indeed. It turns out to be the competitive equilibrium, where price equals marginal cost!

First we note that price can never be less than marginal cost since then either firm would increase its profits by producing less. So let us consider the case where price is greater than marginal cost. Suppose that both firms are selling output at some price $\hat{p}$ greater than marginal cost. Consider the position of firm 1. If it lowers its price by any small amount ϵ and if the other firm keeps its price fixed at $\hat{p}$, all of the consumers will prefer to purchase from firm 1. By cutting its price by an arbitrarily small amount, it can steal all of the customers from firm 2.

If firm 1 really believes that firm 2 will charge a price $\hat{p}$ that is greater than marginal cost, it will always pay firm 1 to cut its price to $\hat{p} - \epsilon$. But firm 2 can reason the same way! Thus any price higher than marginal cost cannot be an equilibrium; the only equilibrium is the competitive equilibrium.

This result seems paradoxical when you first encounter it: how can we get a competitive price if there are only two firms in the market? If we think of the Bertrand model as a model of competitive bidding it makes more sense. Suppose that one firm "bids" for the consumers' business by quoting a price above marginal cost. Then the other firm can always make a profit by undercutting this price with a lower price. It follows that the only price that each firm cannot rationally expect to be undercut is a price equal to marginal cost.

It is often observed that competitive bidding among firms that are unable to collude can result in prices that are much lower than can be achieved by other means. This phenomenon is simply an example of the logic of Bertrand competition.

27.10 Collusion

In the models we have examined up until now the firms have operated independently. But if the firms collude so as to jointly determine their output, these models are not very reasonable. If collusion is possible, the firms would do better to choose the output that maximizes total industry profits and then divide up the profits among themselves. When firms get together and attempt to set prices and outputs so as to maximize total industry profits, they are known as a **cartel**. As we saw in Chapter 24, a cartel is simply a group of firms that jointly collude to behave like a single monopolist and maximize the sum of their profits.

Thus the profit-maximization problem facing the two firms is to choose their outputs y_1 and y_2 so as to maximize total industry profits:

$$\max_{y_1, y_2} p(y_1 + y_2)[y_1 + y_2] - c_1(y_1) - c_2(y_2).$$

This will have the optimality conditions

$$p(y_1^* + y_2^*) + \frac{\Delta p}{\Delta Y}[y_1^* + y_2^*] = MC_1(y_1^*)$$

$$p(y_1^* + y_2^*) + \frac{\Delta p}{\Delta Y}[y_1^* + y_2^*] = MC_2(y_2^*).$$

The interpretation of these conditions is interesting. When firm 1 considers expanding its output by Δy_1, it will contemplate the usual two effects: the extra profits from selling more output and the reduction in profits from forcing the price down. But in the second effect, it now takes into account the effect of the lower price on both its own output and the output of the other firm. This is because it is now interested in maximizing total industry profits, not just its own profits.

The optimality conditions imply that the marginal revenue of an extra unit of output must be the same no matter where it is produced. It follows that $MC_1(y_1^*) = MC_2(y_2^*)$, so that the two marginal costs will be equal in equilibrium. If one firm has a cost advantage, so that its marginal cost curve always lies below that of the other firm, then it will necessarily produce more output in equilibrium in the cartel solution.

The problem with agreeing to join a cartel in real life is that there is always a temptation to cheat. Suppose, for example, that the two firms are operating at the outputs that maximize industry profits (y_1^*, y_2^*) and firm 1 considers producing a little more output, Δy_1. The marginal profits accruing to firm 1 will be

$$\frac{\Delta \pi_1}{\Delta y_1} = p(y_1^* + y_2^*) + \frac{\Delta p}{\Delta Y} y_1^* - MC_1(y_1^*). \tag{27.5}$$

We saw earlier that the optimality condition for the cartel solution is

$$p(y_1^* + y_2^*) + \frac{\Delta p}{\Delta Y} y_1^* + \frac{\Delta p}{\Delta Y} y_2^* - MC_1(y_1^*) = 0.$$

Rearranging this equation gives us

$$p(y_1^* + y_2^*) + \frac{\Delta p}{\Delta Y} y_1^* - MC_1(y_1^*) = -\frac{\Delta p}{\Delta Y} y_2^* > 0. \tag{27.6}$$

The last inequality follows since $\Delta p / \Delta Y$ is negative, since the market demand curve has a negative slope.

Inspecting equations (27.5) and (27.6) we see that

$$\frac{\Delta \pi_1}{\Delta y_1} > 0.$$

Thus, if firm 1 believes that firm 2 will keep its output fixed, then it will believe that it can increase profits by increasing its own production. In the cartel solution, the firms act together to restrict output so as not to "spoil" the market. They recognize the effect on joint profits from producing more output in either firm. But if each firm believes that the other firm will stick to its output quota, then each firm will be tempted to increase its own profits by unilaterally expanding its output. At the output levels that maximize joint profits, it will always be profitable for each firm to unilaterally increase its output—if each firm expects that the other firm will keep its output fixed.

The situation is even worse than that. If firm 1 believes that firm 2 will keep its output fixed, then it will find it profitable to increase its own output. But if it thinks that firm 2 will increase its output, then firm 1 would want increase its output first and make its profits while it can!

Thus, in order to maintain an effective cartel, the firms need a way to detect and punish cheating. If they have no way to observe each other's output, the temptation to cheat may break the cartel. We'll return to this point a little later.

To make sure that we understand the cartel solution, let's calculate it for the case of zero marginal costs and the linear demand curve we used in the Cournot case.

The aggregate profit function will be

$$\pi(y_1, y_2) = [a - b(y_1 + y_2)](y_1 + y_2) = a(y_1 + y_2) - b(y_1 + y_2)^2,$$

so the marginal revenue equals marginal cost conditions will be

$$a - 2b(y_1^* + y_2^*) = 0,$$

which implies that

$$y_1^* + y_2^* = \frac{a}{2b}.$$

Since marginal costs are zero, the division of output between the two firms doesn't matter. All that is determined is the total level of industry output.

This solution is shown in Figure 27.5. Here we have illustrated the isoprofit curves for each of the firms and have highlighted the locus of common tangents. Why is this line of interest? Since the cartel is trying to maximize total industry profits, it follows that the marginal profits from having either firm produce more output must be the same—otherwise it would pay to have the more profitable firm produce more output. This in

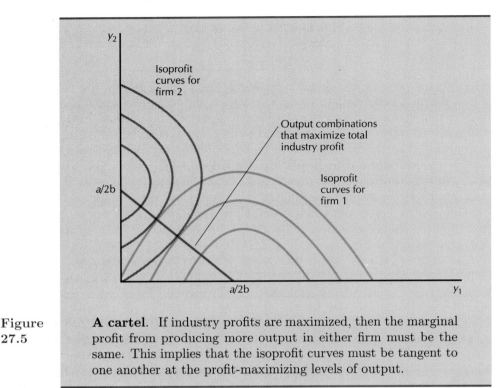

Figure
27.5
A cartel. If industry profits are maximized, then the marginal profit from producing more output in either firm must be the same. This implies that the isoprofit curves must be tangent to one another at the profit-maximizing levels of output.

turn implies that the slopes of the isoprofit curves must be the same for each firm; that is, that the isoprofit curves must be tangent to each other. Hence the output combinations that maximize total industry profits—the cartel solution—are those that lie along the line illustrated in Figure 27.5.

Figure 27.5 also illustrates the temptation to cheat that is present at the cartel solution. Consider, for example, the point where the two firms split the market equally. Think about what would happen if firm 1 believed that firm 2 would keep its output constant. If firm 1 increased its output and firm 2 kept constant output, then firm 1 would move to a lower isoprofit curve—which means that firm 1 would increase its profits. This is exactly the story told in the algebra above. If one firm thinks that the other's output will remain constant, it will be tempted to increase its own output and thereby make higher profits.

27.11 Punishment Strategies

We have seen that a cartel is fundamentally unstable in the sense that it is always in the interest of each of the firms to increase their production above that which maximizes aggregate profit. If the cartel is to operate successfully, some way must be found to "stabilize" the behavior. One way to do this is for firms to threaten to punish each other for cheating on the cartel agreement. In this section, we investigate the size of punishments necessary to stabilize a cartel.

Consider a duopoly composed of two identical firms. If each firm produces half the monopoly amount of output, total profits will be maximized and each firm will get a payoff of, say, π_m. In an effort to make this outcome stable, one firm announces to the other: "If you stay at the production level that maximizes joint industry projects, fine. But if I discover you cheating by producing more than this amount, I will punish you by producing the Cournot level of output forever." This is known as a **punishment strategy**.

When will this sort of threat be adequate to stabilize the cartel? We have to look at the benefits and costs of cheating as compared to those of cooperating. Suppose that cheating occurs, and the punishment is carried out. Since the optimal response to Cournot behavior is Cournot behavior (by definition), this results in each firm receiving a per-period profit of, say, π_c. Of course, the Cournot payoff, π_c is less than the cartel payoff, π_m.

Let us suppose that the two firms are each producing at the collusive, monopoly level of production. Put yourself in the place of one of the firms trying to decide whether to continue to produce at your quota. If you produce more output, deviating from your quota, you make profit π_d, where $\pi_d > \pi_m$. This is the standard temptation facing a cartel member described above: if each firm restricts output and pushes the price up, then each firm has an incentive to capitalize on the high price by increasing its production.

But this isn't the end of the story because of the punishment for cheating. By producing at the cartel amount, each firm gets a steady stream of payments of π_m. The present value of this stream starting today is given by

$$\text{Present value of cartel behavior} = \pi_m + \frac{\pi_m}{r}.$$

If the firm produces more than the cartel amount, it gets a one-time benefit of profits π_d, but then has to live with the breakup of the cartel and the reversion to Cournot behavior:

$$\text{Present value of cheating} = \pi_d + \frac{\pi_c}{r}.$$

When will the present value of remaining at the cartel output be greater than the present value of cheating on the cartel agreement? Obviously when

$$\pi_m + \frac{\pi_m}{r} > \pi_d + \frac{\pi_c}{r},$$

which can also be written as

$$r < \frac{\pi_m - \pi_c}{\pi_d - \pi_m}.$$

Note that the numerator of this fraction is positive, since the monopoly profits are larger than the Cournot profits, and the denominator is positive, since deviation is even more profitable than sticking with the monopoly quota.

The inequality says that as long as the interest rate is sufficiently small, so that the prospect of future punishment is sufficiently important, it will pay the firms to stick to their quotas.

The weakness of this model is that the threat to revert to Cournot behavior forever is not very believable. One firm certainly may believe that the other will punish it for deviating, but "forever" is a long time. A more realistic model would consider shorter periods of retaliation, but the analysis then becomes much more complex. In the next chapter, we discuss some models of "repeated games" that illustrate some of the possible behaviors.

EXAMPLE: Price Matching and Competition

We have seen that there is always a temptation for each member of a cartel to produce more than its quota. In order to maintain a successful cartel, some way must be found to police members' behavior by some form of punishment for deviations from the joint profit-maximizing output. In particular this means that firms must be able to keep track of the prices and production levels of the other firms in the cartel.

One easy way to acquire information about what the other firms in your industry are charging is to use your customers to spy on the other firms. It is common to see retail firms announce that they will "beat any price." In some cases, such an offer may indicate a highly competitive retail environment. But in other cases, this same policy can be used to gather information about other firms' prices in order to maintain a cartel.

Suppose, for example, that two firms agree, either explicitly or implicitly to sell a certain model of refrigerator for $700. How can either of the stores be sure that the other firm isn't cheating on their agreement and selling the refrigerator for $675? One way is to offer to beat any price a customer can find. That way, the customers report any attempts to cheat on the collusive arrangement.

EXAMPLE: Voluntary Export Restraints

During the 1980s, the Japanese automobile companies agreed to a "voluntary export restraint (VER)." This meant that they would "voluntarily" reduce the exports of their automobiles to the United States. The typical U.S. consumer thought that this was a great victory for U.S. trade negotiators.

But if you think about this for a minute, things look quite different. In our examination of oligopoly we have seen that the problem facing firms in an industry is how to *restrict* output in order to support higher prices and discourage competition. As we've seen, there will always be a temptation to cheat on production agreements; every cartel must find a way to detect and prevent this cheating. It is especially convenient for the firms if a third party, such as the government, can serve this role. This is exactly the role that the U.S. government played for the Japanese auto makers!

According to one estimate Japanese imported cars were about $2500 more expensive in 1984 than they would have been without the VERs. Furthermore, the higher prices of imported cars allowed American producers to sell their automobiles at about $1000 more than they would have otherwise.[5]

Due to these higher prices the U.S. consumers paid about $10 billion more for Japanese cars in 1985–86 than they would have otherwise. This money has gone directly into the pockets of the Japanese automobile producers. Much of this additional profit appears to have been invested in increasing productive capabilities, which allowed the Japanese auto producers to reduce the cost of producing new cars in subsequent years. The VERs did succeed in saving American jobs; however, it appears that the cost per job saved was about $160,000 per year.

If the goal of the VER policy was simply to increase the health of the American automobile industry, there was a much simpler way to do this: just impose a $2500 tariff on each imported Japanese car. This way the revenues due to the restriction of trade would accrue to the U.S. government rather than to the Japanese automobile industry. Rather than send $10 billion abroad during 1985–86, the U.S. government could have spent the money on projects designed to increase the long-term health of the U.S. auto industry.

27.12 Comparison of the Solutions

We have now examined several models of duopoly behavior: quantity leadership (Stackelberg), price leadership, simultaneous quantity setting (Cournot), simultaneous price setting (Bertrand), and the collusive solution. How do they compare?

In general, collusion results in the smallest industry output and the highest price. Bertrand equilibrium—the competitive equilibrium—gives us the highest output and the lowest price. The other models give results that are in between these two extremes.

---

[5] Robert Crandall, "Import Quotas and the Automobile Industry: the Costs of Protectionism," *The Brookings Review,* Summer, 1984.

A variety of other models are possible. For example, we could look at a model with differentiated products where the two goods produced were not perfect substitutes for each other. Or we could look at a model where the firms make a sequence of choices over time. In this framework, the choices that one firm makes at one time can influence the choices that the other firm makes later on.

We have also assumed that each firm knows the demand function and the cost functions of the other firms in the industry. In reality these functions are never known for sure. Each firm needs to estimate the demand and cost conditions facing its rivals when it makes its own decisions. All of these phenomena have been modeled by economists, but the models become much more complex.

Summary

1. An oligopoly is characterized by a market with a few firms that recognize their strategic interdependence. There are several possible ways for oligopolies to behave depending on the exact nature of their interaction.

2. In the quantity-leader (Stackelberg) model one firm leads by setting its output, and the other firm follows. When the leader chooses an output, it will take into account how the follower will respond.

3. In the price-leader model, one firm sets its price, and the other firm chooses how much it wants to supply at that price. Again the leader has to take into account the behavior of the follower when it makes its decision.

4. In the Cournot model, each firm chooses its output so as to maximize its profits given its beliefs about the other firm's choice. In equilibrium each firm finds that its expectation about the other firm's choice is confirmed.

5. A Cournot equilibrium in which each firm has a small market share implies that price will be very close to marginal cost—that is, the industry will be nearly competitive.

6. In the Bertrand model each firm chooses its price given its beliefs about the price that the other firm will choose. The only equilibrium price is the competitive equilibrium.

7. A cartel consists of a number of firms colluding to restrict output and to maximize industry profit. A cartel will typically be unstable in the sense that each firm will be tempted to sell more than its agreed upon output if it believes that the other firms will not respond.

REVIEW QUESTIONS

1. Suppose that we have two firms that face a linear demand curve $p(Y) = a - bY$ and have constant marginal costs, c, for each firm. Solve for the Cournot equilibrium output.

2. Consider a cartel in which each firm has identical and constant marginal costs. If the cartel maximizes total industry profits, what does this imply about the division of output between the firms?

3. Can the leader ever get a lower profit in a Stackelberg equilibrium than he would get in the Cournot equilibrium?

4. Suppose there are n identical firms in a Cournot equilibrium. Show that the elasticity of the market demand curve must be greater than $1/n$. (Hint: in the case of a monopolist, $n = 1$, and this simply says that a monopolist operates at an elastic part of the demand curve. Apply the logic that we used to establish that fact to this problem.)

5. Draw a set of reaction curves that result in an unstable equilibrium.

6. Do oligopolies produce an efficient level of output?

CHAPTER **28**

GAME
THEORY

The previous chapter on oligopoly theory presented the classical economic theory of strategic interaction among firms. But that is really just the tip of the iceberg. Economic agents can interact strategically in a variety of ways, and many of these have been studied by using the apparatus of **game theory**. Game theory is concerned with the general analysis of strategic interaction. It can be used to study parlor games, political negotiation, and economic behavior. In this chapter we will briefly explore this fascinating subject to give you a flavor of how it works and how it can be used to study economic behavior in oligopolistic markets.

28.1 The Payoff Matrix of a Game

Strategic interaction can involve many players and many strategies, but we'll limit ourselves to two-person games with a finite number of strategies. This will allow us to depict the game easily in a **payoff matrix**. It is simplest to examine this in the context of a specific example.

Suppose that two people are playing a simple game. Person A will write one of two words on a piece of paper, "top" or "bottom." Simultaneously, person B will independently write "left" or "right" on a piece of paper. After they do this, the papers will be examined and they will each get the payoff depicted in Table 28.1. If A says top and B says left, then we examine the top left-hand corner of the matrix. In this matrix the payoff to A is the first entry in the box, 1, and the payoff to B is the second entry, 2. Similarly, if A says bottom and B says right, then A will get a payoff of 1 and B will get a payoff of 0.

Person A has two strategies: he can choose top or he can choose bottom. These strategies could represent economic choices like "raise price" or "lower price." Or they could represent political choices like "declare war" or "don't declare war." The payoff matrix of a game simply depicts the payoffs to each player for each combination of strategies that are chosen.

What will be the outcome of this sort of game? The game depicted in Table 28.1 has a very simple solution. From the viewpoint of person A, it is always better for him to say bottom since his payoffs from that choice (2 or 1) are always greater than their corresponding entries in top (1 or 0). Similarly, it is always better for B to say left since 2 and 1 dominate 1 and 0. Thus we would expect that the equilibrium strategy is for A to play bottom and B to play left.

In this case, we have a **dominant strategy**. There is one optimal choice of strategy for each player no matter what the other player does. Whichever choice B makes, player A will get a higher payoff if he plays bottom, so it makes sense for A to play bottom. And whichever choice A makes, B will get a higher payoff if he plays left. Hence, these choices dominate the alternatives, and we have an equilibrium in dominant strategies.

A payoff matrix of a game.

Table
28.1

		Player B	
		Left	Right
Player A	Top	1, 2	0, 1
	Bottom	2, 1	1, 0

If there is a dominant strategy for each player in some game, then we would predict that it would be the equilibrium outcome of the game. For a dominant strategy is a strategy that is best no matter what the other player does. In this example, we would expect an equilibrium outcome in which A plays bottom, receiving an equilibrium payoff of 2, and B plays left, receiving an equilibrium payoff of 1.

28.2 Nash Equilibrium

Dominant strategy equilibria are nice when they happen, but they don't happen all that often. For example, the game depicted in Table 28.2 doesn't have a dominant strategy equilibrium. Here when B chooses left the payoffs to A are 2 or 0. When B chooses right, the payoffs to A are 0 or 1. This means that when B chooses left, A would want to choose top; and when B chooses right, A would want to choose bottom. Thus A's optimal choice depends on what he thinks B will do.

A Nash equilibrium.

Table
28.2

		Player B	
		Left	Right
Player A	Top	2, 1	0, 0
	Bottom	0, 0	1, 2

However, perhaps the dominant strategy equilibrium is too demanding. Rather than require that A's choice be optimal for *all* choices of B, we can just require that it be optimal for the *optimal* choices of B. For if B is a well-informed intelligent player, he will only want to choose optimal strategies. (Although, what is optimal for B will depend on A's choice as well!)

We will say that a pair of strategies is a **Nash equilibrium** if A's choice is optimal, given B's choice, *and* B's choice is optimal given A's choice.[1] Remember that neither person knows what the other person will do when he has to make his own choice of strategy. But each person may have some expectation about what the other person's choice will be. A Nash equilibrium can be interpreted as a pair of expectations about each person's choice such that, when the other person's choice is revealed, neither individual wants to change his behavior.

In the case of Table 28.2, the strategy (top, left) is a Nash equilibrium. To prove this note that if A chooses top, then the best thing for B to do is to choose left, since the payoff to B from choosing left is 1 and from choosing right is 0. And if B chooses left, then the best thing for A to do is to choose top since then A will get a payoff of 2 rather than of 0.

[1] John Nash is an American mathematician who formulated this fundamental concept of game theory in 1951.

Thus if A chooses top, the optimal choice for B is to choose left; and if B chooses left, then the optimal choice for A is top. So we have a Nash equilibrium: each person is making the optimal choice, *given* the other person's choice.

The Nash equilibrium is a generalization of the Cournot equilibrium described in the last chapter. There the choices were output levels, and each firm chose its output level taking the other firm's choice as being fixed. Each firm was supposed to do the best for itself, assuming that the other firm continued to produce the output level it had chosen—that is, it continued to play the strategy it had chosen. A Cournot equilibrium occurs when each firm is maximizing profits given the other firm's behavior; this is precisely the definition of a Nash equilibrium.

The Nash equilibrium notion has a certain logic. Unfortunately, it also has some problems. First, a game may have more than one Nash equilibrium. In fact, in Table 28.2 the choices (bottom, right) also comprise a Nash equilibrium. You can either verify this by the kind of argument used above, or just note that the structure of the game is symmetric: B's payoffs are the same in one outcome as A's payoffs are in the other, so that our proof that (top, left) is an equilibrium is also a proof that (bottom, right) is an equilibrium.

The second problem with the concept of a Nash equilibrium is that there are games that have no Nash equilibrium of the sort we have been describing at all. Consider, for example, the case depicted in Table 28.3. Here a Nash equilibrium of the sort we have been examining does not exist. If player A plays top, then player B wants to play left. But if player B plays left, then player A wants bottom. Similarly, if player A plays bottom, then player B will play right. But if player B plays right, then player A will play top.

A game with no Nash equilibrium (in pure strategies).

Table
28.3

		Player B	
		Left	Right
Player A	Top	0, 0	0, −1
	Bottom	1, 0	−1, 3

28.3 Mixed Strategies

However, if we enlarge our definition of strategies, we can find a new sort of Nash equilibrium for this game. We have been thinking of each agent as choosing a strategy once and for all. That is, each agent is making one choice and sticking to it. This is called a **pure strategy**.

Another way to think about it is to allow the agents to *randomize* their strategies—to assign a probability to each choice and to play their choices according to those probabilities. For example, A might choose to play top 50 percent of the time and bottom 50 percent of the time, while B might choose to play left 50 percent of the time and right 50 percent of the time. This kind of strategy is called a **mixed strategy**.

If A and B follow the mixed strategies given above, of playing each of their choices half the time, then they will have a probability of 1/4 of ending up in each of the four cells in the payoff matrix. Thus the average payoff to A will be 0, and the average payoff to B will be 1/2.

A Nash equilibrium in mixed strategies refers to an equilibrium in which each agent chooses the optimal frequency with which to play his strategies given the frequency choices of the other agent.

It can be shown that for the sort of games we are analyzing in this chapter, there will always exist a Nash equilibrium in mixed strategies. Because a Nash equilibrium in mixed strategies always exists, and because the concept has a certain inherent plausibility, it is a very popular equilibrium notion in analyzing game behavior. In the example in Table 28.3 it can be shown that if player A plays top with probability 3/4 and bottom with probability 1/4, and player B plays left with probability 1/2 and right with probability 1/2, this will constitute a Nash equilibrium.

28.4 The Prisoner's Dilemma

Another problem with the Nash equilibrium of a game is that it does not necessarily lead to Pareto efficient outcomes. Consider, for example, the game depicted in Table 28.4. This game is known as the **prisoner's dilemma**. The original discussion of the game considered a situation where two prisoners who were partners in a crime were being questioned in separate rooms. Each prisoner had a choice of confessing to the crime, and thereby implicating the other, or denying that he had participated in the crime. If only one prisoner confessed, then he would go free, and the authorities would throw the book at the other prisoner, requiring him to spend 6 months in prison. If both prisoners denied being involved, then both would be held for 1 month on a technicality, and if both players confessed they would both be held for 3 months. The payoff matrix for this game is given in Table 28.4. The entries in each cell in the matrix represent the utility that each of the agents assigns to the various prison terms, which for simplicity we take to be the negative of the length of their prison terms.

Put yourself in the position of player A. If player B decides to deny committing the crime, then you are certainly better off confessing, since then you'll get off free. Similarly, if player B confesses, then you'll be better off confessing, since then you get a sentence of 3 months rather than a sentence of 6 months. Thus *whatever* player B does, player A is better off confessing.

The prisoner's dilemma.

Table
28.4

		Player B	
		Confess	Deny
Player A	Confess	$-3, -3$	$0, -6$
	Deny	$-6, 0$	$-1, -1$

The same thing goes for player B—he is better off confessing as well. Thus the unique Nash equilibrium for this game is for both players to confess. In fact, both players confessing is not only a Nash equilibrium, it is a dominant strategy equilibrium, since each player has the same optimal choice independent of the other player.

But if they could both just hang tight, they would each be better off! If they both could be sure the other would hold out, and both could agree to hold out themselves, they would each get a payoff of -1, which would make each of them better off. The strategy (deny, deny) is Pareto efficient—there is no other strategy choice that makes both players better off—while the strategy (confess, confess) is Pareto inefficient.

The problem is that there is no way for the two prisoners to coordinate their actions. If each could trust the other, then they could both be made better off.

The prisoner's dilemma applies to a wide range of economic and political phenomena. Consider, for example, the problem of arms control. Interpret the strategy of "confess" as "deploy a new missile" and the strategy of "deny" as "don't deploy." Note that the payoffs are reasonable. If my opponent deploys his missile, I certainly want to deploy, even though the best strategy for both of us is to agree not to deploy. But if there is no way to make a binding agreement, we each end up deploying the missile and are both made worse off.

Another good example is the problem of cheating in a cartel. Now interpret confess as "produce more than your quota of output" and interpret deny as "stick to the original quota." If you think the other firm is going to stick to its quota, it will pay you to produce more than your own quota. And if you think that the other firm will overproduce, then you might as well, too!

The prisoner's dilemma has provoked a lot of controversy as to what is the "correct" way to play the game—or, more precisely, what is a reasonable way to play the game. The answer seems to depend on whether you are playing a one–shot game or whether the game is to be repeated an indefinite number of times.

If the game is going to be played just one time, the strategy of defecting—in this example, confessing—seems to be a reasonable one. After all, whatever the other fellow does, you are better off, and you have no way of influencing the other person's behavior.

28.5 Repeated Games

In the preceding section, the players met only once and played the prisoner's dilemma game a single time. However, the situation is different if the game is to be played repeatedly by the same players. In this case there are new strategic possibilities open to each player. If the other player chooses to defect on one round, then you can choose to defect on the next round. Thus your opponent can be "punished" for "bad" behavior. In a repeated game, each player has the opportunity to establish a reputation for cooperation, and thereby encourage the other player to do the same.

Whether this kind of strategy will be viable depends on whether the game is going to be played a *fixed* number of times or an *indefinite* number of times.

Let us consider the first case, where both players know that the game is going to be played 10 times, say. What will the outcome be? Suppose we consider round 10. This is the last time the game will be played, by assumption. In this case, it seems likely that each player will choose the dominant strategy equilibrium, and defect. After all, playing the game for the last time is just like playing it once, so we should expect the same outcome.

Now consider what will happen on round 9. We have just concluded that each player will defect on round 10. So why cooperate on round 9? If you cooperate, the other player might as well defect now and exploit your good nature. Each player can reason the same way, and thus each will defect.

Now consider round 8. If the other person is going to defect on round 9 ... and so it goes. If the game has a known, fixed number of rounds, then each player will defect on every round. If there is no way to enforce cooperation on the last round, there will be no way to enforce cooperation on the next to the last round, and so on.

Players cooperate because they hope that cooperation will induce further cooperation in the future. But this requires that there will always be the possibility of future play. Since there is no possibility of future play in the last round, no one will cooperate then. But then why should anyone cooperate on the next to the last round? Or the one before that? And so it goes—the cooperative solution "unravels" from the end in a prisoner's dilemma with a known, fixed number of plays.

But if the game is going to be repeated an indefinite number of times, then you *do* have a way of influencing your opponent's behavior: if he refuses to cooperate this time, you can refuse to cooperate next time. As long as both parties care enough about future payoffs, the threat of non-cooperation in the future may be sufficient to convince people to play the Pareto efficient strategy.

This has been demonstrated in a convincing way in a series of experiments run by Robert Axelrod.[2] He asked dozens of experts on game theory to submit their favorite strategies for the prisoner's dilemma and then ran a "tournament" on a computer to pit these strategies against each other. Every strategy was played against every other strategy on the computer, and the computer kept track of the total payoffs.

The winning strategy—the one with the highest overall payoff—turned out to be the simplest strategy. It is called "tit for tat" and goes like this. On the first round, you cooperate—play the "deny" strategy. On every round thereafter, if your opponent cooperated on the previous round, you cooperate. If your opponent defected on the previous round, you defect. In other words, whatever your opponent did the last round, you do on this round. That's all there is to it.

The tit-for-tat strategy does very well because it offers an immediate punishment for defection. It is also a forgiving strategy: it punishes the other player only once for each defection. If he falls into line and starts to cooperate, then tit for tat will reward the other player with cooperation. It appears to be a remarkably good mechanism for achieving the efficient outcome in a prisoner's dilemma that will be played an indefinite number of times.

28.6 Enforcing a Cartel

In Chapter 27 we discussed the behavior of duopolists playing a price-setting game. We argued there that if each duopolist could choose his price, then the equilibrium outcome would be the competitive equilibrium. If each firm thought that the other firm would keep its price fixed, then each firm would find it profitable to undercut the other. The only place where this would not be true was if each firm were charging the lowest possible price, which in the case we examined was a price of zero, since the marginal costs were zero. In the terminology of this chapter, each firm charging a zero price is a Nash equilibrium in pricing strategies—what we called a Bertrand equilibrium in Chapter 27.

---

[2] Robert Axelrod is a political scientist from the University of Michigan. For an extended discussion, see his book *The Evolution of Cooperation* (New York: Basic Books, 1984).

The payoff matrix for the duopoly game in pricing strategies has the same structure as the prisoner's dilemma. If each firm charges a high price, then they both get large profits. This is the situation where they are both cooperating to maintain the monopoly outcome. But if one firm is charging a high price, then it will pay the other firm to cut its price a little, capture the other fellow's market, and thereby get even higher profits. But if both firms cut their prices, they both end up making lower profits. Whatever price the other fellow is charging, it will always pay you to shave your price a little bit. The Nash equilibrium occurs when each fellow is charging the lowest possible price.

However, if the game is repeated an indefinite number of times, there may be other possible outcomes. Suppose that you decide to play tit for tat. If the other fellow cuts his price this week, you will cut yours next week. If each player knows that the other player is playing tit for tat, then each player would be fearful of cutting his price and starting a price war. The threat implicit in tit for tat may allow the firms to maintain high prices.

Real-life cartels sometimes appear to employ tit-for-tat strategies. For example, The Joint Executive Committee was a famous cartel that set the price of railroad freight in the United States in the late 1800s. The formation of this cartel preceded antitrust regulation in the United States, and at the time was perfectly legal.[3]

The cartel determined what market share each railroad could have of the freight shipped. Each firm set its rates individually, and the JEC kept track of how much freight each firm shipped. However, there were several occasions during 1881, 1884, and 1885 where some members of the cartel thought that other member firms were cutting rates so as to increase their market share, despite their agreement. During these periods, there were often price wars. When one firm tried to cheat, all firms would cut their prices so as to "punish" the defectors. This kind of tit-for-tat strategy was apparently able to support the cartel arrangement for some time.

EXAMPLE: Tit for Tat in Airline Pricing

Airline pricing provides an interesting example of tit-for-tat behavior. Airlines often offer special promotional fares of one sort or another; many observers of the airline industry claim that these promotions can be used to signal competitors to refrain from cutting prices on key routes.

A senior director of marketing for a major U.S. airline described a case in which Northwest lowered fares on night flights from Minneapolis to various

[3] For a detailed analysis, see Robert Porter, "A Study of Cartel Stability: the Joint Executive Committee, 1880–1886," *The Bell Journal of Economics*, 14, 2 (Autumn 1983), 301–25.

West Coast cities in an effort to fill empty seats. Continental Airlines interpreted this as an attempt to gain market share at its expense and responded by cutting *all* its Minneapolis fares to Northwest's night-fare level. However, the Continental fare cuts were set to expire one or two days after they were introduced.

Northwest interpreted this as a signal from Continental that it was not serious about competing in this market, but simply wanted Northwest to retract its night-fare cuts. But Northwest decided to send a message of its own to Continental: it instituted a set of cheap fares to the West Coast for its flights departing from Houston, Continental's home base! Northwest thereby signaled that it felt its cuts were justified, while Continental's response was inappropriate.

All these fare cuts had very short expiration dates; this feature seems to indicate that they were meant more as messages to the competition than as bids for larger market share. As the analyst explained, fares that an airline doesn't want to offer "should almost always have an expiration date on them in the hopes that the competition will eventually wake up and match."

The implicit rules of competition in duopoly airline markets seem to be the following: if the other firm keeps its prices high, I will maintain my high prices; but if the other firm cuts its prices, I will play tit for tat and cut my prices in response. In other words, both firms "live by the Golden Rule": do unto others as you would have them do unto you. This threat of retaliation then serves to keep all prices high.[4]

28.7 Sequential Games

Up until now we have been thinking about games in which both players act simultaneously. But in many situations one player gets to move first, and the other player responds. An example of this is the Stackelberg model described in Chapter 27, where one player is a leader and the other player is a follower.

Let's describe a game like this. In the first round, player A gets to choose top or bottom. Player B gets to observe the first player's choice and then chooses left or right. The payoffs are illustrated in a game matrix in Table 28.5.

Note that when the game is presented in this form it has two Nash equilibria: (top, left) and (bottom, right). However, we'll show below that one of these equilibria isn't really reasonable. The payoff matrix hides the fact that one player gets to know what the other player has chosen before he makes his choice. In this case it is more useful to consider a diagram that illustrates the asymmetric nature of the game.

---

[4] Facts taken from A. Nomani, "Fare Warning: How Airlines Trade Price Plans," *Wall Street Journal,* October 9, 1990, B1.

The payoff matrix of a sequential game.

Table
28.5

		Player B	
		Left	Right
Player A	Top	1, 9	1, 9
	Bottom	0, 0	2, 1

Table 28.6 is a picture of the game in **extensive form**—a way to represent the game that shows the time pattern of the choices. First, player A has to choose top or bottom, and then player B has to choose left or right. But when B makes his choice, he will know what A has done.

Table
28.6

A game in extensive form.

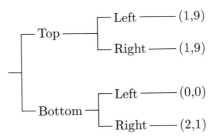

The way to analyze this game is to go to the end and work backward. Suppose that player A has already made his choice and we are sitting in one branch of the game tree. If player A has chosen top, then it doesn't matter what player B does, and the payoff is (1,9). If player A has chosen bottom, then the sensible thing for player B to do is to choose right, and the payoff is (2,1).

Now think about player A's initial choice. If he chooses top, the outcome will be (1,9) and thus he will get a payoff of 1. But if he chooses bottom, he gets a payoff of 2. So the sensible thing for him to do is to choose bottom. Thus the equilibrium choices in the game will be (bottom, right), so that the payoff to player A will be 2 and to player B will be 1.

The strategies (top, left) are not a reasonable equilibrium in this sequential game. That is, they are not an equilibrium given the order in which the players actually get to make their choices. It is true that if player A chooses top, player B could choose left—but it would be silly for player A to ever choose top!

From player B's point of view this is rather unfortunate, since he ends up with a payoff of 1 rather than 9! What might he do about it?

Well, he can *threaten* to play left if player A plays bottom. If player A thought that player B would actually carry out this threat, he would be well advised to play top. For top gives him 1, while bottom—if player B carries out his threat—will only give him 0.

But is this threat credible? After all, once player A makes his choice, that's it. Player B can get either 0 or 1, and he might as well get 1. Unless player B can somehow convince player A that he will really carry out his threat—even when it hurts him to do so—he will just have to settle for the lower payoff.

Player B's problem is that once player A has made his choice, player A expects player B to do the rational thing. Player B would be better off if he could *commit* himself to play left if player A plays bottom.

One way for B to make such a commitment is to allow someone else to make his choices. For example, B might hire a lawyer and instruct him to play left if A plays bottom. If A is aware of these instructions, the situation is radically different from his point of view. If he knows about B's instructions to his lawyer, then he knows that if he plays bottom he will end up with a payoff of 0. So the sensible thing for him to do is to play top. In this case B has done better for himself by *limiting* his choices.

28.8 A Game of Entry Deterrence

In our examination of oligopoly we took the number of firms in the industry as fixed. But in many situations, entry is possible. Of course, it is in the interest of the firms in the industry to try to prevent such entry. Since they are already in the industry, they get to move first and thus have an advantage in choosing ways to keep their opponents out.

Suppose, for example, that we consider a monopolist who is facing a threat of entry by another firm. The entrant decides whether or not to come into the market, and then the incumbent decides whether or not to cut its price in response. If the entrant decides to stay out, it gets a payoff of 1 and the incumbent gets a payoff of 9.

If the entrant decides to come in, then its payoff depends on whether the incumbent fights—by competing vigorously—or not. If the incumbent fights, then we suppose that both players end up with 0. If the incumbent decides not to fight, we suppose that the entrant gets 2 and the incumbent gets 1.

Note that this is exactly the structure of the sequential game we studied earlier, and thus it has a structure identical to that depicted in Table 28.6. The incumbent is player B, while the potential entrant is player A. The top strategy is to stay out, and the bottom strategy is to enter. The left strategy is to fight and the right strategy is not to fight. As we've seen in this game, the equilibrium outcome is for the potential entrant to enter and the incumbent *not* to fight.

The incumbent's problem is that he cannot precommit himself to fighting if the other firm enters. If the other firm enters, the damage is done and the rational thing for the incumbent to do is to live and let live. Insofar as the potential entrant recognizes this, he will correctly view any threats to fight as empty.

But now suppose that the incumbent can purchase some extra production capacity that will allow him to produce more output at the same marginal cost he currently has. Of course, if he remains a monopolist, he won't want to actually use this capacity since he is already producing the profit-maximizing monopoly output.

But, if the other firm enters, the incumbent will now be able to produce so much output that he may well be able to compete much more successfully against the new entrant. By investing in the extra capacity, he will lower his costs of fighting if the other firm tries to enter. Let us assume that if he purchases the extra capacity and if he chooses to fight, he will make a profit of 2. This changes the game tree to the form depicted in Table 28.7.

Table
28.7

The new entry game in extensive form.

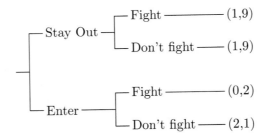

Now, because of the increased capacity, the threat of fighting is credible. If the potential entrant comes into the market, the incumbent will get a payoff of 2 if he fights and 1 if he doesn't; thus the incumbent will rationally choose to fight. The entrant will therefore get a payoff of 0 if he enters, and if he stays out he will get a payoff of 1. The sensible thing for the potential entrant to do is to stay out.

But this means that the incumbent will remain a monopolist and never have to use his extra capacity! Despite this, it is worthwhile for the monopolist to invest in the extra capacity in order to make credible the *threat* of fighting if a new firm tries to enter the market. By investing in "excess" capacity, the monopolist has signaled to the potential entrant that he will be able to successfully defend his market.

Summary

1. A game can be described by indicating the payoffs to each of the players for each configuration of strategic choices they make.

2. A dominant strategy equilibrium is a set of choices for which each player's choices are optimal *regardless* of what the other players choose.

3. A Nash equilibrium is a set of choices for which each player's choice is optimal, given the choices of the other players.

4. The prisoner's dilemma is a particular game in which the Pareto efficient outcome is strategically dominated by an inefficient outcome.

5. If a prisoner's dilemma is repeated an indefinite number of times, then it is possible that the Pareto efficient outcome may result from rational play.

6. In a sequential game, the time pattern of choices is important. In these games, it can often be advantageous to find a way to precommit to a particular line of play.

REVIEW QUESTIONS

1. Consider the tit-for-tat strategy in the repeated prisoner's dilemma. Suppose that one player makes a mistake and defects when he meant to cooperate. If both players continue to play tit for tat after that, what happens?

2. Are dominant strategy equilibria always Nash equilibria? Are Nash equilibria always dominant strategy equilibria?

3. Suppose your opponent is *not* playing her Nash equilibrium strategy. Should you play your Nash equilibrium strategy?

4. We know that the single-shot prisoner's dilemma game results in a dominant Nash equilibrium strategy that is Pareto inefficient. Suppose we allow the two prisoners to retaliate after their respective prison terms. Formally, what aspect of the game would this affect? Could a Pareto efficient outcome result?

5. What is the dominant Nash equilibrium strategy for the repeated prisoner's dilemma game when both players know that the game will end after one million repetitions? If you were going to run an experiment with human players for such a scenario, would you predict that players would use this strategy?

6. Suppose that player B rather than player A gets to move first in the sequential game described in this chapter. Draw the extensive form of the new game. What is the equilibrium for this game? Does player B prefer to move first or second?

CHAPTER **29**

EXCHANGE

Up until now we have generally considered the market for a single good in isolation. We have viewed the demand and supply functions for a good as depending on its price alone, disregarding the prices of other goods. But in general the prices of other goods *will* affect people's demands and supplies for a particular good. Certainly the prices of substitutes and complements for a good will influence the demand for it, and, more subtly, the prices of goods that people sell will affect the amount of income they have and thereby influence how much of other goods they will be able to buy.

Up until now we have been ignoring the effect of these other prices on the market equilibrium. When we discussed the equilibrium conditions in a particular market, we only looked at part of the problem: how demand and supply were affected by the price of the particular good we were examining. This is called **partial equilibrium** analysis.

In this chapter we will begin our study of **general equilibrium** analysis: how demand and supply conditions interact in several markets to determine the prices of many goods. As you might suspect, this is a complex problem, and we will have to adopt several simplifications in order to deal with it.

First, we will limit our discussion to the behavior of competitive markets, so that each consumer or producer will take prices as given and optimize accordingly. The study of general equilibrium with imperfect competition is very interesting but too difficult to examine at this point.

Second, we will adopt our usual simplifying assumption of looking at the smallest number of goods and consumers that we possibly can. In this case, it turns out that many interesting phenomena can be depicted using only two goods and two consumers. All of the aspects of general equilibrium analysis that we will discuss can be generalized to arbitrary numbers of consumers and goods, but the exposition is simpler with two of each.

Third, we will look at the general equilibrium problem in two stages. We will start with an economy where people have fixed endowments of goods and examine how they might trade these goods among themselves; no production will be involved. This case is naturally known as the case of **pure exchange**. Once we have a clear understanding of pure exchange markets we will examine production behavior in the general equilibrium model.

29.1 The Edgeworth Box

There is a convenient graphical tool known as the **Edgeworth box** that can be used to analyze the exchange of two goods between two people.[1] The Edgeworth box allows us to depict the endowments and preferences of two individuals in one convenient diagram, which can be used to study various outcomes of the trading process. In order to understand the construction of an Edgeworth box it is necessary to examine the indifference curves and the endowments of the people involved.

Let us call the two people involved A and B and the two goods involved 1 and 2. We will denote A's consumption bundle by $X_A = (x_A^1, x_A^2)$, where x_A^1 represents A's consumption of good 1 and x_A^2 represents A's consumption of good 2. Then B's consumption bundle is denoted by $X_B = (x_B^1, x_B^2)$. A *pair* of consumption bundles, X_A and X_B, is called an **allocation**. An allocation is a **feasible allocation** if the total amount of each good consumed is equal to the total amount available:

$$x_A^1 + x_B^1 = \omega_A^1 + \omega_B^1$$

$$x_A^2 + x_B^2 = \omega_A^2 + \omega_B^2.$$

A particular feasible allocation that is of interest is the **initial endowment allocation**, (ω_A^1, ω_A^2) and (ω_B^1, ω_B^2). This is the allocation that the consumers start with. It consists of the amount of each good that consumers bring to the market. They will exchange some of these goods with each other in the course of trade to end up at a **final allocation**.

---

[1] The Edgeworth box is named in honor of Francis Ysidro Edgeworth (1845–1926), an English economist who was one of the first to use this analytical tool.

The Edgeworth box shown in Figure 29.1 can be used to illustrate these concepts graphically. We first use a standard consumer theory diagram to illustrate the endowment and preferences of consumer A. We can also mark off on these axes the *total* amount of each good in the economy— the amount that A has plus the amount that B has of each good. Since we will only be interested in feasible allocations of goods between the two consumers, we can draw a box that contains the set of possible bundles of the two goods that A can hold.

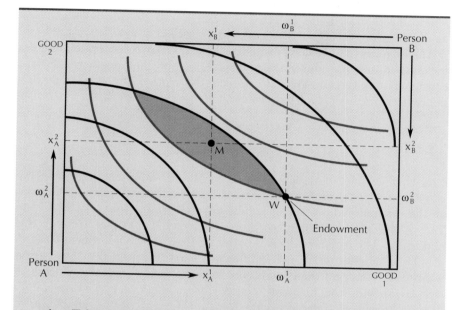

An Edgeworth box. The width of the box measures the total amount of good 1 in the economy and the height measures the total amount of good 2. Person A's consumption choices are measured from the lower left-hand corner while person B's choices are measured from the upper right.

Figure
29.1

Note that the bundles in this box also indicate the amount of the goods that B can hold. If there are 10 units of good 1 and 20 units of good 2, then if A holds (7,12), B must be holding (3,8). We can depict how much A holds of good 1 by the distance along the horizontal axis from the origin in the lower left-hand corner of the box and the amount B holds of good 1 by measuring the distance along the horizontal axis from the upper right-hand corner. Similarly, distances along the vertical axes give the amounts of good 2 that A and B hold. Thus the points in this box give us both the bundles that A can hold and the bundles that B can hold—just measured from different origins. The points in the Edgeworth box can represent all feasible allocations in this simple economy.

We can depict A's indifference curves in the usual manner, but B's indifference curves take a somewhat different form. To construct them we take a standard diagram for B's indifference curves, turn it upside down, and "overlay" it on the Edgeworth box. This gives us B's indifference curves on the diagram. If we start at A's origin in the lower left-hand corner and move up and to the right, we will be moving to allocations that are more preferred by A. As we move down and to the left we will be moving to allocations that are more preferred by B. (If you rotate your book and look at the diagram, this discussion may seem clearer.)

The Edgeworth box allows us to depict the possible consumption bundles for both consumers—the feasible allocations—and the preferences of both consumers. It thereby gives a complete description of the economically relevant characteristics of the two consumers.

29.2 Trade

Now that we have both sets of preferences and endowments depicted we can begin to analyze the question of how trade takes place. We start at the original endowment of goods, denoted by the point W in Figure 29.1. Consider the indifference curves of A and B that pass through this allocation. The region where A is better off than at her endowment consists of all the bundles above her indifference curve through W. The region where B is better off than at his endowment consists of all the allocations that are above—from his point of view—*his* indifference curve through W. (This is *below* his indifference curve from *our* point of view ... unless you've still got your book upside down.)

Where is the region of the box where A and B are *both* made better off? Clearly it is in the intersection of these two regions. This is the lens-shaped region illustrated in Figure 29.1. Presumably in the course of their negotiations the two people involved will find some mutually advantageous trade—some trade that will move them to some point inside the lens-shaped area such as the point M in Figure 29.1.

The particular movement to M depicted in Figure 29.1 involves person A giving up $|x_A^1 - \omega_A^1|$ units of good 1 and acquiring in exchange $|x_A^2 - \omega_A^2|$ units of good 2. This means that B acquires $|x_B^1 - \omega_B^1|$ units of good 1 and gives up $|x_B^2 - \omega_B^2|$ units of good 2.

There is nothing particularly special about the allocation M. Any allocation inside the lens-shaped region would be possible—for every allocation of goods in this region is an allocation that makes each consumer better off than he or she was at the original endowment. We only need to suppose that the consumers trade to *some* point in this region.

Now we can repeat the same analysis at the point M. We can draw the two indifference curves through M, construct a new lens-shaped "region of mutual advantage," and imagine the traders moving to some new point N in this region. And so it goes ... the trade will continue until there are no more trades that are preferred by both parties. What does such a position look like?

29.3 Pareto Efficient Allocations

The answer is given in Figure 29.2. At the point M in this diagram the set of points above A's indifference curve doesn't intersect the set of points above B's indifference curve. The region where A is made better off is disjoint from the region where B is made better off. This means that any movement that makes one of the parties better off necessarily makes the other party worse off. Thus there are no exchanges that are advantageous for both parties. There are no mutually improving trades at such an allocation.

An allocation such as this is known as a **Pareto efficient** allocation. The idea of Pareto efficiency is a very important concept in economics that arises in various guises.

A Pareto efficient allocation. At a Pareto efficient allocation such as M, each person is on his highest possible indifference curve, given the indifference curve of the other person. The
line connecting such points is known as the contract curve.

Figure
29.2

A Pareto efficient allocation can be described as an allocation where:

1. There is no way to make all the people involved better off; or

2. there is no way to make some individual better off without making someone else worse off; or

3. all of the gains from trade have been exhausted; or

4. there are no mutually advantageous trades to be made, and so on.

Indeed we have mentioned the concept of Pareto efficiency several times already in the context of a single market: we spoke of the Pareto efficient level of output in a single market as being that amount of output where the marginal willingness to buy equaled the marginal willingness to sell. At any level of output where these two numbers differed, there would be a way to make both sides of the market better off by carrying out a trade. In this chapter we will examine more deeply the idea of Pareto efficiency involving many goods and many traders.

Note the following simple geometry of Pareto efficient allocations: the indifference curves of the two agents must be tangent at any Pareto efficient allocation in the interior of the box. It is easy to see why. If the two indifference curves are not tangent at an allocation in the interior of the box, then they must cross. But if they cross, then there must be some mutually advantageous trade—so that point cannot be Pareto efficient. (It is possible to have Pareto efficient allocations on the sides of the box—where one consumer has zero consumption of some good—in which the indifference curves are not tangent. These boundary cases are not important for the current discussion.)

From the tangency condition it is easy to see that there are a lot of Pareto efficient allocations in the Edgeworth box. In fact, given any indifference curve for person A, for example, there is an easy way to find a Pareto efficient allocation. Simply move along A's indifference curve until you find the point that is the best point for B. This will be a Pareto efficient point, and thus both indifference curves must be tangent at this point.

The set of *all* Pareto efficient points in the Edgeworth box is known as the **Pareto set**, or the **contract curve**. The latter name comes from the idea that all "final contracts" for trade must lie on the Pareto set—otherwise they wouldn't be final because there would be some improvement that could be made!

In a typical case the contract curve will stretch from A's origin to B's origin across the Edgeworth box, as shown in Figure 29.2. If we start at A's origin, A has none of either good and B holds everything. This is Pareto efficient since the only way A can be made better off is to take something away from B. As we move up the contract curve A is getting more and more well-off until we finally get to B's origin.

The Pareto set describes all the possible outcomes of mutually advantageous trade from starting anywhere in the box. If we are given the starting point—the initial endowments for each consumer—we can look at the subset of the Pareto set that each consumer prefers to his initial endowment. This is simply the subset of the Pareto set that lies in the lens-shaped region depicted in Figure 29.1. The allocations in this lens-shaped region are the possible outcomes of mutual trade starting from the particular initial endowment depicted in that diagram. But the Pareto set itself doesn't depend on the initial endowment, except insofar as the endowment determines the total amounts of both goods that are available and thereby determines the dimensions of the box.

29.4 Market Trade

The equilibrium of the trading process described above—the set of Pareto efficient allocations—is very important, but it still leaves a lot of ambiguity about where the agents end up. The reason is that the trading process we have described is very general. Essentially we have only assumed that the two parties will move to *some* allocation where they are both made better off.

If we have a *particular* trading process, we will have a more precise description of equilibrium. Let's try to describe a trading process that mimics the outcome of a competitive market.

Suppose that we have a third party who is willing to act as an "auctioneer" for the two agents A and B. The auctioneer chooses a price for good 1 and a price for good 2 and presents these prices to the agents A and B. Each agent then sees how much his or her endowment is worth at the prices (p_1, p_2) and decides how much of each good he or she would want to buy at those prices.

One warning is in order here. If there are really only two people involved in the transaction, then it doesn't make much sense for them to behave in a competitive manner. Instead they would probably attempt to bargain over the terms of trade. One way around this difficulty is to think of the Edgeworth box as depicting the average demands in an economy with only two *types* of consumers, but with many consumers of each type. Another way to deal with this is to point out that the behavior is implausible in the two-person case, but it makes perfect sense in the many-person case, which is what we are really concerned with.

Either way, we know how to analyze the consumer-choice problem in this framework—it is just the standard consumer-choice problem we described in Chapter 5. In Figure 29.3 we illustrate the two demanded bundles of the two agents. (Note that the situation depicted in Figure 29.3 is not an equilibrium configuration since the demand by one agent is not equal to the supply of the other agent.)

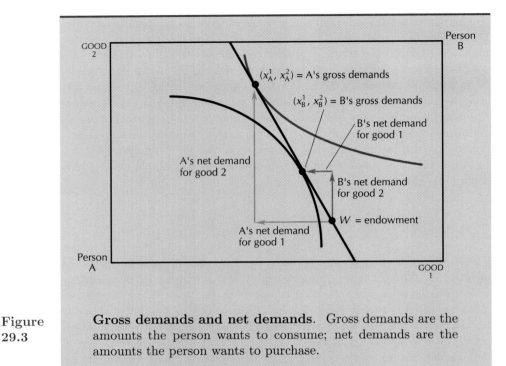

Gross demands and net demands. Gross demands are the amounts the person wants to consume; net demands are the amounts the person wants to purchase.

Figure
29.3

As in Chapter 9 there are two relevant concepts of "demand" in this framework. The **gross demand** of agent A for good 1, say, is the total amount of good 1 that he wants at the going prices. The **net demand** of agent A for good 1 is the difference between this total demand and the initial endowment of good 1 that agent A holds. In the context of general equilibrium analysis, net demands are sometimes called **excess demands**. We will denote the excess demand of agent A for good 1 by e_A^1. By definition, if A's gross demand is x_A^1, and his endowment is ω_A^1, we have

$$e_A^1 = x_A^1 - \omega_A^1.$$

The concept of excess demand is probably more natural, but the concept of gross demand is generally more useful. We will typically use the word "demand" to mean gross demand and specifically say "net demand" or "excess demand" if that is what we mean.

For arbitrary prices (p_1, p_2) there is no guarantee that supply will equal demand—in either sense of demand. In terms of net demand, this means that the amount that A wants to buy (or sell) will not necessarily equal the amount that B wants to sell (or buy). In terms of gross demand, this means that the total amount that the two agents want hold of the goods is not equal to the total amount of that goods available. Indeed, this is true in the example depicted in Figure 29.3. In this example the agents will not be able to complete their desired transactions: the markets will not clear.

We say that in this case the market is in **disequilibrium**. In such a situation, it is natural to suppose that the auctioneer will change the prices of the goods. If there is excess demand for one of the goods, the auctioneer will raise the price of that good, and if there is excess supply for one of the goods, the auctioneer will lower its price.

Suppose that this adjustment process continues until the demand for each of the goods equals the supply. What will the final configuration look like?

The answer is given in Figure 29.4. Here the amount that A wants to buy of good 1 just equals the amount that B wants to sell of good 1, and similarly for good 2. Said another way, the total amount that each person wants to buy of each good at the current prices is equal to the total amount available. We say that the market is in **equilibrium**. More precisely, this is called a **market equilibrium**, a **competitive equilibrium**, or a **Walrasian equilibrium**.[2] Each of these terms refers to the same thing: a set of prices such that each consumer is choosing his or her most-preferred affordable bundle, and all consumers' choices are compatible in the sense that demand equals supply in every market.

We know that if each agent is choosing the best bundle that he can afford, then his marginal rate of substitution between the two goods must be equal to the ratio of the prices. But if all consumers are facing the same prices, then all consumers will have to have the *same* marginal rate of substitution between each of the two goods. In terms of Figure 29.4, an equilibrium has the property that each agent's indifference curve is tangent to his budget line. But since each agent's budget line has the slope $-p_1/p_2$, this means that the two agents' indifference curves must be tangent to each other.

29.5 The Algebra of Equilibrium

If we let $x_A^1(p_1, p_2)$ be agent A's demand function for good 1 and $x_B^1(p_1, p_2)$ be agent B's demand function for good 1, and define the analogous expressions for good 2, we can describe this equilibrium as a set of prices (p_1^*, p_2^*) such that

$$x_A^1(p_1^*, p_2^*) + x_B^1(p_1^*, p_2^*) = \omega_A^1 + \omega_B^1$$

$$x_A^2(p_1^*, p_2^*) + x_B^2(p_1^*, p_2^*) = \omega_A^2 + \omega_B^2.$$

These equations say that in equilibrium the total demand for each good should be equal to the total supply.

[2] Leon Walras (1834–1910) was a French economist at Lausanne who was an early investigator of general equilibrium theory.

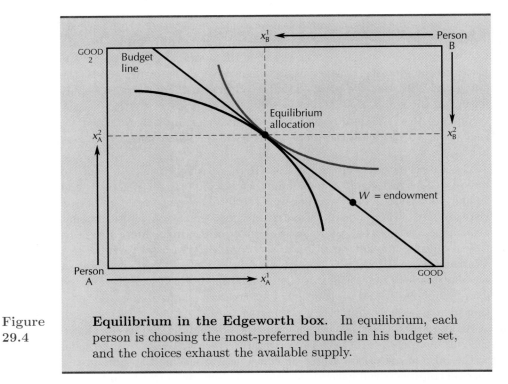

Figure
29.4

Equilibrium in the Edgeworth box. In equilibrium, each person is choosing the most-preferred bundle in his budget set, and the choices exhaust the available supply.

Another way to describe the equilibrium is to rearrange these two equations to get

$$[x_A^1(p_1^*, p_2^*) - \omega_A^1] + [x_B^1(p_1^*, p_2^*) - \omega_B^1] = 0$$
$$[x_A^2(p_1^*, p_2^*) - \omega_A^2] + [x_B^2(p_1^*, p_2^*) - \omega_B^2] = 0.$$

These equations say that the sum of *net demands* of each agent for each good should be zero. Or, in other words, the net amount that A chooses to demand (or supply) must be equal to the net amount that B chooses to supply (or demand).

Yet another formulation of these equilibrium equations comes from the concept of the **aggregate excess demand function**. Let us denote the net demand function for good 1 by agent A by

$$e_A^1(p_1, p_2) = x_A^1(p_1, p_2) - \omega_A^1$$

and define $e_B^1(p_1, p_2)$ in a similar manner.

The function $e_A^1(p_1, p_2)$ measures agent A's **net demand** or his **excess demand**—the difference between what she wants to consume of good 1 and what she initially has of good 1. Now let us add together agent A's net demand for good 1 and agent B's net demand for good 1. We get

$$z_1(p_1, p_2) = e_A^1(p_1, p_2) + e_B^1(p_1, p_2)$$
$$= x_A^1(p_1, p_2) + x_B^1(p_1, p_2) - \omega_A^1 - \omega_B^1,$$

which we call the **aggregate excess demand** for good 1. There is a similar aggregate excess demand for good 2, which we denote by $z_2(p_1, p_2)$.

Then we can describe an equilibrium (p_1^*, p_2^*) by saying that the aggregate excess demand for each good is zero:

$$z_1(p_1^*, p_2^*) = 0$$
$$z_2(p_1^*, p_2^*) = 0.$$

Actually, this definition is stronger than necessary. It turns out that if the aggregate excess demand for good 1 is zero, then the aggregate excess demand for good 2 must necessarily be zero. In order to prove this, it is convenient to first establish a property of the aggregate excess demand function known as **Walras' law**.

29.6 Walras' Law

Using the notation established above, Walras' law states that

$$p_1 z_1(p_1, p_2) + p_2 z_2(p_1, p_2) \equiv 0.$$

That is, *the value of aggregate excess demand is identically zero.* To say that the value of aggregate demand is identically zero means that it is zero for *all* possible choices of prices, not just equilibrium prices.

The proof of this follows from adding up the two agents' budget constraints. Consider first agent A. Since her demand for each good satisfies her budget constraint, we have

$$p_1 x_A^1(p_1, p_2) + p_2 x_A^2(p_1, p_2) \equiv p_1 \omega_A^1 + p_2 \omega_A^2$$

or

$$p_1[x_A^1(p_1, p_2) - \omega_A^1] + p_2[x_A^2(p_1, p_2) - \omega_A^2] \equiv 0$$
$$p_1 e_A^1(p_1, p_2) + p_2 e_A^2(p_1, p_2) \equiv 0.$$

This equation says that the *value of agent A's net demand is zero.* That is, the value of how much A wants to buy of good 1 plus the value of how much she wants to buy of good 2 must equal zero. (Of course the amount that she wants to buy of *one* of the goods must be negative—that is, she intends to sell some of one of the goods to buy more of the other.)

We have a similar equation for agent B:

$$p_1[x_B^1(p_1, p_2) - \omega_B^1] + p_2[x_B^2(p_1, p_2) - \omega_B^2] \equiv 0$$
$$p_1 e_B^1(p_1, p_2) + p_2 e_B^2(p_1, p_2) \equiv 0.$$

Adding the equations for agent A and agent B together and using the definition of aggregate excess demand, $z_1(p_1, p_2)$ and $z_2(p_1, p_2)$, we have

$$p_1[e_A^1(p_1, p_2) + e_B^1(p_1, p_2)] + p_2[e_A^2(p_1, p_2) + e_B^2(p_1, p_2)] \equiv 0$$
$$p_1 z_1(p_1, p_2) + p_2 z_2(p_1, p_2) \equiv 0.$$

Now we can see where Walras' law comes from: since the value of each agent's excess demand equals zero, the value of the sum of the agents' excess demands must equal zero.

We can now demonstrate that if demand equals supply in one market, demand must also equal supply in the other market. Note that Walras' law must hold for all prices, since each agent must satisfy his or her budget constraint for all prices. Since Walras' law holds for all prices, in particular, it holds for a set of prices where the excess demand for good 1 is zero:

$$z_1(p_1^*, p_2^*) = 0.$$

According to Walras' law it must also be true that

$$p_1^* z_1(p_1^*, p_2^*) + p_2^* z_2(p_1^*, p_2^*) = 0.$$

It easily follows from these two equations that if $p_2 > 0$, then we must have

$$z_2(p_1^*, p_2^*) = 0.$$

Thus, as asserted above, if we find a set of prices (p_1^*, p_2^*) where the demand for good 1 equals the supply of good 1, we are guaranteed that the demand for good 2 must equal the supply of good 2. Alternatively, if we find a set of prices where the demand for good 2 equals the supply of good 2, we are guaranteed that market 1 will be in equilibrium.

In general, if there are markets for k goods, then we only need to find a set of prices where $k - 1$ of the markets are in equilibrium. Walras' law then implies that the market for good k will automatically have demand equal to supply.

29.7 Relative Prices

As we've seen above, Walras' law implies that there are only $k - 1$ independent equations in a k-good general equilibrium model: if demand equals supply in $k - 1$ markets, demand must equal supply in the final market. But if there are k goods, there will be k prices to be determined. How can you solve for k prices with only $k - 1$ equations?

The answer is that there are really only $k - 1$ *independent* prices. We saw in Chapter 2 that if we multiplied all prices and income by a positive number t, then the budget set wouldn't change, and thus the demanded bundle wouldn't change either. In the general equilibrium model, each consumer's income is just the value of his or her endowment at the market prices. If we multiply all prices by $t > 0$, we will automatically multiply each consumer's income by t. Thus, if we find some equilibrium set of prices (p_1^*, p_2^*), then (tp_1^*, tp_2^*) are equilibrium prices as well, for any $t > 0$.

This means that we are free to choose one of the prices and set it equal to a constant. In particular it is often convenient to set one of the prices equal to 1 so that all of the other prices can be interpreted as being measured relative to it. As we saw in Chapter 2, such a price is called a **numeraire** price. If we choose the first price as the numeraire price, then it is just like multiplying all prices by the constant $t = 1/p_1$.

The requirement that demand equal supply in every market can only be expected to determine the equilibrium relative prices, since multiplying all prices by a positive number will not change anybody's demand and supply behavior.

EXAMPLE: An Algebraic Example of Equilibrium

The Cobb-Douglas utility function described in Chapter 6 has the form $u_A(x_A^1, x_A^2) = (x_A^1)^a(x_A^2)^{1-a}$ for person A, and a similar form for person B. We saw there that this utility function gave rise to the following demand functions:

$$x_A^1(p_1, p_2, m_A) = a\frac{m_A}{p_1}$$
$$x_A^2(p_1, p_2, m_A) = (1-a)\frac{m_A}{p_2}$$
$$x_B^1(p_1, p_2, m_B) = b\frac{m_B}{p_1}$$
$$x_B^2(p_1, p_2, m_B) = (1-b)\frac{m_B}{p_2},$$

where a and b are the parameters of the two consumers' utility functions.

We know that in equilibrium, the money income of each individual is given by the value of his or her endowment:

$$m_A = p_1\omega_A^1 + p_2\omega_A^2$$
$$m_B = p_1\omega_B^1 + p_2\omega_B^2.$$

Thus the aggregate excess demands for the two goods are

$$z_1(p_1, p_2) = a\frac{m_A}{p_1} + b\frac{m_B}{p_1} - \omega_A^1 - \omega_B^1$$
$$= a\frac{p_1\omega_A^1 + p_2\omega_A^2}{p_1} + b\frac{p_1\omega_B^1 + p_2\omega_B^2}{p_1} - \omega_A^1 - \omega_B^1$$

and

$$z_2(p_1, p_2) = (1-a)\frac{m_A}{p_2} + (1-b)\frac{m_B}{p_2} - \omega_A^2 - \omega_B^2$$
$$= (1-a)\frac{p_1\omega_A^1 + p_2\omega_A^2}{p_2} + (1-b)\frac{p_1\omega_B^1 + p_2\omega_B^2}{p_2} - \omega_A^2 - \omega_B^2.$$

You should verify that these aggregate demand functions satisfy Walras' law.

Let us choose p_2 as the numeraire price, so that these equations become

$$z_1(p_1, 1) = a\frac{p_1\omega_A^1 + \omega_A^2}{p_1} + b\frac{p_1\omega_B^1 + \omega_B^2}{p_1} - \omega_A^1 - \omega_B^1$$

$$z_2(p_1, 1) = (1 - a)(p_1\omega_A^1 + \omega_A^2) + (1 - b)(p_1\omega_B^1 + \omega_B^2) - \omega_A^2 - \omega_B^2.$$

All we've done here is set $p_2 = 1$.

We now have an equation for the excess demand for good 1, $z_1(p_1, 1)$, and an equation for the excess demand for good 2, $z_2(p_1, 1)$, with each equation expressed as a function of the relative price of good 1, p_1. In order to find the *equilibrium* price, we set either of these equations equal to zero and solve for p_1. According to Walras' law, we should get the same equilibrium price, no matter which equation we solve.

The equilibrium price turns out to be

$$p_1^* = \frac{a\omega_A^2 + b\omega_B^2}{(1 - a)\omega_A^1 + (1 - b)\omega_B^1}.$$

(Skeptics may want to insert this value of p_1 into the demand equals supply equations to verify that the equations are satisfied.)

29.8 The Existence of Equilibrium

In the example given above, we had specific equations for each consumer's demand function and we could explicitly solve for the equilibrium prices. But in general, we don't have explicit algebraic formulas for each consumer's demands. We might well ask how do we know that there is *any* set of prices such that demand equals supply in every market? This is known as the question of the **existence of a competitive equilibrium**.

The existence of a competitive equilibrium is important insofar as it serves as a "consistency check" for the various models that we have examined in previous chapters. What use would it be to build up elaborate theories of the workings of a competitive equilibrium if such an equilibrium commonly did not exist?

Early economists noted that in a market with k goods there were $k - 1$ relative prices to be determined, and there were $k - 1$ equilibrium equations stating that demand should equal supply in each market. Since the number of equations equaled the number of unknowns, they asserted that there would be a solution where all of the equations were satisfied.

Economists soon discovered that such arguments were fallacious. Merely counting the number of equations and unknowns is not sufficient to prove that an equilibrium solution will exist. However, there are mathematical tools that can be used to establish the existence of a competitive equilibrium. The crucial assumption turns out to be that the aggregate excess demand function is a **continuous function**. This means, roughly speaking, that small changes in prices should result in only small changes in aggregate demand: a small change in prices should not result in a big jump in the quantity demanded.

Under what conditions will the aggregate demand functions be continuous? Essentially there are two kinds of conditions that will guarantee continuity. One is that each individual's demand function be continuous—that small changes in prices will lead to only small changes in demand. This turns out to require that each consumer have convex preferences, which we discussed in Chapter 3. The other condition is more general. Even if consumers themselves have discontinuous demand behavior, as long as all consumers are small relative to the size of the market, the aggregate demand function will be continuous.

This latter condition is quite nice. After all, the assumption of competitive behavior only makes sense when there are a lot of consumers who are small relative to the size of the market. This is exactly the condition that we need in order to get the aggregate demand functions to be continuous. And continuity is just the ticket to ensure that a competitive equilibrium exists. Thus the very assumptions that make the postulated behavior reasonable will ensure that the equilibrium theory will have content.

29.9 Equilibrium and Efficiency

We have now analyzed market trade in a pure exchange model. This gives us a specific model of trade that we can compare to the general model of trade that we discussed in the beginning of this chapter. One question that might arise about the use of a competitive market is whether this mechanism can really exhaust all of the gains from trade. After we have traded to a competitive equilibrium where demand equals supply in every market, will there be any more trades that people will desire to carry out? This is just another way to ask whether the market equilibrium is Pareto efficient: will the agents desire to make any more trades after they have traded at the competitive prices?

We can see the answer by inspecting Figure 29.4: it turns out that the market equilibrium allocation *is* Pareto efficient. The proof is this: an allocation in the Edgeworth box is Pareto efficient if the set of bundles that A prefers doesn't intersect the set of bundles that B prefers. But at the market equilibrium, the set of bundles preferred by A must lie above her budget set, and the same thing holds for B, where "above" means "above from B's point of view." Thus the two sets of preferred allocations can't intersect. This means that there are no allocations that both agents prefer to the equilibrium allocation, so the equilibrium is Pareto efficient.

29.10 The Algebra of Efficiency

We can also show this algebraically. Suppose that we have a market equilibrium that is *not* Pareto efficient. We will show that this assumption leads to a logical contradiction.

To say that the market equilibrium is not Pareto efficient means that there is some other feasible allocation $(y_A^1, y_A^2, y_B^1, y_B^2)$ such that

$$y_A^1 + y_B^1 = \omega_A^1 + \omega_B^1 \tag{29.1}$$

$$y_A^2 + y_B^2 = \omega_A^2 + \omega_B^2 \tag{29.2}$$

and

$$(y_A^1, y_A^2) \succ_A (x_A^1, x_A^2) \tag{29.3}$$

$$(y_B^1, y_B^2) \succ_B (x_B^1, x_B^2). \tag{29.4}$$

The first two equations say that the y–allocation is feasible, and the next two equations say that it is preferred by each agent to the x–allocation. (The symbols $\succ_A$ and $\succ_B$ refer to the preferences of agents A and B.)

But by hypothesis, we have a market equilibrium where each agent is purchasing the best bundle he or she can afford. If (y_A^1, y_A^2) is better than the bundle that A is choosing, then it must cost more than A can afford, and similarly for B:

$$p_1 y_A^1 + p_2 y_A^2 > p_1 \omega_A^1 + p_2 \omega_A^2$$

$$p_1 y_B^1 + p_2 y_B^2 > p_1 \omega_B^1 + p_2 \omega_B^2.$$

Now add these two equations together to get

$$p_1(y_A^1 + y_B^1) + p_2(y_A^2 + y_B^2) > p_1(\omega_A^1 + \omega_B^1) + p_2(\omega_A^2 + \omega_B^2).$$

Substitute from equations (29.1) and (29.2) to get

$$p_1(\omega_A^1 + \omega_B^1) + p_2(\omega_A^2 + \omega_B^2) > p_1(\omega_A^1 + \omega_B^1) + p_2(\omega_A^2 + \omega_B^2),$$

which is clearly a contradiction, since the left-hand side and the right-hand side are the same.

We derived this contradiction by assuming that the market equilibrium was not Pareto efficient. Therefore, this assumption must be wrong. It follows that all market equilibria are Pareto efficient: a result known as the **First Theorem of Welfare Economics**.

The First Welfare Theorem guarantees that a competitive market will exhaust all of the gains from trade: an equilibrium allocation achieved by a set of competitive markets will necessarily be Pareto efficient. Such an allocation may not have any other desirable properties, but it will necessarily be efficient.

In particular, the First Welfare Theorem says nothing about the distribution of economic benefits. The market equilibrium might not be a "just" allocation—if person A owned everything to begin with, then she would own everything after trade. That would be efficient, but it would probably not be very fair. But, after all, efficiency does count for something, and it is reassuring to know that a simple market mechanism like the one we have described is capable of achieving an efficient allocation.

EXAMPLE: Monopoly in the Edgeworth Box

In order to understand the First Welfare Theorem better, it is useful to consider another resource allocation mechanism that does not lead to efficient outcomes. A nice example of this occurs when one consumer attempts to behave as a monopolist. Suppose now that there is no auctioneer and that instead, agent A is going to quote prices to agent B, and agent B will decide how much he wants to trade at the quoted prices. Suppose further that A knows B's "demand curve" and will attempt to choose the set of prices that makes A as well-off as possible, given the demand behavior of B.

In order to examine the equilibrium in this process, it is appropriate to recall the definition of a consumer's **price offer curve**. The price offer curve, which we discussed in Chapter 6, represents all of the optimal choices of the consumer at different prices. B's offer curve represents the bundles that he will purchase at different prices; that is, it describes B's demand behavior. If we draw a budget line for B, then the point where that budget line intersects his offer curve represents B's optimal consumption.

Thus, if agent A wants to choose the prices to offer to B that make A as well-off as possible, she should find that point on B's offer curve where A has the highest utility. Such a choice is depicted in Figure 29.5.

This optimal choice will be characterized by a tangency condition as usual: A's indifference curve will be tangent to B's offer curve. If B's offer curve cut A's indifference curve, there would be some point on B's offer curve that A preferred—so we couldn't be at the optimal point for A.

Once we have identified this point—denoted by X in Figure 29.5—we just draw a budget line to that point from the endowment. At the prices that generate this budget line, B will choose the bundle X, and A will be as well-off as possible.

Is this allocation Pareto efficient? In general the answer is no. To see this simply note that A's indifference curve will not be tangent to the budget line at X, and therefore A's indifference curve will not be tangent to B's indifference curve. A's indifference curve is tangent to B's *offer curve,*

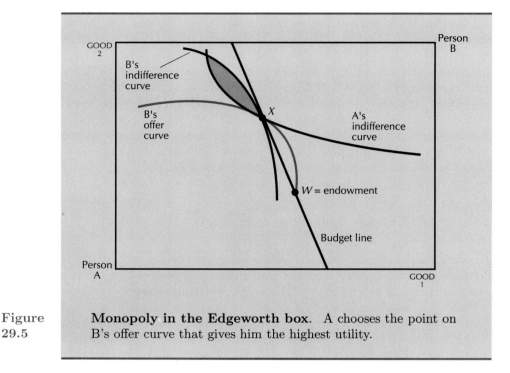

Person
B

GOOD
2

B's
indifference
curve

B's
offer
curve

A's
indifference
curve

X

W = endowment

Budget line

Person
A

GOOD
1

Figure
29.5

Monopoly in the Edgeworth box. A chooses the point on
B's offer curve that gives him the highest utility.

but it cannot then be tangent to B's indifference curve. The monopoly
allocation is Pareto inefficient.

In fact, it is Pareto inefficient in exactly the same way as described in
the discussion of monopoly in Chapter 24. At the margin A would like to
sell more at the equilibrium prices, but she can only do so by lowering the
price at which she sells—and this will lower her income received from all
her inframarginal sales.

We saw in Chapter 24 that a perfectly discriminating monopolist would
end up producing an efficient level of output. Recall that a discriminating
monopolist was one who was able to sell each unit of a good to the person
who was willing to pay the most for that unit. What does a perfectly
discriminating monopolist look like in the Edgeworth box?

The answer is depicted in Figure 29.6. Let us start at the initial endowment, W, and imagine A selling each unit of good 1 to B at a different
price—the price at which B is just indifferent between buying or not buying
that unit of the good. Thus, after A sells the first unit, B will remain on
the same indifference curve through W. Then A sells the second unit of
good 1 to B for the maximum price he is willing to pay. This means that
the allocation moves further to the left, but remains on B's indifference
curve through W. Agent A continues to sell units to B in this manner,
thereby moving up B's indifference curve to find her—A's—most preferred
point, denoted by an X in Figure 29.6.

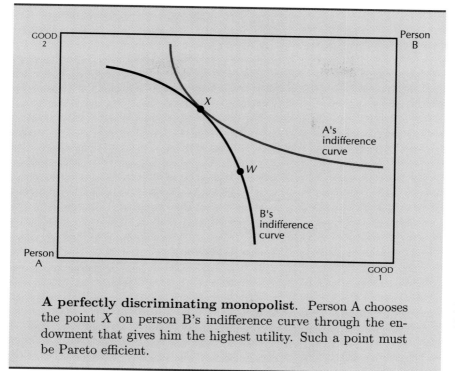

A perfectly discriminating monopolist. Person A chooses the point X on person B's indifference curve through the endowment that gives him the highest utility. Such a point must be Pareto efficient.

Figure
29.6

It is easy to see that such a point must be Pareto efficient. Agent A will be as well-off as possible given B's indifference curve. At such a point, A has managed to extract all of B's consumer's surplus: B is no better off than he was at his endowment.

These two examples provide useful benchmarks with which to think about the First Welfare Theorem. The ordinary monopolist gives an example of a resource allocation mechanism that results in inefficient equilibria, and the discriminating monopolist gives another example of a mechanism that results in efficient equilibria.

29.11 Efficiency and Equilibrium

The First Welfare Theorem says that the equilibrium in a set of competitive markets is Pareto efficient. What about the other way around? Given a Pareto efficient allocation, can we find prices such that it is a market equilibrium? It turns out that the answer is yes, under certain conditions. The argument is illustrated in Figure 29.7.

Let us pick a Pareto efficient allocation. Then we know that the set of allocations that A prefers to her current assignment is disjoint from the set that B prefers. This implies of course that the two indifference curves are

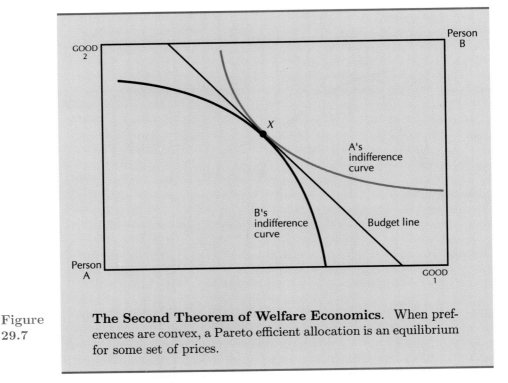

Figure 29.7

The Second Theorem of Welfare Economics. When preferences are convex, a Pareto efficient allocation is an equilibrium for some set of prices.

tangent at the Pareto efficient allocation. So let us draw in the straight line that is their common tangent, as in Figure 29.7.

Suppose that the straight line represents the agents' budget sets. Then if each agent chooses the best bundle on his or her budget set, the resulting equilibrium will be the original Pareto efficient allocation.

Thus the fact that the original allocation is efficient automatically determines the equilibrium prices. The endowments can be any bundles that give rise to the appropriate budget set—that is, bundles that lie somewhere on the constructed budget line.

Can the construction of such a budget line always be carried out? Unfortunately, the answer is no. Figure 29.8 gives an example. Here the illustrated point X is Pareto efficient, but there are no prices at which A and B will want to consume at point X. The most obvious candidate is drawn in the diagram, but the optimal demands of agents A and B don't coincide for that budget. Agent A wants to demand the bundle Y, but agent B wants the bundle X—demand does not equal supply at these prices.

The difference between Figure 29.7 and Figure 29.8 is that the preferences in Figure 29.7 are convex while the ones in Figure 29.8 are not. If the preferences of both agents are convex, then the common tangent will not intersect either indifference curve more than once, and everything will work out fine. This observation gives us the **Second Theorem of Welfare**

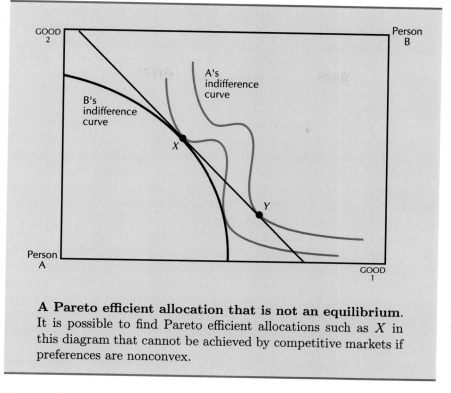

A Pareto efficient allocation that is not an equilibrium.
It is possible to find Pareto efficient allocations such as X in
this diagram that cannot be achieved by competitive markets if
preferences are nonconvex.

Figure
29.8

Economics: if all agents have convex preferences, then there will always
be a set of prices such that each Pareto efficient allocation is a market
equilibrium for an appropriate assignment of endowments.

The proof is essentially the geometric argument we gave above. At a
Pareto efficient allocation, the bundles preferred by agent A and by agent
B must be disjoint. Thus if both agents have convex preferences we can
draw a straight line between the two sets of preferred bundles that separates
one from the other. The slope of this line gives us the relative prices, and
any endowment that puts the two agents on this line will lead to the final
market equilibrium being the original Pareto efficient allocation.

29.12 Implications of the First Welfare Theorem

The two theorems of welfare economics are among the most fundamental
results in economics. We have demonstrated the theorems only in the simple Edgeworth box case, but they are true for much more complex models
with arbitrary numbers of consumers and goods. The welfare theorems
have profound implications for the design of ways to allocate resources.

Let us consider the First Welfare Theorem. This says that any competitive equilibrium is Pareto efficient. There are hardly any explicit assump-

tions in this theorem—it follows almost entirely from the definitions. But there are some implicit assumptions. One major assumption is that agents only care about their own consumption of goods, and not about what other agents consume. If one agent does care about another agent's consumption, we say that there is a **consumption externality**. We shall see that when consumption externalities are present, a competitive equilibrium need not be Pareto efficient.

To take a simple example, suppose that agent A cares about agent B's consumption of cigars. Then there is no particular reason why each agent choosing his or her own consumption bundle at the market prices will result in a Pareto efficient allocation. After each person has purchased the best bundle he or she can afford, there may still be ways to make both of them better off—such as A paying B to smoke fewer cigars. We will discuss externalities in more detail in Chapter 32.

Another important implicit assumption in the First Welfare Theorem is that agents actually behave competitively. If there really were only two agents, as in the Edgeworth box example, then it is unlikely that they would each take price as given. Instead, the agents would probably recognize their market power and would attempt to use their market power to improve their own positions. The concept of competitive equilibrium only makes sense when there are enough agents to ensure that each behaves competitively.

Finally, the First Welfare Theorem is only of interest if a competitive equilibrium actually exists. As we have argued above, this will be the case if the consumers are sufficiently small relative to the size of the market.

Given these provisos, the First Welfare Theorem is a pretty strong result: a private market, with each agent seeking to maximize his or her own utility, will result in an allocation that achieves Pareto efficiency.

The importance of the First Welfare Theorem is that it gives a general mechanism—the competitive market—that we can use to ensure Pareto efficient outcomes. If there are only two agents involved, this doesn't matter very much; it is easy for two people to get together and examine the possibilities for mutual trades. But if there are thousands, or even millions, of people involved there must be some kind of structure imposed on the trading process. The First Welfare Theorem shows that the particular structure of competitive markets has the desirable property of achieving a Pareto efficient allocation.

If we are dealing with a resource problem involving many people, it is important to note that the use of competitive markets economizes on the information that any one agent needs to possess. The only things that a consumer needs to know to make his consumption decisions are the prices of the goods he is considering consuming. Consumers don't need to know anything about how the goods are produced, or who owns what goods, or where the goods come from in a competitive market. If each consumer knows only the prices of the goods, he can determine his demands, and if the market functions well enough to determine the competitive prices, we are guaranteed an efficient outcome. The fact that competitive markets economize on information in this way is a strong argument in favor of their use as a way to allocate resources.

29.13 Implications of the Second Welfare Theorem

The Second Theorem of Welfare Economics asserts that under certain conditions, every Pareto efficient allocation can be achieved as a competitive equilibrium.

What is the meaning of this result? The Second Welfare Theorem implies that the problems of distribution and efficiency can be separated. Whatever Pareto efficient allocation you want can be supported by the market mechanism. The market mechanism is distributionally neutral; whatever your criteria for a good or a just distribution of welfare, you can use competitive markets to achieve it.

Prices play two roles in the market system: an *allocative* role and a *distributive* role. The allocative role of prices is to indicate relative scarcity; the distributive role is to determine how much of different goods different agents can purchase. The Second Welfare Theorem says that these two roles can be separated: we can redistribute endowments of goods to determine how much wealth agents have, and then use prices to indicate relative scarcity.

Policy discussions often become confused on this point. One often hears arguments for intervening in pricing decisions on grounds of distributional equity. However, such intervention is typically misguided. As we have seen above, a convenient way to achieve efficient allocations is for each agent to face the true social costs of his or her actions and to make choices that reflect those costs. Thus in a perfectly competitive market the marginal decision of whether to consume more or less of some good will depend on the price—which measures how everyone else values this good on the margin. The considerations of efficiency are inherently marginal decisions—each person should face the correct marginal tradeoff in making his or her consumption decisions.

The decision about *how much* different agents should consume is a totally different issue. In a competitive market this is determined by the value of the resources that a person has to sell. From the viewpoint of the pure theory, there is no reason why the state can't transfer purchasing power—endowments—among consumers in any way that is seen fit.

In fact the state doesn't need to transfer the physical endowments themselves. All that is necessary is to transfer the purchasing power of the endowment. The state could tax one consumer on the basis of the value of his endowment and transfer this money to another. As long as the taxes are based on the value of the consumer's *endowment* of goods there will be no loss of efficiency. It is only when taxes depend on the *choices* that a consumer makes that inefficiencies result, since in this case, the taxes will affect the consumer's marginal choices.

It is true that a tax on endowments will generally change people's behavior. But, according to the First Welfare Theorem, trade from any initial endowments will result in a Pareto efficient allocation. Thus no matter how one redistributes endowments, the equilibrium allocation as determined by market forces will still be Pareto efficient.

However, there are practical matters involved. It would be easy to have a lump-sum tax on consumers. We could tax all consumers with blue eyes, and redistribute the proceeds to consumers with brown eyes. As long as eye color can't be changed, there would be no loss in efficiency. Or we could tax consumers with high IQs and redistribute the funds to consumers with low IQs. Again, as long as IQ can be measured, there is no efficiency loss in this kind of tax.

But there's the problem. How do we measure people's endowment of goods? For most people, the bulk of their endowment consists of their own labor power. People's endowments of labor consist of the labor that they *could* consider selling, not the amount of labor that they actually end up selling. Taxing labor that people decide to sell to the market is a **distortionary tax**. If the sale of labor is taxed, the labor supply decision of consumers will be distorted—they will likely supply less labor than they would have supplied in the absence of a tax. Taxing the potential value of labor—the endowment of labor—is not distortionary. The potential value of labor is, by definition, something that is not changed by taxation. Taxing the value of the endowment sounds easy until we realize that it involves identifying and taxing something that *might* be sold, rather than taxing something that is sold.

We could *imagine* a mechanism for levying this kind of tax. Suppose that we considered a society where each consumer was required to give the money earned in 10 hours of his labor time to the state each week. This kind of tax would be independent of how much the person actually worked—it would only depend on the endowment of labor, not on how much was actually sold. Such a tax is basically transferring some part of each consumer's endowment of labor time to the state. The state could then use these funds to provide various goods, or it could simply transfer these funds to other agents.

According to the Second Welfare Theorem, this kind of lump-sum taxation would be nondistortionary. Essentially any Pareto efficient allocation could be achieved by such lump-sum redistribution.

However, no one is advocating such a radical restructuring of the tax system. Most people's labor supply decisions are relatively insensitive to variations in the wage rate, so the efficiency loss from taxing labor may not be too large anyway. But the message of the Second Welfare Theorem is important. Prices should be used to reflect scarcity. Lump-sum transfers of wealth should be used to adjust for distributional goals. To a large degree, these two policy decisions can be separated.

People's concern about the distribution of welfare can lead them to advocate various forms of manipulation of prices. It has been argued, for example, that senior citizens should have access to less expensive telephone service, or that small users of electricity should pay lower rates than large users. These are basically attempts to redistribute income through the price system by offering some people lower prices than others.

When you think about it this is a terribly inefficient way to redistribute income. If you want to redistribute income, why don't you simply redistribute income? If you give a person an extra dollar to spend, then he can choose to consume more of any of the goods that he wants to consume—not necessarily just the good being subsidized.

Summary

1. General equilibrium refers to the study of how the economy can adjust to have demand equal supply in all markets at the same time.

2. The Edgeworth box is a graphical tool to examine such a general equilibrium with 2 consumers and 2 goods.

3. A Pareto efficient allocation is one in which there is no feasible reallocation of the goods that would make all consumers at least as well-off and at least one consumer strictly better off.

4. Walras' law states that the value of aggregate excess demand is zero for all prices.

5. A general equilibrium allocation is one in which each agent chooses a most preferred bundle of goods from the set of goods that he or she can afford.

6. Only relative prices are determined in a general equilibrium system.

7. If the demand for each good varies continuously as prices vary, then there will always be some set of prices where demand equals supply in every market; that is, a competitive equilibrium.

8. The First Theorem of Welfare Economics states that a competitive equilibrium is Pareto efficient.

9. The Second Theorem of Welfare Economics states that as long as preferences are convex, then every Pareto efficient allocation can be supported as a competitive equilibrium.

REVIEW QUESTIONS

1. Is it possible to have a Pareto efficient allocation where someone is worse off than he is at an allocation that is not Pareto efficient?

2. Is it possible to have a Pareto efficient allocation where everyone is worse off than they are at an allocation that is not Pareto efficient?

3. True or false? If we know the contract curve, then we know the outcome of any trading.

4. Can some individual be made better off if we are at a Pareto efficient allocation?

5. If the value of excess demand in 8 out of 10 markets is equal to zero, what must be true about the remaining two markets?

APPENDIX

Let us examine the calculus conditions describing Pareto efficient allocations. By definition, a Pareto efficient allocation makes each agent as well-off as possible, given the utility of the other agent. So let us pick $\overline{u}$ as the utility level for agent B, say, and see how we can make agent A as well-off as possible.

The maximization problem is

$$\max_{x_A^1, x_A^2, x_B^1, x_B^2} u_A(x_A^1, x_A^2)$$

$$\text{such that } u_B(x_B^1, x_B^2) = \overline{u}$$

$$x_A^1 + x_B^1 = \omega^1$$

$$x_A^2 + x_B^2 = \omega^2.$$

Here $\omega^1 = \omega_A^1 + \omega_B^1$ is the total amount of good 1 available and $\omega^2 = \omega_A^2 + \omega_B^2$ is the total amount of good 2 available. This maximization problem asks us to find the allocation $(x_A^1, x_A^2, x_B^1, x_B^2)$ that makes person A's utility as large as possible, given a fixed level for person B's utility, and given that the total amount of each good used is equal to the amount available.

We can write the Lagrangian for this problem as

$$L = u_A(x_A^1, x_A^2) - \lambda(u_B(x_B^1, x_B^2) - \overline{u})$$
$$- \mu_1(x_A^1 + x_B^1 - \omega^1) - \mu_2(x_A^2 + x_B^2 - \omega^2).$$

Here λ is the Lagrange multiplier on the utility constraint, and the μ's are the Lagrange multipliers on the resource constraints. When we differentiate with respect to each of the goods, we have four first-order conditions that must hold at the optimal solution:

$$\frac{\partial L}{\partial x_A^1} = \frac{\partial u_A}{\partial x_A^1} - \mu_1 = 0$$

$$\frac{\partial L}{\partial x_A^2} = \frac{\partial u_A}{\partial x_A^2} - \mu_2 = 0$$

$$\frac{\partial L}{\partial x_B^1} = -\lambda \frac{\partial u_B}{\partial x_B^1} - \mu_1 = 0$$

$$\frac{\partial L}{\partial x_B^2} = -\lambda \frac{\partial u_B}{\partial x_B^2} - \mu_2 = 0.$$

If we divide the first equation by the second, and the third equation by the fourth, we have

$$MRS_A = \frac{\partial u_A / \partial x_A^1}{\partial u_A / \partial x_A^2} = \frac{\mu_1}{\mu_2} \tag{29.5}$$

$$MRS_B = \frac{\partial u_B / \partial x_B^1}{\partial u_B / \partial x_B^2} = \frac{\mu_1}{\mu_2}. \tag{29.6}$$

The interpretation of these conditions is given in the text: at a Pareto efficient allocation, the marginal rates of substitution between the two goods must be the same. Otherwise, there would be some trade that would make each consumer better off.

Let us recall the conditions that must hold for optimal choice by consumers. If consumer A is maximizing utility subject to her budget constraint and consumer B is maximizing utility subject to his budget constraint, and both consumers face the same prices for goods 1 and 2, we must have

$$\frac{\partial u_A / \partial x_A^1}{\partial u_A / \partial x_A^2} = \frac{p_1}{p_2} \tag{29.7}$$

$$\frac{\partial u_B / \partial x_B^1}{\partial u_B / \partial x_B^2} = \frac{p_1}{p_2}. \tag{29.8}$$

Note the similarity with the efficiency conditions. The Lagrange multipliers in the efficiency conditions, μ_1 and μ_2, are just like the prices p_1 and p_2 in the consumer choice conditions. In fact the Lagrange multipliers in this kind of problem are sometimes known as **shadow prices** or **efficiency prices**.

Every Pareto efficient allocation has to satisfy conditions like those in equations (29.5) and (29.6). Every competitive equilibrium has to satisfy conditions like those in equations (29.7) and (29.8). The conditions describing Pareto efficiency and the conditions describing individual maximization in a market environment are virtually the same.

CHAPTER **30**

PRODUCTION

In the last chapter we described a general equilibrium model of a pure exchange economy and discussed issues of resource allocation when a fixed amount of each good was available. In this chapter we want to describe how production fits into the general equilibrium framework. When production is possible, the amounts of the goods are not fixed but will respond to market prices.

If you thought the two-consumer two-good assumption was a restrictive framework in which to examine trade, imagine what production is going to look like! The minimal set of players that we can have to make an interesting problem is one consumer, one firm, and two goods. The traditional name for this economic model is the **Robinson Crusoe economy**, after Defoe's shipwrecked hero.

30.1 The Robinson Crusoe Economy

In this economy Robinson Crusoe plays a dual role: he is both a consumer and a producer. Robinson can spend his time loafing on the beach thereby consuming leisure, or he can spend time gathering coconuts. The more coconuts he gathers the more he has to eat, but the less time he has to improve his tan.

Robinson's preferences for coconuts and leisure are depicted in Figure 30.1. They are just like the preferences for leisure and consumption depicted in Chapter 9, except we are measuring labor on the horizontal axis rather than leisure. So far nothing new has been added.

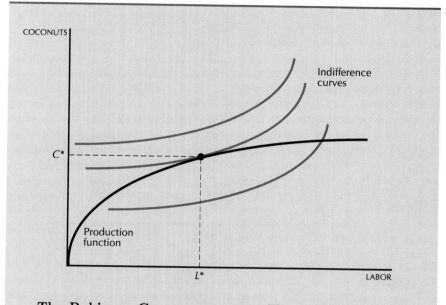

The Robinson Crusoe economy. The indifference curves depict Robinson's preferences for coconuts and leisure. The production function depicts the technological relationship between the amount he works and the amount of coconuts he produces.

Figure
30.1

Now let's draw in the **production function**, the function that illustrates the relationship between how much Robinson works and how many coconuts he gets. This will typically have the shape depicted in Figure 30.1. The more Robinson works, the more coconuts he will get; but, due to diminishing returns to labor, the marginal product of his labor declines: the number of extra coconuts that he gets from an extra hour's labor decreases as the hours of labor increase.

How much does Robinson work and how much does he consume? To answer these questions, look for the highest indifference curve that just touches the production set. This will give the most-preferred combination of labor and consumption that Robinson can get, given the technology for gathering coconuts that he is using.

At this point, the slope of the indifference curve must equal the slope of the production function by the standard argument: if they crossed, there would be some other feasible point that was preferred. This means that the marginal product of an extra hour of labor must equal the marginal rate of substitution between leisure and coconuts. If the marginal product were greater than the marginal rate of substitution, it would pay for Robinson to give up a little leisure in order to get the extra coconuts. If the marginal product were less than the marginal rate of substitution, it would pay for Robinson to work a little less.

30.2 Crusoe, Inc.

So far this story is only a slight extension of models we have already seen. But now let's add a new feature. Suppose that Robinson is tired of simultaneously being a producer and consumer and that he decides to alternate roles. One day he will behave entirely as a producer, and the next day he will behave entirely as a consumer. In order to coordinate these activities, he decides to set up a labor market and a coconut market.

He also sets up a firm, Crusoe, Inc., and becomes its sole shareholder. The firm is going to look at the prices for labor and coconuts and decide how much labor to hire and how many coconuts to produce, guided by the principle of profit maximization. Robinson, in his role as a worker, is going to collect income from working at the firm; in his role as shareholder in the firm he will collect profits; and, in his role as consumer he will decide how much to purchase of the firm's output. (No doubt this sounds peculiar, but there really isn't that much else to do on a desert island.)

In order to keep track of his transactions, Robinson invents a currency he calls "dollars," and he chooses, somewhat arbitrarily, to set the price of coconuts at one dollar apiece. Thus coconuts are the numeraire good for this economy; as we've seen in Chapter 2, a numeraire good is one whose price has been set to one. Since the price of coconuts is normalized at one, we have only to determine the wage rate. What should his wage rate be in order to make this market work?

We're going to think about this problem first from the viewpoint of Crusoe, Inc., and then from the viewpoint of Robinson, the consumer. The discussion is a little schizophrenic at times, but that's what you have to put up with if you want to have an economy with only one person. We're going to look at the economy after it has been running along for some time, and everything is in equilibrium. In equilibrium, the demand for coconuts will equal the supply of coconuts and the demand for labor will equal the supply of labor. Both Crusoe, Inc. and Robinson the consumer will be making optimal choices given the constraints they face.

30.3 The Firm

Each evening, Crusoe, Inc. decides how much labor it wants to hire the next day, and how many coconuts it wants to produce. Given a price of coconuts of 1 and a wage rate of labor of w, we can solve the firm's profit-maximization problem in Figure 30.2. We first consider all combinations of coconuts and labor that yield a constant level of profits, π. This means that

$$\pi = C - wL.$$

Solving for C, we have

$$C = \pi + wL.$$

Just as in Chapter 19, this formula describes the isoprofit lines—all combinations of labor and coconuts that yield profits of π. Crusoe, Inc. will choose a point where the profits are maximized. As usual, this implies a tangency condition: the slope of the production function—the marginal product of labor--must equal w, as illustrated in Figure 30.2.

Profit maximization. Crusoe, Inc. chooses a production plan that maximizes profits. At the optimal point the production function must be tangent to an isoprofit line.

Figure 30.2

Thus the vertical intercept of the isoprofit line measures the maximal level of profits measured in units of coconuts: if Robinson generates π^* dollars of profit, this money can buy π^* coconuts, since the price of coconuts has been chosen to be 1. There we have it. Crusoe, Inc. has done its job. Given the wage w, it has determined how much labor it wants to hire, how many coconuts it wants to produce, and what profits it will generate by following this plan. So Crusoe, Inc. declares a stock dividend of π^* dollars and mails it off to its sole shareholder, Robinson.

30.4 Robinson's Problem

The next day Robinson wakes up and receives his dividend of π^* dollars. While eating his coconut breakfast, he contemplates how much he wants to work and consume. He may consider just consuming his endowment— spend his profits on π^* coconuts and consume his endowment of leisure. But listening to his stomach growl is not so pleasant, and it might make sense to work for a few hours instead. So Robinson trudges down to Crusoe, Inc. and starts to gather coconuts, just as he has done every other day.

We can describe Robinson's labor-consumption choice using standard indifference curve analysis. Plotting labor on the horizontal axis and coconuts on the vertical axis, we can draw in an indifference curve as illustrated in Figure 30.3.

Since labor is a bad, by assumption, and coconuts are a good, the indifference curve has a positive slope as shown in the diagram. If we indicate the maximum amount of labor by $\overline{L}$, then the distance from $\overline{L}$ to the chosen supply of labor gives Robinson's demand for leisure. This is just like the supply of labor model examined in Chapter 9, except we have reversed the origin on the horizontal axis.

Robinson's budget line is also illustrated in Figure 30.3. It has a slope of w and passes through his endowment point $(\pi^*, 0)$. (Robinson has a zero endowment of labor and a π^* endowment of coconuts since that would be his bundle if he engaged in no market transactions.) Given the wage rate, Robinson chooses optimally how much he wants to work and how many coconuts he wants to consume. At his optimal consumption, the marginal rate of substitution between consumption and leisure must equal the wage rate, just as in a standard consumer choice problem.

30.5 Putting Them Together

Now we superimpose Figures 30.2 and 30.3 to get Figure 30.4. Look at what has happened! Robinson's bizarre behavior has worked out all right after all. He ends up consuming at exactly the same point as he would have if he had made all the decisions at once. Using the market system

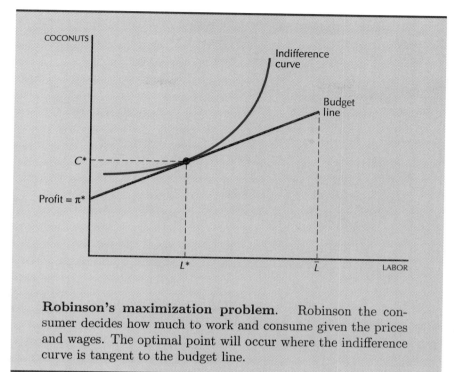

Robinson's maximization problem. Robinson the consumer decides how much to work and consume given the prices and wages. The optimal point will occur where the indifference curve is tangent to the budget line.

Figure
30.3

results in the same outcome as choosing the consumption and production plans directly.

Since the marginal rate of substitution between leisure and consumption equals the wage, and the marginal product of labor equals the wage, we are assured that the marginal rate of substitution between labor and consumption equals the marginal product—that is, that the slopes of the indifference curve and the production set are the same.

In the case of a one-person economy, using the market is pretty silly. Why should Robinson bother to break up his decision into two pieces? But in an economy with many people, breaking up decisions no longer seems so odd. If there are many firms, then questioning each person about how much they want of each good is simply impractical. In a market economy the firms simply have to look at the prices of goods in order to make their production decisions. For the prices of goods measure how much the consumers value *extra* units of consumption. And the decision that the firms face, for the most part, is whether they should produce more or less output.

The market prices reflect the marginal values of the goods that the firms use as inputs and outputs. If firms use the change in profits as a guide to production, where the profits are measured at market prices, then their decisions will reflect the marginal values that consumers place on the goods.

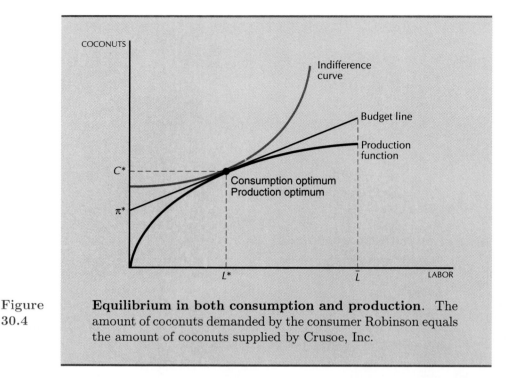

Figure
30.4

Equilibrium in both consumption and production. The amount of coconuts demanded by the consumer Robinson equals the amount of coconuts supplied by Crusoe, Inc.

30.6 Different Technologies

In the above discussion we have assumed that the technology available to Robinson exhibited diminishing returns to labor. Since labor was the only input to production, this was equivalent to decreasing returns to scale. (This is not necessarily true if there is more than one input!)

It is useful to consider some other possibilities. Suppose, for example, that the technology exhibited constant returns to scale. Recall that constant returns to scale means that using twice as much of all inputs produces twice as much output. In the case of a one-input production function, this means that the production function must be a straight line through the origin as depicted in Figure 30.5.

Since the technology has constant returns to scale, the argument in Chapter 19 implies that the only reasonable operating position for a competitive firm is at zero profits. This is because if the profits were ever greater than zero, it would pay for the firm to expand output indefinitely, and if profits were ever less than zero, it would pay the firm to produce zero output.

Thus Robinson's endowment involves zero profits and $\overline{L}$, his initial endowment of labor time. His budget set coincides with the production set, and the story is much the same as before.

The situation is somewhat different with an increasing returns to scale

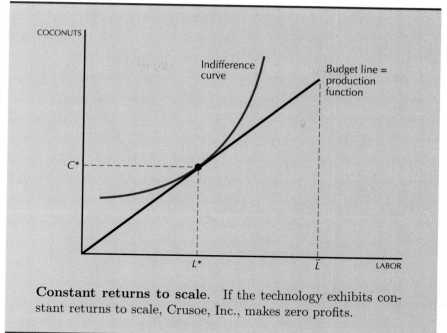

COCONUTS

Indifference
curve

Budget line =
production
function

C^*

L^* $\bar{L}$ LABOR

Constant returns to scale. If the technology exhibits constant returns to scale, Crusoe, Inc., makes zero profits.

Figure
30.5

technology, as depicted in Figure 30.6. There is no difficulty in this simple example in exhibiting the optimal choice of consumption and leisure for Robinson. The indifference curve will be tangent to the production set as usual. The problem arises in trying to support this point as a profit-maximizing point. For if the firm were faced with the prices given by Robinson's marginal rate of substitution, it would want to produce more output than Robinson would demand.

If the firm exhibits increasing returns to scale at the optimal choice, then the average costs of production will exceed the marginal costs of production—and that means that the firm will be making negative profits. The goal of profit maximization would lead the firm to want to increase its output—but this would be incompatible with the demands for output and the supplies of inputs from the consumers. In the case depicted, there is *no* price at which the utility-maximizing demand by the consumer will equal the profit-maximizing supply from the firm.

Increasing returns to scale is an example of a **nonconvexity**. In this case the production set—the set of coconuts and labor that are feasible for the economy—is not a convex set. Thus the common tangent to the indifference curve and the production function at the point (L^*, C^*) in Figure 30.6 will not separate the preferred points from the feasible points as it does in Figure 30.4.

Nonconvexities such as this pose grave difficulties for the functioning of competitive markets. In a competitive market consumers and firms look

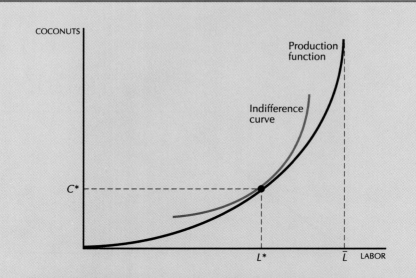

Figure
30.6

Increasing returns to scale. The production set exhibits increasing returns to scale and the Pareto efficient allocation cannot be achieved by a competitive market.

at just one set of numbers—the market prices—to determine their consumption and production decisions. If the technology and the preferences are convex, then the only things that the economic agents need to know to make efficient decisions are the relationship between the prices and the marginal rates of substitution near the points where the economy is currently producing: the prices tell the agents everything that is necessary in order to determine an efficient allocation of resources.

But if the technology and/or the preferences are nonconvex, then the prices do not convey all the information necessary in order to choose an efficient allocation. Information about the slopes of the production function and indifference curves far away from the current operating position is also necessary.

However, these observations apply only when the returns to scale are large relative to the size of the market. Small regions of increasing returns to scale do not pose undue difficulties for a competitive market.

30.7 Production and the First Welfare Theorem

Recall that in the case of a pure exchange economy, a competitive equilibrium is Pareto efficient. This fact is known as the First Theorem of Welfare Economics. Does the same result hold in an economy with production? The diagrammatic approach used above is not adequate to answer this question, but a generalization of the algebraic argument we provided in Chapter 29 does nicely. It turns out that the answer is yes: if all firms act as competitive profit maximizers, then a competitive equilibrium will be Pareto efficient.

This result has the usual caveats. First, it has nothing to do with distribution. Profit maximization only ensures efficiency, not justice! Second, this result only makes sense when a competitive equilibrium actually exists. In particular, this will rule out large areas of increasing returns to scale. Third, the theorem implicitly assumes that the choices of any one firm do not affect the production possibilities of other firms. That is, it rules out the possibility of **production externalities**. Similarly, the theorem requires that firms' production decisions do not directly affect the consumption possibilities of consumers; that is, that there are no **consumption externalities**. More precise definitions of externalities will be given in Chapter 32, where we will examine their effect on efficient allocations in more detail.

30.8 Production and the Second Welfare Theorem

In the case of a pure exchange economy, every Pareto efficient allocation is a possible competitive equilibrium, as long as consumers exhibit convex preferences. In the case of an economy involving production, the same result is true, but now we require not only that consumers' preferences are convex, but also that firms' production sets are convex. As discussed above, this requirement effectively rules out the possibility of increasing returns to scale: if firms have increasing returns to scale at the equilibrium level of production, they would want to produce more output at the competitive prices.

However, with constant or decreasing returns to scale, the Second Welfare Theorem works fine. Any Pareto efficient allocation can be achieved through the use of competitive markets. Of course in general it will be necessary to redistribute endowments among the consumers to support different Pareto efficient allocations. In particular, both the income from endowments of labor and ownership shares of the firm will have to be redistributed. As indicated in the last chapter, there may be significant practical difficulties involved with this sort of redistribution.

30.9 Production Possibilities

We have now seen how production and consumption decisions can be made in a one-input, one-output economy. In this section we want to explore how this model can be generalized to an economy with several inputs and outputs. Although we will deal only with the two-good case, the concepts will generalize naturally to many goods.

So let us suppose that there is some other good that Robinson might produce—say fish. He can devote his time to gathering coconuts or to fishing. In Figure 30.7 we have depicted the various combinations of coconuts and fish that Robinson can produce from devoting different amounts of time to each activity. This set is known as a **production possibilities set**. The boundary of the production possibilities set is called the **production possibilities frontier**. This should be contrasted with the production function discussed earlier that depicts the relationship between the input good and the output good; the production possibilities set depicts only the set of *output* goods that is feasible. (In more advanced treatments, both inputs and outputs can be considered part of the production possibilities set, but these treatments cannot easily be handled with two-dimensional diagrams.)

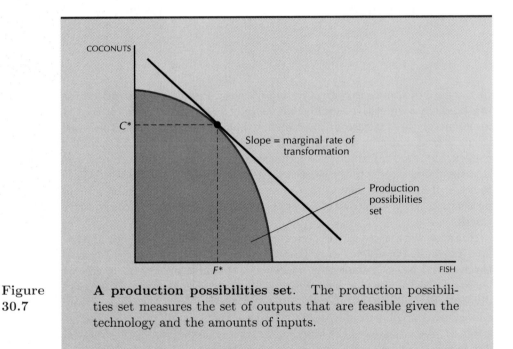

Figure 30.7

A production possibilities set. The production possibilities set measures the set of outputs that are feasible given the technology and the amounts of inputs.

The shape of the production possibilities set will depend on the nature of the underlying technologies. If the technologies for producing coconuts and fish exhibit constant returns to scale the production possibilities set will take an especially simple form. Since by assumption there is only one input to production—Robinson's labor—the production functions for fish and coconuts will be simply *linear* functions of labor.

For example, suppose that Robinson can produce 10 pounds of fish per hour or 20 pounds of coconuts per hour. Then if he devotes L_f hours to fish production and L_c hours to coconut production, he will produce $10L_f$ pounds of fish and $20L_c$ pounds of coconuts. Suppose that Robinson decides to work 10 hours a day. Then the production possibilities set will consist of all combinations of coconuts, C, and fish, F, such that

$$F = 10L_f$$
$$C = 20L_c$$
$$L_c + L_f = 10.$$

The first two equations measure the production relationships, and the third measures the resource constraint. To determine the production possibilities frontier solve the first two equations for L_f and L_c to get

$$L_f = \frac{F}{10}$$
$$L_c = \frac{C}{20}.$$

Now add these two equations together, and use the fact that $L_f + L_c = 10$ to find

$$\frac{F}{10} + \frac{C}{20} = 10.$$

This equation gives us all the combinations of fish and coconuts that Robinson can produce if he works 10 hours a day. It is depicted in Figure 30.8A.

The slope of this production possibilities set measures the **marginal rate of transformation**—how much of one good Robinson can get if he decides to sacrifice some of the other good. If Robinson gives up enough labor to produce 1 less pound of fish, he will be able to get 2 more pounds of coconuts. Think about it: if Robinson works one hour less on fish production, he will get 10 pounds less fish. But then if he devotes that time to coconuts, he will get 20 pounds more coconuts. The tradeoff is at a ratio of 2 to 1.

30.10 Comparative Advantage

The construction of the production possibilities set given above was quite simple since there was only one way to produce fish and one way to produce coconuts. What if there is more than one way to produce each good? Suppose that we add another worker to our island economy, who has different skills in producing fish and coconuts.

To be specific, let us call the new worker Friday, and suppose that he can produce 20 pounds of fish per hour, or 10 pounds of coconuts per hour.

Thus if Friday works for 10 hours, his production possibilities set will be determined by

$$F = 20L_f$$
$$C = 10L_c$$
$$L_c + L_f = 10.$$

Doing the same sort of calculations as we did for Robinson, Friday's production possibilities set is given by

$$\frac{F}{20} + \frac{C}{10} = 10.$$

This is depicted in Figure 30.8B. Note that the marginal rate of transformation between coconuts and fish for Friday is $\Delta C / \Delta F = -1/2$, whereas for Robinson the marginal rate of transformation is -2. For every pound of coconuts that Friday gives up, he can get two pounds of fish; for every pound of fish that Robinson gives up, he can get two pounds of coconuts. In this circumstance we say that Friday has a **comparative advantage** in fish production, and Robinson has a comparative advantage in coconut production. In Figure 30.8 we have depicted three production possibilities sets: Panel A shows Robinson's, panel B shows Friday's, and panel C depicts the joint production possibilities set—how much of each good could be produced in total by both people.

Figure 30.8

Joint production possibilities. Robinson's and Friday's production possibilities sets and the joint production possibilities set.

The joint production possibilities set combines the best of both workers. If both workers are used entirely to produce coconuts, we will get 300 coconuts—100 from Friday and 200 from Robinson. If we want to get more fish, it makes sense to shift the person who is most productive at fish—Friday—out of coconut production and into fish production. For each pound of coconuts that Friday doesn't produce we get 2 pounds of fish; thus the slope of the joint production possibilities set is $-1/2$—which is exactly Friday's marginal rate of transformation.

When Friday is producing 200 pounds of fish, he is fully occupied. If we want even more fish, we have to switch to using Robinson. From this point on the joint production possibilities set will have a slope of -2, since we will be operating along Robinson's production possibilities set. Finally, if we want to produce as much fish as possible, both Robinson and Friday concentrate on fish production and we get 300 pounds of fish, 200 from Friday, and 100 from Robinson.

Since the workers each have a comparative advantage in different goods, the joint production possibilities set will have a "kink," as shown in Figure 30.8. There is only one kink in this example since there are just two different ways to produce output—Crusoe's way and Friday's way. If there are many different ways to produce output, the production possibilities set will have the more typical "rounded" structure, as depicted in Figure 30.7.

30.11 Pareto Efficiency

In the last two sections we saw how to construct the production possibilities set, the set that describes the feasible consumption bundles for the economy as a whole. Here we consider Pareto efficient ways to choose among the feasible consumption bundles.

We will indicate aggregate consumption bundles by (X^1, X^2). This indicates that there are X^1 units of good 1 and X^2 units of good 2 that are available for consumption. In the Crusoe/Friday economy, the two goods are coconuts and fish, but we will use the (X^1, X^2) notation in order to emphasize the similarities with the analysis in Chapter 29. Once we know the total amount of each good, we can draw an Edgeworth box as in Figure 30.9.

Given (X^1, X^2), the set of Pareto efficient consumption bundles will be the same sort as those examined in the last chapter: the Pareto efficient consumption levels will lie along the Pareto set—the line of mutual tangencies of the indifference curves, as illustrated in Figure 30.9. These are the allocations in which each consumer's marginal rate of substitution—the rate at which he or she is just willing to trade—equals that of the other.

These allocations are Pareto efficient as far as the consumption decisions are concerned. If people can simply trade one good for another, the Pareto set describes the set of bundles that exhausts the gains from trade. But in an economy with production, there is another way to "exchange" one good for another—namely, to produce less of one good and more of another.

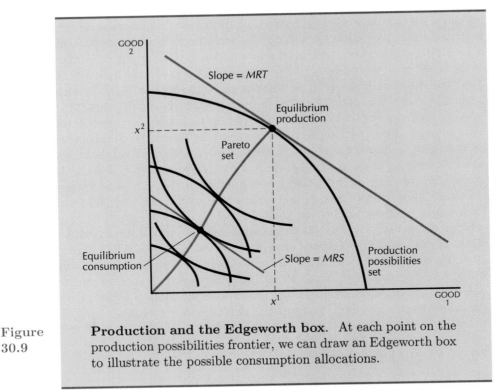

Figure
30.9
Production and the Edgeworth box. At each point on the production possibilities frontier, we can draw an Edgeworth box to illustrate the possible consumption allocations.

The Pareto set describes the set of Pareto efficient bundles *given* the amounts of goods 1 and 2 available, but in an economy with production those amounts can themselves be chosen out of the production possibilities set. Which choices from the production possibilities set will be Pareto efficient choices?

Let us think about the logic underlying the marginal rate of substitution condition. We argued that in a Pareto efficient allocation, the MRS of consumer A had to be equal to the MRS of consumer B: the rate at which consumer A would just be willing to trade one good for the other should be equal to the rate at which consumer B would just be willing to trade one good for the other. If this were not true, then there would be some trade that would make both consumers better off.

Recall that the marginal rate of transformation (MRT) measures the rate at which one good can be "transformed" into the other. Of course, one good really isn't being literally *transformed* into the other. Rather the factors of production are being moved around so as to produce less of one good and more of the other.

Suppose that the economy were operating at a position where the marginal rate of substitution of one of the consumers was not equal to the marginal rate of transformation between the two goods. Then such a position cannot be Pareto efficient. Why? Because at this point, the rate at which the consumer is willing to trade good 1 for good 2 is different from the rate at which good 1 can be transformed into good 2—there is a way to make the consumer better off by rearranging the pattern of production.

Suppose, for example, that the consumer's MRS is 1; the consumer is just willing to substitute good 1 for good 2 on a one-to-one basis. Suppose that the MRT is 2, which means that giving up one unit of good 1 will allow society to produce two units of good 2. Then clearly it makes sense to reduce the production of good 1 by one unit; this will generate two extra units of good 2. Since the consumer was just indifferent between giving up one unit of good 1 and getting one unit of the other good in exchange, he or she will now certainly be better off by getting *two* extra units of good 2.

The same argument can be made whenever one of the consumers has a MRS that is different from the MRT—there will always be a rearrangement of consumption and production that will make that consumer better off. We have already seen that for Pareto efficiency each consumer's MRS should be the same, and the argument given above implies that each consumer's MRS should in fact be equal to the MRT.

Figure 30.9 illustrates a Pareto efficient allocation. The MRSs of each consumer are the same, since their indifference curves are tangent in the Edgeworth box. And each consumer's MRS is equal to the MRT—the slope of the production possibilities set.

30.12 Castaways, Inc.

In the last section we derived the necessary conditions for Pareto efficiency: the MRS of each consumer must equal the MRT. Any way of distributing resources that results in Pareto efficiency must satisfy this condition. Earlier in this chapter, we claimed that a competitive economy with profit-maximizing firms and utility-maximizing consumers would result in a Pareto efficient allocation. In this section we explore the details of how this works.

Our economy now contains two individuals, Robinson and Friday. There are four goods: two factors of production (Robinson's labor and Friday's labor) and two output goods (coconuts and fish). Let us suppose that Robinson and Friday are both shareholders of the firm, which we will now refer to as Castaways, Inc. Of course, they are also the sole employees and customers, but as usual we shall examine each role in turn, and not allow the participants to see the wider picture. After all, the object of the analysis is to understand how a *decentralized* resource allocation system works—one in which each person only has to determine his or her own decisions, without regard for the functioning of the economy as a whole.

Start first with Castaways, Inc., and consider the profit-maximization problem. Castaways, Inc., produces two outputs, coconuts (C) and fish (F), and it uses two kinds of labor, Crusoe's labor (L_C) and Friday's labor

(L_F). Given the price of coconuts (p_C), the price of fish (p_F), and the wage rates of Crusoe and Friday (w_C and w_F), the profit-maximization problem is

$$\max_{C,F,L_F,L_C} p_C C + p_F F - w_C L_C - w_F L_F$$

subject to the technological constraints described by the production possibilities set.

Let us suppose that the firm finds it optimal in equilibrium to hire L_F^* units of Friday's labor and L_C^* units of Crusoe's labor. The question we want to focus on here is how profit maximization determines the pattern of output to produce. Let $L^* = w_C L_C^* + w_F L_F^*$ represent the labor costs of production, and write the profits of the firm, π, as

$$\pi = p_C C + p_F F - L^*.$$

Rearranging this equation, we have

$$C = \frac{\pi + L^*}{p_C} - \frac{p_F F}{p_C}.$$

This equation describes the **isoprofit lines** of the firm, as depicted in Figure 30.10, with a slope of $-p_F/p_C$ and a vertical intercept of $(\pi + L^*)/p_C$. Since L^* is fixed by assumption, higher profits will be associated with isoprofit lines that have higher vertical intercepts.

If the firm wants to maximize its profits, it will choose a point on the production possibilities set such that the isoprofit line through that point has the highest possible vertical intercept. By this stage, it should be clear that this implies that the isoprofit line must be tangent to the production possibilities set; that is, that the slope of the production possibilities set (the MRT) should be equal to the slope of the isoprofit line, $-p_F/p_C$:

$$\text{MRT} = -\frac{p_F}{p_C}.$$

We've described this profit-maximization problem in the case of one firm, but it holds for an arbitrary number of firms: each firm that chooses the most profitable way to produce coconuts and fish will operate where the marginal rate of transformation between any two goods equals the price ratio between those two goods. This holds true even if the firms have quite different production possibilities sets, as long as they face the same prices for the two goods.

This means that in equilibrium the prices of the two goods will measure the marginal rate of transformation—the opportunity cost of one good in terms of the other. If you want more coconuts, you will have to give up some fish. How much fish? Just look at the price ratio of fish to coconuts: the ratio of these economic variables tells us what the technological tradeoff must be.

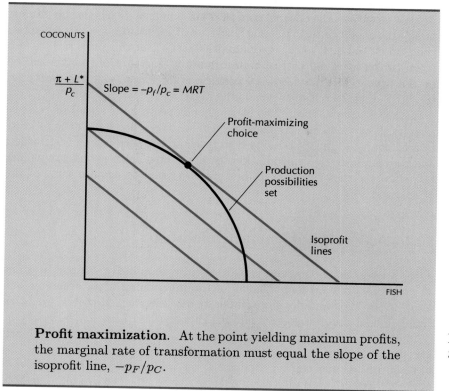

Profit maximization. At the point yielding maximum profits, the marginal rate of transformation must equal the slope of the isoprofit line, $-p_F/p_C$.

Figure
30.10

30.13 Robinson and Friday as Consumers

We've seen how Castaways, Inc., determines its profit-maximizing production plan. In order to do this, it must hire some labor and it may generate some profits. When it hires labor, it pays wages to the labor; when it makes profits, it pays dividends to its shareholders. Either way the money made by Castaways, Inc., gets paid back to Robinson and Friday, either in the form of wages or profits.

Since the firm pays out all of its receipts to its workers and its shareholders, this means that they must necessarily have enough income to purchase its output. This is just a variation on Walras' law discussed in Chapter 29: people get their income from selling their endowments, so they must always have enough income to purchase those endowments. Here people get income from selling their endowments and also receive profits from the firm. But since money never disappears from or is added to the system, people will always have exactly enough money to purchase what is produced.

What do the consumers do with the money from the firm? As usual, they use the money to purchase consumption goods. Each person chooses the best bundle of goods that he can afford at the prices p_F and p_C. As we've seen earlier, the optimal consumption bundle for each consumer must satisfy the condition that the marginal rate of substitution between the two goods must be equal to the common price ratio. But this price ratio is also equal to the marginal rate of transformation, due to profit maximization by the firm. Thus the necessary conditions for Pareto efficiency are met: the MRS of each consumer equals the MRT.

In this economy, the prices of the goods serve as a signal of relative scarcity. They indicate the technological scarcity—how much the production of one good must be reduced in order to produce more of the other; and they indicate the consumption scarcity—how much people are willing to reduce their consumption of one good in order to acquire some of the other good.

30.14 Decentralized Resource Allocation

The Crusoe-Friday economy is a drastically simplified picture. In order to make a start on a larger model of the functioning of an economy, one needs to use substantially more elaborate mathematics. However, even this simple model contains some useful insights.

The most important of these is the relationship between individuals' *private* goals of utility maximization and the *social* goals of efficient use of resources. Under certain conditions, the individuals' pursuit of private goals will result in an allocation that is Pareto efficient overall. Furthermore, any Pareto efficient allocation can be supported as an outcome of a competitive market, if initial endowments—including the ownership of firms—can be suitably redistributed.

The great virtue of a competitive market is that each individual and each firm only has to worry about its own maximization problem. The only facts that need to be communicated among the firms and the consumers are the prices of the goods. Given these signals of relative scarcity, consumers and firms have enough information to make decisions that achieve an efficient allocation of resources. In this sense, the social problems involved in efficiently utilizing resources can be decentralized, and solved at the individual level.

Each individual can solve his or her own problem of what to consume. The firms face the prices of the goods the consumers consume and decide how much to produce of each of them. In making this decision, they are guided by profit signals. In this context, profits serve as exactly the right guide. To say that a production plan is profitable is to say that people are willing to pay more for some good than it costs to produce it—so it is natural to expand the production of such goods. If all firms pursue a competitive profit-maximizing policy, and all consumers choose consumption bundles to maximize their own utility, then resulting competitive equilibrium must be a Pareto efficient allocation.

Summary

1. The general equilibrium framework can be extended by allowing competitive, profit-maximizing firms to produce goods destined for exchange in the economy.

2. Under certain conditions there exists a set of prices for all of the input and output goods in the economy such that the profit-maximizing actions of firms along with the utility-maximizing behavior of individuals results in the demand for each good equaling the supply in all markets—that is, a competitive equilibrium exists.

3. Under certain conditions the resulting competitive equilibrium will be Pareto efficient: the First Welfare Theorem holds in an economy with production.

4. With the addition of convex production sets, the Second Welfare Theorem also holds in the case of production.

5. When goods are being produced as efficiently as possible, the marginal rate of transformation between two goods indicates the number of units of one good the economy must give up to obtain additional units of the other good.

6. Pareto efficiency requires that each individual's marginal rate of substitution be equal to the marginal rate of transformation.

7. The virtue of competitive markets is that they provide a way to achieve an efficient allocation of resources by decentralizing production and consumption decisions.

REVIEW QUESTIONS

1. The competitive price of coconuts is $6 per pound and the price of fish is $3 per pound. If society were to give up 1 pound of coconuts, how many more pounds of fish could be produced?

2. What would happen if the firm depicted in Figure 30.2 decided to pay a higher wage?

3. In what sense is a competitive equilibrium a good or bad thing for a given economy?

4. If Robinson's marginal rate of substitution between coconuts and fish is -2 and the marginal rate of transformation between the two goods is -1, what should he do if he wants to increase his utility?

5. Suppose that Robinson and Friday both want 60 pounds of fish and 60 pounds of coconuts per day. Using the production rates given in the chapter, how many hours must Robinson and Friday work per day if they don't help each other? Suppose they decide to work together in the most efficient manner possible. Now how many hours each day do they have to work? What is the economic explanation for the reduction in hours?

APPENDIX

Let us derive the calculus conditions for Pareto efficiency in an economy with production. We let X^1 and X^2 represent the total amount of good 1 and good 2 produced and consumed, as in the body of this chapter:

$$X^1 = x_A^1 + x_B^1$$
$$X^2 = x_A^2 + x_B^2.$$

The first thing we need is a convenient way to describe the production possibilities frontier—all the combinations of X^1 and X^2 that are technologically feasible. The most useful way to do this for our purposes is by use of the **transformation function**. This is a function of the aggregate amounts of the two goods $T(X^1, X^2)$, such that the combination (X^1, X^2) is on the production possibilities frontier (the boundary of the production possibilities set) if and only if

$$T(X^1, X^2) = 0.$$

Once we have described the technology, we can calculate the marginal rate of transformation: the rate at which we have to sacrifice good 2 in order to produce more of good 1. Although the name evokes an image of one good being "transformed" into another, that is a somewhat misleading picture. What really happens is that other resources are moved from producing good 2 to producing good 1. Thus, by devoting fewer resources to good 2 and more to good 1, we move from one point on the production possibilities frontier to another. The marginal rate of transformation is just the slope of the production possibilities set, which we denote by dX^2/dX^1.

Consider a small change in production (dX^1, dX^2) that remains feasible. Thus we have

$$\frac{\partial T(X^1, X^2)}{\partial X^1} dX^1 + \frac{\partial T(X^1, X^2)}{\partial X^2} dX^2 = 0.$$

Solving for the marginal rate of transformation:

$$\frac{dX^2}{dX^1} = -\frac{\partial T/\partial X^1}{\partial T/\partial X^2}.$$

We'll use this formula in a moment.

A Pareto efficient allocation is one that maximizes any one person's utility, given the level of the other people's utility. In the two-person case, we can write this maximization problem as

$$\max_{x_A^1, x_A^2, x_B^1, x_B^2} u_A(x_A^1, x_A^2)$$

$$\text{such that } u_B(x_B^1, x_B^2) = \overline{u}$$

$$T(X^1, X^2) = 0.$$

The Lagrangian for this problem is

$$L = u_A(x_A^1, x_A^2) - \lambda(u_B(x_B^1, x_B^2) - \overline{u})$$
$$- \mu(T(X_1, X_2) - 0),$$

and the first-order conditions are

$$\frac{\partial L}{\partial x_A^1} = \frac{\partial u_A}{\partial x_A^1} - \mu \frac{\partial T}{\partial X^1} = 0$$

$$\frac{\partial L}{\partial x_A^2} = \frac{\partial u_A}{\partial x_A^2} - \mu \frac{\partial T}{\partial X^2} = 0$$

$$\frac{\partial L}{\partial x_B^1} = -\lambda \frac{\partial u_B}{\partial x_B^1} - \mu \frac{\partial T}{\partial X^1} = 0$$

$$\frac{\partial L}{\partial x_B^2} = -\lambda \frac{\partial u_B}{\partial x_B^2} - \mu \frac{\partial T}{\partial X^2} = 0.$$

Rearranging and dividing the first equation by the second gives

$$\frac{\partial u_A / \partial x_A^1}{\partial u_A / \partial x_A^2} = \frac{\partial T / \partial X^1}{\partial T / \partial X^2}.$$

Performing the same operation on the third and fourth equations gives

$$\frac{\partial u_B / \partial x_B^1}{\partial u_B / \partial x_B^2} = \frac{\partial T / \partial X^1}{\partial T / \partial X^2}.$$

The left-hand sides of these equations are our old friends, the marginal rates of substitution. The right-hand side is the marginal rate of transformation. Thus the equations require that each person's marginal rate of substitution between the goods must equal the marginal rate of transformation: the rate at which each person is just willing to substitute one good for the other must be the same as the rate at which it is technologically feasible to transform one good into the other.

The intuition behind this result is straightforward. Suppose that the MRS for some individual was not equal to the MRT. Then the rate at which the individual would be willing to sacrifice one good to get more of the other would be different than the rate that was technologically feasible—but this means that there would be some way to increase that individual's utility while not affecting anyone else's consumption.

CHAPTER **31**

WELFARE

Up until now we have focused on considerations of Pareto efficiency in evaluating economic allocations. But there are other important considerations. It must be remembered that Pareto efficiency has nothing to say about the distribution of welfare across people; giving everything to one person will typically be Pareto efficient. But the rest of us might not consider this a reasonable allocation. In this chapter we will investigate some techniques that can be used to formalize ideas related to the distribution of welfare.

Pareto efficiency is in itself a desirable goal—if there is some way to make some group of people better off without hurting other people, why not do it? But there will usually be many Pareto efficient allocations; how can society choose among them?

The major focus of this chapter will be the idea of a **welfare function**, which provides a way to "add together" different consumers' utilities. More generally, a welfare function provides a way to rank different distributions of utility among consumers. Before we investigate the implications of this concept, it is worthwhile considering just how one might go about "adding together" the individual consumers' preferences to construct some kind of "social preferences."

31.1 Aggregation of Preferences

Let us return to our early discussion of consumer preferences. As usual, we will assume that these preferences are transitive. Originally, we thought of a consumer's preferences as being defined over his own bundle of goods, but now we want to expand on that concept and think of each consumer as having preferences over the entire allocation of goods among the consumers. Of course, this includes the possibility that the consumer might not care about what other people have, just as we had originally assumed.

Let us use the symbol x to denote a particular allocation—a description of what every individual gets of every good. Then given two allocations, x and y, each individual i can say whether or not he or she prefers x to y.

Given the preferences of all the agents, we would like to have a way to "aggregate" them into one **social preference**. That is, if we know how all the individuals rank various allocations, we would like to be able to use this information to develop a social ranking of the various allocations. This is the problem of social decision making at its most general level. Let's consider a few examples.

One way to aggregate individual preferences is to use some kind of voting. We could agree that x is "socially preferred" to y if a majority of the individuals prefer x to y. However, there is a problem with this method— it may not generate a transitive social preference ordering. Consider, for example, the case illustrated in Table 31.1.

Preferences that lead to intransitive voting.   Table 31.1

Person A	Person B	Person C
x	y	z
y	z	x
z	x	y

Here we have listed the rankings for three alternatives, x, y, and z, by three people. Note that a majority of the people prefer x to y, a majority prefer y to z, and a majority prefer z to x. Thus aggregating individual preferences by majority vote won't work since, in general, the social preferences resulting from majority voting aren't well-behaved preferences, since they are not transitive. Since the preferences aren't transitive, there will be no "best" alternative from the set of alternatives (x, y, z). Which outcome society chooses will depend on the order in which the vote is taken.

To see this suppose that the three people depicted in Table 31.1 decide to vote first on **x** versus **y**, and then vote on the winner of this contest versus **z**. Since a majority prefer **x** to **y**, the second contest will be between **x** and **z**, which means that **z** will be the outcome.

But what if they decide to vote on **z** versus **x** and then pit the winner of this vote against **y**? Now **z** wins the first vote, but **y** beats **z** in the second vote. Which outcome is the overall winner depends crucially on the order in which the alternatives are presented to the voters.

Another kind of voting mechanism that we might consider is rank-order voting. Here each person ranks the goods according to his preferences and assigns a number that indicates its rank in his ordering: for example, a 1 for the best alternative, 2 for the second best, and so on. Then we sum up the scores of each alternative across the people to determine an aggregate score for each alternative and say that one outcome is socially preferred to another if it has a lower score.

In Table 31.2 we have illustrated a possible preference ordering for three allocations **x**, **y**, and **z** by two people. Suppose first that only alternatives **x** and **y** were available. Then in this example **x** would be given a rank of 1 by person A and 2 by person B. The alternative **y** would be given just the reverse ranking. Thus the outcome of the voting would be a tie with each alternative having an aggregate rank of 3.

Table
31.2

The choice between x and y depends on z.

Person A	Person B
x	**y**
y	**z**
z	**x**

But now suppose that **z** is introduced to the ballot. Person A would give **x** a score of 1, **y** a score of 2, and **z** a rank of 3. Person B would give **y** a score of 1, **z** a score of 2, and **x** a score of 3. This means that **x** would now have an aggregate rank of 4, and **y** would have an aggregate rank of 3. In this case **y** would be preferred to **x** by rank-order voting.

The problem with both majority voting and rank-order voting is that their outcomes can be manipulated by astute agents. Majority voting can be manipulated by changing the order on which things are voted so as to yield the desired outcome. Rank-order voting can be manipulated by introducing new alternatives that change the final ranks of the relevant alternatives.

The question naturally arises as to whether there are social decision mechanisms—ways of aggregating preferences—that are immune to this kind of manipulation? Are there ways to "add up" preferences that don't have the undesirable properties described above?

Let's list some things that we would want our social decision mechanism to do:

1. Given any set of complete, reflexive, and transitive individual preferences, the social decision mechanism should result in social preferences that satisfy the same properties.

2. If everybody prefers alternative **x** to alternative **y**, then the social preferences should rank **x** ahead of **y**.

3. The preferences between **x** and **y** should depend only on how people rank **x** versus **y**, and not on how they rank other alternatives.

All three of these requirements seem eminently plausible. Yet it can be quite difficult to find a mechanism that satisfies all of them. In fact, Kenneth Arrow has proved the following remarkable result:[1]

Arrow's Impossibility Theorem.   *If a social decision mechanism satisfies properties 1, 2, and 3, then it must be a dictatorship: all social rankings are the rankings of one individual.*

Arrow's Impossibility Theorem is quite surprising. It shows that three very plausible and desirable features of a social decision mechanism are inconsistent with democracy: there is no "perfect" way to make social decisions. There is no perfect way to "aggregate" individual preferences to make one social preference. If we want to find a way to aggregate individual preferences to form social preferences, we will have to give up one of the properties of a social decision mechanism described in Arrow's theorem.

31.2 Social Welfare Functions

If we were to drop any of the desired features of a social welfare function described above, it would probably be property 3—that the social preferences between two alternatives only depends on the ranking of those two alternatives. If we do that, certain kinds of rank-order voting become possibilities.

---

[1] See Kenneth Arrow, *Social Choice and Individual Values* (New York: Wiley, 1963). Arrow, a professor at Stanford University, was awarded the Nobel Prize in economics for his work in this area.

Given the preferences of each individual i over the allocations, we can construct utility functions, $u_i(\mathbf{x})$, that summarize the individuals' value judgments: person i prefers $\mathbf{x}$ to $\mathbf{y}$ if and only if $u_i(\mathbf{x}) > u_i(\mathbf{y})$. Of course, these are just like all utility functions—they can be scaled in any way that preserves the underlying preference ordering. There is no *unique* utility representation.

But let us pick some utility representation and stick with it. Then one way of getting social preferences from individuals' preferences is to add up the individual utilities and use the resulting number as a kind of social utility. That is, we will say that allocation $\mathbf{x}$ is socially preferred to allocation $\mathbf{y}$ if

$$\sum_{i=1}^{n} u_i(\mathbf{x}) > \sum_{i=1}^{n} u_i(\mathbf{y}),$$

where n is the number of individuals in the society.

This works—but of course it is totally arbitrary, since our choice of utility representation is totally arbitrary. The choice of using the sum is also arbitrary. Why not use a weighted sum of utilities? Why not use the product of utilities, or the sum of the squares of utilities?

One reasonable restriction that we might place on the "aggregating function" is that it be increasing in each individual's utility. That way we are assured that if everybody prefers $\mathbf{x}$ to $\mathbf{y}$, then the social preferences will prefer $\mathbf{x}$ to $\mathbf{y}$.

There is a name for this kind of aggregating function; it is called a **social welfare function**. A social welfare function is just some function of the individual utility functions: $W(u_1(\mathbf{x}), \ldots, u_n(\mathbf{x}))$. It gives a way to rank different allocations that depends only on the individual preferences, and it is an increasing function of each individual's utility.

Let's look at some examples. One special case mentioned above is the *sum* of the individual utility functions

$$W(u_1, \ldots, u_n) = \sum_{i=1}^{n} u_i.$$

This is sometimes referred to as a **classical utilitarian** or **Benthamite** welfare function.[2] A slight generalization of this form is the **weighted-sum-of-utilities welfare function**:

$$W(u_1, \ldots, u_n) = \sum_{i=1}^{n} a_i u_i.$$

---

[2] Jeremy Bentham (1748–1832) was the founder of the utilitarian school of moral philosophy, a school that considers the highest good to be the greatest happiness for the greatest number.

Here the weights, $a_1, \ldots, a_n$, are supposed to be numbers indicating how important each agent's utility is to the overall social welfare. It is natural to take each a_i as being positive.

Another interesting welfare function is the **minimax** or **Rawlsian** social welfare function:

$$W(u_1, \ldots, u_n) = \min\{u_1, \ldots, u_n\}.$$

This welfare function says that the social welfare of an allocation depends only on the welfare of the worst off agent—the person with the minimal utility.[3]

Each of these is a possible way to compare individual utility functions. Each of them represents different ethical judgments about the comparison between different agents' welfares. About the only restriction that we will place on the structure of the welfare function at this point is that it be increasing in each consumer's utility.

31.3 Welfare Maximization

Once we have a welfare function we can examine the problem of welfare maximization. Let us use the notation x_i^j to indicate how much individual i has of good j, and suppose that there are n consumers and k goods. Then the allocation $\mathbf{x}$ consists of the list of how much each of the agents has of each of the goods.

If we have a total amount $X^1, \ldots, X^k$ of goods $1, \ldots, k$ to distribute among the consumers, we can pose the welfare maximization problem:

$$\max \ W(u_1(\mathbf{x}), \ldots, u_n(\mathbf{x}))$$

$$\text{such that } \sum_{i=1}^{n} x_i^1 = X^1$$

$$\vdots$$

$$\sum_{i=1}^{n} x_i^k = X^k.$$

Thus we are trying to find the feasible allocation that maximizes social welfare. What properties does such an allocation have?

The first thing that we should note is that a maximal welfare allocation must be a Pareto efficient allocation. The proof is easy: suppose that

[3] John Rawls is a contemporary moral philosopher at Harvard who has argued for this principle of justice.

it were not. Then there would be some other feasible allocation that gave everyone at least as large a utility, and someone strictly greater utility. But the welfare function is an increasing function of each agent's utility. Thus this new allocation would have to have higher welfare, which contradicts the assumption that we originally had a welfare maximum.

We can illustrate this situation in Figure 31.1, where the set U indicates the set of possible utilities in the case of two individuals. This set is known as the **utility possibilities set**. The boundary of this set—the **utility possibilities frontier**—is the set of utility levels associated with Pareto efficient allocations. If an allocation is on the boundary of the utility possibilities set, then there are no other feasible allocations that yield higher utilities for both agents.

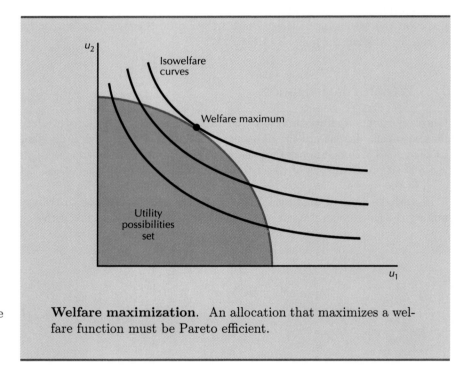

Figure 31.1   **Welfare maximization.** An allocation that maximizes a welfare function must be Pareto efficient.

The "indifference curves" in this diagram are called **isowelfare curves** since they depict those distributions of utility that have constant welfare. As usual, the optimal point is characterized by a tangency condition. But for our purposes, the notable thing about this maximal welfare point is that it is Pareto efficient—it must occur on the boundary of the utility possibilities set.

The next observation we can make from this diagram is that *any* Pareto efficient allocation must be a welfare maximum for some welfare function.

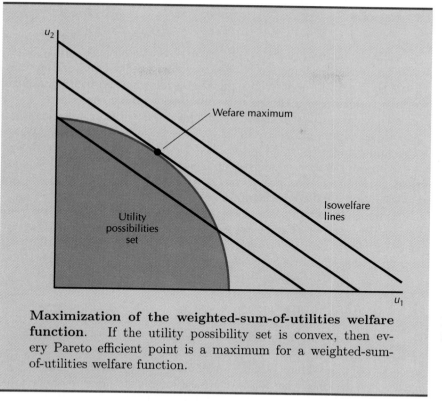

Maximization of the weighted-sum-of-utilities welfare function. If the utility possibility set is convex, then every Pareto efficient point is a maximum for a weighted-sum-of-utilities welfare function.

Figure 31.2

An example is given in Figure 31.2.

In Figure 31.2 we have picked a Pareto efficient allocation and found a set of isowelfare curves for which it yields maximal welfare. Actually, we can say a bit more than this. If the set of possible utility distributions is a convex set, as illustrated, then every point on its frontier is a welfare maximum for a weighted-sum-of-utilities welfare function, as illustrated in Figure 31.2. The welfare function thus provides a way to single out Pareto efficient allocations: every welfare maximum is a Pareto efficient allocation, and every Pareto efficient allocation is a welfare maximum.

31.4 Individualistic Social Welfare Functions

Up until now we have been thinking of individual preferences as being defined over entire allocations rather than over each individual's bundle of goods. But, as we remarked earlier, individuals might only care about their own bundles. In this case, we can use x_i to denote individual $i's$ consumption bundle, and let $u_i(x_i)$ be individual $i's$ utility level using some fixed representation of utility. Then a social welfare function will have the form

$$W = W(u_1(x_1), \ldots, u_n(x_n)).$$

The welfare function is directly a function of the individuals' utility levels, but it is indirectly a function of the individual agents' consumption bundles. This special form of welfare function is known as an **individualistic welfare function** or a **Bergson-Samuelson welfare function**.[4]

If each agent's utility depends only on his or her own consumption, then there are no consumption externalities. Thus the standard results of Chapter 29 apply and we have an intimate relationship between Pareto efficient allocations and market equilibria: all competitive equilibria are Pareto efficient, and, under appropriate convexity assumptions, all Pareto efficient allocations are competitive equilibria.

Now we can carry this categorization one step further. Given the relationship between Pareto efficiency and welfare maxima described above, we can conclude that all welfare maxima are competitive equilibria and that all competitive equilibria are welfare maxima for some welfare function.

31.5 Fair Allocations

The welfare function approach is a very general way to describe social welfare. But because it is so general it can be used to summarize the properties of many kinds of moral judgments. On the other hand, it isn't much use in deciding what kinds of ethical judgments might be reasonable ones.

Another approach is to start with some specific moral judgments and then examine their implications for economic distribution. This is the approach taken in the study of **fair allocations**. We start with a definition of what might be considered a fair way to divide a bundle of goods, and then use our understanding of economic analysis to investigate its implications.

Suppose that you were given some goods to divide fairly among n equally deserving people. How would you do it? It is probably safe to say that in this problem most people would divide the goods equally among the n agents. Given that they are by hypothesis equally deserving, what else could you do?

What is appealing about this idea of equal division? One appealing feature is that it is *symmetric*. Each agent has the same bundle of goods; no agent prefers any other agent's bundle of goods to his or her own, since they all have exactly the same thing.

Unfortunately, an equal division will not necessarily be Pareto efficient. If agents have different tastes they will generally desire to trade away from

---

[4] Abram Bergson and Paul Samuelson are contemporary economists who investigated properties of this kind of welfare function in the early 1940s. Samuelson was awarded a Nobel Prize in economics for his many contributions.

equal division. Let us suppose that this trade takes place and that it moves us to a Pareto efficient allocation.

The question arises: is this Pareto efficient allocation still fair in any sense? Does trade from equal division inherit any of the symmetry of the starting point?

The answer is: not necessarily. Consider the following example. We have three people, A, B, and C. A and B have the same tastes, and C has different tastes. We start from an equal division and suppose that A and C get together and trade. Then they will typically both be made better off. Now B, who didn't have the opportunity to trade with C, will **envy** A—that is, he would prefer A's bundle to his own. Even though A and B started with the same allocation, A was luckier in her trading, and this destroyed the symmetry of the original allocation.

This means that arbitrary trading from an equal division will not necessarily preserve the symmetry of the starting point of equal division. We might well ask if there is any allocation that preserves this symmetry? Is there any way to get an allocation that is both Pareto efficient and equitable at the same time?

31.6 Envy and Equity

Let us now try to formalize some of these ideas. What do we mean by "symmetric" or "equitable" anyway? One possible set of definitions is as follows.

We say an allocation is **equitable** if no agent prefers any other agent's bundle of goods to his or her own. If some agent i does prefer some other agent $j's$ bundle of goods, we say that i **envies** j. Finally, if an allocation is both equitable and Pareto efficient, we will say that it is a **fair** allocation.

These are ways of formalizing the idea of symmetry alluded to above. An equal division allocation has the property that no agent envies any other agent—but there are many other allocations that have this same property.

Consider Figure 31.3. To determine whether any allocation is equitable or not, just look at the allocation that results if the two agents swap bundles. If this swapped allocation lies "below" each agent's indifference curve through the original allocation, then the original allocation is an equitable allocation. (Here "below" means below from the point of view of each agent; from our point of view the swapped allocation must lie between the two indifference curves.)

Note also that the allocation in Figure 31.3 is also Pareto efficient. Thus it is not only equitable, in the sense that we defined the term, but it is also efficient. By our definition, it is a fair allocation. Is this kind of allocation a fluke, or will fair allocations typically exist?

It turns out that fair allocations *will* generally exist, and there is an easy way to see that this is so. We start as we did in the last section, where

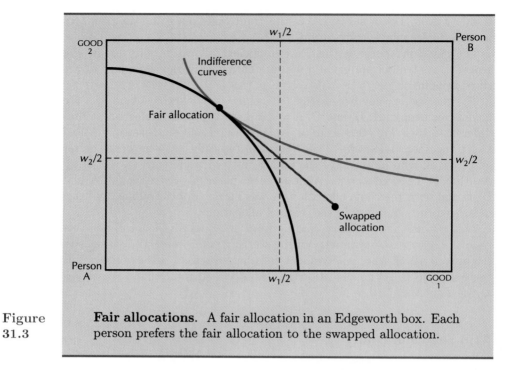

Person
B

$w_1/2$

Indifference
curves

Fair allocation

$w_2/2$

$w_2/2$

Swapped
allocation

Person
A

$w_1/2$

GOOD
1

Figure
31.3

Fair allocations. A fair allocation in an Edgeworth box. Each
person prefers the fair allocation to the swapped allocation.

we had an equal division allocation and considered trading to a Pareto
efficient allocation. Instead of using just any old way to trade, let us use
the special mechanism of the competitive market. This will move us to a
new allocation where each agent is choosing the best bundle of goods he or
she can afford at the equilibrium prices (p_1, p_2), and we know from Chapter
29 that such an allocation must be Pareto efficient.

But is it still equitable? Well, suppose not. Suppose that one of the
consumers, say consumer A, envies consumer B. This means that A prefers
what B has to her own bundle. In symbols:

$$(x_A^1, x_A^2) \prec_A (x_B^1, x_B^2).$$

But, if A prefers B's bundle to her own, and if her own bundle is the
best bundle she can afford at the prices (p_1, p_2), this means that B's bundle
must cost more than A can afford. In symbols:

$$p_1 \omega_A^1 + p_2 \omega_A^2 < p_1 x_B^1 + p_2 x_B^2.$$

But this is a contradiction! For by hypothesis, A and B started with
exactly the same bundle, since they started from an equal division. If A
can't afford B's bundle, then B can't afford it either.

Thus we can conclude that it is impossible for A to envy B in these
circumstances. A competitive equilibrium from equal division must be a

fair allocation. Thus the market mechanism will preserve certain kinds of equity: if the original allocation is equally divided, the final allocation must be fair.

Summary

1. Arrow's Impossibility Theorem shows that there is no ideal way to aggregate individual preferences into social preferences.

2. Nevertheless, economists often use welfare functions of one sort or another to represent distributional judgments about allocations.

3. As long as the welfare function is increasing in each individual's utility, a welfare maximum will be Pareto efficient. Furthermore, every Pareto efficient allocation can be thought of as maximizing some welfare function.

4. The idea of fair allocations provides an alternative way to make distributional judgments. This idea emphasizes the idea of symmetric treatment.

5. Even when the initial allocation is symmetric, arbitrary methods of trade will not necessarily produce a fair allocation. However, it turns out that the market mechanism will provide a fair allocation.

REVIEW QUESTIONS

1. Suppose that we say that an allocation x is socially preferred to an allocation y only if *everyone* prefers x to y. (This is sometimes called the Pareto ordering, since it is closely related to the idea of Pareto efficiency.) What shortcoming does this have as a rule for making social decisions?

2. A Rawlsian welfare function counts only the welfare of the worst off agent. The opposite of the Rawlsian welfare function might be called the "Nietzschean" welfare function—a welfare function that says the value of an allocation depends only on the welfare of the *best off* agent. What mathematical form would the Nietzschean welfare function take?

3. Suppose that the utility possibilities set is a convex set and that consumers care only about their own consumption. What kind of allocations represent welfare maxima of the Nietzschean welfare function?

4. Suppose that an allocation is Pareto efficient, and that each individual only cares about his own consumption. Prove that there must be some individual that envies no one, in the sense described in the text. (This puzzle requires some thought, but it is worth it.)

5. The ability to set the voting agenda can often be a powerful asset. Assuming that social preferences are decided by pair-wise majority voting and that the preferences given in Table 30.1 hold, demonstrate this fact by producing a voting agenda that results in allocation **y** winning. Find an agenda that has **z** as the winner. What property of the social preferences is responsible for this agenda-setting power?

APPENDIX

Here we consider the problem of welfare maximization, using an individualistic welfare function. Using the transformation function described in Chapter 30 to describe the production possibilities frontier, we write the welfare maximization problem as

$$\max_{x_A^1, x_A^2, x_B^1, x_B^2} W(u_A(x_A^1, x_A^2), u_B(x_B^1, x_B^2))$$

such that $T(X^1, X^2) = 0$,

where we use X^1 and X^2 to denote the total amount of good 1 and good 2 produced and consumed.

The Lagrangian for this problem is

$$L = W(u_A(x_A^1, x_A^2), u_B(x_B^1, x_B^2)) - \lambda(T(X^1, X^2) - 0).$$

Differentiating with respect to each of the choice variables gives us the first-order conditions

$$\frac{\partial L}{\partial x_A^1} = \frac{\partial W}{\partial u_A} \frac{\partial u_A(x_A^1, x_A^2)}{\partial x_A^1} - \lambda \frac{\partial T(X^1, X^2)}{\partial X^1} = 0$$

$$\frac{\partial L}{\partial x_A^2} = \frac{\partial W}{\partial u_A} \frac{\partial u_A(x_A^1, x_A^2)}{\partial x_A^2} - \lambda \frac{\partial T(X^1, X^2)}{\partial X^2} = 0$$

$$\frac{\partial L}{\partial x_B^1} = \frac{\partial W}{\partial u_B} \frac{\partial u_B(x_B^1, x_B^2)}{\partial x_B^1} - \lambda \frac{\partial T(X^1, X^2)}{\partial X^1} = 0$$

$$\frac{\partial L}{\partial x_B^2} = \frac{\partial W}{\partial u_B} \frac{\partial u_B(x_B^1, x_B^2)}{\partial x_B^2} - \lambda \frac{\partial T(X^1, X^2)}{\partial X^2} = 0.$$

Rearranging and dividing the first equation by the second, and the third by the fourth, we have

$$\frac{\partial u_A/\partial x_A^1}{\partial u_A/\partial x_A^2} = \frac{\partial T/\partial X^1}{\partial T/\partial X^2}$$

$$\frac{\partial u_B/\partial x_B^1}{\partial u_B/\partial x_B^2} = \frac{\partial T/\partial X^1}{\partial T/\partial X^2}.$$

Note that these are exactly the same equations that we encountered in the Appendix to Chapter 30. Thus the welfare maximization problem gives us the same first-order conditions as the Pareto efficiency problem.

This is obviously no accident. According to the discussion in the text, the allocation resulting from the maximization of a Bergson-Samuelson welfare function is Pareto efficient, and every Pareto efficient allocation maximizes some welfare function. Thus welfare maxima and Pareto efficient allocations have to satisfy the same first-order conditions.

CHAPTER 32

EXTERNALITIES

We say that an economic situation involves a **consumption externality** if one consumer cares directly about another agent's production or consumption. For example, I have definite preferences about my neighbor playing loud music at 3 in the morning, or the person next to me in a restaurant smoking a cheap cigar, or the amount of pollution produced by local automobiles. These are all examples of *negative* consumption externalities. On the other hand, I may get pleasure from observing my neighbor's flower garden—this is an example of a *positive* consumption externality.

Similarly, a **production externality** arises when the production possibilities of one firm are influenced by the choices of another firm or consumer. A classic example is that of an apple orchard located next to a beekeeper, where there are mutual positive production externalities—each firm's production positively affects the production possibilities of the other firm. Similarly, a fishery cares about the amount of pollutants dumped into its fishing area, since this will negatively influence its catch.

The crucial feature of externalities is that there are goods people care about that are not sold on markets. There is no market for loud music at 3 in the morning, or drifting smoke from cheap cigars, or a neighbor who keeps a beautiful flower garden. It is this lack of markets for externalities that causes problems.

Up until now we have implicitly assumed that each agent could make consumption or production decisions without worrying about what other agents were doing. All interactions between consumers and producers took place via the market, so that all the economic agents needed to know were the market prices and their own consumption or production possibilities. In this chapter we will relax this assumption and examine the economic consequences of externalities.

In earlier chapters we saw that the market mechanism was capable of achieving Pareto efficient allocations when externalities were *not* present. If externalities are present, the market will not necessarily result in a Pareto efficient provision of resources. However, there are other social institutions such as the legal system, or government intervention, that can "mimic" the market mechanism to some degree and thereby achieve Pareto efficiency. In this chapter we'll see how these institutions work.

32.1 Smokers and Nonsmokers

It is convenient to start with an example to illustrate some of the main considerations. We'll imagine two roommates, A and B, who have preferences over "money" and "smoke." We suppose that both consumers like money, but that A likes to smoke and B likes clean air.

We can depict the consumption possibilities for the two consumers in an Edgeworth box. The length of the horizontal axis will represent the total amount of money the two agents have, and the height of the vertical axis will represent the total amount of smoke that can be generated. The preferences of agent A are increasing in both money and smoke, while agent B's preferences are increasing in money and clean air—the absence of smoke. We'll measure smoke on a scale from 0 to 1, where 0 is no smoke at all, and 1 is the proverbial smoke-filled room.

This setup gives us a diagram like that depicted in Figure 32.1. Note that the picture looks very much like the standard Edgeworth box, but the interpretation is quite different. The amount of smoke is a good for A and a bad for B, so that B is moved to a more preferred position as A consumes less smoke. Be sure to note the difference in the way things are measured on the horizontal and vertical axes. We measure A's money horizontally from the lower left-hand corner of the box, and B's money horizontally from the upper right-hand corner. But the total amount of smoke is measured vertically from the lower left-hand corner. The difference occurs because money can be divided between the two consumers, so there will always be two amounts of money to measure, but there is only one amount of smoke that they must both consume.

In the ordinary Edgeworth box diagram B is made better off when A reduces his consumption of good 2—but that is because B then gets to consume more of good 2. In the Edgeworth box in Figure 32.1 B is also better off when A reduces his consumption of good 2 (smoke), but for a very different reason. In this example, B is better off when A reduces his consumption of smoke since both agents must consume the same amount of smoke and smoke is a bad for agent B.

We've now illustrated the consumption possibilities of the two roommates and their preferences. What about their endowments? Let's assume that they both have the same amount of money, say $100 apiece, so that their endowments will lie somewhere on the vertical line in Figure 32.1. In order to determine exactly where on this line the endowments lie, we must determine the initial "endowment" of smoke/clean air.

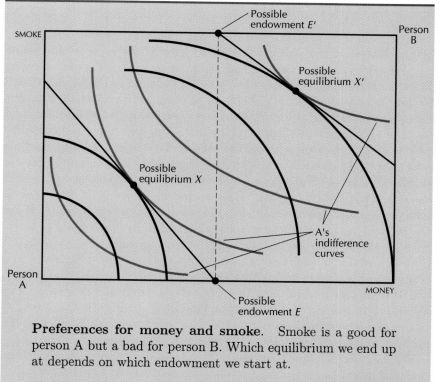

Preferences for money and smoke.   Smoke is a good for person A but a bad for person B. Which equilibrium we end up at depends on which endowment we start at.

Figure
32.1

The answer to this question depends on the legal rights of smokers and nonsmokers. It may be that A has a right to smoke as much as he wants, and B just has to put up with it. Or, it could be that B has a right to clean air. Or the legal right to smoke and clean air could be somewhere between these two extremes.

The initial endowment of smoke depends on the legal system. This is not so different from the initial endowment of ordinary sorts of goods. To say that A has an initial endowment of $100 means that A can decide to consume the $100 himself, or he can give it away or trade it to any other individual. There is a legal definition of property involved in saying that a person "owns" or "has a right to" $100. Similarly if a person has a property right to clean air, it means that he can consume clean air if he wants to, or he can give it away or sell that right to someone else. In this way, having a property right to clean air is no different from having a property right to $100.

Let's start by considering a legal situation where person B has a legal right to clean air. Then the initial endowment in Figure 32.1 is labeled E; it is where A has $(100, 0)$ and B has $(100, 0)$. This means that both A and B have $100, and that the initial endowment—what there would be in the absence of trade—is clean air.

Just as before, in the case with no externalities, there is no reason why the initial endowment is Pareto efficient. One of the aspects of having a property right to clean air is having the right to trade some of it away for other desirable goods—in this case, for money. It can easily happen that B would prefer to trade some of his right to clean air for some more money. The point labeled X in Figure 32.1 is an example of such a case.

As before, a Pareto efficient allocation is one where neither consumer can be made better off without the other being made worse off. Such an allocation will be characterized by the usual tangency condition that the marginal rates of substitution between smoke and money should be the same between the two agents, as illustrated in Figure 32.1. It is easy to imagine A and B trading to such a Pareto efficient point. In effect, B has the right to clean air, but he can allow himself to be "bribed" to consume some of A's smoke.

Of course, other assignments of property rights are possible. We could imagine a legal system where A had a right to smoke as much as he wanted, and B would have to bribe A to reduce his consumption of smoke. This would correspond to the endowment labeled E' in Figure 32.1. Just as before, this would typically not be Pareto efficient, so we could imagine the agents trading to a mutually preferred point such as the one labeled X'.

Both X and X' are Pareto efficient allocations; they just come from different initial endowments. Certainly the smoker, A, is better off at X' than at X, and the nonsmoker, B, is better off at X than at X'. The two points have different distributional consequences, but on grounds of efficiency they are equally satisfactory.

In fact, there is no reason to limit ourselves to just these two efficient points. As usual there will be a whole contract curve of Pareto efficient allocations of smoke and money. If agents are free to trade both of these goods, we know that they will end up somewhere on this contract curve. The exact position will depend on their property rights involving smoke and money and on the precise mechanism that they use to trade.

One mechanism that they could use to trade is the price mechanism. Just as before we could imagine an auctioneer calling out prices and asking how much each agent would be willing to buy at those prices. If the initial endowment point gave A the property rights to smoke, he could consider selling some of his smoking rights to B in exchange for B's money. Similarly, if the property rights for clean air were given to B, he could sell some of his clean air to A.

When the auctioneer manages to find a set of prices where supply equals demand everything is fine: we have a nice Pareto efficient outcome. If there is a market for smoke, a competitive equilibrium will be Pareto efficient. Furthermore, the competitive prices will measure the marginal rate of substitution between the two goods, just as in the standard case.

This is just like the usual Edgeworth box analysis, but described in a slightly different framework. As long as we have well-defined property rights in the good involving the externality—no matter who holds the property rights—the agents can trade from their initial endowment to a Pareto efficient allocation. If we want to set up a market in the externality to encourage trade, that will work as well.

The only problem arises if the property rights are *not* well defined. If A believes that he has the right to smoke and B believes that he has the right to clean air, we have difficulties. *The practical problems with externalities generally arise because of poorly defined property rights.*

My neighbor may believe that he has the right to play his trumpet at 3 in the morning, and I may believe that I have the right to silence. A firm may believe that it has the right to dump pollutants into the atmosphere that I breathe, while I may believe that it doesn't. Cases where property rights are poorly defined can lead to an inefficient production of externalities—which means that there would be ways to make both parties involved better off by changing the production of externalities. If property rights are well defined, and mechanisms are in place to allow for negotiation between people, then people can trade their rights to produce externalities in the same way that they trade rights to produce and consume ordinary goods.

32.2 Quasilinear Preferences and the Coase Theorem

We argued above that as long as property rights were well defined, trade between agents would result in an efficient allocation of the externality. In general, the amount of the externality that will be generated in the efficient solution will depend on the assignment of property rights. In the case of the two roommates, the amount of smoke generated will depend on whether the smoker has the property rights or the nonsmoker has them.

But there is a special case where the outcome of the externality is independent of the assignment of property rights. If the agents' preferences are **quasilinear**, then every efficient solution must have the same amount of the externality.

This case is illustrated in Figure 32.2 for the Edgeworth box case of the smoker versus the nonsmoker. Since the indifference curves are all horizontal translates of each other, the locus of mutual tangencies—the set of Pareto efficient allocations—will be a horizontal line. This means that the amount of smoke is the same in every Pareto efficient allocation; only the dollar amounts held by the agents differ across the efficient allocations.

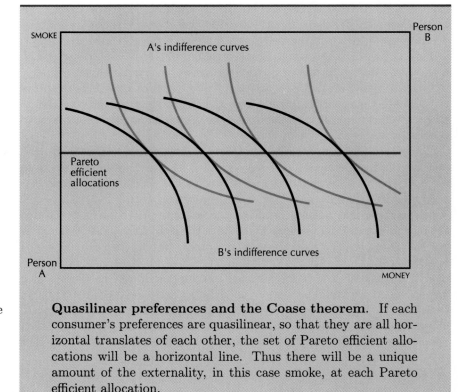

Figure 32.2
Quasilinear preferences and the Coase theorem. If each consumer's preferences are quasilinear, so that they are all horizontal translates of each other, the set of Pareto efficient allocations will be a horizontal line. Thus there will be a unique amount of the externality, in this case smoke, at each Pareto efficient allocation.

The result that under certain conditions the efficient amount of the good involved in the externality is independent of the distribution of property rights is sometimes known as the **Coase Theorem**. However, it should be emphasized just how special these conditions are. The quasilinear preference assumption implies that the demands for the good causing the exter-

nality doesn't depend on the distribution of income. Therefore a reallocation of endowments doesn't affect the efficient amount of the externalities.
This is sometimes expressed by saying that the Coase theorem is valid if
there are no "income effects."[1]

In this case, the Pareto efficient allocations will involve a unique amount
of the externality being generated. The different Pareto efficient allocations
will involve different amounts of money being held by the consumers; but
the amount of the externality—the amount of smoke—will be independent
of the distribution of wealth.

32.3 Production Externalities

Let us now consider a situation involving production externalities. Firm
S produces some amount of steel, s, and also produces a certain amount
of pollution, x, which it dumps into a river. Firm F, a fishery, is located
downstream and is adversely affected by S's pollution.

Suppose that firm S's cost function is given by $c_s(s, x)$, where s is the
amount of steel produced and x is the amount of pollution produced. Firm
F's cost function is given by $c_f(f, x)$, where f indicates the production of
fish and x is the amount of pollution. Note that F's costs of producing a
given amount of fish depend on the amount of pollution produced by the
steel firm. We will suppose that pollution increases the cost of providing
fish $\Delta c_f / \Delta x > 0$, and that pollution *decreases* the cost of steel production,
$\Delta c_s / \Delta x \leq 0$. This last assumption says that increasing the amount of
pollution will decrease the cost of producing steel—that reducing pollution
will increase the cost of steel production, at least over some range.

The steel firm's profit-maximization problem is

$$\max_{s,x} \; p_s s - c_s(s, x)$$

and the fishery's profit-maximization problem is

$$\max_{f} \; p_f f - c_f(f, x).$$

Note that the steel mill gets to choose the amount of pollution that it
generates, but the fishery must take the level of pollution as outside of its
control.

---

[1] Ronald Coase is an emeritus professor at the University of Chicago Law School. His
famous paper, "The Problem of Social Costs," *The Journal of Law & Economics*, 3
(October 1960), has been given a variety of interpretations. Some authors suggest
that Coase only asserted that costless bargaining over externalities achieves a Pareto
efficient outcome, not that the outcome will be independent of the assignment of
property rights. Coase received the 1991 Nobel Prize in Economics for this work.

The conditions characterizing profit maximization will be

$$p_s = \frac{\Delta c_s(s^*, x^*)}{\Delta s}$$
$$0 = \frac{\Delta c_s(s^*, x^*)}{\Delta x}$$

for the steel firm and

$$p_f = \frac{\Delta c_f(f^*, x^*)}{\Delta f}$$

for the fishery. These conditions say that at the profit-maximizing point, the price of each good—steel and pollution—should equal its marginal cost. In the case of the steel firm, one of its products is pollution, which, by assumption, has a zero price. So the condition determining the profit-maximizing supply of pollution says to produce pollution until the cost of an extra unit is zero.

It is not hard to see the externality here: the fishery cares about the production of pollution but has no control over it. The steel firm looks only at the cost of producing steel when it makes its profit-maximizing calculation; it doesn't consider the cost it imposes on the fishery. The increase in the cost of fishing associated with an increase in pollution is part of the **social cost** of steel production, and it is being ignored by the steel firm. In general, we expect that the steel firm will produce too much pollution from a social point of view since it ignores the impact of that pollution on the fishery.

What does a Pareto efficient production plan for steel and fish look like? There is an easy way to see what it should be. Suppose that the fishery and the steel firm merged and formed one firm that produced both fish and steel (and possibly pollution). Then there is no externality! For a production externality only arises when one firm's actions affect another firm's production possibilities. If there is only one firm, then it will take the interactions between its different "divisions" into account when it chooses the profit-maximizing production plan. We say that the externality has been **internalized** by this reassignment of property rights. Before the merger, each firm had the right to produce whatever amount of steel or fish or pollution that it wanted, regardless of what the other firm did. After the merger, the combined firm has the right to control the production of both the steel mill and the fishery.

The merged firm's profit-maximization problem is

$$\max_{s,f,x} \; p_s s + p_f f - c_s(s, x) - c_f(f, x),$$

which yields optimality conditions of

$$p_s = \frac{\Delta c_s(\hat{s}, \hat{x})}{\Delta s}$$

$$p_f = \frac{\Delta c_f(\hat{f}, \hat{x})}{\Delta f}$$

$$0 = \frac{\Delta c_s(\hat{s}, \hat{x})}{\Delta x} + \frac{\Delta c_f(\hat{f}, \hat{x})}{\Delta x}.$$

The crucial term is the last one. This shows that the merged firm will take into account the effect of pollution on the marginal costs of both the steel firm and the fishery. When the steel division decides how much pollution to produce, it considers the effect of this action on the profits of the fish division; that is, it takes the social cost of its production plan into account.

What does this imply about the amount of pollution produced? When the steel firm acted independently, the amount of pollution was determined by the condition

$$\frac{\Delta c_s(s^*, x^*)}{\Delta x} = 0. \tag{32.1}$$

That is, the steel mill produced pollution until the marginal cost was zero:

$$MC_S(s^*, x^*) = 0.$$

In the merged firm, the amount of pollution is determined by the condition

$$\frac{\Delta c_s(\hat{s}, \hat{x})}{\Delta x} + \frac{\Delta c_f(\hat{f}, \hat{x})}{\Delta x} = 0. \tag{32.2}$$

That is, the merged firm produces pollution until the *sum* of the marginal cost to the steel mill and the marginal cost to the fishery is zero. This condition can also be written as

$$-\frac{\Delta c_s(\hat{s}, \hat{x})}{\Delta x} = \frac{\Delta c_f(\hat{f}, \hat{x})}{\Delta x} > 0 \tag{32.3}$$

or

$$-MC_S(\hat{s}, \hat{x}) = MC_F(\hat{f}, \hat{x}).$$

In this latter expression $MC_F(\hat{f}, \hat{x})$ is positive, since more pollution increases the cost of producing a given amount of fish. Hence the merged firm will want to produce where $-MC_S(\hat{s}, \hat{x})$ is positive; that is, it will want to produce *less* pollution than the independent steel firm. When the true social cost of the externality involved in the steel production is taken into account, the optimal production of pollution will be reduced.

When the steel firm considers minimizing its **private costs** of producing steel, it produces where the marginal cost of extra pollution equals zero;

but the Pareto efficient level of pollution requires minimizing the **social costs** of the pollution. At the Pareto efficient level of pollution, the *sum* of the two firm's marginal costs of pollution must be equal to zero.

This argument is illustrated in Figure 32.3. In this diagram $-MC_S$ measures the marginal cost to the steel firm from producing more pollution. The curve labeled MC_F measures the marginal cost to the fishery of more pollution. The profit-maximizing steel firm produces pollution up to the point where its marginal cost from generating more pollution equals zero.

 Figure 32.3

Social cost and private cost. The steel firm produces pollution up to the point where the marginal cost of extra pollution equals zero. But the Pareto efficient production of pollution is at the point where price equals marginal social cost, which includes the cost of pollution borne by the fishery.

But at the Pareto efficient level of pollution, the steel firm pollutes up to the point where the effect of a marginal increase in pollution is equal to the marginal social cost, which counts the impact of pollution on the costs of both firms. At the efficient level of pollution production, the amount that the steel firm is willing to pay for an extra unit of pollution should equal the social costs generated by that extra pollution—which include the costs it imposes on the fishery.

This is perfectly consistent with the efficiency arguments given in earlier chapters. There we assumed that there were no externalities, so that private costs and social costs coincided. In this case the free market will determine a Pareto efficient amount of output of each good. But if the private costs and the social costs diverge, the market alone may not be sufficient to achieve Pareto efficiency.

EXAMPLE: Pollution Vouchers

Everyone wants a clean environment ... as long as someone else pays for it. Even if we reach a consensus on how much we should reduce pollution, there is still the problem of determining the most cost-effective way to achieve the targeted reduction.

Take the case of nitrogen oxide emissions. One emitter may find it relatively inexpensive to reduce its emissions of this pollutant, whereas another may find it very expensive. Should they both be required to reduce their emission of pollutants by the same physical amount, by the same proportional amount, or by some other rule?

Let's look at a simple economic model. Suppose that there are only two firms. Firm 1's emission quota is x_1 and firm 2's is x_2. The cost of achieving an emission quota x_1 is $c_1(x_1)$ and similarly for firm 2. The total amount of emission is fixed at some target level X. If we want to minimize the total costs of achieving the emissions target, subject to the aggregate constraint, we need to solve the following problem:

$$\min_{x_1, x_2} \; c_1(x_1) + c_2(x_2)$$

$$\text{such that } x_1 + x_2 = X.$$

A by now standard economic argument shows that the marginal cost of emission control must be equalized across the firms. If one firm had a higher marginal cost of emission control than the other, then we could lower total costs by reducing its quota and increasing the quota of the other firm.

How can we achieve this outcome? If the government regulators had information on the cost of emissions for all firms, they could calculate the appropriate pattern of production and impose it on all the relevant parties. But the cost of gathering all this information, and keeping it up-to-date, is staggering. It is much easier to characterize the optimal solution than to actually implement it!

Many economists have argued that the best way to implement the efficient solution to the emission control problem is to use a market. It appears that such a market based emissions control system will soon be put into effect in Southern California. Here is how the California plan works.[2]

---

[2] See Richard Stevenson, "Trying a Market Approach to Smog," *New York Times*, March 25, 1992, C1.

Each of the 2700 largest polluters in Southern California is assigned a quota for their emissions of nitrogen oxide. This quota is initially set to be 8 percent less than their previous year's emission. If the firm exactly meets its emissions quota it faces no fines or penalties. However, if it reduces its emissions by *more* than its emissions quota, it can sell the extra "right to emit" on the open market.

Suppose that a firm's quota is 95 tons of nitrogen oxide emissions per year. If it manages to produce only 90 tons in a given year, then it can sell the right to emit 5 tons of nitrogen oxide to some other firm. Each firm can compare the market price of an emission credit to the cost of reducing its emissions and decide whether it was more cost-effective to reduce emissions further or purchase emission credits from other firms.

Firms that find it easy to reduce emissions will sell credits to firms that find it costly to reduce emissions. In equilibrium, the market price of the right to emit one ton of pollution should just equal the marginal cost of reducing emissions by one ton. But this is exactly the condition characterizing the optimal pattern of emissions! The market for emission permits produces the efficient pattern of emissions automatically.

32.4 Interpretation of the Conditions

There are several useful interpretations of the conditions for Pareto efficiency derived above. Each of these interpretations suggests a scheme to correct the efficiency loss created by the production externality.

The first interpretation is that the steel firm faces the wrong price for pollution. As far as the steel firm is concerned, its production of pollution costs it nothing. But that neglects the costs that the pollution imposes on the fishery. According to this view, the situation can be rectified by making sure that the polluter faces the correct social cost of its actions.

One way to do this is to place a tax on the pollution generated by the steel firm. Suppose that we put a tax of t dollars per unit of pollution generated by the steel firm. Then the profit-maximization problem of the steel firm becomes

$$\max_{s,x} p_s s - c_s(s, x) - tx.$$

The profit-maximization conditions for this problem will be

$$p_s - \frac{\Delta c_s(s, x)}{\Delta s} = 0$$

$$-\frac{\Delta c_s(s, x)}{\Delta x} - t = 0.$$

Comparing these conditions to equation (32.3), we see that setting

$$t = \frac{\Delta c_f(\hat{f}, \hat{x})}{\Delta x}$$

will make these conditions the same as the conditions characterizing the Pareto efficient level of pollution.

This kind of a tax is known as a **Pigouvian tax**.[3] The problem with Pigouvian taxes is that we need to know the optimal level of pollution in order to impose the tax. But if we knew the optimal level of pollution we could just tell the steel firm to produce exactly that much and not have to mess with this taxation scheme at all.

Another interpretation of the problem is that there is a missing market— the market for the pollutant. The externality problem arises because the polluter faces a zero price for an output good that it produces, even though people would be willing to pay money to have that output level reduced. From a social point of view, the output of pollution should have a *negative* price.

We could imagine a world where the fishery had the right to clean water, but could sell the right to allow pollution. Let q be the price per unit of pollution, and let x be the amount of pollution that the steel mill produces. Then the steel mill's profit-maximization problem is

$$\max_{s,x} \; p_s s - qx - c_s(s, x),$$

and the fishery's profit-maximization problem is

$$\max_{f,x} \; p_f f + qx - c_f(f, x).$$

The term qx enters with a negative sign in the profit expression for the steel firm since it represents a cost—the steel firm must buy the right to generate x units of pollution. But it enters with a positive sign in the expression for the profits of the fishery, since the fishery gets revenue from selling this right.

The profit-maximization conditions are

$$p_s = \frac{\Delta c_s(s, x)}{\Delta s} \tag{32.4}$$

$$q = -\frac{\Delta c_s(s, x)}{\Delta x} \tag{32.5}$$

$$p_f = \frac{\Delta c_f(f, x)}{\Delta f} \tag{32.6}$$

$$q = \frac{\Delta c_f(f, x)}{\Delta x}. \tag{32.7}$$

[3] Arthur Pigou (1877–1959), an economist at Cambridge University, suggested such taxes in his influential book *The Economics of Welfare*.

Thus each firm is facing the social marginal cost of each of its actions when it chooses how much pollution to buy or sell. If the price of pollution is adjusted until the demand for pollution equals the supply of pollution, we will have an efficient equilibrium, just as with any other good.

Note that at the optimal solution, equations (32.5) and (32.7) imply that

$$-\frac{\Delta c_s(s,x)}{\Delta x} = \frac{\Delta c_f(f,x)}{\Delta x}.$$

This says that the marginal cost to the steel firm of reducing pollution should equal the marginal benefit to the fishery of that pollution reduction. If this condition were not satisfied, we couldn't have the optimal level of pollution. This is, of course, the same condition we encountered in equation (32.3).

In analyzing this problem we have stated that the fishery had a right to clean water and that the steel mill had to purchase the right to pollute. But we could have assigned the property rights in the opposite way: the steel mill could have the right to pollute and the fishery would have to pay to induce the steel mill to pollute less. Just as in the case of the smoker and nonsmoker, this would also give an efficient outcome. In fact, it would give precisely the *same* outcome, since exactly the same equations would have to be satisfied.

To see this, we now suppose that the steel mill has the right to pollute up to some amount $\overline{x}$, say, but the fishery is willing to pay it to reduce its pollution. The profit-maximization problem for the steel mill is then

$$\max_{s,x} \; p_s s + q(\overline{x} - x) - c_s(s,x).$$

Now the steel mill has two sources of income: it can sell steel, and it can sell pollution relief. The price equals marginal cost conditions become

$$p_s - \frac{\Delta c_s(s,x)}{\Delta s} = 0 \tag{32.8}$$

$$-q - \frac{\Delta c_s(s,x)}{\Delta x} = 0. \tag{32.9}$$

The fishery's maximization problem is now

$$\max_{f,x} \; p_f f - q(\overline{x} - x) - c_f(f,x),$$

which has optimality conditions

$$p_f - \frac{\Delta c_f(f,x)}{\Delta f} = 0 \tag{32.10}$$

$$q - \frac{\Delta c_f(f,x)}{\Delta x} = 0. \tag{32.11}$$

Now observe: the four equations (32.8)–(32.11) are precisely the same as the four equations (32.4)–(32.7). In the case of production externalities, the optimal pattern of production is independent of the assignment of property rights. Of course, the distribution of profits will generally depend on the assignment of property rights. Even though the social outcome will be independent of the distribution of property rights, the owners of the firms in question may have strong views about what is an appropriate distribution.

32.5 Market Signals

Finally we turn to the third interpretation of externalities, which in some respects is the most profound. In the case of the steel mill and the fishery there is no problem if both firms merge—so why don't they merge? In fact, when you think about it, there is a definite incentive for the two firms to merge: if the actions of one affect the other, then they can make higher profits together by coordinating their behavior than by each going alone. *The objective of profit maximization itself should encourage the internalization of production externalities.*

Said another way: if the joint profits of the firms with coordination exceed the sum of the profits without coordination, then the current owners could each be bought out for an amount equal to the present value of the stream of profits for their firm, the two firms could be coordinated, and the buyer could retain the excess profits. The new buyer could be either of the old firms, or anybody else for that matter.

The market itself provides a signal to internalize production externalities, which is one reason this kind of production externality is rarely observed. Most firms have *already* internalized the externalities between units that affect each other's production. The case of the apple orchard and the beekeeper mentioned earlier is a case in point. Here there *would* be an externality if the two firms ignored their interaction ... but why would they be so foolish as to do so? It is more likely that one or both of the firms would realize that more profits could be made by coordinating their activities, either by mutual agreement or by the sale of one of the firms to the other. Indeed, it is very common for apple orchards to keep honey bees for the purpose of fertilizing the trees. That particular externality is easily internalized.

32.6 The Tragedy of the Commons

We have argued above that if property rights are well defined, there will be no problem with production externalities. But if property rights are not well defined, the outcome of the economic interactions will undoubtedly involve inefficiencies.

In this section we will examine a particularly well-known inefficiency called "the tragedy of the commons."[4] We will pose this problem in the original context of a common grazing land, although there are many other possible illustrations.

Consider an agricultural village in which the villagers graze their cows on a common field. We want to compare two allocation mechanisms: the first is the private ownership solution where someone owns the field and decides how many cows should graze there; the second is the solution where the field is owned in common by the villagers and access to it is free and unrestricted.

Suppose that it costs a dollars to buy a cow. How much milk the cow produces will depend on how many other cows are grazed on the common land. We'll let $f(c)$ be the value of the milk produced if there are c cows grazed on the common. Thus the value of the milk per cow is just the average product, $f(c)/c$.

How many cows would be grazed on the common if we wanted to maximize the total wealth of the village? In order to maximize the total amount of wealth, we set up the following problem:

$$\max_{c} \ f(c) - ac.$$

It should be clear by now that the maximal production will occur when the marginal product of a cow equals its cost, a:

$$MP(c^*) = a.$$

If the marginal product of a cow were greater than a, it would pay to put another cow on the commons; and if it were less than a, it would pay to take one off.

If the common grazing ground were owned by someone who could restrict access to it, this is indeed the solution that would result. For in this case, the owner of the grazing grounds would purchase just the right amount of cows to maximize his profits.

Now what would happen if the individual villagers decided whether or not to use the common field? Each villager has a choice of grazing a cow or not grazing one, and it will be profitable to graze a cow as long as the output generated by the cow is greater than the cost of a cow. Suppose that there are c cows currently being grazed, so that the current output per cow is $f(c)/c$. When a villager contemplates adding a cow, the total output will be $f(c+1)$, and the total number of cows will be $c+1$. Thus the revenue that the cow generates for the villager will be $f(c+1)/(c+1)$. He must compare this revenue to the cost of the cow, a. If $f(c+1)/(c+1) > a$, it is profitable to add the cow since the value of the output exceeds the cost.

[4] See G. Hardin, "The Tragedy of the Commons," *Science*, 1968, 1243–47.

Hence the villagers will choose to graze cows until the average product of a cow is driven to a. It follows that the total number of cows grazed will be $\hat{c}$, where

$$\frac{f(\hat{c})}{\hat{c}} = a.$$

Another way to derive this result is to appeal to free entry. If it is profitable to graze a cow on the common field, villagers will purchase cows. They will stop adding cows to the common only when the profits have been driven to zero, that is, when

$$f(\hat{c}) - a\hat{c} = 0,$$

which is just a rearrangement of the condition in the last paragraph.

When an individual decides whether or not to purchase a cow, he looks at the extra value he will get $f(c)/c$ and compares this to the cost of the cow, a. This is fine for him, but what has been left out of this calculation is the fact that his extra cow will reduce the output of milk from all the *other* cows. Since he is ignoring this **social cost** of his purchase, too many cows will be grazed on the common ground. (We assume that each individual has a number of cows that is negligible relative to the total number grazed on the common.)

This argument is illustrated in Figure 32.4. Here we have depicted a falling average product curve, since it is reasonable to suppose that the output per cow declines as more and more cows are grazed on the common land.

Since the average product is falling, it must be that the marginal product curve always lies below the average product curve. Thus the number of cows where the marginal product equals a must be less than where the average product equals a. The field will be overgrazed in the absence of a mechanism to restrict use.

Private property provides such a mechanism. Indeed, we have seen that if everything that people care about is owned by someone who can control its use and, in particular, can exclude others from overusing it, then there are by definition no externalities. The market solution leads to a Pareto efficient outcome. Inefficiencies can only result from situations where there is no way to exclude others from using something, a topic that we will investigate in the next chapter.

Of course, private property is not the only social institution that can encourage efficient use of resources. For example, rules could be formulated about how many cows can be grazed on the village common. If there is a legal system to enforce those rules, this may be a cost-effective solution to providing an efficient use of the common resource. However, in situations where the law is ambiguous or nonexistent, the tragedy of the commons can easily arise. Overfishing in international waters and the extermination of several species of animals due to overhunting are sobering examples of this phenomenon.

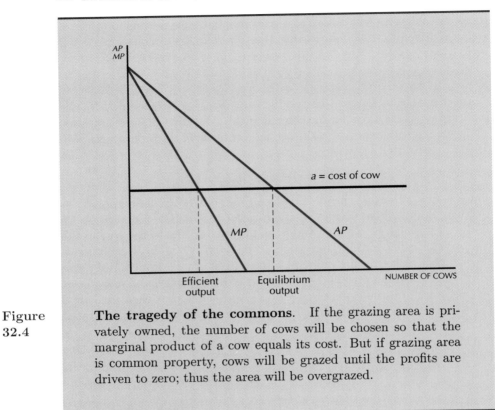

Figure 32.4

The tragedy of the commons. If the grazing area is privately owned, the number of cows will be chosen so that the marginal product of a cow equals its cost. But if grazing area is common property, cows will be grazed until the profits are driven to zero; thus the area will be overgrazed.

EXAMPLE: Overfishing

According to a report in the *New York Times,* "...overfishing has decimated the stocks of cod, haddock and flounder that have sustained New Englanders for centuries."[5] According to one expert, fishermen in New England are taking 50 to 70 percent of the available stock, over twice the sustainable amount.

This overfishing is a prime example of the problem of the commons: each fisherman has a negligible impact on the total stock of fish, but the accumulated efforts of thousands of fishermen results in serious depletion. The New England Fisheries Management Council is attempting to alleviate the problem by banning new entry to the industry, requiring fishermen to limit their days at sea, and increasing the mesh size of their nets.

It appears that the supplies of fish could be restocked in as little as 5 years if conservation measures were undertaken. The present value of profits to the industry as a whole would be larger with regulation to prevent

[5] "Plenty of Fish in the Sea? Not Anymore," *New York Times,* March 25, 1992, A15.

overfishing. However, such measures would almost certainly imply a substantial reduction in the number of fishing boats in the industry, which is highly unpopular with the small fishermen, who would likely be forced to leave the industry.

32.7 Automobile Pollution

As suggested above, pollution is a prime example of an economic externality. The activity of one consumer operating an automobile will typically lower the quality of the air that other consumers breathe. It seems unlikely that an unregulated free market would generate the optimal amount of pollution; more likely, if the consumer bears no cost in generating pollution, too much pollution would be produced.

One approach to controlling the amount of automobile pollution is to require that automobiles meet certain standards in the amount of pollution that they generate. This has been the basic thrust of U.S. antipollution policy since the Clean Air Act of 1963. That act, or, more properly, the subsequent amendments, set automobile emission standards for the manufacturers of vehicles in the United States.

Lawrence White has examined the benefits and costs of this program; most of the following discussion is drawn from this work.[6]

White estimates that the cost of emission control equipment is about $600 per car, the extra maintenance costs are about $180 per car, and the costs of the reduced gasoline mileage and the necessity for unleaded gasoline come to about $670 per car. Thus the total cost per car of the emission control standards is about $1450 over the lifetime of the car. (All figures are in 1981 dollars.)

He argues that there are several problems with the current approach to the regulation of automobile emissions. First, it requires that all automobiles meet the same standards. (California is the only state with different standards for emission control.) This means that *everyone* who buys a car must pay an extra $1450 whether they live in a high pollution area or not. A 1974 National Academy of Sciences study concluded that 63 percent of all U.S. cars did not require the stringent standards now in effect. According to White, "almost two-thirds of car buyers are spending . . . substantial sums for unnecessary systems."

Secondly, most of the responsibility for meeting the standards falls on the manufacturer, and little falls on the user. Owners of cars have little incentive to keep their pollution control equipment in working order unless they live in a state with required inspections.

---

[6] See Lawrence White, *The Regulation of Air Pollutant Emissions from Motor Vehicles* (Washington, D.C.: American Enterprise Institute for Public Policy Research, 1982).

More significantly, motorists have no incentive to economize on their driving. In cities such as Los Angeles, where pollution is a significant hazard, it makes good economic sense to encourage people to drive less. Under the current system, people who drive 2000 miles a year in North Dakota pay exactly the same amount for pollution control as people who drive 50,000 miles a year in Los Angeles.

An alternative solution to pollution would be *effluent fees*. As described by White, effluent fees would require an annual inspection of all vehicles along with an odometer reading and tests that would estimate the likely emissions of the vehicle during the past year. Different communities could then levy fees based on the estimated amount of pollution that had actually been generated by the operation of the vehicle. This method would ensure that people would face the true cost of generating pollution and would encourage them to choose to generate the socially optimal amount of pollution.

Such a system of effluent fees would encourage the vehicle owners themselves to find low-cost ways of reducing their emissions—investing in pollution control equipment, changing their driving habits, and changing the kinds of vehicles that they operate. A system of effluent fees could impose even higher standards than are now in effect in communities where pollution is a serious problem. Any desired level of pollution control can be achieved by appropriate effluent fees ... and it can be achieved at a substantially lower cost than the current system of mandated standards.

Of course, there is no reason why there might not also be some federally mandated standards for the two-thirds of the vehicles that are operated in localities where pollution is not a serious problem. If it is cheaper to impose standards than to require inspections, then by all means that should be the proper choice. The appropriate method of pollution control for automobiles should depend on a rational analysis of benefits and costs—as should all social policies of this nature.

Summary

1. The First Theorem of Welfare Economics shows that a free, competitive market will provide an efficient outcome in the absence of externalities.

2. However, if externalities are present, the outcome of a competitive market is unlikely to be Pareto efficient.

3. However, in this case, the state can sometimes "mimic" the role of the market by using prices to provide correct signals about the social cost of individual actions.

4. More importantly, the legal system can ensure that property rights are well defined, so that efficiency-enhancing trades can be made.

5. If preferences are quasilinear, the efficient amount of a consumption externality will be independent of the assignment of property rights.

6. Cures for production externalities include the use of Pigouvian taxes, setting up a market for the externality, simply allowing firms to merge, or transferring property rights in other ways.

7. The tragedy of the commons refers to the tendency for common property to be overused. This is a particularly prevalent form of externality.

REVIEW QUESTIONS

1. True or false? An explicit delineation of property rights usually eliminates the problem of externalities.

2. True or false? The distributional consequences of the delineation of property rights are eliminated when preferences are quasilinear.

3. List some other examples of positive and negative consumption and production externalities.

4. Suppose that the government wants to control the use of the commons, what methods exist for achieving the efficient level of use?

CHAPTER **33**

LAW AND ECONOMICS

In recent years economic analysis has become commonplace in legal theory and practice. It is easy to see the natural affinity between these two subjects: both have the goal of understanding social institutions. Furthermore, each subject has a strong normative component: both law and economics are concerned not only with how social institutions function but how to improve their operation.

In this chapter we will briefly explore three topics in law and economics. The first has to do with the economic analysis of crime. The second is concerned with liability law. The third focuses on a special topic in antitrust law. These examples are only a small sample of a rich and varied field. The models presented here are simple ones; they omit many real-world complexities. Nevertheless, even these very basic models can yield significant insights into the legal system.

33.1 Crime and Punishment

It is safe to say that nearly everyone commits a crime at some point in his or her life. These crimes range from misdemeanors such as illegal parking to major felonies such as armed robbery. It is clear that many crimes are motivated by economic considerations.[1] The bank robber Willie Sutton was once asked why he robbed banks. His reply was, "That's where they keep the money."

Even minor misdemeanors like illegal parking involve economic consider- ations: the motorist presumably trades off the benefits from a convenient location against the costs of the parking ticket. Such tradeoffs are inher- ently economic in nature, and an economic model can yield useful insights about crimes and punishments.

Consider, for example, the case of shoplifting. The benefit to the shop- lifter is the utility of the items taken, while the cost involve the possibility of arrest and the associated fine and/or imprisonment. Think of a single act of shoplifting, in which the thief is contemplating how valuable an item to take. We write the shoplifter's choice problem as

$$\max_{x} \; B(x) - C(x),$$

where x is the value of the item, $B(x)$ are the benefits of that item to the shoplifter, and $C(x)$ are the expected costs faced by the shoplifter.

The criminal justice system determines the form and magnitude of the costs imposed on the shoplifter. What form should the punishment take in order to discourage shoplifting? Let us focus on the simple case where the punishment is a fine of F dollars. Initially, let us suppose that the fine does not depend on the value of the item taken.

Criminal activities are, by their very nature, often not directly observ- able. Not all criminals are apprehended, so that the fine is imposed only with some probability. This probability is, in turn, determined by the resources devoted to detecting crime, so we use e to denote the level of enforcement and write $\pi(e)$ for the probability of apprehension. Think of e as being the expenditures on crime detection and enforcement by the police.

The shoplifter's problem can now be written as

$$\max_{x} \; B(x) - \pi(e)F. \tag{33.1}$$

The amount of crime that the individual chooses—the value of the items shoplifted—is the x that maximizes this expression.

How should the state set e and F? The criminal, through his choice of x imposes some harm on other people. In the case of theft, this cost includes cost of the items stolen, along with the cost of the locks, security guards,

---

[1] One of the first economists to examine the economic aspects of criminal behavior was Gary Becker, a professor of economics and sociology at the Univeristy of Chicago. In 1992 he was awarded the Nobel Prize in Economics for his work in this and other areas.

and so on that are used to protect against theft. Let the total amount of this harm be denoted by $H(x)$, and let $c(e)$ denote the cost of enforcement. We assume that the state wishes to minimize the net costs of the criminal activity and write its objective function as

$$\min_{F,e} \ H(x) - \pi(e)Fx + c(e). \tag{33.2}$$

The state chooses the degree of enforcement and the fine, recognizing that these choices influence the amount of shoplifting.[2]

The first thing to observe about the problem described in equation (33.1) is that the expected cost of the crime to the criminal, $\pi(e)F$, is independent of the magnitude of the crime, x. This means that the criminal will either choose the level of x that maximizes his net benefits, or choose not to commit the crime at all. If the benefit function is increasing in x, as would be the case for a crime that is motived solely by economic considerations, only the most valuable items would be shoplifted. Since the shoplifter faces the same punishment no matter how expensive an item he shoplifts, it makes sense for him to take the most valuable item. (Assuming, of course, that all of the items being considered are equally difficult to steal.)

This observation emphasizes the important point that an effective deterrent must impose a *marginal* cost on the criminal. If the cost is independent of the magnitude of the crime, the criminal may as well choose to engage in the largest feasible crime. This is a simple observation in the case of shoplifting, but is more sobering when you consider more serious crimes. If the punishment for robbing a bank is the same as the punishment for murder, then a bank robber has every incentive to murder any witnesses to the crime.

These observations show that we want the "punishment to fit the crime" in the sense that the criminal should face higher costs for more severe crimes. Accordingly, we restructure the problem described to equation (33.1) to make the fine facing the criminal proportional to the magnitude of the crime:

$$\max_{x} \ B(x) - \pi(e)Fx. \tag{33.3}$$

The level of the crime chosen will be that which equates marginal benefit to marginal cost:

$$MB(x^*) = \pi(e)F. \tag{33.4}$$

In general, larger levels of enforcement and larger fines should impose larger marginal costs on the criminal, leading to a reduced level of criminal activity.

---

[2] We have counted the fines collected as part of the benefits to the state; some economists argue that since the fine is a transfer from the criminal to the state it should net out of the social cost calculation.

Let us now return to the problem facing the criminal justice system in setting the appropriate level of the fine and enforcement. A complete analysis of this problem is beyond the scope of this book, but we can describe one useful insight. Suppose that the state decides to tolerate a level of criminal activity. How should the state set e and F to enforce this level in the most cost-effective way? Referring to equation (33.4), we see that that state wants to choose the fine so that the criminal's choice, x^*, is equal to the level the state is willing to tolerate.

Note that in equation (33.4) the level of criminal activity depends only on the *expected* cost of the criminal activity, $\pi(e)F$. Increasing the level of enforcement, e, is costly to the state, but increasing the size of the fine imposes no costs. Indeed, increasing the fine is beneficial to the state since the fines can be used to cover the costs of enforcement and apprehension. It follows that the state should set the lowest possible value of e that results in positive probability of apprehension, and the highest possible value of F so that the product of the two satisfies equation (33.4).

Let us review the logic of this argument. The criminal only cares about the expected cost of apprehension. Since it is costly to the state to increase the level of enforcement and there are only benefits to increasing the amount of the fine, the state will want to impose large fines with small probability of enforcement.

This argument shows why many communities charge very high fines for littering—in some cases as much as $1000—despite the fact that a piece of litter does much less than $1000 of damage. It is very hard to catch a litterer in the act; hence a very high fine is necessary to discourage this activity.

33.2 Qualifications

Taken to its extreme this analysis says that the optimal form of parking enforcement is to spend very little on attempting to catch people, but once they are caught subject them to astronomical fines. If we suspect that this policy may not be the best policy in every circumstance, this simply means that this particular model is too simple to describe every sort of criminal activity. If the model appears to give the "wrong" answer, we can still learn a lot by asking why we think the answer is wrong.

For example, it may be that juries or judges may be reluctant to impose very large punishments. In Michigan possession of a fraction of an ounce of cocaine can, in some circumstances, result in more than 10 years in prison. This has caused some Michigan juries to refuse to convict obviously guilty defendants.

Another reason why small probability/large fines may be inappropriate is that criminals may misperceive the probability of getting caught. After all, these probabilities are not readily available to the average criminal.

Most people's determination of how likely it is to get caught depends on the experiences of people they know or have heard about and increasing the level of enforcement will likely increase the accuracy of people's perceptions about the probability of getting caught.

Finally, if the punishment is too severe, then it can lead to an even greater crime. If illegal parking were punishable by death, albeit with a very low probability of getting caught, then people who *were* caught in the act might well attempt to murder the meter maid! As the old English saying puts it, one might as well hang for a cow as for a sheep.

Despite these qualifications, the insights from this simple analysis of crime and punishment are important: the criminal must face a marginal deterrent to crime, and society must recognize the tradeoff between the probability of enforcement and the magnitude of the punishment.

33.3 Liability Law

Suppose that two individuals are involved in an accident and that the injured party attempts to recover damages from the injurer. The body of law governing such situations is known as **liability law** or **tort law**. There is a large literature in the law and economics literature dealing with such cases. What follows is a simple theoretical analysis of liability.[3]

We suppose that there are two individuals, a injurer and a victim. The injurer engages in some activity (e.g., driving down the road) and the victim engages in some related activity (e.g., crossing the street.) The injurer takes a certain amount of care in driving—for example, how slowly he drives. The victim may take a certain amount of care in his activity—for example, the victim may choose to jay-walk or to cross at a crosswalk. To keep the analysis simple, we will suppose that the injurer must drive down the street and that the pedestrian must cross the street. The only choices that they make have to do with the amount of care that they exercise.

Let x denote the amount of care chosen by the injurer—for instance, how slowly he drives the car. In general, exercising more care will be costly to the injurer, and we measure this cost by $c_i(x)$. In the case of the automobile driver, $c_i(x)$ could measure the value of the lost time from driving slowly.

Let $L(x)$ measure the *expected* loss to the victim if the injurer chooses level of care x. Presumably, the higher the level of care taken by the injurer, the lower the expected losses facing the victim, so we expect that $L(x)$ will be a decreasing function of x.

---

[3] The discussion here is based on Steve Shavell's treatise, *Economic Analysis of Accident Law,* Harvard University Press, 1987. One of the first economists to look at these issues was John Prather Brown, "Toward an Economic Theory of Liability," *Journal of Legal Studies,* 2: 323–350, 1973.

The social objective function is to minimize the total losses imposed on both parties:

$$\min_{x} \; c_i(x) + L(x).$$

This leads to a natural condition for the socially optimal choice of care: the marginal cost to the injurer from increasing the level of care should equal the marginal benefit to the victim of this more careful behavior. We'll call the level of care that minimizes the total costs of the accident the **socially optimal level of care** and denote it by x^*.

Liability law imposes certain costs on the injurer in the case of the accident and the way in which these costs are imposed will influence the level of care that the injurer takes. Let us consider the behavior of the injurer under various liability rules.

• No liability. In this case, the injurer wants simply to minimize his own costs, without regard to the harm imposed on the victim. Under our assumptions of increasing cost of care, he will choose the lowest possible level of care, which is not socially optimal.

• Strict liability. Under strict liability, the injurer must pay all costs of accidents that they cause. In this case, the expected cost to the injurer from taking care x is $c_i(x) + L(x)$. Hence the injurer faces the total social costs and will choose the socially optimal level of care.

• Negligence rule. Under this rule, the injurer will be liable for accident losses only if he exercised a level of care less than an amount determined by the court. This amount is called **due care** or **reasonable care** and is denoted by $\overline{x}$. If the injurer exercised due care, he will not be held liable for the costs of the accident. Suppose that the court sets the level of due care equal to the socially optimal level of care, so that $\overline{x} = x^*$. Would the injurer want to choose $x > x^*$? No, since he would also have no liability by choosing $x = x^*$, and it is costly to undertake "excessive" care. Would the injurer want to choose any $x < x^*$? No, since for levels of care less than the due care amount, the injurer faces the total expected costs of the accident. Since total costs are minimized at x^*, it cannot be optimal to choose a level of care less than that amount. Hence the negligence rule results in the socially optimal level of care being taken.

In this case, both the strict liability rule and the negligence rule achieve the socially optimal level of care. However, note that the division of costs between the injurer and the victim are quite different. Under strict liability, the victim recovers the total costs of *all* accidents from the injurer, while under the negligence rule, the victim is compensated only for actions in which the injurer did not exercise due care. We might anticipate that those more likely to be victims prefer the rule of strict liability, while those more likely to be injurers would prefer the negligence rule.

33.4 Bilateral Accidents

It is rare that an accident is due entirely to one party. In many cases, both parties in an accident may contribute to the costs. A motorist is certainly more likely to hit a pedestrian if the pedestrian crosses in the middle of the street, walks on the wrong side of the road, and so on. Let us extend the model described above to the case where the injured party can also exercise some degree of care to avoid an accident.

Let us write y for the level of care taken by the victim, and let $c_v(y)$ be the cost to the victim of taking this level of care. We also assume that the expected loss of the accident depends on the level of care exercised by both parties and write $L(x, y)$. The appropriate social objective is to minimize total costs,

$$\min_{x,y} \ c_i(x) + c_v(y) + L(x, y).$$

There are now two conditions determining the two optimal levels of care: the marginal cost of increasing care by the injurer should equal the marginal benefit enjoyed by the victims from the reduction in the expected cost of the accident. Furthermore, the marginal cost borne by the victim from increasing his level of care must equal the marginal benefit he achieves from the reduction in expected accident costs.

Let us examine how various forms of liability law influence the behavior of the two parties.

• No liability. As before the injurer will choose a zero level of care, and the victim will choose the level of care that minimizes his total costs, recognizing the fact that the injurer has no incentive to take care. As we've seen, this is not socially optimal.

• Strict liability. In this case the victims will be compensated for all costs imposed on them. Therefore, the victims will have no incentive to take care themselves. Their optimal choice is therefore $y = 0$, and injurers will choose the level of care that is optimal for them given the reckless behavior of the victims. Again, this is not socially optimal.

• Strict division of losses. Under this liability rule, the injurer must pay a fraction f of the costs of the accident. He will thus choose x to minimize $c_i(x) + fL(x, y)$, which will generally lead to a lower level of care than the socially optimal amount. The victim will choose y to minimize $c_v(y) + (1 - f)L(x, y)$, which will also result in too low a level of care being chosen from the social point of view.

• Negligence rule. Recall that in this case the injurer is liable unless he can show that he has taken due care. Suppose that the victim happens to choose the socially optimal level of care y^*. If the injurer expects that the victim will exercise appropriate care, the argument for the single-cause accident can be applied to show that the injurer will choose $x = x^*$. If the injurer chooses the due care standard $x = x^*$, he has no liability, and the victim faces the costs $c_v(y) + L(x^*, y)$. Hence the victim will choose the level of care that minimizes this expression, which is the socially optimal amount y^*. This argument shows that each party choosing the socially optimal level of care is a **Nash equilibrium** under the negligence rule.[4] It turns out that under standard assumptions this is the *unique* equilibrium. Hence we may expect that the negligence rule will lead to socially optimal levels of care.

• Strict liability with defense of contributory negligence. In this rule, the injurer is liable for the accident losses unless he can show that the victim's level of care is less than some specified due care amount $\bar{y}$. As you might suspect, if the law sets the due care level for the victim equal to the socially optimal amount, then both parties will choose the socially optimal level of care.

There are a number of other variations on these rules of law that we will not consider here. The general message that emerges is that if the court can determine an appropriate level of due care by *either* party, some variation of the negligence rule will result in socially optimal decisions by *both* parties.

In order to determine the socially optimal level of due care, the courts must have some idea of how much taking care costs the injurer and the victim and how care affects the expected costs of an accident. The court can always seek the advice of experts on these matters, but in many cases it will be very difficult to determine these amounts.

Suppose that the court can determine the loss involved in an accident, $L(x, y)$, but cannot observe how much care either party took, so that the court cannot apply any form of negligence rule. It turns out that there is still a way to ensure that the two parties each exercise the socially optimal level of care. All the court has to do is to impose the cost of the accident on both the victim and the injurer!

For example, suppose that an automobile hits a bicycle and imposes a cost of \$200 on the victim. If the automobile driver is fined an amount equal to the cost he imposes on the other party—in this case, \$200—then he will have appropriate incentives to minimize that cost. Since the victim also bears a cost of \$200 if the accident occurs, he will also have an incentive to avoid the accident.

Note that it is important that the victim is *not* compensated by the injurer, as in the case of strict liability, for that would give the victim

---

[4] See Chapter 28 for a discussion of Nash equilibrium.

too little incentive to avoid the accident. Each of the parties must face the full cost of the accident for this scheme to work. Again our simple economic analysis has yielded an important insight: the optimal damages to encourage due care by an injurer is not necessarily equal to the optimal compensation to the victim. In fact, these two magnitudes may have very little to do with each other.

This is the logic behind no-fault automobile insurance. The courts take care of punishment for violations of traffic safety laws while insurance companies compensate victims of accidents. The roles of deterring people who cause accidents and of compensating people who are injured are distinct. This gives the state more flexibility in setting rules and regulations to discourage accidents while leaving the role of providing insurance to the private sector.

33.5 Treble Damages in Antitrust Law

There is a large body of antitrust law concerned with what constitutes monopolistic practices, unfair competition, price fixing and the like. There are both civil and criminal sanctions for these illegal acts. For example, the maximum criminal sanction for price fixing is imprisonment for 3 years, a $100,000 fine per person, and a fine of $1,000,000 per corporation. In addition to these criminal sanctions, the Sherman Act and the Clayton Act allow a private individual or firm to sue companies who engage in illegal price fixing and recover "threefold the damages by him sustained."

One reason for the civil sanctions is that it gives injured parties an incentive to bring illegal activities to the attention of the governmental bodies. Complaints by customers are one significant way that price-fixing cases are brought to the attention of the U.S. Department of Justice.

Let us consider a simple model of the treble-damages component of antitrust law.[5] Assume that a group of firms with identical and constant marginal costs collude to form a cartel that sets price and industry output. We assume that in the absence of antitrust action the cartel is able to collude well enough to support the monopoly level of output.

Let $x(p)$ be the demand function facing the cartel. Then we can write the profit-maximization problem as

$$\max_{p} \; (p - c)x(p). \tag{33.5}$$

We denote the solution to this monopoly profit-maximization problem by (x_m, p_m).

---

[5] This discussion is based on Stephen W. Salant, "Treble Damage Awards in Private Lawsuits for Price Fixing," *Journal of Political Economy*, 95, 6, 1987, 1326–36.

A customer of the firm can bring suit against the cartel and recover treble damages if she succeeds in proving that the firms conspired to fix prices. For simplicity assume that the probability of winning the suit is π and that if the suit is won, the consumers will receive damages of γ times the profits of the firm. (In the simplest model $\gamma = 3$, but we want to allow for other possibilities.) This means that the expected damages will be

$$D(x) = \pi\gamma(p - c)x. \tag{33.6}$$

The objective function of the firm should now be

$$\max_{p}\ (p - c)x(p) - D(x(p)). \tag{33.7}$$

Note that the firm recognizes that its production choice will influence the penalty that it has to pay. Substituting equation (33.6) into equation (33.7), we have the following profit-maximizing problem

$$\max_{p}\ [1 - \pi\gamma](p - c)x(p). \tag{33.8}$$

In this model the antitrust penalty is equivalent to a profits tax on the firm: some fraction of the expected profits will have to be paid as damages to injured consumers. Such a tax does not affect the behavior of the cartel: the price that maximizes profits also maximizes $(1 - \pi\gamma)$ times profits. Hence, there should be no change in the behavior of the firm at all!

However, this conclusion is subject to the qualification that the cartel actually forms. The antitrust law causes the profits of the cartel to decrease below the monopoly level. The question is, are the profits of the cartel lower than they would be if the firms behaved competitively? If we take a zero-profit competitive equilibrium as our baseline case, we see from equation (33.8) that the antitrust law will make the expected profits of the cartel negative if $\pi\gamma > 1$. This simply says that that the firms will not have the incentive to form a cartel if the probability of detection and the magnitude of the damages are large enough.

Seeking to Be Damaged

The above discussion assumes that consumer demand does not change with the level of damages. However, this is not the only possible assumption. If the level of awards for price-fixing behavior is very high, potential customers may attempt to "get damaged" in order to collect under the treble-damages provision of the antitrust law.

For simplicity, we assume a consumer with quasilinear utility. If there are no civil damages for price fixing, the consumer's utility-maximization problem is

$$\max_{x}\ u(x) + m - px.$$

If the consumer can sue for damages, and only cares about the expected damages from this suit, his utility-maximization problem is

$$\max_{x} \ u(x) + m - px + D(x).$$

Substituting from equation (33.7) we can write this as

$$\max_{x} \ u(x) + m - px + \pi\gamma(p - c)x.$$

Collecting terms we have

$$\max_{x} \ u(x) + m - [p - \pi\gamma(p - c)]x.$$

The nice thing about this last formulation is that the term in brackets behaves just like a price in the ordinary consumer-maximization problem.

Exploiting this analogy, we define $\hat{p} = p - \pi\gamma(p - c)$ to be the *effective price* facing the consumer. Each unit of the good the consumer buys costs p directly, but it also yields $\pi\gamma(p-c)$ of expected damages to the consumer. This possibility of damage awards lowers the effective cost of the good to the consumer.

Recognizing that the consumer's behavior depends on the effective price allows us to write the cartel's profit-maximization problem as

$$\max_{p} \ [1 - \pi\gamma](p - c)x(\hat{p}).$$

Some elementary algebra—which you should do!—shows that this expression can also be written as

$$\max_{\hat{p}} \ (\hat{p} - c)x(\hat{p}). \tag{33.9}$$

Note the remarkably simple form of this profit-maximization problem. The consumer and the cartel face the *same* effective price $\hat{p}$. In equation (33.5) we defined p_m to be the price that maximized monopoly profits in the absence of antitrust law. Hence the *effective price* that maximizes (33.9) must also be p_m. Letting p^* be the price that the cartel actually charges, this means that

$$p_m = p^* - \pi\gamma(p^* - c). \tag{33.10}$$

It is easy to see from equation (33.10) that p^* is larger than p_m. The cartel actually increases its price *above* the monopoly price since it expects to pay some damages to the consumers. The consumers, however, are willing to buy more at this price than they would otherwise since they expect to receive some damages from the firm! Of course the *effective* price to the cartel and the consumers are exactly the same as they would be in the absence of any antitrust law.

33.6 Which Model Is Right?

We've presented two models of the treble-damages provision in antitrust law. The first model presumed that consumers would not change their behavior even if there was a possibility that they might collect legal damages. Here we found that the cartel, assuming it formed, would set the same price and sell the same amount of output as it would with no antitrust law. In the second model, the consumers behaved more strategically. They recognized the fact that the more they consumed, the more damages they would be able to collect if the cartel was found guilty of price fixing. In this case, the actual price charged by the cartel would be higher than the monopoly price, but the effective price would be the same as the monopoly price. We can't answer the question of which is the correct model on purely logical grounds. The answer depends on how the consumers actually behave.

Summary

1. Economics can be used to analyze the choice of criminal activities and to structure incentives to discourage crime.

2. Economics can be used to analyze the impact of different forms of liability law.

3. Economics can be used to asses the impact of legal remedies for price fixing on firm behavior.

REVIEW QUESTIONS

1. Tossing a chewing gum wrapper out of the window on a California freeway may result in a $1000 fine for littering, even though the social cost of the litter is much smaller than $1000. Does this make economic sense?

2. Which party, the injurer or the victim, takes too little care in bilateral accidents under the rule of strict liability?

3. Consider the model of trebble damages where the consumers "seek injury." If $\gamma = 3$, $\pi = 1/6$, $c = 0$ and $p_m = 100$, what will p^* equal?

CHAPTER **34**

INFORMATION TECHNOLOGY

One of the most radical changes in the economy in the last 15 years has been the emergence of the **information economy**. The popular press is filled with stories about advances in computer technology, the Internet, and new software. Not surprisingly, many of these stories are on the business pages of the newspaper, for this *technological* revolution is also an *economic* revolution.

Some observers have gone so far as to put the Information Revolution on a par with the Industrial Revolution. Just as the Industrial Revolution transformed the way *goods* were produced, distributed, and consumed, the Information Revolution is transforming the way *information* is produced, distributed, and consumed.

It has been claimed that these dramatically new technologies will require a fundamentally different form of economics. Bits, it is argued, are fundamentally different than atoms. Bits can be reproduced costlessly and distributed around the world at the speed of light, and they never deteriorate. Material goods, made of atoms, have none of these properties: they are costly to produce and transport, and they inevitably deteriorate.

It is true that the unusual properties of bits require new economic analysis, but I would argue that they do not require a new *kind* of economic analysis. After all, economics is primarily about *people* not *goods*. The models we have analyzed in this book have had to do with how people make choices and interact with each other. We have rarely had occasion to refer to the specific goods that were involved in the transactions. The fundamental concerns were the tastes of the individuals, the technology of production, and the structure of the market, and *these* same factors will determine how markets for information will work ... or not work.

In this chapter we will investigate a few economic models relevant to the information revolution. The first has to do with the economics of networks, the second with switching costs, and the third with rights management for information goods. These examples will illustrate how the fundamental tools of economic analysis can help us to understand the world of bits as well as the world of atoms.

34.1 Systems Competition

Information technology often takes the form of *systems*. Such systems involve several components, often provided by different firms, that only have value if they work together. Hardware and software, video cassettes and video players, and Web servers and browsers are all examples. These components are **complements** in producing value for the end user. Just as a right shoe isn't worth much without a left shoe, the best computer hardware in the world isn't worth much if there is no software for it.

It follows that competition among the providers of these components often have to worry just as much about their "complementors" as their competitors. A key part of Apple's competitive strategy has to involve their relations with software developers. This gives competitive strategy in information technology (IT) industries a different flavor than strategy in traditional industries.[1]

34.2 Lock-In

Since IT components often work together as systems, switching any one component often involves switching others as well. This means that the **switching costs** associated with one component in IT industries may be quite substantial. For example, switching from a Macintosh to a Windows-based PC involves not only the hardware costs of the computer itself, but also involves purchasing of a whole new library of software, and, even more importantly, learning how to use a brand new system.

---

[1] See Shapiro, Carl and Hal R. Varian, *Information Rules: A Strategic Guide to the Network Economy*, Harvard Business School Press, 1998, for a guide to competitive strategy in IT industries.

When switching costs are very high, users may find themselves experiencing **lock-in**, a situation where the cost of changing to a different system is so high that switching is virtually inconceivable. This is bad for the consumers, but is, of course, quite attractive for the seller of the components that make up the system in question. Since the locked-in user has a very *inelastic* demand, the seller(s) can jack up the prices of their components to extract consumer surplus from the user.

Of course, wary consumers will try to avoid such lock-in, or, at the very least, bargain hard to be compensated for being locked in. Even if the consumers themselves are poor at bargaining, competition among sellers of systems will force prices down for the *initial* purchase, since the locked-in consumers can provide them with a steady revenue stream afterwards.

Consider, for example, choosing an Internet service provider (ISP). Once you have committed to such a choice, it may be inconvenient to switch due to the cost of notifying all of your correspondents about your new e-mail address, reconfiguring your Internet access programs, and so on. The monopoly power due to these switching costs means that the ISP can charge more than the marginal cost of providing service, once it has acquired you as a customer. But the flip side of this effect is that the stream of profits of the locked-in customers is a valuable asset, and ISPs will compete up front to acquire such customers by offering discounts and other inducements to sign up with them.

A Model of Competition with Switching Costs

Let's examine a model of this phenomenon. We assume that the cost of providing a customer with Internet access is c per month. We also assume a perfectly competitive market, with many identical firms, so that in the absence of any switching costs, the price of Internet service would simply be $p = c$.

But now suppose that there is a cost s of switching ISPs and that ISPs can offer a discount of size d for the first month to attract new customers. At the start of a given month, a consumer contemplates switching to a new ISP. If he does so, he only has to pay the discounted price, $p - d$, but he also has to endure the switching costs s. If he stays with his old provider, he has to pay the price p. After the first month, we assume that both providers continue to charge the same price p.

The consumer will change if the present value of switching exceeds the present value of staying with the original ISP. Letting r be the (monthly) interest rate, the consumer will switch if

$$(p - d) + \frac{p}{r} + s > p + \frac{p}{r}.$$

Competition between providers ensures that the consumer is indifferent between switching or not switching, which implies

$$(p - d) + s = p.$$

It follows that $d = s$, which means the discount offered just covers the switching cost of the consumer.

On the producer side, we suppose that competition forces the present value of profits to be zero. The present value of profit associated with a single customer is initial discount, plus the present value of the profits in future months. Letting r be the (monthly) interest rate, and using the fact that $d = s$, the zero-profit condition can be written as

$$(p - s) - c + \frac{p - c}{r} = 0. \tag{34.1}$$

Rearranging this equation gives us two equivalent ways to describe the equilibrium price:

$$p - c + \frac{p - c}{r} = s, \tag{34.2}$$

or

$$p = c + \frac{r}{1 + r} s. \tag{34.3}$$

Equation (34.2) says that the present value of the future profits from the consumer must just equal the consumer's switching cost. Equation (34.3) says that the price of service is a markup on marginal cost, with the amount of the markup is proportional to the switching costs.

Adding switching costs to the model raises the *monthly* price of service above cost, but competition for this profit flow forces the *initial* price down. Effectively, the producer is investing in the discount $d = s$ in order to acquire the flow of markups in the future.

In reality many ISPs have other sources of revenue than just the monthly income from their customers. America Online, for example, derives a substantial part of its operating revenue from advertising. It makes sense for them to offer large up-front discounts, in order to capture advertising revenue, even if they have to provide Internet connections at rates at or below cost.

We can easily add this effect to the model. If a is the advertising revenue generated by the consumer each month, the zero-profit condition requires

$$(p - s) + a - c + \frac{p + a - c}{r} = 0. \tag{34.4}$$

Solving for p we have

$$p = c - a + \frac{r}{1 + r} s.$$

This equation shows that what is relevant is the *net* cost of servicing the customer, $c - a$, which involves both the service cost and the advertising revenues.

34.3 Network Externalities

We have already examined the idea of **externalities** in Chapter 32. Recall that economists use this term to describe situations in which one person's consumption directly influences another person's utility. **Network externalities** are a special kind of externalities in which one person's utility for a good depends on the *number* of other people who consume this good.[2]

Take for example a consumer's demand for a fax machine. People want fax machines so they can communicate with each other. If no one else has a fax machine, it certainly isn't worthwhile for you to buy one. Modems have a similar property: a modem is only useful if there is another modem somewhere that you can communicate with.

Another more indirect effect for network externalities arises with complementary goods. There is no reason for a video store to locate in a community where no one owns a video player; but then again, there is little reason to buy a video player unless you have access to pre-recorded video tapes to play in the machine. In this case the demand for video tapes depends on the number of VCRs, and the demand for VCRs depends on the number of video tapes available, resulting in a slightly more general form of network externalities.

34.4 Markets with Network Externalities

Let us try to model network externalities using a simple demand and supply model. Suppose that there are 1000 people in a market for some good and we index the people by $v = 1, \ldots, 1000$. Think of v as measuring the **reservation price** for the good by person v. Then if the price of the good is p, the number of people who think that the good is worth at least p is $1000 - p$. For example, if the price of the good is \$200, then there are 800 people who are willing to pay at least \$200 for the good, so the total number of units sold would be 800. This structure generates a standard, downward-sloping demand curve.

But now let's add a twist to the model. Suppose that the good we are examining exhibits network externalities, like a fax machine or a telephone. For simplicity, let us suppose that the value of the good to person v is vn, where n is the number of people who consume the good—the number of people who are connected to the network. The more people there are who consume the good, the more *each* person is willing to pay to acquire it.[3] What does the demand function look like for this model?

---

[2] More generally, a person's utility could depend on the *identity* of other users; it is easy to add this to the analysis.

[3] We should really interpret n as the number of people who are *expected* to consume the good, but this distinction won't be very important for what follows.

If the price is p, there is someone who is just indifferent between buying the good and not buying it. Let $\hat{v}$ denote the index of this marginal individual. By definition, he is just indifferent to purchasing the good, so his willingness to pay for the good equals its price:

$$p = \hat{v}n. \tag{34.5}$$

Since this "marginal person" is indifferent, everyone with a *higher* value of v than $\hat{v}$ must definitely want to buy. This means that the number of people who want to buy the good is

$$n = 1000 - \hat{v}. \tag{34.6}$$

Putting equations (34.5) and (34.6) together, we have a condition that characterizes equilibrium in this market:

$$p = n(1000 - n).$$

This equation gives us a relationship between the price of the good and the number of users. In this sense, it is a kind of demand curve; if there are n people who purchase the good, then the willingness to pay of the marginal individual is given by the height of the curve.

However, if we look at the plot of this curve in Figure 34.1, we see that it has quite a different shape than a standard demand curve! If the number of people who connect is low, then the willingness to pay of the marginal individual is low, because there aren't many other people out there that he can communicate with. If there are a large number of people connected, then the willingness to pay of the marginal individual is low, because everyone else who valued it more highly has already connected. These two forces lead to the humped shape depicted in Figure 34.1.

Now that we understand the demand side of the market, let's look at the supply side. To keep things simple, let us suppose that the good can be provided by a constant returns to scale technology. As we've seen, this means that the supply curve is a flat line at price equals average cost.

Note that there are three possible intersections of the demand and supply curve. There is a low-level equilibrium where $n^* = 0$. This is where no one consumes the good (connects to the network), so no one is willing to pay anything to consume the good. This might be referred to as a "pessimistic expectations" equilibrium.

The middle equilibrium with a positive but small number of consumers is one where people don't think the network will be very big, so they aren't willing to pay that much to connect to it—and therefore the network isn't very big.

Finally the last equilibrium has a large number of people, n_H. Here the price is small because the marginal person who purchases the good doesn't value it very highly, even though the market is very large.

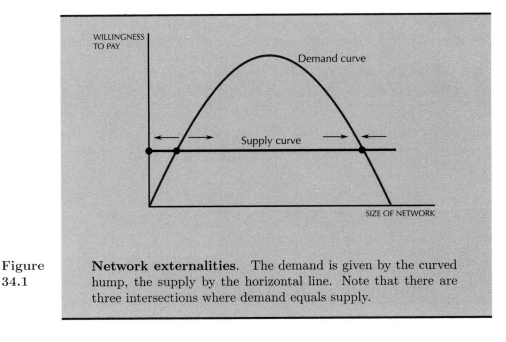

Figure
34.1
Network externalities. The demand is given by the curved
hump, the supply by the horizontal line. Note that there are
three intersections where demand equals supply.

34.5 Market Dynamics

Which of the three equilibria will we see occur? So far the model gives
us no reason to choose among them. At each of these equilibria, demand
equals supply. However, we can add a dynamic adjustment process to help
us decide which equilibrium is more likely to occur.

It is plausible to assume that when people are willing to pay more than
the cost of the good, the size of the market expands and, when they are
willing to pay less, the market contracts. Geometrically this is saying that
when the demand curve is above the supply curve, the quantity goes up
and, when it is beneath the supply curve, the quantity goes down. The
arrows in Figure 34.1 illustrate this adjustment process.

These dynamics give us a little more information. It is now evident
that the low-level equilibrium, where no one connects, and the high-level
equilibrium, where many people connect, are stable whereas the middle
equilibrium is unstable. Hence it is unlikely that the final resting point of
the system will be the middle equilibrium.

We are now left with two possible stable equilibria; how can we tell which
is likely to occur? One idea is to think about how costs might change over
time. For the kinds of examples we have discussed—faxes, VCRs, computer
networks, and so on—it is natural to suppose that the cost of the good starts
out high and then decreases over time due to technological progress. This
process is illustrated in Figure 34.2. At a high unit cost there is only one
stable equilibrium—where demand equals zero. When the cost decreases

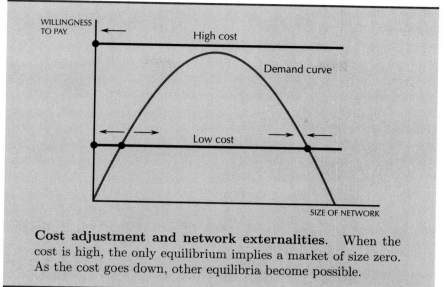

Cost adjustment and network externalities. When the cost is high, the only equilibrium implies a market of size zero. As the cost goes down, other equilibria become possible.

Figure
34.2

sufficiently, there are two stable equilibria.

Now add some noise to the system. Think of perturbing the number of people connected to the network around the equilibrium point of $n^* = 0$. These perturbations could be random, or they could be part of business strategies such as initial discounts or other promotions. As the cost gets smaller and smaller, it becomes increasingly likely that one of these perturbations will kick the system up *past* the unstable equilibrium. When this happens, the dynamic adjustment will push the system up to the high-level equilibrium.

A possible path for the number of consumers of the good is depicted in Figure 34.3.

It starts out at essentially zero, with a few small perturbations over time. The cost decreases, and at some point we reach a critical mass that kicks us up past the low-level equilibrium and the system then zooms up to the high-level equilibrium.

A real-life example of this kind of adjustment is the market for fax machines. Figure 34.4 illustrates the price and number of fax machines shipped over a period of 12 years.[4]

---

[4] This diagram is taken from "Critical Mass and Network Size with Applications to the US Fax Market," by Nicholas Economides and Charles Himmelberg (Discussion Paper no. EC-95-11, Stern School of Business, N.Y.U., 1995). See also Michael L. Katz and Carl Shapiro, "Systems Competition and Network Effects," *Journal of Economic Perspectives*, 8 (1994), 93–116, for a nice overview of network externalities and their implications.

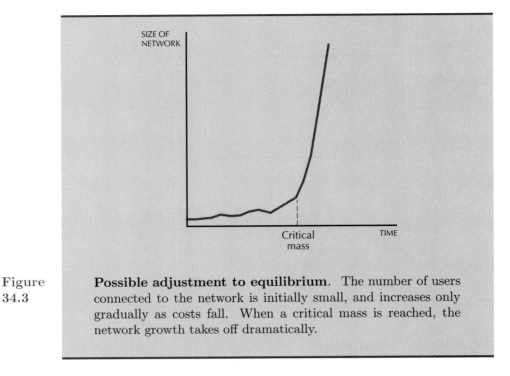

Figure
34.3

Possible adjustment to equilibrium. The number of users connected to the network is initially small, and increases only gradually as costs fall. When a critical mass is reached, the network growth takes off dramatically.

EXAMPLE: Network Externalities in Computer Software

Network externalities arise naturally in the provision of computer software. It is very convenient to be able to exchange data files and tips with other users of the same software. This gives a significant advantage to the largest seller in a given market and leads software producers to invest heavily in acquiring market share.

Examples of this abound. Adobe Systems for example, invested heavily in developing a "page description language" called PostScript for desktop publishing. Adobe realized clearly that no one would invest the time and resources necessary to learn PostScript unless it was the clear "industry standard." So the firm deliberately allowed competitors to "clone" its language in order to create a competitive market in PostScript interpreters. Adobe's strategy paid off: several competitors emerged (including one that gave its product away) and PostScript became a widely used standard for desktop publishing. Adobe kept a few things proprietary—for instance, techniques for displaying fonts at low resolution—and managed to dominate the high end of the market. Ironically, Adobe's market success was due to its ability to encourage entry by its competitors!

In recent years, many software producers have followed this model. Adobe itself gives away several software products, such as the Adobe Acrobat reader. One of the hot new stock issues of 1995, Netscape Communica-

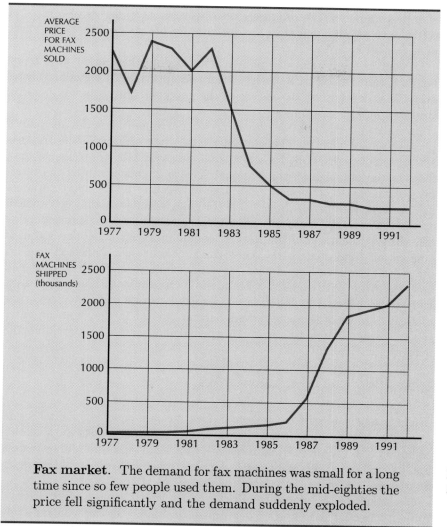

Fax market. The demand for fax machines was small for a long time since so few people used them. During the mid-eighties the price fell significantly and the demand suddenly exploded.

Figure
34.4

tions Corporation, acquired the lion's share of the Web browser market by giving away its main product, making it a prime example of a company that "lost money on every sale, but made up for it in volume."

34.6 Implications of Network Externalities

The model described above, simple though it is, still yields a number of insights. For example, the critical mass issue is very important: if one user's demand depends on how many other users there are, it is very important to try to stimulate growth early in the life cycle of a product. Nowadays it is quite common to see producers offering very cheap access to a piece of software or a communications service in order to "create a market" where none existed before.

Of course, the critical question is how big does the market have to be before it can take off on its own? Theory can provide little guidance here; everything depends on the nature of the good and the costs and benefits the users face in adopting it.

Another important implication of network externalities is the role played by governmental policy. The Internet is a prime example. The Internet was originally used only by a few small research labs to exchange data files. In the mid-eighties the National Science Foundation used the Internet technology to connect several large universities to 12 supercomputers deployed at various locations. The original vision was that researchers at the universities would send data back and forth to the supercomputers. But a fundamental property of communications networks is that if you are all connected to the same thing, you are all connected to each other. This allowed researchers to send email to each other that had nothing to do with the supercomputers. Once a critical mass of users had been connected to the Internet, its value to new users increased dramatically. Most of these new users had no interest in the supercomputer centers, even though this was the original motivation for providing the network.

34.7 Rights Management

There is much interest these days in new business models for intellectual property (IP). IP transactions take a variety of forms: books are sold outright and also borrowed from libraries. Videos can either be sold or rented. Some software is licensed for particular uses; other software is sold outright. Shareware is a form of software in which payment is voluntary.

Choosing the terms and conditions under which a piece of intellectual property is offered is a critical business decision. Should you use copy protection? Should you encourage users to share a news item with a friend? Should you sell to individuals or use site license?

Some simple economics helps to understand the relevant issues. Let's consider a purely digital good, such as an online newspaper, so we don't have to worry about marginal cost of production. First let us consider behavior under some default set of terms and conditions. The owner of the digital good will choose a price and, implicitly, a quantity to sell so as to maximize profit:

$$\max_{y} \ p(y)y \qquad\qquad (34.7)$$

This yields some optimal (p^*, y^*).

Now the seller of the good contemplates liberalizing terms and conditions: let's say extending a trial period of free use from 1 week to 1 month. This has two effects on the demand curve. First, it increases the value of the product to each of the potential users, shifting the demand curve up. But it also may easily result in less of the item being sold, since some users will find the longer trial period enough to meet their needs.

Let us model this by defining the new amount consumed by $Y = by$, where $b > 1$, and the new demand curve by $P(Y) = ap(Y)$, where $a > 1$. The new profit-maximization problem now becomes

$$\max_Y \ P(Y)y.$$

Note that we multiply price times the amount sold, y, not the amount consumed, Y.

Applying the definitions $Y = by$ and $P(Y) = ap(Y)$, we can write this as

$$\max_Y \ ap(Y)\frac{Y}{b} = \max_Y \ \frac{a}{b}p(Y)Y.$$

This maximization problem looks like problem (34.7) except for the constant a/b in front of the max. This will not affect the optimal choice, so we can conclude that $Y^* = y^*$.

This simple analysis allows us to make several conclusions:

- The amount of the good consumed, Y^*, is independent of the terms and conditions.

- The amount of the good produced is y^*/b which is less than y^*.

- The profits could go up or down depending on whether a/b is greater or less than 1. Profits go up if the increase in value to the consumers who buy the product compensates for the reduced number of buyers.

EXAMPLE: Video Rental

Video stores can choose the terms and conditions under which they rent videos. The longer you can keep the video, the more valuable it is to you, since you have a longer period of time during which you can watch it. But the longer you keep the video, the less profit the store makes from it, since it is unable to rent it to someone else. The optimal choice for the rental period involves trading off these two effects.

In practice, this has tended to lead to a form of product differentiation. New releases are rented for short periods, since the the profits from other renters being excluded are very substantial. Older videos are rented for longer periods, since there is less cost to the store from the video being unavailable.

34.8 Sharing Intellectual Property

Intellectual property is often shared. Libraries, for example, facilitate the sharing of books. Video stores help people to "share" videos—and charge a price for doing so. Interlibrary loan helps libraries share books among themselves. Even textbooks—such as the one you are holding—are shared among students from one term to the next via the resale market.

There is considerable debate in the publishing and library communities about the proper role of sharing. Librarians have established an informal "rule of five" for interlibrary loan: an item may be loaned out up to five times before additional royalty payments should be made to the publisher. Publishers and authors have traditionally been unenthusiastic about the resale market for books.

The advent of digital information has made this situation even more acute. Digital information can be perfectly reproduced, and "sharing" can be taken to new extremes. Recently, a well-known country music singer engaged in a vociferous public relations campaign against stores selling used CDs. The problem was that CDs do not deteriorate with replay and it is possible to buy a CD, tape it, and then sell the CD to the used-CD store.

Let us try to construct a model of this sort of sharing phenomenon. We begin with the baseline case in which there is no sharing. In this case a video maker chooses to produce y copies of a video to maximize profit:

$$\max_{y} \ p(y)y - cy - F. \tag{34.8}$$

As usual, $p(y)$ is the inverse demand function, c is the (constant) marginal cost, and F is the fixed cost. Let the profit maximizing output be denoted by y_n, where the n stands for "no sharing."

Now suppose that a video rental market is allowed. In this case the number of videos *viewed* will be distinct from the number of copies produced. If y is the number of videos produced and each video is shared among k viewers, then the number of viewings will be $x = ky$. (For simplicity we are assuming that *all* copies of the video are rented in this case.)

We need to specify how the consumers sort themselves into the "clubs" that share the videos. The simplest assumption is that the consumers with high values associate with each other, and the consumers with low-values associate with each other. That is, one club consists of consumers with the k highest values, another club consists of the consumers with the next k highest values, and so on. (Other assumptions could be used, but this one gives a very simple analysis.)

If y copies of the video are produced, $x = ky$ copies will be viewed, so the willingness to pay of the marginal individual will be $p(x) = p(ky)$. However, it is clearly the case that there is some inconvenience cost to renting a video rather than owning it yourself. Let us denote this "transactions cost" by t, so that the willingness to pay of the marginal individual becomes $p(x) - t$.

Recall that we have assumed that all copies of the video are shared among k users. Therefore the willingness to pay of a *video store* will just be k times the willingness to pay of the marginal individual. That is, if y copies are produced, the willingness to pay of the video store will be

$$P(y) = k[p(ky) - t]. \tag{34.9}$$

Equation (34.9) contains the two key effects that arise from sharing: the willingness to pay goes *down* since more videos are viewed than are produced; but the willingness to pay also goes *up* since the cost of a single video is shared among several individuals.

The profit maximization problem of the producer now becomes

$$\max_{y} P(y)y - cy - F,$$

which can be written as

$$\max_{y} k[p(ky) - t]y - cy - F,$$

or

$$\max_{y} p(ky)ky - \left(\frac{c}{k} + t\right) ky - F.$$

Recalling that the number of viewings, x, is related to the number produced, y, via $x = ky$, we can also write the maximization problem as

$$\max_{x} p(x)x - \left(\frac{c}{k} + t\right) x - F.$$

Note that this problem is identical to problem (34.8), with the exception that the marginal cost is now $(c/k + t)$ rather than c.

The close relationship between the two problems is very useful since it allows us to make the following observation: *profits will be larger when rental is possible than when it is not if and only if*

$$\frac{c}{k} + t < c.$$

Rearranging this condition, we have

$$\left(\frac{k}{k+1}\right) t < c.$$

For large k, the fraction on the left is about 1. Hence the critical issue is the relationship between the marginal cost of production, c, and the transactions cost of renting, t.

If the cost of production is large and the cost of renting is small, then the most profitable thing for a producer to do is to produce a few copies, sell them at a high price, and let the consumers rent. On the other hand, if the transactions cost of renting is larger than the cost of production, it is more profitable for a producer to have renting prohibited: since renting is so inconvenient for the consumers, video stores aren't willing to pay much more for the "shared" videos, and so the producer is better off selling.

Summary

1. Because information technology works together in systems, it is costly to consumers to switch any one component.

2. In equilibrium the discount offered first period is paid for by increased prices in future periods.

3. Network externalities arise when one person's willingness to pay for a good depends on the number of other users of that good.

4. Models with network externalities typically exhibit multiple equilibria. The ultimate outcome often depends on the history of the industry.

5. Rights management involves a tradeoff between increased value and prices versus reduced sales.

6. Information goods like books and videos are often rented or shared as well as purchased. Rental or purchase can be more profitable depending on how transactions costs compare with production costs.

REVIEW QUESTIONS

1. If the cost to a customer from switching long-distance carriers is on the order of $50, how much should a long-distance carrier be willing to pay to acquire a new customer?

2. Describe how the demand for a word processing package might exhibit network externalities.

3. Suppose that the marginal cost of producing an extra video is zero and the transactions cost of renting a video is zero. Does a producer make more money by selling the video or by renting it?

CHAPTER **35**

PUBLIC GOODS

In Chapter 32 we argued that for certain kinds of externalities, it was not difficult to eliminate the inefficiencies. In the case of a consumption externality between two people, for example, all one had to do was to ensure that initial property rights were clearly specified. People could then trade the right to generate the externality in the normal way. In the case of production externalities, the market itself provided profit signals to sort out the property rights in the most efficient way. In the case of common property, assigning property rights to someone would eliminate the inefficiency.

Unfortunately, not all externalities can be handled in that manner. As soon as there are more than two economic agents involved things become much more difficult. Suppose, for example, that instead of the two roommates examined in the last chapter, we had *three* roommates—one smoker and two nonsmokers. Then the amount of smoke would be a negative externality for both of the nonsmokers.

Let's suppose that property rights are well defined—say the nonsmokers have the right to demand clean air. Just as before, although they have the *right* to clean air, they also have the right to trade some of that clean air away in return for appropriate compensation. But now there is a problem involved—the nonsmokers have to agree among themselves how much smoke should be allowed and what the compensation should be.

Perhaps one of the nonsmokers is much more sensitive than the other, or one of them is much richer than the other. They may have very different preferences and resources, and yet they both have to reach some kind of agreement to allow for an efficient allocation of smoke.

Instead of roommates, we can think of inhabitants of a whole country. How much pollution should be allowed in the country? If you think that reaching an agreement is difficult with only three roommates, imagine what it is like with millions of people!

The smoke externality with three people is an example of a **public good**—a good that must be provided in the same amount to all the affected consumers. In this case the amount of smoke generated will be the same for all consumers—each person may value it differently, but they all have to face the same amount.

Many public goods are provided by the government. For example, streets and sidewalks are provided by local municipalities. There are a certain number and quality of streets in a town, and everyone has that number available to use. National defense is another good example; there is one level of national defense provided for all the inhabitants of a country. Each citizen may value it differently—some may want more, some may want less—but they are all provided with the same amount.

Public goods are an example of a particular kind of consumption externality: everyone must consume the same amount of the good. They are a particularly troublesome kind of externality, for the decentralized market solutions that economists are fond of don't work very well in allocating public goods. People can't purchase different amounts of public defense; somehow they have to decide on a common amount.

The first issue to examine is what the ideal amount of the public good should be. Then we'll discuss some ways that might be used to make social decisions about public goods.

35.1 When to Provide a Public Good?

Let us start with a simple example. Suppose that there are two roommates, 1 and 2. They are trying to decide whether or not to purchase a TV. Given the size of their apartment, the TV will necessarily go in the living room, and both roommates will be able to watch it. Thus it will be a public good, rather than a private good. The question is, is it worth it for them to acquire the TV?

Let's use w_1 and w_2 to denote each person's initial wealth, g_1 and g_2 to denote each person's contribution to the TV, and x_1 and x_2 to denote each person's money left over to spend on private consumption. The budget constraints are given by

$$x_1 + g_1 = w_1$$
$$x_2 + g_2 = w_2.$$

We also suppose that the TV costs c dollars, so that in order to purchase it, the sum of the two contributions must be at least c:

$$g_1 + g_2 \geq c.$$

This equation summarizes the technology available to provide the public good: the roommates can acquire one TV if together they pay the cost c.

The utility function of person 1 will depend on his or her private consumption, x_1, and the availability of the TV—the public good. We'll write person 1's utility function as $u_1(x_1, G)$, where G will either be 0, indicating no TV, or 1, indicating that a TV is present. Person 2 will have utility function $u_2(x_2, G)$. Each person's private consumption has a subscript to indicate that the good is consumed by person 1 or person 2, but the public good has no subscript. It is "consumed" by both people. Of course, it isn't really consumed in the sense of being "used up"; rather, it is the *services* of the TV that are consumed by the two roommates.

The roommates may value the services of the TV quite differently. We can measure the value that each person places on the TV by asking how much each person would be willing to pay to have the TV available. To do this, we'll use the concept of the **reservation price**, introduced in Chapter 15.

The reservation price of person 1 is the maximum amount that person 1 would be willing to pay to have the TV present. That is, it is that price, r_1, such that person 1 is just indifferent between paying r_1 and having the TV available, and not having the TV at all. If person 1 pays the reservation price and gets the TV, he will have $w_1 - r_1$ available for private consumption. If he doesn't get the TV, he will have w_1 available for private consumption. If he is to be just indifferent between these two alternatives, we must have

$$u_1(w_1 - r_1, 1) = u_1(w_1, 0).$$

This equation defines the reservation price for person 1—the maximum amount that he would be willing to pay to have the TV present. A similar equation defines the reservation price for person 2. Note that in general the reservation price of each person will depend on that person's wealth: the maximum amount that an individual will be *willing* to pay will depend to some degree on how much that individual is *able* to pay.

Recall that an allocation is Pareto efficient if there is no way to make both people better off. An allocation is Pareto *inefficient* if there *is* some way to make both people better off; in this case, we say that a **Pareto improvement** is possible. In the TV problem there are only two sorts of allocations that are of interest. One is an allocation where the TV is not provided. This allocation takes the simple form $(w_1, w_2, 0)$; that is, each person spends his wealth only on his private consumption.

The other kind of allocation is the one where the public good is provided. This will be an allocation of the form $(x_1, x_2, 1)$, where

$$x_1 = w_1 - g_1$$

$$x_2 = w_2 - g_2.$$

These two equations come from rewriting the budget constraints. They say that each individual's private consumption is determined by the wealth that he has left over after making his contribution to the public good.

Under what conditions should the TV be provided? That is, when is there a payment scheme (g_1, g_2) such that both people will be better off having the TV and paying their share than not having the TV? In the language of economics, when will it be a Pareto improvement to provide the TV?

It will be a Pareto improvement to provide the allocation $(x_1, x_2, 1)$ if both people would be better off having the TV provided than not having it provided. This means

$$u_1(w_1, 0) < u_1(x_1, 1)$$
$$u_2(w_2, 0) < u_2(x_2, 1).$$

Now use the definition of the reservation prices r_1 and r_2 and the budget constraint to write

$$u_1(w_1 - r_1, 1) = u_1(w_1, 0) < u_1(x_1, 1) = u_1(w_1 - g_1, 1)$$
$$u_2(w_2 - r_2, 1) = u_2(w_2, 0) < u_2(x_2, 1) = u_2(w_2 - g_2, 1).$$

Looking at the left- and the right-hand sides of these inequalities, and remembering that more private consumption must increase utility, we can conclude that

$$w_1 - r_1 < w_1 - g_1$$
$$w_2 - r_2 < w_2 - g_2,$$

which in turn implies

$$r_1 > g_1$$
$$r_2 > g_2.$$

This is a condition that must be satisfied if an allocation $(w_1, w_2, 0)$ is Pareto inefficient: it must be that the contribution that each person is making to the TV is less than his willingness to pay for the TV. If a consumer can acquire the good for less than the maximum that he would be willing to pay, then the acquisition would be to his benefit. Thus the condition that the reservation price exceeds the cost share simply says that a Pareto improvement will result when each roommate can acquire the services of the TV for less than the maximum that he would be willing to pay for it. This is clearly a *necessary* condition for purchase of the TV to be a Pareto improvement.

If each roommate's willingness to pay exceeds his cost share, then the *sum* of the willingnesses to pay must be greater than the cost of the TV:

$$r_1 + r_2 > g_1 + g_2 = c. \tag{35.1}$$

This condition is a *sufficient* condition for it to be a Pareto improvement to provide the TV. If the condition is satisfied, then there will be some payment plan such that both people will be made better off by providing the public good. If $r_1 + r_2 \geq c$, then the total amount that the roommates will be willing to pay is at least as large as the cost of purchase, so they can easily find a payment plan (g_1, g_2) such that $r_1 \geq g_1$, $r_2 \geq g_2$, and $g_1 + g_2 = c$. This condition is so simple that you might wonder why we went through all the detail in deriving it. Well, there are a few subtleties involved.

First, it is important to note that the condition describing when provision of the public good will be a Pareto improvement only depends on each agent's *willingness* to pay and on the total cost. If the sum of the reservation prices exceeds the cost of the TV, then there will always *exist* a payment scheme such that both people will be better off having the public good than not having it.

Second, whether or not it is Pareto efficient to provide the public good will, in general, depend on the initial distribution of wealth (w_1, w_2). This is true because, in general, the reservation prices r_1 and r_2 will depend on the distribution of wealth. It perfectly possible that for some distributions of wealth $r_1 + r_2 > c$, and for other distributions of wealth $r_1 + r_2 < c$.

To see how this can be, imagine a situation where one roommate really loves the TV and the other roommate is nearly indifferent about acquiring it. Then if the TV-loving roommate had all of the wealth, he would be willing to pay more than the cost of the TV all by himself. Thus it would be a Pareto improvement to provide the TV. But if the indifferent roommate had all of the wealth, then the TV lover wouldn't have much money to contribute toward the TV, and it would be Pareto efficient *not* to provide the TV.

Thus, in general, whether or not the public good should be provided will depend on the distribution of wealth. But in specific cases the provision of the public good may be independent of the distribution of wealth. For example, suppose that the preferences of the two roommates were quasilinear. This means that the utility functions take the form

$$u_1(x_1, G) = x_1 + v_1(G)$$
$$u_2(x_2, G) = x_2 + v_2(G),$$

where G will be 0 or 1, depending on whether or not the public good is available. For simplicity, suppose that $v_1(0) = v_2(0) = 0$. This says that no TV provides zero utility from watching TV.[1]

In this case the definitions of the reservation prices become

$$u_1(w_1 - r_1, 1) = w_1 - r_1 + v_1(1) = u_1(w_1, 0) = w_1$$
$$u_2(w_2 - r_2, 1) = w_2 - r_2 + v_2(1) = u_2(w_2, 0) = w_2,$$

---

[1] Perhaps watching TV should be assigned a negative utility.

which implies that the reservation prices are given by

$$r_1 = v_1(1)$$
$$r_2 = v_2(1).$$

Thus the reservation prices are independent of the amount of wealth, and hence the optimal provision of the public good will be independent of wealth, at least over some range of wealths.[2]

35.2 Private Provision of the Public Good

We have seen above that acquiring the TV will be Pareto efficient for the two roommates if the sum of their willingnesses to pay exceeds the cost of providing the public good. This answers the question about efficient allocation of the good, but it does not necessarily follow that they will actually decide to acquire the TV. Whether they actually decide to acquire the TV depends on the particular method they adopt to make joint decisions.

If the two roommates cooperate and truthfully reveal how much they value the TV, then it should not be difficult for them to agree on whether or not they should buy the TV. But under some circumstances, they may not have incentives to tell the truth about their values.

For example, suppose that each person valued the TV equally, and that each person's reservation price was greater than the cost, so that $r_1 > c$ and $r_2 > c$. Then person 1 might think that if he said he had 0 value for the TV, the other person would acquire it anyway. But person 2 could reason the same way! One can imagine other situations where both people would refuse to contribute in the hopes that the other person would go out and unilaterally purchase the TV.

In this kind of situation, economists say that the people are attempting to **free ride** on each other: each person hopes that the other person will purchase the public good on his own. Since each person will have full use of the services of the TV if it is acquired, each person has an incentive to try to pay as little as possible toward the provision of the TV.

35.3 Free Riding

Free riding is similar, but not identical, to the prisoner's dilemma that we examined in Chapter 28. To see this, let us construct a numerical example of the TV problem described above. Suppose that each person has a wealth of $500, that each person values the TV at $100, and that the cost of the

---

[2] Even this will only be true for some ranges of wealth, since we must always require that $r_1 \leq w_1$ and $r_2 \leq w_2$—i.e., the willingness to pay is less than the ability to pay.

TV is $150. Since the sum of the reservation prices exceeds the cost, it is Pareto efficient to buy the TV.

Let us suppose that there is no way for one of the roommates to exclude the other one from watching the TV and that each roommate will decide independently whether or not to buy the TV. Consider the decision of one of the roommates, Player A. If he buys the TV, he gets benefits of $100 and pays a cost of $150, leaving him with net benefits of −50. However, if Player A buys the TV, Player B gets to watch it for free, which gives B a benefit of $100. The payoffs to the game are depicted in Table 35.1.

Free riding game matrix.

Table 35.1

		Player B	
		Buy	Don't buy
Player A	Buy	−50, −50	−50, 100
	Don't buy	100, −50	0, 0

The dominant strategy equilibrium for this game is for neither player to buy the TV. If player A decides to buy the TV, then it is in player B's interest to free ride: to watch the TV but not contribute anything to paying for it. If player A decides not to buy, then it is in player B's interest not to buy the TV either. This is similar to the prisoners' dilemma, but not exactly the same. In the prisoners' dilemma, the strategy that maximizes the sum of the players' utilities is for each player to make the *same* choice. Here the strategy that maximizes the sum of the utilities is for just one of the players to buy the TV (and both players to watch it).

If Player A buys the TV and both players watch it, we can construct a Pareto improvement simply by having Player B make a "sidepayment" to Player A. For example, if Player B gives Player A $51, then both players will be made better off when Player A buys the TV. More generally, any payment between $50 and $100 will result in a Pareto improvement for this example.

In fact, this is probably what would happen in practice: each player would contribute some fraction of the cost of the TV. This public goods problem is relatively easy to solve, but more difficult free riding problems can arise in the sharing of other household public goods. For example, what about cleaning the living room? Each person may prefer to see the living room clean and is willing to do his part. But each may also be tempted to free ride on the other—so that neither one ends up cleaning the room, with the usual untidy results.

The situation becomes even worse if there are more than just two people involved—since there are more people on whom to free ride! Letting the other guy do it may be optimal from an *individual* point of view, but it is Pareto inefficient from the viewpoint of society as a whole.

35.4 Different Levels of the Public Good

In the above example, we had an either/or decision: either provide the TV or not. But the same kind of phenomena occurs when there is a choice of *how much* of the public good to provide. Suppose, for example, that the two roommates have to decide how much money to spend on the TV. The more money they decide to spend, the better the TV they can get.

As before we'll let x_1 and x_2 measure the private consumption of each person and g_1 and g_2 be their contributions to the TV. Let G now measure the "quality" of the TV they buy, and let the cost function for quality be given by $c(G)$. This means that if the two roommates want to purchase a TV of quality G, they have to spend $c(G)$ dollars to do so.

The constraint facing the roommates is that the total amount that they spend on their public and private consumption has to add up to how much money they have:

$$x_1 + x_2 + c(G) = w_1 + w_2.$$

A Pareto efficient allocation is one where consumer 1 is as well-off as possible given consumer 2's level of utility. If we fix the utility of consumer 2 at $\overline{u}_2$, we can write this problem as

$$\max_{x_1, x_2, G} u_1(x_1, G)$$

$$\text{such that } u_2(x_2, G) = \overline{u}_2$$

$$x_1 + x_2 + c(G) = w_1 + w_2.$$

It turns out that the appropriate optimality condition for this problem is that the *sum* of the absolute values of the marginal rates of substitution between the private good and the public good for the two consumers equals the marginal cost of providing an extra unit of the public good:

$$|MRS_1| + |MRS_2| = MC(G)$$

or, spelling out the definitions of the marginal rates of substitution,

$$\left| \frac{\Delta x_1}{\Delta G} \right| + \left| \frac{\Delta x_2}{\Delta G} \right| = \frac{MU_G}{MU_{x_1}} + \frac{MU_G}{MU_{x_2}} = MC(G).$$

In order to see why this must be the right efficiency condition, let us apply the usual trick and think about what would be the case if it were violated. Suppose, for example, that the sum of the marginal rates of substitution were less than the marginal cost: say $MC = 1$, $|MRS_1| = 1/4$, and $|MRS_2| = 1/2$. We need to show that there is some way to make both people better off.

Given his marginal rate of substitution, we know that person 1 would be willing to accept 1/4 more dollars of the private good for the loss of 1 dollar of the public good (since both goods cost \$1 per unit). Similarly, person 2 would accept 1/2 more dollars of the private good for a 1-dollar decrease in the public good. Suppose we reduce the amount of the public good and offer to compensate both individuals. When we reduce the public good by one unit we save a dollar. After we pay each individual the amount he requires to allow this change $(3/4 = 1/4 + 1/2)$, we find that we still have 1/4 of a dollar left over. This remaining money could be shared between the two individuals, thereby making them both better off.

Similarly, if the sum of the marginal rates of substitution were greater than 1, we could increase the amount of the public good to make them both better off. If $|MRS_1| = 2/3$ and $|MRS_2| = 1/2$, say, this means that person 1 would give up 2/3 of a dollar of private consumption to get 1 unit more of the public good and person 2 would give up 1/2 of a dollar of private consumption to get 1 unit more of the public good. But if person 1 gave up his 2/3 units, and person 2 gave up his 1/2 unit, we would have more than enough to produce the extra unit of the public good, since the marginal cost of providing the public good is 1. Thus we could give the left-over amount back to both people, thereby making them both better off.

What does the condition for Pareto efficiency mean? One way to interpret it is to think of the marginal rate of substitution as measuring the *marginal* willingness to pay for an extra unit of the public good. Then the efficiency condition just says that the *sum* of the marginal willingnesses to pay must equal the marginal cost of providing an extra unit of the public good.

In the case of a discrete good that was either provided or not provided, we said that the efficiency condition was that the sum of the willingnesses to pay should be at least as large as the cost. In the case we're considering here, where the public good can be provided at different levels, the efficiency condition is that the sum of the *marginal* willingnesses to pay should *equal* the marginal cost at the optimal amount of the public good. For whenever the sum of the marginal willingnesses to pay for the public good exceeds the marginal cost, it is appropriate to provide more of the public good.

It is worthwhile comparing the efficiency condition for a public good to the efficiency condition for a private good. For a private good, each person's marginal rate of substitution must equal the marginal cost; for a public good, the *sum* of the marginal rates of substitution must equal the marginal cost. In the case of a private good, each person can consume a different amount of the private good, but they all must value it the same at the margin—otherwise they would want to trade. In the case of a public good, each person must consume the same amount of the public good, but they can all value it differently at the margin.

We can illustrate the public good efficiency condition in Figure 35.1. We simply draw each person's MRS curve and then add them vertically to get the sum of the MRS curves. The efficient allocation of the public good will occur where the sum of the MRSs equals the marginal cost, as illustrated in Figure 35.1.

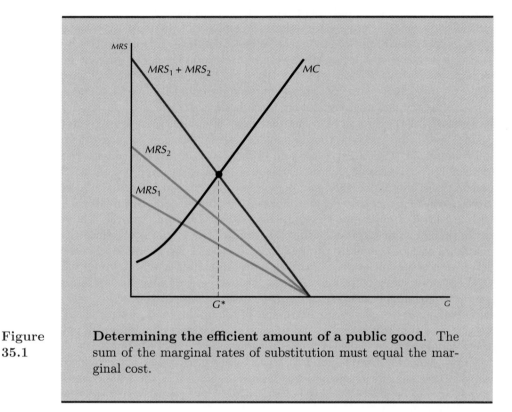

Figure
35.1
Determining the efficient amount of a public good. The sum of the marginal rates of substitution must equal the marginal cost.

35.5 Quasilinear Preferences and Public Goods

In general, the optimal amount of the public good will be different at different allocations of the private good. But if the consumers have quasilinear preferences it turns out that there will be a unique amount of the public good supplied at every efficient allocation. The easiest way to see this is to think about the kind of utility function that represents quasilinear preferences.

As we saw in Chapter 4, quasilinear preferences have a utility representation of the form: $u_i(x_i, G) = x_i + v_i(G)$. This means that the marginal utility of the private good is always 1, and thus the marginal rate of substitution between the private and the public good—the ratio of the marginal utilities—will depend only on G. In particular:

$$|MRS_1| = \frac{\Delta u_1(x_1, G)/\Delta G}{\Delta u_1/\Delta x_1} = \frac{\Delta v_1(G)}{\Delta G}$$

$$|MRS_2| = \frac{\Delta u_2(x_2, G)/\Delta G}{\Delta u_2/\Delta x_2} = \frac{\Delta v_2(G)}{\Delta G}.$$

We already know that a Pareto efficient level of the public good must satisfy the condition

$$|MRS_1| + |MRS_2| = MC(G).$$

Using the special form of the MRSs in the case of quasilinear utility, we can write this condition as

$$\frac{\Delta v_1(G)}{\Delta G} + \frac{\Delta v_2(G)}{\Delta G} = MC(G).$$

Note that this equation determines G without any reference to x_1 or x_2. Thus there is a unique efficient level of provision of the public good.

Another way to see this is to think about the behavior of the indifference curves. In the case of quasilinear preferences, all of the indifference curves are just shifted versions of each other. This means, in particular, that the slope of the indifference curves—the marginal rate of substitution—doesn't change as we change the amount of the private good. Suppose that we find one efficient allocation of the public and private goods, where the sum of the absolute value of the MRSs equals $MC(G)$. Now if we take some amount of the private good away from one person and give it to another, the slopes of both indifference curves stay the same, so the sum of the absolute value of the MRSs is still equal to $MC(G)$ and we have another Pareto efficient allocation.

In the case of quasilinear preferences, all Pareto efficient allocations are found by just redistributing the private good. The amount of the public good stays fixed at the efficient level.

EXAMPLE: Pollution Revisited

Recall the model of the steel firm and the fishery described in Chapter 32. There we argued that the efficient provision of pollution was one which internalized the pollution costs borne by the steel firm and the fishery. Suppose now that there are two fisheries, and that the amount of pollution produced by the steel firm is a public good. (Or, perhaps more appropriately, is a public bad!)

Then the efficient provision of pollution will involve maximizing the sum of the profits of all three firms—that is, minimizing the total social cost of the pollution. Formally, let $c_s(s, x)$ be the cost to the steel firm of producing s units of steel and x units of pollution, and write $c_f^1(f_1, x)$ for the costs for firm 1 to catch f_1 fish when the pollution level is x, and $c_f^2(f_2, x)$ as the analogous expression for firm 2. Then to compute the Pareto efficient amount of pollution, we maximize the sum of the three firms' profits:

$$\max_{s, f_1, f_2, x} \ p_s s + p_f f_1 + p_f f_2 - c_s(s, x) - c_f^1(f_1, x) - c_f^2(f_2, x).$$

The interesting effect for our purposes is the effect on aggregate profits of increasing pollution. Increasing pollution lowers the cost of producing steel but raises the costs of producing fish for each of the fisheries. The appropriate optimality condition from the profit-maximization problem is

$$\frac{\Delta c_s(\hat{s}, \hat{x})}{\Delta x} + \frac{\Delta c_f^1(\hat{f}_1, \hat{x})}{\Delta x} + \frac{\Delta c_f^2(\hat{f}_2, \hat{x})}{\Delta x} = 0,$$

which simply says that the *sum* of the marginal costs of pollution over the three firms should equal zero. Just as in the case of a public consumption good, it is the *sum* of the marginal benefits or costs over the economic agents that is relevant for determining the Pareto efficient provision of a public good.

35.6 The Free Rider Problem

Now that we know what the Pareto efficient allocations of public goods are, we can turn our attention to asking how to get there. In the case of private goods with no externalities we saw that the market mechanism will generate an efficient allocation. Will the market work in the case of public goods?

We can think of each person as having some endowment of a private good, w_i. Each person can spend some fraction of this private good on his own private consumption, or he or she can contribute some of it to purchase the public good. Let's use x_1 for 1's private consumption, and let g_1 denote the amount of the public good he buys, and similarly for person 2. Suppose for simplicity that $c(G) \equiv G$, which implies that the marginal cost of providing a unit of the public good is constant at 1. The total amount of the public good provided will be $G = g_1 + g_2$. Since each person cares about the *total* amount of the public good provided, the utility function of person i will have the form $u_i(x_i, g_1 + g_2) = u_i(x_i, G)$.

In order for person 1 to decide how much he should contribute to the public good, he has to have some forecast of how much person 2 will contribute. The simplest thing to do here is to adopt the Nash equilibrium model described in Chapter 28, and suppose that person 2 will make some contribution $\overline{g}_2$. We assume that person 2 also makes a guess about person 1's contribution, and we look for an equilibrium where each person is making an optimal contribution given the other person's behavior.

Thus person 1's maximization problem takes the form

$$\max_{x_1,g_1} u_1(x_1, g_1 + \overline{g}_2)$$

such that $x_1 + g_1 = w_1$.

This is just like an ordinary consumer maximization problem. The optimization condition is therefore the same: if both people purchase both goods the marginal rate of substitution between the public and the private goods should be 1 for each consumer:

$$|MRS_1| = 1$$

$$|MRS_2| = 1.$$

However, we have to be careful here. It is true that if person 2 purchases any amount of the public good at all, he will purchase it until the marginal rate of substitution equals one. But it can easily happen that person 2 decides that the amount already contributed by person 1 is sufficient and that it would therefore be unnecessary for him to contribute anything toward the public good at all.

Formally, we are assuming that the individuals can only make positive contributions to the public good—they can put money into the collection plate, but they can't take money out. Thus there is an extra constraint on each person's contributions, namely, that $g_1 \geq 0$ and $g_2 \geq 0$. Each person can only decide whether or not he wants to *increase* the amount of the public good. But then it may well be that one person decides that the amount provided by the other is just fine and would prefer to make no contribution at all.

A case like this is depicted in Figure 35.2. Here we have illustrated each person's private consumption on the horizontal axis and his or her public consumption on the vertical axis. The "endowment" of each person consists of his or her wealth, w_i, along with the amount of the public good contribution of the *other* person—since this is how much of the public good will be available if the person in question decides not to contribute. Figure 35.2A shows a case where person 1 is the only contributor to the public good, so that $g_1 = G$. If person 1 contributes G units to the public good, then person 2's endowment will consist of her private wealth, w_2, and the amount of the public good G—since person 2 gets to consume the public good whether or not she contributes to it. Since person 2 cannot reduce the amount of the public good, but can only increase it, her budget constraint is the bold line in Figure 35.2B. Given the shape of 2's indifference curve,

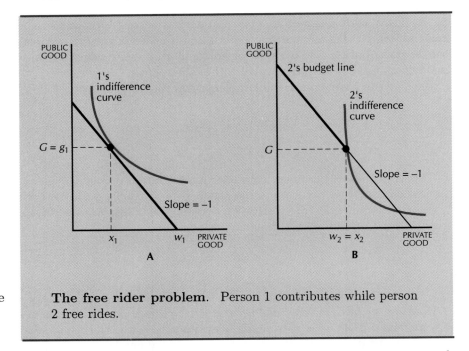

Figure
35.2

The free rider problem. Person 1 contributes while person 2 free rides.

it is optimal from her point of view to free ride on 1's contribution and simply consume her endowment, as depicted.

This is an example where person 2 is free riding on person 1's contribution to the public good. Since a public good is a good that everyone must consume in the same amount, the provision of a public good by any one person will tend to reduce the other peoples' provision. Thus in general there will be too little of the public good supplied in a voluntary equilibrium, relative to an efficient provision of the public good.

35.7 Comparison to Private Goods

In our discussion of private goods, we were able to show that a particular social institution—the competitive market—was capable of achieving a Pareto efficient allocation of private goods. Each consumer deciding for himself or herself how much to purchase of various goods would result in a pattern of consumption that was Pareto efficient. A major assumption in this analysis was that an individual's consumption did not affect other people's utility—that is, that there were no consumption externalities. Thus each person optimizing with respect to his or her own consumption was sufficient to achieve a kind of social optimum.

The situation is radically different with respect to public goods. In this case, the utilities of the individuals are inexorably linked since everyone is required to consume the same amount of the public good. In this case the market provision of *public* goods would be very unlikely to result in a Pareto efficient provision.

Indeed, for the most part we use *different* social institutions to determine the provision of public goods. Sometimes people use a **command mechanism**, where one person or small group of people determines the amount of various public goods that will be provided by the populace. Other times people use a **voting system** where individuals vote on the provision of public goods. One can well ask the same sorts of questions about voting, or other social mechanisms for decision making, that we asked about the private market: are they capable of achieving a Pareto efficient allocation of public goods? Can any Pareto efficient allocation of public goods be achieved by such mechanisms? A complete analysis of these questions is beyond the scope of this book, but we will be able to shed a little light on how some methods work below.

35.8 Voting

Private provision of a public good doesn't work very well, but there are several other mechanisms for social choice. One of the most common mechanisms in democratic countries is **voting**. Let's examine how well it works for the provision of public goods.

Voting isn't very interesting in the case of two consumers, so we will suppose that we have n consumers. Furthermore, so as not to worry about ties, we'll suppose that n is an odd number. Let's imagine that the consumers are voting about the size of some public good—say the magnitude of expenditures on public defense. Each consumer has a most-preferred level of expenditure, and his valuation of other levels of expenditure depends on how close they are to his preferred level of expenditure.

The first problem with voting as a way of determining social outcomes has already been examined in Chapter 31. Suppose that we are considering three levels of expenditure, A, B, and C. It is perfectly possible that there is a majority of the consumers who prefer A to B, a majority who prefer B to C ... and a majority who prefer C to A!

Using the terminology of Chapter 31, the social preferences generated by these consumers are not transitive. This means that the outcome of voting on the level of public good may not be well defined—there is always a level of expenditure that beats every expenditure. If a society is allowed to vote many times on an issue, this means that it may "cycle" around various choices. Or if a society votes only once on an issue, the outcome depends on the order in which the choices are presented.

If first you vote on A versus B and then on A versus C, C will be the outcome. But if you vote on C versus A and then C versus B, B will be the outcome. You can get any of the three outcomes by choosing how the alternatives are presented!

The "paradox of voting" described above is disturbing. One natural thing to do is to ask what restrictions on preferences will allow us to rule it out; that is, what form must preferences have so as to ensure that the kinds of cycles described above cannot happen?

Let us depict the preferences of consumer i by a graph like those in Figure 35.3, where the height of the graph illustrates the value or the net utility for different levels of the expenditure on the public good. The term "net utility" is appropriate since each person cares both about the level of the public good, and the amount that he has to contribute to it. Higher levels of expenditure mean more public goods but also higher taxes in order to pay for those public goods. Thus it is reasonable to assume that the net utility of expenditure on the public good rises at first due to the benefits of the public good but then eventually falls, due to the costs of providing it.

One restriction on preferences of this sort is that they be **single-peaked**. This means that preferences must have the shape depicted in Figure 35.3A rather than that depicted in Figure 35.3B. With single-peaked preferences, the net utility of different levels of expenditure rises until the most-preferred point and then falls, as it does in Figure 35.3A; it never goes up, down, and then up again, as it does in Figure 35.3B.

Figure 35.3

Shapes of preferences. Single-peaked preferences are shown in panel A and multiple peaked preferences in panel B.

If each individual has single-peaked preferences, then it can be shown that the social preferences revealed by majority vote will never exhibit the kind of intransitivity we described above. Accepting this result for the moment, we can ask which level of expenditure will be chosen if everyone has single-peaked preferences. The answer turns out to be the **median expenditure**—that expenditure such that one-half of the population wants to spend more, and one-half wants to spend less. This result is reasonably intuitive: if more than one-half wanted more expenditure on the public good, they would vote for more, so the only possible equilibrium voting outcome is when the votes for increasing and decreasing expenditure on the public good are just balanced.

Will this be an efficient level of the public good? In general, the answer is no. The median outcome just means that half the population wants more and half wants less; it doesn't say anything about *how much more* they want of the public good. Since efficiency takes this kind of information into account, voting will not in general lead to an efficient outcome.

Furthermore, even if peoples' true preferences are single-peaked, so that voting may lead to a reasonable outcome, individuals may choose to misrepresent their true preferences when they vote. Thus people will have an incentive to vote differently than their true preferences would indicate in order to manipulate the final outcome.

EXAMPLE: Agenda Manipulation

We have seen that the outcome of a sequence of votes may depend on the order in which the votes are taken. Experienced politicians are well aware of this possibility. In the U.S. Congress, amendments to a bill must be voted on before the bill itself, and this provides a commonly used way to influence the legislative process.

In 1956 the House of Representatives considered a bill calling for Federal aid to school construction. One representative offered an amendment requiring that the bill would only provide Federal aid to states with integrated schools. There were three more-or-less equally sized groups of representatives with strongly held views on this issue.

• Republicans. They were opposed to Federal aid to education, but preferred the amended bill to the original. Their ranking of the alternatives was no bill, amended bill, original bill.

• Northern Democrats. They wanted Federal aid to education and supported integrated schools, so they ranked the alternatives amended bill, original bill, no bill.

• Southern Democrats. This group wanted Federal aid to education, but would not get any aid under the amended bill due to the segregated schools in the South. Their ranking was original bill, no bill, amended bill.

In the vote on the amendment, the Republicans and the Northern Democrats were in the majority, thereby substituting the amended bill for the original. In the vote on the amended bill, the Republicans and the Southern Democrats were in the majority, and the amended bill was defeated. However, before being amended the original bill had a majority of the votes!

35.9 Demand Revelation

We have seen above that majority voting, even if it leads to a well-defined outcome, will not necessarily provide the correct incentives for people to honestly reveal their true preferences. In general, there will be an incentive to misrepresent preferences in order to manipulate the voting outcome.

This observation leads to the issue of what other methods there might be that would ensure that individuals have the proper incentives to correctly reveal their true preferences about a public good. Are there any procedures that provide the right incentives to tell the truth about the value of a public good?

It turns out that there is a way to ensure that people will correctly reveal their true value for a public good using a kind of market or "auction" process. Unfortunately, this method also requires a special restriction on preferences, namely, that they be quasilinear. As we've seen earlier, quasilinear preferences imply that we will have a unique optimal amount of the public good, and the issue is to discover what it is. In order to keep things simple, we'll just consider the case where there is one level of the public good to be supplied, and the question is whether to supply it or not.

We can think of a neighborhood association that is considering putting up a street light. The cost of providing the street light is known; say it is $100. Each person i places some value on the street light, which we denote by v_i. From our analysis of the public goods problem, we know that it is efficient to provide the street light if the *sum* of the values is greater than or equal to the cost:

$$\sum_{i=1}^{n} v_i \geq \$100.$$

One way to decide whether or not to put up the light is to ask each person how much they value the light, with the understanding that their share of the cost will be proportional to their stated value, if the street light gets built. The trouble with this mechanism is that people will have the incentive to free ride: if each person thinks that the other people are willing to pay enough to provide the street light, why should he contribute? It can easily happen that the street light may not get provided even though it would have been efficient to do so.

The problem with this mechanism is that the declaration of how much a person values the good affects how much he or she has to pay, so there is a natural incentive to shade the true value. Let's try to devise a scheme that doesn't have this fault. Suppose that we decide in advance that if the street light is built, everyone will pay a predetermined amount towards its construction, c_i. Then each person will announce his or her value and we'll see whether the sum of the values exceeds the cost. It is convenient to define the term net value, n_i, as the difference between person i's value, v_i, and his or her cost, c_i:

$$n_i = v_i - c_i.$$

Using this definition, we can think of each person announcing his or her net value, and then we simply sum up the net values to see if the total is positive.

The problem with *this* decision mechanism is that it contains an incentive to exaggerate the statements of the true values. If you value the street light only a little more than your cost, you might as well say that you value it a million dollars more—that won't affect what you have to pay, and it will help to ensure that the sum of the values exceeds the cost. Similarly, if you value the light less than your cost, you might as well say it is worth zero to you. Again, that doesn't affect your payment, and it helps to ensure that the street light *won't* get built.

The problem with both of these schemes is that there is no cost for deviating from the truth. And without some incentive to tell the truth about your true value of the public good, there is an incentive to understate or overstate your true value.

Let's think about a way to correct this. The first important idea is that exaggeration doesn't matter if it doesn't affect the social decision. If the sum of the values of everyone else already exceeds the cost, it doesn't matter if you state an exaggerated value. Similarly, if the sum of the values is already less than the cost, it doesn't matter what value you state, as long as the sum of everyone's values remains below the cost.

The only individuals that matter are those who *change* the sum of the values to be greater or less than the cost of the public good. These are called the **pivotal agents**. There might be no pivotal agents, or everyone might be pivotal. The importance of the pivotal agents is that they are the ones who have to have the right incentives to tell the truth; the nonpivotal people don't really matter. Of course, anybody *might* be pivotal, so in ensuring that the pivotal people have the right incentives, we are making sure that everyone has the right incentives in deciding whether or not to tell the truth.

So let's consider the situation of a pivotal person, one who changes the social decision. When the social decision is changed, there will be some harm imposed on the other agents. If the other agents wanted the street light, and this particular pivotal person voted it down, then the other agents have been made worse off by this agent's decision. Similarly, if the other agents didn't want the street light, and this agent cast the dollar vote that provided it, the other agents have been made worse off.

How much worse off are they? Well, if the sum of the net values was positive without person j, say, and person j made the sum go negative, then person j has imposed a total harm of

$$H_j = \sum_{i \neq j} n_i > 0$$

on the other people. This is because the other people wanted the street light, and person j has ensured that they won't get it.

Similarly, if everyone else didn't want the light on the average, so that the sum of their net values was negative, and j made it go positive, then the harm that j imposed is given by

$$H_j = -\sum_{i \neq j} n_i > 0.$$

In order to give person j the right incentives to decide whether or not to be pivotal, we'll just impose this social cost on him. By doing this we make sure that he faces the true social cost of his decision—namely, the harm that he imposes on the other people. This is much like the Pigovian taxes we considered in regulating externalities; in the case of public good provision, the kind of tax is known as a **Groves-Clarke tax**, or the **Clarke tax**, after the economists who first investigated it.

We can now describe the Groves-Clarke mechanism for making public goods decisions.

1. Assign a cost to each agent, c_i, which the individual will have to pay if it is decided that the public good will be provided.

2. Have each agent state a net value s_i. (This may or may not be his or her *true* net value n_i.)

3. If the sum of the stated net values is positive, the public good will be provided; if it is negative, it won't be.

4. Each pivotal person will be required to pay a tax. If person j changes the decision from provision to no provision, the tax on that person will be

$$H_j = \sum_{i \neq j} s_i.$$

If person j changes the decision from no provision to provision, the tax will be

$$H_j = -\sum_{i \neq j} s_i.$$

The tax is *not* paid to the other agents—it is paid to the state. It doesn't matter where the money goes, as long as it doesn't influence anybody else's decision; all that matters is that it be paid by the pivotal people so that they face the proper incentives to tell the truth.

EXAMPLE: An Example of the Clarke Tax

It is convenient to consider a numerical example to see just how the Clarke tax works. Suppose that we have three roommates who have to decide whether or not to acquire a TV that costs $300. They agree in advance that if they jointly decide to get the TV, then they will each contribute $100 towards the cost. Persons A and B are willing to pay $50 each to have the TV present, while person C is willing to pay $250. This information is summarized in Table 35.2.

Example of the Clarke tax.   Table 35.2

Person	Cost share	Value	Net value	Clarke tax
A	100	50	−50	0
B	100	50	−50	0
C	100	250	150	100

Note that the TV provides a positive net value only to person C. Thus if the roommates voted on whether or not to purchase the TV, a majority would be opposed. Nevertheless, it is Pareto efficient to provide the TV since the *sum* of the values ($350) exceeds the cost ($300).

Let us consider how the Clarke tax works in this example. Consider person A. The sum of the net values *excluding* person A is 100, and person A's net value is −50. Thus person A is not pivotal. Since person A is made worse off in the net by the provision of the public good, he might have a temptation to exaggerate his bid downward. In order to ensure that the public good is *not* provided, A would have to bid −100 or below. But if he did this, then A would become pivotal, and he would have to pay a Clarke tax equal to the amount the other two people bid: −50 + 150 = 100. Thus reducing his bid saves him $50 in net value, but costs him $100 in taxes—leaving him with a net loss of $50.

The same thing goes for person B. What about person C? In the example, person C is pivotal—without his bid the public good would not be supplied, and with his bid the good will be supplied. He receives a net value from the public good of $150, but pays a $100 tax, leaving him with a total value of his actions of $50. Would it be worth it for him to increase his bid above his true value? No, because that doesn't change any of his payoffs. Would it be worth it to reduce his bid? No, because that lowers the chance that the public good will be supplied and doesn't change the amount of tax he has to pay. Thus it is in the interest of each of the parties to truthfully reveal his or her net value of the public good. Honesty is the best policy—at least in a situation involving a Clarke tax![3]

35.10 Problems with the Clarke Tax

Despite the nice features of the Clarke tax it does have some problems. The first problem is that it only works with quasilinear preferences. This is because we can't have the amount that you have to pay influence your demand for the public good. It is important that there is a unique optimal level of the public good.

The second problem is that the Clarke tax doesn't really generate a Pareto efficient outcome. The level of the public good will be optimal, but the private consumption could be greater. This is because of the tax collection. Remember that in order to have the correct incentives, the pivotal people must actually pay some taxes that reflect the harm that they do to the other people. And these taxes cannot go to anybody else involved in the decision process, since that might affect their decisions. The taxes have to disappear from the system. And that's the problem—if the taxes actually have to be paid, the private consumption will end up being lower than it could be otherwise, and therefore be Pareto inefficient.

However, the taxes only have to be paid if someone is pivotal. If there are many people involved in the decision, the probability that any one person is pivotal may not be very large; thus the tax collections might typically be expected to be rather small.

The final problem concerns the equity and efficiency tradeoff inherent in the Clarke tax. Since the payment scheme must be fixed in advance, there will generally be situations where some people will be made worse off by providing the public good, even though the Pareto efficient *amount* of the public good will be provided. To say that it is Pareto preferred to provide the public good is to say that there is *some* payment scheme for which everyone is better off having the public good provided than not having it. But this doesn't mean that for an *arbitrary* payment scheme everyone will be better off. The Clarke tax ensures that if everyone *could* be better off

---

[3] For a more detailed discussion of the Clarke tax, see N. Tideman and G. Tullock, "A New and Superior Process for Making Social Choices," *Journal of Political Economy*, 84, December 1976, pp. 1145–59.

having the good provided, then it will be provided. But that doesn't imply that everyone will actually be better off.

It would be nice if there were a scheme that not only determined whether or not to provide the public good, but also the Pareto efficient way to pay for it—that is, a payment plan that makes everyone better off. However, it does not appear that such a general plan is available.

Summary

1. Public goods are goods for which everyone must "consume" the same amount, such as national defense, air pollution, and so on.

2. If a public good is to be provided in some fixed amount or not provided at all, then a necessary and sufficient condition for provision to be Pareto efficient is that the sum of the willingnesses to pay (the reservation prices) exceeds the cost of the public good.

3. If a public good can be provided in a variable amount, then the necessary condition for a given amount to be Pareto efficient is that the sum of the marginal willingnesses to pay (the marginal rates of substitution) should equal the marginal cost.

4. The free rider problem refers to the temptation of individuals to let others provide the public goods. In general, purely individualistic mechanisms will not generate the optimal amount of a public good because of the free rider problem.

5. Various collective decision methods have been proposed to determine the supply of a public good. Such methods include the command mechanism, voting, and the Clarke tax.

REVIEW QUESTIONS

1. Consider an auction in which people will bid in turn, where each bid has to be at least a dollar higher than the previous bid, and the item is sold to the person who bids the highest. If the value of the good to person i is v_i, what will be the winning bid? Which person will get the good?

2. Consider a sealed bid auction among n people for some good. Let v_i be the value of the good to person i. Prove that if the good is sold to the highest bidder at the *second* highest price bid, it will be in each player's interest to tell the truth.

3. Suppose that 10 people live on a street and that each of them is willing to pay \$2 for each extra streetlight, regardless of the number of streetlights provided. If the cost of providing x streetlights is given by $c(x) = x^2$, what is the Pareto efficient number of streetlights to provide?

APPENDIX

Let's solve the maximization problem that determines the Pareto efficient allocations of the public good:

$$\max_{x_1, x_2, G} u_1(x_1, G)$$

$$\text{such that } u_2(x_2, G) = \overline{u}_2$$

$$x_1 + x_2 + c(G) = w_1 + w_2.$$

We set up the Lagrangian:

$$L = u_1(x_1, G) - \lambda[u_2(x_2, G) - \overline{u}_2] - \mu[x_1 + x_2 + c(G) - w_1 - w_2]$$

and differentiate with respect to x_1, x_2, and G to get

$$\frac{\partial L}{\partial x_1} = \frac{\partial u_1(x_1, G)}{\partial x_1} - \mu = 0$$

$$\frac{\partial L}{\partial x_2} = -\lambda \frac{\partial u_2(x_2, G)}{\partial x_2} - \mu = 0$$

$$\frac{\partial L}{\partial G} = \frac{\partial u_1(x_1, G)}{\partial G} - \lambda \frac{\partial u_2(x_2, G)}{\partial G} - \mu \frac{\partial c(G)}{\partial G} = 0.$$

If we divide the third equation by μ and rearrange, we get

$$\frac{1}{\mu} \frac{\partial u_1(x_1, G)}{\partial G} - \frac{\lambda}{\mu} \frac{\partial u_2(x_2, G)}{\partial G} = \frac{\partial c(G)}{\partial G}. \tag{35.2}$$

Now solve the first equation for μ to get

$$\mu = \frac{\partial u_1(x_1, G)}{\partial x_1},$$

and solve the second equation for μ/λ to get

$$\frac{\mu}{\lambda} = -\frac{\partial u_2(x_2, G)}{\partial x_2}.$$

Substitute these two equations into equation (35.2) to find

$$\frac{\partial u_1(x_1, G)/\partial G}{\partial u_1(x_1, G)/\partial x_1} + \frac{\partial u_2(x_2, G)/\partial G}{\partial u_2(x_2, G)/\partial x_2} = \frac{\partial c(G)}{\partial G},$$

which is just

$$MRS_1 + MRS_2 = MC(G)$$

as given in the text.

CHAPTER **36**

ASYMMETRIC INFORMATION

So far in our study of markets we have not examined the problems raised by differences in information: by assumption buyers and sellers were both perfectly informed about the quality of the goods being sold in the market. This assumption can be defended if it is easy to verify the quality of an item. If it is not costly to tell which goods are high-quality goods and which are low-quality goods, then the prices of the goods will simply adjust to reflect the quality differences.

But if information about quality is costly to obtain, then it is no longer plausible that buyers and sellers have the same information about goods involved in transactions. There are certainly many markets in the real world in which it may be very costly or even impossible to gain accurate information about the quality of the goods being sold.

One obvious example is the labor market. In the simple models described earlier, labor was a homogeneous product—everyone had the same "kind" of labor and supplied the same amount of effort per hour worked. This is clearly a drastic simplification! In reality, it may be very difficult for a firm to determine how productive its employees are.

Costly information is not just a problem with labor markets. Similar problems arise in markets for consumer products. When a consumer buys a used car it may be very difficult for him to determine whether or not it is a good car or a lemon. By contrast, the seller of the used car probably has a pretty good idea of the quality of the car. We will see that this **asymmetric information** may cause significant problems with the efficient functioning of a market.

36.1 The Market for Lemons

Let us look at a model of a market where the demanders and suppliers have different information about the qualities of the goods being sold.[1]

Consider a market with 100 people who want to sell their used cars and 100 people who want to buy a used car. Everyone knows that 50 of the cars are "plums" and 50 are "lemons."[2] The current owner of each car knows its quality, but the prospective purchasers don't know whether any given car is a plum or a lemon.

The owner of a lemon is willing to part with it for $1000 and the owner of a plum is willing to part with it for $2000. The buyers of the car are willing to pay $2400 for a plum and $1200 for a lemon.

If it is easy to verify the quality of the cars there will be no problems in this market. The lemons will sell at some price between $1000 and $1200 and the plums will sell at some price between $2000 and $2400. But what happens to the market if the buyers *can't* observe the quality of the car?

In this case the buyers have to guess about how much each car is worth. We'll make a simple assumption about the form that this guess takes: we assume that if a car is equally likely to be a plum as a lemon, then a typical buyer would be willing to pay the expected value of the car. Using the numbers described above this means that the buyer would be willing to pay $\frac{1}{2}1200 + \frac{1}{2}2400 = \$1800$.

But who would be willing to sell their car at that price? The owners of the lemons certainly would, but the owners of the plums wouldn't be willing to sell their cars—by assumption they need at least $2000 to part with their cars. The price that the buyers are willing to pay for an "average" car is less than the price that the sellers of the plums want in order to part with their cars. At a price of $1800 only lemons would be offered for sale.

But if the buyer was certain that he would get a lemon, then he wouldn't be willing to pay $1800 for it! In fact, the equilibrium price in this market would have to be somewhere between $1000 and $1200. For a price in this range only owners of lemons would offer their cars for sale, and buyers

---

[1] The first paper to point out some of the difficulties in markets of this sort was George Akerlof, "The Market for Lemons: Quality Uncertainty and the Market Mechanism," *The Quarterly Journal of Economics*, 84, 1970, pp. 488-500.

[2] A "plum" is slang for a good car; a "lemon" is slang for a bad car.

would therefore (correctly) expect to get a lemon. In this market, none of the plums ever get sold! Even though the price at which buyers are willing to buy plums exceeds the price at which sellers are willing to sell them, no such transactions will take place.

It is worth contemplating the source of this market failure. The problem is that there is an externality between the sellers of good cars and bad cars; when an individual decides to try to sell a bad car, he affects the purchasers' perceptions of the quality of the average car on the market. This lowers the price that they are willing to pay for the average car, and thus hurts the people who are trying to sell good cars. It is this externality that creates the market failure.

The cars that are most likely to be offered for sale are the ones that people want most to get rid of. The very act of offering to sell something sends a signal to the prospective buyer about its quality. If too many low-quality items are offered for sale it makes it difficult for the owners of high-quality items to sell their products.

36.2 Quality Choice

In the lemons model there were a fixed number of cars of each quality. Here we consider a variation on that model where quality may be determined by the producers. We will show how the equilibrium quality is determined in this simple market.

Suppose that each consumer wants to buy a single umbrella and that there are two different qualities available. Consumers value high-quality umbrellas at $14 and low-quality umbrellas at $8. It is impossible to tell the quality of the umbrellas in the store; this can only be determined after a few rainstorms.

Suppose that some manufacturers produce high-quality umbrellas and some produce low-quality umbrellas. Suppose further that both high-quality and low-quality umbrellas cost $11.50 to manufacture and that the industry is perfectly competitive. What would we expect to be the equilibrium quality of umbrellas produced?

We suppose that consumers judge the quality of the umbrellas available in the market by the *average* quality sold, just as in the case of the lemons market. If the fraction of high-quality umbrellas is q, then the consumer would be willing to pay $p = 14q + 8(1 - q)$ for an umbrella.

There are three cases to consider.

Only low-quality manufacturers produce. In this case then the consumers would be willing to pay only $8 for an average umbrella. But it costs $11.50 to produce an umbrella, so none would be sold.

Only high-quality manufacturers produce. In this case the producers would compete the price of an umbrella down to marginal cost, $11.50. The consumers are willing to pay $14 for an umbrella, so they would get some consumers' surplus.

Both qualities are produced. In this case competition ensures that the price will be $11.50. The average quality available must therefore have a value to the consumer of at least $11.50. This means that we must have

$$14q + 8(1 - q) \geq 11.50.$$

The lowest value of q that satisfies this inequality is $q = 7/12$. This means that if $7/12$ of the suppliers are high-quality the consumers are just willing to pay $11.50 for an umbrella.

The determination of the equilibrium ratio of high-quality producers is depicted in Figure 36.1. The horizontal axis measures q, the fraction of high-quality producers. The vertical axis measures the consumers' willingness to pay for an umbrella if the fraction of high-quality umbrellas offered is q. Producers are willing to supply either quality of umbrella at a price of $11.50, so the supply conditions are summarized by the colored horizontal line at $11.50.

Consumers are willing to purchase umbrellas only if $14q + 8(1 - q) \geq 11.50$; the boundary of this region is illustrated by the dashed line. The equilibrium value of q is between $7/12$ and 1.

In this market the equilibrium price is $11.50, but the value of the average umbrella to a consumer can be anywhere between $11.50 and $14, depending on the fraction of high-quality producers. Any value of q between 1 and $7/12$ is an equilibrium.

However, all of these equilibria are not equivalent from the social point of view. The producers get zero producer surplus in all the equilibria, due to the assumption of pure competition and constant marginal cost, so we only have to examine the consumers' surplus. Here it is easy to see that the higher the average quality, the better off the consumers are. The best equilibrium from the viewpoint of the consumers is the one in which only the high-quality goods are produced.

Choosing the Quality

Now let us change the model a bit. Suppose that each producer can choose the quality of umbrella that he produces and that it costs $11.50 to produce a high-quality umbrella and $11 to produce a low-quality umbrella. What will happen in this case?

Suppose that the fraction of producers who choose high-quality umbrellas is q, where $0 < q < 1$. Consider one of these producers. If it behaves competitively and believes that it has only a negligible effect on the market

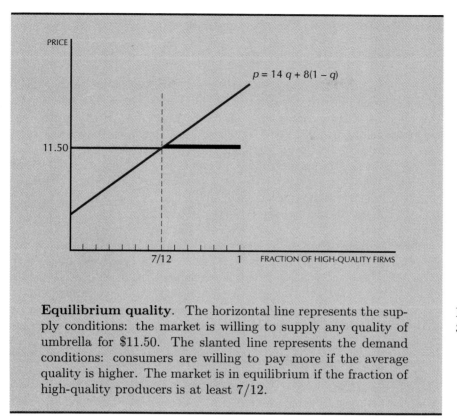

Equilibrium quality. The horizontal line represents the supply conditions: the market is willing to supply any quality of umbrella for $11.50. The slanted line represents the demand conditions: consumers are willing to pay more if the average quality is higher. The market is in equilibrium if the fraction of high-quality producers is at least $7/12$.

Figure
36.1

price *and* quality, then it would always want to produce only low-quality umbrellas. Since this producer is by assumption only a small part of the market, it neglects its influence on the market price and therefore chooses to produce the more profitable product.

But every producer will reason the same way and only low-quality umbrellas will be produced. But consumers are only willing to pay $8 for a low-quality umbrella, so there is no equilibrium. Or, if you will, the only equilibrium involves zero production of *either* quality of umbrella! The possiblity of low-quality production has destroyed the market for *both* qualities of the good!

36.3 Adverse Selection

The phenomenon described in the last section is an example of **adverse selection**. In the model we just examined the low-quality items crowded out the high-quality items because of the high cost of acquiring information. As we just saw, this adverse selection problem may be so severe that it can completely destroy the market. Let's consider a few other examples of adverse selection.

Consider first an example from the insurance industry. Suppose that an insurance company wants to offer insurance for bicycle theft. They do a careful market survey and find that the incident of theft varies widely across communities. In some areas there is a high probability that a bicycle will be stolen, and in other areas thefts are quite rare. Suppose that the insurance company decides to offer the insurance based on the *average* theft rate. What do you think will happen?

Answer: the insurance company is likely to go broke quickly! Think about it. Who is going to buy the insurance at the average rate? Not the people in the safe communities—they don't need much insurance anyway. Instead the people in the communities with a high incidence of theft will want the insurance—they're the ones who need it.

But this means that the insurance claims will mostly be made by the consumers who live in the high-risk areas. Rates based on the *average* probability of theft will be a misleading indication of the actual experience of claims filed with the insurance company. The insurance company will not get an unbiased selection of customers; rather they will get an *adverse* selection. In fact the term "adverse selection" was first used in the insurance industry to describe just this sort of problem.

It follows that in order to break even the insurance company must base their rates on the "worst-case" forecasts and that consumers with a low, but not negligible, risk of bicycle theft will be unwilling to purchase the resulting high-priced insurance.

A similar problem arises with health insurance—insurance companies can't base their rates on the *average* incidence of health problems in the population. They can only base their rates on the average incidence of health problems in the group of potential purchasers. But the people who want to purchase health insurance the most are the ones who are likely to need it the most and thus the rates must reflect this disparity.

In such a situation it is possible that everyone can be made better off by *requiring* the purchase of insurance that reflects the average risk in the population. The high-risk people are better off because they can purchase insurance at rates that are lower than the actual risk they face and the low-risk people can purchase insurance that is more favorable to them than the insurance offered if *only* high-risk people purchased it.

A situation like this, where the market equilibrium is dominated by a compulsary purchase plan, is quite surprising to most economists. We usually think that "more choice is better," so it is peculiar that restricting choice can result in a Pareto improvement. But it should be emphasized that this paradoxical result is due to the externality between the low-risk and high-risk people.

In fact there are social institutions that help to solve this market inefficiency. It is commonly the case that employers offer health plans to their employees as part of the package of fringe benefits. The insurance company can base its rates on the averages over the set of employees and is assured that *all* employees must participate in the program, thus eliminating the adverse selection.

36.4 Moral Hazard

Another interesting problem that arises in the insurance industry is known as the **moral hazard** problem. The term is somewhat peculiar, but the phenomenon is not hard to describe. Consider the bicycle-theft insurance market again and suppose for simplicity that all of the consumers live in areas with identical probabilities of theft, so that there is no problem of adverse selection. On the other hand, the probability of theft may be affected by the *actions* taken by the bicycle owners.

For example, if the bicycle owners don't bother to lock their bikes or use only a flimsy lock, the bicycle is much more likely to be stolen than if they use a secure lock. Similar examples arise in other sorts of insurance. In the case of health insurance, for example, the consumers are less likely to need the insurance if they take actions associated with a healthy lifestyle. We will refer to actions that affect the probability that some event occurs as *taking care*.

When it sets its rates the insurance company has to take into account the incentives that the consumers have to take an appropriate amount of care. If no insurance is available consumers have an incentive to take the maximum possible amount of care. If it is impossible to buy bicycle-theft insurance, then all bicyclists would use large expensive locks. In this case the individual bears the full cost of his actions and accordingly he wants to "invest" in taking care until the marginal benefit from more care just equals the marginal cost of doing so.

But if a consumer can purchase bicycle insurance, then the cost inflicted on the individual of having his bicycle stolen is much less. After all, if the bicycle is stolen then the person simply has to report it to the insurance company and he will get insurance money to replace it. In the extreme case, where the insurance company completely reimburses the individual for the theft of his bicycle, the individual has no incentive to take care at all. This lack of incentive to take care is called **moral hazard**.

Note the tradeoff involved: too little insurance means that people bear a lot of risk, too much insurance means that people will take inadequate care.

If the amount of care is observable, then there is no problem. The insurance company can base its rates on the amount of care taken. In real life it is common for insurance companies to give different rates to businesses that have a fire sprinkler system in their building, or to charge smokers different rates than nonsmokers for health insurance. In these cases the insurance firm attempts to discriminate among users depending on the choices they have made that influence the probability of damage.

But insurance companies can't observe all the relevant actions of those they insure. Therefore we will have the tradeoff described above: full insurance means too little care will be undertaken because the individuals don't face the full costs of their actions.

What does this imply about the types of insurance contracts that will be offered? In general, the insurance companies will not want to offer the consumers "complete" insurance. They will always want the consumer to face some part of the risk. This is why most insurance policies include a "deductible," an amount that the insured party has to pay in any claim. By making the consumers pay part of a claim, the insurance companies can make sure that the consumer always has an incentive to take *some* amount of care. Even though the insurance company would be willing to insure a consumer completely if they could verify the amount of care taken, the fact that the consumer can *choose* the amount of care he takes implies that the insurance company will not allow the consumer to purchase as much insurance as he wants if the company cannot observe the level of care.

This is also a paradoxical result when compared with the standard market analysis. Typically the amount of a good traded in a competitive market is determined by the condition that demand equals supply—the marginal willingness to pay equals the marginal willingness to sell. In the case of moral hazard, a market equilibrium has the property that each consumer would like to buy more insurance, and the insurance companies would be willing to provide more insurance if the consumers continued to take the same amount of care ... but this trade won't occur because if the consumers were able to purchase more insurance they would rationally choose to take less care!

36.5 Moral Hazard and Adverse Selection

Moral hazard refers to situations where one side of the market can't observe the actions of the other. For this reason it is sometimes called a **hidden action** problem.

Adverse selection refers to situations where one side of the market can't observe the "type" or quality of the goods on other side of the market. For this reason it is sometimes called a **hidden information** problem.

Equilibrium in a market involving hidden action typically involves some form of rationing—firms would like to provide more than they do, but they are unwilling to do so since it will change the incentives of their customers. Equilibrium in a market involving hidden information will typically involve too little trade taking place because of the externality between the "good" and "bad" types.

Equilibrium outcomes in this market appear to be inefficient, but one has to be careful in making such a claim. The question to ask is "inefficient relative to what?" The equilibrium will always be inefficient relative to the equilibrium with full information. But this is of little help in making policy decisions: if the firms in the industry find it too costly to collect more information the government would probably find it too costly as well.

The real question to ask is whether some sort of governmental intervention in the market could improve efficiency even if the government had the same information problems as the firms.

In the case of hidden action considered above, the answer is usually "no." If the government can't observe the care taken by the consumers, then it can do no better than the insurance companies. Of course the government might have other tools at its disposal that are not available to the insurance company—it could compel a particular level of care, and it could set criminal punishments for those who did not take due care. But if the government can only set prices and quantities, then it can do no better than the private market can do.

Similar issues arise in the case of hidden information. We have already seen that if the government can *compel* people of all risk classes to purchase insurance, it is possible for everyone to be made better off. This is, on the face of it, a good case for intervention. On the other hand, there are costs to government intervention as well; economic decisions made by governmental decree may not be as cost-effective as those made by private firms. Just because there are governmental actions that *can* improve social welfare doesn't mean that these actions will be taken!

Furthermore, there may be purely private solutions to the adverse selection problems. For example, we have already seen how providing health insurance as a fringe benefit can help to eliminate the adverse selection problem.

36.6 Signaling

Recall our model of the used-car market: the owners of the used cars knew the quality, but the purchasers had to guess at the quality. We saw that this asymmetric information could cause problems in the market; in some cases, the adverse selection problem would result in too few transactions being made.

However, the story doesn't end there. The owners of the good used cars have an incentive to try to convey the fact that they have a good car to the potential purchasers. They would like to choose actions that **signal** the quality of their car to those who might buy it.

One sensible signal in this context would be for the owner of a good used car to offer a **warranty**. This would be a promise to pay the purchaser some agreed upon amount if the car turned out to be a lemon. Owners of the good used cars can afford to offer such a warranty while the owners of the lemons can't afford this. This is a way for the owners of the good used cars to signal that they have good cars.

In this case signaling helps to make the market perform better. By offering the warranty—the signal—the sellers of the good cars can distinguish themselves from the sellers of the bad used cars. But there are other cases where signaling can make a market perform less well.

Let's consider a very simplified model of the education market first examined by Michael Spence.[3] Suppose that we have two types of workers, able and unable. The able workers have a marginal product of a_2, and the unable workers have a marginal product of a_1, where $a_2 > a_1$. Suppose that a fraction b of the workers are able and $1 - b$ of them are unable.

For simplicity we assume a linear production function so that the total output produced by L_2 able workers and L_1 unable workers is $a_1 L_1 + a_2 L_2$. We also assume a competitive labor market.

If worker quality is easily observable, then firms would just offer a wage of $w_2 = a_2$ to the able workers and of $w_1 = a_1$ to the unable workers. That is, each worker would be paid his marginal product and we would have an efficient equilibrium.

But what if the firm can't observe the marginal products? If a firm can't distinguish the types of workers, then the best that it can do is to offer the average wage, which is $w = (1-b)a_1 + ba_2$. As long as the good and the bad workers both agree to work at this wage there is no problem with adverse selection. And, given our assumption about the production function, the firm produces just as much output and makes just as much profit as it would if it could perfectly observe the type of the worker.

However, suppose now that there is some signal that the workers can acquire that will distinguish the two types. For example, suppose that the workers can acquire education. Let e_1 be the amount of education attained by the type 1 workers and e_2 the amount attained by the type 2 workers. Suppose that the workers have different costs of acquiring education, so that the total cost of education for the able workers is $c_2 e_2$ and the total cost of education for the unable workers is $c_1 e_1$. These costs are meant to include not only the dollar costs of attending school, but also includes the opportunity costs, the costs of the effort required, and so on.

Now we have two decisions to consider. The workers have to decide how much education to acquire and the firms have to decide how much to pay workers with different amounts of education. Let us make the extreme assumption that the education doesn't affect worker productivity at all. Of course this isn't true in real life—especially for economics courses—but it helps to keep the model simple.

---

[3] Michael Spence, *Market Signaling* (Cambridge, Mass: Harvard University Press, 1974).

It turns out that the nature of the equilibrium in this model depends crucially on the cost of acquiring education. Suppose that $c_2 < c_1$. This says that the marginal cost of acquiring education is less for the able workers than the unable workers. Let e^* be an education level that satisfies the following inequalities:

$$\frac{a_2 - a_1}{c_1} < e^* < \frac{a_2 - a_1}{c_2}.$$

Given our assumption that $a_2 > a_1$ and that $c_2 < c_1$ there must be such an e^*.

Now consider the following set of choices: the able workers all acquire education level e^* and the unable workers all acquire education level 0, and the firm pays workers with education level e^* a wage of a_2 and workers with less education than this a wage of a_1. Note that the choice of the education level of a worker perfectly signals his type.

But is this an equilibrium? Does anyone have an incentive to change his or her behavior? Each firm is paying each worker his or her marginal product, so the firms have no incentive to do anything differently. The only question is whether the workers are behaving rationally given the wage schedule they face.

Would it be in the interest of an unable worker to purchase education level e^*? The benefit to the worker would be the increase in wages $a_2 - a_1$. The cost to the unable worker would be $c_1 e^*$. The benefits are less than the costs if

$$a_2 - a_1 < c_1 e^*.$$

But we are guaranteed that this condition holds by the choice of e^*. Hence the unable workers find it optimal to choose a zero educational level.

Is it actually in the interest of the able workers to acquire the level of education e^*? The condition for the benefits to exceed the costs is

$$a_2 - a_1 > c_2 e^*,$$

and this condition also holds due to the choice of e^*.

Hence this pattern of wages is indeed an equilibrium: if each able worker chooses education level e^* and each unable worker chooses a zero educational level, then no worker has any reason to change his or her behavior. Due to our assumption about the cost differences, the education level of a worker can, in equilibrium, serve as a signal of the different productivities. This type of signaling equilibrium is sometimes called a **separating equilibrium** since the equilibrium involves each type of worker making a choice that allows him to separate himself from the other type.

Another possibility is a **pooling equilibrium**, in which each type of worker makes the *same* choice. For example, suppose that $c_2 > c_1$, so that the able workers have a higher cost of acquiring education than the unable workers. In this case it can be shown that the only equilibrium involves the workers all getting paid a wage based on their average ability, and so no signaling occurs.

The separating equilibrium is especially interesting since it is inefficient from a social point of view. Each able worker finds it in his interest to pay for acquiring the signal, even though it doesn't change his productivity at all. The able workers want to acquire the signal not because it makes them any more productive, but just because it distinguishes them from the unable workers. Exactly the same amount of output is produced in the (separating) signaling equilibrium as would be if there were no signaling at all. In this model the acquisition of the signal is a total waste from the social point of view.

It is worth thinking about the nature of this inefficiency. As before, it arises because of an externality. If both able and unable workers were paid their *average* product, the wage of the able workers would be depressed because of the presence of the unable workers. Thus they would have an incentive to invest in signals that will distinguish them from the less able. This investment offers a private benefit but no social benefit.

Of course signaling doesn't always lead to inefficiencies. Some types of signals, such as the used-car warranties described above, help to facilitate trade. In that case the equilibrium with signals is preferred to the equilibrium without signals. So signaling can make things better or worse; each case has to be examined on its own merits.

EXAMPLE: The Sheepskin Effect

In the extreme form of the educational signaling model described above education has no effect on productivity: the years spent in school serve only to signal the fixed ability of an individual. This is obviously an exaggeration: a student with 11 years of schooling almost certainly is more productive than one with 10 years of schooling due to the fact that they have acquired more useful skills during the additional year. Presumably part of the returns to schooling are due to signaling, and part are due to the acquisition of useful skills while in school. How can we separate these two factors?

Labor economists who have studied the returns to education have observed the following suggestive fact: the earnings of people who have graduated from high school are much higher than the incomes of people who have only completed 3 years of high school. One study found that graduating from high school increases earnings by 5 to 6 times as much as does completing a year in high school that does not result in graduation. The same discontinuous jump occurs for people who graduate from college. According to one estimate, the economic return to the 16th year of schooling are about three times as high as the return to the 15th year of schooling.[4]

If education imparts productive skills, we might well expect that people with 11 years of education are paid more than people with 10 years of education. What is surprising is that there is a huge jump in earnings associated with high school graduation. Economists have termed this the **sheepskin effect**, in reference to the fact that diplomas were often written on sheepskins. Presumably, graduation from high school is some kind of signal. But what is it a signal of? In the educational signaling model described earlier, educational attainment was a signal of ability. Is that what high school graduation signals? Or is it something else?

Andrew Weiss, a Boston University economist, attempted to answer these questions.[5] He looked at a set of data describing how workers assembled equipment and was able to obtain a measure of how much output they produced in their first month on the job. He found that there was a very small effect of education on output: each year of secondary education increased a worker's output by about 1.3 percent. Furthermore, high school graduates produced essentially the same amount of output as nongraduates. Apparently education contributed only a small amount to the initial productivity of these workers.

Weiss then looked at another data set that described various characteristics of workers in a variety of occupations. He found that high school graduates had significantly lower quit and absentee rates than nongraduates. It seems that high school graduates receive higher wages because they are more productive—but the reason that they are more productive is because they stay with the firm longer and have fewer absences. This suggests that the signaling model does give us insight into real-world labor markets. However, the actual signal sent by educational attainment is considerably more complex than the simplest version of the signaling model suggests.

36.7 Incentives

We turn now to a slightly different topic, the study of **incentive systems**. As it turns out, our investigation of this topic will naturally involve asymmetric information. But it is useful to start with the case of full information.

The central question in the design of incentive systems is "How can I get someone to do something for me?" Let's pose this question in a specific

---

[4] See Thomas Hungerford and Gary Solon, "Sheepskin Effects in the Returns to Education," *Review of Economics and Statistics*, 69, 1987, 175–77.

[5] "High School Graduation, Performance and Wages," *Journal of Political Economy*, 96, 4, 1988, 785–820.

context. Suppose that you own a plot of land but you are unable to work on the land yourself. So you try to hire someone to do the farming for you. What sort of compensation system should you set up?

One plan might involve paying the worker a lump-sum fee independent of how much he produces. But then he would have little incentive to work. In general a good incentive plan will make the payment of the worker depend in some way on the output he produces. The problem of incentive design is to determine exactly how sensitive the payment should be to the produced output.

Let x be the amount of "effort" that the worker expends, and let $y = f(x)$ be the amount of output produced; for simplicity we suppose that the price of output is 1 so that y also measures the value of the output. Let $s(y)$ be the amount that you pay the worker if he produces y dollars worth of output. Presumably you would like to choose the function $s(y)$ to maximize your profits $y - s(y)$.

What are the constraints that you face? In order to answer this question we have to look at things from the worker's perspective.

We assume that the worker finds effort costly, and write $c(x)$ for the cost of effort x. We assume that this cost function has the usual shape: both total and marginal costs increase as effort increases. The utility of the worker who chooses effort level x is then simply $s(y)-c(x) = s(f(x))-c(x)$. The worker may have other alternatives available that give him some utility $\bar{u}$. This could come from working at other jobs or from not working at all. All that is relevant for the design of the incentive scheme is that the utility that the worker gets from this job must be at least as great as the utility he could get elsewhere. This gives us the **participation constraint**:

$$s(f(x)) - c(x) \geq \bar{u}.$$

Given this constraint we can determine how much output we can get from the worker. You want to induce the worker to choose an effort level x that yields you the greatest surplus given the constraint that the worker is willing to work for you:

$$\max_{x} f(x) - s(f(x))$$

$$\text{such that } s(f(x)) - c(x) \geq \bar{u}.$$

In general, you will want the worker to choose x to just satisfy the constraint so that $s(f(x)) - c(x) = \bar{u}$. Substituting this into the objective function we have the unconstrained maximization problem

$$\max_{x} f(x) - c(x) - \bar{u}.$$

But it is easy to solve this problem! Just choose x^* so that the marginal product equals the marginal cost:

$$MP(x^*) = MC(x^*).$$

Any choice of x^* where the marginal benefit is not equal to the marginal cost cannot maximize profits.

This tells us what level of effort the owner wants to achieve; now we have to ask what he has to pay the worker to achieve that effort. That is, what does the function $s(y)$ have to look like to induce the worker to choose to make x^* the optimal choice?

Suppose that you decide that you want to induce the worker to put in x^* amount of effort. Then you must make it in his interest to do so; that is, you must design your incentive scheme $s(y)$ so that the utility from choosing to work x^* is larger than the utility of worker any other amount x. This gives us the constraint

$$s(f(x^*)) - c(x^*) \geq s(f(x)) - c(x) \quad \text{for all } x.$$

This constraint is called the **incentive compatibility constraint**. It simply says that the utility to the worker from choosing x^* must be greater than the utility of any other choice of effort.

So we have two conditions that the incentive scheme must satisfy: first, it must give total utility to the worker of $\bar{u}$, and second, it must make the marginal product of effort equal to the marginal cost of effort at the effort level x^*. There are several ways to do this.

Rent. The landowner could simply rent the land to the worker for some price R, so that the worker gets all the output he produces after he pays the owner R. For this scheme

$$s(f(x)) = f(x) - R.$$

If the worker maximizes $s(f(x)) - c(x) = f(x) - R - c(x)$, he will choose the effort level where $MP(x^*) = MC(x^*)$, which is exactly what the owner wants. The rental rate R is determined from the participation condition. Since the total utility to the worker must be $\bar{u}$ we have

$$f(x^*) - c(x^*) - R = \bar{u},$$

which says $R = f(x^*) - c(x^*) - \bar{u}$.

Wage labor. In this scheme the landowner pays the worker a constant wage per unit of effort along with a lump sum K. This means that the incentive payment takes the form

$$s(x) = wx + K.$$

The wage rate w is equal to the marginal product of the worker at the optimal choice x^*, $MP(x^*)$. The constant K is chosen to just make the worker indifferent between working for the landowner and working elsewhere; that is, it is chosen to satisfy the participation constraint.

The problem of maximizing $s(f(x)) - c(x)$ then becomes

$$\max_{x} \ wx + K - c(x),$$

which means that the worker will choose x so as to set his marginal cost equal to the wage: $w = MC(x)$. Since the wage is $MP(x^*)$, this means that the *optimal* choice of the worker will be x^* such that $MP(x^*) = MC(x^*)$ which is just what the firm wants.

Take-it-or-leave-it. In this scheme the landowner pays the worker B^* if he works x^* and zero otherwise. The amount B^* is determined by the participation constraint $B^* - c(x^*) = \bar{u}$, so $B^* = \bar{u} + c(x^*)$. If the worker chooses any level of effort $x \neq x^*$, he gets a utility of $-c(x)$. If he chooses x^*, he gets a utility of $\bar{u}$. Hence the optimal choice for the worker is to set $x = x^*$.

Each of these schemes is equivalent as far as the analysis goes: each one gives the worker a utility of $\bar{u}$, and each one gives the worker an incentive to work the optimal amount x^*. At this level of generality there is no reason to choose between them.

If all of these schemes are optimal, what could a nonoptimal scheme look like? Here is an example.

Sharecropping. In sharecropping the worker and the landowner each get some fixed percentage of the output. Suppose that the worker's share takes the form $s(x) = \alpha f(x) + F$, where F is some constant and $\alpha < 1$. This is *not* an efficient scheme for the problem under consideration. It is easy to see why. The worker's maximization problem is

$$\max_{x} \ \alpha f(x) + F - c(x),$$

which means that he would choose a level of effort $\hat{x}$ where

$$\alpha MP(\hat{x}) = MC(\hat{x}).$$

Such an effort level clearly cannot satisfy the efficiency condition that $MP(x) = MC(x)$.

Here is a way to summarize this analysis. In order to design an efficient incentive scheme it is necessary to ensure that the person who makes the effort decision is the **residual claimant** to the output. The way the owner can make himself as well off as possible is to make sure that he gets the worker to produce the optimal amount of output. This is the output level where the marginal product of the worker's extra effort equals the marginal cost of putting forth that effort. It follows that the incentive scheme must provide a marginal benefit to the worker equal to his marginal product.

EXAMPLE: Voting Rights in the Corporation

Normally shareholders in a corporation have the right to vote on various issues related to the management of the corporation while bondholders do not. Why is this? The answer comes from looking at the structure of payoffs to stockholders and bondholders. If a corporation produces X dollars of profit in a given years, the bondholders have first claim on these profits, while the amount that is left over goes to the stockholders. If the total claim by the bondholders is B, then the amount that goes to the stockholders is $X - B$. This makes the stockholders the residual claimants—so they have an incentive to make X as large as possible. The bondholders on the other hand only have an incentive to make sure that X is at least B, since that is the most that they are entitled to. Hence giving the stockholders the right to make decisions will generally result in larger profits.

EXAMPLE: Chinese Economic Reforms

Prior to 1979 Chinese rural communes were organized along orthodox Marxist lines. Workers were paid according to a rough estimate of how much they contributed to the commune income. Five percent of the commune's land was set aside for private plots, but peasants were not allowed to travel to cities to sell the output from their private farms. All trade had to take place through a highly regulated government market.

At the end of 1978 the Chinese central government instituted a major reform in the structure of agriculture, known as the "responsibility system." In the responsibility system, any production in excess of a fixed quota was kept by the household and could be sold on private markets. The government removed restrictions on private plots and increased the amount of land devoted to private farming. By the end of 1984, 97 percent of the farmers operated under this responsibility system.

Note that the structure of the system is very much like the optimal incentive mechanism described above: each household makes a lump-sum payment to the commune but can keep anything in excess of this quota. Hence the *marginal* incentives for household production are the economically appropriate ones.

The effect of this new system on agricultural output was phenomenal: between 1978 and 1984, the output of Chinese agriculture increased by over 61 percent! However, not all of this increase is due to better incentives; at the same time these reforms were going on, the Chinese government also changed the controlled prices of agricultural goods, and even allowed some of these prices to be determined on private markets.

Three economists attempted to divide the increase in output into the part due to better incentives and the part due to the change in prices.[6] They found that over three-fourths of the increase was due to the improvement in incentives, and only one-fourth was due to the price reforms.

36.8 Asymmetric Information

The above analysis provides some insights about the use of different sorts of incentive schemes. For example, it shows that renting the land to a worker is better than sharecropping. But this really proves too much. If our analysis is a good description of the world, then we would expect to see rental or wage labor used in agriculture and never see sharecropping used, except by mistake.

Clearly this isn't right. Sharecropping has been used for thousands of years in some parts of the world, so it is likely that it fulfills some kind of need. What have we left out of our model?

Given the title of this section it is not hard to guess the answer: we've left out problems involving imperfect information. We assumed that the owner of the firm could perfectly observe the effort of the worker. In many situations of interest it may be impossible to observe the effort. At best the owner may observe some *signal* of the effort such as the resulting production of output. The amount of output produced by a farmer may depend in part on his effort, but it may also depend on the weather, the quality of the inputs, and many other factors. Because of this kind of "noise," a payment from the owner to the worker based on output will not in general be equivalent to a payment based on effort alone.

This is essentially a problem of asymmetric information: the worker can choose his effort level, but the owner cannot perfectly observe it. The owner has to guess the effort from the observed output, and the design of the optimal incentive scheme has to reflect this inference problem.

Consider the four incentive schemes described above. What goes wrong if effort is not perfectly correlated with output?

Rent. If the firm rents the technology to the worker, then the worker can get all of the output that remains after paying the fixed rental fee. If output has a random component, this means that the worker will have to bear all the risk from the random factors. If the worker is more risk averse than the owner—which is the likely case—this will be inefficient. In general, the worker would be willing to give up some of the residual profits in order to have a less risky income stream.

---

[6] J. McMillan, J. Whalley, and L. Zhu, "The Impact of China's Economic Reforms on Agricultural Productivity Growth," *Journal of Political Economy,* 97, 4, 1989, 781–807.

Wage labor. The problem with wage labor is that it requires observation of the *amount* of labor input. The wage has to be based on the effort put in to production, not just the hours spent in the firm. If the owner can't observe the amount of labor input, then it will be impossible to implement this kind of incentive scheme.

Take-it-or-leave-it. If the incentive payment is based on the labor input, then we have the same problem with this scheme as with wage labor. If the payment is based on *output*, then the scheme involves the worker bearing all the risk. Even missing the "target output" by a small amount results in a zero payment.

Sharecropping. This is something of a happy medium. The payment to the worker depends in part on observed output, but the worker and the owner share the risk of output fluctuations. This gives the worker an incentive to produce output but it doesn't leave him bearing all the risk.

The introduction of asymmetric information has made a drastic change in our evaluation of the incentive methods. If the owner can't observe effort, then wage labor is infeasible. Rent and the take-it-or-leave-it scheme leave the worker bearing too much risk. Sharecropping is a compromise between the two extremes: it gives the worker some incentive to produce, but it doesn't leave him with all the risk.

EXAMPLE: Monitoring Costs

It is not always easy to observe the amount of effort an employee puts into his or her job. Consider, for example, a job as a clerk in a 24-hour convenience store. How can the manager observe the employees' performance when the manager isn't around? Even if there are ways to observe the physical output of the employee (shelves stocked, sales rung up) it is much harder to observe things like politeness to customers.

There is little doubt that some of the worst service in the world was provided in the formerly Communist countries in Eastern Europe: once you managed to attract the attention of a clerk, you were more likely to be greeted by a scowl than a smile. Nevertheless, a Hungarian entrepreneur, Gabor Varszegi, has made millions by providing high-quality service in his photo developing shops in Budapest.[7]

Varszegi says that he got his start as a businessman in the mid-sixties by playing bass guitar and managing a rock group. "Back then," he says, "the only private businessmen in Eastern Europe were rock musicians."

---

[7] See Steven Greenhouse, "A New Formula in Hungary: Speed Service and Grow Rich," *New York Times*, June 5, 1990, A1.

He introduced one-hour film developing to Hungary in 1985; the next best alternative to his one-hour developing shops was the state-run agency that took one month.

Varszegi follows two rules in labor relations: he never hires anyone who worked under Communism, and he pays his workers four times the market wage. This makes perfect sense in light of the above remarks about monitoring costs: there are very few employees per store and monitoring their behavior is very costly. If there were only a small penalty to being fired, there would be great temptation to slack off. By paying the workers much more than they could get elsewhere, Varszegi makes it very costly for them to be fired—and reduces his monitoring costs significantly.

EXAMPLE: The Grameen Bank

A village moneylender in Bangladesh charges over 150 percent interest a year. Any American banker would love a return of that size: why isn't Citibank installing money machines in Bangladesh? To ask the question is to answer it: Citibank would probably not do as well as the moneylender. The village moneylender has a comparative advantage in these small-scale loans for several reasons.

• The village moneylender can deal more effectively with the small scale of lending involved;

• The moneylender has better access to information about who are good and bad credit risks than an outsider does.

• The moneylender is in a better position to monitor the progress of the loan payments to insure repayment.

These three problems—returns to scale, adverse selection and moral hazard—allow the village moneylender to maintain a local monopoly in the credit market.

Such a local monopoly is especially pernicious in an underdeveloped country such as Bangladesh. At an interest rate of 150 percent there are many profitable projects that are not being undertaken by the peasants. Improved access to credit could lead to a major increase in investment, and a corresponding increase in the standards of living.

Muhammad Yunas, an American-trained economist from Bangladesh, has developed an ingenious institution known as the Grameen Bank (village bank) to address some of these problems. In the Grameen plan, entrepreneurs with separate projects get together and apply for a loan as a group. If the loan is approved, two members of the group get their loan and commence their investment activity. If they are successful in meeting the repayment schedule, two more members get loans. If they are also successful the last member, the group leader, will get a loan.

The Grameen bank addresses each of the three problems described above. Since the quality of the group influences whether or not individual members will get loans, potential members are highly selective about who they will join with. Since members of the group can only get loans if other members succeed in their investments, there are strong incentives to help each other out and share expertise. Finally, these activities of choosing candidates for loans and monitoring the progress of the repayments are all done by the peasants themselves, not directly by the loan officers at the bank.

The Grameen bank has been very successful. It makes about 475,000 loans a month with an average size of $70. Their loan-recovery rate is about 98 percent, while conventional lenders in Bangladesh achieve a loan-recovery rate of about 30 to 40 percent. The success of the group responsibility program in encouraging investment has led to its adoption in a number of other poverty-stricken areas in North and South America.

Summary

1. Imperfect and asymmetric information can lead to drastic differences in the nature of market equilbrium.

2. Adverse selection refers to situations where the type of the agents is not observable so that one side of the market has to guess the type or quality of a product based on the behavior of the other side of the market.

3. In markets involving adverse selection too little trade may take place. In this case it is possible that everyone can be made better off by forcing them to transact.

4. Moral hazard refers to a situation where one side of the market can't observe the actions of the other side.

5. Signaling refers to the fact that when adverse selection or moral hazard are present some agents will want to invest in signals that will differentiate them from other agents.

6. Investment in signals may be privately beneficial but publically wasteful. On the other hand, investment in signals may help to solve problems due to asymmetric information.

7. Efficient incentive schemes (with perfect observability of effort) leave the worker as the residual claimant. This means that the worker will equate marginal benefits and marginal costs.

8. But if information is imperfect this is no longer true. In general, an incentive scheme that shares risks as well as providing incentives will be appropriate.

REVIEW QUESTIONS

1. Consider the model of the used-car market presented in this chapter. What is the maximum amount of consumers' surplus that is created by trade in the market equilibrium?

2. In the same model, how much consumers' surplus would be created by *randomly* assigning buyers to sellers? Which method gives the larger surplus?

3. A worker can produce x units of output at a cost of $c(x) = x^2/2$. He can achieve a utility level of $\overline{u} = 0$ working elsewhere. What is the optimal wage-labor incentive scheme $s(x)$ for this worker?

4. Given the setup of the previous problem, what would the worker be willing to pay to rent the production technology?

5. How would your answer to the last problem change if the worker's alternative employment gave him $\overline{u} = 1$?

MATHEMATICAL APPENDIX

In this Appendix we will provide a brief review of some of the mathematical concepts that are used in the text. This material is meant to serve as a reminder of the definitions of various terms used in the text. It is emphatically not a tutorial in mathematics. The definitions given will generally be the simplest, not the most rigorous.

A.1 Functions

A **function** is a rule that describes a relationship between numbers. For each number x, a function assigns a *unique* number y according to some rule. Thus a function can be indicated by describing the rule, as "take a number and square it," or "take a number and multiply it by 2," and so on. We write these particular functions as $y = x^2$, $y = 2x$. Functions are sometimes referred to as **transformations**.

Often we want to indicate that some variable y depends on some other variable x, but we don't know the specific algebraic relationship between the two variables. In this case we write $y = f(x)$, which should be interpreted as saying that the variable y depends on x according to the rule f.

Given a function $y = f(x)$, the number x is often called the **independent variable**, and the number y is often called the **dependent variable**.

The idea is that x varies independently, but the value of y *depends* on the value of x.

Often some variable y depends on several other variables x_1, x_2, and so on, so we write $y = f(x_1, x_2)$ to indicate that both variables together determine the value of y.

A.2 Graphs

A **graph** of a function depicts the behavior of a function pictorially. Figure A.1 shows two graphs of functions. In mathematics the independent variable is usually depicted on the horizontal axis, and the dependent variable is depicted on the vertical axis. The graph then indicates the relationship between the independent and the dependent variables.

However, in economics it is common to graph functions with the independent variable on the vertical axis and the dependent variable on the horizontal axis. Demand functions, for example, are usually depicted with the price on the vertical axis and the amount demanded on the horizontal axis.

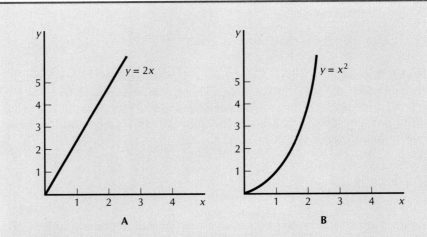

Graphs of functions. Panel A denotes the graph of $y = 2x$, and panel B denotes the graph of $y = x^2$.

A.3 Properties of Functions

A **continuous function** is one that can be drawn without lifting a pencil from the paper: there are no jumps in a continuous function. A **smooth**

function is one that has no "kinks" or corners. A **monotonic** function is one that always increases or always decreases; a **positive monotonic function** always increases as x increases, while a **negative monotonic function** always decreases as x increases.

A.4 Inverse Functions

Recall that a function has the property that for each value of x there is a unique value of y associated with it and that a monotonic function is one that is always increasing or always decreasing. This implies that for a monotonic function there will be a unique value of x associated with each value of y.

We call the function that relates x to y in this way an **inverse function**. If you are given y as a function of x, you can calculate the inverse function just by solving for x as a function of y. If $y = 2x$, then the inverse function is $x = y/2$. If $y = x^2$, then there is no inverse function; given any y, both $x = +\sqrt{y}$ and $x = -\sqrt{y}$ have the property that their square is equal to y. Thus there is not a *unique* value of x associated with each value of y, as is required by the definition of a function.

A.5 Equations and Identities

An **equation** asks when a function is equal to some particular number. Examples of equations are
$$2x = 8$$
$$x^2 = 9$$
$$f(x) = 0.$$
The **solution** to an equation is a value of x that satisfies the equation. The first equation has a solution of $x = 4$. The second equation has two solutions, $x = 3$ and $x = -3$. The third equation is just a general equation. We don't know its solution until we know the actual rule that f stands for, but we can denote its solution by x^*. This simply means that x^* is a number such that $f(x^*) = 0$. We say that x^* **satisfies** the equation $f(x) = 0$.

An **identity** is a relationship between variables that holds for *all* values of the variables. Here are some examples of identities:
$$(x + y)^2 \equiv x^2 + 2xy + y^2$$
$$2(x + 1) \equiv 2x + 2.$$
The special symbol $\equiv$ means that the left-hand side and the right-hand side are equal for *all* values of the variables. An equation only holds for some values of the variables, whereas an identity is true for all values of the variables. Often an identity is true by the definition of the terms involved.

A.6 Linear Functions

A **linear function** is a function of the form

$$y = ax + b,$$

where a and b are constants. Examples of linear functions are

$$y = 2x + 3$$
$$y = x - 99.$$

Strictly speaking, a function of the form $y = ax + b$ should be called an **affine function**, and only functions of the form $y = ax$ should be called linear functions. However, we will not insist on this distinction.

Linear functions can also be expressed implicitly in forms like $ax + by = c$. In such a case, we often like to solve for y as a function of x to convert this to the "standard" form:

$$y = \frac{c}{b} - \frac{a}{b}x.$$

A.7 Changes and Rates of Change

The notation Δx is read as "the change in x." It does *not* mean Δ times x. If x changes from x^* to x^{**}, then the change in x is just

$$\Delta x = x^{**} - x^*.$$

We can also write

$$x^{**} = x^* + \Delta x$$

to indicate that x^{**} is x^* plus a change in x.

Typically Δx will refer to a *small* change in x. We sometimes express this by saying that Δx represents a **marginal change**.

A **rate of change** is the ratio of two changes. If y is a function of x given by $y = f(x)$, then the rate of change of y with respect to x is denoted by

$$\frac{\Delta y}{\Delta x} = \frac{f(x + \Delta x) - f(x)}{\Delta x}.$$

The rate of change measures how y changes as x changes.

A linear function has the property that the rate of change of y with respect to x is constant. To prove this, note that if $y = a + bx$, then

$$\frac{\Delta y}{\Delta x} = \frac{a + b(x + \Delta x) - a - bx}{\Delta x} = \frac{b\Delta x}{\Delta x} = b.$$

For nonlinear functions, the rate of change of the function will depend on the value of x. Consider, for example, the function $y = x^2$. For this function

$$\frac{\Delta y}{\Delta x} = \frac{(x + \Delta x)^2 - x^2}{\Delta x} = \frac{x^2 + 2x\Delta x + (\Delta x)^2 - x^2}{\Delta x} = 2x + \Delta x.$$

Here the rate of change from x to $x + \Delta x$ depends on the value of x and on the size of the change, Δx. But if we consider very small changes in x, Δx will be nearly zero, so the rate of change of y with respect to x will be approximately $2x$.

A.8 Slopes and Intercepts

The rate of change of a function can be interpreted graphically as the **slope** of the function. In Figure A.2A we have depicted a linear function $y = -2x + 4$. The **vertical intercept** of this function is the value of y when $x = 0$, which is $y = 4$. The **horizontal intercept** is the value of x when $y = 0$, which is $x = 2$. The slope of the function is the rate of change of y as x changes. In this case, the slope of the function is -2.

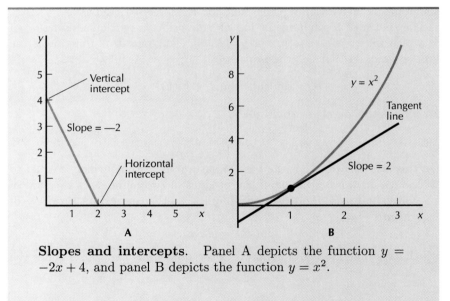

Slopes and intercepts.   Panel A depicts the function $y = -2x + 4$, and panel B depicts the function $y = x^2$.

Figure
A.2

In general, if a linear function has the form $y = ax + b$, the vertical intercept will be $y^* = b$ and the horizontal intercept will be $x^* = -b/a$. If a linear function is expressed in the form

$$a_1 x_1 + a_2 x_2 = c,$$

then the horizontal intercept will be the value of x_1 when $x_2 = 0$, which is $x_1^* = c/a_1$, and the vertical intercept will occur when $x_1 = 0$, which means $x_2^* = c/a_2$. The slope of this function is $-a_1/a_2$.

A nonlinear function has the property that its slope changes as x changes. A **tangent** to a function at some point x is a linear function that has the same slope. In Figure A.2B we have depicted the function x^2 and the tangent line at $x = 1$.

If y increases whenever x increases, then Δy will always have the same sign as Δx, so that the slope of the function will be positive. If on the other hand y decreases when x increases, or y increases when x decreases, Δy and Δx will have opposite signs, so that the slope of the function will be negative.

A.9 Absolute Values and Logarithms

The **absolute value** of a number is a function $f(x)$ defined by the following rule:
$$f(x) = \begin{cases} x & \text{if } x \geq 0 \\ -x & \text{if } x < 0. \end{cases}$$
Thus the absolute value of a number can be found by dropping the sign of the number. The absolute value function is usually written as $|x|$.

The (natural) **logarithm** or **log** of x describes a particular function of x, which we write as $y = \ln x$ or $y = \ln(x)$. The logarithm function is the unique function that has the properties

$$\ln(xy) = \ln(x) + \ln(y)$$

for all positive numbers x and y and

$$\ln(e) = 1.$$

(In this last equation, e is the base of natural logarithms which is equal to $2.7183\ldots$) In words, the log of the product of two numbers is the sum of the individual logs. This property implies another important property of logarithms:
$$\ln(x^y) = y\ln(x),$$
which says that the log of x raised to the power y is equal to y times the log of x.

A.10 Derivatives

The **derivative** of a function $y = f(x)$ is defined to be

$$\frac{df(x)}{dx} = \lim_{\Delta x \to 0} \frac{f(x + \Delta x) - f(x)}{\Delta x}.$$

In words, the derivative is the limit of the rate of change of y with respect to x as the change in x goes to zero. The derivative gives precise meaning to the phrase "the rate of change of y with respect to x for small changes in x." The derivative of $f(x)$ with respect to x is also denoted by $f'(x)$.

We have already seen that the rate of change of a linear function $y = ax + b$ is constant. Thus for this linear function

$$\frac{df(x)}{dx} = a.$$

For a nonlinear function the rate of change of y with respect to x will usually depend on x. We saw that in the case of $f(x) = x^2$, we had $\Delta y / \Delta x = 2x + \Delta x$. Applying the definition of the derivative

$$\frac{df(x)}{dx} = \lim_{\Delta x \to 0} 2x + \Delta x = 2x.$$

Thus the derivative of x^2 with respect to x is $2x$.

It can be shown by more advanced methods that if $y = \ln x$, then

$$\frac{df(x)}{dx} = \frac{1}{x}.$$

A.11 Second Derivatives

The **second derivative** of a function is the derivative of the derivative of that function. If $y = f(x)$, the second derivative of $f(x)$ with respect to x is written as $d^2 f(x)/dx^2$ or $f''(x)$. We know that

$$\frac{d(2x)}{dx} = 2$$

$$\frac{d(x^2)}{dx} = 2x.$$

Thus

$$\frac{d^2(2x)}{dx^2} = \frac{d(2)}{dx} = 0$$

$$\frac{d^2(x^2)}{dx^2} = \frac{d(2x)}{dx} = 2.$$

The second derivative measures the curvature of a function. A function with a negative second derivative at some point is concave near that point; its slope is decreasing. A function with a positive second derivative at a point is convex near that point; its slope is increasing. A function with a zero second derivative at a point is flat near that point.

A.12 The Product Rule and the Chain Rule

Suppose that $g(x)$ and $h(x)$ are both functions of x. We can define the function $f(x)$ that represents their product by $f(x) = g(x)h(x)$. Then the derivative of $f(x)$ is given by

$$\frac{df(x)}{dx} = g(x)\frac{dh(x)}{dx} + h(x)\frac{dg(x)}{dx}.$$

Given two functions $y = g(x)$ and $z = h(y)$, the **composite function** is

$$f(x) = h(g(x)).$$

For example, if $g(x) = x^2$ and $h(y) = 2y + 3$, then the composite function is

$$f(x) = 2x^2 + 3.$$

The **chain rule** says that the derivative of a composite function, $f(x)$, with respect to x is given by

$$\frac{df(x)}{dx} = \frac{dh(y)}{dy}\frac{dg(x)}{dx}.$$

In our example, $dh(y)/dy = 2$, and $dg(x)/dx = 2x$, so the chain rule says that $df(x)/dx = 2 \times 2x = 4x$. Direct calculation verifies that this is the derivative of the function $f(x) = 2x^2 + 3$.

A.13 Partial Derivatives

Suppose that y depends on both x_1 and x_2, so that $y = f(x_1, x_2)$. Then the **partial derivative** of $f(x_1, x_2)$ with respect to x_1 is defined by

$$\frac{\partial f(x_1, x_2)}{\partial x_1} = \lim_{\Delta x_1 \to 0} \frac{f(x_1 + \Delta x_1, x_2) - f(x_1, x_2)}{\Delta x_1}.$$

The partial derivative of $f(x_1, x_2)$ with respect to x_1 is just the derivative of the function with respect to x_1, *holding x_2 fixed*. Similarly, the partial derivative with respect to x_2 is

$$\frac{\partial f(x_1, x_2)}{\partial x_2} = \lim_{\Delta x_2 \to 0} \frac{f(x_1, x_2 + \Delta x_2) - f(x_1, x_2)}{\Delta x_2}.$$

Partial derivatives have exactly the same properties as ordinary derivatives; only the name has been changed to protect the innocent (that is, people who haven't seen the ∂ symbol).

In particular, partial derivatives obey the chain rule, but with an extra twist. Suppose that x_1 and x_2 both depend on some variable t and that we define the function $g(t)$ by

$$g(t) = f(x_1(t), x_2(t)).$$

Then the derivative of $g(t)$ with respect to t is given by

$$\frac{dg(t)}{dt} = \frac{\partial f(x_1, x_2)}{\partial x_1} \frac{dx_1(t)}{dt} + \frac{\partial f(x_1, x_2)}{\partial x_2} \frac{dx_2(t)}{dt}.$$

When t changes, it affects both $x_1(t)$ and $x_2(t)$. Therefore, we need to calculate the derivative of $f(x_1, x_2)$ with respect to each of those changes.

A.14 Optimization

If $y = f(x)$, then $f(x)$ achieves a **maximum** at x^* if $f(x^*) \geq f(x)$ for all x. It can be shown that if $f(x)$ is a smooth function that achieves its maximum value at x^*, then

$$\frac{df(x^*)}{dx} = 0$$

$$\frac{d^2 f(x^*)}{dx^2} \leq 0.$$

These expressions are referred to as the **first-order condition** and the **second-order condition** for a maximum. The first-order condition says that the function is flat at x^*, while the second-order condition says that the function is concave near x^*. Clearly both of these properties have to hold if x^* is indeed a maximum.

We say that $f(x)$ achieves its **minimum** value at x^* if $f(x^*) \leq f(x)$ for all x. If $f(x)$ is a smooth function that achieves its minimum at x^*, then

$$\frac{df(x^*)}{dx} = 0$$

$$\frac{d^2 f(x^*)}{dx^2} \geq 0.$$

The first-order condition again says that the function is flat at x^*, while the second-order condition now says that the function is convex near x^*.

If $y = f(x_1, x_2)$ is a smooth function that achieves its maximum or minimum at some point (x_1^*, x_2^*), then we must satisfy

$$\frac{\partial f(x_1^*, x_2^*)}{\partial x_1} = 0$$

$$\frac{\partial f(x_1^*, x_2^*)}{\partial x_2} = 0.$$

These are referred to as the **first-order conditions**. There are also second-order conditions for this problem, but they are more difficult to describe.

A.15 Constrained Optimization

Often we want to consider the maximum or minimum of some function over some restricted values of (x_1, x_2). The notation

$$\max_{x_1, x_2} f(x_1, x_2)$$

$$\text{such that } g(x_1, x_2) = c.$$

means

find x_1^* and x_2^* such that $f(x_1^*, x_2^*) \geq f(x_1, x_2)$ for all values of x_1 and x_2 that satisfy the equation $g(x_1, x_2) = c$.

The function $f(x_1, x_2)$ is called the **objective function**, and the equation $g(x_1, x_2) = c$ is called the **constraint**. Methods for solving this kind of constrained maximization problem are described in the Appendix to Chapter 5.

ANSWERS

1 The Market

1.1. It would be constant at $500 for 25 apartments and then drop to $200.

1.2. In the first case, $500, and in the second case, $200. In the third case, the equilibrium price would be any price between $200 and $500.

1.3. Because if we want to rent one more apartment, we have to offer a lower price. The number of people who have reservation prices greater than p must always increase as p decreases.

1.4. The price of apartments in the inner ring would go up since demand for apartments would not change but supply would decrease.

1.5. The price of apartments in the inner ring would rise.

1.6. A tax would undoubtedly reduce the number of apartments supplied in the long run.

1.7. He would set a price of 25 and rent 50 apartments. In the second case he would rent all 40 apartments at the maximum price the market would bear. This would be given by the solution to $D(p) = 100 - 2p = 40$, which is $p^* = 30$.

1.8. Everyone who had a reservation price higher than the equilibrium price in the competitive market, so that the final outcome would be Pareto efficient. (Of course in the long run there would probably be fewer new apartments built, which would lead to another kind of inefficiency.)

2 Budget Constraint

2.1. The new budget line is given by $2p_1x_1 + 8p_2x_2 = 4m$.

2.2. The vertical intercept (x_2 axis) decreases and the horizontal intercept (x_1 axis) stays the same. Thus the budget line becomes flatter.

2.3. Flatter. The slope is $-2p_1/3p_2$.

2.4. A good whose price has been set to 1; all other goods' prices are measured relative to the numeraire good's price.

2.5. A tax of 8 cents a gallon.

2.6. $(p_1 + t)x_1 + (p_2 - s)x_2 = m - u$.

2.7. Yes, since all of the bundles the consumer could afford before are affordable at the new prices and income.

3 Preferences

3.1. No. It might be that the consumer was indifferent between the two bundles. All we are justified in concluding is that $(x_1, x_2) \succeq (y_1, y_2)$.

3.2. Yes to both.

3.3. It is transitive, but it is not complete—two people might be the same height. It is not reflexive since it is false that a person is strictly taller than himself.

3.4. It is transitive, but not complete. What if A were bigger but slower than B? Which one would he prefer?

3.5. Yes. An indifference curve can cross itself, it just can't cross another distinct indifference curve.

3.6. No, because there are bundles on the indifference curve that have strictly more of both goods than other bundles on the (alleged) indifference curve.

3.7. A negative slope. If you give the consumer more anchovies, you've made him worse off, so you have to take away some pepperoni to get him back on his indifference curve. In this case the direction of increasing utility is *toward* the origin.

3.8. Because the consumer weakly prefers the weighted average of two bundles to either bundle.

3.9. If you give up one $5 bill, how many $1 bills do you need to compensate you? Five $1 bills will do nicely. Hence the answer is -5 or $-1/5$, depending on which good you put on the horizontal axis.

3.10. Zero—if you take away some of good 1, the consumer needs zero units of good 2 to compensate him for his loss.

3.11. Anchovies and peanut butter, scotch and Kool Aid, and other similar repulsive combinations.

4 Utility

4.1. The function $f(u) = u^2$ is a monotonic transformation for positive u, but not for negative u.

4.2. (1) Yes. (2) No (works for v positive). (3) No (works for v negative). (4) Yes (only defined for v positive). (5) Yes. (6) No. (7) Yes. (8) No.

4.3. Suppose that the diagonal intersected a given indifference curve at two points, say (x, x) and (y, y). Then either $x > y$ or $y > x$, which means that one of the bundles has more of *both* goods. But if preferences are monotonic, then one of the bundles would have to be preferred to the other.

4.4. Both represent perfect substitutes.

4.5. Quasilinear preferences. Yes.

4.6. The utility function represents Cobb-Douglas preferences. No. Yes.

4.7. Because the MRS is measured *along* an indifference curve, and utility remains constant along an indifference curve.

5 Choice

5.1. $x_2 = 0$ when $p_2 > p_1$, $x_2 = m/p_2$ when $p_2 < p_1$, and anything between 0 and m/p_2 when $p_1 = p_2$.

5.2. The optimal choices will be $x_1 = m/p_1$ and $x_2 = 0$ if $p_1/p_2 < b$, $x_1 = 0$ and $x_2 = m/p_2$ if $p_1/p_2 > b$, and any amount on the budget line if $p_1/p_2 = b$.

5.3. Let z be the number of cups of coffee the consumer buys. Then we know that $2z$ is the number of teaspoons of sugar he or she buys. We must satisfy the budget constraint

$$2p_1 z + p_2 z = m.$$

Solving for z we have

$$z = \frac{m}{2p_1 + p_2}.$$

5.4. We know that you'll either consume all ice cream or all olives. Thus the two choices for the optimal consumption bundles will be $x_1 = m/p_1$, $x_2 = 0$, or $x_1 = 0$, $x_2 = m/p_2$.

5.5. This is a Cobb-Douglas utility function, so she will spend $4/(1+4) = 4/5$ of her income on good 2.

5.6. For kinked preferences, such as perfect complements, where the change in price doesn't induce any change in demand.

6 Demand

6.1. No. If her income increases, and she spends it all, she must be purchasing more of at least one good.

6.2. The utility function for perfect substitutes is $u(x_1, x_2) = x_1 + x_2$. Thus if $u(x_1, x_2) > u(y_1, y_2)$, we have $x_1 + x_2 > y_1 + y_2$. It follows that $tx_1 + tx_2 > ty_1 + ty_2$, so that $u(tx_1, tx_2) > u(ty_1, ty_2)$.

6.3. The Cobb-Douglas utility function has the property that

$$u(tx_1, tx_2) = (tx_1)^a (tx_2)^{1-a} = t^a t^{1-a} x_1^a x_2^{1-a} = t x_1^a x_2^{1-a} = tu(x_1, x_2).$$

Thus if $u(x_1, x_2) > u(y_1, y_2)$, we know that $u(tx_1, tx_2) > u(ty_1, ty_2)$, so that Cobb-Douglas preferences are indeed homothetic.

6.4. The demand curve.

6.5. No. Concave preferences can only give rise to optimal consumption bundles that involve zero consumption of one of the goods.

6.6. We know that $x_1 = m/(p_1 + p_2)$. Solving for p_1 as a function of the other variables, we have

$$p_1 = \frac{m}{x_1} - p_2.$$

7 Revealed Preference

7.1. No. This consumer violates the Weak Axiom of Revealed Preference since when he bought (x_1, x_2) he could have bought (y_1, y_2) and vice versa. In symbols:

$$p_1 x_1 + p_2 x_2 = 1 \times 1 + 2 \times 2 = 5 > 4 = 1 \times 2 + 2 \times 1 = p_1 y_1 + p_2 y_2$$

and

$$q_1 y_1 + q_2 y_2 = 2 \times 2 + 1 \times 1 = 5 > 4 = 2 \times 1 + 1 \times 2 = q_1 x_1 + q_2 x_2.$$

7.2. Yes. No violations of WARP are present, since the y-bundle is not affordable when the x-bundle was purchased and vice versa.

7.3. Since the y-bundle was more expensive than the x-bundle when the x-bundle was purchased and vice versa, there is no way to tell which bundle is preferred.

7.4. If both prices changed by the same amount. Then the base-year bundle would still be optimal.

7.5. Perfect complements.

8 Slutsky Equation

8.1. Yes. To see this, use our favorite example of red pencils and blue pencils. Suppose red pencils cost 10 cents a piece, and blue pencils cost 5 cents a piece, and the consumer spends $1 on pencils. She would then consume 20 blue pencils. If the price of blue pencils falls to 4 cents a piece, she would consume 25 blue pencils, a change which is entirely due to the income effect.

8.2. Yes.

8.3. Then the income effect would cancel out. All that would be left would be the pure substitution effect, which would automatically be negative.

8.4. They are receiving tx' in revenues and paying out tx, so they are losing money.

8.5. Since their old consumption is affordable, the consumers would have to be at least as well-off. This happens because the government is giving them back *more* money than they are losing due to the higher price of gasoline.

9 Buying and Selling

9.1. Her gross demands are $(9, 1)$.

9.2. The bundle $(y_1, y_2) = (3, 5)$ costs more than the bundle $(4, 4)$ at the current prices. The consumer will not necessarily prefer consuming this bundle, but would certainly prefer to own it, since she could sell it and purchase a bundle that she would prefer.

9.3. Sure. It depends on whether she was a net buyer or a net seller of the good that became more expensive.

9.4. Yes, but only if the U.S. switched to being a net exporter of oil.

9.5. The new budget line would shift outward and remain parallel to the old one, since the increase in the number of hours in the day is a pure endowment effect.

9.6. The slope will be positive.

10 Intertemporal Choice

10.1. According to Table 10.1, $1 20 years from now is worth 3 cents today at a 20 percent interest rate. Thus $1 million is worth $.03 \times 1,000,000 = \$30,000$ today.

10.2. The slope of the intertemporal budget constraint is equal to $-(1+r)$. Thus as r increases the slope becomes more negative (steeper).

10.3. If goods are perfect substitutes, then consumers will only purchase the cheaper good. In the case of intertemporal food purchases, this implies that consumers only buy food in one period, which may not be very realistic.

10.4. In order to remain a lender after the change in interest rates, the consumer must be choosing a point that he could have chosen under the old interest rates, but decided not to. Thus the consumer must be worse off. If the consumer becomes a borrower after the change, then he is choosing a previously unavailable point that cannot be compared to the initial point (since the initial point is no longer available under the new budget constraint), and therefore the change in the consumer's welfare is unknown.

10.5. At an interest rate of 10%, the present value of $100 is $90.91. At a rate of 5% the present value is $95.24.

11 Asset Markets

11.1. Asset A must be selling for $11/(1+.10) = \$10$.

11.2. The rate of return is equal to $(10,000 + 10,000)/100,000 = 20\%$.

11.3. We know that the rate of return on the nontaxable bonds, r, must be such that $(1 - t)r_t = r$, therefore $(1 - .40).10 = .06 = r$.

11.4. The price today must be $40/(1 + .10)^{10} = \$15.42$.

12 Uncertainty

12.1. We need a way to reduce consumption in the bad state and increase consumption in the good state. To do this you would have to *sell* insurance against the loss rather than buy it.

12.2. Functions (a) and (c) have the expected utility property (they are affine transformations of the functions discussed in the chapter), while (b) does not.

12.3. Since he is risk-averse, he prefers the expected value of the gamble, $325, to the gamble itself, and therefore he would take the payment.

12.4. If the payment is $320 the decision will depend on the form of the utility function; we can't say anything in general.

12.5. Your picture should show a function that is initially convex, but then becomes concave.

12.6. In order to self-insure, the risks must be independent. However, this does not hold in the case of flood damage. If one house in the neighborhood is damaged by a flood it is likely that all of the houses will be damaged.

13 Risky Assets

13.1. To achieve a standard deviation of 2% you will need to invest $x = \sigma_x/\sigma_m = 2/3$ of your wealth in the risky asset. This will result in a rate of return equal to $(2/3).09 + (1 - 2/3).06 = 8\%$.

13.2. The price of risk is equal to $(r_m - r_f)/\sigma_m = (9 - 6)/3 = 1$. That is, for every additional percent of standard deviation you can gain 1% of return.

13.3. According to the CAPM pricing equation, the stock should offer an expected rate of return of $r_f + \beta(r_m - r_f) = .05 + 1.5(.10 - .05) = .125$ or 12.5%. The stock should be selling for its expected present value, which is equal to $100/1.125 = \$88.89$.

14 Consumer's Surplus

14.1. We want to compute the area under the demand curve to the left of the quantity 6. Break this up into the area of a triangle with a base of 6 and a height of 6 and a rectangle with base 6 and height 4. Applying the formulas from high school geometry, the triangle has area 18 and the rectangle has area 24. Thus gross benefit is 42.

14.2. When the price is 4, the consumer's surplus is given by the area of a triangle with a base of 6 and a height of 6; i.e., the consumer's surplus is 18. When the price is 6, the triangle has a base of 4 and a height of 4, giving an area of 8. Thus the price change has reduced consumer's surplus by $10.

14.3. Ten dollars. Since the demand for the discrete good hasn't changed, all that has happend is that the consumer has had to reduce his expenditure on other goods by ten dollars.

15 Market Demand

15.1. The inverse demand curve is $P(q) = 200 - 2q$.

15.2. The decision about whether to consume the drug at all could well be price sensitive, so the adjustment of market demand on the extensive margin would contribute to the elasticity of the market demand.

15.3. Revenue is $R(p) = 12p - 2p^2$, which is maximized at $p = 3$.

15.4. Revenue is $pD(p) = 100$, regardless of the price, so all prices maximize revenue.

15.5. True. The weighted average of the income elasticities must be 1, so if one good has a *negative* income elasticity, the other good must have an elasticity *greater* than 1 to get the average to be 1.

16 Equilibrium

16.1. The entire subsidy gets passed along to the consumers if the supply curve is flat, but the subsidy is totally received by the producers when the supply curve is vertical.

16.2. The consumer.

16.3. In this case the demand curve for red pencils is horizontal at the price p_b, since that is the most that they would be willing to pay for a red pencil. Thus, if a tax is imposed on red pencils, consumers will end up paying p_b for them, so the entire amount of the tax will end up being borne by the producers (if any red pencils are sold at all—it could be that the tax would induce the producer to get out of the red pencil business).

16.4. Here the supply curve of foreign oil is flat at $25. Thus the price to the consumers must rise by the $5 amount of the tax, so that the net price to the consumers becomes $30. Since foreign oil and domestic oil are perfect substitutes as far as the consumers are concerned, the domestic producers will sell their oil for $30 as well and get a windfall gain of $5 per barrel.

16.5. Zero. The deadweight loss measures the value of lost output. Since the same amount is supplied before and after the tax, there is no deadweight loss. Put another way: the suppliers are paying the entire amount of the tax, and everything they pay goes to the government. The amount that the suppliers would pay to avoid the tax is simply the tax revenue the government receives, so there is no excess burden of the tax.

16.6. Zero revenue.

16.7. It raises negative revenue, since in this case we have a net subsidy of borrowing.

17 Auctions

17.1. Since the collectors likely have their own values for the quilts, and don't particularly care about the other bidders' values, it is a private-value auction.

17.2. Following the analysis in the text, there are four equally likely configurations of bidders: (8,8), (8,10), (10,8), and (10,10). With zero reservation price, the optimal bids will be (8,9,9,10), resulting in expected profit of $9. The only candidate for a reservation price is $10, which yields expected profit of $30/4 = $7.50. Hence zero is a profit-maximizing reservation price in this auction.

17.3. Have each person write down a value, then award the two books to the students with the two highest values, but just charge them the bid of the third highest student.

17.4. It was efficient in the sense that it awarded the license to the firm that valued it most highly. But it took a year for this to happen, which is inefficient. A Vickrey auction or an English auction would have achieved the same result more quickly.

17.5. This is a common-value auction since the value of the prize is the same to all bidders. Normally, the winning bidder overestimates the number of pennies in the jar, illustrating the winner's curse.

18 Technology

18.1. Increasing returns to scale.

18.2. Decreasing returns to scale.

18.3. If $a + b = 1$, we have constant returns to scale, $a + b < 1$ gives decreasing returns to scale, and $a + b > 1$ gives increasing returns to scale.

18.4. $4 \times 3 = 12$ units.

18.5. True.

18.6. Yes.

19 Profit Maximization

19.1. Profits will decrease.

19.2. Profit would increase, since output would go up more than the cost of the inputs.

19.3. If the firm really had decreasing returns to scale, dividing the scale of all inputs by 2 would produce more than half as much output. Thus the subdivided firm would make more profits than the big firm. This is one argument why having everywhere decreasing returns to scale is implausible.

19.4. The gardener has ignored opportunity costs. In order to accurately account for the true costs, the gardener must include the cost of her own time used in the production of the crop, even if no explicit wage was paid.

19.5. Not in general. For example, consider the case of uncertainty.

19.6. Increase.

19.7. The use of x_1 does not change, and profits will increase.

19.8. May not.

20 Cost Minimization

20.1. Since profit is equal to total revenue minus total costs, if a firm is not minimizing costs then there exists a way for the firm to increase profits; however, this contradicts the fact that the firm is a profit maximizer.

20.2. Increase the use of factor 1 and decrease the use of factor 2.

20.3. Since the inputs are identically priced perfect substitutes, the firm will be indifferent between which of the inputs it uses. Thus the firm will use any amounts of the two inputs such that $x_1 + x_2 = y$.

20.4. The demand for paper either goes down or stays constant.

20.5. It implies that $\sum_{i=1}^{n} \Delta w_i \Delta x_i \leq 0$, where $\Delta w_i = w_i^t - w_i^s$ and $\Delta x_i = x_i^t - x_i^s$.

21 Cost Curves

21.1. True, true, false.

21.2. By simultaneously producing more output at the second plant and reducing production at the first plant, the firm can reduce costs.

21.3. False.

22 Firm Supply

22.1. The inverse supply curve is $p = 20y$, so the supply curve is $y = p/20$.

22.2. Set $AC = MC$ to find $10y + 1000/y = 20y$. Solve to get $y^* = 10$.

22.3. Solve for p to get $P_s(y) = (y - 100)/20$.

22.4. At 10 the supply is 40 and at 20 the supply is 80. The producer's surplus is composed of a rectangle of area 10×40 plus a triangle of area $\frac{1}{2} \times 10 \times 40$, which gives a total change in producer's surplus of 600. This is the same as the change in profits, since the fixed costs don't change.

22.5. The supply curve is given by $y = p/2$ for all $p \geq 2$, and $y = 0$ for all $p \leq 2$. At $p = 2$ the firm is indifferent between supplying 1 unit of output or not supplying it.

22.6. Mostly technical (in more advanced models this could be market), market, could be either market or technical, technical.

22.7. That all firms in the industry take the market price as given.

22.8. The market price. A profit-maximizing firm will set its output such that the marginal cost of producing the last unit of output is equal to its marginal revenue, which in the case of pure competition is equal to the market price.

22.9. The firm should produce zero output (with or without fixed costs).

22.10. In the short run, if the market price is greater than the average variable cost, a firm should produce some output even though it is losing money. This is true because the firm would have lost more had it not produced since it must still pay fixed costs. However, in the long run there are no fixed costs, and therefore any firm that is losing money can produce zero output and lose a maximum of zero dollars.

22.11. The market price must be equal to the marginal cost of production for all firms in the industry.

23 Industry Supply

23.1. The inverse supply curves are $P_1(y_1) = 10 + y_1$ and $P_2(y_2) = 15 + y_2$. When the price is below 10 neither firm supplies output. When the price is 15 firm 2 will enter the market, and at any price above 15, both firms are in the market. Thus the kink occurs at a price of 15.

23.2. In the short run, the consumers pay the entire amount of the tax. In the long run it is paid by the producers.

23.3. False. A better statement would be: convenience stores can charge high prices because they are near the campus. Because of the high prices the stores are able to charge, the landowners can in turn charge high rents for the use of the convenient location.

23.4. True.

23.5. The profits or losses of the firms that are currently operating in the industry.

23.6. Flatter.

23.7. No, it does not violate the model. In accounting for the costs we failed to value the rent on the license.

24 Monopoly

24.1. No. A profit-maximizing monopolist would never operate where the demand for its product was inelastic.

24.2. First solve for the inverse demand curve to get $p(y) = 50 - y/2$. Thus the marginal revenue is given by $MR(y) = 50 - y$. Set this equal to marginal cost of 2, and solve to get $y = 48$. To determine the price, substitute into the inverse demand function, $p(48) = 50 - 48/2 = 26$.

24.3. The demand curve has a constant elasticity of -3. Using the formula $p[1 + 1/\epsilon] = MC$, we substitute to get $p[1 - 1/3] = 2$. Solving, we get $p = 3$. Substitute back into the demand function to get the quantity produced: $D(3) = 10 \times 3^{-3}$.

24.4. The demand curve has a constant elasticity of -1. Thus marginal revenue is zero for all levels of output. Hence it can never be equal to marginal cost.

24.5. For a linear demand curve the price rises by half the change in cost. In this case, the answer is $3.

24.6. In this case $p = kMC$, where $k = 1/(1 - 1/3) = 3/2$. Thus the price rises by $9.

24.7. Price will be two times marginal cost.

24.8. A subsidy of 50 percent, so the marginal costs facing the monopolist are half the actual marginal costs. This will ensure that price equals marginal cost at the monopolist's choice of output.

24.9. A monopolist operates where $p(y) + y\Delta p/\Delta y = MC(y)$. Rearranging, we have $p(y) = MC(y) - y\Delta p/\Delta y$. Since demand curves have a negative slope, we know that $\Delta p/\Delta y < 0$, which proves that $p(y) > MC(y)$.

24.10. False. Imposing a tax on a monopolist may cause the market price to rise more than, the same as, or less than the amount of the tax.

24.11. A number of problems arise, including: determining the true marginal costs for the firm, making sure that all customers will be served, and ensuring that the monopolist will not make a loss at the new price and output level.

24.12. Some appropriate conditions are: large fixed costs and small marginal costs, large minimum efficient scale relative to the market, ease of collusion, etc.

25 Monopoly Behavior

25.1. Yes, if it can perfectly price discriminate.

25.2. $p_i = \epsilon_i c / (1 + \epsilon_i)$ for $i = 1, 2$.

25.3. If he can perfectly price discriminate, he can extract the entire consumers' surplus; if he can charge for admission, he can do the same. Hence, the monopolist does equally well under either pricing policy. (In practice, it is much easier to charge for admission than to charge a different price for every ride.)

25.4. This is third-degree price discrimination. Apparently the Disneyland administrators believe that residents of Southern California have more elastic demands than other visitors to their park.

26 Factor Markets

26.1. Sure. A monopsonist can produce at any level of supply elasticity.

26.2. Since the demand for labor would exceed the supply at such a wage, we would presumably see unemployment.

26.3. We find the equilibrium prices by substituting into the demand functions. Since $p = a - by$, we can use the solution for y to find

$$p = \frac{3a + c}{4}.$$

Since $k = a - 2bx$, we can use the solution for x to find

$$k = \frac{a + c}{2}.$$

27 Oligopoly

27.1. In equilibrium each firm will produce $(a - c)/3b$, so the total industry output is $2(a - c)/3b$.

27.2. Nothing. Since all firms have the same marginal cost, it doesn't matter which of them produces the output.

27.3. No, because one of the choices open to the Stackelberg leader is to choose the level of output it would have in the Cournot equilibrium. So it always has to be able to do at least this well.

27.4. We know from the text that we must have $p[1 - 1/n|\epsilon|] = MC$. Since $MC > 0$, and $p > 0$, we must have $1 - 1/n|\epsilon| > 0$. Rearranging this inequality gives the result.

27.5. Make $f_2(y_1)$ steeper than $f_1(y_2)$.

27.6. In general, no. Only in the case of the Bertrand solution does price equal the marginal cost.

28 Game Theory

28.1. The second player will defect in response to the first player's (mistaken) defection. But then the first player will defect in response to that, and each player will continue to defect in response to the other's defection! This example shows that tit-for-tat may not be a very good strategy when players can make mistakes in either their actions or their perceptions of the other player's actions.

28.2. Yes and no. A player prefers to play a dominant strategy regardless of the strategy of the opponent (even if the opponent plays her own dominant strategy). Thus, if all of the players are using dominant strategies then it is the case that they are all playing a strategy that is optimal given the strategy of their opponents, and therefore a Nash equilibrium exists. However, not all Nash equilibria are dominant strategy equilibria; for example, see Table 28.2.

28.3. Not necessarily. We know that your Nash equilibrium strategy is the best thing for you to do as long as your opponent is playing her Nash equilibrium strategy, but if she is not then perhaps there is a better strategy for you to pursue.

28.4. Formally, if the prisoners are allowed to retaliate the payoffs in the game may change. This could result in a Pareto efficient outcome for the game (for example, think of the case where the prisoners both agree that they will kill anyone who confesses, and assume death has a very low utility).

28.5. The dominant Nash equilibrium strategy is to defect in every round. This strategy is derived via the same backward induction process that was used to derive the finite 10-round case. The experimental evidence using much smaller time periods seems to indicate that players rarely use this strategy.

28.6. The equilibrium has player B choosing left and player A choosing top. Player B prefers to move first since that results in a payoff of 9 versus a payoff of 1. (Note, however, that moving first is not always advantageous in a sequential game. Can you think of an example?)

29 Exchange

29.1. Yes. For example, consider the allocation where one person has everything. Then the other person is worse off at this allocation than he would be at an allocation where he had something.

29.2. No. For this would mean that at the allegedly Pareto efficient allocation there is some way to make everyone better off, contradicting the assumption of Pareto efficiency.

29.3. If we know the contract curve, then any trading should end up somewhere on the curve; however, we don't know where.

29.4. Yes, but not without making someone else worse off.

29.5. The value of excess demand in the remaining two markets must sum to zero.

30 Production

30.1. Giving up 1 coconut frees up $6 worth of resources that could be used to produce 2 pounds (equals $6 worth) of fish.

30.2. A higher wage would produce a steeper isoprofit line, implying that the profit maximizing level for the firm would occur at a point to the left of the current equilibrium, entailing a lower level of labor demand. However, under this new budget constraint Robinson will want to supply more than the required level of labor (why?) and therefore the labor market will not be in equilibrium.

30.3. Given a few assumptions, an economy that is in competitive equilibrium is Pareto efficient. It is generally recognized that this is a good thing for a society since it implies that there are no opportunities to make any individual in the economy better off without hurting someone else. However, it may be that the society would prefer a different distribution of welfare; that is, it may be that society prefers making one group better off at the expense of another group.

30.4. He should produce more fish. His marginal rate of substitution indicates that he is willing to give up two coconuts for an additional fish. The marginal rate of transformation implies that he only has to give up one coconut to get an additional fish. Therefore, by giving up a single coconut (even though he would have been willing to give up two) he can have an additional fish.

30.5. Both would have to work 9 hours per day. If they both work for 6 hours per day (Robinson producing coconuts, and Friday catching fish) and give half of their total production to the other, they can produce the same output. The reduction in the hours of work from 9 to 6 hours per day is due to rearranging production based on each individual's comparative advantage.

31 Welfare

31.1. The major shortcoming is that there are many allocations that cannot be compared—there is no way to decide between any two Pareto efficient allocations.

31.2. It would have the form: $W(u_1, \ldots, u_n) = \max\{u_1, \ldots, u_n\}$.

31.3. Since the Nietzschean welfare function cares only about the best off individual, welfare maxima for this allocation would typically involve one person getting everything.

31.4. Suppose that this is not the case. Then each individual envies someone else. Let's construct a list of who envies whom. Person A envies someone—call him person B. Person B in turn envies someone—say person C. And so on. But eventually we will find someone who envies someone who came earlier in the list. Suppose the cycle is "C envies D envies E envies C." Then consider the following swap: C gets what D has, D gets what E has, and E gets what C has. Each person in the cycle gets a bundle that he prefers, and thus each person is made better off. But then the original allocation couldn't have been Pareto efficient!

31.5. First vote between **x** and **z**, and then vote between the winner (**z**) and **y**. First pair **x** and **y**, and then vote between the winner (**x**) and **z**. The fact that the social preferences are intransitive is responsible for this agenda-setting power.

32 Externalities

32.1. True. Usually, efficiency problems can be eliminated by the delineation of property rights. However, when we impose property rights we are also imposing an endowment, which may have important distributional consequences.

32.2. False.

32.3. Come on, your roommates aren't all bad ...

32.4. The government could just give away the optimal number of grazing rights. Another alternative would be to sell the grazing rights. (Question: how much would these rights sell for? Hint: think about rents.) The government could also impose a tax, t per cow, such that $f(c^*)/c^* + t = a$.

33 Law and Economics

33.1. It may. The probability of catching someone littering may be very small, so the magnitude of the punishment has to be large to deter this behavior.

33.2. If the victim is *completely* compensated for the costs of the accident, he will have no incentive to take care to avoid the accident.

33.3. Substituting from the formula in the text, we have $100 = p^* - 3 \times \frac{1}{6}p^*$. Solving this for p^*, we find that $p^* = 200$.

34 Information Technology

34.1. They should be willing to pay up to $50, since this is the present value of the profit they can hope to get from that customer in the long run.

34.2. Users would gravitate toward packages with the most users, since that would make it more convenient for them to exchange files and information about how to use the program.

34.3. In this case the profit maximization conditions are identical. If two people share a video, the producer would just double the price and make exactly the same profits.

35 Public Goods

35.1. It will *not* be the highest value. Rather, it will be the *second* highest value plus a dollar. The person who is *willing* to bid the highest gets the good, but he only has to pay the price of the second highest bidder plus a small amount.

35.2. The argument is similar to the argument for the Clarke tax. Consider increasing your bid above your true value. If you were the high bidder anyway, you don't change your chances of getting the good. If you were not the high bidder, then if you increase your bid enough to exceed the actual high bidder, you will get the good, but have to pay the price bid by the second highest bidder—which is more than the value of the good to you. A similar argument can be made for underbidding.

35.3. We want the sum of the marginal rates of substitution to equal the marginal cost of providing the public good. The sum of the MRSs is 20 ($= 10 \times 2$), and the marginal cost is $2x$. Thus we have the equation $2x = 20$, which implies that $x = 10$. So the Pareto efficient number of streetlights is 10.

36 Asymmetric Information

36.1. Since only the low-quality cars get exchanged in equilibrium and there is a surplus of $200 per transaction, the total surplus created is $50 \times 200 = \$10,000$.

36.2. If the cars were assigned randomly, the average surplus per transaction would be the average willingness to pay, $1800, minus the average willingness to sell, $1500. This gives an average surplus of $300 per transaction and there are 100 transactions, so we get a total surplus of $30,000, which is much better than the market solution.

36.3. We know from the text that the optimal incentive plan takes the form $s(x) = wx + K$. The wage w must equal the marginal product of the worker, which in this case is 1. The constant K is chosen so that the worker's utility at the optimal choice is $\bar{u} = 0$. The optimal choice of x occurs where price, 1, equals marginal cost, x, so $x^* = 1$. At this point the worker gets a utility of $x^* + K - c(x^*) = 1 + K - 1/2 = 1/2 + K$. Since the worker's utility must equal 0, it follows that $K = -1/2$.

36.4. We saw in the last answer that the profits at the optimal level of production are $1/2$. Since $\bar{u} = 0$, the worker would be willing to pay $1/2$ to rent the technology.

36.5. If the worker is to achieve a utility level of 1, the firm would have to give the worker a lump-sum payment of $1/2$.

INDEX